P9-DEX-306

In Conflict and Order

UNDERSTANDING SOCIETY

EIGHTH EDITION

D. Stanley Eitzen
Colorado State University

Maxine Baca Zinn
Michigan State University

Allyn and Bacon

BOSTON   LONDON   TORONTO   SYDNEY   TOKYO   SINGAPORE

Editor in Chief, Social Sciences: *Karen Hanson*
Editorial Assistant: *Elissa Schaen*
Marketing Manager: *Joyce Nilsen*
Editorial Production Service: *Chestnut Hill Enterprises, Inc.*
Manufacturing Buyer: *Megan Cochran*
Cover Administrator: *Linda Knowles*

Internet: www.abacon.com
America Online: keyword: College Online

ISBN: 0-205-26469-7

Photo Credits:
Photo credits are found on page 590, which should be considered an extension of the
copyright page.

Printed in the United States of America
10 9 8 7 6 5 4 3 2 1   02 01 00 99 98 97

CONTENTS

PART TWO   The Individual in Society: Society in the Individual

PART FOUR   **Social Institutions**

PREFACE

Many introductory students will be exposed to sociology only once. They should leave that course with a new and meaningful way of understanding themselves, other people, and society. The most fundamental goal of this book is to help the student develop a sociological perspective.

This goal is emphasized explicitly in the first chapter and implicitly throughout *In Conflict and Order: Understanding Society,* Eighth Edition. The sociological perspective focuses on the social sources of behavior. It requires the shedding of existing myths and ideologies by questioning all social arrangements. One of the most persistent questions of the sociologist is, Who benefits from the existing customs and social order and who does not? Because social groups are created by people, such groups are not sacred. Is there a better way? One editorial writer has posed a number of questions that illustrate the critical approach typical of the sociological perspective:

> Must we Americans try to perpetuate our global empire, maintaining far-flung military outposts, spending billions on the machinery of death, meddling in the affairs of other nations—or is there a better way? Must we continue to concentrate power and wealth in the hands of a few, preserving the income gaps that have remained virtually undisturbed through the New Deal, Fair Deal, New Frontier, and Great Society—or is there a better way? Must millions of our people be subjected to the cruel displacements of an irrational economy—or is there a better way? Must we stand by while our liberties are undermined, our resources squandered, our environment polluted—or is there a better way? Must private profit be the nation's driving force—or is there a better way? (*The Progressive,* 1976:5)

Although there will be disagreement on the answers to these questions, the answers are less important, sociologically, than is the willingness to call into question existing social arrangements that many people consider sacred. This is the beginning of the sociological perspective. But being critical is not enough. The sociologist must have a coherent way to make sense of the social world, and this leads us to the second goal of *In Conflict and Order*—the elaboration of a consistent framework from which to understand and interpret social life. *In Conflict and Order,* Eighth Edition, is guided by the assumption that there is an inherent duality in all societies. The realistic analysis of any one society must include both the integrating and stabilizing forces, on the one hand, and the forces that are conducive to mal-integration and change, on the other. Society in the United States is characterized by harmony and conflict, integration and division, stability and change. This synthesis is crucial if the intricacies of social structure, the mechanisms of social change, and the sources of social problems are to be understood fully.

This objective of achieving a balance between the order and the conflict perspectives is not fully realized in this book, however. Although both perspectives are incorporated into each chapter, the scales tend to be tipped toward the conflict perspective. This imbalance is the conscious product of how the authors, as sociologists and teachers, view the structure and mechanisms of society. In addition to presenting what we believe is a realistic analysis of society, this imbalance counters the prevailing view of the order perspective with its implicit sanctification of the status quo. Such a stance is untenable to us, given the spate of social problems that persist in U.S. society. The emphasis of the conflict approach, on the other hand, questions the existing social arrangements, viewing them as sources of social problems, a position with which we agree. Implicit in such a position is the goal of restructuring society along more humane lines.

That we stress the conflict approach over the order model does not suggest that *In Conflict and Order* is a polemic. On the contrary, the social structure is also examined from a sympathetic view. The existing arrangements do provide for the stability and maintenance of the system. But the point is that by including a relatively large dose of the conflict perspective, the discussion is a realistic appraisal of the system rather than a look through rose-colored glasses.

This duality theme is shown primarily at the societal level in this book. But even though the societal level is the focus of our inquiry, the small-group and individual levels are not ignored. The principles that apply to societies are also appropriate for the small social organizations to which we belong, such as families, work groups, athletic teams, religious organizations, and clubs. Just as important, the sociological perspective shows how the individual is affected by groups of all sizes. Moreover, it shows how the individual's identity is shaped by social forces and how in many important ways the individual's thoughts and actions are determined by group memberships. The linkage of the individual to social groups is shown throughout *In Conflict and Order*. The relationship of the individual to the larger society is illustrated in special panels that examine societal changes and forces impinging on individuals and the choices available to us as we attempt to cope with these societal trends.

The book is divided into four parts. In Part One, Chapters 1 through 3 introduce the reader to the sociological perspective, the fundamental concepts of the discipline, and the duality of social life. These chapters set the stage for an analysis of the structure (organization) and process (change) of U.S. society. The emphasis is on the characteristics of societies in general and of the United States in particular.

Part Two (Chapters 4 through 7) describes the way human beings are shaped by society. The topics include the values that direct our choices, the social bases of social identity and personality, the mechanisms that control individual and group behavior, and the violation of social expectations—deviance. Throughout these chapters we examine the forces that, on the one hand, work to make all of us living in the United States similar and those that, on the other hand, make us different.

The remainder of this text is an analysis of society. Part Three (Chapters 8 through 12) focuses on social change and social inequality. This section begins with a chapter new to this edition. This chapter shows how two macro social forces (the economic transformation and the new immigration) affect human behavior and social life. Among other things, these structural changes affect social stratification by class and race. These are the topics of the remaining chapters in this section. We examine how societies rank people in hierarchies. Also examined are the mechanisms that ensure that some people have a greater share of wealth, power, and prestige than do others and the positive and negative consequences of such an arrangement. Other chapters focus on the specific hierarchies of stratification—class, race, and gender.

Part Four (Chapters 13 to 18) discusses another characteristic of all societies— the presence of social institutions. Every society historically has developed a fairly consistent way of meeting its survival needs and the needs of its members. The family, for example, ensures the regular input of new members, provides for the stable care and protection of the young, and regulates sexual activity. In addition to the family, chapters are devoted to education, to the economy, to the polity, and to religion. The understanding of institutions is vital to the understanding of society because these social arrangements are part of its structure, resist change, and have such a profound impact on the public and private lives of people.

Chapter 18 is a new chapter and one unique to introductory textbooks. The goal of this chapter is to combat the strong structural determinism bias of the earlier chapters by focusing on how human beings, individually and collectively, change social structures.

This eighth edition of *In Conflict and Order,* while retaining the structure of the earlier editions, is different and improved. In addition to two new chapters, the latest statistical data and research findings are included. Timely topics, such as corporate crimes, the Bell Curve debate, immigration, and the politics of the religious right, are discussed. Four themes are incorporated throughout. First, although there are separate chapters on race, class, and gender, these fundamental sources of differences are infused throughout the book and in the photographs. This emphasis is important when highlighting the diversity in society as well as furthering our understanding of the structural sources of inequality and injustice. Second, the tendency toward structural determinism is countered by Chapter 18 and various examples of human agency—when the powerless organize to achieve power and positive social changes (e.g., civil rights movement, gay rights, rights for people with disabilities, and efforts to achieve gender equity in sports). Third, the sources and consequences of the structural transformation of the economy are examined. This is a pivotal shift in the U.S. economy with significant implications for individuals, communities, the society, and the global economy. And, fourth, the focus is often shifted away from the United States through descriptions, panels, and tables to other societies. This global perspective is important for at least two reasons: to illustrate the universality of sociological concepts and to help us understand how the world is becoming ever more interdependent.

These four themes—diversity, the struggle by the powerless to achieve social justice, the transformation of the economy, and a global perspective—are important to consider sociologically. We see that social problems are structural in origin and that the pace of social change is increasing, yet society's institutions are slow to change and meet the challenges. The problems of U.S. society are of great magnitude, and solutions must be found. But understanding must precede action—and that is one goal of *In Conflict and Order.*

The analysis of U.S. society is a challenging task. It is frustrating because of the heterogeneity of the population and the complexity of the forces impinging on U.S. social life. It is also frustrating because the diversity within the United States leads to many inconsistencies and paradoxes. Furthermore, it is difficult, if not impossible, for people in the United States to be objective and consistently rational about their society. Nevertheless, the sociological study of U.S. society is fascinating and rewarding. It becomes absorbing as people gain insights into their own actions and into the behavior of other people. Understanding the intricate complex of forces leading to a particular type of social structure or social problem can be liberating and can lead toward collective efforts to bring about social change. This book attempts to give the reader just such a sociological perspective.

Finally, we are unabashedly proud of being sociologists. Our hope is that you will capture some of our enthusiasm for exploring and understanding the intricacies and mysteries of social life.

A Note on Language Usage

In writing this eighth edition of *In Conflict and Order,* we have been especially sensitive to our use of language. Language is used to reflect and maintain the secondary status of social groups by defining them, diminishing them, trivializing them, or excluding them. For example, traditional English uses masculine words (*man, mankind, he*) when referring to people in general. Even the ordering of masculine and feminine, or of Whites and Blacks, with the discussion or reference to one category consistently preceding its counterpart, subtly conveys the message that the one listed first is superior to the other. In short, our goal is to use language so that it does *not* create the impression that one social class, race, or gender is superior to any other. The terms of reference for racial and ethnic categories are changing. Blacks increasingly use the term *African American,* and Hispanics often refer to themselves as *Latinos.* In this book, we use each of these terms for each social category because they often are used interchangeably in popular and scholarly discourse.

Also, we do *not* use the terms *America* or *American society* when referring to the United States. *America* should be used only in reference to the entire Western hemisphere—North, Central, and South America. Its use as a reference to only the United States implies that the other nations of the Western hemisphere have no place in our frame of reference.

Acknowledgments

Our thanks to the following people for their thoughtful comments:

Pat Allen, Los Angeles Valley College; David Alvirez, University of Texas at San Antonio; Barb Brents, University of Nevada, Las Vegas; Levon Chorbajian, University of Massachusetts, Lowell; Pamela Dee Elkind, Eastern Washington University; Kay B. Forest, Northern Illinois University; Harold Nelson, University of Texas—Pan American; Dean A. Purdy, Bowling Green State University; Christa Reiser, East Carolina University; Mark O. Rousseau, University of Nebraska—Omaha; William L. Smith, Georgia Southern University; Anne Szopa, Indiana University East; Steve Talbot, San Joaquin Delta College; and Lawrence D. Weiss, University of Alaska, Anchorage.

D. Stanley Eitzen
Maxine Baca Zinn

CHAPTER 1

PART ONE

The Sociological Perspective

Life appears to be a series of choices for each of us. We decide how much schooling is important and what field to major in. We choose a job, a mate, and a lifestyle. But how free are we? Have you ever felt trapped by events and conditions beyond your control? Your religious beliefs may make you feel guilty for some behaviors. Your patriotism may cost you your life—even willingly. These ideological traps are powerful, so powerful that we usually do not even see them as traps.

Have you ever felt trapped in a social relationship? Have you ever continued a relationship with a friend, group of friends, a lover, or a spouse when you were convinced that this relationship was wrong for you? Have you ever participated in an act because other people wanted you to that later seemed absolutely ridiculous, even immoral? Most likely your answers to these questions are in the affirmative, because those people closest to us effectively command our conformity.

At another level, have you ever felt that because of your race, gender, age, ethnicity, or social class certain opportunities were closed to you? For example, if you are an African American football player, your chances to play certain positions on the team (usually quarterback, center, offensive guard, and kicker) will probably be limited to you regardless of your abilities. If you are a woman, you may want to try certain sports or jobs, but to do so is to call your femininity into question.

Even more remotely, each of us is controlled by decisions made in corporate boardrooms, in government bureaus, and in foreign capitals. Our tastes in style are decided on and manipulated by corporate giants through the media. Rising or declining interest rates can encourage corporate decisions to expand or contract their businesses, thus affecting employment. Those same interest rates can stimulate or deter individuals and families to purchase housing and automobiles. A war in the Middle East reduces the supply of oil, raises the price dramatically, and thus restricts personal use in the United States. That same war may mean that you will be called to action because you are the right age and sex. The weather in China and Russia affects grain prices in the United States, meaning bankruptcy or prosperity for individual farmers and high or low prices for individual consumers.

Finally, we are also trapped by our culture. We do not decide what is right or wrong, moral or immoral. These are decided for us and incorporated inside us. We do not decide what is beautiful and what is not. Even the decision on what is important and what is not is a cultural bias embedded deep inside each of us.

Sociology

Sociology is the science that attempts to understand these social forces—the forces outside us that shape our lives, interests, and personalities. In John Walton's words, "Sociology explores the determinants of individual and collective behavior that are not given in our psychic or biological makeup, but fashioned in the broader arena of social interaction" (Walton, 1990:5). As the science of society and social behavior, sociology is interesting, insightful, and important. This is true because sociology explores and analyzes the ultimate issues of our personal lives, of society, and of the world. At the personal level, sociology investigates the causes and consequences of such phenomena as romantic love, violence, identity, conformity, deviance, personality, and interpersonal power. At the societal level, sociology examines and explains poverty, crime rates, racism, sexism, pollution, and political power. At the global level, sociology researches such phenomena as war, conflict resolution, immigration patterns, and population growth. Other disciplines are also helpful in understanding these social phenomena, but sociology makes a unique contribution.

The insights of sociology are important for the individual because they help us understand why we behave as we do. This understanding is not only liberating but also is a necessary precondition for meaningful social action to bring social change. As a scholarly discipline, sociology is important because it complements and in some cases supersedes other disciplines concerned with understanding and explaining social behavior.

Assumptions of the Sociological Perspective

To discover the underlying order of social life and the principles that explain human behavior, scientists have focused on different levels of phenomena. The result of this division of labor has been the creation of scholarly disciplines, each concentrating on a relatively narrow sphere of phenomena. Biologists interested in social phenomena have focused on the organic bases for behavior. Psychological explanations assume the source of human behavior in the psyches of individuals.

The understanding of human behavior benefits from the emphases of the various disciplines. Each discipline makes important contributions to knowledge. Of the three major disciplines focusing on human behavior, sociology is commonly the least understood. The explicit goal of this book is to remedy this fault by introducing the reader to the sociological ways of perceiving and interpreting the social world. Let us begin by considering the assumptions of the sociological approach that provide the foundation for this unique, exciting, and insightful way of viewing the world.

Individuals are, by their nature, social beings. There are two fundamental reasons for this assumption. First, human babies enter the world totally dependent on other people for their survival. This initial period of dependence means, in effect, that each of us has been immersed in social groups from birth. A second basis for the social nature of human beings is that throughout history people have found it to their advantage to cooperate with other people (for defense, for material comforts, to overcome the perils of nature, and to improve technology).

Individuals are, for the most part, socially determined. This essential assumption stems from the first assumption, that people are social beings. Individuals are products of their social environments for several reasons. During infancy, the child is at the mercy of adults, especially parents. These persons shape the infant in an infinite variety of ways, depending on their proclivities and those of their society. The parents have a profound impact on that child's ways of thinking about himself or herself and about other people. The parents transmit religious views, political attitudes, and attitudes toward how other groups are to be rated. The child is punished for certain behaviors and rewarded for others. Whether that child becomes a bigot or integrationist, traditionalist or innovator, saint or sinner depends in large measure on the parents, peers, and other people who interact with her or him.

The parents may transmit to their offspring some idiosyncratic beliefs and behaviors, but most significantly they act as cultural agents, transferring the ways of the society to their children. Thus, the child is born into a family and also into a society. This society into which the individuals are born shapes their personalities and perceptions. Berger has summarized the impact of society:

> Society not only controls our movements, but shapes our identity, our thoughts and our emotions. The structures of society become the structures of our own consciousness. Society does not stop at the surface of our skins. Society penetrates us as much as it envelops us. (Berger, 1963:121)

The individual's identity is socially bestowed. Who we are, how we feel about ourselves, and how other people treat us are usually consequences of our social location (which is determined by our social class, race/ethnicity, and gender) in society. Individuals' personalities are also shaped by the way we are accepted, rejected, and/or defined by other people. Whether an individual is attractive or plain, witty or dull, worthy or unworthy depends on the values of society and the groups in which the individual is immersed. Although genes determine one's physiology and potential, the social environment determines how those characteristics will be evaluated. Suggesting that human beings are socially determined is another way of saying that they are similar to puppets. They are dependent on and manipulated by social forces. A major function of sociology is to identify the social forces that affect

Parents act as cultural agents, transferring the ways of society to their children.

us so greatly. Freedom, as McGee has pointed out, can come only from a recognition of these unseen forces:

> Freedom consists in knowing what these forces are and how they work so that we have the option of saying no to the impact of their operation. For example, if we grow up in a racist society, we will be racists unless we learn what racism is and how it works and then choose to refuse its impact. In order to do so, however, we must recognize that it is there in the first place. People often are puppets, blindly danced by strings of which they are unaware and over which they are not free to exercise control. A major function of sociology is that it permits us to recognize the forces operative on us and to untie the puppet strings which bind us, thereby giving us the option to be free. (McGee, 1975:3)

Thus, one task of sociology is to learn, among other things, what racism is and to determine how it works. This is often difficult because we typically do not recognize its existence—because we have been puppets, socialized to believe and behave in particular ways.

To say that we are puppets is too strong, however. This assumption is not meant to imply a total **social determinism** (the assumption that human behavior is explained exclusively by social factors).* The puppet metaphor is used to convey the idea that much of who we are and what we do is a product of our social environment. But there are nonconformists, deviants, and innovators. Society is not a rigid, static entity composed of robots. While the members of society are shaped by their social environment, they also change that environment. Human beings are the shapers of society as well as the shapees. This is the third assumption of the sociological approach.

---

*Advocates of social determinism are guilty of oversimplifying complex phenomena, just as are genetic determinists, psychological determinists, geographical determinists, and economic determinists.

Individuals create, sustain, and change the social forms within which they conduct their lives. Even though individuals are largely puppets of society, they are also puppeteers. Chapter 2 describes this process of how people in interaction are the architects of society. In brief, the argument is that social groups of all sizes and types (families, peer groups, work groups, corporations, communities, and societies) are made by people. What interacting persons create becomes a source of control over those individuals (that is, they become puppets of their own creation). But the continuous interaction of the group's members also changes the group.

There are four important implications of this assumption that groups are human-made. First, these social forms that are created have a certain momentum of their own that defies change. The ways of doing and thinking common to the group are natural and right. Although human-made, the group's expectations and structures take on a sacred quality—the sanctity of tradition—that constrains behavior in the socially prescribed ways.

A second implication is that social organizations, because they are created and sustained by people, are imperfect. Slavery benefited some segments of society by taking advantage of other segments. A competitive free enterprise system creates winners and losers. The wonders of technology make worldwide transportation and communication easy and relatively inexpensive but create pollution and waste natural resources. These examples show that there are positive *and* negative consequences of the way people have organized.

The third implication is that individuals through collective action are capable of changing the structure of society and even the course of history. Consider, for example, the social movement in India led by Gandhi that ended colonial rule by Great Britain, or the civil rights movement in the South led by Martin Luther King, Jr., that ended segregationist laws, or the failure of the attempted coup by Communist hardliners in the summer of 1991 because of the refusal of Soviet citizens and soldiers to accept it.

The final significance of this assumption is that individuals are not passive. Rather, they actively shape social life by adapting to, negotiating with, and changing social structures. This process is called **human agency.** Occasional panels will highlight human agency throughout the text. Also, the final chapter is devoted to this meaningful interaction between social actors and their social environment. Whereas most of this book examines social life from the top (social structure) down, human agency provides the crucial vantage point and insights from the bottom up.

Problems with the Sociological Perspective

Sociology is not a comfortable discipline and therefore will not appeal to everyone. To look behind the closed doors of social life is fraught with danger. Sociology frightens some people because it questions what they normally take for granted. Sociologists ask such questions as: How does society really work? Who really has power? Who benefits under the existing social arrangements and who does not? To ask such questions means that the inquirer is interested in looking beyond the commonly accepted official definitions. As Berger has put it, the "sociological perspective involves a process of 'seeing through' the facades of social structures" (Berger, 1963:31). The underlying assumption of the sociologist is that things are not as they seem. Is the mayor of your town the most powerful person in the community? Is the system of justice truly just? Is professional sport free of racism? Is the United States a meritocratic society where talent and effort combine to stratify the people fairly? To make such queries calls into question existing myths, stereotypes, and official dogma. The critical examination of society will demystify and demythologize. It sensitizes the individual to the inconsistencies present in society. Clearly, that will result if you ask: Why does the United States, in the name of freedom, protect dictatorships around the world? Why do we encourage subsidies to the affluent but resent those directed to the poor? How high would Bill Clinton have risen politically if his surname were Garcia? Why are people who have killed Whites more likely to be sentenced to death than people who have killed African Americans? Why are many women opposed to the Equal Rights Amendment? Why in a democracy such as the United States are there so few truly democratic organizations?

The sociological assumption that provides the basis for this critical stance is that the social world is human-made—and therefore not sacred. Belief systems, the economic system, the law, the way power is distributed—all are created and sustained by people. They can, therefore, be changed by people. But if the change is to correct imperfections, then we must understand how social phenomena work. The central task of this book is to aid in such an understanding of United States society.

The sociological perspective is also discomforting to many people because an understanding of society's constraints is liberating. Traditional sex roles, for example, are no longer sacred for many persons. But while this understanding is liberating from the constraints of tradition, it is also freedom from the protection that custom provides. The acceptance of tradition is comfortable because it frees us from choice (and therefore blame) and from ambiguity. Thus, the understanding of society is a two-edged sword—freeing us, but also increasing the probability of frustration, anger, and alienation.

Sociology is also uncomfortable because the behavior of the subjects is not always certain. Prediction is not always accurate, because people can choose among options or can be persuaded by irrational factors. The result is that if sociologists know the social conditions, they can predict, but in terms of probabilities. In chemistry, on the other hand, scientists know exactly what will occur if a certain measure of sodium is mixed with a precise amount of chlorine in a test tube. Civil engineers armed with the knowledge of rock formations, type of soils, wind currents, and temperature extremes know exactly what specifications are needed when building a dam in a certain place. They could not know these, however, if the foundation and building materials kept shifting. That is the problem—and the source of excitement—for the sociologist.

The political proclivities of people in the United States during the past few decades offer a good example of shifting attitudes. In 1964 the Republican candidate for president, Barry Goldwater, was soundly defeated, and many observers predicted the demise of the Republican Party. But in 1968, Richard Nixon, the Republican, won. He won again in 1972 by a record-setting margin, leading to the prognostication that the Democratic Party would no longer be viable. Two years later, however, Nixon resigned in disgrace, and in 1976 the Democratic candidate, Jimmy Carter, was the victor. In 1980 President Carter was defeated by Ronald Reagan, and a number of liberal senators were defeated by conservatives. These wide swings seemed to stop as Reagan was reelected in 1984, and he was succeeded four years later by his loyal vice-president, George Bush. But Bush was defeated by the Democrat Bill Clinton in 1992, leading some observers to predict the end of the Republican era. Then Clinton's first two years in office, and the timidity of the Democratic majorities in the House and Senate, led to the Republicans winning majorities in the House and the Senate in 1994 and ushered in what appeared to be a new era of conservatism. By 1996, however, the Republican blueprint (the "Contract with America") was no longer viable, President Clinton was reelected, although the Republicans held majorities in the House and Senate. What does the future hold? History reveals that as long as human beings are not robots, their behaviors will be somewhat unpredictable. International events, economic cycles, scandals, and other occurrences will lead to shifts in political opinions and shifts in the prevailing political ideology.

In sum, "sociology excites a unique set of reactions—it bores some and frightens others. . . . Sociology is extraordinary because it can be regarded as both trivial and threatening" (Walton, 1990:4). Students tend to react to sociology in either of these ways. One reaction is that sociology is the trivial and tedious examination of the obvious. Sociology for them is boring. After all, they have lived in families, communities, and society. They know social life. To them, we argue, immersion in social life does not equate with understanding social life. As Zygmunt Bauman has written:

> Deeply immersed in our daily routines, though, we hardly ever pause to think about the meaning of what we have gone through; even less often have we the opportunity to compare our private experience with the fate of others, to see the *social* in the *individual*, the *general* in the *particular;* this is precisely what sociologists can do for us. (Bauman, 1990:10)

To understand social life requires more than social experiences. It requires a perspective—the sociological perspective—that leads to sociological questions and analysis. With this perspective, students will find excitement and engagement in looking behind the facades of social life and finding patterns in human behaviors (seeing the general in the particular).

A second common reaction by students to sociology is that they find this inquiry threatening. Sociology is subversive. That is, sociology undermines our foundations because it questions all social arrangements, whether religious, political, economic, or familial. Even though this critical approach may be uncomfortable to some people, it is necessary for the understanding of human social arrangements and for finding solutions to social problems. Thus, we ask that you think sociologically. The process may be scary at first, but the results will be enlightenment, interest, and excitement in all things social.

The Historical Development of Sociology

Sociology emerged in western Europe in the late eighteenth century during the Enlightenment (also known as the Age of Reason). Spurred by dramatic social changes such as the Industrial Revolution, the French Revolution, urbanization, and capitalism, intellectuals during this period promoted the ideals of progress, democracy, freedom, individualism, and the scientific method. These ideas replaced those of the old medieval order, where religious dogma and unquestioned obedience to royal authorities dominated. The new intellectuals believed that human beings could solve their social problems. They also believed that society itself could be analyzed rationally. Out of this intellectual mix, several key theorists laid the foundation for contemporary sociological thought. We will focus briefly on the contributions of four: Auguste Comte, Karl Marx, Emile Durkheim, and Max Weber. We will further elaborate on the sociological explanations of Marx, Durkheim, and Weber throughout this book.

Auguste Comte (1798–1857): The Science of Society

The founder of sociology was a Frenchman, Auguste Comte, who coined the word *sociology* from the Latin *socius* (companion, with others) and the Greek *logos* (study of) for the science of society and group life. Comte sought to establish sociology as a science (his initial name for the discipline was *social physics*) using the Enlightenment's emphasis on **positivism** (knowledge based on systematic observation, experiment, and comparison). Comte was convinced that using scientific principles, sociologists could solve social problems such as poverty, crime, and war.

Emile Durkheim (1858–1917): Social Facts and the Social Bond

Durkheim provided the rationale for sociology by emphasizing social facts. His classic work, *Suicide* (Durkheim, 1951, first published in 1897), demonstrates how social factors explain individual behavior (see Chapter 2). Durkheim focused on **social facts,** social factors that exist external to individuals such as tradition, values, laws, religious ideology, and population density. The key for Durkheim was that these factors affect the behaviors of people, thus allowing for sociological explanations rather than biological and psychological reasoning.

Durkheim was also interested in what holds society together. His works show how belief systems bind people together, how public ceremonies and rituals promote solidarity, how labeling some people as deviant reaffirms what society deems to be right, and how similarities (shared traditions, values, ideology) provide the societal glue in traditional societies and differences (division of labor) provide the social bond in complex societies.

Durkheim made invaluable contributions to such core sociological concepts as social roles, socialization, anomie, deviant behavior, social control, and the social bond. In particular, Durkheim's works provide the foundation for the order model that is found throughout this book (see Chapter 3).

Karl Marx (1818–1883): Economic Determinism

Karl Marx devoted his life to analyzing and criticizing the society he observed. He was especially concerned with the gap between the people at the bottom of society and the elite, between the powerless and the powerful, the dominated and the dominant. Marx reasoned that the type of economy found in a society provides its basic structure (system of stratification, unequal distribution of resources, the bias of the law, and ideology). Thus, he was vitally interested in how the economic system of his day—capitalism—shaped society. The owners of capital exploited their workers to extract maximum profits. They used their economic power to keep the less powerful in their place and to benefit unequally from the educational system, the law, and other institutional arrangements in society. These owners of capital (the ruling class) also determined the prevailing ideas in society because they controlled the political system, religion, and media outlets. In this way, members of the working class accept the prevailing ideology. Marx called this **false consciousness** (believing in ideas that are not in their objective interests but rather in the best interests of the capitalist class). Social change occurs when the contradictions inherent in capitalism (see Chapter 13) cause the working class to recognize their oppression and develop **class consciousness** (recognizing their class interests, common oppression, and an understanding of who the oppressors are), resulting in a revolt against the system.

Marx made extraordinary contributions to such core sociological concepts as systems of inequality, social class, power, alienation, and social movements. Marx's view of the world is the foundation of the conflict perspective, which is infused throughout this book.

Max Weber (1864–1920): A Response to Marx

Although it is an oversimplification, it helps to think of Weber's thought as a reaction to the writings of Marx. Marx in his view was too narrowly deterministic. In response, he showed that the basic structure of society comes from three sources: the political, economic, and cultural spheres, not just the economic as Marx argued. Similarly, social class is not just determined by economic resources, but also includes status (prestige) and power dimensions. Political power does not stem just from economic resources, as Marx argued, but also from the expressive qualities of individual leaders (**charisma**). But power can also reside in organizations (not individuals), as Weber showed in his extensive analysis of bureaucracy (see Chapter 2). Weber countered Marx's emphasis on material economic concerns by showing how ideology shapes the economy. Arguably his most important work, *The Protestant Ethic and the Spirit of Capitalism* (Weber, 1958, first published in 1904), demonstrates how a particular type of religious thought (protestant belief system) made capitalism possible. In sum, Weber's importance to sociology is seen in his mighty contributions to core concepts as power, ideology, charisma, bureaucracy, and social change.

Sociological Methods: The Craft of Sociology

Sociology is dependent on reliable data and logical reasoning. These necessities are possible, but there are problems that must be acknowledged. Before we describe how sociologists gather reliable data and make valid conclusions, let us examine the kinds of questions sociologists ask and the two major obstacles sociologists face in obtaining answers to these questions.

Sociological Questions

To begin, sociologists try to ascertain the facts. For example, let's assume that we want to assess the degree to which the public education system provides equal educational opportunities for all youngsters. To determine this, we need to do an empirical investigation to find the facts concerning such items as the amount spent per pupil by school districts within each state and by each state. Within school districts we need to know the facts concerning the distribution of monies by neighborhood schools. Are these monies appropriated equally regardless of the social class or racial composition of the school? Are curriculum offerings the same for girls and boys within a school? Are extra fees charged for participation in extracurricular activities, and does this affect the participation of children by social class?

Sociologists also may ask comparative questions. That is, how does the situation in one social context compare with that in another? Most commonly, these questions involve the comparison of one society with another. Examples here might be the comparisons among industrialized nations on infant mortality, murder, leisure time, or the mathematics scores of sixteen-year-olds.

A third type of question that a sociologist may ask is historical. Sociologists are interested in trends. What are the facts now concerning divorce, crime, political participation, for example, and how have these patterns changed over time?

The three types of questions of sociologists considered so far determine the way things are. But these types of questions are not enough. Sociologists go beyond the factual to ask why. Why have real wages (controlling for inflation) declined since 1973 in the United States? Why are the poor poor? Why do birth rates decline with industrialization? Why is the United States the most violent (as measured by murder, rape, and assault rates) industrialized society? (See "A Closer Look: Sociological Questions" for an example of sociological questions applied to a particular social occurrence.)

A **sociological theory** is a set of ideas that explains a range of human behavior and a variety of social and societal events. "A sociological theory designates those parts of the social world that are especially important, and offers ideas about how the social world works" (Kammeyer, Ritzer, and Yetman, 1997:21).

Chapter 3 provides two competing theories that guide many sociologists. In that chapter there is a quote from Michael Harrington, which says:

> The data of society are, for all practical purposes, infinite. You need criteria that will provisionally permit you to bring some order into that chaos of data and to distinguish between relevant and irrelevant factors. (Harrington, 1985:1)

Thus, theory not only helps us to explain social phenomena, it also guides research.

Problems in Collecting Data

A fundamental problem with the sociological perspective is that bane of the social sciences—objectivity. We are all guilty of harboring stereotyped conceptions of such social categories as African Americans, hard hats, professors, homosexuals, fundamentalists, business tycoons, communists, the rich, the poor, and jocks. Moreover, we interpret events, material objects, and people's behavior through the perceptual filter of our religious and political beliefs. When fundamentalists oppose the use of certain books in school, when abortion is approved by a legislature, when the president advocates cutting billions from the federal budget by eliminating social services, or when the Supreme Court denies private schools the right to exclude certain racial groups, most of us rather easily take a position in the ensuing debate.

Sociologists are caught in a dilemma. On the one hand, they are members of society with beliefs, feelings, and biases. At the same time, though, their professional task is to study society in a disciplined (scientific) way. This latter requirement is that scientist-scholars be dispassionate, objective observers. In short, if they take sides, they lose their status as scientists.

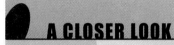

A CLOSER LOOK

Sociological Questions

An article in *The New York Times* (Henneberger and Marriott, 1993) reported a disturbing social trend—male teenagers, apparently to demonstrate their manhood, were abusing or showing disrespect to girls in ever greater numbers. These incidents included verbal abuse, such as yelling explicit propositions, and physical abuse, such as fondling girls and other sexual assaults. This story also reported a nationwide survey of junior high and high school students, which found that more than two-thirds of the girls and 42 percent of the boys reported being touched, grabbed, or pinched on school grounds.

A sociologist interested in adolescence, courtship patterns, or gender might wish to research this apparent trend. The particular research questions of the sociologist depend on his or her interests and theoretical orientation. For our purposes, though, some likely questions might be:

Factual Questions: Is sexually oriented abuse aimed at females by adolescent males common today? The authors of the *New York Times* article interviewed only fifty adolescents. If it is common, is it more an urban phenomenon or is it found in the suburbs and rural areas as well? Is it more concentrated in the Northeast or is it found throughout the United States? Is this behavior pattern more prevalent among the youth in some racial and ethnic groups than others? Is it related to social class? And, if the reported incidents occur most often among the disadvantaged in society, is this an accurate measure or is this the result of the bias of the criminal justice system?

Comparative Questions: Is this trend limited to the United States or is it found in other societies as well?

If so, are these societies similar to the United States in affluence, religious heritage, and economic activities?

Historical Questions: How do the current adolescent behaviors compare with those behaviors at other times in the United States? Have there been times in U.S. history when adolescent gendered behavior was less abusive and more courtly? If so, have the changes become gradually more abusive or has sexual abuse among teenagers varied according to some social condition such as the level of economic affluence or gender inequality?

Theoretical Questions: Assuming that the facts indicate that male teenagers are especially abusive to females now, the important question is why? Sociologists persuaded by the theoretical perspective of the order model (which is discussed in Chapter 3), might ask questions such as: How have the socialization patterns of youth changed from an earlier, more genteel time? Is the loosening of family ties (higher separation/divorce/remarriage) the reason? Are these behavioral changes congruent with the changes in values? Are changing gender roles invoking this hostile response by males? Is this type of violence the result of a culture of poverty that idealizes a tough "macho" image. Conflict theorists, on the other hand, would ask quite different questions: Are patterns of male aggression toward females correlated with poverty rates, unemployment rates, and low wage rates? Is this form of violence related to a changing economy in which opportunities are becoming more limited because of technology and global competition? Does male abuse of females increase as the degree of inequality in a society increases?

This ideal of **value neutrality** (to be absolutely free of bias in research) can be attacked from three positions. The first is that scientists should not be morally indifferent to the implications of their research. Gouldner has argued this in the following statement:

> It would seem that social science's affinity for modeling itself after physical science might lead to instruction in matters other than research alone. Before Hiroshima, physi-

cists also talked of a value-free science; they, too, vowed to make no value judgments. Today many of them are not so sure. If we today concern ourselves exclusively with the technical proficiency of our students and reject all responsibility for their moral sense, or lack of it, then we may someday be compelled to accept responsibility for having trained a generation willing to serve in a future Auschwitz. Granted that science always has inherent in it both constructive and destructive potentialities. It does not follow from this that we should encourage our students to be oblivious to the difference. (Gouldner, 1962:212)

The second argument against the purely neutral position is that such a stance is impossible. Becker, among others, has argued that there is no dilemma—because it is impossible to do research that is uncontaminated by personal and political sympathies (Becker, 1967). This argument is based on several related assumptions. One is that the values of the scholar-researcher enter into the choices of what questions will be asked and how they will be answered. For example, in the study of poverty a critical decision involves the object of the study—the poor or the system that tends to perpetuate poverty among a certain segment of society. Or, in the study of the problems of youth, we can ask either of these questions: Why are some youths troublesome for adults? or, Why do adults make so much trouble for youths? In both illustrations, quite different questions will yield very different results.

Similarly, our values lead us to decide from which vantage point we will gain access to information about a particular social organization. If they want to understand how a prison operates, researchers must determine whether they want a description from the inmates, from the guards, from the prison administrators, or from the state board of corrections. Each view provides useful insights about a prison, but obviously a biased one. If they obtain data from more than one of these levels, researchers are faced with making assessments as to which is the more accurate view, clearly another place in the research process where the values of the observers have an impact.

Perhaps the most important reason the study of social phenomena cannot be value-free is that the type of problems researched and the strategies used tend either to support the existing societal arrangements or to undermine them. Seen in this way, social research of both types is political. Ironically, however, there is a strong tendency to label only the research aimed at changing the system as political. By the same token, whenever the research sides with the powerless, the implication is that the hierarchical system is being questioned—thus, the charge that this type of research is biased. Becker has provided us with the logic of this viewpoint:

> When do we accuse ourselves and our fellow sociologists of bias? I think an inspection of representative instances would show that the accusation arises, in one important class of cases, when the research gives credence, in any serious way, to the perspective of the subordinate group in some hierarchical relationship. In the case of deviance, the hierarchical relationship is a moral one. The superordinate parties in the relationships are those who represent the forces of approved and official morality; the subordinate parties are those who, it is alleged, have violated that morality. . . . It is odd that, when we perceive bias, we usually see it in these circumstances. It is odd because it is easily ascertained that a great many more studies are biased in the direction of the interests of responsible officials than the other way around. (Becker, 1967:240, 242)

In summary, bias is inevitable in the study and analysis of social problems. The choice of a research problem, the perspective from which one analyzes the problems, and the solutions proposed all reflect a bias that either supports the existing social arrangements or does not. Moreover, unlike biologists, who can dispassionately observe the behavior of an amoeba under a microscope, sociologists are participants in the social life they seek to study and understand. As they study race riots in cities, children living in poverty, or urban blight, sociologists cannot escape from their own feelings and values. They must, however, not let their feelings and values render their analysis invalid. In other words, research and reports of research must reflect reality, not as the researcher might want it to be. Sociologists must display scientific integrity, which requires recognizing biases in such a way that these biases do not invalidate the findings (Berger, 1963:5). Properly done in this spirit, an atheist can study a religious sect, a pacifist can study the military-industrial complex, a divorcee can study marriage, and a person who abhors the beliefs of the Ku Klux Klan can study that organization and its members.

In addition to bias, people gather data and make generalizations about social phenomena in a number of faulty ways. In a sense everyone is a scientist seeking to find valid generalizations to guide behavior and make sense of the world. But most people are, in fact, very unscientific about the social world. The first problem, as we have noted, is the problem of bias. The second is that people tend to generalize from their experience. Not only is one's interpretation of things that happen to him or her subjective, but there also is a basic problem of sampling. The chances are that one's experience will be too idiosyncratic to allow for an accurate generalization. For example, if you and your friends agree that abortion is appropriate, that does not mean that other people in the society, even those of your age, will agree with you. Very likely, your friends are quite similar to you on such dimensions as socioeconomic status, race, religion, and geographic location.

Another instance of faulty sampling leading to faulty generalizations is when we make assumptions from a single case. An individual may argue that Blacks can succeed economically in this country as easily as Whites because he or she knows a wealthy Black person. Similarly, one might argue that all Latinos are dumb because the one you know is in the slowest track in high school. This type of reasoning is especially fallacious because it blames the victim (Ryan, 1976). The cause of poverty or crime or dropping out of school or scoring low on an IQ test is seen as a result of the flaw in the individual, ignoring the substantial impact of the economy or school.

Another typical way that we explain social behavior is to use some authority other than our senses. The Bible, for example, has been used by many persons to support or condemn activities such as slavery, capital punishment, war, or monogamy. The media provide other sources of authority for individuals. The media, however, are not always reliable sources of facts. Stories are often selected because they are unusually dramatic, giving the faulty impression of, for example, a crime wave or questionable air safety (see "Research Methods: Minimizing Bias").

Our judgments and interpretations are also affected by prevailing myths and stereotypes. We just "know" certain things to be true, when, actually, they may be contradicted by scientific evidence. As examples, six common beliefs about the poor and racial minorities are presented and discussed.

Research Methods

Minimizing Bias

S ocial scientists must contend with the essential problem of credibility of their research. How is objectivity possible, though, when they cannot escape their personal values, biases, and opinions? The answer lies in the norms of science.

Sociologists share with other scientists norms for conducting research that minimize personal bias. Their research must reflect the standards of science before it is accepted in scholarly journals. These journals function as gate-keepers for a discipline. What they accept for publication is assumed by their readers to be scientific. The editors of scholarly journals send manuscripts to referees who are unaware of the identity of the authors. This system of anonymity allows the referees to make objective judgments about the credibility of the studies. They review, among other things, the methods used to assess validity and reliability. Validity is the degree to which a study actually measures what it purports to measure. Reliability is the degree to which another study repeating the same methods would yield the same results.

To guide sociologists, their professional association— the American Sociological Association—has a code of ethics, which includes a number of standards for objectivity and integrity in sociological research.

1. Sociologists should adhere to the highest possible technical standards in their research, teaching and practice.

2. Since individual sociologists vary in their research modes, skills, and experience, sociologists should always set forth ex ante the limits of their knowledge and the disciplinary and personal limitations that condition the validity of findings which affect whether or not a research project can be successfully completed.

3. In practice or other situations in which sociologists are requested to render a professional judgment, they should accurately and fairly represent their areas and degrees of expertise.

4. In presenting their work, sociologists are obligated to report their findings fully and should not misrepresent the findings of their research. When work is presented, they are obligated to report their findings fully and without omission of significant data. To the best of their ability, sociologists should also disclose details of their theories, methods and research designs that might bear upon interpretations of research findings.

5. Sociologists must report fully all sources of financial support in their publications and must note any special relations to any sponsor.

6. Sociologists must not accept grants, contracts or research assignments that appear likely to require violation of the principles enunciated in this Code, and should dissociate themselves from research when they discover a violation and are unable to achieve its correction.

7. Sociologists have the obligation to disseminate research findings, except those likely to cause harm to clients, collaborators and participants, or those which are proprietary under a formal or informal agreement.

8. In their roles as practitioners, researchers, teachers, and administrators, sociologists have an important social responsibility because their recommendations, decisions, and actions may alter the lives of others. They should be aware of the situations and pressures that might lead to the misuse of their influence and authority. In these various roles, sociologists should also recognize that professional problems and conflicts may interfere with professional effectiveness. Sociologists should take steps to insure that these conflicts do not produce deleterious results for clients, research participants, colleagues, students and employees.

Source: Excerpted from American Sociological Association, "Code of Ethics," (Washington, D.C.: American Sociological Association, August 14, 1989), pp. 2–3.

1. *Most homeless people are disabled by drugs, mental disease, or physical afflictions.* The facts show, however, that the homeless, for the most part, are not "deficient and defective" but rather not much different than the nonhomeless. People are

not homeless because of their individual flaws but because of structural arrangements and trends that result in extreme impoverishment and a shortage of affordable housing (Timmer, Eitzen, and Talley, 1994).

2. *Adolescent Blacks are more likely than adolescent Whites to use drugs.* The truth
is that Black youth are *less* likely to use drugs than White youth. In 1992 Louis Sullivan, then Secretary of Health and Human Services said, "Our studies show that
contrary to many misconceptions, these youngsters [African Americans] are less
likely to use alcohol and other drugs than are kids from other ethnic groups"
(quoted in Sklar, 1993b:55).

3. *Welfare makes people dependent, lazy, and unmotivated.* Contrary to this image,
however, the evidence is that most daughters of welfare recipients do *not* become
welfare recipients as adults (Sklar, 1993a). Put another way, most women on welfare did not receive welfare as children (Center on Social Welfare and Law, 1996).

4. *Welfare is given more generously to the poor than to the nonpoor.* Farm subsidies, tax deductibility for taxes and interest on homes, low-interest loans to students
and victims of disasters, and pork-barrel projects are examples of government welfare and even the dependency of nonpoor people on government largesse. Most significant, these government handouts to the nonpoor are significantly greater than
the amounts given to the poor (see Chapters 10 and 14).

5. *Blacks are similar in their behaviors.* Blacks are *not* a monolithic group, with
members acting more or less alike. A study by the Rand Corporation, for example,
found that about one in one hundred young, high-ability, affluent Black women
from homes with two parents become single, teenage mothers (for White women
in this category, the chances were one in one thousand, explained, in part, by the
much greater willingness to use abortion). In contrast, a poor Black teenager from
a female-headed household who scores low on standardized tests has a one in four
probability of becoming an unwed teenage mother (for White women in this category, the odds were one in twelve) (cited in Luker, 1991:76–77). In the words of
Kristin Luker, "Unwed motherhood thus reflects the intersecting influences of race,
class, and gender; race and class each has a distinct impact on the life histories of
young women" (Luker, 1991:77).

6. *Unmarried women are having children to increase their welfare payments.* Three
facts show that this belief of political conservatives is a myth (Carville, 1996:23–24;
Males, 1996): (*a*) Since 1972, the value of the average Aid to Families with Dependent Children (AFDC) check has declined by 40 percent, yet the ratio of out-of-wedlock births has risen in the same period by 140 percent; (*b*) states that have lower
welfare benefits usually have more out-of-wedlock births than states with higher
benefits; and (*c*) the teen out-of-wedlock birth rate in the United States is much
higher than the rate in countries where welfare benefits are much more generous.

Conventional wisdom is not always wrong, but when it is it can lead to faulty
generalizations and bad public policy. Therefore, it is imperative to know the facts,
rather than accept myths as real.

A similar problem occurs when we use aphorisms to explain social occurrences. The problem with this common tactic is that society supplies us with ready

explanations that fit contradictory situations and are therefore useless. For instance, if we know a couple who are alike in religion, race, socioeconomic status, and political attitudes, that makes sense to us because "birds of a feather flock together." But the opposite situation also makes sense. If partners in a relationship are very different on a number of dimensions, we can explain this by the obvious explanation—"opposites attract." We use a number of other proverbs to explain behavior. The problem is that there is often a proverb or aphorism to explain the other extreme:

- Absence makes the heart grow fonder.
  Out of sight, out of mind.
- Look before you leap.
  He who hesitates is lost.
- Familiarity breeds contempt.
  To know her is to love her.
- Women are unpredictable.
  Isn't that just like a woman.
- You can't teach an old dog new tricks.
  It's never too late to learn.
- Above all, to thine own self be true.
  When in Rome, do as the Romans do.
- Variety is the spice of life.
  Never change horses in the middle of the stream.
- Two heads are better than one.
  If you want something done right, do it yourself.
- You can't tell a book by its cover.
  Clothes make the man.
- Many hands make light work.
  Too many cooks spoil the broth.
- Better safe than sorry.
  Nothing ventured, nothing gained.
- Haste makes waste.
  Strike while the iron is hot.
- Work, for the night is coming.
  Eat, drink, and be merry for tomorrow you may die.
- There's no place like home.
  The grass is always greener on the other side of the fence.

These contradictory explanations are commonly used and, of course, explain nothing. The job of the sociologist is to specify under what conditions certain rates of social behaviors occur.

Sources of Data

Sociologists do not use aphorisms to explain behavior, nor do they speculate based on faulty samples or authorities. Because we are part of the world that is to be explained, sociologists must obtain evidence that is beyond reproach. In addition to observing scrupulously the canons of science, there are four basic sources of data that yield valid results for sociologists: survey research, experiments, observation, and the use of existing documents. We describe these techniques only briefly here.*

Survey Research. Sociologists are interested in obtaining information about certain kinds of persons. They may want to know how political beliefs and behaviors are influenced by differences in sex, race, ethnicity, religion, and social class. Or sociologists may wish to know whether religious attitudes are related to racial antipathy. They may want to determine whether poor people have different values from other people in society, the answer to which will have a tremendous impact on the ultimate solution to poverty.

To answer these and similar questions, the sociologist may use personal interviews or written questionnaires to gather the data. The researcher may obtain information from all possible subjects or from a selected **sample** (a representative part of a population). Because the former method is often impractical, a random sample of subjects is selected from the larger population. If the sample is selected scientifically, a relatively small proportion can yield satisfactory results—that is, the inferences made from the sample will be reliable about the entire population. For example, a probability sample of only 2,000 from a total population of 1 million can provide data very close to what would be discovered if a survey were taken of the entire 1 million.

Typically with survey research, sociologists use sophisticated statistical techniques to control the contaminating effects of confounding variables to determine whether the findings could have occurred by chance or not, to determine whether variables are related, and to see whether such a relationship is a causal one. A **variable** is an attitude, behavior, or condition that can vary in magnitude and significance from case to case.

Experiments. To understand the cause-and-effect relationship among a few variables, sociologists use controlled experiments. Let us assume, for example, that we want to test whether White students in interracial classrooms have more positive attitudes toward Blacks than Whites in segregated classrooms have toward them. Using the experimental method, the researcher would take a number of White students previously unexposed to Blacks in school and randomly assign a subset to an integrated classroom situation. Before actual contact with the Blacks, however, all the White students would be given a test of their racial attitudes. This pretest establishes a benchmark from which to measure any changes in attitudes. One group, the control group, continues school in segregated classrooms. (The **control group** is a group of subjects not exposed to the independent variable.) The other group, the experimental group, now has Blacks as classmates. (The **experimental group** is a group of subjects who are exposed to the independent variable.) Otherwise, the

---

*See the bibliography at the end of the chapter for references on the methods of sociology. Methodological footnotes and "Research Methods" panels focusing on methodological issues and procedures appear occasionally throughout this book to give insight into how sociologists obtain, analyze, and interpret data.

two groups are the same. Following a suitable period of time, the Whites in both groups are tested again (posttest) for their racial attitudes. If the experimental group is found to differ from the control group in racial attitudes (the dependent variable), then it is assumed that interracial contact (the independent variable) is the source of the change. (The **dependent variable** is a variable that is influenced by the effect of another variable. The **independent variable** is a variable that affects another variable.) As an example of a less contrived experiment, a researcher can test the results of two different treatments on the subsequent behavior of juvenile delinquents. Delinquent boys who had been adjudicated by the courts can be randomly assigned to a boys' industrial school or a group home facility in the community. After release from incarceration, records are kept on the boys' subsequent behavior in school (grades, truancy, formal reprimands) and in the community (police contacts, work behavior). If the boys from the two groups differ appreciably, then we can say with assurance, because the boys were randomly assigned to each group, that the difference in treatment (the independent variable) was the source of the difference in behavior (the dependent variable).

Observation.   The researcher, without intervention, can observe as accurately as possible what occurs in a community, group, or social event. This type of procedure is especially helpful in understanding such social phenomena as the decision-making process, the stages of a riot, the attraction of cults for their members, or the depersonalization of patients in a mental hospital. Case studies of entire communities have been very instrumental in the understanding of power structures (e.g., Hunter, 1953; Dahl, 1961) and the complex interaction patterns of cities (Whyte, 1988). Long-time participant observation studies of slum neighborhoods and gangs have been insightful in showing the social organization present in what the casual observer might think of as disorganized activity (e.g., Whyte, 1956; Gans, 1962; Liebow, 1967).

Existing Sources.   The sociologist can also use existing data to test theories. The most common sources of information are the various agencies of the government. Data are provided for the nation, regions, states, communities, and census tracts on births, deaths, income, education, unemployment, business activity, health delivery systems, prison populations, military spending, poverty, migration, and the like. Important information can also be obtained from such sources as business firms, athletic teams and leagues, unions, and professional associations. Statistical techniques can be used with these data to describe populations and the effects of social variables on various dependent variables.

CHAPTER REVIEW

1. Sociology is the science dealing with social forces—the forces outside us that shape our lives, interests, and personalities. Sociologists, then, work to discover the underlying order of social life and the principles regarding it that explain human behavior.

2. The assumptions of the sociological perspective are that (*a*) individuals are, by their nature, social beings; (*b*) individuals are socially determined; and (*c*) individuals create, sustain, and change the social forms within which they conduct their lives.

3. Sociology is uncomfortable for many people because it looks behind the facades of social life. This requires a critical examination of society that questions the existing myths, stereotypes, and official dogma.

4. The basis for the critical stance of sociologists is that the social world is not sacred because it is made by human beings.

5. Sociological research involves four types of questions: factual, comparative, historical, and theoretical.

6. The development of sociology was dependent on four European intellectuals: (*a*) Auguste Comte was the founder of sociology. His emphasis was on a rigorous use of the scientific method. (*b*) Emile Durkheim emphasized social facts (sociological explanation for human behavior) and the social bond. (*c*) Karl Marx wrote about the importance of economics in understanding social stratification, power, and ideology. (*d*) Max Weber, in reaction to Marx, demonstrated that social life is multidimensional and that ideology shapes the economy.

7. Sociology is dependent on reliable data and logical reasoning. Although value neutrality is impossible in the social sciences, bias is minimized by the norms of science.

8. Survey research is a systematic means of gathering data to obtain information about people's behaviors, attitudes, and opinions.

9. Sociologists may use experiments to assess the effects of social factors on human behavior. One of two similar groups—the experimental group—is exposed to an independent variable. If this group later differs from the control group, then the independent variable is known to have produced the effect.

10. Observation is another technique for obtaining reliable information. Various social organizations such as prisons, hospitals, schools, churches, cults, families, communities, and corporations can be studied and understood through systematic observation.

11. Sociologists also use existing sources of data to test their theories.

12. Sociology is a science, and the rules of scientific research guide the efforts of sociologists to discover the principles of social organization and the sources of social constraints on human behavior.

KEY TERMS

Sociology	Class consciousness	Control group
Social determinism	Charisma	Experimental group
Human agency	Sociological theory	Dependent variable
Positivism	Value neutrality	Independent variable
Social facts	Sample	
False consciousness	Variable	

STUDY QUESTIONS

1. How would sociologists differ from psychologists in studying such phenomena as divorce or racism?

2. Peter Berger has said that "the sociological perspective involves a process of 'seeing through' the facades of social structure." What does this mean? Give examples.

3. To what extent are you shaped by your social environment? Provide examples of the social facts (Durkheim) that affect you.

4. Speculate (sociologically) on why sociology developed where and when it did.

5. Are you comfortable or uncomfortable with the sociological perspective? Elaborate.

6. How do sociologists minimize bias in their research activities?

FOR FURTHER READING

The Sociological Perspective

Zygmunt Bauman, *Thinking Sociologically* (Cambridge, MA: Basil Blackwell, 1990).

Bennett M. Berger (ed.), *Authors of Their Own Lives: Intellectual Autobiographies by Twenty American Sociologists* (Berkeley: University of California Press, 1990).

Peter L. Berger, *Invitation to Sociology: A Humanistic Perspective* (Garden City, NY: Doubleday Anchor Books, 1963).

Peter Berger and Hansfried Kellner, *Sociology Reinterpreted* (Garden City, NY: Doubleday Anchor Books, 1981).

Randall Collins, *Sociological Insight,* 2nd ed. (New York: Oxford University Press, 1992).

Ann Game and Andrew Metcalfe, *Passionate Sociology* (Thousand Oaks, CA: Sage Publications, 1996).

C. Wright Mills, *The Sociological Imagination* (New York: Oxford University Press, 1959).

John Walton, *Sociology and Critical Inquiry: The Work, Tradition, and Purpose,* 2nd ed. (Belmont, CA: Wadsworth, 1990).

The Historical Development of Sociology

Tom Campbell, *Seven Theories of Human Society* (New York: Oxford University Press, 1981).

Randall Collins and Michael Makowsky, *The Discovery of Society,* 3rd ed. (New York: Random House, 1984).

R. P. Cuzzort, *Humanity and Modern Sociological Thought* (New York: Holt, Rinehart and Winston, 1969).

Charles Lemert (ed.), *Social Theory: The Multicultural & Classic Readings* (Boulder, CO: Westview Press, 1993).

Ken Morrison, *Marx, Durkheim, Weber: Formations of Modern Social Thought* (Thousand Oaks, CA: Sage Publications, 1995).

George Ritzer, *Sociological Theory,* 3rd ed. (New York: McGraw-Hill, 1992).

The Craft of Sociology

Earl R. Babbie, *The Practice of Social Research,* 6th ed. (Belmont, CA: Wadsworth, 1992).

Kenneth R. Hoover, *The Elements of Social Scientific Thinking,* 5th ed. (New York: St. Martin's, 1991).

Robert B. Smith, *An Introduction to Social Research:* Volume I of *Handbook of Social Science Methods* (Cambridge, MA: Ballinger, 1983).

CHAPTER 2

The Structure of Social Groups

An experiment was conducted some years ago when twenty-four previously unacquainted boys, age twelve, were brought together at a summer camp (Sherif and Sherif, 1966). For three days the boys, who were unaware that they were part of an experiment, participated in campwide activities. During this period the camp counselors (actually, they were research assistants) observed the friendship patterns that emerged naturally. The boys were then divided into two groups of twelve. The boys were deliberately separated in order to break up the previous friendship patterns. The groups were then isolated from each other for five days. During this period the boys were left alone by the counselors so that what occurred was the spontaneous result of the boys' behavior. The experimenters found that in both groups there developed (1) a division of labor; (2) a hierarchical structure of ranks—that is, differences among the boys in power, prestige, and rewards; (3) the creation of rules; (4) punishments for violations of the rules; (5) argot—that is, specialized language such as nicknames and group symbols that served as positive ingroup identifications; and (6) member cooperation to achieve group goals.

This experiment illustrates the process of social organization. The counselors did not insist that these phenomena occur in each group. They seemed to occur naturally. In fact, they happen universally (see Whyte, 1956; Liebow, 1967). The goals of this chapter are to understand the components of social structure that emerge and how these components operate to constrain behavior. Although the process is generally the same regardless of group size, we examine it at two levels—the micro level and the societal level.

The Micro Level

The Process of Social Organization

Social organization refers to the ways in which human conduct becomes socially organized, that is, the observed regularities in the behavior of people that are due to the social conditions in which they find themselves rather than to their physiological or psychological characteristics as individuals (Blau and Scott, 1962:2). The social conditions that constrain behavior can be divided into two types: (1) **social structure**—the structure of behavior in groups and society; and (2) **culture**—the shared beliefs of group members that unite them and guide their behavior.

Social Structure. **Sociology** is the study of the patterns that emerge when people interact over time. The emphasis is on the linkages and networks that emerge and that transform an aggregate of individuals into a group. (An **aggregate** is a collection of individuals who happen to be at the same place at the same time. A **group** is a collection of people who, because of sustained interaction, have evolved a common structure and culture.) We begin, then, with social interaction. When the actions of one person affect another person, **social interaction** occurs. The most common method is communication through speech, the written word, or a symbolic act such as a wink, a wave of the hand, or the raising of a finger (which one is often crucial).

Behavior can also be altered by the mere presence of other people. The way we behave (from the way we eat to what we think) is affected by whether we are alone or with other people. Even physical reactions such as crying, laughing, or passing gas are controlled by the individual because of the fear of embarrassment. It could even be argued that, except in the most extreme cases, people's actions are always oriented toward other human beings whether other people are physically present or not. We, as individuals, are constantly concerned about the expected or actual reactions of other people. Even when alone, an individual may not act in certain ways because of having been taught that such actions are wrong.

Social interaction may be either transitory or enduring. Sociologists are interested in the latter type because only then does patterned behavior occur. A case of enduring social interaction is a **social relationship.** Relationships occur for a number of reasons: sexual attraction, familial ties, a common interest (for example, collecting coins or growing African violets), a common political or religious ideology, cooperation to produce or distribute a product, or propinquity (neighbors). Regardless of the specific reasons, the members of a social relationship are united at least in some minimal way with the other members. Most important, the members of a social relationship behave quite differently than they would as participants in a fleeting interaction.

Once the interaction is perpetuated, the behavior of the participants is profoundly altered. An autonomous individual is similar to an element in chemistry.

As soon as there is a chemical reaction between them, however, the two elements become parts of a new entity, as Olsen has noted.

> The concepts of "elements" and "parts" are analogous to terms in chemistry. By themselves, chemical elements— sodium and chlorine, for instance—exhibit characteristics peculiarly their own, by which each can be separately identified. This condition holds true even if elements are mixed together, as long as there is no chemical reaction between them. Through a process of chemical interaction, however, the elements can join to form an entirely new substance—in this case, salt. The elements of sodium and chlorine have now both lost their individual identities and characteristics, and have instead become parts of a more inclusive chemical compound, which has properties not belonging to either of its component parts by themselves. In an emergent process such as this, the original elements are transformed into parts of a new entity. (Olsen, 1976:37)

Olsen's description of a chemical reaction is also appropriate for what arises in a social relationship. Most sociologists assume that the whole is not identical to the sum of its parts—that is, through the process of enduring interaction something is created with properties different from the component parts.* The two groups of boys artificially formed at the summer camp, for example, developed similar structural properties regardless of the unique personalities of the boys in each group. Although groups may differ in size or purpose, they are similar in structure and in the processes that create the structure. In other words, one group may exist to knit quilts for charity while another may do terrorist bombings, but they will be alike in many important ways. Their social structure involves the patterns of interaction that emerge, the division of labor, and the linking and hierarchy of positions. The social structure is an emergent phenomenon bringing order and predictability to social life within the group.

Culture.   The other component of social organization is culture—the shared beliefs of a group's members that serve to guide conduct. Through enduring social interaction common expectations emerge about how people should act. These expectations are called **norms.** Criteria for judging what is appropriate, correct, moral, and important also emerge. These criteria are the **values** of the group. Also part of the shared beliefs are the expectations group members have of individuals occupying the various positions within the group. These are **social roles.** The elements of culture are described briefly below for the micro and macro levels and in detail in Chapter 4. To summarize, social organization refers to both culture and social structure. Blau and Scott describe how they operate to constrain human behavior:

> The prevailing cultural standards and the structure of social relations serve to organize human conduct in the collectivity. As people conform more or less closely to the

---

*This assumption—the **realist position**—is one side of a fundamental philosophical debate. The **nominalist position,** on the other hand, argues that to know the parts is to know the whole. In sociology the realist position is dominant and is found especially in the works of Emile Durkheim (1958) and the contemporary classic by Charles Warriner (1956). The minority nominalist position in sociology is represented most prominently by George Homans (1964).

expectations of their fellows, and as the degree of their conformity in turn influences their relations with others and their social status, and as their status in turn further affects the inclinations to adhere to social norms and their chances to achieve valued objectives, their patterns of behavior become socially organized. (Blau and Scott, 1962:4–5)

Norms

All social organizations have rules (norms) that specify appropriate and inappropriate behaviors. In essence, norms are the behavioral expectations that members of a particular group collectively share. They ensure that action within social organizations is generally predictable.

Some norms are not considered as important as others and consequently are not severely punished if violated. These minor rules are called **folkways.** Folkways vary, of course, from group to group. A particular fraternity may expect its members to wear formal dress on certain occasions. In a church, wine may be consumed by the parishioners at the appropriate time—communion. To bring one's own bottle of wine to communion, however, would be a violation of the folkways of that church. (Could you imagine an announcement in your church bulletin that communion will be next Sunday—B.Y.O.B.?) These examples show that folkways involve etiquette, customs, and regulations that, if violated, do not threaten the fabric of the social organization.

The violation of the group's mores, on the other hand, is considered important enough that it must be punished severely. (**Mores** are important norms, the violation of which results in severe punishment.) This type of norm involves morality—in fact, mores can be thought of as moral imperatives. In a sorority, for instance, examples of the mores might be disloyalty, stealing from a sister, and conduct that brings shame to the organization, such as blatant sexual promiscuity.

Status and Role

One important aspect of social structure is comprised of the positions of a social organization. If one determines what positions are present in an organization and how they are interrelated (hierarchy, reciprocal pairs, etc.), then the analyst has a structural map of that social group. The existence of positions in organizations has an important consequence for individuals—the bestowing of a social identity. Each of us belongs to a number of organizations, and in each we occupy a position, or **status.** If you were asked, "Who are you?," chances are you would respond by listing your various statuses. An individual may at the same time be a student, sophomore, daughter, sister, friend, female, Baptist, Sunday school teacher, Democrat, sales clerk, U.S. citizen, and secretary-treasurer of the local chapter of Weight Watchers.

The individual's social identity, then, is a product of the particular matrix of statuses that she or he occupies. Another characteristic of statuses that has an important influence on social identity is that these positions in organizations tend to be differentially rewarded and esteemed. This element of **hierarchy** (the arrangement of people in order of importance) of status reinforces the positive or negative image individuals have of themselves depending on placement in various organizations. Some individuals consistently hold prestigious positions (bank president, deacon, Caucasian, male, chairman of United Fund), while others may hold only those statuses negatively esteemed (welfare recipient, aged, Latino, janitor), and some people occupy mixed statuses (bus driver, 32nd-degree Mason, union member, church trustee).

Group memberships are vital sources of our notion of our own identity. Similarly, when they know of our status in various organizations, other people assign a social identity to us. When we determine a person's age, race, religion, and occupation, we tend to stereotype that person—that is, we assume that the individual is a certain type. Stereotyping has the effect of conferring a social identity on that person, raising expectations for certain behaviors that, very often, result in a self-fulfilling prophecy.

The mapping of statuses provides important clues about the social structure of an organization, but the most important aspect of status is the behavior expected of the occupant of a status. To determine that an individual occupies the status of father does not tell us much about what the group expects of a father. In some societies, for example, the biological father has no legal, monetary, or social responsibility for his children, who are cared for by the mother and her brother. In U.S. society, there are norms (legal and informal) that demand that the father be responsible for his children. Not only must he provide for them, but he must also, depending on the customs of the family, be a disciplinarian, buddy, teacher, Santa Claus, and tooth fairy.

The behavior expected of a person occupying a status in a group is that person's **role*** (the behavioral expectations and requirements attached to a position in a social organization). The norms of the social organization constrain the incumbents in a status to behave in prescribed and therefore predictable ways, regardless of their particular personalities. Society insists that we play our roles correctly (see "Other Societies: Women in Moslem Societies"). To do otherwise is to risk being judged by other people as abnormal, crazy, incompetent, and/or immature. These pressures to conform to role demands ensure that there is stability in social groups even though member turnover occurs. For example, ministers to a particular congregation come and go, but certain actions are predictable in particular incumbents because of the demands on their behavior. These demands come from the hierarchy of the denomination, from other ministers, and most assuredly from the members of the parish. The stability imposed by role is also seen with other statuses, such as professor, janitor, police officer, student, and even president of the United States.

The organizational demands on members in the various statuses do not make behavior totally predictable, however. Occupants of the statuses can vary within limits. There are at least three reasons for this. First, personality variables can

---

*This section introduces the concept of role as it is appropriate to the context of social organization. We elaborate on it in Chapter 4.

Other Societies
Other Ways

Women in Moslem Societies

Wearing a headscarf and a floor-length dress under her white lab coat, Majida Agal seems out of place in the hi-tech lab of a Persian Gulf scientific institute. But the 23-year-old physics graduate finds nothing incompatible in working with lasers and fundamentalist Islam.

"People are afraid of Moslems, and they should be," she says. "Our real strength is in Islam. We are nothing without it."

Part of that strength must be needed to wear an *abbayah*—the head-to-toe black cloak that is mandatory religious apparel for women—in the 110-degree inferno that is Kuwait. For Majida, the apparent restrictions of her costume are a symbol of freedom. "I wasn't born like this. I decided to wear this uniform. It means I will not respond to just anyone."

Although Kuwaiti women are among the most highly educated in the Middle East, she doesn't believe they deserve the right to vote. "There are not so many really enlightened women," she sighs. "I don't care whether women are treated equally with men, because in this life we don't see justice. We live and die being tested."

Majida is chided by friend and chemist Anal Al-Mosler for taking her devotion to Islam only so far. Anal, who wears a skirt and jacket, says she would wear traditional Islamic dress only if she believed in a few basic rules.

"First, I should not work with men. I shouldn't go outside. Actually, if a man hears my voice, it is not good."

A World of Difference

But such "basic rules"—and their interpretation—vary from country to country. "Women in Indonesia

have a different attitude to themselves than women in Saudi Arabia, Morocco, Africa or China. They may have this common denominator of religion, but the way it is practiced is extremely different."

And it is changing—for many reasons, including the Persian Gulf War. Just how did the war affect these women? According to Moslem historian Rana Kabbani, there are no pat answers.

"Some women will become more fundamental because of their experience, others will move politically to the left. The view that somehow in these countries women have a homogeneously repressed time is a very superficial view of what Moslem women's lives are like."

While life is hard for women in Yemen, where female mortality is high because men traditionally control health care, in Iraq, women are doctors, pharmacists, teachers and civil servants. In Saudi Arabia, not all women are banned from driving—only the educated and upper class Bedouin women drive pick-up trucks and other work vehicles.

Even when religious laws regarding women seem straightforward, they are not. Under the law School of the Twelve Shi'ia, Iranian women can be publicly flogged and stoned to death for adultery. Yet, the practice of *mut'a,* or temporary marriage—which can last from one hour to 99 years and requires neither a witness nor a legal document—has resurfaced in the past decade. Although acceptable to Shi'ite religious scholars, in other countries it is considered legalized prostitution.

Veiled References

Moslem women were thrown into the international spotlight during the Gulf War, as their veiled visages

account for variations in the behavior of persons holding identical status. People can be conformist or unconventional, manipulated or manipulators, passive or aggressive, followers or inspirational leaders, cautious or impetuous, ambitious or

peered nightly from the television screen. For most Westerners, the veil is a symbol of oppression. But for Moslem women—especially today—the meaning of the veil runs the gamut.

In Kabbani's Syrian family, the veil was something her grandmother, inspired by Western suffragettes, tore off in the beginning of this century. Kabbani's secular mother raised her daughter in a similar way. In many countries, however, women of Kabbani's generation and younger are voluntarily donning the *hijab,* or Islamic headdress.

"A lot of these women are not from families that traditionally wore the *hijab.* For want of a better reason, I think you could call it Islamic militantism, but it is more of a disappointment with Western culture and with local government's inability to solve outstanding problems like the economy and the Palestinian issue. These societies are not what everybody hoped they would become after independence. This is why a lot of women across the Moslem world—from Malaysia to Morocco—have taken on the *hijab* in large numbers."

Like the names that describe it, the Islamic dress for women has many variations. Called the *chadoor* in Iran, the *milayah* in Egypt, the *yashmak* in Turkey and the *djellbah* and *haik* in North Africa, the veil has become a chic radical fashion statement. In Egypt, young women professionals are voluntarily wearing it in such great numbers that Cairo fashion shows introduce the latest styles. Polls have shown that for many Moslem women, choosing the traditional headdress is more a matter of style than the symbol of repression Westerners see. Meanwhile, in Turkey and Western countries such as Britain and France, Moslem schoolgirls clamour to wear traditional dress in public schools.

With more than 800 million adherents, Islam is the world's fastest-growing religion. Through conquest and trade, it spread as far west as Spain and east as Malaysia and the Philippines. There are Moslem Iranian and Turkish speakers in the Balkans and the Central Asian Republic, as well as along China's Silk Route. In Pakistan, Bangladesh and north India, Islam has already influenced Sikh and Hindu conventions. Twenty years ago in Africa, it was mainly located in the north. Now, the religion stretches throughout the continent.

Contentious Clothing

Contrary to popular belief, there was no concept of veiling in 7th-century Arabia, the debauched society that gave birth to Islam. Like Christianity and Judaism, the Islamic *Qur'an* calls for modesty in both sexes. Women were told to cover that which was uncovered—their breasts.

The wives of the Prophet Mohammed first adopted veiling after being insulted at the mosque by worshippers who mistook them for slaves. By donning the veil, a custom initially from China and Persia, they immediately set themselves apart and the twinned concept of family honor and sexual modesty became the basis of Islamic society.

But, as Angela Davis noted when she visited Egypt in the '70s, the veil was an indication of class as well. Rural women rejected it due to its impracticality for work in the fields. It is no longer a common denominator among Moslem countries.

Source: Excerpt from Malu Halasa, "Beyond the Veil," *In These Times* (November 20–26, 1991), pp. 12–13. Reprinted from *In These Times,* a weekly newspaper published in Chicago.

lackadaisical. The particular configuration of personality traits can make obvious differences in the behavior of individuals, even though they may face identical group pressures.

A second reason role does not make social actors robots is that the occupants of a status may not receive a clear, consistent message as to what behavior is expected. A minister, for example, may find within his or her congregation individuals and cliques that make conflicting demands. One group may insist that the minister be a social activist. Another may demand that the pastor be apolitical and spend time exclusively meeting the spiritual needs of the members.

Another circumstance leading to conflicting expectations—and unpredictability of action—results from multiple group memberships. The statuses we occupy may have conflicting demands on our behavior. When a Black politician, for example, is elected as mayor of a large city, as has been the case in Los Angeles, Chicago, Detroit, Philadelphia, Baltimore, and Atlanta, he or she is faced with the constraints of the office, on the one hand, and the demands of the Black constituency, on the other. Other illustrations of conflicting demands because of occupying two quite different statuses are daughter and lover, son and peer-group member, and businessperson and church deacon. Being the recipient of incompatible demands results in hypocrisy, secrecy, guilt, and, most important for our consideration, unpredictable behavior.

Although role performance may vary, stability within organizations remains. The stability is a consequence of the strong tendency of persons occupying sta-

The power of the role to shape behavior is seen as one moves from one status to another. Consider this couple. When they are together their behavior varies with the setting (church service, football game, party) or who they are with (parents, other couples, strangers, or alone).

tuses in the organization to conform. Let us look briefly at just how powerfully roles shape behavior. First, the power of role over personal behavior is seen dramatically as one moves from one status to another. If you could observe a parent's behavior, for example, at work, at parties, at church, and at a convention in a far-away city, chances are that the behavioral patterns would be inconsistent. Or, even closer to home, what about your own behavior at home, at church, at school, in the dorm, or in a parked car? In each of these instances the same individual occupies multiple statuses and faces conflicting role expectations, resulting in overall inconsistent behavior but likely behavior that is expected for each separate role.

The power of role to shape behavior is also demonstrated as one changes status within an organization. The Amish, for instance, select their minister by lot from among the male adults of the group. The eligible members each select a Bible. The one choosing the Bible with the special mark in it is the new pastor. His selection is assumed to be ordained by God. This individual now has a new status in the group—the leader with God's approval. Such an elevation in status will, doubtless, have a dramatic effect on that person's behavior. Without special training (the Amish rarely attend school beyond the eighth grade), the new minister will in all likelihood exhibit leadership, self-confidence, and wisdom. Less dramatically, but with similar results nonetheless, each of us undergoes shifts in status within the organizations to which we belong—from freshman to senior, bench warmer to first team, assembly-line worker to supervisor, and from adolescent to adult. These changes in status mean, of course, a concomitant shift in the expectations for behavior (role). Not only does our behavior change but so too do our attitudes, perceptions, and perhaps even our personalities.

A dramatic example of the power of role over behavior is provided by an experiment conducted by Philip Zimbardo, who wanted to study the impact of prison life on guards and prisoners. Using student volunteers, Zimbardo randomly assigned some to be guards and others to be inmates. By using subjects who were unassociated with a prison, the researcher could actually study the effects of social roles on behavior without the confounding variables of personality traits, character disorders, and the like.

Zimbardo constructed a mock prison in the basement of the psychology building at Stanford University. The students chosen as prisoners were arrested one night without warning, dressed in prison uniforms, and locked in the cells. The guards were instructed to maintain order. Zimbardo found that the college students assigned the roles of guard or inmate actually *became* guards and inmates in just a few days. The guards showed brutality and the prisoners became submissive, demonstrating that roles effectively shape behavior because they have the power to shape consciousness (thinking, feeling, and perceiving). Interestingly, Zimbardo, who is a psychologist, concluded that social factors superseded individual ones: "Individual behavior is largely under the control of social forces and environmental contingencies rather than personality traits, character, will power or other empirically unvalidated constructs" (Zimbardo, 1972:6).

Finally, roles have the power to protect individuals. The constraints on behavior implied in the role provide a blueprint that relieves the individual from the responsibility for action. Thus, the certainty provided by role makes us comfortable. Gay rights and the women's movement, to name two contemporary movements, are aimed at liberation from the constraints of narrowly prescribed gender roles. But to be free of these constraints brings not only freedom but also problems. So, too, when one is freed from the constraints of a particular community, job, or marriage, the newfound liberty, independence, and excitement are countered by the frustrations involving ambiguity, choice, loneliness, and responsibility.

Social Control

Although they vary in the degree of tolerance for alternative behaviors, social groups universally demand conformity to some norms. In the absence of such demands, groups would not exist because of the resulting anarchy. The mechanisms of social control are varied. They can occur subtly in the socialization process (see Chapter 5), so that persons feel guilty or proud, depending on their actions. They can occur in the form of rewards (medals, prizes, merit badges, gold stars, trophies, praise) by family members, peers, neighbors, fellow workers, employers, and the community to reinforce certain behaviors. Also common are negative sanctions such as fines, demerits, imprisonment, and excommunication that are used to ensure conformity. More subtle techniques, such as gossip or ridicule, are also successful in securing conformity because of the common fear of humiliation before one's friends, classmates, co-workers, or neighbors.

An example of a particularly devastating and effective technique is the practice of shunning the sinner used by some of the Amish and Mennonite religious sects. No one in the religious community, not even the guilty party's spouse and children, is to recognize his or her existence. In one celebrated case, Robert Bear was the victim of shunning. He took the case to court on the grounds that this practice was unconstitutional because it was too severe. Since the shun had been invoked, Bear's wife had not slept with him, his six children were alienated from him, and his farm operation was in ruin because no one would work for him or buy his produce. The courts ruled, however, that it was within the province of the church to punish its members for transgressions. The severity of the shun is an extremely effective social control device for the Amish community, guaranteeing, except in rare cases, conformity to the dictates of the group.

Whatever the mechanism used, social control efforts tend to be very effective, whether within a family, peer group, organization, community, or a society. Most of the people, most of the time, conform to the norms of their groups and society. Otherwise, the majority of the poor would riot, most of the starving would steal, and more young men would refuse to fight in wars. The pressure to conform comes from within us (internalization of the group's norms and values from the socialization process) and from outside us (**sanctions** (or the threat of sanctions), social rewards or punishments for approved or disapproved behavior), and we obey. In fact, what we consider self-control is really the consequence of social control. These constraints are usually not oppressive to the individual. Indeed, we want to obey the rules.

Primary and Secondary Groups

A **social group** is an organization created through enduring and patterned interaction. It consists of people who have a common identity, share a common culture, and define themselves as a distinct social unit. Groups may be classified in a number of ways, the most significant of which involves the kind and quality of relationships that members have with each other. Sociologists have delineated two types of groups according to the degrees of intimacy and involvement among the members—primary and secondary.

Primary groups are groups whose members are the most intimately involved with each other. These groups are small and display face-to-face interaction. They are informal in organization and long-lasting. The members have a strong identification, loyalty, and emotional attachment to the group and its members. Examples are the nuclear family, a child's play group, a teenage gang, and close friends. Primary groups are crucial to the individual because they provide members with a sense of belonging, identity, purpose, and security. Thus, they have the strongest influence on the attitudes and values of members.

Secondary groups, in contrast to primary groups, are much larger and more impersonal. They are formally organized, task oriented, and relatively nonpermanent. The individual member is relatively unimportant. The members may vary considerably in beliefs, attitudes, and values. Americans are greatly affected by this type of group. The government at all levels deals with us impersonally. So, too, does our school, where we are a number in a computer. We live in large dormitories or in neighborhoods where we are barely acquainted with people near us. We work in large organizations and belong to large religious organizations.

One significant impact of their impersonal nature is that secondary groups spawn the formation of primary groups. Primary groups emerge at school, at work,

Kirk Anderson

in an apartment complex, in a neighborhood, in a church, or in an army. In other words, intensely personal groups develop and are sustained by their members in largely impersonal settings.

The existence of primary groups within secondary groups is an important phenomenon that has ramifications for the goals of the secondary group. Two examples from military experience make this point. In World War II the German army was organized to promote the formation of primary groups. The men were assigned to a unit for the duration of the war. They trained together, fought together, went on furloughs together, and were praised or punished as a group. This was a calculated organizational ploy to increase social solidarity in the small fighting units. This worked to increase morale, loyalty, and a willingness to die for the group. In fact, individuals often became more loyal to their fighting unit than to the nation (Shils and Janowitz, 1948).

In contrast, the U.S. army in Vietnam was organized in such a way as to minimize the possibility of forming primary groups. Instead of being assigned to a single combat unit until the war was over, soldiers were given a twelve-month tour of duty in Vietnam. This rotation system meant that in any fighting unit, soldiers were continually entering and leaving. This constant rotation prevented the development of close relationships and a feeling of all for one and one for all. Because each soldier had his own departure date, his goal was not to win the war but to survive until he was eligible to go home. This individualism made morale difficult to maintain and loyalty to one's unit difficult if not impossible to achieve. It also made the goal of winning the war less attainable than would a system that fostered primary groups (Moskos, 1975).

Bureaucracy: The Ultimate Secondary Group

A **bureaucracy** is a hierarchical formal organization characterized by rationality and efficiency—that is, improved operating efficiency and more effective attainment of common goals. As an organization grows in size and complexity, there is a greater need for coordination if efficiency is to be maintained or improved. Organizational efficiency would be maximized (ideally) under the following conditions:

- When the work is divided into small tasks performed by specialists.
- When there is a hierarchy of authority (chain of command) with each position in the chain having clearly defined duties and responsibilities.
- When behaviors are governed by standardized, written, and explicit rules.
- When all decisions are made on the basis of technical knowledge, not personal considerations.
- When the members are judged solely on the basis of proficiency, and discipline is impartially enforced. (Weber, 1947:329–341)

In short, a bureaucracy is an organization designed to perform like a machine. The push toward increased bureaucratization pervades nearly all aspects of U.S. life, including government (at all levels), the church (for example, the Catholic church and the Methodist church), education (all school systems), sports (NCAA, athletic departments at big-time schools, professional teams), health care (hospitals, health maintenance organizations, Blue Cross/Blue Shield), corporations (General Motors, IBM), and even crime (Mafia) and fast-food chains. The increasing bureaucratization in social life is called **McDonaldization** by George Ritzer. By this he means "the process by which the principles of the fast-food restaurant are coming to dominate more and more sectors of American Society as well as the rest of the world" (Ritzer, 1996:1).

The benefits of bureaucracy include a division of labor that promotes efficiency, specific expectations of members, rewards based on achievement rather than favoritism, and expertise for specific tasks coordinated to accomplish complex goals.

There is also a significant downside to bureaucracy. Ironically, while created for efficiency, bureaucracies often foster the opposite result by having too many regulations—individuals evade responsibility by passing the buck, and creativity is stifled by rules. Blind obedience to rules and the unquestioned following of orders mean that new and unusual situations cannot be handled efficiently because the rules do not apply. Rigid adherence to the rules creates automatons. Robert Merton observed that "adherence to the rules, originally conceived as a means, becomes transformed into an end-in-itself" (1957:199). Most significant, there is the danger that Max Weber feared from the **"iron cage" of rationality.** That is, bureaucracies can be dehumanizing. As summarized by Ritzer:

> In Weber's view, bureaucracies are cages in the sense that people are trapped in them, their basic humanity denied. Weber feared most that these systems would grow more and more rational and that rational principles would come to dominate an accelerating number of sectors of society. Weber anticipated a society of people locked into a series of rational structures, who could move only from one rational system to another. Thus, people would move from rationalized educational institutions to rationalized work places, from rationalized recreational settings to rationalized homes. Society would become nothing more than a seamless web of rationalized structures; there would be no escape. (Ritzer, 1996:21)

Power of the Social Group

We have seen that primary and secondary groups structure the behavior of their members by providing rules, roles, and mechanisms of social control. The result is that most of us, most of the time, conform to the expectations of social groups. Let us examine some illustrations of the profound influence of social groups on individuals, beginning with the classic study of suicide by Emile Durkheim.

Group Affects Probability of Suicide.   One's attachment to social groups affects the probability of suicide. Suicide would appear on the surface to be one area that could strictly be left to psychological explanations. An individual is committing the ultimate individual act—ending one's own life—presumably because of excessive guilt, anxiety, and/or stress. Sociologists, however, are interested in this seemingly individual phenomenon because of the social factors that may produce the feelings of guilt or the undue psychological stress. Sociologists are not interested, however, in the individual suicide case, as psychologists are, but in a number of people in the same social situation. Let us look at how sociologists would study suicide by examining in some detail the classic study by the nineteenth-century French sociologist Emile Durkheim (1951). Durkheim was the consummate sociologist. He reacted to what he considered the excessive psychologism of his day by examining suicide rates (the number of suicides per 100,000 people in a particular category) sociologically. Some of the interesting results of his study were that single people had higher rates than married people, childless married people had a higher rate than those with children, the rate of city dwellers exceeded that of rural people, and Protestants were more likely to be self-destructive than Catholics or Jews. Societal conditions were also correlated with suicide rates. As expected, rates were higher during economic depressions than in periods of economic stability, although surprisingly high rates were found during economic booms.

Durkheim went an important step beyond just noting that social factors were related to suicide rates. He developed a theory to explain these facts—a theory based on the individual's relationship to a social organization. Durkheim posited three types of suicide—the egoistic, altruistic, and anomic—to illustrate the effect of one's attachment to a group (society, religion, family) on self-preservation. **Egoistic suicide** occurs when an individual has minimal ties to a social group. The person is alone, lacking group goals and group supports. This explains why married people are less likely to commit suicide than are single people, and why married people with children are not as likely to kill themselves as are married people who are childless. Being an important part of a group gives meaning and purpose to life. This lack of group supports also explains why Protestants during Durkheim's day had a higher suicide rate than did Catholics. The Catholic religion provided believers with many group supports, including the belief in the authority of religious leaders to interpret the scriptures. Catholics also believed that through the confessional, sinners could be redeemed. Protestants, on the other hand, were expected to be their own priests, reading and interpreting God's word. When guilty of sin, Protestants again were alone. There was no confessional where a priest would assure one of forgiveness. The differences in theology left individual Protestants without religious authority and with a greater sense of uncertainty. This relatively greater isolation left Protestants without the group of believers and the authority of priests in times of stress.

Altruistic suicide occurs in a completely different type of group setting. When groups are highly cohesive, the individual member of such a collectivity tends to be group oriented. Such a group might expect its members to kill themselves for the good of the group under certain conditions. Soldiers may be expected to leave the relative safety of their foxholes and attack a strategic hill even though the odds are against them. The strong allegiance to one's group may force an act which would otherwise seem irrational. The kamikaze attacks by Japanese pilots during World War II were suicide missions in which the pilot guided his ammunition-laden plane into a target. These pilots gave their lives because of their ultimate allegiance to a social group—clearly an example of altruistic suicide. Another example of obligatory suicide for the good of the group is found among Eskimos. Because life is so tenuous in their harsh environment, Eskimos are expected to carry their full burden in providing for the survival of the group. When individuals become too old and feeble to provide their share, they provide for the survival of the group by taking their own lives.

The third type of suicide—**anomic suicide**—is also related to the individual's attachment to a group. It differs from the other two types in that it refers especially to the condition in which the expectations of a group are ambiguous or they conflict with other sets of expectations. Typically, behavior is regulated by a clear set of rules (norms). But there are times when these rules lose their clarity and certainty for individuals. This is a condition of anomie (normlessness). Anomie usually occurs in a situation of rapid change. Examples of anomic situations are emigration from one society to another, movement from a rural area to an urban one, rapid loss of status, overnight wealth, widowhood, divorce, and drastic inflation or deflation. In all these cases, people are often not sure how to behave. They are not certain of their goals. Life may appear aimless. Whenever the constraints on behavior are suddenly lifted, the probability of suicide increases. The irony is that we tend to be comfortable under the tyranny of the group and that freedom from such constraints is often intolerable. The sexual freedom of married persons in U.S. society, for example, is highly regulated. There is only one legitimate sex partner. The unmarried person is not limited. But even though married persons might fantasize that such a life is nirvana, the replacement of regulated sexual behavior with such freedom is a condition of normlessness conducive to higher suicide rates.

Group Affects Perceptions.   The group may affect our perceptions. Apparently, our wish to conform is so great that we often give in to group pressure. Solomon Asch, a social psychologist, has tested this proposition by asking the subjects in an experiment to compare the length of lines on cards (Asch, 1958). The subjects were asked one at a time to identify verbally the longest line. All the subjects but one were confederates of the experimenter, coached to give the same wrong answer, placing the lone subject in the awkward position of having the evidence of his senses unanimously contradicted. Each experiment consisted of eighteen trials, with the confederates giving wrong responses on twelve and correct ones on six. For the fifty subjects going through this ordeal, the average number of times they went along with the majority with incorrect judgments was 3.84. Thirteen of the fifty were independent and gave responses in accord with their perceptions, but thirty-seven (74 percent) gave in to the group pressure at least once (twelve did eight or more times). In other experiments in which the confederates were not unanimous in their responses, the subjects were freed from the overwhelming group pressure and generally had confidence enough in their perceptions to give the correct answer.

Muzafer Sherif also conducted a series of experiments to determine the extent of conformity among individuals (Sherif, 1958). An individual subject was placed in a dark room to observe a pinpoint of light. The subject was asked to describe how many inches the light moved (the light appears to move, even though it is stationary, because of what is called the autokinetic effect). In repeated experiments each subject tended to be consistent as to how far he or she felt the light had moved. When placed in a group, however, individuals modified their observations to make them more consistent with those of the other people in the room. After repeated exposures, the group arrived at a collective judgment. The important point about this experiment is that the group, unlike the one in the Asch experiment, was composed entirely of naive subjects. Therefore, the conclusion about group pressure on individual members is more valid, reflecting natural group processes.

Group Affects Convictions.   Sectarians with group support maintain their conviction despite contrary evidence. Leon Festinger and his associates at the University of Minnesota carefully studied a group that believed that a great flood would submerge the West Coast from Seattle to Chile on December 21 of that year (Festinger, Riecken, and Schachter, 1956). On the eve of the predicted cataclysm the leader received a message that her group should be ready to leave at midnight in a flying saucer that had been dispatched to save them. The group of ten waited expectantly at midnight for the arrival of the saucer. It did not appear, and finally at 4:45 A.M. the leader announced that she had received another communication. The message was that the world had been spared the disaster because of the force of good found among this small band of believers. Festinger was especially interested in how the group would handle this disconfirmation of prophecy. But this group, like other millennial groups of history, reacted to the disconfirmation by reaffirming their beliefs and doubling their efforts to win converts.

Group Affects Health and Life.   Membership in a group may have an effect on one's health and even on life itself. Pakistan has a caste system; children are destined to occupy the stratum of society into which they are born. Their occupation will be that of their parents with no questions asked. One of the lowest castes is that of beggar. Because the child of a beggar will be a beggar and because the most successful beggars are deformed, the child will be deformed by his family (usually by an uncle). Often the method is to break the child's back because the resulting deformity is so wretched. All parents wish success for their children, and the beggar family wishing the same is forced by the constraints of the rigid social system to physically disable their child for life.

A religious sect in Cortez, Colorado, the Church of the First Born, does not believe in traditional medical care. A three-year-old boy, whose mother belonged to this sect, died of diphtheria. The boy had never been immunized for this disease. Moreover, the mother refused medical treatment for her son after the illness had been diagnosed. The mother knew the consequences of her refusal of medical treatment because her nephew had died of diphtheria, but her faith and the faith of the other members kept her from saving her son's life. This is dramatic evidence for the power of the group to curb what we erroneously call maternal instinct.

A few religious congregations in the United States use snakes in their worship services. Members handle poisonous snakes to show their ultimate faith. Thus, religious ideology takes precedence over rational behavior.

Another example of a group demanding hazardous behavior of its members is found among some religious sects of Appalachia that encourage the handling of poisonous snakes (rattlesnakes, water moccasins, and copperheads) as part of worship. Members pick up handfuls of poisonous snakes, throw them on the ground, pick them up again, thrust them under their shirts and blouses, and even cover their heads with clusters of snakes. The ideology of the group thus encourages members literally to put their faith to the ultimate test—death. The ideology is especially interesting because it justifies both death by snakebite and being spared the bite or recovering if bitten.

> The serpent-handlers say the Lord causes a snake to strike in order to refute scoffers' claims that the snakes' fangs have been pulled. They see each recovery from snakebite as a miracle wrought by the Lord—and each death as a sign that the Lord "really had to show the scoffers how dangerous it is to obey His commandments." Since adherents believe that death brings one to the throne of God, some express an eagerness to die when He decides they are ready. Those who have been bitten and who have recovered seem to receive special deference from other members of the church. (Gerrard, 1968:23)

Group Affects Behavior.   The group can alter the behavior of members, even behaviors that involve basic human drives. Human beings are biologically programmed to eat, drink, sleep, and engage in sexual activity; but human groups significantly shape how these biological drives are met. How we eat, when we eat, and what we eat are all greatly influenced by social groups. Some groups have rigid rules that require periods of fasting. Others have festivals at which huge quantities of food and drink are consumed. Sexual behavior is also controlled. Although the sex drive is universal, mating is not a universal activity among adults. Some persons, because of their group membership, take vows of chastity. Some persons, because they have certain physical or mental traits, are often labeled by groups as undesirable and are therefore involuntarily chaste. Some societies are obsessed with sex; others are not. An example of the latter is the Dani tribe of New Guinea. Sexual intercourse is delayed between marriage partners until exactly two years after the ceremony. After the birth of a child there is a five-year period of abstinence.

These dramatic examples of the power of groups over individuals should not keep us from recognizing the everyday and continual constraints on behavior. Our everyday activities, our perceptions and interpretations, and our attitudes are the products of our group memberships. The constraints, however, are for the most part subtle and go unrecognized as such. In short, what we think of as autonomous behavior is generally not autonomous at all.

In summary, social groups undergo a universal process—the process of social organization. Through enduring social interaction, a matrix of social expectations emerges that guides behavior in prescribed channels, making social life patterned and therefore predictable. Thus, social organizations tend to be stable. But this is also a process, as Figure 2.1 indicates.

Interaction among the social actors in a social organization is constant and continuous, reinforcing stability but also bringing about change. Social organizations are never static. New ideas and new expectations emerge over time. Social change, however, is generally gradual. This is because, as shown in Figure 2.1, while social organizations are humanmade, the creation, like Frankenstein's monster, to an important degree controls the creator. The culture that emerges takes on a sacred quality (the sanctity of tradition) that is difficult to question. This quality profoundly affects the attitudes and behaviors of the social actors in the social organization and the organization itself. As Wilbert Moore, the late distinguished sociologist, has put it,

> man is an inevitably social animal, and one whose social behavior is scarcely guided by instinct. He learns social behavior, well or poorly of one sort or another. As a member

FIGURE 2.1

Process of Social Organization

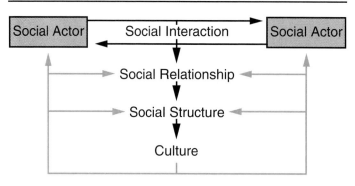

Source: This scheme is adapted from that developed by Marvin E. Olsen, *The Process of Social Organization*, 2nd ed. (New York: Holt, Rinehart and Winston, 1976).

of social groups he invents values for himself and his collectivities, rules for his conduct, knowledge to aid him in predicting and controlling his environment, gods to reward and punish him, and other ingenious elements of the human condition. . . .Once [the products of this activity] are established in the human consciousness, they become, in turn, guides to behavior. (Moore, 1969:283)

The Social Structure of Society

Primary and secondary groups illustrate nicely the process and the components of social organization. But each of these groups exists in a larger social setting—a context that is also structured with norms, statuses, roles, and mechanisms of social control. These are the components of social structure through which society affects our attitudes and behaviors regardless of our other group memberships.

A **society** is the largest social organization to which persons owe their allegiance. It is an aggregate of people, united by a common culture, who are relatively autonomous and self-sufficient and who live in a definite geographical location. It is difficult to imagine a society undergoing the same processes as other, smaller, social organizations because societies are typically composed of so many different persons and groups, none of whom were present at the beginning of the society. But the conceptual scheme for the process of social organization shown in Figure 2.1 is also applicable at the societal level. Continuing interaction among the members reinforces stability but also is a source of change. At any given time, the actors in the society are constrained by the norms, values, and roles that are the results of hundreds of years of evolution.

Society as a Social System

A society is a **social system,** composed of interdependent parts that are linked together into a boundary-maintaining whole. This concept of system implies that there is order and predictability within. Moreover, there are clear boundaries to a system in terms of membership and territory. Finally, the parts are independent.

The U.S. economy illustrates this interdependence nicely. There is a division of labor in society that provides a wide range of products and services meeting the needs of society's members. The presence of economic booms and depressions further illustrates the interdependence in society. For example, a depression comes about (in overly simplistic terms) when the flow of money is restricted by high taxes, high interest rates, high unemployment, and restricted buying practices by individuals. When large numbers of persons delay buying items such as a new car or refrigerator because they are uncertain of the future, the sales of these items decline dramatically. This decrease itself is a source of further pessimism, thereby further dampening sales. The price of stocks in these companies will, of course, plummet under these conditions, causing further alarm. Moreover, many workers in these industries will be laid off. These newly unemployed persons, in turn, will purchase only necessities, thereby throwing other industries into panic as their sales decline. A depression, then, is the result of actions by individual consumers, boards of directors of corporations, banks and savings and loan associations, individual and institutional investors, and the government. Additionally, the actions of the United States and the actions of other nations greatly affect the economic conditions of each other because nations, too, form an interdependent network.

Culture of Society

Culture explains much individual and group behavior, as well as the persistence of most aspects of social life. Social scientists studying a society foreign to them must spend months, perhaps years, learning the culture of that group. They must learn the meanings for the symbols (written and spoken language, gestures, and rituals) used by the individuals in that society. They must know the feelings people share as to what is appropriate or inappropriate behavior. Additionally, they need to know the rules of the society: which activities are considered important, the skills members have in making and using tools, as well as the knowledge members need to exist in that society. In short, analysts must discover all the knowledge that people share—that is, they must know the culture. Culture and its transmission are discussed fully in Chapters 4 through 7.

Social Classes

A structural component of societies is **social stratification,** the hierarchical arrangement of people in terms of power, prestige, and resources. This universal phenomenon of social inequality is so important for the understanding of individual behavior and the structure of society that Chapters 9 through 12 are devoted to it. At the individual level, one's placement in the hierarchy directly affects self-perception, motivation, political attitudes, and the degree of advantage or disadvantage in school, in the economy, in the courts, and even for life itself. At the societal level, the extent of inequality affects the types and magnitude of social problems, societal stability, and economic growth.

Social Institutions

One distinguishing characteristic of societies is the existence of a set of institutions. The popular usages of this term are imprecise and omit some important sociological considerations. An institution is not anyone or anything that is established and traditional (for example, a janitor who has worked at the same school for forty-five years). An institution is not limited to specific organizations, such as a school or a prison or a hospital. An institution is much broader in scope and importance than a person, a custom, or a social organization.

Institutions are social arrangements that channel behavior in prescribed ways in the important areas of social life. They are interrelated sets of normative elements—norms, values, and role expectations—that the persons making up the society have devised and passed on to succeeding generations in order to provide permanent solutions to society's perpetually unfinished business. Institutions are cultural imperatives. They serve as regulatory agencies, channeling behavior in culturally prescribed ways.

> Institutions provide procedures through which human conduct is patterned, compelled to go, in grooves deemed desirable by society. And this trick is performed by making the grooves appear to the individual as the only possible ones. (Berger, 1963:87)

For example, a society instills in its members predetermined channels for marriage. Instead of allowing the sexual partners a host of options, it is expected in U.S. society that the couple, composed of a man and a woman, will marry and set up a conjugal household. Although the actual options are many, the partners choose what society demands. In fact, they do not consider the other options as valid (for example, polygymy, polyandry, or group marriage). The result is a patterned arrangement that regulates sexual behavior and attempts to ensure a stable environment for the care of dependent children. The current demand by state legislatures that gays should not be allowed to marry illustrates the strict institutional demands of society over individual behavior (see "Diversity: The Societal Reaction to Gay Marriage").

Diversity

The Societal Reaction to Gay Marriages

In 1996 Hungary's Parliament by a vote of 207 to 73 recognized common-law relationships between homosexuals (Denmark, Sweden, and Norway are the only other nations to recognize homosexual marriages). The response by politicians in the United States is different—much different. In 1996 a conservative Congress and a centrist president signed the so-called Defense of Marriage Act, which allowed states to deny recognition to same-sex marriages that might be accorded full legal status in other states. This is in direct opposition to the "Full Faith and Credit" clause of the Constitution, which requires that each state recognize "the public acts, records, and judicial proceedings of every other state" (Tribe, 1996:11E). Despite this, as of September 1996, fifteen states had passed legislation to ban same-sex marriages.

This move by Congress and the various state legislatures is prompted by the fear that Hawaii's courts will legalize same-sex marriages, inducing gay couples from throughout the United States to travel to Hawaii to marry, which then their home states would have to accept as legal.

Public opinion in the United States opposes same-sex marriage. Most Christian religious leaders and denominations resist homosexual marriage because they believe that it violates biblical commands for sex to be heterosexual and within marriages, with procreation as the goal. Most politicians, whether Republican or Democrat, favor a ban on same-sex marriages. Conservative, pro-family advocates oppose gay marriage, even though it would promote stable, monogamous relationships among couples who seek to have their loving and committed relationships legitimated by the state. They oppose homosexual marriage because it will change the American family as we know it (Rotello, 1996). The institution of the family is by definition conservative, holding to the traditional demands of heterosexual unions only. Seen in this light, same-sex marriage is subversive and therefore an intolerable idea that must be stopped.

Institutions arise from the uncoordinated actions of multitudes of individuals over time. These actions, procedures, and rules evolve into a set of expectations that appear to have a design, because the consequences of these expectations provide solutions that help maintain social stability. The design is accidental, however; it is a product of cultural evolution.

All societies face problems in common. Although the variety of solutions is almost infinite, there is a functional similarity in their consequence, which is stability and maintenance of the system. Table 2.1 cites a number of common societal problems and the resulting institutions. This partial list of institutions shows the type of societal problems for which solutions are continually sought. All societies, for instance, have some form of the family, education, polity, economy, and religion. The variations on each theme that are found in societies are almost beyond imagination. These variations, while most interesting, are beyond the scope of this book. By looking at the interrelated norms, values, and role expectations that provide pat solutions to fundamental societal problems we can begin to understand U.S. society.

Institutions are, by definition, conservative. They are the answer of custom and tradition to questions of survival. Although absolutely necessary for unity and stability, institutions in contemporary U.S. society are often outmoded, inefficient, and unresponsive to the incredibly swift changes brought about by technological advances, population shifts, and increasing worldwide interdependence.

As we look at the institutions of U.S. society, we must not forget that institutions are made by people and can therefore be changed. We should be guided by the insight that even though institutions appear to have the quality of being sacred, they are not. They can be changed, but critical examination is imperative. Social sci-

TABLE 2.1

Common Societal Problems and Their Institutions

SOCIETAL PROBLEMS	INSTITUTION
Sexual regulation; maintenance of stable units that ensure continued births and care of dependent children	Family
Socialization of the newcomers to the society	Education
Maintenance of order; the distribution of power	Polity
Production and distribution of goods and services; ownership of property	Economy
Understanding the transcendental; the search for meaning of life and death and the place of humankind in the world	Religion
Understanding the physical and social realms of nature	Science
Providing for physical and emotional health care	Medicine

entists must look behind the facades. They must not accept the patterned ways as the only correct ways. This is in the U.S. heritage—as found in the Declaration of Independence. As Skolnick and Currie have put it,

> Democratic conceptions of society have always held that institutions exist to serve man, and that, therefore, they must be accountable to men. Where they fail to meet the tests imposed on them, democratic theory holds that they ought to be changed. Authoritarian governments, religious regimes, and reformatories, among other social systems, hold the opposite: in case of misalignment between individuals or groups and the "system," the individuals and groups are to be changed or otherwise made unproblematic. (Skolnick and Currie, 1970:15)

CHAPTER REVIEW

1. Social organization refers to the observed regularities in the behavior of people that are due to social conditions rather than the physiology or psychology of individuals.

2. Social organization includes both social structure and culture. These emerge through enduring social interaction.

3. Social structure involves the linkages and networks that transform individuals into a group. It includes the patterns of interaction that emerge, the division of labor, and the links and hierarchy of positions.

4. Culture, the shared beliefs of a group's members, guides conduct. The elements of culture include the norms (rules), roles (behavioral expectations for the occupants of the various positions), and values (the criteria for judging people, things, and actions).

5. Norms are rules specifying appropriate and inappropriate behaviors. The important norms are called *mores;* the less important ones, *folkways.*

6. Each of us belongs to a number of social organizations, and in each we occupy a position (status). These statuses are a major source of identity for individuals.

7. The behavior expected of a person occupying a status in a social organization is the role. The pressures to conform to role demands ensure that there is stability and predictability in social groups even though member turnover occurs.

8. There are three reasons, however, that role expectations do not make behavior totally predictable:

(*a*) personality differences, (*b*) inconsistent messages as to what behavior is expected, and (*c*) multiple group memberships resulting in conflicting demands.

9. Social organizations use positive sanctions (rewards) and negative sanctions (punishments) to enforce conformity to the norms, values, and roles of the group.

10. Two ways to classify social groups are on the basis of size and the quality of interaction. Primary groups are those whose members are involved in intimate, face-to-face interaction, with strong emotional attachments. The organization is informal and long-lasting. The members identify strongly with each other and with the group. In contrast, secondary groups are large, impersonal, and formally organized. The individual member is relatively unimportant.

11. Primary groups often emerge within secondary groups.

12. Bureaucracies are complex organizations designed to increase efficiency by dividing work into small tasks performed by specialists, by having a chain of command in which each position has clearly defined responsibilities, by making decisions based on technical knowledge, and by judging performancy by proficiency.

13. Positively, bureaucracies accomplish coordination, reliability, efficiency, stability, and continuity. Negatively, they create inefficiency through blind obedience to the rules and authority, stifling creativity, and too many regulations. Also, bureaucracies can be dehumanizing (Weber's iron cage of rationality).

14. Social groups have enormous power over their members and affect their beliefs, behaviors, perceptions, and even health.

15. A society is the largest social organization to which persons owe their allegiance. The society provides the social context for primary and secondary groups. Society places constraints on these groups and their members through its own norms, values, roles, and mechanisms for social control.

16. A society is a social system composed of interdependent parts that are linked together in a boundary-maintaining whole. There is order and predictability within. There is a division of labor providing for self-sufficiency.

17. A society, like other social organizations, has a culture involving norms, roles, values, symbols, and technical knowledge.

18. Unlike other social organizations, a society has a set of institutions. These are social arrangements that channel behavior in prescribed ways in the important areas of social life.

19. Institutions are conservative, providing the answers of custom and tradition to questions of social survival. Even though they are absolutely necessary for unity and stability, institutions can be outmoded, inefficient, and unresponsive to the swift changes of contemporary life.

KEY TERMS

Social organization	Values	Bureaucracy
Social structure	Social roles	McDonaldization
Culture	Folkways	"Iron cage" of rationality
Sociology	Mores	Egoistic suicide
Aggregate	Status	Altruistic suicide
Group	Hierarchy	Anomic suicide
Social interaction	Role	Society
Social relationship	Sanctions	Social system
Realist position	Social group	Social stratification
Nominalist position	Primary groups	Institutions
Norms	Secondary groups	

STUDY QUESTIONS

1. What is meant by social organization? Describe the social organization of a group to which you belong, using the appropriate sociological concepts.

2. Define the related concepts of status and role. What do they have to do with social organization?

3. Using the information in the panel on Moslem women, illustrate the concepts of norm, status, role, and social control. Illustrate also the power of the group over individual behaviors.

4. Illustrate McDonaldization with some bureaucracy with which you are familiar.

5. Emile Durkheim made a sociological analysis of the most private of acts—suicide. Describe this sociological analysis. How would psychologists differ from sociologists in their explanations of this phenomenon?

6. What are social institutions? Explain the apparent anomaly that they are both sources of stability in society as well as sources of social problems.

FOR FURTHER READING

The Process of Social Organization

Robert K. Merton, *Social Theory and Social Structure* (New York: Free Press, 1968).

S. F. Nadel, *The Theory of Social Structure* (New York: Free Press, 1957).

Marvin E. Olsen, *The Process of Social Organization,* 2nd ed. (New York: Holt, Rinehart and Winston, 1976).

Charles Perrow, *Complex Organizations: A Critical Essay,* 3rd ed. (New York: Random House, 1986).

George Ritzer, *The McDonaldization of Society: An Investigation into the Changing Character of Social Life,* revised edition (Thousand Oaks, CA: Pine Forge Press, 1996).

Max Weber, *The Theory of Social and Economic Organization,* A. M. Henderson and Talcott Parsons, trans. (New York: Free Press, 1947).

Micro Structure

Elliot Aronson, *The Social Animal,* 3rd ed. (San Francisco: W. H. Freeman, 1980).

Harold Garfinkel, *Studies in Ethnomethodology* (Englewood Cliffs, NJ: Prentice-Hall, 1967).

Erving Goffman, *Presentation of Self in Everyday Life* (Garden City, NY: Doubleday Anchor Books, 1957).

A. Paul Hare, Robert F. Bales, and Edward Borgatta, eds., *Small Groups* (New York: Alfred A. Knopf, 1965).

Macro Structure

Gerhard Lenski and Jean Lenski, *Human Societies: An Introduction to Macrosociology,* 5th ed. (New York: Mc-Graw-Hill, 1987).

Stephen K. Sanderson, *Macrosociology: An Introduction to Human Societies* (New York: Harper and Row, 1988).

Robin Williams, Jr., *American Society: A Sociological Interpretation,* 3rd ed. (New York: Alfred A. Knopf, 1970).

3

The Duality of Social Life: Order and Conflict

What is violence? The answer depends on one's vantage point in the power structure, because violence is defined as such if the act threatens the power structure. Protesting Blacks in South Africa, for example, are perceived by Whites as violent, whereas the actions of the police to maintain order are seen as violent by the protestors. Similarly, in the spring of 1989, the students in Tiananmen Square in Beijing who demonstrated for increased freedoms were viewed by the Chinese government as a threat and were forcibly defeated. The students' actions were depicted on government television as being illegitimate (violent), whereas the actions to maintain order were defined as legitimate. From the perspective of the victimized group, however, the actions of the police were illegitimate and, therefore, amounted to police brutality.

Violence always refers to a disruption of some condition of order; but order, like violence, is also politically defined. Order itself can be destructive to some categories of persons. In South Africa the normal way that society is organized does harm to Blacks (poor health care, low wages, segregated facilities, unfair system of justice, inferior education). Somehow, the term *violence* is not applied to high infant mortality and rates of preventable disease that prevail among the poor and powerless in every society. Critics of this type of societal violence might call such harmful outcomes "institutional violence," to imply that the system itself injures and destroys (Skolnick, 1969:3–8).

Violence is also defined politically through the selection process. Some acts of force (to injure persons or to destroy property) are not always forbidden or condemned in U.S. society. Property damaged during celebrations (winning the crucial football game, on Halloween, or during Mardi Gras) is often overlooked. Even thousands of drunken, noisy, and sometimes destructive college students on the Florida beaches during spring break are usually tolerated because they are just boisterous youth on a binge (and the money they spend helps the local economy). But if these same thousands of students were to destroy the same amount of property in a demonstration of which the goal was to change the system, then the acts would be defined as violent and the police would be called to restore order by force if necessary (which, of course, would not be defined as violence by the authorities). Thus, violence is condoned or condemned through political pressures and decisions. The basic criterion is whether the acts are in approved channels or are supportive of existing social and political arrangements. If not supportive, then the acts are, by definition, to be condemned and punished.

In sum, there is a relationship between the power structure and violence. The perception of how violence is defined provides insight toward a greater understanding of the role of conflict and order in society.

Social Systems: Order and Conflict

The analysis of society begins with a mental picture of its structure. This image (or **model**) influences what scientists look for, what they see, and how they explain the phenomena that occur within the society.

One of the characteristics of societies—the existence of segmentation—is the basis for the two prevailing models of society. Every society is composed of parts. This differentiation may result from differences in age, race, sex, physical prowess, wisdom, family background, wealth, organizational membership, type of work, or any other characteristic considered to be salient by the members. The fundamental question concerning differentiation is this: What is the basic relationship among the parts of society? The two contradictory answers to this question provide the rationale for the two models of society—order and conflict.

One answer is that the parts of society are in harmony. They cooperate because of similar or complementary interests and because they need each other to accomplish those things beneficial to all (for example, production and distribution of goods and services, protection). Another answer is that the subunits of society are basically in competition with each other. This view is based on the assumption that the things people desire most (wealth, power, autonomy, resources, high status) are always in short supply; hence, competition and conflict are universal social phenomena. (See "Research Methods: Social Scientists and Values.")

The Order Model

The **order model** (sometimes referred to as **functionalism**) attributes to societies the characteristics of cohesion, consensus, cooperation, reciprocity, stability, and persistence. Societies are viewed as social systems, composed of interdependent parts that are linked together into a boundary-maintaining whole. The parts of the

Research Methods

Social Scientists and Values

S ocial scientists are not value neutral. Whether they admit it or not, they take sides by adopting a way of perceiving and interpreting the social world. This does not render social science useless, as the late Michael Harrington, a highly esteemed social scientist and political activist, argues in the following excerpt:

> Truths about society can be discovered only if one takes sides. . . . You must stand somewhere in order to see social reality, and where you stand will determine much of what you see and how you see it. The data of society are, for all practical purposes, infinite. You need criteria that will provisionally permit you to bring some order into that chaos of data and to distinguish between relevant and irrelevant factors or, for that matter, to establish that there are facts in the first place. These criteria cannot be based upon the data for they are the precondition of the data. They represent—and the connotations of the phrase should be savored—a "point of view." That involves intuitive choices, a value-laden sense of what is meaningful and what is not. . . .

> The poor, I suggest, see a different social world from the rich—and so do those who think, whether consciously or not, from the vantage point of the poor or the rich. I was born into and have lived my life in the middle class. But I have tried to write from the point of view of the poor and excluded, those in the United States and elsewhere. I am therefore a deeply biased man, a taker of sides; but that is not really distinctive at all. Everyone else is as biased as I am, including the most "objective" social scientist. The difference between us is that I am frank about my values while many other analysts fool both themselves and their audiences with the illusion that they have found an intellectual perch that is free of Earth's social field of gravity.

Source: From *Taking Sides* by Michael Harrington © 1985 by Michael Harrington. Reprinted by permission of Henry Holt and Company, Inc.

system are basically in harmony with each other. The high degree of cooperation (and societal integration) is accomplished because there is a high degree of consensus on societal goals and on cultural values. Moreover, the different parts of the system are assumed to need each other because of complementary interests. Because the primary social process is cooperation and the system is highly integrated, all social change is gradual, adjustive, and reforming. Societies are therefore basically stable units.

For order theorists, the central issue is: What is the nature of the social bond? What holds groups together? This was the focus of Emile Durkheim, the French social theorist of the early 1900s (see Chapter 1). The various forms of integration were used by Durkheim to explain differences in suicide rates (see Chapter 2), social change, and the universality of religion (Durkheim, 1951; 1960; 1965).

For Durkheim there are two types of societies, based on the way the members are bonded. In smaller, less complex societies, solidarity among the members occurs through the collective holding of beliefs (ideologies, moral sentiments, traditions). Social integration, therefore, occurs because the members are alike. Modern, complex societies, in contrast, achieve social integration through differentiation. Society is based on the division of labor, in which the members involved in specialized tasks are united by their dependence on others.

One way to focus on integration is to determine the manifest and latent consequences of social structures, norms, and social activities. Do these consequences contribute to the integration (cohesion) of the social system? Durkheim, for example, noted that the punishment of crime has the **manifest consequences** (intended) of punishing and deterring the criminal. The **latent consequence** (unintended) of punishment, however, is the societal reaffirmation of what is to be considered moral. The society is thereby integrated through belief in the same rules (Durkheim, 1958).

Taking Durkheim's lead, sociologists of the order persuasion have made many penetrating and insightful analyses of various aspects of society. By focusing on *all* the consequences of social structures and activities—intended and unintended, as well as negative (malintegrative functions or **dysfunctions**)—we can see behind the facades and thereby understand more fully such disparate social arrangements and activities as ceremonials (from rain dances to sporting events), social stratification, fashion, propaganda, and even political machines.

The Conflict Model

The assumptions of the **conflict model** (the view of society that posits conflict as a normal feature of social life, influencing the distribution of power and the direction and magnitude of social change) are opposite from those of the order model. The basic form of interaction is not cooperation but competition, which often leads to conflict. Because the individuals and groups of society compete for advantage, the degree of social integration is minimal and tenuous. Social change results from the conflict among competing groups and therefore tends to be drastic and revolutionary. The ubiquitousness of conflict results from the dissimilar goals and interests of social groups. It is, moreover, a result of social organization itself. The most famous conflict theorist was Karl Marx. He theorized that there exists in every society (except, Marx believed, in the last historical stage of communism) a dynamic tension between two groups—those who own the means of production and those who work for the owners. Contrary to Durkheim, who saw modern industry and its required division of labor as promoting social solidarity, Marx viewed these groups as the sources of division and exploitation (Walton, 1990:20). Marx focused on inequality—the oppressors and the oppressed, the dominant and the dominated, the powerful and the powerless. For him, the powerful protect their privileges by supporting the status quo. The laws, religion, education, and the mass media all work for the advantage of the advantaged. The powerful will use and abuse the powerless, thereby sowing the seeds of their own destruction. The destruction of the elite is accomplished when the dominated people unite and overthrow the dominants.

Ralf Dahrendorf, a contemporary conflict theorist, has also viewed conflict as a ubiquitous phenomenon, not because of economic factors as Marx believed, but because of other aspects of social organization. Organization means, among other things, that power will be distributed unequally. The population will therefore be separated into the haves and the have-nots with respect to power. Because organization also means constraint, there will be a situation in all societies in which the constraints are determined by the powerful, thereby further ensuring that the have-nots will be in conflict with the haves—thus, the important insight that conflict is endemic to social organization.*

One other emphasis of conflict theorists is that the unity present in society is superficial, because it results not from consensus but from coercion. The powerful, it is asserted, use force and fraud to keep society running smoothly, with benefits mostly accruing to those in power.

The Duality of Social Life

The basic duality of social life can be seen by summarizing the opposite ways in which order and conflict theorists view the nature of society. If asked, "What is the fundamental relationship among the parts of society?" the answers of order and conflict theorists would disagree. This disagreement leads to and is based on a number of related assumptions about society. These assumptions are summarized in Table 3.1.

One interesting but puzzling aspect of Table 3.1 is that these two models are held by different scientific observers *of the same phenomenon.* How can such different

TABLE 3.1

Duality of Social Life: Assumptions of the Order and Conflict Models of Society

	ORDER MODEL	CONFLICT MODEL
Question:	What is the fundamental relationship among the parts of society?	
Answer:	Harmony and cooperation.	Competition, conflict, domination, and subordination.
Why:	The parts have complementary interests. Basic consensus on societal norms and values.	The things people want are always in short supply. Basic dissensus on societal norms and values.
Degree of integration:	Highly integrated.	Loosely integrated. Whatever integration is achieved is the result of force and fraud.
Type of social change:	Gradual, adjustive, and reforming.	Abrupt and revolutionary.
Degree of stability.	Stable.	Unstable.

*This description is a very superficial account of a complex processs that has been fully described by Ralf Dahrendorf (1959).

assumptions be derived by experts on society? The answer is that both models are partially correct. Each model focuses on reality—but on only *part* of that reality. Scientists have tended to accept one or the other of these models, thereby focusing on only part of social reality, for at least two reasons: (1) one model or the other was in vogue at the time of the scientist's intellectual development; or (2) one model or the other made the most sense for the analysis of the particular problems of interest—for example, the interest of Emile Durkheim, who devoted his intellectual energies to determining what holds society together, or the fundamental concern of Karl Marx, who explored the causes of revolutionary social change.

The analyses of sport and of social problems are two important areas in which sociologists have been influenced by the order and the conflict models. Let us turn to these contrary ways to view these two social phenomena before examining a synthesis of the two models.

Sport from the Order and the Conflict Perspectives.   Order theorists examining any aspect of society emphasize the contribution that aspect makes to the stability of society (this section is dependent on Coakley, 1994; and Eitzen and Sage, 1997). Sport, from this perspective, preserves the existing social order in several ways. To begin, sport symbolizes the American way of life—competition, individualism, achievement, and fair play. Not only is sport compatible with basic American values, but it also is a powerful mechanism for socializing youth to adopt desirable character traits, such as the acceptance of authority, obeying rules, and striving for excellence.

Sport also supports the status quo by promoting the unity of society's members through patriotism (e.g., national anthem, militaristic displays, and other nationalistic rituals accompanying sports events). Can you imagine, for example, a team that espouses antiestablishment values in its name, logo, mascot, and pageantry? Would Americans, for example, tolerate a major league team called the Atlanta Atheists? the Boston Bigamists? the Pasadena Pacifists? or the Sacramento Socialists? Finally, sport inspires us through the excellent and heroic achievements of athletes, the magical moments in sport when the seemingly impossible happens, and the feelings of unity in purpose and of loyalty of fans.

Clearly, then, sport from the order perspective is good. Sport socializes youth into proper channels; sport unites; and sport inspires. Thus, to challenge or to criticize sport is to challenge the foundation of our society's social order.

Conflict theorists argue that the social order reflects the interests of the powerful. Sport is organized at every level—youth, high school, college, and professional—to exploit athletes and meet the goals of the powerful (e.g., public relations, prestige, and profits).

Sport inhibits the potential for revolution by society's have-nots in three ways. First, sport validates the prevailing myths of capitalism, such as anyone can succeed if he or she works hard enough. If a person fails, it's his or her fault and not that of the system. Second, sport serves as an opiate of the masses by diverting attention away from the harsh realities of poverty, unemployment, and dismal life chances by giving them a "high" (Hoch, 1972). And, third, sport gives false hope to African Americans and other oppressed members of society, because they see sport as a realistic avenue of upward social mobility. The high visibility of wealthy athletes provides proof that athletic ability translates into monetary success. The reality, of course, is that only an extremely small percentage of aspiring athletes ever achieves professional status. In basketball, for example, there are about 500,000 high school players in any one year, about 4,000 college seniors playing, and only about 50 of them will play as rookies at the professional level.

Conflict theorists agree with order theorists on many of the facts but differ significantly in interpretation. Both agree that sport socializes youth, but conflict theorists view this socialization negatively, because they see sport as a mechanism to get youth to follow orders, work hard, and fit into a system that is not necessarily beneficial to them. Both agree that sport maintains the status quo. But instead of this being interpreted as good, as the order theorists maintain, conflict theorists view this as bad because it reflects and reinforces the unequal distribution of power and resources in society.

Social Problems from the Order and the Conflict Perspectives. Social problems are societally induced conditions that harm any segment of the population or acts or conditions that violate the norms and values of society (Eitzen and Baca Zinn, 1997). Under this rubric fall such phenomena as poverty, homelessness, crime, gender inequality, and discrimination.

The order and conflict perspectives constrain their adherents to view the causes, consequences, and remedies of social problems in opposing ways. The order perspective focuses on deviants themselves. This approach (which has been the conventional way of studying social problems) asks, Who are the deviants? What are their social and psychological backgrounds? With whom do they associate? Deviants somehow do not conform to the standards of the dominant group; they are assumed to be out of phase with conventional behavior. This is believed to occur most often as a result of inadequate socialization. In other words, deviants have not internalized the norms and values of society because they either are brought up in an environment of conflicting value systems (as are children of immigrants or the poor in a middle-class school) or are under the influence of a deviant subculture such as a gang. Because the order theorist uses the prevailing standards to define and label deviants, the existing practices and structures of society are accepted implicitly. The remedy is to rehabilitate the deviants so that they conform to the societal norms.

The conflict theorist takes a different approach to social problems. The adherents of this perspective criticize order theorists for blaming the victim (Ryan, 1976). To focus on the individual deviant locates the symptom, not the disease. Deviants are a manifestation of a failure of society to meet the needs of individuals. The sources of crime, poverty, drug addiction, and racism are found in the laws, the customs, the quality of life, the distribution of wealth and power, and in the accepted practices of schools, governmental units, and corporations. In this view, then, the schools are the problem, not the dropouts; the quality of life, not the mentally ill; the maldistribution of wealth, not the poor; the roadblocks to success for minority-group members, not apathy on their part. The established system, in this view, is not sacred. Because the system is the primary source of social problems, it, not the individual deviant, must be restructured.

Although most of this book attempts to strike a balance between the order and the conflict perspectives, the conflict model is clearly favored when social problems are brought into focus. This is done explicitly for two reasons. The subject matter of sociology is not individuals, who are the special province of psychology, but society. If sociologists do not make a critical analysis of the social structure, who will? Also, we are convinced that the source of social problems is found within the institutional framework of society. Thus, a recurrent theme of this book is that social problems are societal in origin and not the exclusive function of individual pathologies.

Synthesis of the Order and the Conflict Models

The assumptions of both models are contradictory for each comparison shown in Table 3.1, and their contradictions highlight the duality of social life. Social interaction can be harmonious or acrimonious. Societies are integrated or divided, stable or unstable. Social change can be fast or slow, revolutionary or evolutionary.

Taken alone, each of these perspectives fosters a faulty perception and interpretation of society, but taken together, they complement each other and present a complete and realistic model. A synthesis that combines the best of each model would appear, therefore, to be the best perspective for understanding the structure and process of society (see van den Berghe, 1963; Lenski, 1966).

The initial assumption of a synthesis approach is that the *processes of stability and change are properties of all societies.* There is an essential paradox to human societies: They are always ordered; they are always changing. These two elemental properties of social life must be recognized by the observer of society. Within any society there are forces providing impetus for change, and there are forces insisting on rooted permanence. Allen Wheelis (1958) has labeled these two contrary tendencies as the instrumental process and the institutional process, respectively.

The **instrumental process** is based on the desire for technological change—to find new and more efficient techniques to achieve goals. The **institutional process,** on the other hand, designates all those activities that are dominated by the quest for certainty. We are bound in our activities, often by customs, traditions, myths, and religious beliefs. So there are rites, taboos, and mores that persons obey without thinking. There also are modern institutions such as monotheism, monogamy, private property, and the sovereign state, all of which are coercive in that they limit freedom of choice, but they are assumed proper by almost all individuals in U.S. society.

These two processes constitute the **dialectic** (opposing forces) of society. As contrary tendencies, they generate tension because the instrumental forces are constantly prodding the institutions to change when it is not their nature to do so.

The second assumption is that *societies are organized, but the process of organization generates conflict.* Organization implies, among other things, the differential allocation of power. Inequalities in power are manifested in at least two conflict-generating ways: differentials in decision making, and inequalities in the system of social stratification (social classes and minority groups). Scarce resources can never be distributed equally to all persons and groups in society. The powerful are always differentially rewarded and make the key decisions as to the allocation of scarce resources.

A third basic assumption for a synthesis model is that *society is a social system.* The term *social system* has three important implications: (1) that there is not chaos but some semblance of order—that action within the unit is, in a general way, predictable; (2) that boundaries exist that may be in terms of geographical space or membership; and (3) that there are parts which are interdependent—thus conveying the reality of differentiation and unity. A society is a system made up of many subsystems (for example, groups, organizations, communities). Although these subsystems are all related in some way, some are strongly linked to others, whereas others have only a remote linkage. The interdependence of the parts implies further that events and decisions in one sector may have a profound influence on the entire system. A strike in the transportation industry, for example, eventually impinges on all individuals and groups. Some events, however, have little or no effect on all of U.S. society. Most important for the synthesis approach is the recognition that the parts of the system may have complementary interests with other parts but may also have exclusive, incompatible interests and goals. There is generally some degree of cooperation and harmony found in society because of consensus over common goals and because of similar interests (for example, defense against external threats). Some degree of competition and dissensus is also present because of incompatible interests, scarcity of resources, and unequal rewards. Societies, then, are imperfect social systems.

A fourth assumption is that *societies are held together by complementary interests, by consensus on cultural values, and also by coercion.* Societies do cohere. There are forces that bind diverse groups together into a single entity. The emphasis of both order and conflict models provides twin bases for such integration—consensus and coercion.

Finally, *social change is a ubiquitous phenomenon in all societies. It may be gradual or abrupt, reforming or revolutionary.* All social systems change. Order theorists have tended to view change as a gradual phenomenon occurring either because of innovation or because of differentiation (for example, dividing units into subunits to separate activities and make the total operation more efficient). This view of change is partially correct. Change can also be abrupt; it can come about because of internal violence, or it can result from forces outside the society (that is, as a reaction to events outside the system, or an acceptance of the innovations of others).

To summarize, a synthesis of the order and the conflict models views society as having "two faces of equal reality—one of stability, harmony, and consensus and one of change, conflict, and constraint" (Dahrendorf, 1968:127).

The remainder of this chapter illustrates the duality of social life by examining the society of the United States from the perspectives of the conflict and the order theorists. We consider the sources of disunity in the United States and the major instances of violence that have occurred throughout U.S. history. Despite the existence of division and violence, the United States is unified, at least minimally. We therefore also consider the factors that work to unify.

Division and Violence

Societies are integrated, but disunity and disharmony also exist to some degree in all societies. It is especially important to examine the segmenting influences in U.S. society, for they aid in explaining contemporary conflict and social change.

Social scientists studying the divisive forces in U.S. society have found that in small groups, the more heterogeneous the group, the more likely cliques will form. A group composed of members of one religion, for example, cannot form cliques on the basis of religion, but one with three religions represented has the potential of subdividing into three parts (Davies, 1966). This principle applies to larger organizations as well, including societies. The United States, then, has the potential of many, many subgroups because it is so diverse. The United States is, in effect, a mosaic of different groups—different on a number of dimensions, such as occupation, racial and ethnic backgrounds, education, and economic circumstances. Let us briefly examine these and other dimensions and the manner in which they bring about segmentation in U.S. society.

Size.   The United States is large in size, in both number of people and expanse of land. Both of these facts have a segmenting influence in U.S. society. With respect to population size, an accepted sociological proposition states: "As the population of a social organization increases, the number of its parts and the degree of their specialization also increases" (Mott, 1965:50). If, as in the United States, there is not only a large population (more than 265 million in July 1996) but also a high level of technology, then the division of labor becomes very refined. This division is so refined that more than 30,000 different occupations are recognized and catalogued by the Bureau of the Census.

If they have specialized occupations, the people will probably interact most often with persons like themselves. Because of similar interests, they will tend to cooperate with each other and perhaps compete with other groups for advantage. An important social theorist of the early 1900s, Robert Michels, wrote about this tendency for exclusion and conflict as a universal tendency in all social organizations.

> By a universally applicable social law, every organ of the collectivity, brought into existence through the need for the division of labor, creates for itself, as soon as it becomes consolidated, interests peculiar to itself. The existence of these special interests involves a necessary conflict with the interests of collectivity. (Michels, 1966:389, originally published in 1915)

A second segmenting factor related to size has to do with land rather than population. The United States, excluding Alaska and Hawaii, has an area of 3,615,123 square miles. Found within this large territory is a wide range in topography and climate. Some areas are sparsely settled, others densely populated. Some regions are attracting new residents at a much faster rate than others; some are declining in population.

Traditionally, there have been pronounced regional differences (and sometimes rivalries), because each region had its own economic specialization (that is, its own industry and agriculture) and each was relatively isolated from the influences of the others. The revolutions in manufacturing, transportation, and communication have helped to break down this regionalism.

Although regionalism has been declining, it remains a force that sometimes divides peoples. As evidence of this, many votes in Congress show that regional considerations often outweigh national ones, and many nonsoutherners have stereotyped ideas of southerners. Consequently, communication within U.S. society is often blocked and interaction stifled because persons from one region feel not only physically separate from but also superior to persons from other regions. The residents of some states feel divided from each other in economic function, geography, and power. Northern California, for example, is making a serious attempt to become a separate state because many residents feel that they are different from Californians from the south and because the California legislature is dominated by southern Californians who vote against the interests of the north.

Social Class.   Economic differences provide important sources of division in U.S. society. There is a natural resentment of persons without the necessities of life toward those with a bountiful supply of not only the necessities but luxuries as well. There is also hostility toward a system that provides excessive benefits (or excessive hurdles) to persons not on the basis of demonstrated skills but on family background.

The United States has the most unfair distribution of wealth and income in the industrialized world (Bradsher, 1995). Moreover, the rate of growth in inequality is faster than in any other industrialized country. The facts concerning **economic inequality** (the gap between the rich and the poor) include:

- In 1975 about 20 percent of the nation's net worth was held by the top 1 percent of households; today 36 percent is (Budiansky, 1996:13).
- In 1960, the average chief executive officer earned about as much as 41 factory workers. In 1992 that CEO made as much as 157 factory workers (Sklar, 1995).

Status (prestige) differentials also divide. Organizations, residential areas, and social clubs sometimes exclude certain persons and groups because of their supposed social inferiority.

Race.   Throughout human history race has been used as a criterion for differentiation. If any factor makes a difference in the United States, it is race. African Americans, Native Americans, Latinos, Asian Americans, and other minority racial groups have often been systematically excluded from residential areas, occupations, and organizations, and even sometimes denied equal rights under the law. Although the overt system of racial discrimination has changed, racist acts by individuals and organizations continue in the United States, with the result that members of these disadvantaged groups continue to be treated as second-class citizens.

Racial strife has occurred throughout American history. Slave revolts, Indian battles, race riots, and lynchings have occurred with regularity. Racial conflict continues today not only in the ghettos of large cities but also in most neighborhoods where the minority group is large enough to be perceived by the majority as a threat, in universities and secondary schools, in factories and other places of work, and in the armed forces.

Many members of racial minorities want justice now. It is equally clear that many majority-group members will do virtually anything to keep the status quo (that is, to retain an advantageous position for themselves). Some minority persons seeking to shake the status quo may participate in various acts of violence. This violence brings repression by the powerful, which further angers and frustrates the minority—thus, a treadmill of violence and division.

The racial composition of the United States is changing, and this change will likely lead to increased tension and conflict. The two largest racial minorities are increasing in number faster than the rest of the population. By the year 2000, Blacks will number nearly 36.4 million (13.0 percent of the population) and Latinos, the fastest growing minority, will likely number 29 million (10 percent of the population—up from 4 percent in 1970).

Also in recent years legal and illegal (undocumented) immigrants in great numbers have entered the United States. During the 1980s about 7.4 million immigrants entered the United States legally, and an estimated 10 million entered illegally (Meisler, 1993). These refugees have brought problems that have led to growing hostility. Jobs are in short supply (hostility toward immigrants rises and falls with the availability of jobs). Taxes are already high, and these groups require large amounts of aid, especially for health services and education. The poor people fear that these new refugees will take jobs, increase demands on cheap housing, and decrease welfare currently allocated to themselves. Schools and other public agencies cannot meet the demands of these new groups.

Ethnic Groups. The United States is inhabited by a multitude of ethnic groups that migrated to this country in different waves and that continue to do so. These groups have distinctive lifestyles and customs. One reason for this is that they have retained a cultural heritage brought to this country from another society. Another important reason for their continued distinctiveness is the structure of U.S. society. The persistence of subordination, discriminatory housing and work patterns, and other forms of structured inequality encourages solidarity among the disadvantaged. The uniqueness and strong ethnic identification of immigrant groups are sources of internal strength for them but cause resentment, negative stereotypes, competition, hatred, and conflict as other ethnic groups or members of the dominant majority question their loyalty, resent their success, fear being displaced by them in the job market, and worry about maintaining the integrity of their schools and neighborhoods. There is plenty of evidence for increasing racial tensions. Some examples:

- In the 1996 presidential campaign, a candidate for the Republican nomination, Patrick Buchanan, used anti-immigrant themes in his speeches.
- The Anti-Defamation League of B'nai B'rith reported that skinheads were responsible for seven deaths in 1992 and constituted a bigger racial threat than the Ku Klux Klan (reported in Biema, 1993).
- Leaders of the Latino and African American communities have become increasingly hostile to each other, rather than working together for common goals (Chavira, 1991).

■ During an eighteen-month period from 1995 to mid-1996, more than thirty-five Black churches in the South were burned.

Sexual Orientation.   Estimates vary, but approximately 2 to 5 percent of the U.S. population is homosexual. This small minority, however, is the object of considerable hostility from the dominant heterosexual population.

■ In 1996 the U.S. Senate by a 50-49 vote *rejected* legislation that would have extended workplace discrimination protections to homosexuals.

■ In 1996 Congress passed and the president signed a bill that allowed states to ban same-sex marriages. A *USA Today*/CNN/Gallup Poll in April 1996 found that two-thirds of adult Americans opposed same sex marriages (*USA Today*, 1996).

■ Prior to 1993 the armed forces discharged about 1,400 homosexuals annually because of their sexual orientation. President Clinton attempted to open the military to gays and lesbians, but this effort was defeated by a coalition of political conservatives. The compromise that resulted was that people entering the military will not be asked their sexual orientation. If, however, someone declares himself or herself a homosexual or if they engage in homoerotic activities, they will be discharged from the service.

■ A 1992 study of five major cities—New York, San Francisco, Minneapolis–St. Paul, Chicago, and Boston—found a total of 1,898 incidents of gay bashing (assault, murder, police abuse, harassment, vandalism, and arson). This was a 4 percent increase over the number reported in 1991 (*New York Times*, 1993a).

■ The Republican Party has obstructed all efforts by gays and lesbians to receive fair treatment.

■ In 1996 the Southern Baptist Convention voted to boycott the Walt Disney Corporation because it supported paying benefits to partners of their gay employees.

Religion.   A wide variety of religious beliefs abound in the United States. Although 59 percent of Americans are Protestants, the variations among them include snake handlers in Appalachia; the Amish, who refuse to use modern conveniences; sects that refuse medical help; literalists who are dogmatic in their narrow views of the Scriptures; and other groups that accept religious pluralism. Among the 28 percent of the U.S. population who are Roman Catholics, great differences exist in beliefs and lifestyles. The same is true when comparing Orthodox, Conservative, and Reformed Jews. Outside the Judeo–Christian tradition are Muslims (an estimated 5 million), Buddhists, and many other religious organizations and faiths.

Religion, like race and ethnicity, evokes an emotional response in individuals. It is difficult to be neutral about religion. It is almost impossible to accept the idea that religious beliefs other than one's own are equally legitimate. Religion also has a polarizing effect because it is often the basis for selecting (or rejecting) mates, friends, neighbors, schools, and employees. Therefore, religious differences in the United States not only differentiate persons but also may provide the basis for conflict.

Religious intolerance is not unknown in U.S. history. Although the nation was founded on the principle of religious freedom, at various times and places Jews, Catholics, Quakers, Mennonites, and atheists have been targets of religious bigotry. There have been political parties (Know-Nothing Party), organizations (Ku Klux Klan and the American Nazi Party), and demagogues who have been anti-Catholic and anti-Semitic. Their moderate success in attracting followers demonstrates that some people in the United States are susceptible to such appeals. The effects of their success have been to lessen the probability of interfaith cooperation and enhance the likelihood of conflict.

These segmenting factors create some groups in society that are advantaged and others that are disadvantaged. The former work to perpetuate their advantages, while the latter sometimes organize to protest and change the system they consider unfair. But how can these persons change the system if they are self-defined as powerless? A first step is legitimate, polite protest, which usually takes the form of voting, petitions, or writing to public officials. A second option is to use impolite, yet legitimate forms of protest (for example, peaceful demonstrations, picket lines, boycotts, and marches). The third alternative, used when others fail, is to use illegitimate forms of protest (for example, civil disobedience, riots, bombings, and guerrilla warfare).

Dissident groups select illegitimate protest because of the intransigence of the people in power toward change. The dissident groups consider their actions legitimate because they are for a just cause ("the ends justify the means"), but these protests are perceived as illegitimate by those in power. The people in authority resort to force, often intensifying the zeal and purpose of the protesters and frequently rallying previously uncommitted persons to the cause of the dissidents.

Implicit in this section is the notion that highly differentiated social systems, like that in the United States, must cope with the realities of disharmony, conflict of interest, and even violence. There is no alternative to conflict because of the diverse conditions of the U.S. social structure. This is not to say that conflict is altogether bad. There can be positive consequences of conflict for both parties to the conflict and for society as well (Coser, 1966).

All societies have the potential for cleavage and conflict because of the differential allocation of power. Concomitant with having power is the holding of other advantages (prestige, privilege, and economic benefits). Persons with advantage almost invariably wish to keep it, and those without typically want to change the reward system.

Coupled with the stratification system (the structured inequality of categories of people; see Chapter 9) in the United States are other aspects of social structure that increase the probability of conflict. The United States, perhaps more than any other society, is populated by a multitude of ethnic groups, racial groups, and religious groups. (For a similar situation in India, see "Other Societies: Division and Violence in India.") The diversity is further increased by the existence of regional differences and by a generation gap. Although assimilation has occurred to some degree, the different groups and categories have not blended into a homogeneous mass but continue to remain separate—often with a pride that makes assimilation unlikely and conflict possible.

Violence and the Myth of Peaceful Progress

Two beliefs held typically by Americans combine to make the **myth of peaceful progress**—the incorrect belief that throughout U.S. history disadvantaged groups have gained their share of power, prosperity, and respectability without violence (see Skolnick, 1969; Graham and Gurr, 1969; Rubenstein, 1970). First, there is a widely held notion that the United States is made up of diverse groups that have learned to compromise differences in a peaceful manner. Second, there is the belief that any group in the United States can gain its share of power, prosperity, and respectability merely by playing the game according to the rules. Hence, there is no need for political violence in the United States because the system works for the advantage of all.

Because these beliefs are widely shared, most people in the United States do not understand dissent by minority groups. Their opinions are believed to be aberrations and are explained away by saying that they are communist inspired, or that some groups are exceptions to the rule because they are basically immoral and irrational. Perhaps the most prevalent explanation locates the source of all violence in the individual psyches of the persons involved.

These explanations are incomplete because they locate the blame outside the system itself. United States history shows that, with few exceptions, powerless and downtrodden groups seeking power have not achieved it without a struggle. United States institutions, Rubenstein has noted, are better designed to facilitate the upward mobility of talented individuals than of oppressed groups. "Most groups which have engaged in mass violence have done so only after a long period of fruitless, relatively nonviolent struggle in which established procedures have been tried and found wanting" (Rubenstein, 1970:8). The problem is that the United States, like all other societies, has not and does not allow for the nonviolent transfer of power.

Throughout the history of the United States groups that were oppressed resorted to various legitimate and illegitimate means to secure rights and privileges that they believed to be rightfully theirs. Those in power typically reacted either by doing nothing or by repression—the choice depending on the degree to which the minority groups' actions were perceived as a real threat. The following discussion is a partial list of groups that at various times in U.S. history have resorted to violence to achieve social, economic, or political objectives.

Revolutionary Colonists.   A notable case of violence by a minority in the New World was the American Revolutionary War. The United States was literally born through violence. The colonists first petitioned the King of England to redress grievances, and when this failed they turned to acts of civil disobedience and finally to eight years of war. "The Declaration of Independence," clearly a revolutionary document, provided the rationale for mass violence:

> We hold these truths to be self-evident, that all men are created equal, that they are endowed by their Creator with certain unalienable Rights, that among these are Life, Liberty, and the pursuit of Happiness. That to secure these rights, Governments are instituted among Men, deriving their just powers from the consent of the governed.

Other Societies **O**ther Ways

Division and Violence in India

Although well-known for a strong socioreligious tradition of nonviolence, India has been beset by many forms of collective violence stemming from the particular divisions that characterize that society.

1. Religious Violence

The formation of India and Pakistan in 1947 into predominantly Hindu and Muslim states, respectively, was accompanied by numerous riots between both communities, and a bloody, massive transfer of population. In recent times, Hindu–Muslim riots have taken place centering on issues such as the conversion of lower-caste Hindus to Islam, processions on the holy days of each faith, and over mosques which some Hindus claim were built on the sites of pre-existing temples and places holy to Hinduism. Violence in Punjab that can be traced to demands by Sikhs, and in Kashmir by Muslims who live in those states, also has religious connotations.

2. Caste Violence

Caste is a traditional form of stratification that determines one's social position at birth; narrows choices with regard to occupation, marriage, etc.; and rigidly controls mobility. In an effort to do away with the resulting discriminatory and degrading treatment of the lower castes, government policies provide for preferential treatment in education and employment to some of these groups. Caste violence was traditionally a rural phenomenon, pitting members of the upper

castes against those of the lower castes. Such violence has recently been seen in urban areas as a result of the opposition of upper castes to the continuance and extension of these preferential policies.

3. Partisan Violence

For about thirty years following independence, the major political party in India was the Indian National Congress (known as the Congress). However, the domination of the Congress has declined in the national parliament, where it now supports a coalition government of fifteen other smaller parties. In various state legislatures, the Congress is generally in the opposition or shares power with other regional parties. Given the proliferation of parties with narrow and conflicting agendas, collective violence over political issues has taken place regularly. Demands for increased autonomy to a particular area, governmental assistance to certain groups, subsidies, power sharing, resource allocation, demarcation of state borders, and elections have been issues that have generated political violence.

4. Linguistic Violence

India has fifteen officially recognized languages (including Hindi, the "national" language) along with English, which is used for a number of official purposes. Recent censuses have enumerated thirty-three languages that are spoken by at least 100,000 people each. Although often unrecognized outside India, lan-

That whenever any Form of Government becomes destructive of these ends, it is the Right of the People to alter or to abolish it, and to institute new Government, laying its foundation on such principles and organizing its powers in such form as to them shall seem most likely to effect their Safety and Happiness. Prudence, indeed, will dictate that Governments long established should not be changed for light and transient causes; and accordingly all experiences hath shewn that mankind are more disposed to suffer, while evils are sufferable, than to right themselves by abolishing the forms to which they are accustomed. But when a long train of abuses and usurpations, pursuing invariably the

guage has been a potent divisive factor in Indian life and complicates educational, media, and governmental policies. States in India were demarcated according to linguistic criteria in the late 1950s. This has enabled, for example, political parties in these "linguistic" states to be formed around, and claim to represent the interests of speakers of, those languages. While the number of such incidents has dwindled, demands for and against the recognition of particular languages as "official" or as a medium of instruction crop up from time to time.

5. Ethnic Violence

Race/ethnicity has not been considered a major factor in collective violence in India. Most of India's population represents an intermingling of various racial groups. However, perceived differences between the "Aryan" dominated north and "Dravidian" dominated south resulted in a number of riots in the southern state of Tamil Nadu in the early sixties. In recent times, the northeastern states of India have witnessed separatist violence based on "pan-Mongolism," a professed identification with similar ethnic groups in Nagaland, Mizoram, Manipur (border states in India), and neighboring Myanmar (Burma), as well as among various tribal groups.

6. Economic Violence

There are two forms of collective violence, rural and urban, that can be traced to the economic structure. Around 70 percent of the population of India live in rural areas, where caste norms still hold sway, and economic violence in these settings is often confused with intercaste violence. Violent confrontations between peasants and landowners (or their hirelings) on issues related to inadequate pay, debts, putative land ownership reforms, and other work-related conditions typify rural economic violence. These confrontations result from the structured inequality of traditional village life in India.

Urban economic violence also revolves around a number of issues such as union strikes, lockouts, specific grievances such as price rises, job terminations of fellow employees and privatization efforts, or are instigated by factional disputes. Close to 30 percent of India's population live below the official poverty line, which in 1990 was set at an annual income of $370. In terms of both absolute and relative deprivation, there is a large segment of the rural and urban population who have not shared in the fruits of economic development and are willing to engage in the violence of protest to highlight their conditions. This in turn provokes counterviolence from those whose interests are threatened.

Source: N. Prabha Unnithan, 1996. This is a revision of the essay written for the sixth and seventh editions of *In Conflict and Order.* Used with permission. See also N. Prabha Unnithan (1995) "Explaining Collective Violence in India: Social Cleavages and their Consequences." *Studies in Conflict and Terrorism* 18: 93–109.

same Object evinces a design to reduce them under absolute Despotism, it is their right, it is their duty, to throw off such Government, and to provide new Guards for their future security.

This document, a cornerstone of the heritage of the United States, legitimates the use of violence by oppressed peoples. It could have been written by a modern-day revolutionary. While still revered, its content is no longer taken literally by the bulk of U.S. citizenry.

Native Americans. Long before the Revolutionary War and continuing to the present day, Native Americans attempted to change the order established by Whites. When White settlers took their land, ruined their hunting, and imprisoned them on reservations, the Native Americans fought these occurrences and were systematically suppressed by the U.S. government (Brown, 1971). In recent years Native Americans have occasionally boycotted, used violence, or used legal offensives to regain former Indian lands. The last tactic has become especially popular. More than half of the 266 federally recognized tribes have claims in various federal courts.

Exploited Farmers. Farmers have used violence on occasion to fight economic exploitation. Between the Revolutionary War and 1800, for example, three such revolts took place—Shays's Rebellion, the Whiskey Rebellion, and Fries's Rebellion. Protesting farmers have used various forms of violence (destruction of property, looting, and killing) throughout U.S. history. Some modern farmers have resorted to acts of violence to publicize their demands and to terrorize other farmers in order to present a united front against their opponents.

Slaveholders. Feeling the threat of the abolitionist movement, White southerners beginning in about 1820 used violent means to preserve slavery. In the early stages this amounted to civil disobedience, and later it burst out into fighting in places like

"bleeding Kansas." Eventually the South seceded, and the Civil War was waged—a classic example of a minority group using violence to force a change and being suppressed by the power of the majority.

WASP Supremacists.   Following the Civil War and continuing to the present day, some Whites have engaged in guerrilla warfare, arson, terrorism, and lynching in order to maintain the subjugation of Blacks. From 1882 to 1903, for example, 1,985 Blacks were killed by southern lynch mobs (Cutler, 1905:177).

Riots, lynchings, and mob actions are not solely southern phenomena. Many people from other sections of the United States have used these techniques against various alien groups (usually Catholics and immigrants from non-Teutonic Europe) in order to maintain their superiority. United States history is rife with examples of this phenomenon: "native" Americans tore apart the Irish section of Philadelphia in 1844; a Roman Catholic church and homes of Irish Catholics were destroyed in Boston in 1854; Chinese and Japanese immigrants were victims of both riots and discrimination, particularly on the West Coast; Japanese, even those who were U.S. citizens, were put in concentration camps during World War II because their patriotism was suspect; and Jews have been the objects of physical attack, boycotts, intimidation, and discrimination throughout U.S. history.

Perhaps the best contemporary example of mob violence against intruders can be seen in some communities where an all-White neighborhood is faced with one or more Haitian or Vietnamese families moving in. Threats, burning crosses, ostracism, and occasional physical violence have occurred with alarming regularity where Black invasion of previously all-White areas has taken place. This is not a southern phenomenon, but one that is found throughout the United States.

Ethnic Minorities.   Immigrant groups (that is, those groups most recently immigrant), as well as racial groups, because they have been the target of discrimination, threats, and physical violence, have themselves participated in violence. Sometimes gangs have attacked the groups responsible for their deprived condition. Most often, however, hostility by immigrants has been aimed at groups with less power, either toward Blacks or toward more recently arrived immigrants. Violence by Blacks has occurred throughout U.S. history. Always the victims, they have sometimes responded to violence in kind. During the years of slavery more than 250 insurrections took place. Mass Black violence has occurred in many major cities (for example, Chicago and Washington, DC, in 1919, Detroit in 1943 and again in 1967, Los Angeles in 1965 and again in 1992, Newark in 1967, and Miami in 1987).

The rage that racial minorities feel against Whites has surfaced sporadically in small and diffuse ways as well. Most commonly it has been manifested in individual crimes (murder, theft, and rape) or in gang assaults on Whites or in destruction of property owned by Whites.

Labor Disputants.   Another relatively powerless group resorting to violence to achieve its aims has been organized labor. In the 1870s workers attempted to organize for collective action against unfair policies of the industrialists. Unions, such as the Knights of Labor, American Federation of Labor, and the Industrial Workers of the World, formed. Their primary tactic was the strike, which in itself is nonviolent. But strikers often used force to keep persons from crossing the picket lines. Nor were the owners blameless. Their refusal to change existing wages, hours, and working conditions was the source of grievance. They sometimes turned to violence themselves to suppress the unions (for example, hiring persons to physically break up picket lines). The intransigent refusal of the owners to change the awful conditions of nineteenth-century workers resulted in considerable violence in many industries, particularly in the coal mining, steel, timber, and railroad industries. Labor violence, as in other cases mentioned previously, was ultimately effective. Working conditions, wages, and security of the workers improved. Legislation was passed providing for arbitration of differences and recognition of unions. Clearly, the use of force was necessary to gain advances for laboring men and women.

Given the evidence just cited, it is remarkable that people still believe in the myth of peaceful progress. Violence was necessary to give birth to the United States. Violence was used both to keep the Blacks in servitude and to free them. Violence was used to defeat rebellious Native Americans and to keep them on reservations. Additionally, violence has been a necessary means for many groups in the United States to achieve equality or something approaching parity in power and in the rights that all citizens and residents are supposed to enjoy.

The powerful have not been munificent in giving a break to the powerless. To the contrary, much effort has been expended by the powerful to keep the powerless in that condition. Many times in the history of the United States, violence has been the only catalyst for change. Relatively powerless groups in the United States (for example, African Americans, women, farmers) have repeatedly gone outside of existing law. To these groups, the use of force was justified because of the need to right insufferable wrongs—the reason the colonists gave for breaking from England.

We should note, however, that violence does not always work. The revolts of Native Americans were not beneficial in any way to the Indians. Moreover, some groups, such as the Jews, have advanced with comparatively little violence. Historically, however, violence is as American as cherry pie. The Presidential Commissions on Civil Disorders and Violence have laid bare the inaccuracies of the peaceful progress idea held by so many people. The uniform remedy suggested by these commissions for minimizing violence is to eliminate the causes of social unrest and perceived injustice. It cannot be a surprise that minority groups occasionally use violence because they are reacting against a system that systematically disadvantages them with little hope for change through peaceful means.

The Integrative Forces in Society

Order theorists recognize that conflict, disharmony, and division occur within societies, particularly in complex, heterogeneous societies. They stress, however, the opposite societal characteristics of cooperation, harmony, and solidarity. They see United States society as "We the people of the United States" rather than as a conglomerate of sometimes hostile groups.

In particular, order theorists focus on what holds society together. What are the forces that somehow keep anarchy from becoming a reality—or as the English philosopher Thomas Hobbes asked long ago, "Why is there not a war of all against all?" The answer to this fundamental question is found in the combined effects of a number of factors.

Functional Integration.   Probably the most important unifying factor is the phenomenon of **functional integration** (the unity among divergent elements of society resulting from a specialized division of labor, noted by Durkheim). In a highly differentiated society such as the United States, with its specialized division of labor, interaction among different segments occurs with some regularity. Interdependence often results because no group is entirely self-sufficient. The farmer needs the miller, the processor, and retail agents, as well as the fertilizer manufacturer and the agricultural experimenters. Manufacturers need raw materials, on the one hand, and customers, on the other. Management needs workers, and the workers need management.

These groups, because they need each other, because each gains from the interaction, work to perpetuate a social framework that maximizes benefits to both parties and minimizes conflict or the breaking of the relationship. Written and unwritten rules emerge to govern these relationships, usually leading to cooperation rather than either isolation or conflict and to linkages between different (and potentially conflicting) groups.

Consensus on Societal Values.   A second basis for the unification of diverse groups in the United States is that almost all people hold certain fundamental values in common. Order theorists assume that commonly held values are like social glue binding otherwise diverse people in a cohesive societal unit. Unlike functional integration, unity is achieved here through similarity rather than through difference.

Most of us believe that democracy is the best possible government. We accept the wishes of the majority on election day. Defeated candidates, for example, do not go off into the hills with their followers to blow up bridges and otherwise harass the government. Most people are patriotic. They revere the heritage of the United States and believe strongly in individualism and free enterprise and in the Judeo–Christian ethic.

Many symbols epitomize the consensus of people in the United States with respect to basic values. One such unifying symbol is the national flag. Although a mere piece of cloth, the flag clearly symbolizes something approaching the sacred. Reverence for the flag is evidenced by the shock shown when it is defiled and by the punishment given to defilers. The choice of the flag as an object to spit on or burn is a calculated one by dissident groups. They choose to defile it precisely because of what it represents and because most citizens revere it so strongly.

In 1989, the Supreme Court ruled that an individual who had desecrated the flag was guaranteed the right to do so because the Constitution protects the freedom of political expression. This decision outraged the majority of citizens, and politicians seized the opportunity to pass legislation making flag desecration an illegal act.

Similarly, such documents as the Declaration of Independence and the Constitution are held in high esteem and serve to unify citizens. The heritage of the United States is also revered through holidays such as Thanksgiving and Independence Day. Consensus is also achieved through the collective reverence of such leaders as George Washington, Abraham Lincoln, and John F. Kennedy.

The U.S. flag is an important unifying symbol in U.S. society.

The Social Order.   A third factor that unifies people in the United States, at least minimally, is that they are all subject to similar influences and rules of the game. United States inhabitants are answerable to the same body of law (at the national level), and they are under the same government. Additionally, they use the same system of monetary exchange, the same standards for measurement, and so on. The order in society is evidenced by the taking for granted such assorted practices as obeying traffic lights, the use of credit, and the acceptance of checks in lieu of money.

Group Membership.   A source of unity (as well as of cleavage) is group memberships. Some groups are exclusive because they limit membership to people of a particular race, ethnic group, income category, religion, or other characteristic. The existence of exclusive organizations creates tension if persons are excluded who want to be included, because exclusiveness generally implies feelings of superiority. Country clubs, fraternities, some churches, and some neighborhoods are based on the twin foundations of exclusiveness and superiority. There are other groups, however, whose membership consists of persons from varying backgrounds (that is, the membership includes rich and poor or Black and White). Consequently, heterogeneous organizations such as political parties, religious denominations or churches, and veterans' organizations allow members the chance not only to interact with persons unlike themselves but also to join together in a common cause.

Many, if not most, Americans who belong to several organizations belong to organizations with different compositions by race, religion, or other salient characteristics. To the extent that these crosscutting memberships and allegiances exist, they tend to cancel out potential cleavages along social class, race, or other lines. Individuals belonging to several different organizations will probably feel some cross-pressures (that is, pulls in opposite directions), thereby preventing polarization.

Additionally, most people belong to at least one organization such as a school, church, or civic group with norms that support those of the total society. These organizations support the government and what it stands for, and they expect their members to do the same.

International Competition and Conflict.   External threats to the society's existence unify. The advice Machiavelli gave his prince is a regrettable truth: "If the Prince is in trouble, he should promote a war." This was the advice that Secretary of State Seward gave to President Lincoln prior to the Civil War. Although expedient advice from the standpoint of preserving unity, it was, Lincoln noted, only a short-term solution.

A real threat to security unifies those groups, no matter how diverse, that feel threatened. Thus, a reasonable explanation for the lack of unity in the U.S. involvement in an Indochina war was that the Viet Cong were not perceived by most Americans as a real threat to their security. The Soviet buildup in armaments in the 1980s, on the other hand, was perceived as a real threat, unifying many Americans in a willingness to sacrifice in order to catch up with and surpass the Soviets. Now that the Soviet Union has been dismantled and the Cold War is a thing of the past, we no longer are united by the possible attack by Communists. The Persian Gulf War in 1991, however, was an instance when most Americans were unified against a dictator who threatened democracy and stability in the Middle East.

The Mass Media.   The world is in the midst of a communications revolution. Television, for example, has expanded to encompass virtually every home in the United States. This phenomenon—universal exposure to television—has been blamed, among other things, for rising juvenile delinquency, lowering cultural tastes, declining test scores, contributing to general moral deterioration, and suppressing creativity. These criticisms are countered by order theorists, who see television and the other forms of mass media as performing several integrative functions. Government officials, for example, can use the media to shape public opinion (for example, to unite against an enemy or to sacrifice by paying higher taxes). The media also reinforce the values and norms of society. Newspaper editorials extol certain persons and events while decrying others. Soap operas are stories involving moral dilemmas, with virtue winning out. Newspaper and magazine stories under the caption, "It Could Only Have Happened in America," abound. The media do not usually rock the boat. The heroes of the United States are praised and its enemies vilified. Our way of life is the right way; the ways of others are considered incorrect, or downright immoral. (For an example of how the media tend to ignore the realities of race and class, see "Diversity: The Media's Selective Perception of Race and Class.")

Planned Integration.   Charismatic figures or other persons of influence may work to unite segmented parts of the system (conversely, they can promote division). Thus, a union leader or the archbishop of a Catholic diocese can, through personal exhortation or by example, convince group members to cooperate rather than compete, or to open membership requirements rather than maintain exclusiveness.

Public officials on the local, state, and national levels can use their power to integrate the parts of the society in three major ways: by passing laws to eliminate barriers among groups, by working to solve the problems that segment the society, and by providing mediators to help negotiate settlements between such feuding groups as management and labor (Mott, 1965:283–284). High officials such as the president use various means of integration. First, there is the technique of **co-optation** (appointing a member of a dissident group to a policy-making body to appease the dissenting group). Second, they can use their executive powers to enforce and interpret the laws in such a way as to unite groups within the society. Finally, the president and other high officials can use the media to persuade the people. The president, for example, can request television time on all networks during prime time, thereby reaching most of the adult population in order to use full presidential powers of persuasion to unite diverse groups.

False Consciousness.   Most Americans do not feel oppressed. Even many persons who do not have many material blessings tend to believe in the American creed that anyone can be upwardly mobile—if not themselves, then at least their children (Sennett and Cobb, 1973). According to Marxian theory, when oppressed people hold beliefs damaging to their interests, they have **false consciousness.**

Thus, contrary to Karl Marx's prediction more than a century ago that capitalism would be overthrown by an oppressed majority, most of us today consider ourselves as haves or as could-be haves rather than as have-nots. There has been little polarization along purely economic lines because of a relatively large middle class. This may be changing, however, as more and more of the middle class are moving downward (see Chapter 10).

The Use of the Order and the Conflict Models in this Book

There are two contradictory models of society—the order and the conflict models. The order model views society as basically cooperative, consensual, and stable. The system works. Any problems are the faults of people, not of society. At the other extreme, the adherents of the conflict model assume that society is fundamentally competitive, conflictual, coercive, and radically changing. Social problems are the faults of society, not of individuals, in this view.

Diversity

The Media's Selective Perception of Race and Class

From the window that I wake at, most of my city is untouched. Houses stand stately after the 7.1 earthquake.

Everyone knows from watching television that earthquake damage in the Bay Area has been restricted to a relatively few neighborhoods. But not everyone may realize that considerations of race and class shaped the images that Americans saw on their TV screens.

The Marina district of San Francisco is a stately, upper-middle-class neighborhood. Homes sit alongside the Bay. People here lived well, and they faced tragedy with dignity after their neighborhood was devastated. Marina residents on TV were articulate, focused. No wonder television crews set up their cameras at this neighborhood's periphery and interviewed the residents who, even in anger and frustration, remained gentle.

But why have so few of the television crews chosen to go to the Moscone Center where those who lost homes in the city's low-income neighborhoods are now bedded down? Many of those who sleep at Moscone do not speak in tones modulated with good humor. Many of them possessed little to begin with, and they lost that little bit with the earthquake. Some had nothing and now have to redefine what nothing means.

Why were so few of the camera crews talking to people who live in West Oakland's projects, a stone's throw away from the Interstate 880 freeway that collapsed? These people now live under the same sort of stress that affects those of the Marina district.

Despite the fact that the stench of dead bodies permeates the air around the Cypress projects, help was slow in coming to those people. Not until I-880 was threatened with further collapse did the social service system that sheltered the Marina even reach out to those who lived in the midst of the Cypress deaths.

Why didn't Bryant Gumbel and Jane Pauley venture down to Watsonville, where the population is mostly Mexican and poor, where average family income is about $15,000 a year? Are the losses there less painful, the survival tales less moving?

Or do the media value white life over all by ignoring the fact that the lives of far too many people of color were also shattered by the earthquake?

TV's silence about the earthquake's impact on the non-white and the poor is reminiscent of the Depression when aid was more available to whites than to blacks; when the employment expansion resulting from World War II only included blacks after a March on Washington was threatened.

At every tragedy we are told to pull together and ignore our differences. We should not complain that the Marina was more televised than the Cypress neighborhoods because earthquake relief will finally assist both areas. We must not point out that Hispanics in Watsonville have been largely ignored because they, too, will gain from regional awareness.

But when the urgency abates, we become separate again: black, white, yellow, brown. Some have the skills to lobby for press attention or emergency aid, while others merely have the fortitude to survive and pray for help.

This is not the time to speak of race and class, a friend of mine cautions. Our television anchors reflect this point with pithy cliches: "We are all in this together." Together or not, it rankles that some people's suffering generates more concern than that of others.

The fact is that the earth shrugged, concrete tumbled and people lost their lives. But once again, race and class determined the focus of the news and our national concern.

Source: Julianne Malveaux, "Race and Class Shape TV Images of Earthquake," *Rocky Mountain News* (November 4, 1989):57.

The order and the conflict models of society are both significant, and they are used in the remainder of this book. While each model, by itself, is important, a realistic analysis must include both. The order model must be included because there is integration, order, and stability; because the parts are more or less interdependent;

and because most social change is gradual and adjustive. The conflict model is equally important because society is not always a harmonious unit. To the contrary, much of social life is based on competition. Societal integration is fragile; it is often based on subtle or blatant coercion.

A crucial difference between the two models is the implicit assumption of each as to the nature of the social structure (rules, customs, institutions, social stratification, and the distribution of power). The order perspective assumes that the social structure is basically right and proper because it serves the fundamental function of maintaining society. There is, therefore, an implicit acceptance of the status quo, assuming that the system works. As we examine the major institutions of society in this book, one task is to determine how each institution aids in societal integration.

Although order theorists also look for the dysfunctions of institutions, rules, organizations, and customs (dysfunctions refer to negative consequences), the critical examination of society is the primary thrust of conflict theorists. While this book describes the way the United States is structured and how this arrangement works for society integration, a major consideration centers on the question of who benefits under these arrangements and who does not. Thus, the legitimacy of the system is always to be doubted.

CHAPTER REVIEW

1. Sociologists have a mental image (model) of how society is structured, how it changes, and what holds it together. Two prevailing models—order and conflict—provide contradictory images of society.

2. Order-model theorists view society as ordered, stable, and harmonious, with a high degree of cooperation and consensus. Change is gradual, adjustive, and reforming. Social problems are seen as the result of problem individuals.

3. Conflict-model theorists view society as competitive, fragmented, and unstable. Social integration is minimal and tenuous. Social change, which can be revolutionary, results from clashes among conflicting groups. Social problems are viewed as resulting from society's failure to meet the needs of individuals. Indeed, the structure of society is seen as the problem.

4. The order and the conflict models present extreme views of society. Taken alone, each fosters a faulty perception and interpretation of society. A realistic model of society combines the strengths of both models. The assumptions of such a synthesis are that (a) the processes of stability and change are properties of all

societies; (b) societies are organized, but the very process of organization generates conflict; (c) society is a social system, with the parts linked through common goals and similar interests, and competitive because of scarce resources and inequities; (d) societies are held together by both consensus on values and by coercion; and (e) social change may be gradual or abrupt, reforming or revolutionary.

5. The divisive forces bringing about segmentation in U.S. society are size, social class, race, ethnic groups, sexual orientation, and religion. Thus, society has the potential for cleavage and conflict.

6. There is a widespread belief in the myth of peaceful progress—that disadvantaged groups throughout history have gained prosperity and equality without violence. The evidence, however, is that oppressed groups have had to use force or the threat of force to achieve gains.

7. The integrative forces in the United States are functional integration, consensus on values, the social order, group memberships, threats from other societies, the mass media, planned integration, and false consciousness.

KEY TERMS

Model
Order model (functionalism)
Manifest consequences
Latent consequences
Dysfunctions

Conflict model
Social problems
Instrumental process
Institutional process
Dialectic

Economic inequality
Myth of peaceful progress
Functional integration
Co-optation
False consciousness

STUDY QUESTIONS

1. What is the order model of society? On what kinds of social phenomena does it focus? What social phenomena are neglected from this perspective?

2. What is the conflict model of society? On what kinds of social phenomena does it focus? What social phenomena are neglected from this perspective?

3. What are the potentially divisive forces in society?

4. Contrary to popular belief, throughout much of U.S. history, oppressed groups have used violence to achieve progress. What is the evidence to support this refutation of the myth of peaceful progress?

5. What are the integrative forces of society?

FOR FURTHER READING

Sociological Theories: General

Thomas J. Bernard, *The Consensus-Conflict Debate* (New York: Columbia University Press, 1983).

Tom Campbell, *Seven Theories of Human Society* (New York: Oxford University Press, 1981).

Randall Collins, *Three Sociological Traditions* (New York: Oxford University Press, 1985).

R. P. Cuzzort, *Using Social Thought: The Nuclear Issue and Other Concerns* (Mountain View, CA: Mayfield, 1989).

George Ritzer, *Sociological Theory* (New York: Knopf, 1983).

The Order Model

Mark Abrahamson, *Functionalism* (Englewood Cliffs, NJ: Prentice-Hall, 1978).

Kingsley Davis, *Human Society* (New York: Macmillan, 1937).

Robert K. Merton, *Social Theory and Social Structure,* rev. ed. (New York: Free Press, 1968).

Talcott Parsons, *Sociological Theory and Modern Society* (New York: Free Press, 1967).

Jonathan Turner and Alexandra Maryanski, *Functionalism* (Menlo Park, CA: Benjamin Cummings, 1979).

Robin Williams, Jr., *American Society: A Sociological Interpretation,* 3rd ed. (New York: Knopf, 1970).

The Conflict Model

Carol Andreas, *Meatpackers and Beef Barons* (Niwot: University Press of Colorado, 1994).

William J. Chambliss, ed., *Sociological Readings in the Conflict Perspective* (Reading, MA.: Addison-Wesley, 1973).

Ralf Dahrendorf, *Class and Class Conflict in Industrial Society* (Stanford, CA: Stanford University Press, 1958).

Karl Marx and Friedrich Engels, *The Communist Manifesto,* Eden Paul and Cedar Paul, trans. (New York: Russell and Russell, 1963).

C. Wright Mills, *The Power Elite* (New York: Oxford University Press, 1956).

Michael Parenti, *Power and the Powerless* (New York: St. Martin's Press, 1978).

Michael Parenti, *Dirty Truths: Reflections on Politics, Media, Ideology, Conspiracy, Ethnic Life and Class Power* (San Francisco: City Lights Books, 1996).

John Walton, *Sociology and Critical Inquiry: The Work, Tradition, and Purpose,* 2nd ed. (Belmont, CA: Wadsworth, 1990).

PART TWO

CHAPTER 4

Culture

What is the meaning of a kiss? The meaning varies within a society depending on the situation and differs widely from society to society. As argued in the following excerpt, the kiss is a cultural creation.

Nothing seems more natural than a kiss. Consider the French kiss, also known as the soul kiss, deep kiss, or tongue kiss (to the French, it was the Italian kiss, but only during the Renaissance). Western societies regard this passionate exploration of mouths and tongues as an instinctive way to express love and to arouse desire. To a European who associates deep kisses with erotic response, the idea of one without the other feels like summer without sun.

Yet soul kissing is completely absent in many cultures of the world, where sexual arousal may be evoked by affectionate bites or stinging slaps. Anthropology and history amply demonstrate that, depending on time and place, the kiss may or may not be regarded as a sexual act, a sign of a friendship, a gesture of respect, a health threat, a ceremonial celebration, or disgusting behavior that deserves condemnation. . . .

One of the first modern studies to dispel the belief that sexual behavior is universally the same (and therefore instinctive) was *Patterns of Sexual Behavior,* written in 1951 by Clellan Ford and Frank Beach. Ford and Beach compared many of the sexual customs of 190 tribal societies that were recorded in the Human Relations Area Files at Yale University.

Unfortunately, few of the field studies mentioned kissing customs at all. Of the twenty-one that did, some sort of kissing accompanied intercourse in thirteen tribes—the Chiricahua, Cree, Crow, Gros Ventre, Hopi, Huichol, Kwakiutl, and Tarahumara of North America; the Alorese, Keraki, Trobrianders, and Trukese of Oceania; and in Eurasia, among the Lapps. Ford and Beach noted some variations: The Kwakiutl, Trobrianders, Alorese, and Trukese kiss by sucking the lips and tongue of their partners; the Lapps like to kiss the mouth and nose at the same time. (I would add Margaret Mead's observation of the Arapesh. They "possess the true kiss," she wrote; they touch lips, but instead of pressing, they mutually draw the breath in.)

But sexual kissing is unknown in many societies including the Balinese, Chamorro, Manus, and Tinguian of Oceania; the Chewa and Thonga of Africa; the Siriono of South America; and the Lepcha of Eurasia. In such cultures the mouth-to-mouth kiss is considered dangerous, unhealthy, or disgusting, the way most Westerners would regard a custom of sticking one's tongue into a lover's nose. Ford and Beach report that when the Thonga first saw Europeans kissing they laughed, remarking, "Look at them—they eat each other's saliva and dirt."

Deep kissing apparently has nothing to do with the degree of sexual inhibition or repression in a culture. Donald S. Marshall, an anthropologist who studied a small Polynesian island he called Mangaia, found that all Mangaian women are taught to be orgasmic and sexually active; yet kissing, sexual and otherwise, was unknown until Westerners (and their popular films) arrived on the island. In contrast, John C. Messenger found that on a sexually repressed Irish island where sex is considered dirty, sinful, and, for women, a duty to be endured, tongue kissing was unknown as late as 1966. . . .

Small tribes and obscure Irish islanders are not the only groups to eschew tongue kissing. The advanced civilizations of China and Japan, which regard sexual proficiency as high art, apparently cared little about it. In their voluminous production of erotica—graphic displays of every possible sexual position, angle of intercourse, variation of partner and setting—mouth-to-mouth kissing is conspicuous by its absence. Japanese poets have rhapsodized for centuries about the allure of the nape of the neck, but they have been silent on the mouth; indeed, kissing is acceptable only between mother and child. (The Japanese have no word for kissing—though they recently borrowed from English to create "kissu.") Intercourse is "natural"; a kiss, pornographic. When Rodin's famous sculpture, *The Kiss,* came to Tokyo in the 1920s as part of a show of European art, it was concealed from public view behind a bamboo curtain.

Among cultures of the West, the number of nonsexual uses of the kiss is staggering. The simple kiss has served any or all of several purposes: greeting and farewell, affection, religious or ceremonial symbolism, deference to a person of higher status. (People also kiss icons, dice, and other objects, of course, in prayer, for luck, or as part of a ritual.) Kisses make the hurt go away, bless sacred vestments, seal a bargain. In story and legend a kiss has started wars and ended them, and awakened Sleeping Beauty and put Brunnhilde to sleep.*

Introduction to Culture

An important focus of sociology is on the social influences on human behavior. As people interact over time, two fundamental sources of constraints on individuals emerge—social structure and culture. As noted in Chapter 2, *social structure* refers to the linkages and network among the members of a social organization. **Culture,** the subject of this chapter, as defined in Chapter 1, is the knowledge that the members of a social organization share. Because this shared knowledge includes ideas about what is right, how one is to behave in various situations, religious beliefs, and

*Source: Excerpts from "The Kiss" by Leonore Tiefer in *Human Nature* Volume 1, No. 7, copyright 1978 by Human Nature, Inc., reprinted by permission of the publisher.

communication, culture constrains not only behavior but also how people think about and interpret their world.

This chapter is divided into two parts. The first part describes the nature of culture and its importance for understanding human behavior. The second part focuses on one aspect of culture—values. This discussion is especially vital for understanding the organization and problems of society, in this case, U.S. society.

Culture: The Knowledge That People Share

Social scientists studying a society foreign to them must spend months, perhaps years, learning the culture of that group. They must learn the meanings for the symbols (written and spoken language, gestures, and rituals) the individuals in that society employ. They must know the feelings people share as to what is appropriate or inappropriate behavior. Additionally, they need to know the rules of the society: which activities are considered important, the skills members have in making and using tools, as well as the knowledge members need to exist in that society. In short, the analyst must discover all the knowledge that people share—that is, he or she must know the culture. Let us examine each characteristic of this important social concept.

Characteristics of Culture

An Emergent Process. As individuals interact on any kind of sustained basis, they exchange ideas about all sorts of things. In time they develop common ideas, common ways of doing things, and common interpretations for certain actions. In so doing, the participants have created a culture. The emergent quality of culture is an ongoing process; it is built up slowly rather than being present at the beginnings of social organization. The culture of any group is constantly undergoing change because the members are in continuous interaction. Culture, then, is never completely static.

A Learned Behavior. Culture is not instinctive or innate in the human species; it is not part of the biological equipment of human beings. The biological equipment of humans, however, makes culture possible. That is, we are symbol-making creatures capable of attaching meaning to particular objects and actions and communicating these meanings to other people. When a person joins a new social organization, he or she must learn the culture of that group. This is true for the infant born into a society as well as for a college woman joining a sorority or a young man inducted into the armed forces, or for immigrants to a new society. This process of learning the culture, called **socialization**, is the subject of the next chapter.

When we learn the culture of a society, or a group within society, we share with others a common understanding of words and symbols, we know the rules, what is appropriate and inappropriate, what is moral and immoral, and what is beautiful and what is ugly. Even the down-deep emotions of disgust, anger, and shame are related to the culture. A food that makes one gag in one society (eating insects, for example) may be considered a delicacy in another.

A Channel for Human Behavior.   Culture, because it emerges from social interaction, is an inevitable development of human society. More important, it is essential in the maintenance of any social system because it provides two crucial functions—predictability of action and stability. To accomplish these functions, however, culture must restrict human freedom (although, as we shall see, cultural constraints are not normally perceived as such); through cultural patterns, the individual is expected to conform to the expectations of the group.

How does culture work to constrain individuals? Or stated another way, how does culture become internalized in people so that their actions are controlled? Culture operates not only outside individuals but also inside them. Sigmund Freud recognized this process when he conceptualized the **superego** as the part of the personality structure that internalizes society's morals and thus inhibits people from committing acts considered wrong by their parents, a group, or the society.

The process of **internalization** (where society's demands become part of the individual, acting to control his or her behavior) is accomplished mainly in three ways. First, culture becomes part of the human makeup through the belief system into which a child is born. This belief system, provided by parents and those persons immediately in contact with youngsters, shapes their ideas about the surrounding world and also gives them certain ideas about themselves. The typical child in the United States, for example, is taught to accept Christian beliefs without reservation. These beliefs are literally force-fed, since alternative belief systems are considered unacceptable. It is interesting to note that after Christian beliefs are internalized by the child, they are often used as levers to keep the child in line.

Second, culture is internalized through psychological identification with the groups to which individuals belong (membership groups), or to which they want to belong (**reference groups**). Individuals want to belong; they want to be accepted by other people. Therefore, they tend to conform to the behavior of their immediate group as well as to the wishes of society at large.

Finally, culture is internalized by providing the individual with an identity. People's age, sex, race, religion, and social class have an effect on the way others perceive them and the way they perceive themselves. Berger has said, "in a sociological perspective, identity is socially bestowed, socially sustained, and socially transformed" (Berger, 1963:98; see also Cuzzort, 1969:203–204).

Culture, then, is not freedom but rather constraint. Of the entire range of possible behaviors (which probably are considered appropriate by some society somewhere), the person of a particular society chooses only from a narrow range of alternatives. The paradox, as Berger has pointed out, is that while society is like a prison to the persons trapped in its cultural demands and expectations, it is not perceived as limiting to individual freedom. Berger states it well in the following passage:

> For most of us the yoke of society seems easy to bear. Why? . . . because most of the time we ourselves desire just what society expects of us. We *want* to obey the rules. We *want* the parts that society has assigned to us. (Berger, 1963:93)

Individuals do not see the prisonlike qualities of culture because they have internalized the culture of their society. From birth, children are shaped by the culture of the society into which they are born. They retain some individuality because of the configuration of forces unique to their experience (gene structure, peers, parents' social class, religion, and race), but the behavioral alternatives deemed appropriate for them are narrow.

Culture even shapes thought and perception. What we see and how we interpret what we see are determined by culture. Many White Americans believe that Blacks tend toward criminal activity. This stereotype can, therefore, negatively affect the interpretation of a socially acceptable act such as Black males walking down the street.

For a dramatic illustrative case of the kind of mental closure that may be determined by culture, consider the following riddle about a father and son driving down a highway:

> There is a terrible accident in which the father is killed, and the son, critically injured, is rushed to a hospital. There the surgeon approaches the patient and suddenly cries, "My God, that's my son!"

How is it possible that the critically injured boy is the son of the man in the accident as well as the son of the surgeon? Answers might involve the surgeon being a priest, or a stepfather, or even artificial insemination. The correct answer to this riddle is that the surgeon is the boy's mother. Americans, male and female alike, have been socialized to think of women as occupying roles less important than physician/surgeon. If Russians were given this riddle, they would almost uniformly give the correct answer because approximately three-fourths of Russian physicians are women. Culture thus can be confining, not liberating. It constrains not only actions but also thinking.

A Maintainer of Boundaries.   Culture not only limits the range of acceptable behavior and attitudes, it also instills in its adherents a sense of naturalness about the alternatives peculiar to a given society (or other social organization). Thus, there is a universal tendency to deprecate the ways of persons from other societies as wrong, old-fashioned, inefficient, or immoral, and to think of the ways of one's own group as superior (as the only right way). The concept for this phenomenon is **ethnocentrism.** The word combines the Greek word *ethnikos,* which means nation or people, and the English word for center. One's own race, religion, or society is the center of all and therefore superior to all.

Ethnocentrism is demonstrated in statements such as "My fraternity is the best," "Reincarnation is a weird belief," "We are God's chosen people," "Polygamy is immoral," or the Bible is "the greatest book ever written." To call the playoff between the American and National Leagues the World Series implies that baseball outside the United States (and Canada) is inferior. Religious missionaries provide a classic example of one among several typical groups convinced that their own faith is the only correct one (see "A Closer Look: Is the United States Culturally Superior?" for an egregious example of ethnocentrism).

A resolution passed at a town meeting in Milford, Connecticut, in 1640 is a blatant example of ethnocentrism. It stated:

> Voted, the earth is the Lord's and the fullness thereof
>
> Voted, the earth belongs to the saints
>
> Voted, we are the saints.

Further examples of ethnocentrism from U.S. history are manifest destiny, White man's burden, exclusionary immigration laws such as the Oriental Exclusion Act, and Jim Crow laws. A current illustration of ethnocentrism can be seen in the activities of the United States as it engages in exporting the so-called American way of life because it is believed that democracy and capitalism are necessities for the good life and therefore best for all peoples.

A CLOSER LOOK

Is the United States Culturally Superior?

In 1994 the Lake County (Florida) school board enacted a new school policy for the 22,000 children in the district. The policy: teachers will be required to teach their students that America's political system, its values, and its culture in general are superior to other cultures in every regard. Specifically, it stated:

> Any instruction about other cultures shall also include and instill in our students an appreciation of our American heritage and culture such as: our republican form of government, capitalism, a free enterprise system, patriotism, strong family values, freedom of religion and other basic values that are superior to other foreign or historic cultures (cited in Buchanan, 1994:7B).

This school policy is clearly ethnocentric. It is a reaction by political conservatives (three members of the five person school board of Lake County are members of the Christian Coalition) to the Florida law mandating that teaching about other cultures should "eliminate personal and national ethnocentrism so that children understand that a specific culture is not intrinsically superior or inferior to any other" (cited in Buchanan, 1994:7B).

Supporters of the Board's decision believe that schools should promote the culture of the U.S. because *it is superior.* The country was founded on Christian principles, its economic and political systems are the best possible, and its values without peer. Thus, to teach that all nations are equal, all lifestyles equal, and that political and economic systems are equal "is to teach children a moral equivalence that amounts to a moral lie" (Buchanan, 1994:7B).

Opponents argue that the blatant teaching of "We're Number One" masks our flaws, mistakes, immoral acts. To believe in one's superiority is also to believe in the inferiority of others. This has racist overtones, it hinders cooperation among nations, and it fosters exclusionary policies in such areas as immigration, segregation, and school prayer.

Schools in all societies foster a love of country through their teaching of history and other subjects. But, as political observer Dave Rossie has suggested: "forcing teachers to become cheerleaders at best and propagandists at worst to serve the Christian Coalition's agenda is not the way to teach children to appreciate and love their country" (Rossie, 1994:6B).

Ethnocentrism, because it implies feelings of superiority, leads to division and conflict among subgroups within a society and among societies, each of which feels superior.

Ethnocentric ideas are real because they are believed and they influence perception and behavior. Analysts of U.S. society (whether they are Americans or not) must recognize their own ethnocentric attitudes and the way these attitudes affect their own objectivity.

To summarize, culture emerges from social interaction. The paradox is that although culture is human-made, it exerts a tremendous complex of forces that *constrain* the actions and thoughts of human beings. The analyst of any society must be cognizant of these two qualities of culture, for they combine to give a society its unique character. Culture explains social change as well as stability; culture explains existing social arrangements (including many social problems); culture explains a good deal of individual behavior because it is internalized by the individual members of society and therefore has an impact (substantial but not total) on their actions and personalities.

Types of Shared Knowledge

The concept of culture refers to knowledge that is shared by the members of a social organization. In analyzing any social organization and, in this case, any society, it is helpful to conceive of culture as combining six types of shared knowledge—symbols, technology, ideologies, societal norms, values, and roles.

Symbols.   By definition, language refers to symbols that evoke similar meanings in different people. Communication is possible only if persons attribute the same meaning to such stimuli as sounds, gestures, or objects. Language, then, can be written, spoken, or unspoken. A shrug of the shoulders, a pat on the back, the gesturing with a finger (which finger can be *very* significant), a wink, or a nod are examples of unspoken language and vary in meaning from society to society. Consider the varying meaning for two common gestures:

> When displayed by the Emperor, the upright-thumb gesture spared the lives of gladiators in the Roman Coliseum. Now favored by airline pilots, truck drivers and others who lean out of windows, it means "all right" in the United States and most of Western Europe. In other places, including Sardinia and Northern Greece, it is the insulting "up yours." . . . ; [The "A-Okay" gesture with the thumb and forefinger making a circle means "everything is fine" in the United States but it] has very different meanings in parts of Europe. In Southern Italy, for instance, it means "you asshole" or signifies that you desire anal sex. It can mean "you're worth nothing" in France and Belgium. (Ekman, Friesen, and Bear, 1984:67–68)

While president, George Bush on a trip to Australia unknowingly used the wrong symbolic gesture. While riding in his limousine, the president flashed a "V" sign with the back of his hand. In Australia, this does not mean victory—it is the equivalent of flashing the middle finger in the United States.

Technology.   Technology refers to the information, techniques, and tools used by people to satisfy their varied needs and desires. For analytic purposes, two types of technology can be distinguished—material and social. **Material technology** refers to knowledge of how to make and use things. It is important to note that the things produced are not part of the culture. They represent the knowledge that people share and that make it possible to build and use the object. The knowledge is culture, not the object.

Social technology is the knowledge about how to establish, maintain, and operate the technical aspects of social organization. Examples of this are procedures for operating a university, a municipality, or a corporation through such operations as Robert's Rules of Order, bookkeeping, or the kind of specialized knowledge citizens must acquire to function in society (knowing the laws, how to complete income tax forms, how to vote in elections, how to use credit cards and banks) (Olsen, 1976:60; Lenski, 1970:37–38).

Ideologies.   Ideologies are shared beliefs about the physical, social, and metaphysical worlds. They may, for example, be statements about the existence of supernatural beings, the best form of government, or racial pride.

Ideologies help individuals interpret events. They also provide the rationale for particular forms of action. They can justify the status quo or demand revolution. A number of competing ideologies exist within U.S. society—for example, fundamentalism and atheism, capitalism and socialism, and White supremacy and Black supremacy. Clearly, ideology unites as well as divides and is therefore a powerful human-made (cultural) force within societies.

Societal Norms.   Norms are societal prescriptions for how one is to act in given situations—for example, at a football game, concert, restaurant, church, park, or classroom. We also learn how to act with members of the opposite sex, with our elders, with social inferiors, and with equals. Thus, behavior is patterned. We know how to behave, and we can anticipate how other people will behave. This knowledge allows interaction to occur smoothly.

Ethnomethodology is a subdiscipline in sociology that is the scientific study of the commonplace activities of daily life. Its goals are to discover and understand the underpinnings of relationships (the shared meanings that implicitly guide social behavior). The assumption is that much of social life is scripted; that is, the players act according to society's rules (the script). The conduct in the family, in the department store between customer and salesperson, between doctor and patient, between boss and secretary, between coach and player is, in a sense, determined by societal scripts.

What happens when persons do not play according to the common understandings (the script)? Ethnomethodologist Harold Garfinkel (1967) has used this technique to discover the implicit bases of social interaction. Examples of possible rule breaking include the following: (1) when answering the phone, you remain silent; (2) when selecting a seat in the audience, you ignore the empty seats and choose rather to sit next to a stranger (violating that person's privacy and space); (3) you act as a stranger in your family; (4) in talking with a friend, you insist that he or she clarify the sense of commonplace remarks; and (5) you bargain with clerks over the price of every item of food you wish to purchase. These behaviors violate the rules of interaction in our society. When the rules are violated, the other persons in the situation do not know how to respond. Typically, they become confused, anxious, and angry. These behaviors buttress the notion that most of the time social life is very ordered and orderly. We behave in prescribed ways, and we anticipate that other people will do the same. The norms are strong, and we tend to follow them automatically.

In addition to being necessary for the conduct of behavior in society, societal norms vary in importance, as we saw in our discussion of norms at the micro level. Norms that are less important (the folkways) are not severely punished if violated. Examples of folkways in U.S. society are the following: It is expected that men should rise when a woman enters the room (unless she is the maid); people should not wear curlers to the opera; and a person does not wear a business suit and go barefoot.

Violation of the mores of society is considered important enough by society to merit severe punishment. This type of norm involves morality. Some examples of mores are the following: A person must have only one spouse at a time; thou shalt not kill (unless defending one's country); and one must be loyal to the United States.

There is a problem, however, for many Americans in deciding the degree of importance for some norms. Figure 4.1 shows the criteria for deciding whether norms should be classified as folkways or mores.

Figure 4.1 shows that on the basis of the two defining criteria, there are four possibilities, not just two. It is difficult to imagine cases that would be located in cell *b*. The only possibilities are activities that have only recently been designated as very harmful but against which laws have not yet been passed for strict punishment (either because of the natural lag in the courts and legislatures or because powerful groups have been influential in blocking the necessary legislation). The best current example of cases that would fall in cell *b* is the pollution of lakes, streams, and air by large commercial enterprises. These acts are recognized as having serious consequences for present and future generations, but either go unpunished or receive only minor fines.

Cell *c*, on the other hand, is interesting because there are acts not important to the survival of society or the maintenance of its institutions that receive severe punishments (at least relative to the crime). Some examples include a male police offi-

FIGURE 4.1

Classification of Norms

		Severity of Punishment	
		High	Low
Degree of Importance	High	Mores (a)	(b)
	Low	(c)	Folkways (d)

cer being suspended for wearing earrings; and persons caught smoking marijuana being sentenced to a jail term.

Both criteria used to delineate types of norms—degree of importance and severity of the punishments—are determined by the people in power. Consequently, activities that the powerful people perceive as being disruptive of the power structure or institutional arrangements that benefit some people and not others are viewed as illegitimate and punished severely. For example, if 10,000 young persons protest against the political system with marches, speeches, and acts of civil disobedience, they are typically perceived as a threat and are jailed, beaten, gassed, and harassed by the police and the National Guard. Compare the treatment of these young people with another group of 10,000 on the beaches of Florida during their annual spring college break. These people often drink to excess, are sexually promiscuous, and are destructive of property. Generally, the police consider these behaviors as nonthreatening to the system and therefore treat them relatively lightly.

Norms are also situational. Behavior expected in one societal setting may be inappropriate for another. Several examples should make this point clear. One may ask for change from a clerk, but one would not put money in a church collection plate and remove change. Clearly, behavior considered acceptable by fans at a football game (yelling, booing authority figures, even destroying property) would be inexcusable behavior at a poetry reading. Behavior allowable in a bar probably would be frowned on in a bank. Or doctors may ask patients to disrobe in the examining room but not in the subway.

Finally, because they are properties of groups, norms vary from society to society and from group to group within societies. Thus, behavior appropriate in one group of society may be absolutely inappropriate in another. Some examples of this include the following:

Earrings for males are becoming more acceptable. However, some organizations (e.g., police departments) have specifically forbidden males to wear earrings.

■ *Item:* The couvade is a practice surprisingly common throughout the world but in sharp contrast to what occurs in the United States. This refers to the time when a woman is in childbirth. Instead of the wife suffering, the husband moans and groans and is waited on as though he were in greater pain. After his wife has had the baby, she will get up and bring her husband food and comfort. The husband is so incapacitated by the experience that in some societies he stays in bed for as many as forty days.

■ *Item:* Among the Murgin of Australia, a woman giving birth to twins kills one of the babies because it makes her feel like a dog to have a litter instead of one baby. A tribe along the Niger Delta puts both the mother and the twins to death. With the Bankundo of the Congo Valley, on the other hand, the mother of twins is the object of honor and veneration.

■ *Item:* In some Latin American countries high-status males are expected to have a mistress. This practice is even encouraged by their wives because it implies high status (given the cost of maintaining two households). In the United States, such a practice is grounds for divorce.

■ *Item:* In Pakistan one never reaches for food with her or his left hand. To do so would make the observers physically sick. The reason is that the left hand is used to clean oneself after a bowel movement. Hence, the right hand is symbolically the only hand worthy of accepting food.

Values.   Another aspect of society's structure are its values, which are the bases for the norms. **Values** are the criteria used in evaluating objects, acts, feelings, or events as to their relative desirability, merit, or correctness (see Chapter 2). Values are extremely important, for they determine the direction of individual and group behavior, encouraging some activities and impeding others. For example, efforts to get people in the United States to conserve energy and other resources run counter to the long-held values of growth, progress, and individual freedom. Consequently, the prevailing values have thwarted the efforts of various presidents and other people to plan carefully about future needs and to restrict use and the rate of growth now.

Roles.   Societies, like other social organizations, have social positions (**statuses**) and behavioral expectations for the people who occupy these positions (**roles**). There are family statuses (son or daughter, sibling, parent, husband, wife); age statuses (child, adolescent, adult, aged); sex statuses (male, female); racial statuses (African American, Latino, Native American, White); and socioeconomic statuses (poor, middle class, wealthy). For each of these statuses there are societal constraints on behavior. To become sixty-five years old in U.S. society is a traumatic experience for many people. The expectations of society dramatically shift when one reaches this age. The aged are forced into a situation of dependence rather than independence. To be a male or female in U.S. society is to be constrained in a relatively rigid set of expectations. Similarly, African Americans and other minorities, because of their minority status, have been expected to know their place. The power of the social role is best illustrated, perhaps, by the person who occupies two relevant statuses—for example, the Black physician or the woman airline pilot. Although each of these persons is a qualified professional, both will doubtless encounter many situations in which other people will expect them to behave according to the dictates of the traditional role expectations of their **ascribed status** (race, sex, age, statuses over which the individual has no control) rather than of their **achieved status** (that is, their occupation).

The Social Construction of Reality

How are we to define what we see, feel, and hear? The important sociological insight is that meaning is not inherent in an object. Rather, people learn how to define reality from other people in interaction and by learning the culture. This process is called the **social construction of reality.**

Neurologist Oliver Sacks (1993) tells of a patient, "Virgil," blinded since age three who has his sight restored 45 years later.

> Virgil told me later that in this first moment he had no idea what he was seeing. There was light, there was movement, there was color, all mixed up, all meaningless, a blur. . . . The rest of us, born sighted, can scarcely imagine such confusion. For we, born with a full complement of senses, and correlating these, one with the other, create a sight world from the start, a world of visual objects and concepts and meanings. When we open our eyes each morning, it is upon a world we have spent a lifetime *learning* to see. We are not given the world, we make our world through incessant experience, categorization, memory, reconnection. But when Virgil opened his eyes, after being blind for forty-five years . . . there were no visual memories to support a perception, there was no world of experience and meaning awaiting him. He saw, but what he saw had no coherence. His retina and optic nerve were active, transmitting impulses, but his brain could make no sense of them. . . . (Sacks, 1993:61)

The point is that what we see does not have meaning until we learn from others and our own experiences how to interpret and thus make sense out of our perceptions.

A society's culture determines how the members of that society interpret their environment (Berger and Luckman, 1967). Language, in particular, influences the ways in which the members of a society perceive reality. Two linguists, Edward Sapir and Benjamin Whorf, have shown this by the way the Hopi Indians and Anglos differ in the way each speak about time (Carroll, 1956). The Hopi language has no verb tenses and no nouns for times, days, or years. Consequently, the Hopi think of time as continuous and without breaks. The English language, in sharp contrast, divides time into seconds, minutes, hours, days, weeks, months, years, decades, centuries, and the like. The use of verb tenses in English clearly informs everyone whether an event occurred in the past, present, or future. (See "Other Societies: Cultural Time" for other examples of how time is conceived of in various societies.) Clearly, precision regarding time is important to English-speaking peoples, whereas it is unimportant to the Hopi.

There is an African tribe that has no word for the color gray. This implies that they do not see gray even though we know that there is such a color and readily see it in the sky and in hair. The Navajo do not distinguish between blue and green, yet they have two words for different kinds of black.

The Aimore tribe in eastern Brazil has no word for two. The Yancos, an Amazon tribe, cannot count beyond *poettarrarorincoaroac,* their word for three. The Temiar people of West Malaysia also stop at three (McWhirter and McWhirter,

Other Societies Other Ways

Cultural Time

To find social time it is necessary to look beyond the individual perceptions and attitudes, to the temporal construct of the society or culture. Temporal constructs are not to be found in human experience, but rather in the cultural symbols and institutions through which human experience is construed. Our own Indo-European language imposes the concept of time on us at a very early age, so it is difficult to identify with the concept of timelessness. Societies do exist without a consciousness of time. But most societies possess a concept of time. Conceptualizations of time are as varied as the cultures, but most can be categorized by one of three images. Time in the broad sense is viewed as a line (linear), a wheel (cyclical), or as a pendulum (alternating phenomenon). But within these central images, numerous other distinctions must be made. One is tense. Is there a past or present or future, or all three? If more than one, to which is the society oriented and in what way? Another is continuity. Is time continuous or discontinuous? Does the continuity or hiatus have regularity? Another is progressiveness. Is evolutionary transformation expected with the passage of time? Still another is use. Is time used for measuring duration or is it for punctuality? The metaphysical distinctions are numerous. Is there a mode for measuring time? Is it reversible or irreversible? Subjective or objective, or both? Unidirectional? Rectilinear?

These distinctions come into focus when one studies various cultures. The Pawnee Indians, for example, have no past in a temporal sense; they instead have a timeless storehouse of tradition, not a historical record. To them, life has a rhythm but not a progression. To the Hopi, time is a dynamic process without past, present, or future. Instead, time is divided vertically between subjective and objective time. Although Indo-European languages are laden with tensed verbs and temporal adjectives indicating past, present, and future, the Hopi have no such verbs, adjectives, or any other similar linguistic device. The Trobriander is forever in the present. For the Trobriander and the Tiv, time is not continuous throughout the day. Advanced methods of calculating sun positions exist for morning and evening, but time does not exist for the remainder of the day. For the Balinese, time is conceived in a punctual rather than a durational sense. The Balinese calendar is marked off, not by even duration intervals, but rather by self-sufficient periods which indicate coincidence with a period of life. Their descriptive calendar indicates the *kind* of time, rather than what time it is. The Maya had probably the most complicated system of time yet discovered. Their time divisions were regarded as burdens carried by relays of divine carriers—some benevolent, some malevolent. They would succeed each other, and it was very important to determine who was currently carrying in order to know whether it was a good time or a bad time.

Source: Excerpted from F. Gregory Hayden, "A Critical Analysis of Time Stream Discounting for Social Program Evaluation." *The Social Science Journal* 17 (January 1980): 26–27. Reprinted by permission.

1972:167). Can you imagine how this lack of numbers beyond two or three affects how these people perceive reality?

Our language helps us to make order out of what we experience. Our particular language allows us to perceive differences among things or to recognize a set of things to be alike even when they are not identical. Language permits us to order these unlike things by what we think they have in common. As Bronowski has put it:

Habit makes us think the likeness obvious: it seems to us obvious that all apples are somehow alike, or all trees, or all matter. Yet there are languages in the Pacific Islands in which every tree on the island has a name, but which have no word for tree. To these islanders, trees are not at all alike; on the contrary, what is important to them is that the trees are different. (Bronowski, 1978:21)

The social interpretation of reality is not limited to language. For example, some people believe that there is such a thing as holy water. There is no chemical difference between water and holy water, but some people believe that the differences in properties and potential are enormous. To understand holy water, we must examine priests and parishioners, not water (Szasz, 1974:17). Similarly, consider the difference between saliva and spit (Brouillette and Turner, 1992). There is no chemical difference between them; the only difference is that in one case the substance is inside the mouth and in the other it is outside. We swallow saliva continuously and think nothing about it, yet one would not gather his or her spit in a container and then drink it. Saliva is defined positively and spit negatively, yet the only difference is a social definition. Similarly, some items are defined as edible, whereas others are not.

There is a debate in philosophy and sociology on this issue of reality. One position—**ontology**—accepts the reality of things because their nature cannot be denied (a chair, a tree, the wind, a society). The opposite side—**epistemology**—argues that all reality is socially constructed. In this view all meaning is created out of a world that generates no meanings of its own (Edgley and Turner, 1975:6). The world is absurd, and human beings make sense out of it to fit their situation. Two sociologists express this extreme position in the following quotation:

> Fundamental to our view is the assumption that the universe has no intrinsic meaning—it is, at bottom, absurd—and that the task of the sociologist is to discover the various imputed or fabricated meanings constructed by [people] in society. Or, to put it another way, the sociologist's job is to find out *by what illusions people live*. Without these artifacts, these delicately poised fantasies, most of us would not survive. Society, as we know it, could not exist. Meaninglessness produces terror. And terror must be dissipated by participating in, and believing in, collective fictions. They constitute society's "noble lie," the lie that there is some sort of inherent significance in the universe. It is the job of sociology to understand how people impute meaning to the various aspects of life. (Farberman and Goode, 1973:2)

Cultural Relativity.   This chapter has so far described a number of customs from around the world. They may seem to us to be weird, cruel, or stupid. Anthropologists, though, have helped us to understand that in the cultural context of a given society, the practice may make considerable sense. For example, anthropologist Marvin Harris has explained why sacred cattle are allowed to roam the countryside in India while the people may be starving (Harris, 1975). Outsiders see cow worship as the primary cause of India's hunger and poverty—cattle do not contribute meat, but they do eat crops that would otherwise go to human beings. Harris, however, argues that cattle must not be killed for food because they are the most efficient producer of fuel and food. To kill them would cause the economy to collapse. Cattle contribute to the Indian economy in a number of significant ways. They are the source of oxen, which are the principal traction animals for farming. Their milk helps to meet the nutritional needs of many poor families. India's cattle annually excrete 700 million tons of recoverable manure, half of which is used for fertilizer and the rest for fuel. Cow dung is also used as a household flooring material. If cows were slaughtered during times of famine, the economy would not recover in good times. To Western experts it looks as if Indians would rather starve to death than to eat their cows. But as Harris has argued, "They don't realize that the farmer would rather eat his cow than starve, but that he will starve if he does eat it" (Harris, 1975:21).

The practice of cow worship also allows for a crude redistribution of wealth. The cattle owned by the poor are allowed to roam freely. In this way the poor are able to let their cows graze the crops of the rich and come home at night to be milked. As Harris has concluded:

> The sacredness of the cow is not just an ignorant belief that stands in the way of progress. Like all concepts of the sacred and the profane, this one affects the physical world; it defines the relationships that are important for the maintenance of Indian society.
>
> Indians have the sacred cow; we have the "sacred" car and the "sacred" dog. It would not occur to us to propose the elimination of automobiles and dogs from our society without carefully considering the consequences, and we should not propose the elimination of zebu cattle without first understanding their place in the social order of India.
>
> Human society is neither random nor capricious. The regularities of thought and behavior called culture are the principal mechanisms by which we human beings adapt to the world around us. Practices and beliefs can be rational or irrational, but a society that fails to adapt to its environment is doomed to extinction. Only those societies that draw the necessities of life from their surroundings, inherit the earth. The West has much to learn from the great antiquity of Indian civilization, and the sacred cow is an important part of that lesson. (Harris, 1978:36)

This extended example is used to convey the idea that the customs of a society should be evaluated in the light of the culture and their functions for that society. These customs should *not* be evaluated by our standards, but by theirs. This is called **cultural relativity.** The problem with cultural relativity, of course, is ethnocentrism—the tendency for the members of each society to assume the rightness of their own customs and practices and the inferiority, immorality, or irrationality of those found in other societies.

Values

Because all the components of culture are essential for an understanding of the constraints on human behavior, perhaps the quickest way to reach this understanding is to focus on its values. These are the criteria the members of society use to evaluate objects, ideas, acts, feelings, or events as to their relative desirability, merit, or correctness.

Human beings are valuing beings. They continually evaluate themselves and other people. What objects are worth owning? What makes people successful? What activities are rewarding? What is beauty? Of course, different societies have distinctive criteria (values) for evaluating. People are considered successful in the United States, for example, if they accumulate many material things as a result of hard work. In other societies people are considered to be successful if they attain total mastery of their emotions or if they totally reject materialism.

One objective common to any social science course is the hope that students will become aware of the various aspects of social life in an analytical way. For people studying their own society, this means that while immersed in the subject matter, they also become participant observers. This implies an objective detachment (as much as possible) so that one may understand better the forces that in large measure affect human behavior, both individually and in groups.

The primary task for the participant observer interested in societal values is to determine what the values are. A number of clues are helpful for such a task (Williams, 1970:444–446). The first clue is to determine what most preoccupies people in their conversations and actions. One might ask: Toward what do people most often direct their action? Is it, for example, contemplation and meditation or physical fitness or the acquiring of material objects? In other words, what gives individuals high status in the eyes of their fellows?

A second technique that might help delineate the values is to determine the choices that people make consistently. The participant observer should ascertain what choices tend to be made in similar situations. For example, how do individuals dispose of surplus wealth? Do they spend it for self-aggrandizement or for altruistic reasons? Is there a tendency to spend it for the pleasure of the present, to save it for security in the future, or to spend it on other people?

A third procedure is used typically by social scientists—to find out through interviews or written questionnaires what people say is good, bad, moral, immoral, desirable, or undesirable. There often is a difference between what people say and what people do. A problem in the study of values exists because there are sometimes discrepancies between values and actual behavior. Even if there is a difference between what they write on a questionnaire or say in an interview and their actual behavior, people will probably say or write those responses they feel are appropriate, and this response by itself is a valid indicator of what the values of the society are.

One may also observe the reward–punishment system of the society. What behavior is rewarded with a medal, or a bonus, or public praise? Alternatively, what behavior brings condemnation, ridicule, public censure, or imprisonment? The greater the reward or the punishment, the greater the likelihood that important societal values are involved. Consider, for example, the extraordinary punishment in the United States given to people who willfully destroy the private property of others (for example, a cattle rustler, a thief, a looter, or a pyromaniac). Closely related to the reward–punishment system are the actions that cause individuals to feel guilt or shame (losing a job, living on welfare, declaring bankruptcy) or actions that bring about ego enhancement (a better-paying job, receiving an educational degree, owning a business). Individuals feel guilt or shame because they have internalized the norms and values of society. When values and behavior are not congruent, feelings of guilt are a typical response.

Another technique is to examine the principles that are held as part of the so-called American way of life. These principles are enunciated in historical documents such as the Constitution, the Declaration of Independence, and the Bible. We are continually reminded of these principles in speeches by elected officials, by editorials in the mass media, and from religious pulpits. The United States has gone to war to defend such principles as democracy, equality, freedom, and the free enterprise system. One question the analyst of values should ask, therefore, is, "For what principles will the people fight?" The remainder of this chapter describes the system of values prevalent in the United States. Understanding these values is essential to the analysis of society, for they provide the basis for this country's uniqueness as well as the source of many of its social problems.

Values as Sources of Societal Integration and Social Problems

United States society, while similar in some respects to other advanced industrial societies, is also fundamentally different. Given the combination of geographical, historical, and religious factors found in the United States, it is not surprising that the cultural values found there are unique.

Geographically, the United States has remained relatively isolated from other societies for most of its history. The United States has also been blessed with an abundance of rich and varied resources (land, minerals, and water). Until only recently, the inhabitants of the United States were unconcerned with conservation and the careful use of resources (as many societies must be to survive) because there was no need. The country provided a vast storehouse of resources so rich they were often used wastefully.

Historically, the United States was founded by a revolution that grew out of opposition to tyranny and aristocracy. Hence, people in the United States have verbally supported such principles as freedom, democracy, equality, and impersonal justice.

Another historical factor that has led to the particular nature of the culture in the United States is that the society has been peopled largely by immigrants. This fact has led, on the one hand, to a blending of many cultural traits, such as language, dress, and customs; and alternatively, to the existence of ethnic enclaves that resist assimilation.

A final set of forces that has affected the culture of the United States stems from its religious heritage. First is the Judeo–Christian ethic that has prevailed throughout U.S. history. The strong emphases on humanitarianism, the inherent worth of all individuals, a morality based on the Ten Commandments, and even the Biblical injunction to "have dominion over all living things" have had a profound effect on how Americans evaluate each other. Another aspect of religious heritage, the **Protestant ethic,** has been an important determinant of the values believed to typify most people in the United States (see Weber, 1958). (The Protestant ethic is the religious belief emphasizing hard work and continual striving to prove that one is saved.) The majority of early European settlers in the New World tended to believe in a particular set of religious beliefs that can be traced back to two individuals, Martin Luther and John Calvin. Luther's contribution was essentially twofold: each person was considered to be his or her own priest (stressing the person's individuality and worth), and each person was to accept his or her work as a calling. To be called by God to do a job, no matter how humble, was to give the job and the individual dignity. It also encouraged everyone to work very hard to be successful in that job.

The contribution of John Calvin was based on his belief in predestination. God, because He is all-knowing, knows who will be saved. Unfortunately, individuals do not know whether they are saved or not, and this is very anxiety-producing. Calvinists came to believe that God would look with more favor on people preordained to be saved than on people who were not. Consequently, success in one's business became a sign that one was saved, and this was therefore anxiety-reducing. Calvinists worked very hard to be successful. As they prospered, the capital they accumulated could be spent only on necessities, for to spend on luxuries was another sign that one was not saved. The surplus capital was therefore invested in the enterprise (purchasing more property or better machinery, or hiring a larger work force, for example).

Luther's and Calvin's beliefs led to an ethic that flourished in the United States. This ethic stressed the traits of self-sacrifice, diligence, and hard work. It stressed achievement, and most important, it stressed a self-orientation rather than a collectivity orientation. Indirectly, this ethic emphasized private property, capitalism, rationality, and growth.

Thus, geography, religious heritage, and history have combined to provide a distinctive set of values for Americans. However, before we describe these dominant values, several caveats should be mentioned. First, the tremendous diversity of the United States precludes any universal holding of values. The country has persons and groups that reject the dominant values. Moreover, there are differences in emphasis for the dominant values by region, social class, age, and religion. Second, the system of American values is not always consistent with behavior. Third, the values themselves are not always consistent. How does one reconcile the coexistence of individualism with conformity? or competition and cooperation? Robin Williams, an eminent analyst of U.S. society, has concluded that

Drawing by Ross; © 1993 The New Yorker Magazine, Inc.

"Maybe they didn't try hard enough."

we do not find a neatly unified "ethos" or an irresistible "strain toward consistency." Rather, the total society is characterized by diversity and change in values. Complex division of labor, regional variations, ethnic heterogeneity, and the proliferation of specialized institutions and organizations all tend to insulate differing values from one another. (Williams, 1970:451)

To minimize the problem with inconsistencies, this section examines, in turn, only the most dominant of American values.

Success (Individual Achievement).   The highly valued individual in U.S. society is the self-made person, the person who has achieved money and status through personal efforts in a highly competitive system. Our cultural heroes are persons like Abe Lincoln, John D. Rockefeller, and Sam Walton, each of whom rose from humble origins to the top of his profession.

Success can be achieved, obviously, by outdoing all other people, but it is often difficult to know exactly the extent of one's success. Hence, economic success (one's income, personal wealth, and type of possessions) is the most commonly used measurement. Economic success, moreover, is often used to measure personal worth. As sociologist Robin Williams has stated, "The comparatively striking feature of American culture is its tendency to identify standards of personal excellence with competitive occupational achievement" (Williams, 1970:454–455).

Competition.   Competition is highly valued in U.S. society. Most people believe it is the one quality that has made the United States great because it motivates individuals and groups to be discontented with the status quo and with being second best. Motivated by the hope of being victorious in competition, or put another way, by fear of failure, Americans must not lose a war or the Olympics or be the second nation to land its citizens on the moon.

Competition pervades almost all aspects of U.S. society. The work world, sports, courtship, organizations like the Cub Scouts, and schools all thrive on competition. The pervasiveness of competition in schools is seen in how athletic teams, cheerleading squads, debate teams, choruses, bands, and casts are composed. Competition among classmates is used as the criterion for selection. Of course, the grading system is also often based on the competition of individuals.

The Cub Scouts, because of its reliance on competition, is an all-American organization. In the first place, individual status in the den or pack is determined by the level one has achieved through the attainment of merit badges. Although all boys can theoretically attain all merit badges, there is competition as the boys are pitted against each other to see who can obtain the most. Another example of how the Cub Scouts use competition is their annual event—the Pinewood Derby. Each boy in a Cub pack is given a small block of wood and four wheels that he is to shape into a racing car. The race is held at a pack meeting, and one boy eventually is the winner. The event is rarely questioned even though nearly all the boys go home disappointed losers. Why is such a practice accepted and publicized? The answer is that it is symbolic of how things are done in virtually all aspects of American life.

An important consequence of this emphasis on the survival of the fittest is that some persons take advantage of their fellows to compete successfully. In the business world, we find some people who use theft, fraud, interlocking directorates, and price-fixing to get ahead dishonestly. A related problem, abuse of nature for profit, while not a form of cheating, nevertheless takes advantage of other people, while one person pursues economic success. The current ecology crisis is caused by individuals, corporations, and communities that find pollution solutions too expensive. Thus, in looking out for themselves, they ignore the short- and long-range effects on social and biological life. In other words, competition, while a constant spur for individuals and groups to succeed, is also the source of some illegal activities and hence of social problems in U.S. society.

Similar scandals are also found in the sports world. The most visible type of illegal activity in sports is illegal recruiting of athletes by colleges and universities. In the quest to succeed (i.e., to win), some coaches have violated NCAA regulations by altering transcripts to ensure an athlete's eligibility, allowing substitutes to take admissions tests for athletes of marginal educational ability, paying athletes for nonexistent jobs, illegally using government work-study monies for athletes, and offering money, cars, and clothing to entice athletes to their schools (Eitzen and Sage, 1997). For other negative consequences of competition in sport, see "A Closer Look: The Negative Consequences of Overemphasizing Competition in Sport."

The Valued Means to Achieve.   There are three related highly valued ways to succeed in U.S. society. The first is through hard work. Americans, from the early Puritans to the present day, have elevated persons who were industrious and denigrated those who were not. Most Americans, therefore, assume that poor people deserve to be poor because they are allegedly unwilling to work as hard as persons in the middle and upper classes. This type of explanation places the blame on the victim rather than on the social system that systematically thwarts efforts by the poor. Their hopelessness, brought on by their lack of education, or by their being Black, or by their lack of experience, is interpreted as their fault and not as a function of the economic system. The two remaining valued means to success are con-

Beauty is not inherent in a person. What is beautiful is a "social construction" of a society that its inhabitants learn.

tinual striving and deferred gratification. Continual striving has meaning for both the successful and the not-so-successful. For the former, a person should never be content with what he or she has; there is always more land to own, more money to make, or more books to write. For the poor, continual striving means a never-give-up attitude, a belief that economic success is always possible through hard work, if not for yourself, at least for your children.

Deferred gratification refers to the willingness to deny immediate pleasure for later rewards. The hallmark of the successful person in U.S. society is just such a willingness—to stay in school, to moonlight, or to go to night school. One observer has asserted that the difference between the poor and the nonpoor in this society is whether they are future- or present-time oriented (Banfield, 1974). Superficially, this assessment appears accurate, but we argue that this lack of a future-time orientation among the poor is not a subcultural trait but basically a consequence of their hopeless situation.

Progress.   Societies differ in their emphasis on the past, the present, and the future. United States society, while giving some attention to each time dimension, stresses the future. Americans neither make the past sacred nor are they content with the present. They place a central value on progress—on a brighter tomorrow, a better job, a bigger home, a move to the suburbs, college education for their children, and on self-improvement. People in the United States are not satisfied with the status quo; they want growth (bigger buildings, faster planes, bigger airports, more business moving into the community, larger profits, and new world's records). They want to change and conquer nature (dam rivers, clear forests, rechannel rivers, seed clouds, and spray insecticides).

Although the implicit belief in progress is that change is good, some things are not to be changed, for they have a sacred quality (the political system, the economic system, American values, and the nation-state). Thus, Americans, while valuing technological change, do not favor changing the system (revolution).

The commonly held value of progress has also had a negative effect on contemporary life in the United States. Progress is typically defined to mean either growth or new technology. Every city wants to grow. Chambers of Commerce want more industry and more people (and more consumers). No industry can afford to keep sales at last year's figures. Everyone agrees that the gross national product (GNP) must increase each year. If all these things are to grow as people wish, then concomitant with such growth must be increased population, more products turned out (using natural resources), more electricity, more highways, and more waste. Continued growth will inevitably throw the tight ecological system out of balance because there are limited supplies of air, water, and places to dump waste materials. Not only are these resources limited, but they also diminish as the population increases.

Progress also means a faith in technology. It is commonly believed in the United States that scientific knowledge will solve problems. Scientific breakthroughs and new technology have solved some problems and do aid in saving labor. But new technology often creates problems that were unanticipated.* Although the automobile is

*Sociologists call this phenomenon *latent functions,* which means, in effect, unintended consequences. The intended consequences of an activity or social arrangement are called *manifest functions.*

A CLOSER LOOK

The Negative Consequences of Overemphasizing Competition in Sport

When winning is the primary standard for evaluation, several negative outcomes result. Let me enumerate these, using sport for examples. First, in a competitive society there is a tendency to evaluate people by their accomplishments rather than their character, personality, and other human qualities. When "winning is everything," then losers are considered just that. One successful university basketball coach once counseled prospective coaches that if they wanted to be winners, then they should associate only with winners. Is this an appropriate guiding principle for conducting our lives?

Second, when winning is paramount, schools and communities organize sports for the already gifted. This elitist approach means that the few will be given the best equipment, the best coaching, and prime time reserved for their participating, while the less able will be denied participation altogether or given very little attention. If sports participation is a useful activity, then it should be for the many, not the few, in my view.

A third problem with the emphasis on winning is that parents may push their children beyond the normal to succeed. . . . In 1972 the national record for one-year-olds in the mile run was established by Steve Parsons of Normal, Illinois (the time was 24:16.6). [Is this an example] of child abuse or what?

A fourth problem with the primacy of winning is that coaches may push their charges too hard. Coaches may be physically or emotionally abusive. They may limit their players' civil rights. And, they may play their injured athletes by using pain killers without regard for their long-term physical well-being.

Fifth, when the desire to win is so great, the "end may justify the means." Coaches and players may use illegal tactics. Athletes may use performance enhancing drugs such as steroids and amphetamines to achieve a "competitive edge" or more subtly, but nonetheless unethical, using such means as blood doping or getting pregnant to get positive hormonal changes and then having an abortion. Both of these practices occur among endurance athletes. . . . So much, I would argue, for the myth that "sport builds character."

Sixth, when winning is all important, there may be a tendency to crush the opposition. This was the case when Riverside Poly High School girls basketball team played Norte Vista several years ago. Riverside won by a score of 179–15 with one player, Cheryl Miller, scoring a California record of 105 points. Was the Riverside coach ethical? . . . Will the Norte Vista girls be motivated to improve their performance or will this humiliating experience crush their spirit?

Seven, many people in a competitive society have difficulty with coming in second. . . . [For example, a few years back, a football team, composed of fifth-graders, in Florida was] undefeated going into the state finals but lost there in a close game. At a banquet following that season each player on this team was given a plaque on which was inscribed a quote from Vince Lombardi:

> There is no room for second place. I have finished second twice at Green Bay and I never want to finish second again. There is a second place bowl game but it is a game for losers played by losers. It is and always will be an American zeal to be first in anything we do and to win and to win and to win.

In other words, the parents and coaches of these boys wanted them to never be satisfied with being second. Second is losing. The only acceptable placement is first.

Finally, when "winning is the only thing" the joy in participation is lost. I have observed that organized sport from youth programs to the professional level is mostly devoid of playfulness. When the object is to win, then the primacy of the activity is lost. . . . In other words, it's the process that is primary, not the outcome. White water rafters and mountain climbers understand this. So, too, do players in a pickup touch football game. Why can't the rest of us figure out this fundamental truth?

Source: Excerpts from D. Stanley Eitzen, "The Dark Side of Competition in American Society," *Vital Speeches*, 56 (January 1, 1990), pp. 185–186.

of fantastic help to humankind, it has polluted the air, and each year it kills about 60,000 people in the United States in accidents. It is difficult to imagine life without electricity, but the creation of electricity pollutes the air and causes the thermal pollution of rivers. Insecticides and chemical fertilizers have performed miracles in agriculture, but they have polluted food and streams (and even killed some lakes). Obviously, the slogan of the DuPont Corporation (better living through chemistry) is not entirely correct.

Material Progress.   A belief of people in the United States holds that work pays off. The payoff is not only success in one's profession but also in economic terms—income and the acquisition and consumption of goods and services that go beyond adequate nutrition, medical care, shelter, and transportation. The superfluous things that we accumulate or strive to accumulate, such as country club memberships, jewelry, stylish clothes, lavish homes, boats, second homes, pool tables, electric toothbrushes, and season tickets to the games of our favorite teams or orchestras, are symbols of success in the competitive struggle. But these acquisitions have more than symbolic value because they are elements of what people in the United States consider the good life and, therefore, a right.

This emphasis on having things has long been a facet of U.S. life. This country, the energy crisis notwithstanding, has always been a land of opportunity and abundance. Although many persons are blocked from full participation in this abundance, the goal for most people is to accumulate things that bring status and that provide for a better way of life by saving labor or enhancing pleasure in our leisure.

Individual Freedom.   Americans value individualism. They believe that people should generally be free from government interference in their lives and businesses and free to make their own choices. Implied in this value is the responsibility of each individual for personal development. The focus on individualism places responsibility on the individual for his or her acts—not on society or its institutions. Being poor is blamed on the individual, not on the maldistribution of wealth and other socially perpetuated disadvantages that blight many families generation after generation. The aggressive behavior of minority youth is blamed on them, not on the limits placed on their social mobility by the social system. Dropping out of high school before graduation is blamed on individual students, not on the educational system that fails to meet their needs. This attitude helps explain the reluctance by persons in authority to provide adequate welfare, health care, and compensatory programs to help the disadvantaged. This common tendency of individuals to focus on the deviant (blaming the victim) rather than on the system that produces deviants has also been true of U.S. social scientists analyzing social problems.

Individual freedom is, of course, related to capitalism and private property. The economy is supposed to be competitive. Individuals, through their own efforts, business acumen, and luck can (if successful) own property and pyramid profits.

The belief that private property and capitalism are not to be restricted has led to several social problems: (1) unfair competition (monopolies, interlocking directorates, price-fixing); (2) a philosophy held by many entrepreneurs of caveat emptor (let the buyer beware), whereby the aim is profit with total disregard for the welfare of the consumer; and (3) the current ecology crisis, which is due in great

Reprinted courtesy of the Rocky Mountain News.

measure to the standard policy of many people and most corporations in the United States to do whatever is profitable—thus a neglect for conservation of natural resources.

These practices have led the federal and state governments to enact and enforce regulatory controls. Clearly, Americans have always tended to abuse nature and their fellows in the name of profit. Freedom, if so abused, must be curtailed, and the government (albeit somewhat reluctantly, given the pressures from various interest groups) has done this.

The related values of capitalism, private property, and self-aggrandizement (individualism) have also led to an environmental crisis. Industries fouling the air and water with refuse and farmers spraying pesticides that kill weeds and harm animal and human life are two examples of how individual persons and corporations look out for themselves with an almost total disregard for the short- and long-range effects of their actions on life.

As long as people in the United States hold a narrow self-orientation rather than a collectivity orientation, this crisis will continue and steadily worsen. The use people make of the land (and the water on it or running through it, and the air above it) has traditionally been theirs to decide because of the belief in private property. This belief in private property has meant, in effect, that individuals have had the right to pave a pasture for a parking lot, tear up a lemon grove for a housing development, put down artificial turf for a football field, and dump waste products into the air and water. Consequently, individual decisions have had the collective effect of taking millions of acres of arable land out of production permanently, polluting the air and water, covering land where vegetation once grew with asphalt, concrete buildings, and astroturf even though green plants are the only source of oxygen.

Values and Behavior

The discrepancy between values and behavior has probably always existed in the United States. Inconsistencies have always existed, for example, between the Christian ethic of love, brotherhood, and humanitarianism, on the one hand, and the realities of religious bigotry, the maximization of self-interest, and property rights over human rights on the other. The gap may be widening because of the tremendous rate of social change taking place (the rush toward urbanization, and the increased bureaucratization in all spheres of social life). Values do not change as rapidly as do other elements of the culture. Although values often differ from behavior, they remain the criteria for evaluating objects, persons, and events. It is important, however, to mention behaviors that often contradict the values because they demonstrate the hypocrisy prevalent in U.S. society that so often upsets young people (and others) who, in turn, develop countercultures (a topic that we discuss later in this chapter).

Perhaps the best example of the inconsistency between values and behavior is the belief in the American creed held by most people in the United States—generally assumed to encompass equality of all persons, freedom of speech and religion, and the guarantees of life, liberty, and prosperity—as against the injustices perpetuated by the system and individuals in the system on members of minority groups.

Americans glorify individualism and self-reliance. These related traits, however, are not found in bureaucracies, where the watchword is that to get along you have to go along. Rather than individualism, the way to get ahead in corporations and other large bureaucracies is to be a team player.

There is a myth that successful persons in the United States have always been self-made. Of course, some individuals have achieved wealth, fame, and power through their own achievements, but many have inherited their advantages. The irony is that the wealthy are considered successful whether they made the money or not. People in the United States tend to give great weight to the opinions expressed by wealthy people, as evidenced by the voters' tendency to elect them to public office.

Americans have always placed high value on the equality of all persons (in the courts or in getting a job). This value is impossible to reconcile with the racist and superiority theories held by some individuals and groups. It is also impossible to reconcile with many of the formal and informal practices on jobs, in the schools, in the lending procedures by banks, and in the courts.

Related to the stated belief in equality are the other fundamental beliefs enunciated by the Founding Fathers: the freedoms guaranteed in the Bill of Rights and the Declaration of Independence. Ironically, although the United States was founded by a revolution, the same behavior (called for by the Declaration of Independence) by dissident groups is now squelched (in much the same way as by King George III).

In the United States, people value law and order. This reverence for the law has been overlooked throughout American history whenever law-abiding groups, such as vigilante groups, took the law in their own hands (by threatening that anyone who disobeys vigilante law will be lynched). Currently, the groups to make the loudest demands for law and order are ones who disobey certain laws—for example, southern politicians blocking federal court orders to integrate schools; American Legion posts that notoriously ignore local, state, and federal laws about gambling and liquor; and school administrators allowing prayer in public school functions despite the ruling of the Supreme Court.

A final example of disparity between values and behavior in the United States involves the pride people have in solving difficult problems. Americans are inclined to be realists. They are pragmatic, down-to-earth problem solvers ready to apply scientific knowledge and expertise to handle such technical problems as getting human beings to and from the moon safely. This realism tends to be replaced by mere gestures, however, when it comes to social problems. In the United States, people have a compulsive tendency to avoid confrontation with chronic social problems. They tend to think that social problems will be solved if one has nice thoughts, such as "just say no" or "just don't do it." The verbal level is mistaken for action. If we hear our favorite television personality end the program with a statement against pollution or crime, we think the problem will somehow be solved. This is evidenced at another level by proclaiming a war on drugs, or by setting up a commission to study stock-market fraud, cost overruns in the Pentagon, or youth gangs. Philip Slater has said that the typical U.S. approach to social problems is to decrease their visibility—out of sight, out of mind.

> When these discarded problems rise to the surface again—a riot, a protest, an expose in the mass media—we react as if a sewer has backed up. We are shocked, disgusted, and angered. We immediately call for the emergency plumber (the special commission, the crash program) to ensure that the problem is once again removed from consciousness. (Slater, 1970:15)

The examples just presented make clear that while people in the United States express some values, they often behave differently. The values do, however, still provide the standards by which individuals are evaluated. These inconsistencies are sometimes important in explaining individual behavior (guilt, shame, aggression), and the emergence of insulating personal and social mechanisms such as compartmentalization and racial segregation.

Not only is there an inconsistency between values and behavior, but there is also a lack of unity among some of the values themselves. Some examples of this phenomenon, which has been called ethical schizophrenia, are individualism versus humanitarianism, materialism versus idealism, and pragmatism versus utopianism (Record and Record, 1965).

Cultural Diversity

In the United States, people are far from unanimous on a number of public issues (e.g., gun control, abortion, the death penalty, or prayer in schools). Despite inconsistencies and ambiguities, Americans do tend to believe in certain things—for example, that democracy is the best form of government; that capitalism is the best economic system; that success can be defined in terms of hard work, initiative, and the amassing of wealth and property; that Christianity should be the country's dominant religion; and that there should be equality of opportunity and equal justice before the law. But even though these values are held generally by the U.S. populace, there is never total agreement on any of them. The primary reason for this is the tremendous diversity found within the United States.

The United States is composed of many people who differ on important social dimensions: age, sex, race, region, social class, ethnicity, religion, rural/urban, and so on. These variables suggest that groups and categories will differ in values and behavior because certain salient social characteristics imply differential experiences and expectations. These are noted often in the remainder of this book.

Let us examine a few differences held by various groups and categories to illustrate the lack of consistency among people in the United States. Values are the criteria used to determine, among other things, morality. Public opinion polls show that the vast majority accept the legality of abortion, at least under certain circumstances. When these data are examined according to the age, income, and education of the respondents, we find systematic differences. The older the individual and the lower a person's income or education, the more likely to be anti-abortion.

The rural–urban differences in U.S. society are well known. An interesting example is the probability that rural people are more humanitarian, yet more intolerant of deviance among their neighbors, than are urban dwellers. There also are variations among rural communities, as there are among urban places on these and other differences.

Region of the country accounts for some variation in values held. But the generalizations made about southerners, easterners, and midwesterners, while having some validity, gloss over many real differences. Within any one region there are differences among rural and urban people, among different religious groups, and among different ethnic groups.

The concept **subculture** has been defined typically as a relatively cohesive cultural system that varies in form and substance from the dominant culture. Under the rubric subculture, then, there are ethnic groups, delinquent gangs, and religious sects (for a technique to study subculture, see "Research Methods: Participant Observation"). Milton Yinger (1962) has proposed that the concept *subculture* be defined more precisely. He has suggested that it be used for one type of group and *counterculture* for another type that has been previously called a subculture. For Yinger the concept *subculture* should be limited to relatively cohesive cultural systems that differ from the dominant culture in such things as language, values, religion, and style of life.

Typically, a group that is a subculture differs from the larger group because it has immigrated from another society and, because of physical or social isolation, has not been fully assimilated. The cultural differences, then, are usually based on ethnicity. Tradition keeps the culture of this group somewhat unique from the dominant culture. Examples of such subcultures in the United States include the Amish, the Hutterites, some Orthodox Jewish sects, many Native American tribes,

Research Methods

Participant Observation

A common method of data collection is **participant observation**—the direct observation of social phenomena in natural settings. One way to accomplish this is for the researcher to become part of what he or she is studying. There are several roles that observers may take in this regard. One is to hide the fact that one is a researcher and participate as a member of the group being studied. Another is to let the subjects know that you are a scientist but remain separate and detached from the group. A third option is to identify oneself as a researcher and become friends with those being studied. Each of these alternatives has its problems, such as the ethics of deceiving subjects and the fundamental problem of subjects altering their behavior if they know they are being investigated.

Elliot Liebow—a White, Jewish, and middle-class researcher—investigated the subculture of poor black males in one section of the Washington, DC ghetto.* From the beginning Liebow identified himself as a researcher. He became deeply involved with his subjects.

He partied with them, visited in their homes, gave them legal advice, and just generally hung around with them in their leisure hours. As the research progressed, he became more and more a part of the street-corner life he was investigating. As a White, though, he never escaped completely being an outsider.

At first, Liebow's field notes concentrated on individuals: what they said, what they did, and the contexts in which they said or did them. Through this beginning he ultimately saw the patterns of behavior and how the subjects perceived and understood themselves. He was able to understand the social structure of street-corner life. More important, his research enabled him to see the complexity of the social network of society's losers and how they continuously slip back and forth between the values and beliefs of the larger society and those of their own social system.

Tally's Corner (Boston: Little, Brown, 1967).

Appalachian snake handlers, and Poles, Croatians, Hungarians, Italians, Greeks, and Irish groups at one time or another in U.S. history. The existence of numerous subcultures within the United States explains much of the lack of consistency with respect to U.S. values.

A **counterculture**, as defined by Yinger, is a culturally homogeneous group that has developed values and norms that differ from the larger society because the group opposes the large society. This type of group is in conflict with the dominant culture. The particular values and norms can be understood only by reference to the dominant group.

The values held by delinquent gangs such as the Crips and the Bloods are commonly believed to be a reaction against the values held by the larger society (and hence would represent a counterculture). Albert K. Cohen (1955) has noted, for example, that lower-class juvenile gangs not only reject the dominant value system, but they also exalt opposite values. These boys, Cohen argues, are ill-equipped because of their lower-class origins and other related drawbacks to be successful in the game as it is defined by the dominant society. They therefore repudiate the commonly held values for new values that have meaning for them and under which they can perform satisfactorily. These values differ from the values of the larger culture because the delinquents actually want the larger values but cannot attain them. If

Cohen's thesis is correct, then delinquent gangs form a counterculture (although Cohen specifically names them subcultures).

Values from the Order and the Conflict Perspectives

Values are sources of both societal integration and social problems. Order theorists assume that sharing values solves the most fundamental problem of societal integration. The values are symbolic representations of the existing society and therefore promote unity and consensus among Americans. They must, therefore, be preserved.

Conflict theorists, on the other hand, view the mass acceptance of values as a form of cultural tyranny that promotes political conservatism, inhibits creativity, and gets people to accept their lot because they believe in the system rather than joining with others to try and change it. Thus, conflict theorists believe that slavish devotion to society's values inhibits necessary social change. Moreover, conflict theorists assume that U.S. values are the actual source of social problems such as crime, conspicuous consumption, planned obsolescence, the energy crisis, pollution, and the artificial creation of winners and losers.

Regardless of which side one may take on the consequences of U.S. values, most people would agree that the traditional values of individual freedom, capitalism, competition, and progress have made the United States relatively affluent. The future, however, will probably be very different from the past, requiring a fundamental change in these values. The future of slow growth or no growth, lower levels of affluence, and resource shortages will require that people adapt by adopting values that support cooperation rather than competition, that support group goals over individual goals, and a mode of making do rather than the purchasing of unnecessary products and the relentless search for technological solutions.

CHAPTER REVIEW

1. Culture, the knowledge the members of society or other social organizations share, constrains behavior and how people think about and interpret their world.

2. Culture emerges as a result of continued social interaction.

3. Culture is learned behavior. The process of learning the culture is called *socialization*.

4. Through the socialization process, individuals internalize the culture. Thus, the control that culture has over individuals is seen as natural.

5. Culture channels behavior by providing the rules for behavior and the criteria for judging.

6. Culture is boundary-maintaining. One's own culture seems right and natural. Other cultures are considered inferior, wrong, or immoral. This tendency to consider the ways of one's own group superior is called *ethnocentrism*.

7. Six types of shared knowledge constitute the culture—symbols, technology, ideologies, norms, values, and roles.

8. Norms are divided into two types by degree of importance and severity of punishment for their violation. Folkways are less important. Mores are considered more vital and thereby are more severely punished if violated.

9. Roles are the behavioral expectations of people who occupy the statuses in a social organization.

10. Through language and other symbols, culture determines how the members of a society will interpret

their environment. The important point is that through this construction of reality the members of a society make sense out of a world that may have no inherent meaning.

11. The variety of customs found throughout the world is staggering. The members of one society typically view the customs found elsewhere as weird, cruel, and immoral. If we understand the cultural context of a given society, however, their practices generally make sense. This is called *cultural relativity.*

12. Knowing the values (the criteria for evaluation) of a society is an excellent way of understanding that society.

13. Values in the United States are the result of three major factors: (*a*) geographical isolation and being blessed with abundant resources; (*b*) founding of the nation in opposition to tyranny and aristocracy and supporting freedom, democracy, equality, and impersonal justice; and (*c*) a religious heritage based on the Judeo–Christian ethic and the Protestant work ethic.

14. The dominant U.S. values are success through individual achievement, competition, hard work, progress through growth and new technology, material progress, and individual freedom.

15. These values are the sources of societal integration as well as social problems.

16. Despite the power of culture and U.S. values over individual conduct, the diversity present in U.S. society means that for many people there are inconsistencies between values and actual behavior. There are clear variations in how people feel on public issues based on their different social situations.

17. A major source of cultural variation in the United States is the existence of subcultures. Because of different religions and ethnicity some groups retain a culture different from the dominant one. Other groups form a culture because they oppose the larger society. The latter are called *countercultures.*

18. Order theorists assume that the sharing of values promotes unity among the members of society. The values therefore must be preserved.

19. Conflict theorists view the mass acceptance of values as a form of cultural tyranny that promotes political conservatism, inhibits creativity, and encourages false consciousness.

KEY TERMS

Culture	Ethnomethodology	Epistemology
Socialization	Values	Cultural relativity
Superego	Status(es)	Protestant ethic
Internalization	Roles	Deferred gratification
Reference groups	Ascribed status	Subculture
Ethnocentrism	Achieved status	Participant observation
Material technology	Social construction of reality	Counterculture
Social technology	Ontology	

STUDY QUESTIONS

1. Because individuals internalize the culture, they tend to assume that its control over one's behavior is not control but natural. Assess your ideas and behaviors to determine which of them, if any, are culture-free.

2. What is meant by the social construction of reality? Provide examples.

3. How are U.S. values sources of both societal integration and social problems?

4. How do order theorists and conflict theorists differ in their interpretation of values?

FOR FURTHER READING

Culture: General

Ruth Benedict, *Patterns of Culture* (Baltimore: Penguin, 1946).

Peter L. Berger and Thomas Luckman, *The Social Construction of Reality* (Garden City, NY: Doubleday Anchor Books, 1967).

Marvin Harris, *Cows, Pigs, Wars, and Witches: The Riddles of Culture* (New York: Random House Vintage Books, 1974).

Jeremy Rifkin, *Time Wars: The Primary Conflict in Human History* (New York: Henry Holt, 1987).

American Values

Robert N. Bellah, Richard Madsen, William M. Sullivan, Ann Swidler, and Steven M. Tipton, *Habits of the Heart: Individualism and Commitment in American Life,* updated edition (Berkeley: University of California Press, 1996).

Stephen Butterfield, *Amway: The Cult of Free Enterprise* (Boston: South End Press, 1985).

Charles Derber, *The Wilding of America: How Greed and Violence Are Eroding Our Nation's Character* (New York: St. Martin's Press, 1996).

Marvin Harris, *America Now: The Anthropology of a Changing Culture* (New York: Simon & Schuster, 1981).

Seymour Martin Lipset, *American Exceptionalism: A Double-Edged Sword* (New York: W. W. Norton, 1996).

Philip Slater, *Wealth Addiction* (New York: E. P. Dutton, 1980).

Ben J. Wattenberg, *Values Matter Most: How Republicans or Democrats or a Third Party Can Win and Renew the American Way of Life* (New York: The Free Press, 1995).

Robin Williams, *American Society: A Sociological Interpretation,* 3rd ed. (New York: Alfred A. Knopf, 1970).

Subcultures

Sue Bender, *Plain and Simple: A Woman's Journey to the Amish* (San Francisco: Harper & Row, 1989).

William M. Kephart and William W. Zellner, *Extraordinary Groups: The Sociology of Unconventional Life-Styles,* 4th ed. (New York: St. Martin's, 1991).

Elliot Liebow, *Tally's Corner* (Boston: Little, Brown, 1967).

Jay MacLeod, *Ain't No Makin' It: Aspirations & Attainment in a Low-Income Neighborhood,* revised ed. (Boulder, CO: Westview, 1995).

Felix M. Padilla, *The Gang as an American Enterprise* (New Brunswick, NJ: Rutgers University Press, 1992).

J. Milton Yinger, *Countercultures: The Promise and Peril of a World Turned Upside Down* (New York: Free Press, 1982).

William W. Zellner, *Countercultures: A Sociological Analysis* (New York: St. Martin's Press, 1995).

CHAPTER 5

Socialization

Oscar Stohr and Jack Yufe are identical twins separated as babies by their parents' divorce. Oscar was raised by his maternal grandmother in the Sudetenland of Czechoslovakia. He was a strict Catholic. As a loyal Nazi, he hated Jews. His brother, Jack, was raised by his Jewish father in Trinidad. During World War II he was loyal to the British and hated the Germans.

The twins were united briefly in 1954, but Jack was warned by the translator to not tell his brother that he was Jewish. In 1979, at age 47, the brothers were reunited by scientists who wished to establish the degree to which environment shapes human behavior. Because they had the same genes, any differences between the brothers must result from how they were raised.

The scientists found not only that they were physically alike but also that the twins were strikingly similar in temperament, tastes, tempo, and the way they did things. Both had been excellent athletes. Both had trouble in school with mathematics. But the twins also differed in many important respects. Jack was a workaholic, whereas Oscar enjoyed his leisure time. Jack was a political liberal; Oscar a traditionalist. This difference was seen in Jack's tolerance of feminism and Oscar's resistance to that movement. Jack was proud of being Jewish; Oscar never mentioned his Jewish heritage.

Introduction to Socialization

In this chapter we examine this process of socialization that is so powerful in shaping human thought and behavior as to make identical twins different.

Every day thousands of newborns arrive in the U.S. society. How do these newborns become members of society? How do they become what we term *human?* The answer to these questions is that they learn to be human by acquiring the meanings, ideas, and actions appropriate for that society. This process of learning the culture is called **socialization.***

Children are born with the limits and potential established by their unique genetic compositions. Their physical features, size and shape, rate of physical development, and even temperament unfold within predetermined boundaries (Franklin, 1989). The limits of their intellectual capabilities are also influenced by biological heritage. But even though children are biologically human, they do not have the instincts or the innate drives that will make them human. They acquire their humanness through social interaction. Their concepts of themselves, personality, love, freedom, justice, right and wrong, and interpretation of reality are all products of social interaction. In other words, human beings are essentially the social creations of society.

Evidence for this assertion is found by examining the traits and behaviors of children raised without much human contact. There have been occasional accounts of **feral children** throughout history—children alleged to have been raised by animals. When found, they look human but act like the animals with whom they have had contact. One case involved a Tarzan-like child reported to have been raised by monkeys in the jungles of central Africa. The boy was discovered in 1974 at about the age of six with a troop of gray monkeys. Two years later after painstaking efforts to rehabilitate him, he remained more monkey than human. "He is unable to talk and communicates by 'monkey' grunts and chattering. He will eat only fruit and vegetables, and when excited or scared jumps up and down uttering threatening monkey cries" (Associated Press, May 15, 1976). If a child's personality were largely determined by biological heritage, this child would have been much more human than simian. But there is a consistent finding in all cases that feral children are not normal. They cannot talk and have great difficulty in learning human speech patterns. They do not walk or eat like human beings. They express anger differently. In essence, the behavior that arises in the absence of human contact is not what we associate with human beings.

While the reported cases of feral children should be viewed with considerable skepticism, the cases of children living in human settings but kept isolated from most human contact reveal much about the importance of human interaction in becoming human. The most famous case of a child who was raised with only min-

---

*That this chapter focuses on how children learn the culture should not be interpreted to mean that the socialization process stops at the end of adolescence. To the contrary, socialization is a lifelong process occurring within each social group within the society.

imal human contact was a girl named Anna (Davis, 1940, 1948). Anna was an illegitimate child. Her grandfather refused to acknowledge her existence, and to escape his ire, the mother put her in an attic room and, except for minimal feeding, ignored her. Anna was discovered by a social worker at about age six, and she was placed in a special school. When found, Anna could not sit up or walk. She could not talk and was believed to be deaf. She was immobile and completely indifferent to the people around her. She did not laugh, show anger, or smile. Staff members worked with Anna (during one year a single staff member had to receive medical attention more than a dozen times for bites she received from Anna). Eventually, Anna learned to take care of herself and to walk, talk, and play with other children.

> By the time Anna died of hemorrhagic jaundice approximately four and a half years [after she was found], she had made considerable progress as compared with her condition when found. She could follow directions, string beads, identify a few colors, build with blocks, and differentiate between attractive and unattractive pictures. She had a good sense of rhythm and loved a doll. She talked mainly in phrases but would repeat words and try to carry on a conversation. She was clean about clothing. She habitually washed her hands and brushed her teeth. She would try to help other children. She walked well and could run fairly well, though clumsily. Although easily excited, she had a pleasant disposition. Her involvement showed that socialization, even when started at the late age of six, could still do a great deal toward making her a person. Even though her development was no more than that of a normal child of two or three years, she had made noteworthy progress. (Davis, 1948:205)

The conclusion from the people who had observed Anna and other cases of isolated children is that being deprived of social interaction during one's formative years deprives individuals of their humanness.

The second essential to socialization is language. Language is the vehicle through which socialization occurs. In Anna's case, what little human contact she had during her first six years was physical and not communicative interaction. As Kingsley Davis has noted, Anna's case illustrates "that communicative contact is the core of socialization" (Davis, 1948:205). This principle is also illustrated by Helen Keller. This remarkable person became deaf and blind as a result of illness during infancy. She was locked into her own world until her teacher, Anne Sullivan, was able to communicate to her that the symbol she traced on Helen's hand represented water. That was the beginning of language for Helen Keller and the beginning of her understanding of who she was and the meaning of the world and society in which she was immersed (Keller, 1954).

Learning language has profound effects on how individuals think and perceive. Through their languages, societies differ in how they conceive of time, space, distance, velocity, action, and specificity. To illustrate this last dimension, specificity, let us consider the Navajo language. With respect to rain, the Navajo language makes much finer distinctions than English speakers who generally say, "It has started to rain," "It is raining," and "It has stopped raining." When the Navajo reports personal experiences,

> he uses one verb form if he himself is aware of the actual inception of the rain storm, another if he has reason to believe that the rain has been falling for some time in his

locality before the occurrence struck his attention. One form must be employed if rain is general round about within the range of vision; another if, though it is raining about, the storm is plainly on the move. Similarly, the Navaho must invariably distinguish between the ceasing of rainfall (generally), and the stopping of rain in a particular vicinity because the rain clouds have been driven off by the wind. The people take the consistent noticing and reporting of such differences . . . as much for granted as the rising of the sun. (Kluckhohn and Leighton, 1946:194)

In short, the languages of different societies are not parallel methods for expressing the same reality. Our perception of reality depends on our language (this is the *social construction of reality,* as discussed in the previous chapter). In this way experience itself is a function of language. As the distinguished linguist B. L. Whorf has put it, "no individual is free to describe nature with absolute impartiality but is constrained to certain modes of interpretation even while he thinks himself most free" (Whorf, 1956:1).

In learning language, we discover the meaning of symbols not only for words but also for objects such as the cross, the flag, and traffic lights. Through language we can think about the past and the future. Language symbolizes the values and norms of the society, thus enabling the user to label and evaluate objects, acts, individuals, and groups. The words we use in such instances can be positive, such as *beautiful, wise, moral, friend,* and *appropriate,* or negative, such as *ugly, dumb, immoral, enemy,* or *inappropriate.* Moreover, the description of the same act can portray a positive or a pejorative image. This can be seen in the sports world, as reported by syndicated columnist Jim Murray:

- On our side, a guy is "colorful." On their side, a "hotdog."
- Our team is "resourceful." Theirs is "lucky."
- Our guys are "trusted associates." Theirs are "henchmen."
- Our team gives "rewards." Theirs, "bribes."
- Our team plays "spirited" football. Theirs plays "dirty."
- Our team is "opportunistic." Theirs gets all the "breaks."
- Our guy is "confident." Theirs is ["cocky"]. (Murray, 1976:150)

Thus, language is a powerful labeling tool, clearly delineating who is in and who is out.

Finally, children learn who they are by using words to describe themselves. The words they use are those that other people, in turn, have used in talking about them and their actions.

The Personality as a Social Product

Chapter 2 notes the dialectic character of society. Society is at once a product of social interaction, yet that product continuously acts back on its producers. As Berger (1975:234) has put it, "Society is a product of man. . . . Yet it may also be stated that man is a product of society." In this section, the emphasis is on this second process—human beings as a product of society. In particular, we examine the emergence of the human personality as a social product.

We develop a sense of **self** (our personality) in interaction with other people. Newly born infants have no sense of self-awareness. They are unable to distinguish between themselves and their surroundings. They cry spontaneously when uncomfortable. They eventually become aware that crying can be controlled and that its use can bring a response from other people. In time, and especially with the use of language, the child begins to distinguish between "I" and "you" and "mine" and "yours"—signs of self-awareness. But this is just the beginning of the personality-formation process. Let us look now at several classical theories of how children develop personalities and how they learn what is expected of them in the community and society.

Charles H. Cooley: The Looking-Glass Self

Cooley (1864–1929) believed that children's conceptions of themselves arise through interaction with other people (Cooley, 1964). He used the metaphor of a **looking-glass self** to convey the idea that all persons understand themselves through the way in which other people act toward them. They judge themselves on how they think others judge them. Cooley believed that each of us imagines how we look to others and what their judgment of us is. Bierstedt has summarized this process: "I am not what I think I am and I am not what you think I am. I am what I think you think I am" (Bierstedt, 1974:197).

The critical process in Cooley's theory of personality development, then, is the feedback the individual receives from other people. Others behave in particular ways with regard to an individual. The individual interprets these behaviors positively or negatively. When the behaviors of other people are perceived as consistent, the individual accepts this definition of self, which in turn has consequences for his or her behavior. In sum, there is a self-fulfilling prophecy—the individual is as defined by other people. Suppose, for example, that whenever you entered a room and approached a small knot of people conversing with each other, they promptly melted away with lame excuses. This experience, repeated many times, would affect your feelings about yourself. Or, if wherever you appeared, a conversational group quickly formed around you, would not such attention tend to give you self-confidence and ego strength?

Cooley's insight that our self-concepts are a product of how other people react to us is important in understanding behavior. Why are some categories of persons more likely to be school dropouts or criminals or malcontents or depressed while others fit in? As we see in Chapter 7, deviance is the result of the successful application of a social label, a process akin to the looking-glass self. So, too, does this concept help us to understand the tendency of minority-group members to have low self-esteem. If African American children, for example, receive a consistent message from Whites that they are inferior, that they are incapable of success in intellectually demanding tasks, and that they are not trustworthy, the probability is that they will have these traits. Many Black children and adults fulfill this prophecy, thereby reinforcing the stereotypes of the majority and the low self-esteem of the Blacks.

George Herbert Mead: Taking the Role of the Other

Mead (1863–1931) theorized about the relationship of self and society (Mead, 1934). In essence, he believed that children find out who they are as they learn about society and society's expectations. This occurs in several important stages. Infants learn to distinguish between themselves and others from the actions of their parents. By the age of two or so, children have become self-conscious. By this Mead meant that the children are able to react to themselves as others will react to them. For example, they will tell themselves "no-no," as they have been told many times by their parents, and not touch the hot stove. The importance of this stage is that the children have internalized the feelings of other people. What others expect has become a part of them. They have become conscious of themselves by incorporating the way other people are conscious of them.

The next stage is the play stage. Children from ages four to seven spend many hours a day in a world of play. Much of this time is spent in pretending to be mothers, teachers, doctors, police officers, ministers, grocers, and other roles. Mead called this form of play "taking the role of the others." As they play at a variety of social roles, children act out the behavior associated with these social positions and thus develop a rudimentary understanding of adult roles and why people in those positions act the way they do. They also see how persons in these roles interact with children. Thus, children learn to look at themselves as other people see them. As McGee has put it, "he learns who he is by 'being' who he is not" (McGee, 1975:74–75). The play stage, then, accomplishes two things. It provides further clues for children as to who they are, and it prepares them for later life.

The game stage, which occurs at about age eight, is the final stage of personality development in Mead's scheme. In the play stage the children's activities were

According to George Herbert Mead, during the play stage (ages four to seven), children spend much of their free time pretending to be mothers, teachers, doctors, police officers, ministers, and other roles. As they "take the role of the others," children act out the behavior associated with these social positions, and thus develop a rudimentary understanding of adult roles.

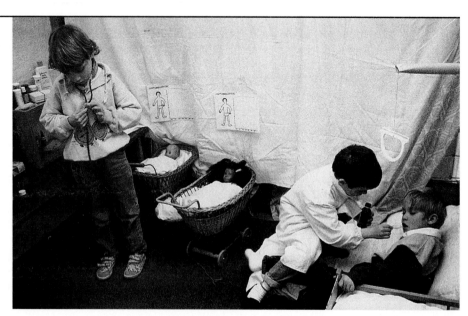

fluid and spontaneous. The game stage, in contrast, involves activities that are structured. There are rules that define, limit, and constrain the participants. Mead used baseball to illustrate what occurs in the game stage. In baseball children must understand and abide by the rules. They must also understand the entire game—that is, when playing second base what they and the other players must do if there is a player on first, one out, and the batter bunts down the first base line. In other words, the various individuals in a game must know the roles of all the players and adjust their behavior to that of the others. The assessment of the entire situation is what Mead called the discovery of the "generalized other." In the play stage, children learn what is expected of them by **significant others** (parents, relatives, teachers). The game stage provides children with constraints from many other people, including people they do not know. In this way children incorporate and understand the pressures of society—the **generalized other.** By passing through these stages children have finally developed a social life from the expectations of parents, friends, and society. The important insight of Mead is that the self emerges as the result of social experience. Thus, the self does not exist at birth but is a social creation.

Sigmund Freud: The Psychoanalytic View

Freud (1856–1939) emphasized the biological dimension along with social factors in personality development (Freud, 1946). For Freud, the infant's first years are totally egocentric, with all energies directed toward pleasure. This is an expression of a primitive biological force—the **id** that dominates the infant. The id, although a force throughout life, is gradually stifled by society. Parents, as the agents of society, hamper children's pleasure-seeking by imposing schedules for eating, punishing them for messy behavior and masturbation, forcing them to control their bowels, and the like.

The process of socialization is, in Freud's view, the process of society controlling the id. Through this process children develop egos. The **ego** is the rational part of the personality that controls the id's basic urges, finding realistic ways of satisfying these biological cravings. The individual also develops a **superego** (conscience) (Chapter 4), which regulates both the id and ego. The superego is the consequence of the child's internalizing the parents' morals. A strong superego represses the id and channels behavior in socially acceptable ways.

Freud presented a view of socialization that differs significantly from the theories of Mead and Cooley. Whereas Mead and Cooley saw the socialization process as a complete and nonconflictual one, Freud believed the process to be incomplete and accomplished by force. Freud saw the person pulled by two contradictory forces—the natural impulses of biology and the constraints of society—resulting in the imperfection and discontent of human beings. Mead and Cooley, in contrast, did not view the child as one who is repressed, led kicking and screaming into adulthood. For Mead, the child passed through natural stages as a willing apprentice to become a conforming member of society. Thus, Mead's conception of the socialization process is deterministic—the individual is a creature of society. Freud's view is quite different.

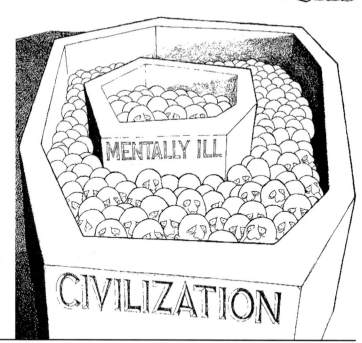

To Freud a human being is a *social* animal without being entirely a *socialized* animal. His or her very social nature is the source of conflicts and antagonisms that create resistance to socialization by the norms of any of the societies which have existed in the course of human history (Wrong, 1969: 130).

Society's Socialization Agents

Two themes stand out in this section. First, the personality of the child is, to a large degree, socially created and sustained. Second, through the process of socialization, the child internalizes the norms and values of society. In a sense, the child learns a script for acting, feeling, and thinking that is in tune with the wishes of society. Before we leave this topic, let us look briefly at the special transmitters of the cultural patterns—the family, the schools, and the media.

The Family. Aside from the obvious function of providing the child with the physical needs of food, clothing, and shelter, the family is the primary agent of socialization. The family indoctrinates the child in the ways of society. The parents equip the child with the information, etiquette, norms, and values necessary for the functioning member of society. Parents in blatant and subtle ways emit messages of what is important, appropriate, moral, beautiful, and correct—and what is not. There is no option for young children. They must accept the messages of their parents of what is and what ought to be. As Everett Wilson has put it:

But when [the child] enters the human group, he is quite at the mercy of parents and siblings. They determine both what and when he shall eat and wear, when he shall sleep and wake, what he shall think and feel, how he shall express his thoughts and feelings (what language he shall speak and how he shall do it), what his political and religious commitments shall be, what sort of vocation he shall aspire to. Not that parents are ogres. They give what they have to give: their own limited knowledge, their prejudices and passions. There is no alternative to this giving of themselves; nor for the receiver is there any option. Neither can withhold the messages conveyed to the other. (Wilson, 1966:92)

Thus, the children learn from their parents. They learn from them the meaning of physical objects such as the Bible, poison, and the police officer's badge. They also learn the relative worth of social groups such as Jews or Blacks. "A Closer Look: Learning to Hate" provides an example of how one young man was raised to hate Blacks.

The Schools.   In contrast to families who may differ somewhat in their attitudes, interests, and emphases, the schools provide a more uniform indoctrination of youth in the culturally prescribed ways. Formal education in any society serves to enculturate young persons. The schools have the avowed goal of preparing persons for their adult roles. Youngsters in school must learn appropriate skills and incorporate character traits and attitudes (such as patriotism) that pay off. In the United States some character traits are competitiveness, ambition, and conformity.

As we see in Chapter 16, the formal system of education is conservative; it transmits the attitudes, values, and training necessary for the maintenance of society.

A CLOSER LOOK

Learning to Hate

In July 1993, eight skinheads from three subgroups (The Fourth Reich Skins, the White Youth Alliance, and the White Aryan Resistance) were arrested for conspiring to kill several well-known Black leaders and plotting to blow up the First African Methodist Episcopal Church in Los Angeles and gun down its parishioners in the hope of starting a race war.

Greg Withrow is widely acknowledged as the founder of the U.S. version of the so-called skinhead movement in 1978. Since then this White supremacy organization has grown to an active membership of 3500 in forty states, doubling since 1988. The motivation to become a member is extreme hatred for minorities. In addition to physical assaults on racial and ethnic minorities, these groups print and distribute thousands of pieces of hate literature, blaming racial minorities and Jews for all manner of social problems.

What makes one a candidate for skinhead membership? Why would one hate others so fiercely? In the case of its founder, Greg Withrow, he was brought up to be racist. In his words, "Some fathers raise their sons to be doctors, some fathers raise their sons to be lawyers. I was raised to be the Fuhrer" (quoted in Mulvaney, 1993:22A). His father made him study the life of Hitler and read hate literature. At age fourteen he joined the Ku Klux Klan. Later he was arrested for heading a group that mugged Japanese tourists and homosexuals. While in college he formed the White Students Union and the Aryan Youth Movement. From these roots came the hatred of one individual for racial minorities *and* the skinhead movement.

"*We can be proud of our little Attila. He has totally absorbed the Hun ethic.*"

Thus, schools are preoccupied with order and control. This emphasis on order teaches the norms and prepares the youth for the organizational life they are expected to experience as adults. Unlike the family, where the child is part of a loving relationship, the school is impersonal. The rules are to be obeyed. Activities are regimented rather than spontaneous. Thus, the child learns how to function in the larger society by learning the formal prescriptions of society and by learning that to get along one must go along.

The Media.   The mass media—consisting of newspapers, magazines, movies, radio, and television—play a vital role in promoting the existing values and practices of society. For example, the mass media provide us with most of the information that helps us to define sociopolitical reality. As Parenti has suggested,

> for many people, an issue does not exist until it appears in the news media. Indeed, what we even define as an issue or event, what we see and hear, and what we do *not* see and hear are greatly determined by those who control the communications world. . . . Even when we don't believe what the media say, we are still hearing or reading their viewpoints rather than some other. They are still setting the agenda, defining what it is we must believe or disbelieve, accept, or reject. The media exert a subtle, persistent influence in defining the scope of respectable political discourse. (Parenti, 1993:1)

The media promote traditional U.S. values. In his study of "CBS Evening News," "NBC Nightly News," *Newsweek,* and *Time,* sociologist Herbert Gans found that these news sources portrayed eight clusters of enduring values: ethnocentrism, altruistic democracy, responsible capitalism, small-town pastoralism, individualism, moderatism, social order, and national leadership (Gans, 1979). The promotion of these values is especially effective because it appears to the consumers as independent and objective.

Television, through its entertainment shows, also functions to promote the status quo. Stereotypes of the aged, women, and minorities are promoted on these programs. Crime shows, for example, provide a series of morality plays in which

> wrongs are righted, victims avenged, and victimizers awarded for just deserts. The timing is the same, the rhythm, the choreography, the cast, the denouement—everyone has learned just what to expect. On the top of the heap are television's Good Guys, for years mainly mature white males. On the bottom of the heap lie the Victims—piled up bodies of children, old people, poor people, nonwhites, young people, lone women—all done in by Bad Guys recruited principally from the lower social strata many of the so-called victims come from. . . . Our modern morality plays . . . point the finger at the social strata from which evil emanates and signal the conditions that make it quite proper to shoot, kill, maim, hurt, rip, smash, slash, crush, tear, burn, bury, excise. What starts out as shocking becomes routine then is converted into ritual. (Goldsen, 1977:223–224, 234; see also Parenti, 1992)

The hard news side of the media also has a class, race, and gender bias, which serves the privileged and the powerful (the following is from Parenti, 1993:9–13). There are few programs with poverty as the subject, and these rarely explain poverty by low wages, high rents, regressive taxes, and other structural reasons. Rather, the poor are seen as poor because of their behaviors, such as a lack of motivation and a dependence on welfare. This consistent message from the media says, in effect, that the problem lies in bad people, not in a bad system. A class bias is also seen in the way crime is reported. The attention of the media is focused on street crimes rather than on white-collar crimes or crimes by corporations. Affluent victims of street crimes receive more media attention than do victims who are poor and non-White.

Blacks, Latinos, and other minorities are disproportionately depicted by the media as criminals, drug addicts, and the homeless. Rare is the news coverage on the injustices that racial minorities face in obtaining loans, receiving fairness in the criminal justice system, desegregating neighborhoods, and getting a fair shake in employment, pay, and advancement.

Women are also treated unfairly by the media, which, subtly, work to maintain male dominance in society. Women, along with racial minorities, are drastically underrepresented as employees in the communications industry. The people in print and broadcast news stories are women only about 11 percent of the time. Women make the news as victims of male violence, but they seldom appear as the victims of public policy. Summing up the biased stories of women in the media, Parenti says:

> Women of accomplishment are very likely to make the news if they are unusual "firsts." . . . However, the more general battle for economic, social, and sexual equality and for the material betterment and health care that women have been waging is slighted. Women make up 65 percent of the minimum-wage work force; but as with

The messages children receive from television are consistent: they are bombarded with materialism and consumerism, what it takes to be a success, sex, violence, and the value of law and order.

the Black struggle, the *class* dimensions of the women's struggle is not a fit subject for the mainstream media. The press regularly ignores issues of desperate concern to working-class women and women of color. (Parenti, 1993:12–13)

The messages children receive are consistent: They are bombarded with materialism and consumerism, what it takes to be a success, sex, violence, and the value of law and order. In short, the media have tremendous power to influence us all, but particularly our youth. This influence can be in the direction of acceptance or criticism of the system. Overwhelmingly, the media are supportive of that system.

Let's consider another possible socialization impact of the media—the bombardment of violence and violent themes in the movies, television, and rap music. By the time a child in the United States graduates from high school, he or she will have spent more time in front of the tube than in class. This means that "by the age of eighteen, the average American child will have seen 200,000 violent acts on television, including 40,000 murders" (Plagens, 1991:51). Or put another way, a study by *TV Guide* in 1992 recorded 1,846 acts of violence during a single day of television with WTBS (a Turner Broadcasting superstation) averaging 18 an hour, HBO 14 an hour, USA Network 12 an hour, 11 an hour on MTV, and 10 an hour on Fox and CBS (reported in *Wall Street Journal*, 1992b:B6). Does watching violence explain the high rate of teenage violence? There are conflicting views on this.

Politicians are fond of blaming Hollywood for violence. The American Medical Association has demanded tighter movie regulations concerning violence. The American Psychological Association lists four experiences crucial to the development of violent behavior: access to guns, involvement with alcohol or other drugs, involvement in antisocial groups, and exposure to violence in the mass media (American Psychological Association, 1993). Similarly, various news magazines and politicians have often pointed to various forms of music that teenagers listen to and watch (MTV), such as rap music, rock-and-roll, and heavy metal, as responsible for youth violence.

But this argument does not hold up, as Mike Males (1996) has argued forcefully. If the media are a significant cause of youth violence, then we should find similar levels of violence among different subgroups of youth, since they are all exposed to similar amounts of media influence. But, as Males points out, youth violence levels are extremely dissimilar: Black youths are twelve times more likely to commit murders than White youths; males are nine times more violent than females; teens from Washington, DC, are twenty-two times more likely to be arrested for homicide than teens from Washington State; inner-city youth are much more violent than youth from the suburbs. Males presents the following compelling argument:

> Thirty-one suburban and rural California counties with a population of 2.5 million, in which a quarter-million teenagers reside, experienced zero murders in 1993. Zero. . . . Same rock'n'roll furies, same rap concerts, same TV barbarism (worse, since suburban and rural families are more likely to subscribe to graphic cable channels), same guns on every block (more in rural towns), no shortage of drug and alcohol involvement, no lack of opportunity to form anti-social groups for youths who so desire, the same teenagers bearing whatever innate "high risk" teenage qualities and "crises" of growing up experts offer as all-purpose explanations. But no killings.
>
> Yet central Los Angeles census tracts with the same youth population as these 31 counties experienced more than 200 murders. (Males, 1996:127)

What are the reasons for this dramatic difference for two categories of youth from the same state? Clearly the media, which is full of gratuitous violence, sexual degradation, and bad taste, are *not* to blame, since both the violent and the nonviolent watch them. Males points to the different conditions in which youth grow up. The Los Angeles census tracts with 200 teenage murders have high concentrations of poverty, compared to the more affluent suburban and rural counties where no youth murders occurred. Growing up in poverty is brutalizing. Children there see real shootings, not just the make-believe violence on television. Again, Males argues:

> [The media devote] far more attention to the oft-repeated assertion that "the average American child sees 8,000 murders and 10,000 acts of violence on television before he or she is out of grammar school" than to the rarely-examined fact that millions of American children experience real rapes and beatings before they are old enough to get out of grammar school. (Males, 1996:123)

Similarities and Differences among the Members of Society

Modal Personality Type

Chapter 2 describes the condition that Durkheim called anomie. This refers to a situation in which an individual is unsure of his or her social world—the norms are ambiguous or conflicting. In other words, an anomic situation lacks consistency, predictability, and order. Because this condition is upsetting, individuals and groups seek order. Every society provides a common **nomos** (meaningful order) for its members (Berger and Luckman, 1967). "Every society has its specific way of defining and perceiving reality—its world, the universe, its overarching organization of symbols" (Berger and Kellner, 1975:219). Through the socialization process, the newcomer to society is provided a reality that makes sense. By learning the language and the ready-made definitions of society, the individual is given a consistent way to perceive the world. We take for granted the order that is created for each of us; it is the only world that we can conceive of; it is the only system in which we feel comfortable.

> This order, by which the individual comes to perceive and define his world, is thus not chosen by him, except perhaps for very small modifications. Rather it is discovered by him as an external datum, a ready-made world that simply is *there* for him to go ahead and live in, though he modifies it continually in the process of living in it. (Berger and Kellner, 1975:220)

Each society has its unique way of perceiving, interpreting, and evaluating reality. This common culture, and nomos, is internalized by the members of society through the process of socialization—thus, people are a product of their culture. It follows, then, that the members of a society will be similar in many fundamental respects. Although there are individual exceptions and subcultural variations, we can say that Americans differ fundamentally from Mexicans, Germans, the French, Malaysians, and others. Let us illustrate how people in a society develop similarly by briefly characterizing two categories of Native Americans of North America (taken from Barnouw, 1979:59–75).

■ **The Pueblo of the Southwest**   The Zuni and Hopi are submissive and gentle peoples. Children are treated with warmth and affection. They live in highly cooperative social structures where individualism is discouraged. One who thirsts for power is ridiculed. Life in these societies is highly structured. The rules are extremely important, and order is highly valued. They never brew intoxicants and reject the use of drugs. In these orderly and cooperative settings, people are trusted. Life is pleasant and relatively free from hatred. The kind of person that develops in these societies tends to be confident, trusting, generous, polite, cooperative, and emotionally controlled.

■ **The Northern Plains**   The Native Americans of this area are aggressive peoples. They are fierce warriors exhibiting almost suicidal bravado in battle. They stress individuality with fierce competition for prestige. They boast of their exploits. They stress individual ecstasy in their religious experiences, brought about by fasting, self-torture, and the use of drugs (peyote and alcohol). The Plains tribes, in contrast to the Pueblo, are more individualistic, competitive, and aggressive. They are more expressive as individuals and less orderly in group life.

These examples show that each society tends to produce a certain type of individual—a **modal personality type.** The individual growing up in the United States, with its set of values, tends to be individualistic, competitive, materialistic, and oriented toward work, progress, and the future. Even though this characterization is generally correct, there are some problems with the assumption that socialization into a culture is all-powerful. First, the power of socialization can vary by the type of society. Small, homogeneous societies like those of Native American tribes provide the individual member of society with a consistent message, whereas in a heterogeneous society like the United States, individuals are confronted with a number of themes, variations, and counterthemes.

A second problem is more fundamental, though: Is the socialization process completely deterministic? The views of Cooley and Mead noted earlier would seem to suggest this. Dennis Wrong has criticized this position. He has argued that, from a Freudian position, the individual and society are never completely in harmony. Even though individuals are socialized and generally comply with the demands of society, the process is never complete (Wrong, 1969:130). The distance from complete socialization is maximized in modern, heterogeneous societies.

Why We Are Not All Alike

Every society has its deviants. Clearly, people are not robots. Given the power of society, through the socialization process, what are the forces that allow for differences in people in the United States? We begin with a discussion of the major agencies of socialization.

Family.   We have said that the family is the ultimate societal agency for socialization. Families teach their children the language, etiquette, and skills that enable the child to find his or her niche in society. But families differ in a variety of important ways (for example, in religion, political views, optimism, and affluence). Some parents tend to be authoritarian, demanding control of their youngsters and providing punishment for failure to comply. Authority figures are to be obeyed without questions. In contrast, other parents allow their children to explore, experiment, and question. The family is democratic. Rules are not necessarily absolute. Clearly, children growing up in authoritarian and permissive families differ in their acceptance of authority, political proclivities, and views of the world.

The family may have little influence on the child if the parents disagree on politics, religion, and/or values. Or, if they are consistent, the parents' views may be neutralized by contrary values held by friends. This neutralization process is facilitated by the decreasing amount of time that the parents spend with the children compared to the time spent in previous generations (Boocock, 1975). As parents spend less and less time raising and influencing their children, their youngsters are influenced more and more not only by their peers but also by baby-sitters, schools, and television.

Some families may have little or negative influence on their children because they are hopelessly disorganized. One or both parents may be alcoholics, unstable, or uncommunicative. In sum, although children raised in the United States are affected by a common culture, family experiences and emphases can vary enough to result in behavioral and attitudinal differences. That children and families can be fundamentally different is seen in the occasional value conflicts between parents and school authorities on sex education, the use of certain literature, rules, and the proper way to enforce rules. But the schools themselves also vary, resulting in different products by type of school.

Schools.   United States schools, as are schools in all societies, are conservative. But there are differences that have a substantial impact on students. In some schools, for example, the curriculum, schedule, and philosophy are very rigid. Children sit in straight rows, may talk only with permission, wear the prescribed clothing, and accept without question the authority of the teacher. In other schools, however, the curriculum, schedules, teachers, and rules are flexible. The products of these two types of schools are likely to differ in much the same way as do the children of autocratic or permissive homes.

Religion.   In general, organized religion in the United States reinforces U.S. values and the policies of the government (see Chapter 17). But significant differences exist among and within the various religious bodies. There are religious disagreements on morality, birth control, abortion, capital punishment, evolution, and other volatile issues. Moreover, religious ideas can conflict with those of one's peers and with what is taught in school. The more salient one's religion, then, the more likely one will differ from people who do not share one's religious views.

Social Location.   Each of us is located in society, not only geographically, but also socially. Depending on our wealth, occupation, education, ethnic or racial heritage, and family background, we see ourselves (and other people see us) as being superior to some persons and inferior to others. Our varying positions in this hierarchy have an effect on our attitudes and perceptions. In particular, people who are highly placed tend to be supportive of the status quo, whereas those who are less advantaged are likely to be more antagonistic to the way things are and desirous of changes beneficial to them.

Generation Cohort.   An **age cohort** is a category of people of the same age. The life experiences of people typically vary depending on when they were born. In other words, people of the same age tend in a general way to be alike in behavior and attitudes, because they were influenced by the same major events such as the Great Depression, World War II, or the antiwar protest of the 1960s. Similarly, the members of age cohorts such as the baby boomers and the post-baby boomers ("Generation X") differ from each other because of differing opportunities, changing economic realities, and the circumstances of their parents.

Contradictory Influences.   We have seen that youngsters may experience pulls in opposite directions from family, church, and school. Other sources of contradictory attractions are peer groups and the media. Parents may insist, for instance, that their children not fight. Yet, their peers might demand such behavior. Moreover, children are bombarded by violence (much of which is considered appropriate) in the movies and on television. How are these children to behave, faced with such opposing and powerful stimuli? Some will follow their parents' dictates; others will succumb to other pressures.

Conflicts in Role Definition.   Some societies are clear and consistent in their expectations for members' behavior. There is no such consensus in the United States.

An examination of a few fundamental social roles illustrates the disagreement on the expectations of the occupants. Adolescents are often unsure of what is expected of them. The law sometimes defines them as children and at other times as adults. Parents and other adults often lack consistency in what they expect of teenagers.

The elderly are another category that experiences ill-defined expectations. At times they are treated as adults, and at other times they are not taken seriously. Some people must retire from work at age sixty-five; others may continue.

Gender roles provide another example of varying expectations depending on the individual, audience, and community. Traditional masculine and feminine roles are in flux. What precisely is expected of a man and woman as they enter a building? Does the man open the door for the woman? This was appropriate behavior in the past and it may be now, but one is never sure, for some women find such behavior offensive. What are the expectations of a newly married husband and wife? How will they divide the household chores? Who is to be the breadwinner? And later, if there is a divorce, who will take the children? Twenty years ago, or even five years ago, the answers to these questions were much more certain.

To conclude, the emphasis of this chapter is on how the individual is shaped by powerful social forces, but we must remember that people are not utterly predictable. Moreover, human beings are actively involved in shaping the social landscape. In sum, the person is, as Kenneth Westhues has said, "a two-sided being, at once created and creating, predictable and surprising" (Westhues, 1982:viii).

Both order and conflict theorists acknowledge the power of the socialization process. They differ, however, in their interpretation of this universal process. The order theorists view this process as necessary to promote stability and law-abiding citizens. Conflict theorists, on the other hand, view the process as one in which persons are led to accept the customs, laws, and values of society uncritically and therefore become willing participants in a society that may be in need of change. In other words, the members of society are taught to accept the way things are, even though the social order benefits some people and disadvantages others. This process is so powerful that most of the powerless and disadvantaged in our society do not rebel because they actually believe in the system that systematically keeps them down. Karl Marx explained this irony through the concept of *false consciousness*.

CHAPTER REVIEW

1. Socialization is the process of learning the culture. Children must learn the culture of the society in which they are born. Socialization, however, is a lifelong process and occurs in all social groups.

2. Infants become human only through learning the culture.

3. The socialization of youth requires social interaction.

4. Another essential to socialization is language, which has profound effects on how individuals think and perceive.

5. The personality emerges as a social product. We develop a sense of self only through interaction with other people.

6. One theory of how personality develops is Cooley's "looking-glass self." Through interaction, children define themselves according to how they interpret how other people think of them.

7. Mead's theory of self-development involves several stages. Through interaction with their parents, infants are able to distinguish between themselves and other people. By age two they are able to react to themselves as others react to them. In the play stage (from ages four to seven) children pretend to be in a variety of adult roles (taking the role of the other). In the game stage (about age eight) children play at games with rigid rules. They begin to understand the structure of the entire game with the expectations for everyone involved. This understanding of the entire situation is called the "generalized other."

8. According to Freud's theory, socialization is the process by which society controls the id (the biological needs for pleasure). Through this process children develop egos (the control of the id by finding appropriate ways to satisfy biological urges). A superego also emerges, which is the internalization of the morals of the parents, further channeling behavior in socially acceptable ways.

9. Through interaction, children internalize the norms and values of society. Three special transmitters of the cultural patterns are the family, the schools, and the media.

10. Because the socialization agents of society present a relatively consistent picture, the members of a society tend to be alike in fundamental ways (modal personality type). The smaller and more homogeneous the society, the more alike the members of that society will be.

11. Despite the tendency for the members to be alike, people, especially in large, heterogeneous societies, are not all similar. The sources of deviation are the differences found in families (e.g., in social class, religion, ethnic background), schools with differing philosophies (rigid or flexible, public or sectarian), religions, social locations, age cohorts, contradictory influences, and conflicts in role definitions.

12. Both order and conflict theorists acknowledge the power of the socialization process, but differ in their interpretation of it. Order theorists view socialization as necessary to promote stability and law-abiding citizens. Conflict theorists, in contrast, view the process as one in which persons are led to accept the customs, laws, and values of society uncritically. This process is so powerful that disadvantaged people may accept the system that disadvantages them (false consciousness).

KEY TERMS

Socialization	Significant others	Superego
Feral children	Generalized other	Nomos
Self	Id	Modal personality type
Looking-glass self	Ego	Age cohort

STUDY QUESTIONS

1. To what extent is "humanness" a social product rather than instinctual?

2. What is meant by the assertion "human beings are social animals"?

3. How do order and conflict theorists differ in their evaluation and interpretation of the role of the media in the socialization process?

4. The forces that socialize us are powerful, but they are not totally deterministic. Why aren't they?

FOR FURTHER READING

The Socialization Process

Charles Horton Cooley, *Human Nature and the Social Order* (New York: Schocken, 1964).

Erik Erikson, *Childhood and Society* (New York: W. W. Norton, 1950).

Frances Fitzgerald, *America Revised* (Boston: Atlantic-Little Brown, 1979).

Sigmund Freud, *Civilization and Its Discontents,* Joan Riviere, trans. (London: Hogarth, 1946).

Herbert J. Gans, *Deciding What's News* (New York: Pantheon, 1979).

Erving Goffman, *The Presentation of Self in Everyday Life* (Garden City, NY: Doubleday, 1959).

Judith Rich Harris and Robert Liebert, *Infancy and the Child* (Englewood Cliffs, NJ: Prentice-Hall, 1992).

Mike Males, *The Scapegoat Generation: America's War on Adolescents* (Monroe, ME: Common Courage Press, 1996).

George Herbert Mead, *Mind, Self and Society* (Chicago: University of Chicago Press, 1934).

Michael Parenti, *Inventing Reality: The Politics of the News Media,* 2nd ed. (New York: St. Martin's Press, 1993).

Jean Piaget and Barbara Inhelder, *The Psychology of the Child* (New York: Basic Books, 1969).

Modal Personality

Victor Barnouw, *Culture and Personality,* 3rd ed. (Homewood, IL: Dorsey, 1979).

Ruth Benedict, *Patterns of Culture* (Baltimore: Penguin Books, 1946).

Urie Bronfenbrenner, *Two Worlds of Childhood: U.S. and U.S.S.R.* (New York: Simon & Schuster Pocket Books, 1973).

Stanley Elkins, *Slavery: A Problem of American Institutional and Intellectual Life* (New York: Universal Library, 1963).

Margaret Mead, *Sex and Temperament in Three Primitive Societies* (New York: William Morrow,1935).

David Reisman, *The Lonely Crowd* (New York: Doubleday, 1953).

Social Control

At 9:34 P.M. on July 13, 1977, the electricity went out in New York City and in some areas did not work again for twenty-five hours. Under the cover of darkness many areas of the city were pillaged. More than two thousand stores were broken into, with property losses estimated at $1 billion. The plunderers were of all ages. They stole appliances, jewelry, shoes, groceries, clothes, furniture, liquor, and automobiles (fifty new Pontiacs from one dealer). The atmosphere was a mixture of revenge, greed, and festival. Observers characterized the looting binge as a carnival atmosphere in which the actors had no concept of morality. It was as if they were immune from the law and from guilt. All of society's constraints were removed, resulting in anarchy. When the lights went out, the social controls on behavior left as well for many people.

Introduction to Social Control

Social control is a central fact of social organization (Eitzen, forthcoming). As Ray Cuzzort asserts:

> A sociocultural system cannot rely on random individual responses to create the structure and the cohesiveness required of organized effort. A society cannot, in other words, rely on people simply "doing their thing." A society must, in effect, generate ways that ensure that what gets done is "society's thing." (Cuzzort, 1989:179)

All social groups have mechanisms to ensure conformity—mechanisms of **social control.** The socialization process is one of these ways by which individuals internalize the norms and values of the group. Persons are taught what is proper, moral, and appropriate. This process is generally so powerful that individuals conform, not out of fear of punishment, but because they *want* to. In other words, group demands *out there* become demands *inside* us. But socialization is never perfect—we are not all robots. As we see in Chapter 7, people deviate. To cope with this, social groups exert external control over their members. These controls are the subject of this chapter.

The focus of this chapter is on social control at the societal level. The dominant modes of socialization vary by type of society. Small, homogeneous societies, for example, are dominated by tradition, whereas large, modern societies are less affected by the force of tradition. Traditional societies tend to have an overriding consensus on societal values; therefore, the family, religion, and the community convey to each individual member a consistent message about which behaviors are appropriate and which ones are not. Although the formal punishment of norm violators does occur in traditional societies, informal controls are usually quite effective and more typical.

In a complex society such as the United States, social control is more difficult to attain because of the existence of different groups with values that are often competing. Therefore, social control tends to be more formal and appears more repressive (because it is more overt) than that found in traditional societies. It occurs in many forms and disguises. Social control is accomplished in the home and school and through various other institutions. It is attained through the overt and covert activities of political agencies, psychotherapists, and even genetic engineers. Efforts to manipulate the masses through various techniques of persuasion also keep deviance in check.

The remainder of this chapter is devoted to an extensive examination of the various agents of social control in U.S. society. These agents are divided into two types by the means used to achieve social control: ideological and direct intervention.

Agents of Ideological Social Control

All social groups have mechanisms to ensure conformity—mechanisms of social control. Peter Berger (1963:68–78) has identified eight sources of social control: (*a*) *force,* the use of violence or threats of violence; (*b*) *economic rewards or punish-*

ments, the promise or denial of material rewards; (*c*) *ridicule and gossip,* fear of being belittled for outside group expectations; (*d*) *ostracism,* the threat or actual removal from the group; (*e*) *fraud and deception,* actions to manipulate (trick) others to conform; (*f*) *belief systems,* the use of ideology to induce individuals to conform; (*g*) *the sphere of intimates,* pressures from close friends, peers, relatives to conform; and (*h*) *the contract,* actions controlled by the stipulations of a formal agreement.

The mechanisms of social control can be divided into two broad types by the means to achieve it: ideological control (belief system from Berger's list) and direct intervention (seven of the eight mechanisms listed by Berger). The former aims at control through manipulation of ideas and perceptions; the latter controls the actual behavior of individuals.

Ideological social control is the attempt to manipulate the consciousness of citizens so that they accept the ruling ideology and refuse to be moved by competing ideologies. Other goals are to persuade the members of society to comply willingly with the law and to accept without question the existing distribution of societal power and rewards. These goals are accomplished in at least three ways. First, ideological social control is accomplished through the socialization of youth. Young people, for example, are taught the values of individualism, competition, patriotism, and respect for authority at home, in school, in scouting organizations, in sports, and through the media. The socialization process could be referred to as cultural control, because the individual is given authoritative definitions of what should and should not be done, which make it appear as if there were no choice (Stivers, 1975). Second, ideological conformity occurs by frontal attacks on competing ideologies by politicians, pastors, teachers, and other persons in authority. Finally, there are propaganda efforts by political authorities to persuade the public what actions are moral, who the enemies are, and why certain courses of governmental action are required.

Ideological social control is more effective than overt social control measures because individuals impose controls upon themselves (Collins, 1992:63–85). Through the socialization process we learn not only the rules of a social organization but also the supporting ideology. The norms are internalized in this process. To the degree that this process works, individuals are not forced to conform, they want to conform. Let us examine this process by describing the agents of social control that are especially important in accomplishing the goal of ideological conformity.

Family

The primary responsibility of parents is to teach their children the attitudes, values, and behaviors considered appropriate by the parents (and society). Parents universally want their children to succeed. Success is measured in terms not only of monetary achievement but also whether the child fits in society. Fitting in requires that the child learn to behave and think in the ways that are deemed proper. Although, as noted in Chapter 5, there is a wide latitude in the actual mode of socialization in the family, most children do behave in acceptable ways.

Education

The formal system of education is an important societal agent for conformity. The school insists that the behavioral standards of the community be maintained in speech, dress, and demeanor. More than this, the schools indoctrinate their pupils in the correct attitudes about work, respect for authority, and patriotism. The textbooks used in schools have typically not provided an accurate account of history, for example, but rather an account that is biased in the direction the authorities wish to perpetuate. The treatment given minorities in these texts is one indicator of the bias. Another indicator is the contrast between descriptions of the behavior of the United States and the behavior of its enemies in wars (see Fitzgerald, 1979).

One critic of the schools is concerned with the problem of conformity, which taken to the extreme results in blind obedience to such malevolent authority figures as Adolph Hitler, Charles Manson, and David Koresh. Rather than turning out conformists, the schools should be turning out individuals with the ability to recognize false prophets and the courage to disobey them.

> The power of socialization can conceivably be harnessed so as to develop individuals who are rational and skeptical, capable of independent thought, and who can disobey or disagree at the critical moment. Our society, however, continues systematically to instill exactly the opposite. The educational system pays considerable lip service to the development of self-reliance, and places huge emphasis on lofty concepts of individual differences. Little notice is taken of the legions of overly obedient children in the schools; yet, for every overly disobedient child, there are probably twenty who are obeying too much. There is little motivation to encourage the unsqueaky wheels to develop as noisy, creative, independent thinkers who may become bold enough to disagree. (McCarthy, 1979:34)

Religion

Religious groups are in many ways involved with social control. Most noticeably, they typically have guidelines for the behavior of members and punishments for disobedience. As an extreme example, see "Diversity: The Amish and Social Control."

© G. Olliver

Diversity

The Amish and Social Control

The Amish are a religious sect found mainly in Pennsylvania, Indiana, and Kansas. They are farmers who resist modern technology. They forbid the use of motorcycles, automobiles, and electricity. They wear simple clothes of the nineteenth century. They believe that they are only temporary visitors on earth, and hence remain aloof from it. This explains why they insist on being different. Most important, the Amish insist on conformity within their community.

The Amish descend from Jacob Amman, a Mennonite preacher in Switzerland. The Mennonites and other Anabaptists of that day differed from mainstream Protestants because they believed in the separation of church and state, adult baptism, refusal to bear arms and take oaths. Amman and his followers split away from the Mennonites in 1700 over an issue of church discipline—the *Meidung.* Amman felt that the Mennonites were too lax in their discipline of deviants and that the *Meidung* must be enforced in severe cases. The *Meidung* is one of the most potent of all social control mechanisms. The following is a description by William M. Kephart and William W. Zellner:

> The ultimate sanction is imposition of the *Meidung,* also known as the "shunning" or "ban," but because of its severity, it is used only as a last resort. The followers of Jacob Amman have a strong religious orientation and a finely honed conscience—and the Amish community relies on this fact. Actions such as gossip, reprimand, and the employment of confession are usually sufficient to bring about conformity. The *Meidung* would be imposed only if a member were to leave the church, or marry an outsider, or break a major rule (such as buying an auto) without full repentance.
>
> Although the *Meidung* is imposed by the bishop, he will not act without the near unanimous vote of the congregation. Generally speaking, however, the ban is total. No one in the district is permitted to associate with the errant party, including members of his or her own family. Even normal marital relations are forbidden. Should any member of the community ignore the *Meidung,* that person would also be placed under the ban. In fact, the *Meidung* is honored by all Amish districts, *including those which are not in full fellowship with the district in question.* There is no doubt that the ban is a mighty weapon. Jacob Amman intended it to be.
>
> On the other hand, the ban is not irrevocable. If the shunned member admits the error of his or her ways—and asks forgiveness of the congregation—the *Meidung* will be lifted and the transgressor readmitted to the fold. No matter how serious the offense, the Amish never look upon someone under the ban as an enemy, but only as one who has erred. And while they are firm in their enforcement of the *Meidung,* the congregation will pray for the errant member to rectify his or her mistake.
>
> Although imposition of the ban is infrequent, it is far from rare. Males are involved much more often than females, the younger more frequently than the old. The *Meidung* would probably be imposed on young males more often were it not for the fact that baptism does not take place until the late 'teens. Prior to this time, young males are expected to be—and often are—somewhat on the wild side, and allowances are made for this fact.
>
> Baptism changes things, however, for this is the rite whereby the young person officially joins the church and makes the pledge of obedience. Once the pledge is made, the limits of tolerance are substantially reduced. More than one Amish youth has been subjected to the *Meidung* for behavior which, prior to his baptism, had been tolerated.

Source: William M. Kephart and William W. Zellner, *Extraordinary Groups: An Examination of Unconventional Life-Styles,* 4th ed. (New York: St. Martin's Press, 1991), p. 25.

Established religion in the United States tends to reinforce the status quo. Few clergy and their parishioners work actively to change the political and economic system. Instead, they preach sermons extolling the virtues of "the American Way of Life," and "giving unto Caesar the things which are Caesar's." Directly or indirectly, there has been a strong tendency for religious groups throughout U.S. history to

The Amish use a special and very effective social control device— absolute shunning ("Meidung") of deviants.

accept existing government policies, whether they are slavery, war, or the conquest of the Native Americans.

Religious groups also preserve the status quo by teaching that people should accept an imperfect society (poverty, racism, and war) because they are born sinners. In this way, religion, as Marx suggested, *is* an opiate of the masses because it convinces them to accept an unjust system rather than work to change it. The downtrodden are advised to accept their lot because they will be rewarded in the next life. Thus, they have no need to change the system from below. As Szymanski has argued:

> The doctrine of the omnipotence of God and total submission to His will pervades the general world views of religious people, and hence is sublimated as submission to political rulers and the upper class. Religion provides a consolation for the suffering of people on earth and a deflection of one's hopes into the future. Combined with its advocacy of the earthly status quo, religion thus typically serves as a powerful legitimatizing force for upper-class rule. Further, most religions, especially the religions of the working class and the poor—Baptism, Methodism, the Messianic sects, and Catholicism—in their sermons typically condemn radical political movements and preach instead either political abstention or submission to government authority. (Szymanski, 1978:253)

Sport

School and professional sports work to reinforce conforming attitudes and behaviors in the populace in several ways (Eitzen and Sage, 1997; Eitzen, forthcoming).

First, there is the strong relationship between sport and nationalism. Success in international sports competition tends to trigger pride among that nation's citizens. The Olympics and other international games tend to promote an us-versus-them feeling among athletes, coaches, politicians, the press, and fans. It can be argued, then, that the Olympic games are a political contest, a symbolic world war in which nations win or lose. Because this interpretation is commonly held, citizens of the nations involved unite behind their flag and their athletes.

The integral interrelationship of sport and nationalism is easily seen in the blatantly militaristic pageantry that surrounds sports contests. The playing of the national anthem, the presentation of the colors, the jet aircraft flyovers, and the band forming a flag or a liberty bell are all political acts supportive of the existing political system.

For whatever reason, sport competition and nationalism are closely intertwined. When U.S. athletes compete against athletes of another country, national unity is the result (for both sides, unless one's athletes do poorly). Citizens take pride in their representatives' accomplishments, viewing them as collective achievements. This identification with athletes and their cause of winning for the nation's glory tends to unite a nation's citizens regardless of social class, race, and regional differences. Thus, sport can be used by political leaders whose nations have problems with divisiveness.

As mentioned in Chapter 3, sport can serve as an opiate of the masses in several ways. Virtually all homes have television sets, making it possible for almost everyone to participate vicariously in and identify with local and national sports teams. Because of this, the minds and energies of the viewers are deflected away from the hunger and misery that are disproportionately the lot of the lower classes in U.S. society. The status quo is thereby preserved.

Sport also acts as an opiate by perpetuating the belief that persons from the lowest classes can be upwardly mobile by success in sports. Clearly this is a myth; for every major leaguer who has come up from poverty, tens of thousands of poor people have not become professional athletes. The point, however, is that most people in the United States *believe* that sport is a mobility escalator and that it is merely a reflection of the opportunity structure of the society in general. Again, poor youth who might otherwise invest their energies in changing the system work instead on a jump shot. The potential for revolution is thus impeded by sport.

Another way that sport serves to control persons ideologically is by reinforcing U.S. values among the participants. Sport is a vehicle by which the values of success in competition, hard work, perseverance, discipline, and order are transmitted. This is the explicit reason given for the existence of Little League programs for youngsters and the tremendous emphasis on sports in U.S. schools. Coaches commonly place signs in locker rooms to inspire certain traits in their athletes. Some examples include (taken from Snyder, 1972):

- "The will to win is the will to work."
- "By failing to prepare yourself you are preparing to fail."
- "Winners never quit and quitters never win."
- "United we stand, divided we fall."

One explicit goal of sports is to build character. The assumption is that participation in sports from the Little Leagues through the Big Leagues (professional ranks) provides the athletes with those values that are American: achievement in competitive situations through hard work, materialism, progress, and respect for authority. As David Matza (1964a:207) has put it: "The substance of athletics contains within itself—in its rules, procedures, training, and sentiments—a paradigm of adult expectations regarding youth." Schools want individuals to follow rules, to be disciplined, to work hard, and to fit in; and sports accomplish these goals.

Not only do schools insist that athletes behave a certain way during practice and games, but they also strictly monitor the behavior of the athletes in other situations. The athletes must conform to the school's norms in dress, speech, demeanor, and grades if they want to continue to participate. In this way, school administrators use athletes as models of decorum. If other people in the school and community admire athletes, then athletes serve to preserve the community and school norms.

Media

The movies, television, newspapers, and magazines also serve to reinforce the system. There is clearly a conservative bias among the various corporations involved because their financial success depends on whether the public will buy their product and whether advertisers will use their vehicles. As Parenti has argued,

> along with products, the corporations sell themselves. By the 1970s, for the first time since the Great Depression, the legitimacy of big business was being called into question by large sectors of the public. Enduring inflation, unemployment, and a decline in real wages, the American people became increasingly skeptical about the blessings of the corporate economy. In response, corporations intensified their efforts at the kind of "advocacy advertising," designed to sell the entire capitalist system rather than just one of its products. . . . *Today, one-third of all corporate advertising is directed at influencing the public on political and ideological issues as opposed to pushing consumer goods.* (That portion is tax deductible as a "business expense," like all other advertising costs.) Led by the oil, chemical, and steel companies, big business fills the airwaves and printed media with celebrations of the "free market," and warnings of the baneful effects of government regulation. (Parenti, 1986:67)

That the media reinforce the values and norms of society is seen in newspaper editorials that extol certain persons and events while decrying others and in stories under the caption, "It Could Only Have Happened in America." Soap operas also accomplish this because they are stories involving moral dilemmas, with virtue winning out. Television, in particular, has had a significant impact on the values of people in the United States. The average two- to eleven-year-old child watches television twenty-five hours a week (Plagens, 1991:51). What are the consistent messages that television emits?

Michael Parenti's book *Make-Believe Media: The Politics of Entertainment* (1992) demonstrates that films and television programs promote images and ideologies that support imperialism, capitalism, racism, sexism, militarism, authoritarian violence, vigilantism, and anti-working-class attitudes. More specifically, he argues that media dramas teach us that:

- Individual effort is preferable to collective action.
- Free enterprise is the best economic system in the world.

- Private monetary gain is a central and worthy objective of life.
- Affluent professionals are more interesting than blue-collar or ordinary service workers.
- All Americans are equal, but some (the underprivileged) must prove themselves worthy of equality.
- Women and ethnic minorities are not really as capable, effective, or interesting as White males.
- The police and everyone else should be given a freer hand in combatting the large criminal element in the United States, using generous applications of force and violence without too much attention to constitutional rights.
- The ills of society are caused by individual malefactors and not by anything in the socioeconomic system.
- There are some unworthy persons in our established institutions, but they usually are dealt with and eventually are deprived of their positions of responsibility.
- United States military force is directed only toward laudable goals, although individuals in the military may sometimes abuse their power.
- Western industrial and military might, especially that of the United States, has been a civilizing force for the benefit of "backward" peoples throughout the Third World.
- The United States and the entire West have long been threatened from abroad by foreign aggressors, such as Russians, Communist terrorists, and swarthy hordes of savages, and at home by un-American subversives and conspirators. These threats can be eradicated by vigilant counterintelligence and by sufficient doses of force and violence (Parenti, 1992:2–3).

In short, the media shape how we evaluate ourselves and other people. Just as important, they affect directly the way viewers or readers perceive and interpret events. The media, therefore, have tremendous power to influence us to accept or question the system. Although the media do investigative reporting and occasionally question the system, the overall impact of the media is supportive of it.

Government

Governmental leaders devote a great deal of energy toward ideological social control. One governmental effort is to convince the public that capitalism is good and socialism is bad. This is done in political speeches and books. Sometimes state legislatures have tried to control the ideological content in schools by requiring certain course content (patriotism, procapitalism, anticommunism). Another example of ideological control is seen in government agencies such as the Defense Department and the Departments of Agriculture, Commerce, and Education. Each department maintains active public relations programs that spend millions of dollars to persuade the public of their views.

The public can also be manipulated by being convinced that their security is threatened by an enemy. This could be done to unify a nation troubled by internal strife. Efforts to unite by suggesting an external threat, although short of declaring war, have been tried by various U.S. political leaders or candidates for office.

Perhaps the most obvious way that government officials attempt to shape public opinion is through speeches, especially on television. The president can request free prime-time television to speak to the public. These efforts are typically intended to unite the people against an enemy (inflation, the deficit, the energy crisis, Saddam Hussein).

We have described how the various agents of ideological social control operate. Perhaps the best evidence that they are successful is that few of the downtrodden in U.S. society question the legitimacy of the political and economic system. Karl Marx theorized that the have-nots in a capitalist society (the poor, the minority group members, the workers) would eventually feel their common oppression and unite to overthrow the owners of capital. That this has not happened in the United States is due, in large part, to the success of the various agents of ideological social control (Parenti, 1978).

Agents of Direct Social Control

Direct social control refers to attempts to punish or neutralize (render powerless) organizations or individuals who deviate from society's norms. The deviant targets here are essentially four: the poor, the mentally ill, criminals, and political dissidents. This section is devoted to three agents of social control whose efforts are directed at these targets—social welfare, science/medicine, and the government.

Welfare

Piven and Cloward, in their classic study of public welfare, have argued that public assistance programs serve a social control function in times of mass unemployment by defusing social unrest (Piven and Cloward, 1993). When large numbers of people are suddenly barred from their traditional occupations, the legitimacy of the system itself may be questioned. Crime, riots, looting, and social movements bent on changing the existing social and economic arrangements become more widespread. Under this threat, relief programs are initiated or expanded by the government. Piven and Cloward show how during the Great Depression, for example, the government remained aloof from the needs of the unemployed until there was a great surge of political disorder. The function of social welfare, then, is to defuse social unrest through direct intervention of the government. Added proof for Piven and Cloward's thesis is the contraction or even abolishment of public assistance programs when political stability is restored.*

---

*The second function of welfare mentioned by Piven and Cloward is more subtle (and fits more logically as an agent of ideological social control). Even in good times some people must live on welfare (the disabled; the husbandless who must care for dependent children). By having a category of persons on welfare who live in wretched conditions and who are continuously degraded, work is legitimized. Thus, the poor on welfare serve as an object lesson—keeping even those who work for low wages relatively satisfied with their lot. As Piven and Cloward have concluded:

> In sum, market values and market incentives are weakest at the bottom of the social order. To buttress weak market controls and ensure the availability of marginal labor, an outcast class—the

The conditions of the 1990s should provide an interesting test of Piven and Cloward's theory. Current trends indicate that the middle class is shrinking and that the gap between the haves and the have-nots is increasing (see Chapters 10, 11, and 13). As long as these increasing numbers of the deprived are docile, government programs to alleviate their suffering will be meager; but should the outrage of the oppressed be manifested in urban riots (e.g., the 1992 Los Angeles riots), acts of terrorism (the Montana Freemen), or in social movements aimed at political change, then, if Piven and Cloward are correct, government welfare programs to aid the poor will become more generous.

Science and Medicine

The practitioners and theoreticians in science and medicine (physicians, psychotherapists, geneticists, electrical engineers, and public health officials) have devised a number of techniques for shaping and controlling the behavior of nonconformists. In the words of Michael Parenti:

> In their never-ending campaign to contain the class struggle and control behavior unacceptable to the existing order, authorities have moved beyond clubs, bullets, and eavesdropping devices and are resorting to such things as electroshock, mind-destroying drugs, and psychosurgery. Since the established powers presume that the present social system is virtuous, then those who are prone to violent or disruptive behavior, or who show themselves to be manifestly disturbed about the conditions under which they live, must be suffering from *inner* malfunctions that can best be treated by various mind controls. Not only are political and social deviants defined as insane, but sanity itself has a political definition. The sane person is the obedient one who lives in peace and goes to war on cue from his leaders, is not too much troubled by the inhumanities committed against people, is capable of fitting into one of the mindless job slots of a profit-oriented hierarchical organization, and does not challenge the established rules and conventional wisdom. Since authorities accept the present politico-economic system as a good one, then anything that increases its ability to control dissident persons is also seen as good. (Parenti, 1988:150–151)*

Psychologists and psychotherapists are clearly agents of social control. Their goal is to aid persons who do not follow the expectations of the society. In other words, they attempt to treat persons considered abnormal in order to make them normal. By focusing on the individual and his or her adjustment, the mental health practitioners validate, enforce, and reinforce the established ways of society. The implicit assumption is that the individual is at fault and needs to change, not that society is the root cause of mental suffering.

More generally, the labeling of mental illness works as a system of social control. As Scarpitti and Andersen have argued,

dependent poor—is created by the relief system. This class, whose members are of no productive use, is not treated with indifference but with contempt. Its degradation at the hands of relief officials serves to celebrate the virtue of all work and deters actual or potential workers from seeking aid. (Piven and Cloward 1971:52)

*Copyright © 1988. From *Democracy for the Few,* 5th edition. By Michael Parenti. Reprinted with permission of St. Martin's Press, Incorporated.

those who are labeled mentally ill are often the outgroups of society. In fact, labeling groups or individuals as mentally ill can work to contain social and political protest, if those who are disturbed are institutionalized, treated with drug therapy, or otherwise incapacitated. The historic identification of homosexuality with mental illness is a case in point. As long as gay men and women were defined as "sick," then it was less likely that other people in society would challenge the heterosexual privilege characteristic of economic, social, and political institutions. (Scarpitti and Andersen, 1992:384)

In short, this application of the medical model to individuals exhibiting certain behaviors personalizes the problem and deflects attention *away* from the social sources for the behaviors.

Another application of the medical model is the control of violent people. The National Institute of Mental Health has considered a National Violence Initiative. Under this plan, researchers would use genetic and biochemical indicators to identify potentially violent children as young as five for biological and behavioral interventions such as drug therapy or even possibly psychosurgery (Horne, 1992–93). This proposal specifically rejected any examination of social and economic factors such as racism, poverty, or unemployment.

Psychosurgery is another method with important implications for social control. As with drug therapy or psychotherapy, individuals who are considered abnormal are treated to correct the problem, but this time through brain surgery. With modern techniques, surgeons can operate on localized portions of the brain that govern particular behaviors (for example, sex, aggression, appetite, or fear).

An extreme example of how psychosurgery might be used for social control was presented by a former Colorado state legislator in 1989. In a letter sent to the governor and all 100 legislators, he proposed that violent criminals be given frontal lobotomies to reduce Colorado's prison population. He argued:

There is a new medical procedure which is humane, safe and permanent; one which will eliminate the violent criminals from our society, reduce our prison population by 10 to 15 percent and provide for early release of all individuals. This procedure is "frontal lobotomy," a procedure done through the eye cavity, leaving no scars and rendering the patient docile, yet able to follow simple commands and to function on their [sic] own. It is accepted as standard medical practice for the violently insane in our sanitariums today. Why not for violent and dangerous criminals? (Quoted in Associated Press, June 22, 1989)

Eugenics, the improvement of the human race through control of hereditary factors, is an ultimate form of social control. That is, if society decided that certain types of people should be sterilized, then those types would be eliminated in a generation. This practice was tried in Nazi Germany, where Jews, gypsies, and the so-called feebleminded were sterilized. It has also occurred in the United States. From 1907 to 1964, for instance, more than 64,000 persons in thirty states were legally sterilized for perceived abnormalities such as drunkenness, criminality, sexual perversion, and feeblemindedness.

The sterilization of the poor, especially racial minorities, has also occurred. Parenti, summarizing recent findings, asserts:

One of every four Native American women of childbearing age is sterilized. One of every three women in Puerto Rico has been sterilized, most of them involuntarily. In Los Angeles and parts of the southwest, Chicano women have been forcibly sterilized.

And in parts of the South, Black girls whose mothers are on welfare are routinely sterilized when they turn fifteen. While the federal government limits funding for Medicaid abortions, thus depriving low-income women of access to medically safe abortions, the government continues to fund sterilization operations for low-income people. (Parenti, 1988:152–153)*

The potential for eugenics will progress dramatically in the near future through biotechnology. Scientists are now capable of manipulating, recombining, and reorganizing living tissue into new forms and shapes. Cells have been fused from different species. Genes have been isolated and mapped, that is, the genes responsible for various physical traits have been located at specific sites on specific chromosomes. Moreover, scientists have been able to change the heredity of a cell. These breakthroughs have positive consequences. Prospective parents, for example, can have the genes of their unborn fetus checked for abnormalities. If an hereditary disorder such as hemophilia or sickle-cell anemia is found, the fetus could be aborted or the genetic makeup of the fetus could be altered before birth.

Even though this new technology has useful applications, it raises some serious questions. Will parents, doctors, and scientists only correct genetic defects, or will they intervene to make genetic improvements? Should dark skin be eliminated? Should aggression be omitted from the behavior traits of future people? If so, passive subjects could be totally controlled without fear of revolution. The social-political-economic system, whatever its composition, would go unchallenged, and society would be tranquil. The logic of genetic engineering, while positive in the sense of ridding future generations of hereditary diseases, is frightening in its basic assumption that problems arise, not from the faults of society, but from the genes of individuals in society. The Human Genome Project raises a number of fears regarding eugenics and social control. (See "A Closer Look: Big Money, Bad Science?")

Similar questions can be raised about the other techniques in this section. The creativity of the scientific community has presented the powerful people in society with unusually effective means to enforce conformity. The aggressive individuals in schools, prisons, mental hospitals, and in society can be anesthetized. But what is aggressive behavior? What is violence?

More than fifteen years ago, the Justice Department proposed a test of 2,000 boys ages nine to twelve who have already had their first contact with the police. The goal of this test is to identify the chronic offender. Proponents of the proposal argued that chronic offenders have certain characteristics that the tests could identify—such as left-handedness, dry or sweaty palms, below normal reactions to noise and shocks, high levels of the male hormone testosterone, abnormalities in alpha waves emitted by their brains, and physical anomalies such as malformed ears, high steepled palate, furrowed tongue, curved fingers, and a wide gap between the first and second toes (reported in Anderson, 1983).

Such a plan, if implemented, has frightening implications. Would these tests actually separate chronic offenders from one-time offenders? Is criminal behavior actually related to the formation of one's tongue, ears, and toes? And, if the tests do

A CLOSER LOOK

Big Money, Bad Science?

Genetic research is big business. Government agencies, industrialists, venture capitalists, insurance companies, pharmaceutical companies, patent lawyers, university researchers, and others approach genes with the same fervor once reserved for high technology and microelectronics. The focus of this attention is on what has come to be recognized as the "holy grail" of biology: the human genome. Comprised of the genetic material that controls an individual's heredity, the genome is believed to hold the key to human disease, aging, and death.

Under the auspices of the National Institutes of Health and the Department of Energy, the Human Genome Project (HGP) promises to uncover the genetic origin of such pernicious diseases as muscular dystrophy, Alzheimer's, diabetes, and even cancer. By mapping and sequencing the more than 100,000 genes making up the genome, researchers believe that new gene treatments and therapies can be developed to impact not only human disease, but also the genetic roots of height, weight, and possibly intelligence.

As a multibillion dollar, publicly financed effort, the HGP is comparable to the space program in scope and expense. Unlike NASA, the HGP has captured the attention of innumerable private investors and enterprises intent on capitalizing on its findings. The relationship between private capital and the HGP means there are definite expectations that genetic research can reap profits through the development of drugs, hormones, modified genes, and diagnostic tests. While the potential benefits of genetic research are obvious, there are also problems that must be considered.

Genetic research raises important questions concerning privacy. Should employers, insurance companies, schools, or the government have access to an individual's genetic information? Diagnostic tests are already on the market that are designed to predict the likelihood of physical or psychological problems. These tests have been used to deny individuals employment and insurance, and are currently used in many elementary and high schools to identify children with learning problems. The scientific evidence supporting genetic testing is negligible, but since so many HGP researchers serve as directors, consultants, or shareholders in biotechnology companies producing these products, knowledgeable and vocal critics are hard to find.

Most important is the question of how much information about human disease, behavior, and potential is genetic in origin in the first place. There is a definite reductionist character to scientific genetic discourse which assumes that biological inheritance holds sway over social and environmental factors on individuals. While genes are certainly important, dismissing the impact of other elements in the development of individuals and disease directs attention away from pressing social and economic causes. A focus on genes neglects the significance of poor preventative health care, smoking, drug abuse, accidents, neglected schools, poverty, pollution, and violence on our health, development, and well-being.

Linking genetic research with private industry only exacerbates the problem. When scientific research is profit-driven, advances are necessarily made in areas conducive to widespread manufacturing, marketing, and promotion. Since biotechnical, pharmaceutical, and insurance companies have inextricably linked their futures to genetic research, it makes sense that the commercial uses of genome research are of paramount importance when scientists go about the business of gene exploration.

Source: Craig S. Leedham, Colorado State University. This essay was written expressly for the eighth edition of *In Conflict and Order.* Used with permission.

identify potential problem people accurately, should such persons be punished for their potential behaviors rather than for their actual behaviors? Most significant, what are the negative effects of being labeled a *chronic offender*? Such a label would doubtless have a self-fulfilling prophecy effect as those people who interact with labeled persons do so on the basis of that label.

Currently, more than 1.5 million people are in U.S. prisons or jails.

Government

The government, as the legitimate holder of power in society, is directly involved in the control of its residents. A primary objective of the government is to provide for the welfare of its citizens. This includes protection of their lives and property. It requires, further, that order be maintained within the society. There is a clear mandate, then, for the government to apprehend and punish criminals. The various levels of government currently have 1.5 million people in prison or jail. Millions more are under the jurisdiction of the criminal justice system, either on probation or parole. The 1995 incarceration rate was 600 inmates per 100,000 people, up from 313 in 1985. The U. S. rate is the highest in the industrialized world. For an example of a society tightly controlled by its government, see "Other Societies: Government Control in Singapore."

Less clear, however, is the legitimacy of a government in a democracy to stifle dissent, which is done in the interests of preserving order. The U.S. heritage, best summed up in the Declaration of Independence, provides a clear rationale for dissent:

> Governments are instituted among men, deriving their just powers from the consent of the governed. That whenever any form of government becomes destructive of these ends, the rights of life, liberty, and the pursuit of happiness, it is the right of the people to alter or to abolish it, and to institute a new government, laying its foundation on such principles and organizing its powers in such form as to them shall seem most likely to effect their safety and happiness.

The U.S. government, then, is faced with a dilemma. American tradition and values affirm that dissent is appropriate. Two facts of political life work against this principle, however. First, for social order to prevail, a society needs to ensure that existing

Other Societies Other Ways

Government Control in Singapore

Singapore is a small country (244 square miles) with 2,700,000 residents. The population is culturally diverse (76 percent Chinese, 15 percent Malay, and 7 percent Indian). It is a prosperous nation known for its efficiency and cleanliness. There is a very strict security system with the largest army per capita in Asia, a relatively large police force, and the Internal Security Department. Since Singapore gained its independence from Great Britain in 1959, it has been ruled by Lee Kuan Yew "in much the way a strict father might rear what he feels are errant children" (Sesser, 1992:37). The authoritarian government has many rules for its citizens and strict punishments if they are broken. Some examples:

- There is censorship, with magazines such as *Cosmopolitan* and *Playboy* banned, as well as the monitoring and censorship of newspapers, books, movies, music, and television.

- Anyone caught littering must pay a fine of up to $620 and undergo counseling.

- Eating or drinking on the subway costs the equivalent of $310.

- Smoking is illegal in public buses, elevators, restaurants, theaters, cinemas, and government offices ($300 fine).

- Video game centers are outlawed because they allegedly harm children.

- Driving without a seatbelt costs $120.

- Jaywalkers are fined $30.

- Beginning in 1988 a law required the flushing of toilets and urinals, with violators fined.

- At the end of 1991 the government banned the import of chewing gum because it is a "perennial nuisance" in public facilities.

- Trucks and commercial vans are required to install a yellow roof light that flashes when the vehicle exceeds the speed limit.

- Cameras mounted above stop lights at intersections photograph the license plates of cars that pass through a red light, with the drivers receiving bills for the offense in the mail (fine of $150).

- Illegal immigrants, burglars, and car thieves are subject to imprisonment and lashes with a cane. As described by the Bar Association, "When the rattan hits the bared buttocks, the skin disintegrates, leaving initially a white line and then a flow of blood. The victim must lie on his front for three weeks to a month because the buttocks are so sore" (reported in Sesser, 1992:56).

- Anyone trafficking a controlled drug receives ten years in prison and five lashes with a cane. Anyone caught with more than fifteen grams of heroin or thirty grams of morphine is *hanged.*

- During the Vietnam War, when long hair was believed to be linked to drug use and political dissent, Singapore police would detain long-haired male youths and give them involuntary haircuts. There is still a regulation that hair must not reach below an ordinary shirt collar.

- Except for social gatherings, assemblies of more than five people in public must have police permission.

- In 1990, Parliament passed the Religious Harmony Act, which gave the government the power to arrest religious workers who it believed were engaged in politics. This act barred judicial review of these cases (i.e., the courts cannot rule on the government's actions).

- Renewal of appointments and tenure in the universities are refused to academics whose work deviates from government views.

- Political dissidents, as a condition for release from detention, must make a public confession.

power relationships are maintained over time (otherwise anarchy will result). Second, the well-off in society benefit from the existing power arrangements, so they use their influence (which is considerable, as noted in the previous chapter) to encourage the repression of challenges to the government. The evidence is strong that the U.S. government has opted for repression of dissent. Let us examine this evidence.

To begin, we must peruse the processes of law enactment and law enforcement. These two processes are both directly related to political authority. Some level of government determines what the law will be (that is, which behaviors are to be allowed and which ones are to be forbidden). The agents of political authorities then apprehend and punish violators. Clearly, the law is employed to control behaviors that might otherwise endanger the general welfare (for example, the crimes of murder, rape, and theft). But laws also promote certain points of view at the expense of others (for example, the majority instead of the minority, or the status quo rather than change). With this in mind, let us turn to the two schools of thought on the function of the law—the prevailing liberal view and the Marxist interpretation (Quinney, 1970:18–25; 1973).

The dominant view in U.S. society is based on liberal democratic theory and is congruent with the order model. The state exists to maintain order and stability. Law is a body of rules enacted by representatives of the people in the interests of the people. The state and law, therefore, are essentially neutral, dispensing rewards and punishments without bias. A basic assumption of this view is that the political system is pluralistic—that is, made up of the existence of a number of interest groups of more-or-less equal power. The laws, then, reflect compromise and consensus among these various interest groups. In this way the interests of all people are protected.

Contrary to the prevailing view of law based on consensus for the common good is the view of the radical criminologists, which is based on conflict theory. The assumptions of this model are that (1) the state exists to serve the ruling class (the owners of large corporations and financial institutions), (2) the law and the legal system reflect and serve the needs of the ruling class, and (3) the interests of the ruling class are served by the law when domestic order prevails and challenges to changing the economic and political system are successfully thwarted. In other words, the law does not serve society as a whole, but the interests of the ruling class prevail.

Closely related to the Marxian view of the role of law in capitalist societies is the interest-group theory of Richard Quinney (1970:29–42). The essence of this theory is that a crime is behavior that conflicts with the interests of the segments of society that have the power to shape criminal policy.

> Law is made by men, representing special interests, who have the power to translate their interests into public policy. Unlike the pluralist conception of politics, law does not represent a compromise of the diverse interests of society, but supports some interests at the expense of others. (Quinney, 1970:35)

Quinney's view is in the conflict-model tradition. Society is held together by some segments coercing other segments. Interest groups are unequal in power. The conflict among interest groups results in the powerful getting their way in determining public policy. Evidence for this position is seen in the successful efforts of certain interest groups to get favorable laws passed: the segregation laws imposed by Whites on Blacks, the repression of political dissidents whose goal is to transform society, and the passage of income tax laws that benefit the rich at the expense of wage earners.

Quinney's model makes a good deal of sense. The model is not universally applicable, however, because certain crimes—burglary, murder, and rape—would be regarded as crimes no matter which interest group was in power. A very important part of his theory that does fit almost universally is this proposition: *"The probability that criminal definitions will be applied varies according to the extent to which the behaviors of the powerless conflict with the interests of the power segments"* (Quinney,1970:18).

The law, of course, provides the basis for establishing what is criminal behavior. Enforcement of the law is accomplished by the police and the courts. The evidence is overwhelming that the law is unequally enforced in U.S. society. Let us direct our attention here, rather, to the efforts of other agencies in the political system to control deviance, especially political deviance.

Government agencies have a long history of surveillance of people in the United States. The pace quickened in the 1930s and increased further with the Communist threat in the 1950s. Surveillance reached its peak during the height of antiwar and civil rights protests of the late 1960s and early 1970s. The FBI's concern with internal security, for example, dates back to 1936, when President Roosevelt directed J. Edgar Hoover to investigate domestic Communist and Fascist organizations in the United States. In 1939, as World War II began in Europe, President Roosevelt issued a proclamation that the FBI would be in charge of investigating subversive activities, espionage, and sabotage, and directed that all law enforcement offices should give the FBI any relevant information on suspected activities. These directives began a pattern followed by the FBI under the administrations of Presidents Truman, Eisenhower, Kennedy, Johnson, Nixon, Ford, Carter, Reagan, Bush, and Clinton.

The scope of these abuses by the FBI and other government agencies such as the CIA, the National Security Agency, and the Internal Revenue Service is enormous. In the name of national security, the following actions have been taken against U.S. citizens:

- The Internal Revenue Service (IRS) monitored the activities of 99 political organizations and 11,539 individuals during the period from 1969 to 1973. During and since that period, the IRS has used a variety of methods to invade the private lives of individuals, including the use of seizure—liens, assessments, penalties, wiretaps, and even hiring prostitutes to occupy suspects while agents photocopied the contents of briefcases (Fleetwood, 1980; Burnham, 1989).
- From 1967 to 1973 the NSA (National Security Agency) monitored the overseas telephone calls and cables of approximately 1,650 Americans and U.S. organizations, as well as of almost 6,000 foreign nationals and groups (*Newsweek*, November 10, 1975).
- The CIA opened and photographed nearly 250,000 first-class letters in the United States between 1953 and 1973 (Ermann and Lundman, 1978:18).
- As director of the CIA, William Colby acknowledged to Congress that the organization opened the mail of private citizens and accumulated secret files on more than 10,000 people (Ermann and Lundman, 1978).

■ The FBI over the years conducted about 1,500 break-ins of foreign embassies and missions, mob hangouts, and the headquarters of such organizations as the Ku Klux Klan and the American Communist Party (*Newsweek,* July 28, 1975).

■ Beginning in 1957, the FBI monitored the activities of civil rights leader Martin Luther King, Jr. The efforts included physical and photographic surveillance and the placement of electronic listening devices in his living quarters.

■ In its annual report for 1982, on electronic surveillance by federal and state officials, the Office of the U.S. Courts stated that the FBI and the Drug Enforcement Administration installed 129 taps and bugs in 1981 (Schwartz, 1983).

■ The FBI consistently monitored the activities of hundreds of U.S. writers including Nelson Algren, Pearl Buck, Truman Capote, William Faulkner, Ernest Hemingway, Sinclair Lewis, Archibald MacLeish, Carl Sandburg, John Steinbeck, Thornton Wilder, Tennessee Williams, James Baldwin, and Thomas Wolfe (Robins, 1992). The question is, Why? Was it because the most acclaimed writers in the United States were part of a conspiracy or were individual lawbreakers, or was it, as has been suggested by Natalie Robins, "an *unconscious* effort on the FBI's part to control writers with a chilling effect that really adds up to intimidation?" (Robins, 1987:367).

■ Beginning in late 1981 the FBI conducted a massive investigation of more than 1,300 organizations and individuals who were opposed to President Reagan's South American Policy. The main target was the Committee in Solidarity with the People of El Salvador (CISPES). For just that one organization, "although no terrorist connection was found, hundreds of people were surveilled and photographed, their meetings infiltrated, their families, friends, and employers questioned, their trash and financial and telephone records examined" (Gentry, 1991:759).

■ An organization of progressive lawyers, the National Lawyers Guild, was under FBI surveillance for fifty years, yet was never found to engage in illegal activity (Parenti, 1995:153).

■ Two recent events reveal government aggression against its citizens. The first was a 1992 raid by the Bureau of Alcohol, Tobacco, and Firearms (ATF) on Randy Weaver, a White supremacist in Idaho, for guns violations. In the process Weaver's wife and son were killed by ATF snipers. The second event was the 1993 assault by ATF on David Koresh and the Branch Davidians near Waco, Texas. This siege, again over guns violations, ended with the deaths of 86 men, women, and children.

■ The Watergate scandal, which involved Nixon's White House, included the Executive Branch's use of the FBI, the IRS, and government granting agencies to punish its enemies. During President Clinton's first term the White House improperly obtained confidential FBI background files on more than 400 Republicans. While not approaching the scale of Nixon's crimes, this act was wrong. Both the FBI and the White House conceded to having committed "egregious violations of privacy."

These are a few examples of government abuses against its people. Actually, the extent of the government's monitoring of the country's residents is much greater than these examples indicate. A survey of 142 federal agencies by the Office of Technology found that one-fourth of them conducted some form of electronic surveillance. The Drug Enforcement Administration, for example, uses ten separate surveillance technologies, and the FBI uses seventeen. Moreover, various federal and state agencies use computerized record systems used for law enforcement, investigative, and intelligence purposes.

One should remember that the government *must* exert some control over its population. There must be a minimum of control if the fabric of society is to remain intact. But in exerting control, serious problems came to the forefront during the Nixon years. First, there is the problem of the violation of individual rights as guaranteed in the Constitution. Under what conditions can these rights be violated by the government—if ever? A closely related problem can be framed in the form of a question: Who monitors the monitors? The problem inherent in this question is not only the tactics of the monitors but also the criteria used to assess who should be controlled or who should not.

A most serious charge is that the government squelches protest, which Thomas Jefferson said is the hallmark of a democracy. The implication is that the government is beyond questioning—the dissidents are the problem. But as Donner has put it,

> to equate dissent with subversion, as intelligence officials do (the FBI, CIA, IRS, Justice Department, and the Department of Defense), is to deny that the demand for change is based on real social, economic, or political conditions. (Donner, 1971:35)

Implications for Contemporary Social Life

In 1949 George Orwell wrote a novel about life as he envisioned it to be in the year 1984. The essence of his prediction was that every word, every thought, and every facial expression of citizens would be monitored by government using sophisticated electronic devices. The computer age has in part fulfilled Orwell's prophecy. The federal government has an average of eighteen computer files on each person in the United States; each state has an average of fifteen files per person, and local governments average six files. In the private sector (e.g., credit, insurance, banks, employers) we have another forty files. There are companies that gather financial records, medical history, credit card purchases, and other personal information that they sell to marketers, mortgage lenders, and businesses. For example, two giant credit bureaus—TRW and Equifax—each have files on 150 million individuals (Lacayo, 1991).

The privacy of workers is also in question. Some employers require prospective employees to be given drug tests and psychological tests that ask about, among other things, sexual behavior, religious beliefs, and political attitudes. Workers using telephones and computers may find their work watched, measured, and analyzed in detail by supervisors. Employers can (and do) peruse employees' E-mail, tap their telephones, examine confidential medical information, and even secretly film them in the restroom (Smith, 1993; Meadow, 1993). Regarding E-mail, for example, the policy of the Kmart Corporation states that the company can review all

WE MONITOR OUR EMPLOY-
EES' WORK HABITS, VOICE-
MAIL AND E-MAIL TO MAKE
SURE THEY DON'T BREACH
OUR BOND OF TRUST.

Kirk Anderson

E-mail messages: "electronic mail sent from Kmart travels on Kmart's electronic stationery" and is thus the same as if it were sent on Kmart's letterhead (cited in Samuels, 1996).

This computer-stored knowledge especially from centralized and increasingly interrelated databases (credit bureaus, banks, marketing companies, stock brokerage firms, health insurers and other insurance companies, and governments) is a threat to privacy (Ritzer, 1995). "The danger is that employers, banks, and government agencies will use data bases to make decisions about our lives without our knowing about it" (Lacayo, 1991:36). Most especially, if the government has access to these data, it can use modern technology to monitor closely the activities of those people who threaten it. And, as we have seen in this chapter, the government is strongly inclined to do so. But the political dissident is not the only person whose freedoms are being threatened; all of us are threatened by the power of large organizations. As Jeffrey Rothfeder says:

> Increasingly people are at the whim of . . . large organizations—direct marketers, credit bureaus, the government, and the entire information economy—that view individuals as nothing but lifeless data floating like microscopic entities in vast electronic chambers, data that exist to be captured, examined, collated and sold, regardless of the individual's desire to choose what should be concealed and what should be made public. (Rothfeder, 1992:30)

The technology for *1984* exists in drugs, psychosurgery, telecommunications, and telemetry. Currently, various arms of the government have used some of these techniques in their battle to fight crime, recidivism, political dissidence, and other forms of nonconformity. But at what point does the government go too far in its control of nonconformity? The critical question, as stated earlier, is who monitors the monitors? One can easily envision a future when the government, faced with anarchy or political revolution, might justify ultimate control of its citizens—in the name of national security. If this were to take place, then, obviously, the freedoms rooted in 200 years of history will have been washed away.

The future may resemble Orwell's vision, however, not because of a tyrannical government, but rather because it is in the interests of society that people be controlled. The time may come when people, because human survival depends on it, will not have the freedom to have as many children as they want or the freedom to squander energy on eight-cylinder cars or air-conditioned homes or to own a gun. B. F. Skinner, the famous behavioral psychologist, has argued that we must give up our outmoded notions of freedom and dignity and build a society in which the behavior of people will be controlled for their own good—for the sake of their survival, happiness, and satisfaction (Skinner, 1972). In other words, if not enough people exercise self-control, the government, for the common good, may be forced to impose controls from the outside. With the technology available to the government, absolute control is a real threat.

Social Control from the Order and the Conflict Perspectives

A perennial question for many sociologists is: How is social order possible? Order theorists and conflict theorists answer this question quite differently. For order theorists the answer to this question is that the vast majority of members of any social organization share a concensus on the norms, laws, and values. In premodern societies social order occurs because the norms and values are shared and legitimized by deeply held religious authority. In modern complex societies social order is maintained as citizens accept the legal order and the state, which are believed to serve the common good.

Conflict theorists, on the other hand, reject the assumption of normative consensus, arguing rather that social order is the result of government force or the threat of force, economic dominants using the law, the media, or other institutions to hold power over the relatively powerless.

CHAPTER REVIEW

1. All societies have mechanisms to ensure conformity—mechanisms of social control.

2. The socialization process through which the demands of the group become internalized is a fundamental mechanism of social control. This process is never complete, however; otherwise, we would be robots.

3. Ideological social control is the attempt to manipulate the consciousness of citizens so they accept the status quo and ruling ideology.

4. The agents of ideological social control are the family, education, religion, sport, and the media.

5. Direct social control refers to attempts to punish or neutralize organizations or individuals who deviate from society's norms, especially the poor, the mentally ill, criminals, and political dissidents.

6. According to Piven and Cloward, public assistance programs serve a direct social control function in times of mass unemployment by defusing social unrest.

7. Science and medicine provide the techniques for shaping and controlling the behavior of nonconformists. Drugs, psychosurgery, and genetic engineering are three such techniques.

8. The government is directly involved in the control of its citizens. It apprehends and punishes criminals. It is also involved in the suppression of dissent, which, while important for preserving order, runs counter to the U.S. democratic heritage.

9. Order theorists argue that social order results from a shared consensus on the norms, laws, and values. In modern complex societies citizens accept the legal order and the state because they are believed to serve the common good. In this view, the state and the law are neutral, dispensing rewards and punishments without bias. Conflict theorists, however, believe that the state and the law (as well as the other institutions) exist to serve the ruling class. Squelching political dissent, therefore, benefits the powerful.

KEY TERMS

Social control
Ideological social control

Direct social control
Eugenics

STUDY QUESTIONS

1. How do order and conflict theorists differ in their interpretation of the role of sport and social control?

2. What is the relationship of ideological social control to what we learned about socialization in the previous chapter?

3. What is Piven and Cloward's thesis concerning the social control function of welfare assistance programs?

4. How do order theorists and conflict theorists differ in their views of the state and the law?

FOR FURTHER READING

Ideological Social Control

Martin Carnoy, *Education as Cultural Imperialism* (New York: Longman, 1974).

Jules Henry, *Culture Against Man* (New York: Random House [Vintage Books], 1963).

Donald B. Kraybill, *Our Star-Spangled Faith* (Scottsdale, PA: Herald Press, 1976).

Michael Parenti, *Inventing Reality: The Politics of the News Media,* 2nd ed. (New York: St. Martin's Press, 1993).

Michael Parenti, *Make-Believe Media: The Politics of Entertainment* (New York: St. Martin's Press, 1986).

Direct Social Control

Ward Churchill and Jim Vander Wall, *Agents of Repression: The FBI's Secret Wars against the Black Panther Party and the American Indian Movement* (Boston: South End Press, 1988).

Steven R. Donziger (ed.), *The Real War on Crime: The Report of the National Criminal Justice Commission* (New York: Harper Perennial, 1996).

Jerome G. Miller, *Search and Destroy: African-American Males in the Criminal Justice System* (Cambridge: Cambridge University Press, 1996).

Frances Fox Piven and Richard A. Cloward, *Regulating the Poor: The Functions of Public Welfare,* Updated Edition (New York: Random House, 1993).

Richard Quinney, *Critique of Legal Order: Crime Control in Capitalist Society* (Boston: Little, Brown, 1973).

George Ritzer, *Expressing America: A Critique of the Global Credit Card Society* (Thousand Oaks, CA: Pine Forge Press, 1995).

David R. Simon and D. Stanley Eitzen, *Elite Deviance,* 4th ed. (Boston: Allyn and Bacon, 1993).

B. F. Skinner, *Beyond Freedom and Dignity* (New York: Alfred A. Knopf, 1972).

Thomas Szasz, *The Manufacture of Madness* (New York: Harper & Row, 1970).

CHAPTER 7

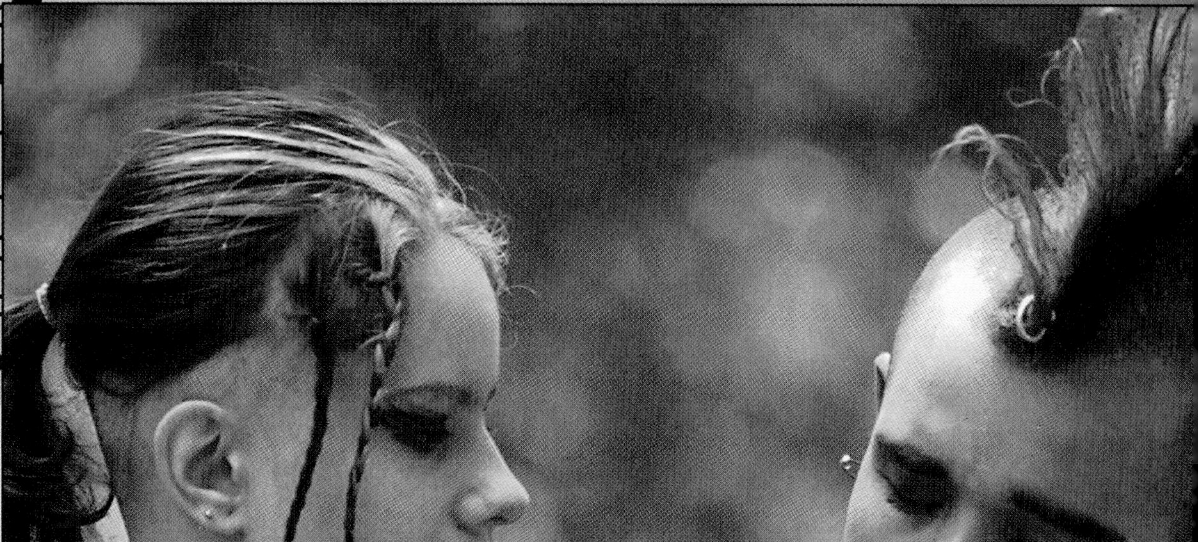

Deviance

Who are the deviants in U.S. society? There is considerable evidence that most of us at one time or another break the laws. For example:

- Surveys by the Internal Revenue Service consistently find that three out of ten persons cheat on their income taxes. This does *not* include the monies received from the selling of goods or services for cash and tips received that go unreported to the government. An estimated 25 percent of the total labor force does not report all or part of its income from these otherwise legal practices.
- Otherwise law-abiding citizens routinely copy computer software and photocopy copyrighted music, even though these activities are against the law.
- Employees embezzle and pilfer an estimated $10 billion from their employers. Time theft by employees (i.e., faked illnesses, excessive breaks, and long lunches) costs U.S. business as much as $200 billion annually.
- Marijuana may be the country's largest cash crop, with annual harvests valued at anywhere between $10 billion and $33 billion. The Justice Department's Drug Enforcement Agency (DEA) estimates the number of commercial growers at between 90,000 and 150,000, with another million people growing marijuana for their personal use.
- The value of federal student loan defaults exceeds $3.5 billion.
- The Transit Authority of New York City estimated that 4.8 million riders annually sneak onto the subway trains without paying. Another estimated $10 million a year is lost by thieves who "jam the turnstiles and steal the tokens by sucking them out with their mouths or by using homemade sleeves, or metal tubes, to catch tokens that riders place in fare boxes" (Sims, 1990:E22).

What Is Deviance?

These illustrations indicate that many of us are guilty of cheating and stealing—behaviors clearly considered wrong. But are those of us who commit these illegal or immoral acts deviant? The complexities of the designation of *deviant* are the topics of this chapter.

The previous three chapters analyzed the ways in which human beings, as members of society, are constrained to conform. We have seen how society is not only outside of us, coercing us to conform, but also inside of us, making us *want* to behave in the culturally prescribed ways. But despite these powerful forces, people deviate from the norms. These acts and actors are the subjects of this chapter.

Deviance is behavior that does not conform to social expectations. It violates the rules of a group (custom, law, role, or moral code). Deviance, then, is *socially created* (Becker, 1963:8–9). Social organizations create right and wrong by originating *norms*, the infraction of which constitutes deviance. This means that nothing inherent in a particular act makes it deviant. Whether an act is deviant depends on how other people react to it. As Kai Erikson has put it, "Deviance is not a property *inherent* in any particular kind of behavior; it is a property *conferred upon* that behavior by the people who come into direct or indirect contact with it" (Erikson, 1966:6). This means that *deviance is a relative, not an absolute, notion.* Evidence for this is found in two sources: inconsistencies among societies as to what is deviance, and inconsistencies in the labeling of behavior as deviant within a single society.

There is abundant anthropological evidence that what is right or wrong varies from society to society. The following are a few examples:

- The Ila of Africa encourage sexual promiscuity among their adolescents. After age ten girls are given houses of their own during harvest time, where they can play at being a wife with boys of their choice. In contrast, the Tepoztlan Indians of Mexico do not allow girls to speak to or encourage a boy after the time of the girl's first menstruation.
- Egyptian royalty were required to marry their siblings, whereas this was prohibited as incestuous and sinful for European royalty.
- Young men of certain Native American tribes are expected, after fasting, to have a vision. This vision will be interpreted by the tribal elders to decide that young man's future occupation and status in the tribe. If an Anglo youth were to tell his elders that he had such a vision, he would likely be considered mentally ill.

Differential treatment for similar behavior by different categories of persons within a single society provides further proof that deviance is *not* a property of the act but depends on the reaction of the particular audience. Several examples illustrate that it is not the act but the situation that determines whether the behavior is interpreted by others as deviant:

In some societies bare female breasts are acceptable in public. Similar behavior in the United States would be regarded as deviant.

- Unmarried fathers escape the degree of public censure that unmarried mothers typically receive.
- Sexual intercourse between consenting adults is not deviant except if one partner pays another for his or her services, and then the deviant is the recipient of the money, not the giver.
- Murder is a deviant act, but the killing of an enemy during wartime is rewarded with praise and medals.
- A father would be considered a deviant if he removed his bathing suit at a public beach, but his two-year-old son could do this with impunity. The father can smoke a cigar and drink a martini every night, but if his young son did, the boy (and his parents, if they permitted this) would be considered deviant (Weinstein and Weinstein, 1974:271).
- Smoking tobacco, long considered appropriate for adult males and only in recent decades for females, is now considered deviant by more and more people.

In a heterogeneous society there will often be widespread disagreement on what the rules are and therefore on what constitutes deviance. There are differences over, for example, sexual activities between consenting adults (regardless of sex, marital status), smoking marijuana, public nudism, pornography, drinking alcohol, remaining seated during the national anthem, and refusal to fight in a war. Concerning this last instance, who is the deviant in a war, for example, the person who kills the enemy or the person who refuses to kill them?

This point leads to a further insight about deviance: *the majority determines who is a deviant.* If most people believe that the Iraqis are the enemy, then bombing their villages is appropriate and refusal to do so is deviant. If most people believe there is a God you may talk to, then such a belief is not deviance (in fact, the refusal to believe in God may be deviant). But if the majority are atheists, then those few who believe in God would be deviant and subject to ridicule, job discrimination, and treatment for mental problems.

Another example of this safety-in-numbers principle is the effort by some parents to deprogram their children if they have adopted a different religion—for example, pentecostal Christian, Children of God, or Hare Krishna. These parents had their children kidnapped away from the religious group. The children were confined for days with little food or sleep and badgered by hired experts into recanting their beliefs. As Mewshaw has described it:

> Euphemistically called "deprogramming," the process amounts to little more than a methodical and sometimes violent attempt to exorcise not Satan, but unpopular, misunderstood, or inarticulate notions about God. (Mewshaw, 1976:32)

Erikson has summarized how deviance is a relative rather than an absolute notion in the following statement:

> Definitions of deviance vary widely as we range over the various classes found in a single society or across the various cultures into which mankind is divided, and it soon becomes apparent that there are no objective properties which all deviant acts can be said to share in common—even within the confines of a given group. *Behavior which qualifies one man for prison may qualify another for sainthood, since the quality of the act itself depends so much on the circumstances under which it was performed and the temper of the audience which witnessed it.* [italics added] (Erikson, 1966:5–6)

An insight of the order theorists is important to note. Deviance is an integral part of all healthy societies (Durkheim, 1958; 1960; Dentler and Erikson, 1959). Deviant behavior, according to Durkheim, actually has positive consequences for society, because it gives the nondeviants a sense of solidarity. By punishing the deviant, the group expresses its collective indignation and reaffirms its commitments to the rules.

> Crime brings together upright consciences and concentrates them. We have only to notice what happens, particularly in a small town, when some moral scandal has just been

Reprinted by permission of United Feature Syndicate.

committed. They stop each other on the street, they visit each other, they seek to come together to talk of the event and to wax indignant in common. From all the similar expressions which are exchanged, for all the temper that gets itself expressed, there emerges a unique temper . . . which is everybody's without being anybody's in particular. That is the public temper. (Durkheim, 1960:102)

Durkheim believed that the true function of punishment was not the prevention of future crimes. He asserted, rather, that the basic function of punishment is to reassert the importance of the rule being violated. It is not that a murderer is caught and put in the electric chair to keep potential murderers in line. That argument assumes people to be more rational than they really are. Instead, the extreme punishment of a murderer reminds each of us that murder is wrong. In other words, the punishment of crimes serves to strengthen our belief as individuals and as members of a collectivity in the legitimacy of society's norms. This enhances the solidarity of society as we unite in opposition to the deviant.

Crime, seen from this view, has positive functions for society. In addition to reaffirming the legitimacy of the society, defining certain acts as crimes creates the boundaries for what is acceptable behavior in the society.

Deviance, from the order perspective, is not only a consequence of social order (a violation of society's rules) but also is necessary for social order. As Rubington and Weinberg have said, "Each [social order and deviance] presupposes the other. And from studying one, sociologists frequently learn more about the other" (Rubington and Weinberg, 1973:1).

The conflict theorists have pointed out that all views of rule violations have *political* implications (Becker, 1963:4). When persons mistreat rule breakers, they are saying, in effect, that the norms are legitimate. Thus, the bias is conservative, serving to preserve the status quo, which includes the current distribution of power. The opposite view, that the norms of society are wrong and should be rejected, is also political. When people and groups flout the laws and customs (for example, the draft, racial segregation, and marijuana smoking) they are not only rejecting the status quo but also are questioning the legitimacy of those in power. As Edwin Schur has argued,

> deviance issues are inherently political. They revolve around some people's assessments of other people's behavior. And power is a crucial factor in determining which and whose assessments gain an ascendancy. Deviance policies, likewise, affect the distribution of power and always have some broad political significance. (Schur, 1980:xi)

Traditional Theories for the Causes of Deviance

The Individual as the Source of Deviance

Biological, psychological, and even some sociological theories have assumed that the fundamental reason for deviance is a fatal flaw in certain people. The criminal, the dropout, the homosexual, the addict, the schizophrenic, have something wrong with them. These theories are deterministic, arguing that the individual ultimately has no choice but to be different.

Biological Theories.   Biological explanations for deviance have focused on physiognomy (the determination of character by facial features), phrenology (the determination of mental abilities and character traits from the configuration of the skull), somatology (the determination of character by physique), genetic anomalies (for example, XYY chromosome in males), and brain malfunctions.

Some of these theories have been discredited (for example, the theory of Caesare Lombroso [1835–1909] that criminals were physically different—with low foreheads, protruding ears, long arms, and hairy. These distinct characteristics suggested that criminals were throwbacks to an earlier stage of human development—closer to the ape stage than are nondeviants). Other biological theories have shown a statistical link between certain physical characteristics and deviant behavior. Chances are, though, that when such a relationship is found, it will be also related to social factors. The learning disability known as dyslexia, for example, is related to school failure, emotional disturbance, and juvenile delinquency. This disability is a brain malfunction in which visual signs are scrambled. Average skills in reading, spelling, and arithmetic are impossible to attain if the malady remains undiagnosed. Teachers and parents often are unaware that the child is dyslexic and assume, rather, that she or he is retarded, lazy, or belligerent. The child (who actually may be very bright—Thomas Edison and Woodrow Wilson were dyslexic) finds school frustrating. Such a child is therefore much more likely than those not affected to be a troublemaker, to be alienated, to be either pushed out of school or a dropout, and never to reach full intellectual potential.

Psychological Theories.   These theories also consider the source of deviance to reside within the individual, but they differ from the biological theories in that they assume conditions of the mind or personality to be the fault. Deviant individuals, depending on the particular psychological theory, are psychopaths (asocial, aggressive, impulsive) as a result of a lack of affection during childhood, Oedipal conflict, psychosexual trauma, or other early life experience (Cohen, 1966:41–45). Using Freudian assumptions, the deviant is a person who has not developed an adequate ego to control deviant impulses (the *id*). Or, alternatively, deviance can result from a dominating *superego*. Persons with this condition are so repulsed by their own feelings (such as sexual fantasies or ambivalence toward parents and siblings) that they may commit deviant acts in order to receive the punishment they deserve. Freudians, therefore, place great stress on the relationship between children and their parents. The parents, in this view, can be too harsh or too lenient, or too inconsistent in their treatment of the child. Each situation leads to inadequately socialized children and immature, infantile behavior by adolescents and adults.

Because the fundamental assumption of the biological and psychological theories of deviance is that the fault lies within the individual, the solutions are aimed at changing the individual. Screening of the population for individuals with the presumed flaws is considered the best preventative. Doctors could routinely determine which boys had the XXY or XYY chromosome pattern. Psychological testing in the schools could find out which students were unusually aggressive, guilt-ridden, or fantasy-oriented. Although the screening for potential problem people may make some sense (to detect dyslexics, for example), there are some fundamental problems with this type of solution. First, the screening devices likely will not be perfect, thereby mislabeling some persons. Second, screening is based on the assumption that there is a direct linkage between certain characteristics and deviance. If identified as a predeviant by these methods, the subsequent treatment of that individual, who has a new definition of self, would likely lead to a self-fulfilling prophecy and a false validation of the screening procedures, increasing their use and acceptability.

A related problem with these screening procedures is the tendency to overpredict. In one attempt to identify predelinquents, a panel of experts examined a sample of youths already in the early stages of troublemaking and made predictions regarding future delinquency. Approximately 60 percent of the cases were judged to be predelinquents. A follow-up twenty years later revealed, however, that less than one-third actually became involved in difficulties with the law (Powers and Witmer, 1951).

For people identified as potential deviants or who are actually deviants, the kinds-of-people theorists advocate solutions aimed at changing the individuals. The person is treated by drug therapy, electrical stimulation of the brain, electronic monitoring, surgery, operant conditioning, counseling, psychotherapy, probation with guidance of a psychiatric social worker, or incarceration. The assumption is clearly that deviants are troubled and sick persons who must be changed to conform to the norms of society.

The Sociological Approach. A number of sociological theories are also kinds-of-people explanations for deviance. Instead of individual characteristics distinguishing the deviant from the nondeviant, these theories focus on differing objective social and economic conditions. These theories are based on the empirical observations that crime and mental illness rates, to name two forms of deviance, vary by social class, ethnicity, race, place of residence, and sex.

> From these gross differences, the sociologist infers that something beyond the intimacy of family surroundings is operative in the emergence of delinquent patterns; something in the cultural and social atmosphere apparent in certain sectors of society. (Matza, 1964b:17)

Let us look at some of these theories, which emphasize that certain social conditions are conducive to the internalization of values that encourage deviance.

Cultural Transmission. Sutherland's theory of differential association sought to explain why some persons are criminals while others are not, even though both may share certain social characteristics, such as social class position (Sutherland and Cressey, 1966:81–82). Sutherland believed that through interaction, one learns to be a criminal. If our close associates are deviants, there is a strong probability that we will learn the techniques and the deviant values that make criminal acts possible.

The significant feature of Sutherland's theory is his claim that procriminal sentiments are acquired, as are all others, by association with other individuals in a process of social interaction. Criminal orientations do not, thus, stem from faulty metabolism, inadequate superego development, or even poverty. (Hartjen, 1974:51)*

Societal Goals and Differential Opportunities. Robert Merton (1957) has presented an explanation for why the lower classes (who, coincidentally, live in the cities) disproportionately commit criminal acts. In Merton's view, societal values determine both what are the appropriate goals (success through the acquisition of wealth) and the approved means for achieving these goals. The problem, however, is that some people are denied access to the legitimate means of achieving these goals. The poor, especially those from certain racial and ethnic groups, in addition to the roadblocks presented by negative stereotypes, often receive a second-class education or have to drop out of school prematurely because of financial exigencies, all of which effectively exclude them from high-paying and prestigious occupations. Because legitimate means to success are inaccessible to them, they often resort to certain forms of deviant behavior to attain success. Viewed from this perspective, deviance is a result of social structure and not the consequence of individual pathology. McGee makes this point in his analysis of Merton's scheme. In each of the deviant adaptations,

> the individuals are behaving as they have been taught by their societies. They are not sinful or weak individuals who choose to deviate. They are, in fact, doing what they have learned they are supposed to do in order to earn the rewards which their society purports to offer its members. But either because their positions in the social structure do not permit them access to the means through which to seek the rewards they have learned to want, or because the means do not in fact guarantee goal attainment, they become frustrated and experience loss of self-esteem. In a final attempt to do and be what they have been taught they must, they engage in what is called deviant behavior. Such behavior is simply an attempt to gain the same self-esteem which others are presumed to have and which the society has made it intolerable to be without. (McGee, 1975: 211–212)

Although Merton's analysis provides many important insights, the emphasis is on the adjustments people make to the circumstances of society. Deviance is a property of people because they cannot adapt to the discrepancy between the goals and the means of society. The problem is that Merton accepts the U.S. success ethic. In the words of Doyle and Schindler,

> What is missing is the perspective that the winner, firster, money mentality could be a pathology rather than a [positive] value in America, a pathology that so powerfully corrupts our economy, polity, and way of life that it precludes any possibility of a cohesive, healthy, community. Certainly it is valid and worthwhile to explore the situation of the deprived in a success oriented society, but it is also valid to question the viability of a social system with such a "value" at its core. The sociology of deviance has turned too quickly and too exclusively to hypotheses about "bad" people. The analysis of "bad" societies has been neglected. (Doyle and Schindler, 1974:2)

*From *Crime and Criminalization* by Clayton A. Hartjen. Copyright © 1974 by Praeger Publishers. Reprinted by Permission of Praeger Publishers, a Division of Holt, Rinehart and Winston.

"Other Societies: Capitalism and Crime in the Former Soviet Bloc Countries" shows how changing the economic system affects crime.

Subcultural Differences by Social Class. We explore the culture of poverty hypothesis in Chapter 9. (The **culture of poverty** is the view that the poor are qualitatively different in values and lifestyles from the rest of society and that these cultural differences explain their poverty.) Because it has special relevance for explaining differential crime rates, we briefly characterize it here with that emphasis. The argument is that people, because of their social class position, differ in resources, power, and prestige and hence have different experiences, lifestyles, and ways of life. The lower-class culture has its own values, many of which run counter to the values of the middle and upper classes. There is a unique morality (a right action is one that works and can be got away with) and a unique set of criteria that make a person successful in the lower-class community (Miller, 1958; Banfield, 1974).

Edward Banfield (1974) argues, for example, that lower-class individuals have a propensity toward criminal behavior. He asserts that a person in the lower class

Other Societies Other Ways

Capitalism and Crime in the Former Soviet Bloc Countries

Among the many problems facing the nations that were once in the Soviet orbit is rising crime. Under totalitarian communism, crime was largely curtailed because of three factors: (1) the people were encouraged constantly to work for the collective good; (2) there was a fear of the police (the strong police presence and the KGB—secret police); and (3) the goods and services of society (such as food, clothing, shelter, and health care) were more or less available to everyone.

With the downfall of communism in Eastern Europe and the republics of the former Soviet Union, there are increased freedom and a greater reliance on a market economy (capitalism). Unlike the previous economic system in which the government maintained a stable currency and full employment and set artificially low prices, the new capitalism emphasizes the market to set prices, companies that must make profits, and individuals working to maximize their own situation. The new system brings advantages, such as more motivated workers and efficient companies. Increased freedom also means fewer police.

There is also a dark side to these changes. Unemployment has risen dramatically. Poverty and homelessness have increased. The prices of goods have risen rapidly (e.g., in early 1992, on the first day that Russia and the Ukraine removed price controls, the prices of some goods increased as much as 500 percent). What appears to be happening in these countries is the development of two-tiered societies. That is, each society is becoming divided into the haves (those who can afford the new, very high prices) and the have-nots (those who cannot pay these exorbitant prices). As a result, many individuals in these countries (certainly many more than was the case under totalitarian communism) have turned to crime in order to survive in what for them is a hostile economic environment. Thus, the rates for prostitution, robbery, burglary, and smuggling have increased dramatically. Gangs of youths are now common in the large cities, as is organized crime.

does not have a strong sense of morality and thus is not constrained by legal rules. These persons, according to Banfield, have weak ego strength, a present-time orientation, a propensity for taking risk, and a willingness to inflict injury. Many scholars accept Banfield's assertions about the "lower-class culture," but there is strong evidence that it is incorrect (see Chapter 9). Even if Banfield's characterization of the lower-class propensity to crime is correct, the critical question is whether these differences are durable or not. Will a change in monetary status or peer groups make a difference because the individual has a dual value system—one that is a reaction to his or her deprived situation and one that is middle class? This is a key research question because the answer determines where to attack the problem—at the individual or the societal level.

The Blaming-the-Victim Critique of the Individual-Oriented Explanations for Deviance

Although the socialization theories focus on forces external to individuals that push them toward deviant behavior, they, like the biological and psychological theories, are kinds-of-people theories that find the fault within the individual. The deviant has an acquired trait—the internalization of values and beliefs favorable to deviance—that is social in origin. The problem is that this results in *blaming the victims,* as William Ryan has forcefully argued:

> The new ideology attributes defect and inadequacy to the malignant nature of poverty, injustice, slum life, and racial difficulties. The stigma that marks the victim and accounts for his victimization is acquired stigma, a stigma of social, rather than genetic origin. But the stigma, the defect, the fatal difference—though derived in the past from environmental forces—is still located within the victim, inside his skin. With such an elegant formulation, the humanitarian can have it both ways. He can, all at the same time, concentrate his charitable interest on the defects of the victim, condemn the vague social and environmental stresses that produced the defect (some time ago), and ignore the continuing effect of victimizing social forces (right now). It is a brilliant ideology for justifying a perverse form of social action designed to change, not society, as one might expect, but rather society's victim. (Ryan, 1976:7)*

Let us contrast, then, two ways to look at deviance—blaming the victim or blaming society. The fundamental difference between these two approaches is whether the problems emanate from the pathologies of individuals or because of the situation in which deviants are immersed. The answer is doubtless somewhere between these two extremes; but because the individual blamers have held sway, let us look carefully at the critique of this approach (Ryan, 1976; Caplan and Nelson, 1973).

We begin by considering some victims. One group of victims is composed of children in slum schools who are failures. Why do they fail? Victim blamers point

---

*William Ryan, *Blaming the Victim,* rev. ed. (New York: Pantheon, 1976), p. 7. Reprinted by permission of the publisher.

to the children's **cultural deprivation.*** They do not do well in school because their families speak a different dialect, because their parents are uneducated, because they have not been exposed to all the education experiences of middle-class children (for example, visits to the zoo, extensive travel, attendance at cultural events, exposure to books, exposure to correct English usage). In other words, the defect is in the children and their families. System blamers, however, look elsewhere for the sources of failure. They ask, What is there about the schools that make slum children more likely to fail? The answer for them is found in the irrelevant curriculum, the class-biased IQ tests, the tracking system, the overcrowded classrooms, the differential allocation of resources within the school district, and insensitive teachers whose low expectations for poor children comprise a prophecy that is continually fulfilled.

Another victim is the criminal. Why is the **recidivism** rate (reinvolvement in crime) of criminals so high? The individual blamer would point to the faults of the individual criminals: their greed, feelings of aggression, weak impulse control, and lack of a conscience (superego). The system blamers' attention is directed to very different sources for this problem. They would look, rather, at the penal system, the employment situation for ex-criminals, and the schools. For example, studies have shown that 20 to 30 percent of inmates are functionally illiterate. This means they cannot meet minimum reading and writing demands in U.S. society, such as filling out job applications. Yet these persons are expected to leave prison, find a job, and stay out of trouble. Because they are illiterate and ex-criminals, they face unemployment or at best the most menial jobs (where there are low wages, no job security, and no fringe benefits). The system blamer would argue that these persons are not to blame for their illiteracy, but rather that the schools at first and later the penal institutions have failed to provide the minimum requirements for productive membership in society. Moreover, the lack of employment and the unwillingness of potential employers to train functional illiterates force many to return to crime in order to survive.

African Americans (and other racial minorities) constitute another set of victims in U.S. society. What accounts for the greater probability for Blacks than Whites to be failures in school, to be unemployed, to be criminals, and to be heroin addicts? The individualistic approach places the blame on the Blacks themselves. They are culturally deprived, they have high rates of illegitimacy and a high proportion of transient males, and a relatively high proportion of Black families have a matriarchal structure. This approach neglects the pervasive effects of racism in the United States, which limits the opportunities for African Americans, provides them with a second-class education, and renders them powerless to change the system through approved channels.

---

*The term *cultural deprivation* is a loaded ethnocentric term. It implies that the culture of the group in question is not only deficient but also inferior. This label is applied by members of the majority to the culture of the minority group. It is not only a malicious putting down of the minority, but the concept itself also is patently false because no culture can be inferior to another; it can only be different. The concept does remind us, however, that people can and do make invidious distinctions about cultures and subcultures. Furthermore, they act on these definitions as if they were true.

Why is there a strong tendency to place the blame for deviance on individuals rather than on the social system? The answer lies in the way that persons tend to define deviance. Most people define deviance as behavior that deviates from the norms and standards of society. Because people do not ordinarily question the norms or the way things are done in society, they tend to question the exceptions. The system is not only taken for granted, but it also has, for most people, an aura of sacredness because of the traditions and customs behind it. Logically, then, the people who deviate are the source of trouble. The obvious question, then, is why do these people deviate from the norms? Because most persons abide by society's norms, the deviation of the exceptions must be the result of some kind of unusual circumstance—accident, illness, personal defect, character flaw, or maladjustment (Ryan, 1976:10–18). The key to this approach, then, is that the flaw is within the deviant and not a function of societal arrangements.

The position taken in this debate has important consequences. Let us briefly examine the effects of interpreting social problems solely within a person-blame framework (Caplan and Nelson, 1973). First, this interpretation of social problems frees the government, the economy, the system of stratification, the system of justice, and the educational system from any blame. The established order is protected against criticism, thereby increasing the difficulty encountered in trying to change the dominant economic, social, and political institutions. A good example is found in the strategy of social scientists studying the origins of poverty. Because the person-blamer studies the poor rather than the nonpoor, the system of inequality (buttressed by the tax laws, welfare rules, and employment practices) goes unchallenged. A related consequence of the person-blame approach, then, is that the relatively advantaged segments of society retain their advantages.

Not only is the established order protected from criticism by the person-blame approach, but the authorities also can control dissidents under the guise of being helpful. Caplan and Nelson provide an excellent illustration of this in the following quote:

> Normally, one would not expect the Government to cooperate with "problem groups" who oppose the system. But if a person-blame rather than system-blame action program can be negotiated, cooperation becomes possible. In this way, the problem-defining process remains in the control of the would-be benefactors, who provide "help" so long as their diagnosis goes unchallenged.
>
> In 1970, for example, while a group of American Indians still occupied Alcatraz Island in San Francisco Bay, a group of blacks took over Ellis Island in New York Harbor. Both groups attempted to take back lands no longer used by the Federal Government. The Government solved the Ellis Island problem by getting the blacks to help establish a drug-rehabilitation center on it. They solved the Alcatraz problem by forcibly removing the Indians. Had the Indians been willing to settle for an alcoholism-treatment center on Alcatraz, thereby acknowledging that what they need are remedies for their personal problems, we suspect the Government would have "cooperated" again. (Caplan and Nelson, 1973:104)

Another social control function of the person-blame approach is that troublesome individuals and groups are controlled in a publicly acceptable manner. Deviants, whether they be criminals, homosexuals, or social protesters, are controlled by incarceration in prison or mental hospital, drugs, or other forms of therapy. In this manner, not only is blame directed at individuals and away from the system, but the problems (individuals) are in a sense also eliminated.

A related consequence is how the problem is to be treated. A person-blame approach demands a person-change treatment program. If the cause of delinquency, for example, is defined as the result of personal pathology, then the solution lies clearly in counseling, behavior modification, psychotherapy, drugs, or some other technique aimed at changing the individual deviant. Such an interpretation of social problems provides and legitimates the right to initiate person-change rather than system-change treatment programs. Under such a scheme, norms that are racist or sexist, for example, will go unchallenged.

The person-blame ideology invites not only person-change treatment programs but also programs for person control. The typical result is that the overwhelming emphasis of government programs is on more police, courts, and prisons, rather than on changing criminogenic social conditions.

A final consequence of person-blame interpretations is that they reinforce social myths about the degree of control we have over our fate. Such interpretations provide justification for a form of **Social Darwinism**—that is, a person's placement in the stratification system is a function of ability and effort. By this logic, the poor are poor because they *are* the dregs of society. In short, they deserve their fate, as do the successful in society. Thus, there is little sympathy for governmental programs to increase welfare to the poor.

We should recognize, however, that the contrasting position—the system-blame orientation—also has its dangers. First, it is only part of the truth. Social problems and deviance are highly complex phenomena that have both individual and systemic origins. Individuals, obviously, can be malicious and aggressive for purely psychological reasons. Perhaps only a psychologist can explain why a particular parent is a child abuser, or why a sniper shoots at cars passing on the freeway. Clearly, society needs to be protected from some individuals. Moreover, some persons require particular forms of therapy, remedial help, or special programs on an individual basis if they are to participate in society. But much that is labeled deviant is the end product of social conditions.

A second danger in a dogmatic system-blame orientation is that it presents a rigidly deterministic explanation for social problems. Taken too far, this position views individuals as robots controlled totally by their social environment. A balanced view of people is needed, because human beings have autonomy most of the time to choose between alternative courses of action. This raises the related question as to the degree to which people are responsible for their behavior. An excessive system-blame approach absolves individuals from the responsibility for their actions. To take such a stance argues that society should never restrict deviants. This extreme view invites anarchy.

Despite the problems just noted, the system-blame approach is emphasized in this chapter. The rationale for this is, first, that the contrasting view (individual-blame) is the prevailing view in U.S. society. Because average citizens, police personnel, legislators, judges, and social scientists tend to interpret social problems from an individualistic perspective, a balance is needed. Moreover, as noted earlier in this section, to hold a strict person-blame perspective has many negative consequences, and citizens must realize the effects of their ideology.

A second basis for the use of the society-blaming perspective is that the subject matter of sociology is not the individual, who is the special province of psychology, but society. If sociologists do not emphasize the social determinants of behavior, and if they do not make a critical analysis of the social structure, then who will? As noted in Chapter 1, an important ingredient of the sociological perspective is the development of a critical stance toward societal arrangements. The job of the sociologist is to look behind the facade to determine the positive and negative consequences of societal arrangements. The persistent question is, Who benefits under these arrangements, and who does not? This is why there should be such a close fit between the sociological approach and the societal-blaming perspective. Unfortunately, this has not always been the case.

Society as the Source of Deviance

We have seen that the traditional explanations for deviance, whether biological, psychological, or sociological, have located the source of deviance in individual deviants, their families, or their immediate social settings. The basic assumption of these theories is that because deviants do not fit in society, something is wrong with them. This section provides an antidote to the medical analogy implicit in those theories by focusing instead on two theories that place the blame for deviance on the role of society—labeling theory and conflict theory.

Labeling Theory

All the explanations for deviance described so far assume that deviants differ from nondeviants in behavior, attitude, and motivation. This assumption is buttressed by the commonly held belief that deviance is the actions of a few weird people who are either criminals, insane, or both. In reality, however, most persons break the rules of society at one time or another. The evidence is that the members of all social classes commit thefts, assaults, and use illegal drugs. Summarizing a number of studies on the relationship between socioeconomic class and crime, Travis Hirschi has said:

> While the prisons bulge with the socioeconomic dregs of society, careful quantitative research shows again and again that the relation between socioeconomic status and the commission of delinquent acts is small, or nonexistent. (Hirschi, 1969:66)

These studies do not mesh with our perceptions and the apparent facts. Crime statistics *do* show that the lower classes are more likely to be criminals. Even data on mental illness demonstrate that the lower classes are more likely than the middle classes to have serious mental problems (Hollingshead and Redlich, 1958; Myers and Bean, 1968). The difference is that most persons break the rules at one time or another, even serious rules for which they could be placed in jail (for example, theft, statutory rape, vandalism, violation of drug or alcohol laws, fraud, violations of the Internal Revenue Service), but only some get the *label* of deviant (Becker, 1963:14). As one adult analyzed his ornery but normal youth:

> I recall my high school and college days, participating in vandalism, entering locked buildings at night, drinking while under age—even while I made top grades and won athletic letters. I was normal and did these things with guys who now are preachers, professors, and businessmen. A few school friends of poorer families somehow tended to get caught and we didn't. They were failing in class, and we all believed they were too dumb not to know when to have fun and when to run. Some of them did time in jail and reformatories. *They* were "delinquents" and *we* weren't. (Janzen, 1974:390; see also Chambliss, 1973)

This chapter begins with the statement that society creates deviance by creating rules, the violation of which constitutes deviance. But rule breaking itself does not make a deviant. The successful application of the label *deviant* is crucial (Schur, 1971). This is the essence of **labeling theory,** the view of deviant behavior that stresses the importance of the society in defining what is illegal and in assigning a deviant status to particular individuals, which in turn dominates their identities and behaviors.

Who gets labeled as a deviant (criminal, psychotic, faggot, or junkie) is not just a matter of luck or random selection but the result of a systematic societal bias against the powerless. Chambliss has summarized the empirical evidence for criminals:

> The lower-class person is (1) more likely to be scrutinized and therefore be observed in any violation of the law, (2) more likely to be arrested if discovered under suspicious circumstances, (3) more likely to spend the time between arrest and trial in jail, (4) more likely to come to trial, (5) more likely to be found guilty, (6) if found guilty, more likely to receive harsh punishment than his middle- or upper-class counterpart. (Chambliss, 1969:86)

That there is a bias is beyond dispute (see "Diversity: Is the Drug War Racist?"), because the studies compare defendants by socioeconomic status or race, *controlling* for type of crime, number of previous arrests, type of counsel, and the like. In short, the well-to-do are much more likely to avoid the label of *criminal.* If they are found guilty, they are much less likely to receive a punishment of imprisonment, and those who are imprisoned receive advantages over the lower-class and minority inmates.

The most blatant example of this is found by examining what type of person actually receives the death penalty and, even more particularly, those who are executed by the state. The data on capital punishment show consistently that people from disadvantaged categories (racial minorities, the poor, the illiterate, the mentally retarded) are disproportionately given the death penalty as well as disproportionately killed by the state (Greenfeld, 1991). A good example is the difference in sentence when a White person is found guilty of killing a Black person, compared to when a Black person is the perpetrator and a White person the victim. The behavior is the same, one individual found guilty of killing another, yet juries and judges make a difference—Blacks receive the harsher sentence and punishment.

Diversity

Is the Drug War Racist?

Justice is, by definition, fair. But is this the case with the U.S. criminal justice system when it comes to race? The disparities between what happens to Whites compared to Blacks in the drug crimes indicate that the system is unfair to African Americans. Let's examine the facts (from Meddis, 1993; Cauchon, 1993).

An immediate contradiction is that even though Black adults were slightly more likely than White adults in 1991 to have used illegal drugs (16 percent to 12 percent), Blacks were four times more likely than Whites to be arrested for drug charges. The arrest rate for illegal drugs was 1,609 per 100,000 for Blacks and 408 per 100,000 for Whites. Moreover, in thirty major cities Blacks were at least ten times more likely to be arrested for drugs as Whites. The disparity in rates by race was greatest in the suburbs (six times greater for Blacks), followed by four times more in the central cities, and three times greater in rural areas.

African Americans are also much more likely than Whites to be imprisoned on drug charges. A 1992 survey found that in a given month about 8.7 million Whites used an illicit drug compared to 1.6 million Blacks. Yet, the number of Whites in state prisons on drug charges was 30,000 compared to 80,000 Blacks.

The law views some drugs more seriously than others, and these differences have implications for racial inequities in the justice system. In 1986 the federal government passed mandatory sentencing procedures, which included this telling difference: the possession of crack cocaine is punished much more severely than is having powder cocaine. One gram of crack is equal to 100 grams of powder in the sentencing rules. This means, in effect, that people found guilty of possessing 5 grams of crack cocaine will receive a five-year sentence whereas those found with 5 grams of powder cocaine will receive probation.

This difference has racial implications. As one observer noted, "The law is racist. Crack cocaine and powder cocaine are essentially the same drug. What's different is how it's ingested and the race of the people who use it" (Cauchon, 1993:A1). The point is that although the law concerning sentencing for cocaine may appear race neutral, it is not because crack is the drug of choice for Blacks (of those defendants accused of possessing crack, 91.5 percent were Black, compared to only 3.0 percent of Whites). Powder cocaine, on the other hand, was a drug used much more by Whites and Latinos.

The police and other authorities are much more likely to assume drug and other illegal behaviors by African Americans than they are by Whites. The police patrol neighborhoods where conspicuous drug-use occurs. This targets low-income areas, while bypassing more affluent areas where drug use is more hidden, with sales occurring at parties and in offices.

The police stop suspicious drivers on Interstates such as I-95 along the East Coast, where drugs travel north from Florida. Who are these suspicious drivers? Typically, they are people of color driving expensive cars. The authorities also use suspect "profiles" that include type of clothing and cash on hand to search questionable persons in airline, train, and bus terminals. These "profiles" disproportionately target racial minorities. There is an assumption of guilt that misses most Whites who also might be driving expensive cars and dress in a particular way.

Is there a conspiracy against African Americans? Most Blacks would argue that there is. Police officials, typically, argue that this is not a racist conspiracy. They are doing their job, responding to citizen complaints, arresting criminals where they find them regardless of race. Other individuals, including Jesse Jackson, say "It just shows how deep racism is institutionalized in American criminal justice" (quoted in Meddis, 1993:A2). Whether a conspiracy or not, the individual and collective actions by the police, Drug Enforcement Administration, judges, and legislators have the effect of treating African Americans unfairly.

Who gets paroled is another indicator of a bias in the system. Parole is a conditional release from prison that allows prisoners to return to their communities under the supervision of a parole officer before the completion of their maximum sentence. Typically, parole is granted by a parole board set up for the correctional institution or for the state. Often, the parole-board members are political appointees without training. The parole board reviews a prisoner's social history, past offenses, and behavior in prison and makes its judgment. The decision is rarely subject to review and can be made arbitrarily or discriminatorily.

The bias that disadvantages minorities and the poor throughout the system of justice continues as parole-board members, corrections officers, and others make judgments that often reflect stereotypes. What type of prisoner represents the safest risk, a Latino or a White? An uneducated or an educated person? A white-collar worker or a chronically unemployed unskilled worker? The evidence is overwhelming and consistent—the parole system, just as the rest of the criminal justice system, is biased against people of color and those of low socioeconomic status.

The state and federal prisons contain more than 1 million inmates. As a society, the United States has 426 prisoners per 100,000 people (the highest incarceration rate in the world). Even more striking, the number of Black males imprisoned per 100,000 in the United States in 1992 was 3,370, which far surpasses the incarceration rate for Blacks of 681 in the Union of South Africa (*Harper's Magazine,* 1993). In fact, nearly one in four Black males in the United States between the ages of twenty and twenty-nine is either incarcerated, on probation, or on parole. This statistic shows that the underdogs in society (the poor and the minorities) are disproportionately represented in the prison population. An important consequence of this representation is that it reinforces the negative stereotypes already present in the majority of the population. The large number of Blacks and the poor in prison prove that they have criminal tendencies. This belief is reinforced further by the high recidivism rate of 70 percent of ex-prisoners.

At least four factors relative to the prison experiences operate to fulfill the prophecy that the poor and racial minorities are likely to behave criminally. The first is that the entire criminal justice system is viewed by the underdogs as unjust. There is a growing belief among prisoners that because the system is biased against them, all prisoners are, in fact, political. This consciousness-raising increases the bitterness and anger among them.

A second reason for the high rate of crime among those processed through the system of criminal justice is the accepted fact that prison is a brutal, degrading, and altogether dehumanizing experience. Mistreatment by guards, sexual assaults by fellow prisoners, overcrowding, and unsanitary conditions are commonplace in U.S. jails and prisons. Prisoners cannot escape the humiliation, anger, and frustration. These feelings, coupled with the knowledge that the entire system of justice is unjustly directed at certain categories of persons, creates within many ex-cons the desire for revenge.

A third factor is that prisons provide learning experiences for prisoners in the art of crime. Through the interaction of the inmates, individuals learn the techniques of crime from the masters and develop the contacts that can be used later.

Finally, the ex-con faces the problems of finding a job and being accepted again in society. Long-termers face problems of adjusting to life without regimentation. More important, since good-paying jobs, particularly in times of economic recession, are difficult for anyone to find, the ex-con who is automatically assumed to be untrustworthy is faced with either unemployment or those jobs nobody else will take. Even the law works to his disadvantage by prohibiting certain jobs to ex-cons.

The result of nonacceptance by society is often to return to crime. Previous offenders, on the average, are arrested for crime within six weeks after leaving prison. This, of course, justifies the beliefs by police officers, judges, parole boards, and other authorities that certain categories of persons should receive punishment whereas others should not.

The Consequences of Labeling.   We have just seen that the labeling process is a crucial factor in the formulation of a deviant career. In other words, the stigma of the label leads to subsequent deviance. This is what Lemert (1951) meant by the concept of secondary deviance. **Primary deviance** is the rule-breaking that occurs before labeling. **Secondary deviance** is that behavior resulting from the labeling process. Being labeled a criminal means being rejected by society, by employers, by friends, and even by relatives. There is a high probability that such a person will turn to behavior that fulfills the prophecies of others. Put another way, persons labeled as deviants tend to become locked into a deviant behavior pattern ("deviant career"). Looking at deviance this way turns the tables on conventional thought.

> Instead of assuming that it is the deviant's difference which needs explanation, [the labeling perspective] asks why the majority responds to this difference as it does. This shift of the question reverses the normal conception of causation; the labeling school suggests that the other person's peculiarity has not caused us to regard him as different so much as our labeling hypothesis has caused his peculiarity. (Nettler, 1974:203)

Ex-mental patients, like ex-convicts, usually have difficulty in finding employment and establishing close relationships because of the stigma of the label. This difficulty, of course, leads to frustration, anger, low self-esteem, and other symptoms of mental illness. Moreover, the consistent messages from other people (remember Cooley's looking-glass self) that one is sick are likely to lead the individual to behavior in accord with these expectations. Even while a patient is in a mental hospital, the actions of the staff may actually foster in the person a self-concept of deviant behavior consistent with that definition. Patients who show insight about their illness confirm the medical and societal diagnosis and are positively rewarded by psychiatrists and other personnel (see Scheff, 1966). The opposite also occurs, as illustrated so vividly by the character R. P. McMurphy in the novel *One Flew over the Cuckoo's Nest* (Kesey, 1962). Although the fictitious McMurphy fought this tendency to confirm the expectations of powerful others, the pressures to conform were great. Cole has summarized this process of how the deviant role is sustained in the following:

> After someone is labeled as deviant, he often finds it rewarding to accept the label and act deviant. Consider, for example, a patient in a mental hospital who has been diagnosed as a schizophrenic. If the patient refuses to accept the diagnosis, claims that he

is not mentally ill, and demands to be immediately released, the staff will consider him to be hostile and uncooperative. He may be denied privileges and treated as hopelessly insane. After all, the person who cannot even recognize that he is ill must be in a mental state in which he has no perception of reality! On the other hand, if the patient accepts the validity of the diagnosis, admits his illness, and tries to cooperate with the staff in effecting a cure, he will be rewarded. He will be defined as a good cooperative patient who is sincerely trying to get better. Any weird or unusual behavior he engages in will be ignored; after all, he is mentally ill, and such types of behavior should be expected from a person in his mental state. He may even be rewarded for engaging in behavior which is considered to be characteristic of schizophrenia. Such behavior serves to reassure the staff that the patient is indeed mentally ill and that the social organization of the mental hospital makes sense. (Cole, 1975:141–142)

The labeling perspective is especially helpful in understanding the bias of the criminal justice system. It shows, in summary, that when society's underdogs are disproportionately singled out for the criminal label, the subsequent problems of stigmatization and segregation they face result in a tendency toward further deviance, thereby justifying the society's original negative response to them. This tendency for secondary deviance is especially strong when the imposition of the label is accompanied by a sense of injustice. Lemert (1967) argued that a stronger commitment to a deviant identity is greatest when the negative label (stigma) is believed by the individual to be inconsistently applied by society. The evidence of such inconsistency is overwhelming.

From this perspective, then, the situations showing that society's underdogs engage in more deviance than do persons from the middle and upper classes are invalid because they reflect the differential response of society to deviance at every phase in the process of criminal justice. Hartjen has provided an excellent statement that summarizes this process.

Criminal sanctions are supposedly directed toward a person's behavior—what he does, not what kind of person he is. Yet, the research on the administration of criminal justice . . . reveals that just the opposite occurs. A person is likely to acquire a social identity as a criminal precisely because of what he is—because of the kind of personal or social characteristics he has the misfortune to possess. Being black, poor, migrant, uneducated, and the like increases a person's chances of being defined as a criminal. . . . What I am suggesting here is that the very structure and operation of the judicial system, which was created to deal with the problem called crime, are not only grounded in an unstated image of the criminal but also—merely because the system exists—serve to produce and perpetuate the "thing" it was created to handle. That is to say, the criminal court (and especially the juvenile court) does not exist in its present form because the people it deals with are what they are. Rather, the criminals and delinquents become the way they are characterized by others as being because the court (and the world view it embodies) exists in the form that it does. *The criminal, thus, is a "product" of the structural and procedural characteristics of the judicial system.* (Hartjen, 1974: 120–121)*

*From *Crime and Criminalization* by Clayton A. Hartjen. Copyright © 1974 by Praeger Publishers. Reprinted by permission of Praeger Publishers, a Division of Holt, Rinehart and Winston.

"Solutions" for Deviance from the Labeling Perspective.   The labeling theorist's approach to deviance leads to unconventional solutions (Schur, 1971). The assumption is that deviants are not basically different—except that they have been processed (and labeled) by official sources (judges and courts; psychiatrists and mental hospitals). The primary target for policy, then, should be neither the individual nor the local community setting, but the process by which some persons are singled out for the negative label. From this approach, organizations produce deviants. Speaking specifically about juvenile delinquency, Schur has argued that the solution should be what he has called **radical nonintervention** (the strategy of leaving juvenile delinquents alone as much as possible rather than giving them a negative label).

> We can now begin to see some of the meanings of the term "radical nonintervention." For one thing, it breaks radically with conventional thinking about delinquency and its causes. Basically, radical nonintervention implies policies that accommodate society to the widest possible diversity of behaviors and attitudes, rather than focusing on as many individuals as possible to "adjust" to supposedly common societal standards. This does not mean that anything goes, that all behavior is socially acceptable. But traditional delinquency policy has proscribed youthful behavior well beyond what is required to maintain a smooth-running society or to protect others from youthful depredations.
>
> Thus, the basic injunction for public policy becomes: *leave kids alone wherever possible.* This effort partly involves mechanisms to divert children away from the courts but it goes further to include opposing various kinds of intervention by diverse social control and socializing agencies. . . . Subsidiary policies would favor collective action programs instead of those that single out specific individuals; and voluntary programs instead of compulsive ones. Finally, this approach is radical in asserting that major and intentional sociocultural change will help reduce our delinquency problems. Piecemeal socioeconomic reform will not greatly affect delinquency; there must be thorough-going changes in the structure and the values of our society. If the choice is between changing youth and changing society (including some of its laws), the radical noninterventionist opts for changing the society. (Schur, 1973: 154–155)

One way to accomplish this "leave the deviants alone whenever possible" philosophy would be to treat fewer acts as criminal or deviant. For adults, this could be accomplished by decriminalizing victimless crimes, such as gambling, drug possession, prostitution, and homosexual acts by consenting adults. Youth should not be treated as criminals for behavior that is legal if one is old enough. Truancy, running away from home, curfew violations, and purchasing alcohol are acts for which persons below the legal age can receive the label *delinquent,* yet they are not crimes for adults. Is there any wonder, then, why so many youthful rule breakers outgrow their so-called delinquency, becoming law-abiding citizens as adults?

Acts dangerous to society do occur, and they must be handled through legal mechanisms. But when a legal approach is required, justice must be applied evenly. Currently, the criminal label is disproportionately applied to individuals from the other side of the tracks. This procedure increases the probability of further deviance by these persons because of secondary deviance and justifies further stern punishment for this category. This unfair cycle must be broken. "Human Agency: The Gay Rights Movement" provides an example of one effort to break that cycle.

Gays and lesbians have organized to protest injustices and to achieve equality under the law.

The strengths of labeling theory are (1) that it concentrates on the role of societal reactions in the creation of deviance, (2) the realization that the label is applied disproportionately to the powerless, and (3) that it explains how deviant careers are established and perpetuated. There are problems with the theory, however (see Warren and Johnson, 1973; Gibbs, 1966; Davis, 1975; Liazos, 1972). First, it avoids the question of causation (primary deviance). Labeling, by definition, occurs after the fact. It disregards undetected deviance. As Charles McCaghy has put it,

> by minimizing the importance of explaining initial (primary) deviance, whatever meaning the behavior originally had for the deviant is ignored as a contributor to subsequent behavior. Although societal reaction may become a crucial factor in behavior, it is questionable that whatever purpose or reward the behavior first held is invariably replaced. For example, if a person first steals for thrills, do thrills fail to be a factor once societal reaction has taken its toll? (McCaghy, 1976:87)

Another problem with labeling involves the assumption that deviants are really normal—because we are all rule breakers. Thus, it overlooks the possibility that some persons are unable to cope with the pressures of their situation. Some people are dangerous. Individuals who are disadvantaged tend to be more angry, frustrated, and alienated than are their more fortunate fellows. The result may be differences in quantity and quality of primary deviance.

This perspective also relieves the individual deviant from blame. The underdog is seen as victimized by the powerful labelers. Further, individuals enmeshed in the labeling process are so constrained by the forces of society that they are incapable of choice. Once again, McCaghy has put it well: "Although it is true that deviants may be pawns of the powerful, this does not mean that deviants are powerless to resist, to alter their behavior, or to acquire power themselves" (McCaghy, 1976:88).

AGENCY

HUMAN

The Gay Rights Movement

The forces of society converge to restrict the behavior of individuals to those activities considered socially acceptable. But occasionally some individuals who find these demands too confining organize to change society. One contemporary example is the Gay Rights Movement.

Although homosexuals have been accepted by some societies (e.g., ancient Greece and Rome), they have never been accepted in the United States. The erotic sexual attraction and behaviors between members of the same sex have always been severely sanctioned in our society. Formal laws forbidding such behaviors have been enacted. Employers, typically, have not knowingly hired homosexuals. Persons assumed to have such aberrant proclivities have been the objects of ridicule throughout society—in the media, on playgrounds, in factories, and in boardrooms. Because of discrimination against them, fear of social ostracism, and other forms of rejection even by friends and family, most homosexuals have felt it necessary to conceal their sexual preference.

These compelling fears have kept homosexuals for most periods of American history from organizing to change a repressive situation. A few homosexual organizations were formed (the first in 1925 and others in the 1950s) for mutual support, but a relatively few homosexuals were willing at these times to declare publicly their deviance from the norm of society.

The 1960s provided a better climate for change as youths, Blacks, women, pacifists, and other groups questioned the norms and ideologies of the dominant society. This time clearly was one of heightened awareness among the oppressed of their oppression and of the possibility that through collective efforts they could change what seemed before as unchangeable.

The precipitating event for homosexual unity occurred at 3 A.M. on June 28, 1969, when police raided the Stonewall Inn in New York's Greenwich Village. But instead of dispersing, the 200 homosexual patrons, who had never collectively resisted the police before, threw objects at the police and set fire to the bar. The riot lasted 45 minutes, but it gave impetus to a number of collective efforts by gays to publicize police harassment of the gay community, job discrimination, and other indignities that homosexuals face. Gay liberation groups emerged in numerous cities and on university cam-

Perhaps its most serious deficiency, though, is that labeling theory focuses on certain types of deviance but ignores others. The attention is directed at society's underdogs, which is good. But the forms of deviance emanating from the social structure or from the powerful are not considered a very serious omission. As Liazos has put it, the themes of labeling theory focus attention on people who have been successfully labeled as deviants ("nuts, sluts, and perverts"), the deviant subculture, and the self-fulfilling prophecy that perpetuates their deviant patterns (Liazos, 1972). Even though this is appropriate and necessary, it concentrates on the powerless. The impression is that deviance is an exclusive property of the poor in the slum, the minorities, and street gangs.

But what of the deviance of the powerful members of society, and even of society itself? Liazos (1972) has chronicled these acts for us:

1. The unethical, illegal, and destructive actions found in the corporate world, such as robbery through price-fixing, low wages, pollution, inferior and dangerous products, deception, and outright lies in advertising.

puses. By 1980 more than 4,000 homosexual organizations existed in the United States. Many neighborhoods in major cities became openly homosexual—most notably the Castro district in San Francisco, New Town in Chicago, and Greenwich Village in New York City. Gay organizations now include churches, associations of professionals, health clinics, and networks of gay-owned businesses to supply the gay community's needs. The proliferation of these organizations for homosexuals has provided a supportive climate allowing many of them to come out of the closet.

The increased numbers of public homosexuals have provided the political base for changing the various forms of oppression that homosexuals experience. A Gay Media Task Force promotes accurate and positive images of gays in television, films, and advertising: a Gay Rights National Lobby promotes favorable legislation; and a National Gay Task Force serves to further gay interests by attacking the minority group status of homosexuals in a variety of political and ideological arenas.

The positive results of these political activities, although limited, have been encouraging to the gay community. Since 1983, the state of Wisconsin and most of the larger cities in the United States have enacted gay-rights laws. The Civil Service Reform Act of 1978 prohibits federal agencies from discriminating against gays in employment practices. And, although still rare, a few avowed homosexuals have been elected to public office.

The successes of gay-rights political activists have not yet achieved their ultimate goal—the full acceptance of homosexuality as an alternative life-style. Homosexuals are still not allowed to marry in all but a very few cities. Discrimination in housing and jobs still occurs. Gays are allowed in the military as long as they "stay in the closet," that is, live a lie. Polls show that only about one-third of people in the United States consider it an acceptable life-style. Gay-rights movements also have met fierce resistance by fundamentalist religious groups who believe homosexuality to be morally offensive and dangerous. But clearly during the past twenty years, the collective efforts of homosexuals and their supporters have had an enormous and positive impact for homosexuals (see Kopkind, 1993).

2. The covert institutional violence committed against the poor by the institutions of society: schools, hospitals, corporations, and the government.

3. The political manipulators who pass laws that protect the interests of the powerful and disadvantage the powerless.

4. The power of the powerful is used to deflect criticism, labeling, and punishment even when deserved.

In short, labeling overlooks the deviant qualities of the society and its powerful members. Although social structure should be central to sociologists, the labeling theorists have minimized its impact on deviance. Liazos has summarized the problem this way:

> We should banish the concept of "deviance" and speak of oppression, conflict, persecution, and suffering. By focusing on the dramatic forms, as we do now, we perpetuate most people's beliefs and impressions that such "deviance" is the basic cause of many of our troubles, that these people (criminals, drug addicts, political dissenters, and others)

are the real "troublemakers"; and, necessarily, we neglect conditions of inequality, powerlessness, institutional violence, and so on, which lie at the bases of our tortured society. (Liazos, 1972:119)

Another way to explain deviance—conflict theory—extends labeling theory by focusing on social structure, thereby overcoming the fundamental criticisms of Liazos and others.

Conflict Theory

Why is certain behavior defined as deviant? The answer, according to conflict theorists, is that powerful economic interest groups are able to get laws passed and enforced that protect their interests (Quinney, 1970, 1974). We must begin, then, with the law.

Of all the requirements for a just system, the most fundamental is the foundation of nondiscriminatory laws. Many criminal laws are the result of a consensus among the public as to what kinds of behaviors are a menace and should be punished (for example, murder, rape, theft). The laws devised to make these acts illegal and the extent of punishment for violators are nondiscriminatory (although, as we have seen, the administration of these laws is discriminatory), because they do not single out a particular social category as the target.

There are laws, however, that do discriminate, because they result from special interests using their power to translate their interests into public policy. These laws may be discriminatory in that some segments of society (for example, the poor, minorities, youth, renters, debtors) rarely have access to the lawmaking process and therefore often find the laws unfairly aimed at them. Vagrancy, for example, is really a crime that only the poor can commit.

Not only is the formation of the law political, but so, too, is the administration of the law. This is true because at every stage in the processing of criminals, authorities make choices based on personal bias, pressures from the powerful, and the constraints of the status quo. Some examples of the political character of law administration are these: (1) the powerful attempt to coerce other people to their view of morality, hence laws against homosexuality, pornography, drug use, and gambling; (2) the powerful may exert pressure on the authorities to crack down on certain kinds of violators, especially individuals and groups who are disruptive (protesters); (3) there may be political pressure exerted to keep certain crimes from public view (embezzlement, stock fraud, the Iran-contra affair); (4) there may be pressure to protect the party in power, the elected officials, the police, CIA, and FBI; and (5) any effort to protect and preserve the status quo is a political act. Hartjen has summarized why the administration of justice is inherently political:

> Unless one is willing to assume that law-enforcement agents can apply some magic formula to gauge the opinions of the public they serve, unless one is willing to assume that citizens unanimously agree on what laws are to be enforced and how enforcement is to be carried out, unless one is willing to assume that blacks, the poor, urbanites, and the young are actually more criminalistic than everyone else, it must be concluded, at least, that discriminatory law enforcement is a result of differences in power and that actual decisions as to which and whose behavior is criminal are expressions of this power. One

need only ask himself why some laws, such as those protecting the consumer from fraud, go largely unenforced while the drug addict, for example, is pursued with a paranoiac passion. (Hartjen, 1974:11)*

The conflict approach is critical of the kinds-of-people explanations of order theorists and the focus of labeling theorists because both explanations center on individual deviants and their crimes. Order theorists and labeling theorists tend to emphasize street crimes and ignore the crimes of the rich and powerful, such as corporate crimes (which go largely unpoliced) and crimes by governments (which are not even considered crimes, unless they are committed by enemy governments). Conflict theorists, in contrast, emphasize corporate and political crimes, which cause many times more the economic damage and harm to people than do street crimes. **Corporate crime** refers to the "illegal and/or socially harmful behaviors that result from deliberate decision making by corporate executives in accordance with the operative goals of their organizations" (Kramer, 1982:75). This definition focuses attention on corporations, rather than on individuals, as perpetrators, and it goes beyond the criminal law to include "socially harmful behaviors."

Both of these elements are critical to conflict theorists. First, deviance is not limited to troubled individuals, as is the traditional focus in sociology. Organizations, too, can be deviant. Moreover, research has shown that corporations have a higher criminality rate than do individuals (and the law does not define most harmful corporate behavior as illegal). For example, one study of the 1,000 largest U.S. corporations found that 11 percent had been convicted of at least one illegal act over a ten-year period (Ross, 1980). As Simon and Eitzen have commented:

> Imagine for a moment that, between 1970 and 1979, 11 percent of the adult population of the United States had been convicted of some illegal offense and sentenced to prison. As a result, approximately 12 million people would be placed in a prison system that is overcrowded with a mere half million inmates. At such a point, liberals and conservatives alike would call crime an epidemic—an institutionalized phenomenon in U.S. society. However, when the same level of corporate crime is discussed, the problem is not considered to be serious. (Simon and Eitzen, 1993:358)

The second part of the definition of corporate crime stresses "socially harmful behaviors," whether criminal or not. This means that conflict theorists ask such questions as:

> What about selling proven dangerous products (e.g., pesticides, drugs, or food) overseas, when it is illegal to do so within the United States? What about promoting an unsafely designed automobile such as the Ford Pinto? Or, what about being excessively slow to promote a safe work environment for workers? (Timmer and Eitzen, 1989:85)

See "A Closer Look: Corporate Crime."

The definition of **political crime** separates order and conflict theorists. Because order theorists assume that the law and the state are neutral, they perceive political

*From *Crime and Criminalization* by Clayton A. Hartjen. Copyright © 1974 by Praeger Publishers. Reprinted by permission of Praeger Publishers, a Division of Holt, Rinehart and Winston.

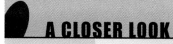

A CLOSER LOOK

Corporate Crime

Chevron Corporation reaped $1.2 billion in profits on $37 billion in revenues in 1991. An integrated petroleum company with production activities in the United States, Canada, Angola, Australia, Indonesia and the United Kingdom, Chevron is no benevolent giant. This year, law enforcement officials and citizen activists began to catch up with this huge corporate criminal.

In June, community activists in San Francisco initiated proceedings for a class-action law suit against Chevron for health and property damage allegedly caused by toxic dust released from a Chevron refinery in Richmond, California in December 1991. The West County Toxics Coalition (WCTC) charges that the release blew at least 40 tons of toxic dust, containing the heavy metal vanadium and cancer-causing nickel, into a 16-square mile area of residential neighborhoods.

"This is only one of a continuing slew of accidents from the plant," says Michael Stein of the Pesticide Action Network. "Every couple of months there's another accident there, usually involving the release of airborne toxics into the surrounding community."

"People were dusted, their property was dusted, lawn furniture was affected," says Michael Leedie of Citizens for a Better Environment. "It fell in their gardens and it fell in their soil." According to Leedie, local citizens have suffered various health effects as a result of the accident, including skin rashes, difficulty with breathing, the taste of metal in their mouths and redness in their eyes. "These are typical symptoms of nickel exposure," Leedie says.

According to Leedie, Chevron was forced to release the dust to relieve pressure and prevent a larger accident when a valve in the fluid catalytic cracking unit failed to open. Local community groups are trying to build a group tort case against Chevron. So far, over 7,000 people have signed up for the class-action lawsuit.

Environmentalists have criticized Chevron's advertising campaign, which portrays the company as environmentally responsible. "Chevron spends millions of dollars advertising itself as an environmentally responsible company when it comes to butterflies, eagles and foxes," WCTC wrote in a letter to Chevron.

"But when it comes to the company's damage to human beings, who are your neighbors, you have ignored your responsibilities. Many people were sick as a result of the accident and deserve to have their health costs paid."

This year, Chevron has continued to prove that it is one of the dirtiest of the giant oil companies.

In August, Chevron entered a guilty plea to 65 Clean Water Act violations, and was ordered to pay $6.5 million in criminal fines and $1.5 million in civil fines. Chevron committed the crimes on Platform Grace, an oil drilling platform in the Pacific Ocean off the coast of Los Angeles.

Chevron admitted to a pattern of unlawfully discharging oil and grease into the ocean in excess of its permit limit. Some of the violations involved releases of substances in amounts as high as three to four times above the discharge limits. Chevron also admitted that on some days, it bypassed its wastewater treatment facility, allowing wastewater to enter the ocean untreated.

Chevron's record overseas is no better than in the United States.

Anti-apartheid activists have long denounced the company for maintaining operations in South Africa despite calls for disinvestment by citizen leaders.

In Papua New Guinea, Chevron is developing two oil fields which the company expects will yield 130,000 barrels a day. Local leaders are "totally disillusioned with Chevron," according to the Rainforest Action Network, because Chevron is not delivering promised infrastructure services, such as health clinics and water. Island residents are also concerned about environmental issues associated with Chevron's operations and whether those operations will threaten their culture. [See "Chevron: The Big Oil Boys," *Multinational Monitor*, April 1992 and "Assault on Papua New Guinea," *Multinational Monitor,* June 1992].

Source: Russell Mokhiber, Julie Gozan, and Holley Knaus, "The Corporate Rap Sheet: The 10 Worst Corporations of 1992," *Multinational Monitor* 13 (December 1992): 10–11. Reprinted with permission from *Multinational Monitor*, PO Box 19405, Washington, DC 20036. Individual subscription $25/yr.

crimes as activities against the government, such as acts of dissent and violence whose purpose is to challenge and change the existing political order. Conflict theorists, in sharp contrast, assume that the law and the state are tools of the powerful used to keep them in power. Thus, the political order itself may be criminal because it can be unjust. Moreover, government, like a corporation, may follow policies that go against democratic principles and that do harm. Examples of political crimes from this perspective are CIA interventions in the domestic affairs of other nations, Watergate, the Iran-contra affair, war crimes, slavery, imperialism (such as forcibly taking the land from the Indians), police brutality, and using citizens experimentally without their knowledge and consent.

An extreme example of using human subjects as guinea pigs is a study begun in 1932 by the U.S. Public Health Service. The subjects were 400 Black male syphilis patients in Macon County, Alabama. The patients did not know that they had syphilis and were never informed of that fact. Because the purpose of the study was to assess the consequences of not treating the disease, the men were not treated, nor were their wives—and when their children were born with congenital syphilis, they, too, were not treated. The experiment lasted forty years, until 1972 (Jones, 1981).

In sum, the focus of the conflict perspective is on the political and economic setting in society. The power of certain interests determines what gets defined as deviance (and who, then, is a deviant), and how this "problem" is to be solved. Because the powerful benefit from the status quo, they vigorously thwart efforts to reform society. The solution, from the conflict theorists, however, requires not only reform of society but also its radical transformation. *The structure of society is the problem.*

The strengths of the conflict perspective on deviance are (Sykes, 1974): (1) its emphasis on the relationship between political order and nonconformity; (2) the understanding that the most powerful groups use the political order to protect their interests; (3) that it emphasizes how the system of justice is unjust and the distribution of rewards in society is skewed; and (4) the realization that the institutional framework of society is the source of so many social problems (for example, racism, sexism, pollution, unequal distribution of health care, poverty, and economic cycles).

There are some problems with this perspective, also. First, there is the tendency to assume a conspiracy by the well-to-do. Because the empirical evidence is overwhelming that the poor, the uneducated, and the members of minority groups are singled out for the deviant label, some persons make the too facile imputation of motive.

Second, the answer of the conflict theorists is too utopian. The following quotation by Quinney is representative of this naivete:

> The alternative to the contradictions of capitalism is a truly democratic society, a socialist society in which human beings no longer suffer the alienation inherent in capitalism. When there is no longer the need for one class to dominate another, when there is no longer the need for a legal system to secure the interests of a capitalist ruling class, then there will no longer be the need for crime. (Quinney, 1974:25)

But would crime and other forms of deviance disappear under such a socialist system? This, like Marx's final stage of history, is a statement of faith rather than one based on proof.

Deviance from the Order and the Conflict Perspectives

The two contrasting theoretical perspectives in sociology—the order model (functionalism) and the conflict model—constrain their adherents to view the causes, consequences, and remedies of deviance in opposing ways (see Table 7.1). The order perspective focuses on deviants themselves. This approach (which has been the conventional way of studying social problems) asks, Who are the deviants? What are their social and psychological backgrounds? With whom do they associate? Deviants somehow do not conform to the standards of the dominant group; they are

TABLE 7.1

Assumptions of the Order and the Conflict Models about Deviance*

ORDER MODEL	CONFLICT MODEL
Who is deviant? Those who break the rules of society.	Those who break the rules but also those who make the rules. Deviance is created by the powerful, who make the rules. Enactment and enforcement of these rules are used by the powerful to control potentially dissident groups and to maintain their own interests at the expense of those being ruled.
The legitimacy of deviance: Deviance is illegitimate, by definition.	Deviance of rule breakers can be legitimate because the rules are arbitrarily made and reflect a class bias. Deviance is also necessary to change an unjust society.
The causes of deviance: People are deviant because they have not been socialized to accept and obey the customs of society.	Deviance is caused by society, which makes the rules, the violation of which consititutes deviance. The inequities of society generate the behavior that the powerful label as deviant.
The solutions for deviance: Control by punishment and rehabilitation of deviant individuals (therapy, behavior modification, incarceration).	Restructure society (eliminate inequities, provide adequately for the needs of all members, a fair system of justice, laws that reflect the interest of all groups).

*See Davis, 1975; Sykes, 1974; Horton, 1966; Skolnick and Currie, 1970; Chambliss, 1974, 1976.

assumed to be out of phase with conventional behavior. This is believed to occur most often as a result of inadequate socialization. In other words, deviants have not internalized the norms and values of society because they are either brought up in an environment of conflicting value systems (as are children of immigrants or the poor in a middle-class school) or under the influence of a deviant subculture, such as a gang. Because the order theorist uses the prevailing standards to define and label deviants, the existing practices and structures of society are accepted implicitly. The remedy is to rehabilitate the deviants so that they conform to the societal norms.

The conflict theorist takes a different approach to social problems. The adherents of this perspective criticize order theorists for blaming the victim. To focus on the individual deviant is to locate the symptom, not the disease. Individual deviants are a manifestation of a failure of society to meet the needs of individuals. The sources of crime, poverty, drug addiction, and racism are found in the laws, the customs, the quality of life, the distribution of wealth and power, and in the accepted practices of schools, governmental units, and corporations. The established system, in this view, is not sacred. Because it is the primary source of social problems, it, not the individual deviant, must be restructured.

Because this is a text on society, we emphasize the conflict approach. The insights of this approach are clarified further in the remainder of this book as we examine the structure and consequences of social inequality in the next five chapters, followed by six chapters describing the positive and negative effects of institutions.

CHAPTER REVIEW

1. Deviance is behavior that violates the laws and expectations of a group. This means that deviance is not a property inherent in a behavior but a property conferred on that behavior by other people. In short, deviance is socially created.

2. What is deviant varies from society to society, and within a society the same behavior may be interpreted differently when it is done by different categories of persons.

3. The norms of the majority determine what behaviors are considered deviant.

4. Order theorists point out that deviant behavior has positive consequences for society, because it gives the nondeviants a sense of solidarity and reaffirms the importance of society's rules.

5. Conflict theorists argue that all views of rule violations have political implications. Punishment of de-

viants reflects a conservative bias by legitimating the norms and the current distribution of power. Support of the deviant behavior is also political, because it rejects the legitimacy of the people in power and their rules.

6. Several traditional theories for the causes of deviance assume the source as a fatal flaw in certain people. These theories focus on physical or psychological reasons for deviant behavior.

7. Kinds-of-people explanations for deviance also apply to some theories by sociologists. One theory argues that crime results from the conditions of city life. Another theory blames the influences of peers. A third focuses on the propensity of the poor to be deviants because of the gap between the goal of success and the lack of the means for these people to attain it. A fourth theory argues that people deviate when their internal or external controls are weak. Finally, some people have argued that lower-class culture is responsible.

8. These kinds-of-people theories have been criticized for blaming the victim. Because they blame the victim, the society (government, system of justice, education) is freed from blame. Since the established order is thus protected from criticism, necessary social change is thwarted.

9. An alternative to person-blame theories is labeling theory. This approach argues that even though most people break the rules on occasion, the crucial factor in establishing a deviant career is the successful application of the label *deviant*.

10. Who gets labeled as a deviant is not a matter of luck but the result of a systematic societal bias against the powerless.

11. Primary deviance is the rule-breaking that occurs prior to labeling. Secondary deviance is behavior resulting from the labeling process.

12. Labeling theorists argue that because deviants are not much different from nondeviants, the problem lies in organizations that label. Thus, these organizations should (*a*) leave the deviants alone whenever possible

and (*b*) apply justice fairly when the legal approach is required.

13. Labeling theory has been criticized because it (*a*) disregards undetected deviance, (*b*) assumes that deviants are really normal because we are all rule-breakers, (*c*) relieves the individual from blame, and (*d*) focuses on certain types of deviance but ignores deviance by the powerful.

14. Conflict theory focuses on social structure as the source of deviance. There is an historical bias in the law that favors the powerful. The administration of justice is also biased. In short, the state is a political organization controlled by the ruling class for its own advantage. The power of powerful interests in society determines what and who is deviant.

15. From the conflict perspective, the only real and lasting solution to deviance is the radical transformation of society.

16. Order theorists focus on individual deviants. Because this perspective uses the prevailing standards to define and label deviants, the existing practices and structures of society are accepted implicitly. The remedy is to rehabilitate the deviants so they conform to the societal norms.

KEY TERMS

Deviance
Culture of poverty
Cultural deprivation
Recidivism

Social Darwinism
Labeling theory
Primary deviance
Secondary deviance

Radical nonintervention
Corporate crime
Political crime

STUDY QUESTIONS

1. Are there universal criteria that determine what is deviant at all times and places? Explain.

2. Most of us at one time or another behave in deviant ways. Why, then, aren't we considered deviants?

3. Explain how deviant behavior has *positive* social consequences for the group.

4. What is labeling theory? What are its strengths and weaknesses in understanding deviant behavior?

5. Contrast the order and the conflict interpretations of deviance.

FOR FURTHER READING

Howard S. Becker, *The Outsiders: Studies in the Sociology of Deviance,* 2nd ed. (New York: Free Press, 1973).

D. Stanley Eitzen and Doug A. Timmer, *Criminology: Crime and Criminal Justice* (New York: John Wiley, 1985).

Kai Erikson, *Wayward Puritans: A Study in the Sociology of Deviance* (New York: John Wiley, 1966).

Erving Goffman, *Stigma: Notes on the Management of Spoiled Identity* (Englewood Cliffs, NJ: Prentice-Hall, 1963).

Frank E. Hagan, *Political Crime: Ideology and Criminality* (Boston: Allyn and Bacon, 1997).

Edwin M. Lemert, *Human Deviance, Social Problems, and Social Control,* 2nd ed. (Englewood Cliffs, NJ: Prentice-Hall, 1972).

Jerome G. Miller, *Search and Destroy: African-American Males in the Criminal Justice System* (Cambridge: Cambridge University Press, 1996).

Richard Quinney, *The Social Reality of Crime* (Boston: Little, Brown, 1970).

Jeffrey H. Reiman, *The Rich Get Richer and the Poor Get Prison: Ideology, Class, and Criminal Justice,* 4th ed. (Boston: Allyn and Bacon, 1995).

Earl Rubington and Martin S. Weinberg, *The Study of Social Problems: Six Perspectives,* 4th ed. (New York: Oxford University Press, 1989).

William Ryan, *Blaming the Victim,* rev. ed. (New York: Vintage Books, 1976).

Edwin M. Schur, *The Politics of Deviance* (Englewood Cliffs, NJ: Prentice-Hall, 1980).

David R. Simon and D. Stanley Eitzen, *Elite Deviance,* 4th ed. (Boston: Allyn and Bacon, 1993).

PART THREE

CHAPTER 8

Structural Sources of Societal Change: Economic and Demographic

We are in the midst of two societal "earthquakes." For most of the twentieth century, the U.S. economy was primarily industrial and its population overwhelmingly White and of European heritage. Now two massive changes are in progress: (1) the "transformation of the economy" that combines deindustrialization, globalization, computer chip technology, and the rapid movement of capital; and (2) "the new immigration," which is changing the racial composition of the United States, as Latino, African American, and Asian American populations increase dramatically (they will soon outnumber Whites in California and Texas and will be the numerical majority throughout the United States before 2050). Each of these trends is profound in its implications for U.S. society and its members. Peter F. Drucker describes the historical import of such transformations (he refers specifically to economic transformations, but his description applies to other changes as well):

> Every few hundred years in Western history there occurs a sharp transformation. We cross . . . a "divide." Within a few short decades, society rearranges itself—its worldview; its basic values; its social and political structure; its arts; its key institutions. Fifty years later, there is a new world. And the people born then cannot even imagine the world in which their grandparents lived and into which their own parents were born. We are currently living through just such a transformation. (Drucker, 1993:1)

The present generation is in the midst of social changes that are more far-reaching and are occurring faster than at any other time in human history.

The purpose of this chapter is to understand these two macro social forces and how they affect social life. We will examine these two societal upheavals: the structural transformation of the economy and new immigration and the changing racial landscape. Both of these trends have external (global) and internal (domestic) origins. Both have extraordinary consequences for individuals, families, communities, and for the institutions of society.

The Structural Transformation of the Economy

There have been two fundamental turning points in human history, and we are in the midst of the third. The Neolithic revolution began about 8000 B.C., marking the transition from nomadic pastoral life, where the animal and vegetable sources of food were hunted and gathered, to life in settlements based on agriculture. During this phase of human existence cities were built, tools were created and used, language, numbers, and other symbols became more sophisticated, and mining and metal working were developed.

The second fundamental change, the Industrial Revolution, began in Great Britain in the 1780s. While the Neolithic agricultural revolution took almost ten thousand years to run its course, the second lasted but two hundred years. And the Industrial Revolution really involved three distinct but related technological revolutions, each of which brought fundamental changes to the economy, the relationship of people and work, family organization, and the like. The first phase lasted about sixty years in Great Britain and involved primarily the application of steam power to textiles, mining, manufacturing, and transportation.

The second phase in the Industrial Revolution occurred between 1860 and 1910 largely in the United States, Great Britain, and Germany. It was marked by a significant cluster of inventions and discoveries—the use of oil and electricity as energy sources for industry and transportation, the telephone and telegraph, motor cars and airplanes, and the first plastics. The final stage of the Industrial Revolution, which is still in progress, involves the major technological breakthroughs of atomic fission and fusion, supersonic aircraft and missiles, television, biotechnology, and computers.

This third phase of the Industrial Revolution is giving way to a new era, which is referred to as the **structural transformation of the economy.** This new era combines the shift from manufacturing to a service/information economy with microchip technology, the global economy, and the rapid movement of capital.

Each of the previous surges in invention and technological growth had major implications for the economy and other societal institutions and for individuals and families within society.

The next two sections describe the forces transforming U.S. society and the special conditions that are making this turning point in history different, much different, from the previous two.

The Interrelated Forces Transforming the U.S. Economy

Several powerful forces converging in the United States are transforming its economy, redesigning and redistributing jobs, exacerbating inequality, reorganizing cities and regions, and profoundly affecting families and individuals. These forces are (1) technological breakthroughs in microelectronics, (2) the globalization of the economy, (3) capital flight, and (4) the shift from an economy based on the manufacture of goods to one based on information and services.

The New Technologies Based on Microelectronics.   The computer chip is the technology transforming the United States toward a service/information economy. Computer transactions are measured in multiples of piecioseconds (ten to the twelfth power). Microelectronic-based systems of information allow for the storage, manipulation, and retrieval of data with speed and accuracy unimagined just a few years ago. Information can be sent instantaneously via communications satellite throughout the world in microseconds. Parallel processing with supercomputers gives machines the ability to reason and make judgments.

Globalization of the Economy.   Because of the size of the domestic market, the relative insulating effects of the Pacific and Atlantic Oceans, and superior technological expertise, the U.S. economy throughout most of the twentieth century has been relatively free from the competitive pressures from abroad. This has changed dramatically since about 1970. The United States, once the world's industrial giant, now employs about 15 percent of the workforce in manufacturing. Many of the goods now used in the United States are produced in low-wage societies.

The shift to a global economy has been accelerated by the tearing down of tariff barriers. The North American Free Trade Agreement (NAFTA) and the General Agreement on Tariffs and Trade (GATT), both passed by Congress in 1994, are two examples of agreements that increased the flow of goods across national boundaries.

> When tariff barriers come crashing down . . . how can the West's workers compete with low-wage economies? In 1993, West Germany's manufacturing labor costs were $24.90 per hour; Japan's $16.90; the U.S. costs were $16.40; France's $16.30; and the United Kingdom's $12.40. Compare those with South Korea's manufacturing labor costs of $4.90 per hour; Hungary's of $1.80; and China's at 40 cents! (Hines and Lang, 1994:26)

Capital Flight.   Private businesses in their search for profit make crucial investment decisions. **Capital flight** refers to the investment choices that involve the movement of corporate monies from one investment to another. This movement takes several forms: (1) investment overseas, (2) plant relocation within the United States, and (3) mergers. While these investment decisions may be positive for the recipients of the move, they also take investment away (disinvestment) from others (workers and their families, communities, and suppliers).

Overseas Investment by U.S. Firms   Multinational corporations based in the United States have invested heavily in foreign countries. Corporate capital is invested overseas because manufacturing overseas is profitable, mainly because of cheap and nonunionized labor and the relative lack of the kind of regulations found

U.S. corporations have located plants in Northern Mexico close to the U.S. border to take advantage of cheap labor and tax advantages.

in the United States. The companies believe that these regulations—on pollution and worker saftey, for instance—are excessive and expensive.

The main reason for overseas investment, though, is greater profit from lower wages. For example, more than 1,100 U.S.-owned plants—owned by corporations such as Ford, General Motors, RCA, Zenith, and Westinghouse—are located in Northern Mexico close to the U.S. border (these plants are called *maquiladoras*). United States corporations are allowed to ship raw materials, components, equipment, and machinery to Mexico duty-free. They are delivered to factories in Mexico and then assembled by low-wage workers. The finished products are then exported back to the United States with duty paid only on the value added to the product. Obviously, the corporations profit greatly from such an arrangement; U.S. workers do not.

Relocation of Business   Corporate administrators may decide to move their business to another locality. Such decisions involve what is called plant migration or, more pejoratively, "runaway shops." The decision may be to move the plant to Mexico (as we have seen), to the Caribbean, to Central America (all baseballs for major league baseball, for example, are manufactured in Costa Rica), or to the Far East, where many U.S. plants involved in textiles, electronics assembly, and other labor-intensive industries are located (such as the manufacture of Nike shoes).

United States corporations are also moving some of their operations to other English-speaking countries such as Ireland, Barbados, Jamaica, the Philippines, and Singapore, where cheap labor does such tasks as data entry for accounting, medical transcription, airline and hotel reservations, and telemarketing.

Capital is also moved within the United States as corporations shut down operations in one locality and start up elsewhere. Profit is the motivation for investment in a new place and disinvestment in another. Corporations move their plants into communities and regions where wages are lower, unions are weaker or nonexistent, and the business climate is more receptive (that is, there are lower taxes and greater government subsidies to the business community).

Mergers   Another type of capital flight occurs when corporations use their capital to purchase companies in related or unrelated enterprises rather than to expand and modernize their plants. In 1995 there were almost 9,000 mergers and acquisitions worth a record $465 billion.

This trend toward mergers has at least three negative consequences: (1) It increases the centralization of capital, which reduces competition and raises prices for consumers; (2) as corporations become fewer and larger, they have increased power over workers, unions, and governments; and (3) it diminishes the number of jobs.

From Manufacturing to Services.   Manufacturing, the backbone of the U.S. economy in this century, is no longer dominant. In 1947 employment in the service sector of the economy reached 50 percent, and now it is over 78 percent. Whereas in the past people mostly worked at producing goods, now they tend to be doing work in offices, banking, insurance, retailing, health care, education, custodial work, restaurant work, security, and transportation.

Peter Drucker has described the rapid rise and fall of the blue-collar worker in this century (Drucker, 1994). Before World War I farmers composed the largest single occupational group. Industrial workers at that time received no pensions, no paid vacation, no overtime pay, and no health or retirement benefits. Fifty years later, in the 1950s, unionized industrial workers in mass-production industry had attained upper-middle-class income levels with job security, pensions, and other comprehensive benefits, and political power.

> Thirty-five years later, in 1990, industrial workers and their unions were in retreat. They had become marginal in numbers. Whereas industrial workers who make or move things had accounted for two-fifths of the American work force in the 1950s, they accounted for less than one-fifth in the early 1990s—that is, for no more than they had accounted for in 1900, when their meteoric rise began. (Drucker, 1994:56)
>
> There . . . is no parallel in history to the abrupt decline of the blue-collar worker during the past 15 years. As a proportion of the working population, blue-collar workers in manufacturing have already decreased to less than a fifth of the American labor force from more than a third. By the year 2010 . . . they will constitute no larger a proportion of the labor force of every developed country than farmers do today—that is, a 20th of the total. The decline will be greatest precisely where the highest-paid jobs are. . . . Yesterday's blue-collar workers in manufacturing were society's darlings; they are fast becoming stepchildren. (Drucker, 1987:36)

There are far fewer of these workers now because we have shifted from a labor-intensive to a knowledge-intensive society. The need is for workers who design, control, and service products and who manage information, not operators who do unskilled, repetitive work, hence the rapid decline of the blue-collar worker.

Overall manufacturing has remained relatively stable, but within this sector about twenty industries have experienced steady declines since 1975. These so-called **sunset industries** (for example, steel, tires, shoes, and the various defense industries) have declined in both output and employment. Over 1,500 plants in these industries have closed permanently since 1975. And, literally millions of jobs have been lost that will not be replaced. "The *Fortune* 500 industrial companies employed 3.7 million fewer workers [in 1991] than the top 500 firms did in 1981, a loss of about one job in four" (O'Reilly, 1992:65). Overall, between 1981 and 1991, a time when the population sixteen and older increased by 19.4 million persons, *the number of manufacturing jobs shrank by 1.8 million* (Barlett and Steele, 1992:xi). Additionally, from 1987 to 1997, some 2.8 million defense-related jobs were lost.

The **sunrise industries,** which are characterized by increased output and employment, are involved in the production of high-tech products (computers, communications equipment, medical instruments, fiber optics, bioengineering, and robotics). These industries are creating many new and exciting products, and their employees are typically highly skilled, but most of the jobs are routine, with labor-saving technologies causing workers to be "deskilled." The production workers in high tech, unlike those in heavy industry, tend to be nonunionized with relatively low wages and benefits.

The third category of manufacturing involves industries that have gained in output but have lost employment (for example, food processing, metal products, industrial machinery, and automobiles). The source of this seeming incongruity (high productivity with a loss in employment) is automation, a topic discussed shortly.

To repeat, the manufacturing sector of the economy overall has been relatively stable. But this stability masks a massive redistribution of job opportunities with declines in some industries (blue-collar manufacturing, for example) and increases in the high-tech industries. But the redistribution of jobs and opportunities occurs not only within the manufacturing sector. The major change is in the growth of the service sector of the economy where wages and benefits tend to be lower.

Another source of low-wage jobs is the proliferation of **contingent employment.** This employment arrangement refers to employees who work for an employer as "temporaries" or as "independent contractors." Employers like to hire temporary workers because they save money on salaries, unemployment compensation, training, and career advancement. It also means avoiding antidiscrimination laws, health-care costs, paid vacations, and pension costs. This "temping of the work force" is a significant trend.

> The U.S. is increasingly becoming a nation of part-timers and free-lancers, of temps and independent contractors. This "disposable" work force is the most important trend in business today, and it is fundamentally changing the relationship between Americans and their jobs. (Castro, 1993:43)

Some negative consequences for workers are a lower standard of living, less security, and treatment as second-class citizens by both employers and permanent staff. Significantly, this trend and its consequences are especially detrimental to women. *Two-thirds of all part-time workers are women.*

Another strategy by management to increase profits by limiting the number of permanent workers is to increase their workload. If labor works overtime, then productivity is increased with relatively few workers.

> In another sign of how hard it is to create jobs, American manufacturers are paying record amounts of overtime and factory workers are putting in more extra hours than ever before. By relying on so much overtime, companies have avoided hiring and jobs in manufacturing have continued to disappear. (Uchitelle, 1993:1)

In 1993 the average overtime for a factory worker was 4.3 hours a week, the highest level since the Bureau of Labor Statistics began keeping records on overtime in 1948.

The Economic Transformation and Jobs

Every new era poses new problems of adjustment, but this one differs from the agricultural and industrial eras. The earlier transformations were gradual enough for adaptation to take place over several decades, but conditions are significantly different now. The rate of change is phenomenal and unprecedented. In today's global economy communication is instantaneous and capital is incredibly mobile. The types of work and the characteristics of the work force in the United States are changing. These factors, which we discuss in this section, result in considerable discontinuity and disequilibrium, especially job loss (see Table 8.1).

Technology and Jobs.   Several aspects regarding technology make this era different. First, new technologies, some quite revolutionary, are being developed rapidly. These technologies have potentials that can be positive and negative and many that are unforeseen. Lasers and fiber optics, for example, have a wide variety of applications as components in telecommunications systems, information processing, and entertainment (three-dimensional television). Fiber optics will increase the capacity of communications networks and make them more efficient. These technologies will generate considerable investment, render other technologies obsolete, generate new jobs, and destroy others.

Biotechnology is just beginning to effect changes in a wide range of industries—foods, agriculture, fuel, pharmaceuticals, chemicals, waste treatment, and natural resource recovery. The changes occurring in this field are rapid and far reaching. This is a field of tremendous growth potential. Its future consequences for the economy and jobs are unknown.

TABLE 8.1

Corporate Downsizing: 1993–1996

COMPANY	EMPLOYEE CUTBACKS
IBM	63,000
AT&T	55,000
Sears	50,000
Digital Equipment	20,000
Delta	18,800
GTE	17,000
Eastman Kodak	16,800
Nynex	16,800
Lockheed Martin	15,000
Chase Manhattan	12,000
Tenneco	11,000

Of greatest significance for our purposes are the technological changes directly affecting work and workers. For the most part, the new technologies—especially those related to computers—are reducing jobs and wages. The cost of technology in the microchip field has fallen dramatically relative to the cost of labor. The incredible storage and speed capabilities of modern computers are almost beyond comprehension.

Microprocessors, of course, are programmable, making robots possible. Robots can, for example, cut materials, weld, paint, and assemble. These robots, unlike human workers, do not get bored or tired, go on strike, require cost of living increases, or bicker among themselves.

> Robots do not require heating or air-conditioning; they can work in the dark, and save electricity; they do not become sloppy or tired. They contribute to a greater flexibility in manufacturing, since they can be reprogrammed for different tasks or to assemble different models. Because their movements are perfectly controlled, they do not waste materials—robot spray painters, for example, use up to 30 percent less paint than human workers. (Kennedy, 1993:89)

Not surprisingly, corporate managers are purchasing robots to replace workers at an accelerating rate. Robots are drastically altering the workplace. For example, robots perform more than 98 percent of the spot welding on Ford's Taurus and Sable cars. The results of this trend, of course, are fewer and fewer industrial jobs and, for the workers who remain, less and less leverage in bargaining with management.

Robots are not just mechanical menials. They can be equipped with a multitude of sensors for vision, touch, and proximity. They can react to these sensory inputs and adapt. Even more incredible, they can be linked (computer-integrated manufacturing, or CIM) into one comprehensive, integrated manufacturing system. In short, robots and computer-controlled machines will work together to plan, schedule, transport, control inventory, and perform many, if not most, of the manufacturing operations that used to require human skills.

The elimination of jobs because of superautomation is not limited to industrial factories. Offices are increasingly electronic. Primarily because of voice-mail, laser printers, and word processors, 776,000 secretarial and clerical jobs were eliminated between 1989 and 1994. Engineers and architects now draw three-dimensional designs, update them, test them, and store them almost instantaneously in a computer. Bank tellers are being replaced by ATMs; telephone operators are being supplanted by automation (the number of telephone operators has declined from 120,000 to 60,000 since 1984). Agriculture employs robot fruit pickers and sheep shearers, computerized irrigation systems that use sensors to calculate water and fertilizer needs in different parts of a field, and automated chicken houses. Retail stores, banks, and brokerage houses use on-line transaction processing to obtain instant information and to conduct transactions. Laser scanning and bar codes are transforming the physical handling of goods by retailers and wholesale distributors. A final example of technological change affecting jobs is the widespread use of televisions, telephones, and personal computers for the purposes of home banking and shopping.

Today's technology is different from that occurring at other stages in history. We now have smart machines that can exercise judgment and intuition. As Jones has put it:

The new technology, for the first time in human history, does not merely extend or replace physical capacity but may also involve a degree of judgment, like humans. . . . Computers can be programmed to parallel human mental processes—including low-level judgment such as rejecting oranges because of unsatisfactory shape or color. (Jones, 1990:37–38)

Throughout history technological changes have tended to increase overall productivity. Although there were considerable dislocations to workers in some fields, employment actually increased overall. In the past the introduction of machines extended the capacity of the labor force. The machines of the past (for example, sewing machines, typewriters, telephones, and motor vehicles) were designed to have one operator for each machine. In addition, they required other workers to make, sell, and maintain them. Now, however, there has been a significant shift toward technology and machines designed to reduce and even eliminate human labor. In Jones's words:

Much technological innovation in the past was "labor-complementing"—it extended the capacity of the existing labor force, and the machines themselves changed the nature of work. *But there has been a significant shift to "labor-displacing" technology where low-cost machines are specifically intended to reduce, if not eliminate, labor inputs.* (Jones, 1990:39) [emphasis added]

Companies, typically, reduce their labor costs by downsizing and by keeping wages and benefits as low as possible. Today's technology permits them to replace many workers with machines *that increase productivity and profits.*

The Global Economy and Domestic Jobs.   The profound transformation in the international economy is another factor making this era in history different from the previous transition periods. For thousands of years caravans have moved across the land, and ships have sailed along the winds and currents. People explored, conquered, and exploited other peoples and their resources; but the pace was slow, and the interaction among different nations muted by time and space. Now, however, there is instant communication around the globe, and transportation anywhere is only a day away rather than six months or more.

These dramatic advances in communication and transportation mean that technological advances now diffuse rapidly. During the Industrial Revolution technological change was quite slow (although rapid compared to previous epochs). The first steam-powered cotton mill in the United States, for example, began in 1847, sixty-three years after its adoption in Britain. Now technological breakthroughs in one country rapidly spread to other nations. The advances in transportation and communications also enhance the mobility of capital as never before.

Corporations of almost any size now make plans regarding raw materials, workers, and markets across national boundaries. Corporations seek cheap labor, which means a transfer of jobs—millions of jobs—to other nations. Consider Nike, the largest sports shoe and sports apparel company: There are 8,000 U.S. employees involved in management, sales, and advertising and 75,000, mostly Asian, employees who actually make the products. "Indonesian girls and young women who sew the shoes start at an entry-level rate of $1.35 a day" (Barnet, 1994:F11).

People in the United States now buy more foreign goods than foreigners buy ours, driving down the number of U.S. jobs and the wages of U.S. workers. Arthur Macewan raises some interesting questions in this regard.

> My morning coffee came from Brazil. A GM subsidiary in Mexico produced the wiring system for my car. Three items in my medicine cabinet were produced in a German-owned plant in the United States. My son's new tape recorder is from Japan. My clothes arrive from ten or more different countries, produced mostly through subcontracting arrangements with large U.S. retailers.
>
> What difference does it make where my coffee came from or where the wiring system for my car was assembled? Does it matter to me whether my clothes come from Brazil, Bangladesh, or from a local factory? What about the Brazilian, Bangladesh, and local workers? How are they affected by the international movement of goods? And does the nationality of the factory owners matter? Should I care whether a U.S., Japanese, German, or Brazilian owner profits from my purchases? (Macewan, 1994:8)

Capital Flight and Jobs. Regardless of whether plants are moved within the United States or to foreign countries, there are consequences to individuals and communities. Plant closures are devastating. Workers in the affected plants are suddenly unemployed—and so, too, may be many other people in the affected communities whose jobs were directly and indirectly tied to that plant (such as transportation, supplies, and services). Also, real estate, banking, schools, and other areas are ad-

Drawing by Toles. U.S. News & World Report (October 9, 1995), p. 34.

versely affected. The local governments can no longer provide the same level of services because of a lower tax base. The recipient communities benefit from the increase in jobs, greater tax revenues, and the image of growth and progress. The boom communities, however, often cannot meet the greater demand for new roads, sewage treatment, schools, hospitals, recreation facilities, and housing that the new plants engender.

The Consequences of the Economic Transformation

The transformation of the economy brought about by new technologies, the globalization of the economy, capital flight, and deindustrialization has profoundly affected individuals, families, and communities and will continue to do so for the foreseeable future. Michael Parenti summarizes the bleak picture:

> We [are] witnessing the gradual Third-Worldization of the United States, involving the abolition of high-wage jobs, a growth of low-wage and part-time employment, an increase in permanent unemployment, a shrinking middle-income population, a growing number of mortgage delinquencies, greater concentrations of wealth for the few and more poverty and privation for the many. (Parenti, 1995:24)

Families are affected when their resources are reduced, when they face economic and social marginalization, and when family members are unemployed or underemployed. This section explores these and related consequences of the economic transformation for families and family members. It focuses on the social price of downsizing, the jobs/skills mismatch, the shrinking middle class, the working poor, and the new poor.

The Social and Personal Costs of Downsizing.   About three million workers and their families are affected by layoffs each year. Firing workers is "natural" in capitalism because of the twin business goals of efficiency and profit. Thus, companies such as AT&T (123,000 jobs cut in the 1990s) reduce labor costs to increase profits and to meet the needs of changing markets and technology. But while downsizing is a fact of life in a capitalist society, the magnitude and contours of the current downsizing are different now than in earlier times (Uchitelle and Kleinfield, 1996).

First, the numbers of workers affected or fearful of downsizing are much greater than before. Second, whereas unskilled and semiskilled workers (especially minorities) have always had the most insecure jobs, now the pool of victims has been widened to include middle-class workers. Corporations are scaling back at all levels, including management. Governments (federal, state, and local) are erasing many jobs that historically elevated the poor. Colleges and universities are replacing retired tenured professors more and more often by temporary instructors. Hospitals are decreasing their staffs, as are HMOs and doctors' offices. As a result, better-paid workers—those making at least $50,000—account for twice the share of the lost jobs than they did in the 1980s. As a consequence "White-collar, middle-class Americans in mass numbers are coming to understand first-hand the chronic insecurity on which the working class and the poor are experts" (Uchitelle and Kleinfield, 1996:8) Third, while the downsized in previous generations usually found work that paid as much as before, now 65 percent do not (U.S. Labor Department, cited in Uchitelle and Kleinfield, 1996:6). More jobs are being added than lost, but many of these jobs are low-paid with scant benefits, and often part-time. The fourth reason why the downsizing now differs from the past is that a large percentage of the jobs are lost to "outsourcing"—contracting work to another (usually low-cost, nonunionized) company.

What are the consequences for individuals and families when a worker loses his or her job? Many find the loss of status intolerable. Their self-esteem is wounded. As a result, they may react by withdrawing from social relationships and from community and civic life, everything from marriages, involvement in school support groups, Rotary Clubs, and in churches, to voting. The divorce rate, for example, is as much as 50 percent higher than the national average in families where the husband has lost a job and cannot quickly find an equivalent one. There is evidence that job loss increases the likelihood of alcohol abuse and of spouse and child abuse. A study in Wisconsin found, for example, that cases of child abuse increased an average of 123 percent in nine counties where the unemployment rate had increased by at least 3.1 percent. In contrast, those counties in which unemployment declined tended to have reduced reports of child abuse (cited in White, 1983:9).

Also, when workers are involuntarily unemployed, they tend, when compared to the employed, to have more hypertension, high cholesterol, ulcers, respiratory diseases, and hyperallergic reactions. Similarly, they are more prone to headaches, upset stomachs, depression, anxiety, and aggression.

Katherine Newman has suggested that the behaviors associated with downward mobility are somewhat normal, given the persistent tensions generated by this condition. Many families experience some degree of these problems and yet they somehow endure. But some families disintegrate completely under the pressure, with serious problems of physical brutality, incapacitating alcoholism, desertion, and even suicide (Newman, 1988:134–140).

The recently downsized are also susceptible to the politics of paranoia and hate, as they search for groups to blame for their plight.

> Millions of middle- and working-class Americans, worried about their own eroding economic fortunes, including loss of job security and falling real wages, may become easy prey to the nascent fascist rhetoric of the extreme right. The politics of scapegoating is already in ascendance, as right-wing politicians blame affirmative action programs, feminists, illegal aliens and immigrants, cheap labor abroad, the "international banking conspiracy" and the United Nations for the deepening economic malaise. (Rifkin, 1996:12)

The Jobs/Skills Mismatch. Changing demography points to some important shifts as the United States moves toward the twenty-first century. First, because the baby-boom generation, which swelled the labor force for the past two decades, is aging and is being replaced by a smaller age cohort (the baby-bust generation), the supply of workers for good jobs will soon not meet the demand. Second, one of three new entrants to the labor force by the year 2000 will be non-White. Third, about two-thirds of the new workers will be women.

When these trends are combined with technological changes, which are continually upgrading the work required for most jobs, the result is that the United States will be running out of workers with the job skills needed for the year 2000 and beyond. In effect, there will be a mismatch between the number of people wanting jobs and the skills required for the new jobs.

These trends and their consequences present reasons for hope and despair. On the hopeful side, there will be room for people without privilege (minorities and women) for upward mobility, if they have the skills. A second reason for hope is that the powerful people in government and business will realize that their past decisions to emphasize technology rather than the maximization of human capital were wrong and must be rectified.

Commonly, the argument is advanced in the business community that the schools must do a better job of educating all students and that businesses must also work at retraining their workforce and at training new employees for the skills required for the new and ever changing technology. Also, businesses will have to provide more benefits to workers with families (flexible work schedules, maternity leaves, provision of day care) in order to expand the pool of workers. Thus, there is a chance that class, race, and gender barriers to privilege will be reduced.

As these trends converge, however, there is also a strong negative potential. If history is a guide, the education and business communities will not educate the disadvantaged for the highly skilled jobs. The children of the poor will continue to receive inferior educations. Many of them will see no hope in the mainstream of schools and jobs because the rewards are not there.

But this conventional argument misses the crucial point. The problem is *not* a lack of education among workers but *a lack of jobs*. Walda Katz-Fishman makes this point forcefully.

> Today the factory system of production with machine technology, that was the basis of expansion of educational opportunities for the working class during the 20th century, no longer exists. The revolution in technology has transformed the production process. Human labor is being displaced permanently by electronically based automated production. . . . As the masses of workers, i. e., "human capital," are replaced by forms of automated production, the capitalist system no longer needs to educate them. *It should thus be clear that the reason more and more working class youth are not getting good jobs with decent wages is not because they do not have a college degree. Rather, the reason they cannot get a college education is precisely because there are not enough good jobs that pay decent wages in our society to warrant the college education of the majority of the working class.* [Emphasis added.] (Katz-Fishman, 1990:23)

The Shrinking Middle Class. The American Dream, in effect a middle-class dream, is that one's family will own a home, own at least one late-model car, and be able to provide a college education for the children. Through the 1950s and 1960s, this dream was realized by more and more Americans as average real wages (i.e., wages adjusted for inflation) and family incomes expanded and the economy created new jobs and opportunities. The result was that many Americans after World War II were able to move up into a growing and vibrant middle class. This trend peaked in 1973, and since then wages have declined (see Figure 8.1).

FIGURE 8.1

Wages in the United States

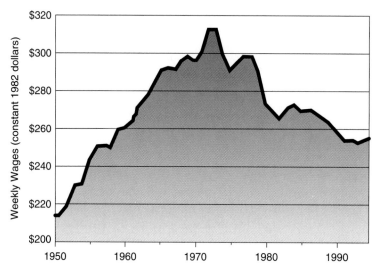

Inflation-Adjusted Weekly Wages 1950–1994

Source: Reprinted with the permission of The Free Press, a division of Simon & Schuster, from *The State of Americans: This Generation and the Next* by Urie Bronfenbrenner, Peter McClelland, Elaine Wethington, Phyllis Moen, and Stephen J. Ceci, p. 56. Copyright © 1996 by Urie Bronfenbrenner, Peter McClelland, Elaine Wethington, Phyllis Moen, and Stephen J. Ceci.

A few facts make this point:

- The median (middle by number) hourly wage of production workers has fallen by 13 percent since 1973 (Herman, 1995:45).
- Unemployment and underemployment both increased from 1973 to 1993 (the combined rate increasing from 8.2 percent to 12.6 percent) (Herman, 1995:45).
- In 1990, "compared to twenty years earlier, U.S. workers . . . had fewer paid days off, fewer benefits, less sick leave, shorter vacations, and less discretionary income. In short, people are experiencing a declining standard of living" (Parenti, 1995:25).
- After adjusting for inflation, the pay of all private sector employees fell 4 percent, to $13.39 an hour, between 1988 and 1994 (Economic Policy Institute, reported in Bernstein, 1996:122).
- From 1988 to 1993, "1.7 million higher wage, mostly blue-collar manufacturing jobs vanished, many in defense. One million other new jobs came in the lowest-paid service occupations, such as cleaning and food preparation" (Bernstein, 1994:122).
- From 1989 to 1993 the median household income declined by 7 percent (Herman, 1995:45).

In short, over the past two and one-half decades there has been a fundamental shift in the income distribution with the middle shrinking and the gap between the affluent and the unfortunate expanding. This shift is the result of powerful forces—technological changes, the global economy, and the shift from manufacturing to service jobs—that have combined to reduce labor's bargaining power, lowered wages and workers' benefits, and increased job insecurity.

The Increase in the Working Poor.   The greatest increase in the number of poor since 1979 has been among the working poor. This increase is the result of declining wages, the rise in the number of working women who head households (who must bear the cost of child care but who earn low wages), and a minimum wage that remained at $3.35 from 1981 to 1991, when it increased to $4.25, where it stayed until 1997 when it was increased to $5.15. Even with this last increase, a full-time worker working for minimum wages was approximately $3,000 short of what a family of four needs to exceed the poverty line.

The Census Bureau reported that there was a sharp rise between 1979 and 1990 in the proportion of full-time workers with low earnings (defined as less than a poverty-level income for a family of four), with the poverty rate rising from 12.1 percent to 18 percent (reported in *Chicago Tribune*, 1991). In other words, nearly one worker in five was in the low-pay category in 1990. When race is considered, the poverty rate for White workers in 1990 was 17.1 percent, compared to 25.3 percent among Black workers and 31.4 percent among Latino workers.

The New Poor.   Millions of blue-collar workers have lost their jobs as obsolete plants have closed and as companies have moved overseas in search of cheaper labor, or when they were replaced by robots or other forms of automation. Many of these displaced workers find other work, but usually at lower-paying jobs (65 percent of laid-off, full-time workers end up in jobs that pay less than did their previous jobs) (Uchitelle and Kleinfield, 1996:6). They are poorer but not poor. Many others, though, especially those who are over 40, find employment difficult because their skills are no longer needed and they are considered too old to retrain.

These **new poor** are quite different from the "old poor." The "old poor"—that is, the poor of the other generations—had hopes of breaking out of poverty; if they did not break out themselves, at least they believed their children would. This hope was based on the presence of a rapidly expanding economy. There were jobs for immigrants, farmers, and grade-school dropouts because of the needs of mass production. The "new poor," however, are much more trapped in poverty (Harrington, 1984). A generation ago, those who were unskilled and uneducated could usually find work and could even do quite well financially if the work place was unionized. But now these people are displaced or misplaced. Hard physical labor is rarely needed in a high-tech society. This phenomenon undercuts the efforts of the working class, especially African Americans, Latinos, and other minorities who face the additional burden of institutional racism (Harrington, 1984:10).

Government data reveal the contours of the "new poor." Tens of millions of Americans have lost their jobs in the past two decades because of plant closings and layoffs. Almost half of these newly unemployed were longtime workers (workers who had held their previous jobs at least three years), and seven out of ten of them found new jobs. Of those reemployed full time, slightly less than half make less money than before. These workers were downwardly mobile but likely not poor. About 15 percent, however, did not find employment and they constitute the "new poor."

Social Agency: Coping Strategies

Lifestyle Changes.   Many Americans, the unemployed as well as those who fear being unemployed, are downsizing their lifestyles and their expectations due to their real or threatened economic marginality. They are scaling back on material comforts as well as their hopes for their future and the future of their children.

Other downsized workers live in denial, resisting reining in their lives. These people increase their debt (usually through credit cards), which in the long run increases their economic fears. Total credit card debt almost quadrupled from 1984 to 1995 (from $108 billion to $414 billion). The outstanding credit card debt increased 14 percent from 1994 to 1995, a period when people's income increased by only 3 percent (Bleifuss, 1995b). In 1994 consumer installment debt increased by about $4 billion *each month*. Total household borrowing stood at a record $1.14 trillion in 1996, an amount equal to Britain's entire gross domestic product. The estimated number of individuals filing for bankruptcy was approximately 1 million (Greenwald, 1996).

Behavioral Changes.   Family changes result when a breadwinner loses a job. Younger families may delay having children during such a crisis. Also, more families choose to limit the number of children for fear of what the future may hold. Families in economic distress may move in with other family members—adult children with parents or parents with adult children.

Dual-Earner Families.   A common coping strategy when the breadwinner is unemployed or reemployed at a low-income job is for the spouse to enter the workforce. Thus, making a living has become a family enterprise, since most families now require two incomes to get by, when a generation ago one income was usually sufficient to maintain a middle-class lifestyle. For example, about 68 percent of families in 1992 whose youngest child was school-aged (6 to 17 years old) had an employed mother (Benett and Jones, 1993:25).

This shift toward dual-income families is important in at least five ways. First, there is the *necessity* of two incomes to maintain an adequate lifestyle, which limits the choice for those women or men who would rather stay at home to raise their children. Second, women's work tends to be poorly paid (approximately 72 cents for every dollar a man makes). Women workers are, for the most part, second-class citizens in the occupational world. Third, although dual-earner families bring in more family income, the amount left after expenses is lowered considerably by the additional costs for such items as transportation, clothing, and child care. Fourth, it increases the burden on women who work for wages and who continue to do most of the housework and child-raising. And, fifth, two-worker families have less time for wife–husband interaction and parent–child interaction as well as for household chores and leisure pursuits.

Increased Workload.   In 1989 the average fully employed U.S. worker worked 138 hours more than in 1969—158 hours more if rising commuter time is included (Moberg, 1992; Schorr, 1991; Yates, 1994). There are three reasons for this increase. Many choose to work overtime or at a second job to maintain or increase their slumping living standards. Second, many companies seek a reduced labor force so that they can limit their costs. The fewer the permanent workers the fewer who need costly pensions, medical, and other benefits. Thus, businesses downsize their workforce and then overwork their core workers to maintain high production. These squeezed workers have few options if they wish to keep their jobs. The third reason for the increased workload has to do with unpaid labor, as working wives now do double duty—work outside the home plus most of the domestic chores at home. The result of this increased workload, of course, is decreased leisure and decreased family time.

Home-based Work.   The structural transformation of the economy has changed the patterns of work in profound ways. The redistribution of jobs has displaced many workers and has placed many millions, as we have seen, in low-wage service jobs, often without traditional benefits. Included in this last category is the new emphasis on contingent work arrangements such as part-time work, temporary work, and home-based work, much of which are jobs held disproportionately by women. We will focus here on women who work for pay in their homes (the following discussion is from Christensen, 1988).

Home-based work includes word processing, typing, editing, accounting, telemarketing, sewing, laundry, and child care. Women often opt for home-based work because the flexibility permits them to combine work and family obligations. Others choose it because of the autonomy—working on their own, at their own pace, and on their own schedule. Others have no option; they need the money, and some form of home-based work is all that is available. Employers contract women to do home work because money is saved—the employers pay only for work delivered, they avoid unions, and they do not pay benefits such as health insurance, paid leaves, and pensions.

The consequences of home-based work are mixed. On the positive side, home-based work allows flexibility and independence not found in most jobs. This type of work allows women to supplement their incomes and maintain skill levels without working full time. It permits women to stay in the work force at times when they could not or would not work full time outside the home. For some, especially single parents on the economic margin, home-based work is the only way they can earn an income and provide for child care. The dark side of this is that the pay is typically low, and the strains engendered from combining the work and parent roles may be excessive and overwhelming. Home-based workers are often frustrated because they cannot work for long uninterrupted periods. An office environment is designed to maximize work, but a home is not. Children, spouses, neighbors, the telephone, household tasks, and other home distractions hinder productivity—and pay. "Working at home eliminates the boundary between work and family, so that women often find they never can leave their work" (Christensen, 1988:5). Thus, the combination of work and family in the home setting engenders a form of claustrophobia for some. This is exacerbated further by the common

problem of isolation. Home-based workers usually work alone, separated from social networks. Aside from not realizing the social benefits of personal interaction
with colleagues, isolation means being cut off from pooled information and the collective power that might result in higher pay, fringe benefits, and supportive legislation and legal decisions. Working alone and doing work for powerful others mean
that home-based workers will continue to be denied fair pay and appropriate fringe
benefits that most other workers receive.

To reiterate, the changing economy is a major societal upheaval that is transforming society and its members in many profound ways.

The New Immigration and the Changing Racial Landscape

A major population shift is transforming U.S. society—the "new immigration." This
new immigration represents two trends that set it apart from past immigration.
First, the volume of immigration is relatively large. For example, in the ten years
from 1963–1972 there were about 3.5 million legal immigrants; from 1973 to 1982
there were slightly less than 5 million; and *there were 9 million added* in the next ten
years (Heer, 1996:1). Second, the racial landscape and rate of population growth
are greatly affected as approximately 1 million immigrants annually set up permanent residence in the United States. These new residents are primarily Latino and
Asian, not European as was the case of earlier immigration eras. This demographic
transition has significant implications for United States society, communities, families, and individuals. The facts, myths, and consequences of these two demographic changes are the subjects of this section.

Newsweek's special issue anticipating the new millennium puts it this way:

> Immigration's vital to understanding the United States today. Americans now aged
> around 50 built their suburban dreams in places like the San Fernando Valley, the heart-
> land of support for California's Proposition 187 [the successful 1994 vote initiative that
> opposed education, welfare, and health services for illegal immigrants]. The world of
> their youth was one in which immigration was rare. . . . Now the Valley's 40 percent
> Latino and Asian . . . And it isn't just southern California that's been changed. . . . Just
> like their predecessors a century ago, today's immigrants will struggle with the twin urges
> to assimilate and to remember their roots. Just like their forebears, they will be accused
> of Balkanizing the country and stealing jobs from "real" Americans. (Elliott, 1994/95:131)

This **demographic** force—the new immigration—is challenging the cultural
hegemony of the White European tradition; creating incredible diversity in race,
ethnicity, language, religion, and culture; rapidly changing the racial landscape; and
leading, often, to division and hostility.

Immigration Patterns

Historically, there have been four major waves of immigration, which were major
sources of population growth and ethnic diversity in the United States (Martin and

Widgren, 1996:20–22). The first wave of immigrants arrived between 1790 and 1820 and consisted mainly of English-speaking Britons. The second wave, mostly Irish and German, came in the 1840s and 1850s and challenged the dominance of Protestantism, which led to a backlash against Catholics. The third wave, between 1880 and 1914, brought over 20 million, mostly southern and eastern Europeans who found factory jobs in large cities. In the 1920s, the United States placed limits on the number of immigrants it would accept, the operating principle being that the new immigrants should resemble the old ones. The "national origins" rules were designed to limit severely the immigration of Eastern Europeans and to deny the entry of Asians.

The fourth immigration wave began in 1965 and continues. The Immigration Act amendments of 1965 abandoned the quota system that had preserved the European character of the United States for nearly half a century. The new law encouraged a new wave of immigrants, only this time the migrants arrived not from northern Europe but from the Third World, especially Asia and Latin America. Put another way, 100 years ago Europeans were 90 percent of immigrants to the United States; now 90 percent of immigrants are from non-European countries. The result, obviously, is a dramatic alteration of the ethnic composition of the U.S. population (see Figure 8.2).

In addition to the legal migrants (about 800,000 each year in the 1990s), an estimated 300,000 unauthorized aliens enter and stay (an estimated 1.5 million to 2.5 million people enter the United States illegally each year, but most return to their native countries) for a net gain of U.S. immigrants of about 1 million annually (Martin and Midgley, 1994). Although the number who enter clandestinely is impossible to determine, the best estimate is that approximately 5 million resided in the United States in 1997 and is rising by 275,000 annually (Immigration and Naturalization Service data, cited in Branigin, 1997).

FIGURE 8.2

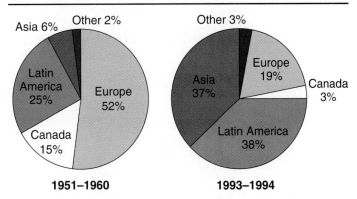

U.S. Immigrants by Region of Origin, 1950s and Mid-1990s

Source: Used with permission from Carol J. De Vita, "The United States at Mid-Decade," *Population Bulletin* 50 (Washington, DC: Population Reference Bureau, March 1996), p. 25.

The settlement patterns of this new migration differ from previous flows into the United States. Whereas previous immigrants settled primarily in the industrial states of the Northeast and Middle Atlantic region, or in the farming areas of the Midwest, immigrants today are much more dispersed geographically. Recent migrants have tended to locate on the two coasts and in the south. Nearly three-fourths of the 20 million foreign-born residents counted in the 1990 Census lived in one of six states: California, (where 64 percent of the nation's Asians and 35 percent of the country's Latinos live), followed by New York, Texas, Florida, Illinois, and New Jersey. Asians have tended to settle on the West Coast; Mexicans are most likely found in the Southwest, with other Latinos widely scattered (for example, Cubans in Florida and Puerto Ricans in New York). The foreign-born population has also tended to locate in large cities. In 1990 the greatest number of foreign-born people lived in New York City (2.08 million), Los Angeles (1.34 million), Chicago (469,000), Houston (290,000), and San Francisco (246,000) (U.S. Bureau of the Census, 1993:4).

California has been uniquely affected. In 1990, the non-White public school population in California constituted a majority—51.3 percent. Whites of all ages account for 58 percent of the population in California (down from 67 percent in 1980). "In San Jose bearers of the Vietnamese surname Nguyen outnumber the Joneses in the telephone directory 14 columns to eight" (Henry, 1990:29). In one political district of East Los Angeles only 15,000 of the 360,000 people are White. Included among the non-Whites are Blacks, Japanese, Chinese, Koreans, Vietnamese, Mexicans, Central Americans, and Filipinos (Mydans, 1991). The Los Angeles metro area, which is home to 12 percent of the nation's total minority population, added 20 percent of the nation's minority population growth in the 1980s—2.8 million new minority residents (Frey, 1991). The diverse population of southern California speaks

Despite their common condition as racial minorities, tensions among Blacks, Asians, and Latinos are heightened as they fight each other for relative advantage. This was clearly in evidence in the 1992 riots in South Los Angeles.

88 languages and dialects. This phenomenon, when coupled with cultural differences, causes great problems for the schools, governmental service agencies, and businesses. For all this diversity, though, southern California is becoming more and more Latino. "By the year 2010, southern California will have become a Latino subcontinent—demographically, culturally and economically distinct from the rest of America" (Meyer, 1992:32).

The population growth of recent immigrants is a consequence of two factors (Burke, 1995). First, those who chose to migrate tend to be young. Between 1970 and 1992, California's population of Latino women of childbearing age (ages 15 to 44) quadrupled, increasing from one-half million to 2.1 million. Second, the **fertility rate** (average lifetime births per woman in a given social category) of migrant women is higher than for women born in the United States.

> The 1992 [fertility rate] of Hispanic women was 3.5 children—twice that of white women (1.7 children). Thus, although there were roughly twice as many non-Hispanic white women of childbearing age in 1992 (3.9 million) as Hispanic women (2.1 million), the number of births to Hispanic women exceeded births to whites. (Burke, 1995:4)

The Consequences of the New Immigration

Although there are many consequences of the new immigration, we will concentrate on three: (1) increasing diversity; (2) the reaction of the hosts to the new immigrants; and (3) the effects of immigration on the immigrants.

Immigration and Increasing Diversity.   The United States is shifting from an Anglo-White society rooted in western culture to a society with three large racial-ethnic minorities, each of them growing in size while the White majority declines in population (this section is taken from Baca Zinn and Eitzen, 1993b). Five facts show the magnitude of this demographic transformation.

■ *One-fourth of the people in the United States are African American, Latino, Asian, or Native American.* The non-White population is numerically significant, comprising one-fourth of the population (up from 15 percent in 1960). In some places they outnumber Whites. The 1990 Census, for example, found that more than 2,000 counties, cities, and towns have racial and ethnic majorities. Minorities make up the majority in six of the eight U. S. cities with more than a million people—New York, Los Angeles, Chicago, Houston, Detroit, and Dallas.

■ *Racial minorities are increasing faster than the majority population.* While one-fourth of Americans are non-Whites, in 25 years, about one in three Americans will come from a minority background, and by 2050 minorities will be equal in size to the White population.

> During the first half of the 1990s, the minority population grew by 15 percent, compared with 3 percent growth in the non-Hispanic white population. The Hispanic and Asian populations grew fastest, expanding by 20 and 31 percent, respectively, while the African American population increased by 8 percent. . . .
>
> Immigration and relatively high fertility rates among most minority groups are expected to add to the size of the minority population. By 2020, 118 million Americans

are projected to be of minority backgrounds [up from 70 million in 1995]. The two fastest growing groups will be Asians and Hispanics. Asians will have the most rapid *rate* of growth; Hispanics will add the most *numbers*. Between 1995 and 2020, the Asian American population is expected to more than double in size—to 21 million. . . . Hispanics, on the other hand, will add more than 24 million people. . . . By 2020, the Hispanic population is expected to exceed 50 million. (De Vita, 1996:19) (See Figure 8.3.)

■ *African Americans are losing their position as the most numerous racial minority.* In 1990, for the first time, Blacks were less than half of all minorities, "a precursor of the flip-flop expected by 2010, when Hispanics replace them as the largest minority" (Usdansky, 1992:A1). In 1996 Latino children outnumbered African American children, 12 million to 11.4 million (Jones, 1996). By 2010, in a historic shift, Latinos will outnumber African Americans.

■ *Immigration now accounts for a large share of the nation's population growth.* The largest 10-year wave of immigration in U.S. history occurred in the 1980s with the arrival of almost 9 million (plus however many undocumented immigrants). Legislation enacted in 1986 and 1990 ensures that this record-high number will be easily surpassed in the 1990s (Portes, 1992). At present immigration accounts for about one-third of the annual population increase. By 2020, immigrants will become more important to the U.S. population growth than natural increase (Waldrop, 1990:23).

■ *New patterns of immigration are changing the racial composition of society.* Among the expanded population of first-generation immigrants "the Asian-born now outnumber the European-born. Those from Latin America—predominantly Mexicans—outnumber both" (Barringer, 1992:2). This contrasts sharply with what occurred as recently as the 1950s when two-thirds of legal immigrants were from Europe and Canada.

FIGURE 8.3

U.S. Population by Race and Ethnicity, 1995 and 2020

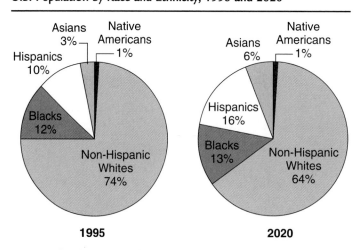

1995   **2020**

Source: Used with permission from Carol J. De Vita, "The United States at Mid-Decade," *Population Bulletin* 50 (Washington, DC: Population Reference Bureau, March 1996), p. 19.

These trends signal a transformation from a White majority to a multiracial/ multicultural society:

> Without fully realizing it, we have left the time when the non-White, non-Western part of our population could be expected to assimilate to the dominant majority. In the future, the White Western majority will have to do some assimilating of its own. (Riche, 1991:28)

The Reaction of the Hosts to the New Immigrants.   The latest wave of immigration has taken place in a historical context that includes the restructuring of the U.S. economy and an increasingly conservative political climate. New immigrants have always been seen as a threat to those already in place. The typical belief is that immigrants, because they will work for lower wages, drive down wages and take jobs away from those already settled here. These fears increase during economic hard times. That is the problem now as businesses downsize, pay lower wages, and replace workers with technology as they adapt to the economic transformation. The hostility toward migrants is also the result of the common belief that the new migrants increase taxes because they require services (education, health care, and welfare) that cost much more than the taxes they produce.

Previous immigration waves were White, coming mostly from Ireland, England, Germany, Italy, and Eastern Europe. Today's immigrants, in sharp contrast, are coming from Latin America and Asia. They are non-White and have distinctly non-European cultures. When these racial and ethnic differences are added to economic fears, the mix is very volatile.

The situation is worsened further by where the new migrants locate. Typically, they situate where migrants like themselves are already established. For example, 20 percent of the 90,000 Hmong living in the United States live in Minnesota, mostly around Minneapolis–St. Paul. One in 12 Asian Indians lives in Illinois, primarily in the Chicago area. Approximately 40 percent of all Asian Americans live in California (De Vita, 1996:21–22). The concentration of migrants by race/ethnicity provides them with a network of friends and relatives who provide them with support when needed. This pattern of clustering in certain areas tends to increase the fear of nonmigrants toward them. It also increases the tax burden as a community increases its population of relatively poor workers, whose children have special needs in school, and who likely do not have health insurance.

A second tendency is for new migrants to locate where other poor people live for the obvious advantage of cheaper housing and the like. The problem here is that two or three minorities often live side by side. Despite their common condition, tensions in such a situation are heightened as groups disadvantaged by society often fight each other for relative advantage. The tensions between African Americans and Asian immigrants was evidenced, for example, during the South Los Angeles riots in 1992 when roughly 2,000 Korean-owned business were looted or damaged by fire.

The result of these factors is often an anti-immigrant backlash. Opinion polls taken over the past 50 years report consistently that Americans want to reduce immigration. A 1992 *Business Week*/Harris Poll found that 68 percent of the respondents believed that the present immigration is bad for the country (Mandel and Farrell, 1992). A 1993 Yankelovich poll reflects the depth of resentment.

Sixty-four percent of those polled think most immigrants enter the United States illegally, 64 percent believe they take jobs from Americans, and 59 percent believe they add to the crime problem. Equally important, voters want the government to take steps to combat immigration. Seventy-three percent of the nation want strict limits on immigration, 50 percent want all U.S. citizens to be required to carry a national I.D. card, and 65 percent want the government to spend more money to tighten the border between the United States and Mexico. (Mills, 1996:38)

The states with the most immigrants have the highest levels of anti-immigrant feeling. This is based on the fears that migrants depress wages and take jobs away from nonmigrants (we will return to these fears later) and to the high costs of providing services to new immigrants. The federal government receives the most tax income, yet the cost of providing services (education, health care, job training) is typically the responsibility of the individual states. The most affected states do not feel that they are adequately compensated for the full cost of immigrants who are in the United States because of federal policy. Several states have filed suit against the federal government that seek reimbursement for services. Some politicians have exploited anti-immigrant feelings. Some 22 states have made English the official state language. California's Proposition 187, passed in 1994 by a 3-to 2- popular vote margin, denied public welfare such as non-emergency medical care, prenatal clinics, and public schools to undocumented immigrants. Many observers feel this anti-immigrant sentiment will fuel similar voter initiatives in other states, more restrictive federal legislation, and greater attempts to control the borders. The Senate in 1996, for example, voted to deny most federal benefits to *legal* immigrants who have not become citizens.

Are the fears toward migrants warranted? Let's examine the evidence that de-mythologizes immigration (the following is taken from Cole, 1994; Barkley, 1995; Rohter, 1993; Defreitas, 1994; and Loeb, et al., 1993):

■ *Myth: Immigrants take jobs from U.S. citizens.* Numerous studies have found that immigrants actually *create* more jobs than they fill. In a study of the 400 largest U.S. counties, the Urban Institute found that for every 100-person increase in adult immigrants, the number of new jobs rose by 46, compared to an increase of 25 jobs for every 100 new native-born Americans (cited in Barkley, 1995). Other studies show that immigrants are more likely than the rest of the population to be self-employed and start their own businesses (Rohter, 1993).

> New immigrants have not worsened the lot of the native born because their arrival has increased not only the supply of workers, but also domestic job growth. Immigrants have above-average self-employment rates, and the new businesses they create mean new jobs, tax revenue, and often new life for marginal and declining urban areas. In addition, they spend their earnings on local consumer goods, cars, and houses, generating multiplier effects that spur more labor demand. And many fill the harshest, low-wage jobs spurned by natives, instead of competing for similar work. (Defreitas, 1994:33)

This last point requires emphasis. Recent immigrants (legal and undocumented) often work for low wages and in dangerous conditions (sweatshops, stoop field work and the like), work that many poor U.S. citizens are unwilling to do. The Human Agency box starting on page 212 describes the immigrant laborers and their attempt to secure better working conditions.

■ *Myth: Immigrants are a drain on society's resources.* The evidence is that immigrants generate more in taxes paid than they cost in services received. Moreover, because recent immigrants tend to be young, they make few demands on Social Security. Julian Simon has even contended that a large flow of young adult immigrants will help solve the forthcoming crisis in the Social Security system (i. e., when the Baby Boom generation reaches retirement age, the relatively young immigrants will help to fund the Social Security recipients) (Simon, 1989). Recent immigrants, however, do present a problem—they are most likely to lack the English language skills and the work skills to be eligible for good jobs. The data show that time takes care of this problem—after ten years, immigrants, on average, take home wages comparable to those of nonimmigrant Americans (Loeb, et al., 1993). Similarly, the use of welfare diminishes as foreign-born residents become more established. In 1994, recent arrivals were almost twice as likely as native-borns to receive public assistance. "The percentages drop quickly, however, as the length of stay increases. Immigrants who entered the United States before 1970 had the lowest rate of public assistance . . . even lower than the U.S.-born population" (De Vita, 1996:29). Finally, research shows that Latino and Asian immigrants in California ten years or more after immigration had poverty rates lower than the non-immigrant population (*New York Times,* 1995).

Proposition 187 was based on the erroneous assumption that illegal immigrants cost more than they pay in. Four facts are pertinent here: (1) Most of those who are in the United States illegally do not seek government services because they fear that they will be deported; (2) most undocumented immigrants are from Mexico here for labor, and when the jobs are not forthcoming, they return to Mexico; and (3) the workers, documented and undocumented, must pay income and social security taxes; all pay local property taxes as owners or indirectly through rents, and all consumers pay sales taxes; and (4) illegal immigrants are not eligible for many public services, including welfare, unemployment insurance, and most tax-paid health care services (Martin and Midgley, 1994:32).

The conclusion is inescapable—the fears that so many Americans have about the new immigrants are unfounded. Yet, the prevailing myths are real for many, and they can have dangerous consequences.

The Effects of Migration on Immigrants: Ethnic Identity or Assimilation?

Martin and Midgley sum up the universal dilemma for immigrants:

> All groups of immigrants arriving in America have grappled with two countervailing forces: the newcomers' need and wish to fit into their new surroundings, and their desire to keep alive the organizing principles of the community they left behind. (Martin and Midgley, 1994:36)

Assimilation is the process in which individuals or groups adopt the culture of another group, losing their original identity. A principal indicator of assimilation is language. In the 1990 Census, about 80 percent of newcomers spoke a language other than English at home, compared with about 8 percent of the native-born population.

AGENCY

HUMAN

Immigrants Fight Back Through Workers Centers

They have the invisibility blues, these low-wage workers in New York's black market of labor. On Long Island, they are Central American women who work as maids, or men who wait on the street corners to be picked up for day jobs as gardeners or in construction. In New York City, they are Mexican workers laboring behind deli and pizza counters, delivery men dropping off takeout food, or sweatshop workers competing with low-wage garment factories abroad. Even working long hours, their weekly pay may reach only $150. Sometimes a boss doesn't pay them at all.

Workers in the growing unregulated economy have been invisible to the labor department inspectors who are supposed to enforce minimum wage and hour laws for all, documented and undocumented workers alike. They are largely invisible to the unions. It seems that the only government agency eager to find them is the Immigration and Naturalization Service (INS), which won extra funding from President Clinton and Congress last year to conduct workplace sweeps in search of undocumented—"illegal"—workers to deport. The INS gets help of course, as it did from Albany-area construction workers who called its agents in this summer to deport nonunion workers removing asbestos from schools.

For the past 15 years, though, these workers have been visible to workers centers. The organizers and fast-growing membership of these centers reach out to low-income immigrants and native-born Americans to build campaigns for fair and legal working conditions, and sometimes for affordable housing. While small, with handfuls of paid staff and at most 1000 members each, the centers are on the front lines of a battle against harmful, sub-minimum-wage work that depresses the labor conditions of all workers—a battle that most other combatants, from unions to labor investigators, have not been effectively fighting.

It is hard to pinpoint what makes four workers centers in the New York area—and the hundreds elsewhere in the country—distinctive from other organizing. Their tactics are not new, but are particularly suited to reaching the low wage workers most abused by the system. Campaigns target one high profile employer for years and build upon ethnic or racial solidarity. Women organize women. Pickets, education, media zaps; these time-worn tactics have an impact because members deploy them in long community-based campaigns and not just workplace struggles.

Among 20th-century immigrants, the shift to English as an individual's chief language typically occurred over three generations. Immigrants rarely learned English well during their lifetimes. Their children were often bilingual, using their parents' language at home and English at school, with English often dominant as they entered the workplace. Their children—the third generation in the United States—are typically monolingual English speakers. The three-generation shift to English may shrink to two generations by 2000. Most immigrants go to U.S. cities, where they are more apt to be exposed to English than were immigrants on farms and in factories earlier in the century. (Martin and Midgley, 1994:37–38)

If the past is a guide, the new immigrants will assimilate. "Our society exerts tremendous pressure to conform, and cultural separatism rarely survives more than a generation" (Cole, 1994:412). There are pressures to assimilate, but the lack of structural supports, especially for immigrants of color, makes assimilation difficult if not impossible for many.

In a storefront office in Brooklyn, you can see the impact as the women's committee of New York's oldest workers center, Chinese Staff and Workers Association (CSWA), campaign for safety on the job. "Occupational health and safety" is not a bureaucratic turn of phrase for the women, but a need to live without crippling back pain, or without the tips of their fingers peeling off from contact with toxic dyes. One evening in June, they photographed each other's injuries, earned working 60 or 70 hours a week in Brooklyn or Manhattan sweatshops. Glued on plasterboard, the photos would soon be displayed on a sidewalk information table and at a neighborhood meeting called to challenge garment bosses.

"We're adopting the older models to new circumstances," says Jennifer Gordon, a Harvard-trained lawyer who four years ago helped found a Long Island workers center, the Workplace Project. "You can't pretend we're making this up."

In some cases, the workers centers' community-based tactics have challenged unions to become more active in organizing or promoting to leadership people they were neglecting. And unions are finding workers centers' innovations worth borrowing. Five years ago the International Ladies Garment Workers Union (ILGWU) began establishing their own workplace justice centers to reach out to undocumented or unorganized workers, and the Service Employees International Union will soon follow with its own in New York.

The workers centers' impact can also be seen in the news every day, as exploitative labor conditions receive more attention. This year, designer Jessica McClintock bowed to the four-year campaign of Oakland's Asian Immigrant Women's Advocates and agreed to subcontract only to bonded manufacturers obeying labor law. Restaurants in Manhattan's Chinatown now pay overtime (even though most still confiscate waiters' tips) as a result of Chinese Staff's decade-long campaign targeting Silver Palace, the largest restaurant in the neighborhood.

Now the question is: Can the isolated, tiny offices, staffed by three or four activists, help build a widespread movement?

Source: Excerpted from Abby Scher, "Immigrants Fight Back: Workers Centers Lead Where Others Don't," *Dollars and Sense,* No. 207 (September/October 1996), pp. 30–35.

An argument countering the assumption that the new immigrants will assimilate as did previous generations of immigrants is that the new immigrants are racial/ethnics, not Whites. As such, they face individual and institutional racism that exclude them from full participation, just as it has excluded African Americans and Native Americans (O'Hare, 1993:2). The current political mood is to reduce or eliminate welfare programs and to eliminate affirmative action (policies aimed at helping the disadvantaged). The courts and legislatures have begun to weaken or eliminate affirmative action programs. Congress and the state legislatures are tightening eligibility requirements for welfare programs and diminishing their benefits. These actions mean that the new immigrants will have a more difficult time than their predecessors to assimilate, should they wish to do so.

Another factor facing this generation of migrants is that they enter the United States during a critical economic transformation where the middle-class is shrinking and the working-class faces difficult economic hurdles. A possible result is that

© G. Olliver

the new immigrants, different in race and culture, will be used as scapegoats for the difficulties that so many face.

In sum, the new immigration, occurring at a time of economic uncertainty and reduced governmental services, is having three pronounced effects that will accelerate in the foreseeable future: (1) an increased bifurcation between the "haves" and the "have nots"; (2) increased racial diversity; and (3) a heightened tension among the races.

The Two Structural Transformations of Society

This chapter focuses on two major transformations occurring in society—economic and demographic. These macro forces have huge consequences for society, for communities, for families, and for individuals. These contemporary economic forces have brought about a fundamental transformation in the nature of work. Fewer and fewer workers are engaged in mass assembly-line production, jobs that paid well and had good benefits. Many assumed that new jobs in the service sector and along the information superhighway and cyberspace would absorb those downsized from changing industries. This occurred but to only a limited extent, since the skills required are very different from the industrial age, and these high-tech corporations also downsize their workers as they automate and use low-cost labor worldwide. As a result, only 35 percent of displaced workers have found work that equalled or surpassed their previous wage/benefits. In effect, the economic transformation has caused millions of workers to transfer from good wage jobs to lower wage jobs or to temporary or to contingent work or to no work at all. Also, the unskilled and semi-skilled workers have been either left out or working at low wages without benefits.

Thus, wages have stagnated or declined for many millions. The results, among others, are a declining middle class, an ever-greater gap between the "haves" and the "have-nots," and changes in family structure.

Society is also undergoing a racial transformation, fueled especially by massive immigration from Latin America and Asia. Most of these immigrants arrive without the work and language skills to fit into a knowledge society. Past immigrants have succeeded economically, but the realities of the economic transformation increase the likelihood that they will be left on the margins. Moreover, the political climate fosters the elimination of affirmative action and other compensatory programs to aid minorities, as well as the downsizing of public supports to the poor, and the neglect of urban blight and inner city schools. All of these occur as racial minorities move toward becoming the numerical majority by mid-twenty-first century.

The consequences for society, then, of the convergence of these two powerful macro social forces are: (1) An increasing wealth/income gap; (2) the downward spiral for racial minorities; (3) an increased proportion of people on the economic margins; (4) growing social unrest by the "have-nots" but also by those workers who fear for their economic future; and (5) an increase in scapegoating as animosities intensify because of economic tough times and a revival of racism.

CHAPTER REVIEW

1. The economy of the United States is in the midst of a major structural transformation. This fundamental shift is the consequence of several powerful converging forces: (*a*) technological change; (*b*) the globalization of the economy; (*c*) capital flight; and (*d*) the shift from an industrial economy to a service/information economy.

2. These forces combine to create considerable discontinuity and disequilibrium in society. In particular, they have reduced the number of jobs that provided a middle-class standard of living and have expanded the number of lower standard-of-living jobs. Moreover, low-wage labor outside the United States has depressed wages and weakened unions. The result is a declining middle class, downward social mobility for many, and the creation of the new poor and changing family forms.

3. The nature of work is shifting as employers downsize their workforce and utilize more part-time or temporary workers. Two-thirds of these contingent workers are women.

4. The economic transformation has expanded the numbers of the working poor. This growth is a result of unemployment and underemployment (wages that do not lift a family above the poverty line).

5. The new poor are those blue-collar workers who lost manufacturing jobs with good pay and benefits because their companies closed or moved elsewhere, or they were replaced by automation. These "new poor" are much more trapped in poverty than were the "old poor" of other generations.

6. In the face of downward mobility, many individuals and families devise coping strategies such as downsizing their lifestyles, increasing their debt, two-earner families, increasing the workload, and home-based work.

7. The second societal upheaval that is shaking up society and families is massive immigration. This wave of immigration (adding about 1 million immigrants annually) differs from previous waves because the immigrants come primarily from Latin America and Asia rather than Europe.

8. Racial and ethnic diversity ("the browning of America") is increasing, with the influx of immigrants and differential fertility. The two fastest growing minorities are Latinos and Asian Americans.

9. The reaction of Americans to the new immigrants is typically negative. This is based on two myths: (*a*) that immigrants take jobs away from those already here; and (*b*) that immigrants are a drain on society's resources.

10. Immigrants face a dilemma: do they fit into their new society or do they retain the traditions of the society they left. Immigrants in the past, for the most part, assimilated. But conditions are different for the new immigrants: (*a*) They are racial/ethnics not Whites; (*b*) the current political mood is to eliminate affirmative action programs and welfare programs; and (*c*) they have entered during difficult economic times brought about by the economic transformation.

11. The consequences of the convergence of these two powerful forces—the structural transformation of the economy and the changing racial composition of society because of immigration—are: (*a*) an increasing wealth/income gap; (*b*) the downward spiral for racial minorities; (*c*) an increased proportion of people on the economic margins; (*d*) growing social unrest; and (*e*) an increase in scapegoating.

KEY TERMS

Structural transformation
   of the economy
Capital flight
Sunset industries

Sunrise industries
Contingent employment
New poor
New immigration

Demographic
Fertility rate
Assimilation

STUDY QUESTIONS

1. The structural transformation of the economy is having dramatic consequences. What social categories are most disadvantaged by these changes? Why?

2. A common argument is that unemployment is the consequence of individuals lacking the proper values of initiative, hard work, and a success orientation. Write an essay making the opposite case, that the fundamental reasons for unemployment are structural.

3. Compare the immigrants entering the United States in the late nineteenth century with the immigrants

today. In your comparison, consider personal characteristics, where they located, the jobs available to them, and their chances for upward mobility.

4. Are the fears toward immigrants warranted?

5. What are the sociological reasons for the contemporary rise in the numbers in such groups as "skin heads," self-appointed state militias, and other "hate" groups?

6. Why is the analysis of these two macro social forces important sociologically?

FOR FURTHER READING

The Structural Transformation of the Economy

Stanley Aronowitz and William DiFazio, *The Jobless Future: Sci Tech and the Dogma of Work* (Minneapolis: University of Minnesota Press, 1994).

Donald L. Barlett and James B. Steele, *America: What Went Wrong?* (Kansas City: Andrews and McMeel, 1992).

Peter F. Drucker, *Post-Capitalist Society* (New York: HarperCollins, 1993).

D. Stanley Eitzen and Maxine Baca Zinn, eds., *The Reshaping of America: Social Consequences of the Changing Economy* (Englewood Cliffs, NJ: Prentice-Hall, 1989).

David M. Gordon, *Fat and Mean: The Corporate Squeeze of Working Americans and the Myth of Managerial "Downsizing"* (New York: The Free Press, 1996).

Barry Jones, *Sleepers Awake! Technology and the Future of Work*, 2nd ed. (Melbourne: Oxford University Press, 1990).

Rachel Kamel, *The Global Factory: Analysis and Action for a New Economic Era* (Philadelphia: American Friends Service Committee, 1990).

Paul Kennedy, *Preparing for the Twenty-First Century* (New York: Random House, 1993).

Philip Mattera, *Prosperity Lost* (Reading, MA: Addison-Wesley, 1991).

New York Times, The Downsizing of America (New York: Times Books, 1996).

Robert B. Reich, *The Work of Nations: Preparing Ourselves for 21st Century Capitalism* (New York: Alfred A. Knopf, 1991).

Jeremy Rifkin, *The End of Work: The Decline of the Global Labor Force and the Dawn of the Post-Market Era* (New York: G. P. Putnam's Sons, 1995).

Lester Thurow, *The Future of Capitalism: How Today's Economic Forces Shape Tomorrow's World* (New York: William Morrow, 1996).

The New Immigration and the Changing Racial Landscape

George J. Borhas, *Friends or Strangers: The Impact of Immigrants on the U.S. Economy* (New York: Basic Books, 1990).

David Heer, *Immigration in America's Future: Social Science Findings and the Policy Debate* (Boulder, CO: Westview Press, 1996).

Pierrette Hondagneu-Sotelo, *Gendered Transitions: Mexican Experiences of Immigration* (Berkeley: University of California Press, 1994).

Philip Martin and Elizabeth Midgley, "Immigration to the United States: Journey to an Uncertain Destination," *Population Bulletin* 49 (September 1994), entire issue.

Philip Martin and Jonas Widgren, "International Migration: A Global Challenge," *Population Bulletin* 51 (April 1996), entire issue.

Thomas Muller, *Immigrants and the American City* (New York: New York University Press, 1993).

Silvia Pedraza and Ruben G. Rumbaut, *Origins and Destinies: Immigration, Race, and Ethnicity in America* (Belmont, CA: Wadsworth, 1996).

Alejandro Portes and Ruben G. Rumbaut, *Immigrant America: A Portrait* (Berkeley: University of California Press, 1990).

David M. Reimers, *Still the Golden Door: The Third World Comes to America,* 2nd ed. (New York: Columbia University Press, 1992).

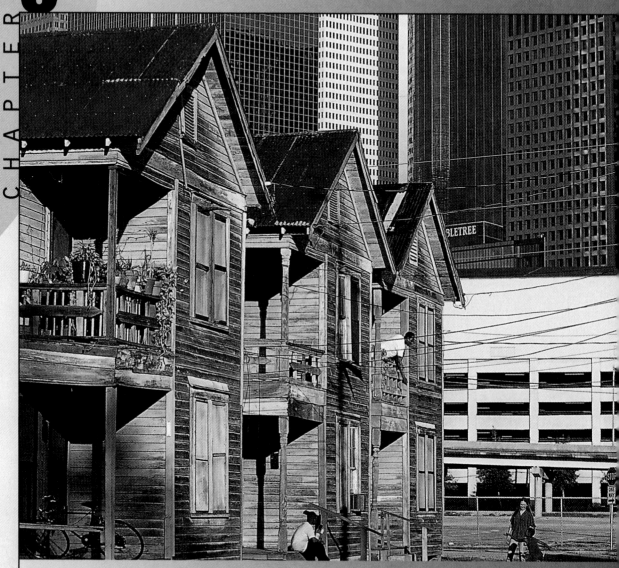

Social Stratification

Inequality is a fact of social life. All known societies have some system of ranking individuals and groups along a superiority–inferiority scale. Consider the following examples:

In India, birth into a particular family determines one's caste position, which in turn establishes one's social position, work, and range of marriage partners. At the bottom of this system is one group—the untouchables—that is so low that its members are not even part of the caste system. There is even a hierarchy among the untouchables with one category so sullied that they cannot be seen by others during the daylight hours. (See "Other Societies: The Caste System in India.")

In South Africa there is an unofficial caste system based on race (just a few years ago it was the official state policy). There are four racial castes: Whites, Blacks, Coloureds (mixed races), and Asians. The conditions for housing, work, pay, and schooling in this apartheid system are decidedly unequal by race.

In Saudi Arabia men have higher status than women. By law, custom, and religious beliefs, women are restricted from certain jobs, from driving automobiles, and from positions of authority.

Brazil was the last nation in the Western Hemisphere to abolish slavery (1888). However, a form of slavery continues as workers in some situations are virtually imprisoned by their employers, working for food and shelter with no hope of paying off their debts (Brooks, 1993).

Introduction

These examples indicate a range of patterned social inequality in various societies. Variations on these themes are also found in the United States, where people are divided and ranked by family of origin, race, gender, and economic position.

The pattern of structured inequities is called *social stratification,* the subject of this and the following three chapters. This chapter examines these ranking systems. These structured systems of inequality are crucial to the understanding of human groups because they are important determinants of human behavior and because they have significant consequences for society and its members.

This chapter is divided into three sections. First, the important concepts are introduced. Second, the three major hierarchies—class, race, and gender—are described briefly. The third section describes and critiques the theories used to explain the universality of stratification systems and how hierarchies of dominant and subordinate groups are established and maintained.

Major Concepts

People differ in age, physical attributes, and in what they do for a living. The process of categorizing persons by age, height, occupation, or some other personal attribute is called **social differentiation.** When people are ranked in a vertical arrangement (hierarchy) that differentiates them as superior or inferior, we have **social stratification.** The key difference between differentiation and stratification is that the process of ranking or evaluation occurs only in the latter. What is ranked and how it is ranked are dependent on the values of the society.

Social stratification refers, in essence, to structured social inequality. The term *structured* refers to stratification being socially patterned. This implies that inequalities are not caused by biological differences (for example, sex or race). Biological traits do not become relevant in patterns of social superiority or inferiority until they are socially recognized and given importance by being incorporated into the beliefs, attitudes, and values of the people in the society. People in the United States, for example, tend to believe that sexual and racial characteristics make a difference—therefore, they do.

The social patterning of stratification is also found in the distribution of rewards in any community or society, because that distribution is governed by social norms. In the United States few individuals seriously question the income differential between medical doctors and nurses or college professors and primary school teachers because the norms and values of society dictate that such inequalities are just.

Patterned behavior is also achieved through the socialization process. Each generation is taught the norms and values of the society and of its social class. The chil-

Other Societies Other Ways

The Caste System in India

The caste system in India was outlawed in 1950. Modern commerce and transportation diminished its force in urban India. It remains in force, however, in many rural villages where tradition retains a powerful grip. This essay depicts this traditional caste system that still holds in some Indian villages and regions.

A caste system is a system of social stratification based on ascription. In such a system birth into a particular family determines one's destiny—social position, type of work, and range of marriage partners—for life. In principle there is no social mobility.

There are four major castes (*varnas*) in hierarchical order (and thousands of subcastes—*jatis*—within them). One category—the untouchables—is considered so low that it is below the caste system, thus its members are outcasts. Each subcaste is identified with an occupation, such as priests, barbers, sweepers, or leather workers.

Because the family transmits social position from one generation to the next, a rigid system requires that marriage occur only between social equals. Thus, a caste system mandates endogamous marriage (to marry within one's group).

An integral part of the Indian caste system is the concern for ritual purity. Because it is believed that the higher the caste, the more pure the members, there are elaborate rules of etiquette governing social distance between the castes. Untouchables, for example, pollute their superiors by their touch or even their presence. They are required to hide whenever anyone from a higher caste is present or, if this is not possible, they must bow with their faces downward. Highborns must not take food or water from an untouchable because it pollutes them. Untouchables must take water only from their own well because to draw water from the same well as the other castes pollutes all others. If polluted there are a number of practices used for ritual purification (the use of fire, bathing, family shrine or temple).

The caste system is supported by powerful cultural beliefs. The Hindu religion emphasizes a strong concern for duty (dharma). This involves one's duty to family, caste, age, and sex. In effect, there is a moral duty to accept one's fate. Moreover, if one does not fulfill the requirements of their particular caste position, there are dire consequences. Central to the Hindu religion is the belief in reincarnation—that souls are reborn after death. Thus, for people who do not observe the moral laws of their particular caste, after death their souls will be reborn in a lower caste. Conversely, faithful obedience to caste duties will result in rebirth into a higher caste. Brahmins (the highest caste), then, are being rewarded for excellence in previous lives while untouchables are being punished. This belief system provides a very strong mechanism for maintaining the rigid stratification system. "No one wants to be reborn as an untouchable, least of all the untouchables, who best know the miseries of this position. Furthermore, we can understand the contempt received by untouchables: they are those believed to have sinned most in a previous life" (Kerbo, 1983:20).

dren of slaves and the children of the ruling family in a society are each taught the behavior proper for persons of their station in life.

Finally, the system of stratification is always connected with other aspects of the society. The existing stratification arrangements are affected by and have effects on such matters as politics, marriage and the family, economics, education, and religion.

Harold Kerbo has summarized what is meant by social stratification:

> *Social stratification* means that inequality has been hardened or *institutionalized,* and there is a *system* of social relationships that determines who gets what, and why. When we say *institutionalized* we mean that a system of layered hierarchy has been established. People have come to expect that individuals and groups with certain positions will be able to demand more influence and respect and accumulate a greater share of goods and services. Such inequality may or may not be accepted equally by a majority in the society, but it is recognized as the way things are. (Kerbo, 1983:11)

The hierarchies of stratification—class, race, and gender—place groups, individuals, and families in the larger society. The crucial consequence of this so-called placement is that the rewards and resources of society such as wealth, power, and privilege are unequally distributed. And, crucially, differential access to these societal resources and rewards produces different life experiences and different life chances. **Life chances** refer to the chances throughout one's life cycle to live and to experience the good things in life. Life chances are most significant because they are those things that "(1) . . . better-off people can purchase (good education, good medical care, comfortable homes, fine vacations, expert services of all kinds, safe and satisfying occupations) and which poor people would also purchase if they had the money; and (2) . . . make life easier, longer, healthier, and more enjoyable" (Tumin, 1973:104). The converse, of course, is that people at the low end of the stratification hierarchies will have inadequate health care, shelter, and diets. Their lives will be more miserable and they will die sooner.

Economic advantages translate into better life chances, that is, the chances throughout life to experience the good things in life.

To understand the U.S. society we must understand the hierarchies of class, race, and gender. Class, race, and gender are macro structures of inequality that shape our micro worlds. These structures organize society as a whole and create varied environments for individuals and families through their unequal distribution of social opportunities.

These structures of inequality array the resources and advantages of society in patterned ways. These hierarchies are also structured systems of exploitation and discrimination in which the affluent dominate the poor, men dominate women, and Whites dominate people of color (Feagin, 1986:21).

Traditionally, the family has been viewed as the principal unit in the class system because it passes on wealth and resources from generation to generation. Even though the family is basic in maintaining stratification, life chances are affected by race and gender inequalities as well as by social class. In most families, men have greater socioeconomic resources and more power and privileges than do women even though all family members are viewed as members of the same social class. While a family's placement in the class hierarchy does determine rewards and resources, hierarchies based on sex create different conditions for women and men even within the same family (Acker, 1973). Systems of sex stratification cut across class and racial divisions to distribute resources differently to men and women (Baca Zinn and Eitzen, 1996: Ch. 3).

Class

When a number of persons occupy the same relative economic rank in the stratification system, they form a **social class.** Social class "implies having or not having

Drawing by Weber;
© 1993 The New
Yorker Magazine,
Inc.

"The caterers haven't shown up, the musicians are late, and the elevator is broken.
We might as well be living in a Third World country."

the following: individual rights, privileges, power, rights over others, authority, life style choices, self-determination, status, wealth, access to services, comfort, leisure, etc." (Comer, 1978:171). Persons are socially located in a class position on the basis of income, occupation, and education, either alone or in combination. In the past, the occupation, income, and education of the husband determined the class location of the family. But family behavior is better explained by locating families according to the more prestigious occupation, regardless of whether it is the husband's or the wife's (Yorburg, 1983:189). Occupations are part of the larger opportunity structure of society. Those that are highly valued and carry high income rewards are unevenly distributed. The amount of income determines how well a given household can acquire the resources needed for survival and perhaps for luxury. The job or occupation that is the source of the paycheck connects families with the opportunity structure in different ways. This connection generates different kinds of class privileges for families. **Privilege** refers to the distribution of goods and services, situations, and experiences that are highly valued and beneficial (Jeffries and Ransford, 1980:68). Class privileges are those advantages, prerogatives, and options that are available to those in the middle and upper classes. They involve help from the system: banks, credit unions, medical facilities, and voluntary associations. Class privileges are based on the systematic linkages between families and society. Class privilege creates many differences in family patterns.

Race and Ethnicity

Racial and ethnic stratification refers to systems of inequality in which some fixed group membership, such as race, religion, or national origin, is a major criterion for ranking social positions and their differential rewards. Like the class system, this hierarchy represents institutionalized power, privilege, and prestige. Racial and ethnic hierarchies generate domination and subordination, often referred to as majority–minority relations. Minority groups are those that are dominated by a more powerful group and stigmatized and singled out for differential treatment.

   Race is socially defined on the basis of a presumed common genetic heritage resulting in distinguishing physical characteristics. **Ethnicity** refers to the condition of being culturally rather than physically distinctive. Ethnic peoples are bound together by virtue of a common ancestry and a common cultural background.

   A racial group that has a distinctive culture or subculture, shares a common heritage, and has developed a common identity is also an ethnic group. Both race and ethnicity are traditional bases for systems of inequality, although there are historical and contemporary differences in the societal placement of racial-ethnics and White-ethnics in this society. We examine how racial stratification deprives people of color of equal access to society's resources and thereby creates family patterns that are different from the idealized family model.

   The most important feature of racial stratification is the exclusion of people of color from equal access to society's valued resources. People of color or racial-ethnics have less power, wealth, and social status than do other people in the United States. African Americans, Latinos, and Asian Americans constitute the largest of the racial minorities in the United States.

Gender

Gender, like race and class, is a basic organizing principle of society. From the macro level of the societal economy, through the institutions of society, to interpersonal relations, gender shapes activities, perceptions, roles, and rewards. **Gender** is the patterning of difference and domination through distinctions between women and men (Acker, 1992:565).

The stratification system that assigns women's and men's roles unequally is the **sex-gender system.** It consists of two complementary yet mutually exclusive categories into which all human beings are placed. The sex-gender system combines biologically based sex roles with socially created gender roles. In everyday life, the terms *sex role* and *gender role* are used interchangeably. This use obscures important differences and underlying issues in the study of women's and men's experiences. **Sex roles** refer to behaviors determined by an individual's biological sex. **Gender roles** are social constructions; they contain self-concepts, psychological traits, as well as family, occupational, and political roles assigned dichotomously to each sex. For example, the traditional female gender role includes expectations for females to be passive, nurturant, and dependent. The standard male gender role incorporates alternative expectations—behaviors that are aggressive, competitive, and independent (Lipman-Blumen, 1984:1–2).

Patriarchy is the term for forms of social organization in which men are dominant over women. As described in Chapter 12 patriarchy is infused throughout U.S. society. Generally, men have more power than women, and they also tend to have greater power over women as well. Even though there is considerable class and racial variation here, men in general gain some privilege at the expense of women. In sum, *the sex-gender system* distributes power, resources, prestige, and privilege unequally.

The Intersection of Class, Race, and Gender

The hierarchies of class, race, and gender do not stand alone. They are interrelated systems of stratification. Economic resources, the bases of class, are not randomly distributed but vary systematically by race and sex. For example, people of color and women have fewer occupational choices than do White males. People of color and women often experience separate and unequal education and receive less income for the work they do, resulting in different life chances.

These systems of inequality form what Patricia Hill Collins calls a **matrix of domination** in which each of us exists (Collins, 1990). The existence of these intersections has several important implications (Baca Zinn and Dill, 1996). First, people experience race, class, gender, and sexuality differently depending upon their social location in these structures of inequality. For example, people of the same race will experience race differently depending upon their location in the class structure as poor, working class, or professional/managerial class, or unemployed and their location in the gender structure as female or male, and in the sexuality system as heterosexual or homosexual.

Second, class, race, and gender are components of both social structure and social interaction. As a result, individuals because of their social locations experience different forms of privilege and subordination. In short, these intersecting forms of inequality produce both oppression and opportunity.

A third implication of the inequality matrix has to do with the relational nature of dominance and subordination. Power is embedded in each system of stratification, determining whether one is dominant or subordinate. The intersectional nature of hierarchies means that power differentials are linked in systematic ways, reinforcing power differentials across hierarchies.

Theories of Stratification

Sociologists and other observers of society have pondered two fundamental questions about stratification. The first is, Why are societies stratified? The second is, Within stratified societies, why are certain categories ranked as superior while others are considered inferior? There are alternative theoretical explanations for each question, and each explanation has important implications. Let's begin with the two sociological theories for the more general and logically prior question.

All societies have some form of stratification. How is this universal phenomenon to be explained? Sociologists answer this question from either the order or the conflict perspective. The position of the order theorists is basically supportive of inequality, because the unequal distribution of rewards is assumed to be not only inevitable but also necessary. Conflict theorists, on the other hand, tend to denounce the distributive system as basically unjust, unnecessary, and the source of many social problems.

Order Theory

Adherents of the order model begin with the fact that social inequality is a ubiquitous and apparently unavoidable phenomenon. They reason that inequality must, therefore, serve a useful function for society. The argument, as presented in the classic statement by Kingsley Davis and Wilbert Moore, is as follows (Davis and Moore, 1945). The smooth functioning of society requires that various tasks be accomplished through a division of labor. There is a universal problem, then, of allocation—of getting the most important tasks done by the most talented people. Some jobs are more important for societal survival than are others (typically persons involved in decision making, medicine, religion, teaching, and the military). The societal problem is how to get the most talented people motivated to go through the required long periods of training and to do these important tasks well. The universally found answer, according to Davis and Moore, is differential rewards. Society must provide suitable rewards (money, prestige, and power) to induce individuals to fill these positions. The rewards must, it is argued, be distributed unevenly to various positions because the positions are not equally pleasant or equally important. Thus, a differential reward system guarantees that the important societal functions are fulfilled, thereby ensuring the maintenance of society. In this way, differential ranks actually serve to unify society through a division of labor (functional integration) and through the socialization of persons to accept their positions in the system.

Although there probably is some truth to this argument, the analyst of society must also ask: Is inequality primarily integrative or divisive? Is it necessary? Must the poor always be with us? (see Tumin, 1953; Huaco, 1966).

Conflict Theory

Conflict theorists view stratification in a wholly different manner from the order theorists. Rather than accepting stratification as a source of societal integration, the conflict perspective assumes that stratification reflects the distribution of power in society and is therefore a major source of discord and coercion. It is a source of discord because groups compete for scarce resources and because the powerless, under certain conditions, resent their lowly position and lack of rewards. Coercion results from stratification as the powerful (who are coincidentally male, White, and wealthy) prey on the weak. From this view, then, the unequal distribution of rewards reflects the interests of the powerful and not the basic survival needs of society, as the order theorists contend.

A major contention of the conflict theorists is that the powerful people use ideology to make their value system paramount. Karl Marx argued that the dominant ideology in any society is always the ideology of the ruling class. The ruling class uses the media, schools, religion, and other institutions to legitimate systems of inequality. So powerful is this socialization process that even oppressed peoples tend to accept their low status as natural. Marx called this tendency of the oppressed to accept their oppression **false consciousness** (see Marx and Engels, 1959; Parenti, 1978:15–18). The working class and the poor in the United States, for example, tend to accept their lack of monetary rewards, power, and prestige because they believe that the system is truly meritocratic—and that they lack the skills and brains to do the better-rewarded tasks in society. In short, they believe that they deserve their fate (see Sennett and Cobb, 1973). Consequently, they accept a differential reward system and the need for supervision and decision making left to experts. False consciousness thus inhibits efforts by the disadvantaged to change an oppressive system. Marx argued, however, that when the oppressed become aware of their common oppression and that they have been manipulated by the powerful to serve the interests of the powerful, they will develop a **class consciousness**—an objective awareness of their common exploitation—thus becoming unified in a cause to advance their class interests.

Even though it is true that social stratification is an important source of societal friction, conflict theorists have not answered the important question as to its necessity (neither have the order theorists, for that matter, although they address themselves directly to that question). Both theoretical perspectives have important insights that must be considered. The order theorists see stratification serving the useful function of societal maintenance by providing a mechanism (differential rewards) to ensure that all the slots in the division of labor are filled. Conflict theorists are equally valid in their contention that stratification is unjust, divisive, and a source of social instability or change.

Deficiency Theories

Some categories of people are systematically disadvantaged in the United States, most especially the poor, non-Whites, and women. Is there some flaw within these groups—perhaps biological or cultural—that explains their inferiority? Or, is it the structure of society that blocks their progress while encouraging the advancement of others? To answer these questions, we examine the various explanations for poverty. The specific explanations for inequities by race and gender are addressed in detail in Chapters 11 and 12, using the same explanatory categories used to understand poverty.

Who or what is to blame for poverty? There are two very different answers to these questions (Barrera, 1979:174–219). One is that the poor are in that condition because of some deficiency: Either they are biologically inferior or their culture fails them by promoting character traits that impede their progress in society. The other response places the blame on the structure of society: Some persons are poor because society has failed to provide equality in educational opportunity, because institutions discriminate against minorities, because private industry has failed to provide enough jobs, because automation has made some jobs obsolete, and so forth. In this view, society has worked in such a way as to trap certain persons and their offspring in a condition of poverty.

Biological Inferiority

In 1882 the British philosopher and sociologist Herbert Spencer came to the United States to promote a theory later known as *Social Darwinism*. He argued that the poor were poor because they were unfit. Poverty was nature's way of

> excreting . . . unhealthy, imbecile, slow, vacillating, faithless members" of society in order to make room for the "fit," who were duly entitled to the rewards of wealth. Spencer preached that the poor should not be helped through state or private charity, because such acts would interfere with nature's way of getting rid of the weak. (*The Progressive*, 1980b)

Social Darwinism has generally lacked support in the scientific community, although it has continued to provide a rationale for the thinking of many individuals. Recently, however, the concept has resurfaced in the work of three scientists. They suggest that the poor are in that condition because they do not measure up to the more well-to-do in intellectual endowment.

Arthur Jensen, professor of educational psychology at the University of California, has argued that there is a strong possibility that Blacks are less well endowed mentally than are Whites. From his review of the research on IQ, he claimed that approximately 80 percent of IQ is inherited, while the remaining 20 percent is attributable to environment. Because Blacks differ significantly from Whites in achievement on IQ tests and in school, Jensen claimed that it is reasonable to hypothesize that the sources of these differences are genetic as well as environmental (Jensen, 1969; 1980).

The late Richard Herrnstein, a Harvard psychologist, agrees with Jensen that intelligence is largely inherited. He goes one step further, positing the formation of hereditary castes based on intelligence (Herrnstein, 1971; 1973). For Herrnstein, social stratification by inborn differences occurs because (1) mental ability is inherited and (2) success (prestige of job and earnings) depends on mental ability. Thus, a **meritocracy** (social stratification by ability) develops through the sorting process. This reasoning assumes that persons close in mental ability are more likely to marry and reproduce, thereby ensuring castes by level of intelligence. According to this thesis, "in times to come, as technology advances, the tendency to be unemployed may run in the genes of a family about as certainly as bad teeth do now" (Herrnstein, 1971:63). This is another way of saying that the bright people are in the upper classes and the dregs are at the bottom. Inequality is justified, just as it was years ago by the Social Darwinists.

Charles Murray, along with Herrnstein, wrote *The Bell Curve* (1994), the latest revival of Social Darwinism. Their claim, an update of Herrnstein's earlier work, is that the economic and social hierarchies reflect a single dimension—cognitive ability, as measured by IQ tests.

Notwithstanding the flaws in the logic and in the evidence used by Jensen, Herrnstein, and Murray (for excellent critiques of the Herrnstein and Murray work, see Gould, 1994; Herman, 1994; Reed, 1994; and the symposium appearing in *Contemporary Sociology*, 1995), we must consider the implications of their biological determinism for dealing with the problem of poverty.

Jensen and Herrnstein have argued that dispassionate study is required to determine whether intelligence is inherited to the degree that they state. Objectivity is the *sine qua non* of scientific inquiry, and one cannot argue with its merits, although science, all science, is tainted (see "Research Methods: How Science Is Affected by the Political Climate"). We should recognize, however, the important social consequences implied by the Jensen-Herrnstein argument. First, biological determinism is a classic example of blaming the victim. The individual poor person is blamed instead of schools, culturally biased IQ tests, low wages, corporate downsizing, or social barriers of race, religion, or nationality. By blaming the victim, this thesis claims a relationship between lack of success and lack of intelligence. This relationship is spurious because it ignores the advantages and disadvantages of ascribed status. According to William Ryan, "Arthur Jensen and Richard Herrnstein confirm regretfully that Black folks and poor folks are born stupid, that little rich kids grow up rich adults, not because they inherited Daddy's stock portfolio, but rather because they inherited his brains" (Ryan, 1972:54).

The Jensen–Herrnstein–Murray thesis divides people in the United States further by appealing to bigots. It provides "scientific justification" for their beliefs in the racial superiority of some groups and the inferiority of others. By implication, it legitimates the segregation and unequal treatment of so-called inferiors. The goal of integration and the fragile principle of egalitarianism are seriously threatened to the degree that members of the scientific community give this thesis credence or prominence.

Another serious implication of the biological determinism argument is the explicit validation of the IQ test as a legitimate measure of intelligence. The IQ test attempts to measure innate potential, but to do this is impossible, because the testing

Research Methods

How Science Is Affected by the Political Climate

The following essay is by Stephen Jay Gould, Harvard professor of evolutionary biology. Gould argues that scientists—all scientists—are enmeshed in a web of personal and social circumstances that affect their science. Leftist geneticists, for example, are more likely to combat biological determinism just as politically conservative geneticists favor interpretations of inequality as the reflection of genetic inadequacies of people.

Social Disparities as "A Product of Nature"

The rise and fall in popularity of scientific theories correlates with changes in the political and social climate. That's why, as the nation moves to the right politically, arguments for biological determinism are bound to become popular. The determinists' message is that existing inequalities in society are a reflection of the intrinsic character of people and are not the fault of social institutions. Determinists are saying that disparities are a product of nature and therefore cannot be alleviated by very expensive social programs.

Similarly, the hereditarian version of IQ, which holds that you are measuring something that's inherited and unchangeable, flourished in the 1920s, the age of Sacco and Vanzetti and of jingoism inspired by World War I. The hereditarians argued that the single number called IQ could capture the multifarious complexities of the concept of intelligence and that you could rank races, classes and sexes on the basis of their average scores. To think that a whole host of abilities could be encompassed in a meaningful way by a single number is fundamentally fallacious. An approach which recognizes that *intelligence* is a word we give to an irreducible set of multifarious abilities might lead to a more adequate assessment.

The "Grievous Consequences" of IQ Testing

I don't deny there is biology involved in some human abilities. I'd never be a marathon runner no matter how hard I trained, and I'll certainly never be a basketball player, because I am too short. But it is one thing to acknowledge that there is biology behind a lot of what we do; it is quite another to say that abilities are the result of intrinsic and unalterable heredity.

Yet today there are still many people, including some scientists, who think, in their heart of hearts, that IQ

process must inevitably reflect some of the skills that develop during the individual's lifetime. For the most part, intelligence tests measure educability—that is, the prediction of conventional school achievement. Achievement in school is, of course, also associated with a cluster of other social and motivational factors, as Joanna Ryan observes.

> The test as a whole is usually validated, if at all, against the external criterion of school performance. It therefore comes as no surprise to find that IQ scores do in fact correlate highly with educational success. IQ scores are also found to correlate positively with socio-economic status, those in the upper social classes tending to have the highest IQs. Since social class, and all that this implies, is both an important determinant and also an important consequence of educational performance, this association is to be expected. (Ryan, 1972:54)

tests are measuring something intrinsic and permanent. That kind of thinking has had grievous social consequences for many groups in American society.

"Scientists reflect the prejudices of their lives." In evaluating these and other arguments by scientists, it is important that people be wary of the claim that science stands apart from other human institutions because its methodology leads to objective knowledge. People need to realize that scientists are human beings like everybody else and that their pronouncements may arise from their social prejudices, as any of our pronouncements might. The public should avoid being snowed by the scientist's line: "Don't think about this for yourself because it's all too complicated."

I wish scientists scrutinized more rigidly the sources of justification for their beliefs. If they did, they might realize that some of their findings do not derive from a direct investigation of nature but are rooted in assumptions growing out of experience and beliefs.

But don't draw from what I have said the negative implication that science is a pack of lies—that it's merely social prejudice. On the one hand, science is embedded in society, and scientists reflect the social prejudices of their own lives and those of their class and culture. On the other hand, I believe that there are correct answers to questions, and science, in its own bumbling, socially conditioned manner, stumbles toward those answers.

Gauging "the truth value of an idea." In evaluating science, a distinction has to be drawn between where an idea comes from and how worthy it is. The truth value of an idea is independent of its source, but when you know its source, you might get more suspicious about its potential truth value.

Darwin's theory of natural selection, for example, came directly out of a social context: It was essentially Adam Smith's economics read into nature. Without Adam Smith and the whole school of Scottish economics, I doubt that Darwin would ever have thought of it. Yet Darwin was right, in large measure. So social conditioning doesn't make an idea wrong; it does mean you have to scrutinize it.

Source: Stephen Jay Gould, "How Science Changes with the Political Climate." Reprinted from *U.S. News & World Report* issue of March 1, 1982. Copyright 1982, U.S. News & World Report, p. 62. Reprinted by permission of the publisher.

The Jensen–Herrnstein–Murray thesis overlooks the important contribution of social class to achievement on IQ tests. This oversight is crucial, because most social scientists feel that these tests are biased in favor of people who have had middle- and upper-class environment and experiences. IQ tests discriminate against the poor in many ways. They discriminate obviously in the language that is used, in the instructions that are given, and in the experiences they assume the subjects have had. The discrimination can also be more subtle. For minority-group examinees, the race of the person administering the test influences the results. Another, less well-known fact about IQ tests is that in many cases they provide a self-fulfilling prophecy, as Ryan notes:

IQ scores obtained at one age often determine how an individual is subsequently treated, and, in particular, what kind of education he receives as a consequence of IQ testing will in turn contribute to his future IQ, and it is notorious that those of low and high IQ do not get equally good education. (Ryan, 1972:44)

Another implication is the belief that poverty is inevitable. The "survival of the fittest" capitalist ideology is reinforced, justifying both discrimination against the poor and continued privilege for the advantaged. Inequality is rationalized so that little will be done to aid its victims. Herrnstein and Murray argue that public policies to ameliorate poverty are a waste of time and resources. "Programs designed to alter the natural dominance of the 'cognitive elite' are useless, the book argues, because the genes of the subordinate castes invariably doom them to failure" (Muwakkil, 1994:22). The acceptance of this thesis, then, has obvious consequences for what policy decisions will be made or not made in dealing with poverty. If their view prevails, then welfare programs will be abolished, as will programs such as Head Start.

This raises the serious question: Is intelligence immutable or is there the possibility of boosting cognitive development? A number of studies have shown that Head Start type programs raise scores among poor children by as much as 9 points. These results, however, fade out entirely by the sixth grade. Yet this rise and fall of IQ scores makes the case for the role of environmental factors in cognitive development. As Beth Maschinot has argued:

> [The critics of Head Start] ignore the obvious fact that once they leave Head Start, poor students typically attend substandard schools from the first grade onward. The fact that IQ scores drop again after this experience should lead one logically to conclude that intelligence as defined by IQ tests is highly responsive to environmental manipulations, not the reverse. (Maschinot, 1995:33)

Research on programs other than Head Start makes the same point. The Abecedarian Project conducted by the University of North Carolina studied high-risk children from 120 families. The conclusion:

> The most important policy implication of these findings is that early educational intervention for impoverished children can have long-lasting benefits, in terms of improved cognitive performance. This underscores the critical importance of good early environments and suggests that the focus of debate should now be shifted from whether government should play a role in encouraging good early environments to how these environments can be assured. (Campbell and Ramey, 1994:694–695)

Another study, by the Robert Wood Johnson Foundation, of low-birthweight infants followed their development for three years. The researchers found that the infants who had a stimulating day-care environment had, on average, a 13-point higher IQ score than the babies who did not have those experiences (reported in Richmond, 1994).

As a final example, high-risk African American children in Ypsilanti, Michigan were randomly divided into two groups. One group received a high-quality active learning program as 3- and 4-year olds. The other groups received no preschool education. The two groups were compared when they were age 27, with these results:

By age 27, those who had received the preschool education had half as many arrests as the comparison group. Four times as many were earning $2,000 or more a month. Three times as many owned their own homes. One-third more had graduated from high school on schedule. One-fourth fewer of them needed welfare as adults. And they had one-third fewer children born out of wedlock. (Beck, 1995:7B)

The Jensen–Herrnstein–Murray thesis also provides justification for unequal schooling. Why should school boards allot comparable sums of money for similar programs in middle-class schools and lower-class schools if the natural endowments of children in each type of school are so radically different? Why should teachers expect the same performance from poor children as from children from the more well-to-do? Why spend extra money on disadvantaged children in Head Start programs if these children are doomed by the genetic inferiority? The result of such beliefs is, of course, a self-fulfilling prophecy. Low expectations beget low achievement.

Finally, the Jensen–Herrnstein–Murray thesis encourages policy makers either to ignore poverty or to attack its effects rather than its causes in the structure of society itself.

Cultural Inferiority

The **culture of poverty** hypothesis (see Chapter 7) contends that the poor are qualitatively different in values and lifestyles from the rest of society *and that these cultural differences explain continued poverty.* In other words, the poor, in adapting to their deprived condition, are found to be more permissive in raising their children, less verbal, more fatalistic, less apt to defer gratification, and less likely to be interested in formal education than are the more well-to-do. Most important is the contention that this deviant cultural pattern is transmitted from generation to generation. Thus, there

According to the culture of poverty argument, the poor have a culture that dooms them and their children to living in poverty.

is a strong implication that poverty is perpetuated by defects in the lifeways of the poor. If poverty itself were to be eliminated, the former poor would probably continue to prefer instant gratification, be immoral by middle-class standards, and so on. This reasoning blames the victim. From this view, the poor have a subculture with values that differ radically from the values of the other social classes. And, this explains their poverty.

Edward Banfield, an eminent political scientist and advisor to Republican presidents, has argued that the difference between the poor and the nonpoor is cultural—the former have a present-time orientation while the nonpoor have a future-time orientation (Banfield, 1974). He does not see the present-time orientation of the poor as a function of the hopelessness of their situation. Yet it seems highly unlikely that the poor see little reason to complain about the slums: What about the filth, the rats, the overcrowded living conditions, the high infant mortality? What about the lack of jobs and opportunity for upward mobility? This feeling of being trapped seems to be the primary cause of hedonistic present-time orientation. If the structure were changed so that the poor could see that hard work and deferred gratification really paid off, they could adopt a future-time orientation.

Critics of the culture-of-poverty hypothesis argue that the poor are an integral part of U.S. society; they do not abandon the dominant values of the society, but rather, retain them while simultaneously holding an alternative set of values. This alternative set is a result of adaptation to the conditions of poverty. Elliot Liebow, in his classic study of lower-class Black men, has taken this view. For him, street corner men strive to live by American values but are continually frustrated by externally imposed failure:

> From this perspective, the street corner man does not appear as a carrier of an independent cultural tradition. His behavior appears not so much as a way of realizing the distinctive goals and values of his own subculture, or of conforming to its models, but rather as his way of trying to achieve many of the goals and values of the larger society, of failing to do this and of concealing his failure from others and from himself as best he can. (Liebow, 1967:222)

Most people in the United States, however, believe that the poor are poor because they have a deviant system of values that encourages behaviors leading to poverty. To illustrate, a 1989 Gallup Poll asked a national sample: "In your opinion, which is more often to blame if a person is poor—lack of effort, or circumstances beyond his or her control?" Thirty-eight percent responded "lack of effort," 42 percent answered "circumstances," and 17 percent felt that both lack of effort and circumstances were to blame (Gallup report, 1989a:4) Those most likely to choose "lack of effort" were men, young adults, Whites, people making over $30,000, and Republicans.

Current research shows that this prevailing view is a myth. If there were a culture of poverty, then there would be a relatively large proportion of the poor that would constitute a permanent underclass. The deviant values and resulting behaviors of the poor would doom them and their children to continuous poverty. But the University of Michigan's Panel Study of Income Dynamics (Duncan, 1984) followed 5,000 representative households for ten years and found that only 2.6 percent fit the stereotype of permanent poverty. Contrary to common belief, most poor people are poor only temporarily; their financial fortunes rise and fall with widowhood, divorce, remarriage, acquiring a job with decent pay or losing one, or other changes affecting economic status. The 2.6 percent who are persistently poor are different from the temporarily poor: 62 percent are Black, compared with 19 percent of the temporarily poor; 39 percent are disabled, compared with 17 percent; one-third are elderly, compared with 14 percent; and 61 percent were female heads of households, compared with 28 percent of the temporarily poor. Examining just the two-thirds of the persistently poor who are not elderly, 65 percent live in households headed by women and almost three-quarters of these women are Black (Duncan, 1984:48–52). These facts show once again the interconnections of race and gender in understanding inequality in U.S. society and, as discussed in the next section, how inequality is structured by race and gender. The other important implication of these findings is that inequality negates the culture of poverty. Duncan and his colleagues find little evidence that poverty is a consequence of the way poor people think. Economic success is not a function of "good" values and behaviors and failure the result of "bad" ones. Thus, the solution to poverty is not to change the attitudes of "flawed persons" but to change the opportunity structures in society (Duncan, 1984:65).

Structural Theories

In contrast to blaming the biological or cultural deficiencies of the poor, there is the view that how society is organized creates poverty and makes certain kinds of people especially vulnerable to being poor.

Institutional Discrimination

Michael Harrington, whose book *The Other America* was instrumental in sparking the federal government's War on Poverty, has said, "The real explanation of why the poor are where they are is that they made the mistake of being born to the wrong parents, in the wrong section of the country, in the wrong industry, or in the wrong racial or ethnic group" (Harrington, 1963:21). This is another way of saying that the society is to blame for poverty, not the poor. When the customary ways of doing things, prevailing attitudes and expectations, and accepted structural arrangements work to the disadvantage of the poor, it is called **institutional discrimination.** Let us look at several examples of how the poor are trapped by this type of discrimination.

© 1976 Ron Cobb. All rights reserved. Used with the permission of Wild & Wooley, publishers of Cobb Again.

Most good jobs require a college degree, but the poor cannot afford to send their children to college. Scholarships go to the best-performing students. Children of the poor usually do not perform well in school, primarily because of low expectations for them among teachers and administrators. This is reflected in the system of tracking by ability as measured on class-biased examinations. Further evidence is found in the disproportionately low amounts of money given to schools in impoverished neighborhoods. All of these acts result in a self-fulfilling prophecy—the poor are not expected to do well in school, and they do not. Because they are failures as measured by so-called objective indicators (such as the disproportionately high number of dropouts and discipline problems and the very small proportion who desire to go to college), the school feels justified in its discrimination toward the children of the poor.

The poor also are trapped because they get sick more often and stay sick longer than do the more well-to-do. The reasons, of course, are that they cannot afford preventive medicine, proper diets, and proper medical attention when ill. The high incidence of sickness among the poor means either that they will be fired from their jobs or that they will not receive money for the days missed from work (unlike the more well-to-do, who usually have jobs with such fringe benefits as sick leave and paid-up medical insurance). Not receiving a paycheck for extended periods means that the poor will have even less money for proper health care—thereby ensuring an even higher incidence of sickness. Thus, there is a vicious cycle of poverty. The poor will tend to remain poor, and their children tend to perpetuate the cycle.

The traditional organization of schools and jobs in the United States has limited the opportunities of racial minorities and women. Chapters 11 and 12 describe at length how these social categories are systematically disadvantaged by the prevailing laws, customs, and expectations of society. Suffice it to say in this context that:

- Racial minorities are deprived of equal opportunities for education, jobs, and income.
- Women typically work at less prestigious jobs than do men, and when working at equal status jobs receive less pay and fewer chances for advancement.

The Political Economy of Society

The basic tenet of capitalism—that who gets what is determined by private profit rather than by collective need—explains the persistence of poverty. The primacy of maximizing profit works to promote poverty in several ways. First, employers are constrained to pay their workers the least possible in wages and benefits. Only a portion of the wealth created by the laborers is distributed to them; the rest goes to the owners for investment and profit. Therefore, employers must keep wages low. That they are successful in this is demonstrated by the more than 2.2 million persons *who work full-time but remain under the poverty level.*

A second way that the primacy of profit promotes poverty is by maintaining a surplus of laborers, because a surplus depresses wages. Especially important for employers is to have a supply of undereducated and desperate people who will work for very low wages. A large supply of these marginal people (such as minorities, women, undocumented workers) aids the ownership class by depressing the wages for all workers in good times and provides the obvious category of people to be laid off from work in economic downturns.

A third impact of the primacy of profits in capitalism is that employers make investment decisions without regard for their employees (potential or actual). If costs can be reduced, employers will purchase new technologies to replace workers (such as robots to replace assembly-line workers and word processors to replace secretaries). Similarly, owners may shut down a plant and shift their operations to a foreign country where wages are significantly lower.

In sum, the fundamental assumption of capitalism is individual gain without regard for what the resulting behaviors may mean for other people. The capitalist system, then, should not be accepted as a neutral framework within which goods and services are produced and distributed, but rather as an economic system that perpetuates inequality.

A number of political factors complement the workings of the economy to perpetuate poverty. Political decisions to fight inflation with high interest rates, for example, hurt several industries, particularly automobiles and home construction, causing high unemployment.

The powerful in society also use their political clout to keep society unequal. Clearly, the affluent in a capitalist society will resist efforts to redistribute their wealth to the disadvantaged. Their political efforts are, rather, to increase their benefits at the expense of the poor and the powerless (see "Diversity: Who Benefits from Poverty?"). In short, they work for laws beneficial to them, sympathetic elected and appointed officials, policies based on trickle-down economics, and favorable tax laws such as low capital-gains taxes and regressive taxes.

In sum, this chapter has examined three stratification systems—the social class system, the system based on race and ethnicity, and the sex-gender system. By definition, in each stratification system certain categories of people are considered inferior and treated unfairly. Various theories have provided the rationales for this alleged inferiority. A review of these explanations is found in Table 9.1, which summarizes the theories used to explain why the poor are poor as discussed in this chapter and which anticipates the discussion of racial and gender inequalities found in Chapters 11 and 12.

Diversity

Who Benefits from Poverty?

Herbert Gans, a sociologist, has some interesting insights about the benefits of poverty. He begins with the assumption that if some social arrangement persists, it must be accomplishing something important (at least in the view of the powerful in society). What, then, does the existence of a relatively large number of persons in a condition of poverty accomplish that is beneficial to the powerful?

1. Poverty functions to provide a low-wage labor pool that is willing (or unable to be unwilling) to do society's necessary "dirty work." The middle and upper classes are subsidized by the existence of economic activities that depend on the poor (low wages to many workers in restaurants, hospitals, and in truck farming).

2. The poor also subsidize a variety of economic activities for the affluent by supporting, for example, innovations in medicine (as patients in research hospitals or as guinea pigs in medical experiments) and providing servants, gardeners, and house cleaners who make life easier for the more well-to-do.

3. The existence of poverty creates jobs for a number of occupations and professions that serve the poor or protect the rest of society from them (penologists, social workers, police, pawn shop owners, numbers racketeers, and owners of liquor stores). The presence of poor people also provides incomes for doctors, lawyers, teachers, and others who are too old, poorly trained, or incompetent to attract more affluent clients.

4. Poor people subsidize merchants by purchasing products that others do not want (seconds, dilapidated cars, deteriorated housing, day-old bread, fruit, and vegetables) and that otherwise would have little or no value.

5. The poor serve as a group to be punished in order to uphold the legitimacy of conventional values (hard work, thrift, honesty, and monogamy). *The poor provide living proof that moral deviance does not pay,* and thus, an indirect rationale for blaming the victim.

6. Poverty guarantees the status of those who are not poor. The poor, by occupying a position at the bottom of the status hierarchy, provide a reliable and relatively permanent measuring rod for status comparison, particularly by those just above them (that is, the working class, whose politics, for example, are often influenced by the need to maintain social distance between themselves and the poor).

7. The poor aid in the upward mobility of others. A number of persons have entered the middle class through the profits earned from providing goods and services in the slums (pawn shops, second-hand clothing and furniture stores, gambling, prostitution, and drugs).

8. The poor, being powerless, can be made to absorb the costs of change in society. In the nineteenth century they did the backbreaking work that built the railroads and the cities. Today they are the ones pushed out of their homes by urban renewal, the building of expressways, parks, and stadiums. Many economists assume that a degree of unemployment is necessary to fight inflation. The poor, who are "first to be fired and the last to be hired," are the ones who make the sacrifice for the economy.

Gans notes:

> This analysis is not intended to suggest that because it is often functional, poverty *should* exist, or that it *must* exist. For one thing, poverty has many more dysfunctions than functions; for another, it is possible to suggest functional alternatives. For example, society's dirty work could be done without poverty, either by automation or by paying "dirty workers" decent wages. Nor is it necessary for the poor to subsidize the many activities they support through their low-wage jobs. This would, however, drive up the costs of these activities, which would result in higher prices to their customers and clients. . . .

In sum, then, many of the functions served by the poor could be replaced if poverty were eliminated, but almost always at higher costs to others, particularly more affluent others. Consequently a functional analysis equivalent to the order model must conclude that poverty persists not only because many of the functional alternatives to poverty would be quite dysfunctional for the affluent members of society. . . . Poverty can be elimi- nated only when they become dysfunctional for the affluent or powerful, or when the powerless can obtain enough power to change society. (p. 24)

Source: Herbert J. Gans, "The Uses of Power: The Poor Pay All." *Social Policy* 2 (July-August 1971):20–24. Copyright © 1971 by Social Policy Corporation. Reprinted by permission of the publisher.

TABLE 9.1

Varying Explanations of Inequality by Class, Race, and Gender

EXPLANATIONS FOR INEQUALITY	Structures of Inequality		
	CLASS	RACE	GENDER
Biological inferiority	Social Darwinism: the poor are unfit.	Jensen/Herrnstein: Blacks are less endowed mentally than Whites.	Women are biologically different from men: weaker, less aggressive, more nurturant, less able in mathematics and spatial relationships but better in language.
Cultural inferiority	Culture of poverty: the poor have a maladaptive value system that dooms them and their children.	Blacks have loose morals, unstable families, do not value education, and lack motivation.	Gender role socialization leads females to accept society's devalued roles, to be passive, and to be secondary to males.
Structural discrimination	The dominant use their power to maintain advantage. The poor are trapped by segmented labor markets, tracking in schools, and other structural arrangements.	Institutional racism blocks opportunities. Segmented labor markets, use of biased tests for jobs, school placement, residential segregation.	Institutional sexism limits women's chances in legal system, job markets, wages, etc. Patriarchy where men are dominant over women through organizational norms.

CHAPTER REVIEW

1. The process of categorizing people on some dimension(s) is called social differentiation.

2. When people are ranked in a hierarchy that differentiates them as superior or inferior, this is called social stratification.

3. The three hierarchies of stratification—class, race, and gender—place groups, families, and individuals in the larger society. The rewards and resources of society are unequally distributed according to this placement. Most crucially, this social location determines for people the chances for a longer, healthier, and more enjoyable life.

4. Order-model theorists accept social inequality as universal and natural. They believe that inequality serves a basic function by motivating the most talented people to perform the most important tasks.

5. Conflict theorists tend to denounce social inequality as basically unjust, unnecessary, and the source of many social problems. The irony is that the oppressed often accept their deprivation. Conflict theorists view this as the result of false consciousness—the acceptance through the socialization process of an untrue belief that works to one's disadvantage.

6. The explanations for why some categories of people are ranked at the bottom of the various hierarchies of stratification are biological, cultural, or structural.

7. The biological explanation for poverty is that the poor are innately inferior. Arthur Jensen, Richard Herrnstein, and Charles Murray, for example, have argued that certain categories of people are disadvantaged because they are less well endowed mentally (a theoretical variation of Social Darwinism).

8. Another explanation that blames the poor for their poverty is the culture-of-poverty hypothesis. This theory contends that the poor are qualitatively different in values and lifestyles from the successful and that these differences explain the persistence of poverty from generation to generation.

9. Critics of innate inferiority and culture-of-poverty explanations charge that, in blaming the victim, both theories ignore how social conditions trap individuals and groups in poverty. The source of the problem lies not in the victims but in the way society is organized to advantage some and disadvantage others.

KEY TERMS

Social differentiation
Social stratification
Life chances
Social class
Privilege
Race
Ethnicity
Gender
Sex-gender system
Sex roles
Gender roles
Patriarchy
Matrix of domination
False consciousness
Class consciousness
Meritocracy
Culture of poverty
Institutional discrimination

STUDY QUESTIONS

1. Explain what is meant by this statement: "The structures of inequality—class, race, and gender—array the resources and advantages of society in patterned ways."

2. Within your college community is there a system of stratification? What appear to be the criteria used in this ranking of individuals and groups on your campus?

3. Contrast the views of order theorists and conflict theorists on social stratification.

4. What are the sociological criticisms of the deficiency theories of social inequality? How do structural theories of inequality meet these criticisms?

5. Summarize Gans's argument in "Diversity: Who Benefits from Poverty?" Is this analysis from the order or the conflict perspective? Elaborate.

FOR FURTHER READING

Margaret L. Andersen and Patricia Hill Collins, eds., *Race, Class, and Gender: An Anthology* (Belmont, CA: Wadsworth, 1992).

Maxine Baca Zinn and D. Stanley Eitzen, *Diversity in Families,* 4th ed. (New York: HarperCollins, 1996).

Virginia Cyrus, ed., *Experiencing Race, Class, and Gender in the United States* (Mountain View, CA: Mayfield, 1993).

Greg J. Duncan, *Years of Poverty, Years of Plenty* (Ann Arbor: Institute for Social Research, University of Michigan, 1984).

Claude S. Fischer, Michael Hout, Martin Sanchez Jankowski, Samuel R. Lucas, Ann Swidler, and Kim Voss, *Inequality by Design: Cracking the Bell Curve Myth* (Princeton, NJ: Princeton University Press, 1996).

Stephen Jay Gould, *The Mismeasure of Man* (New York: W. W. Norton, 1981).

David B. Grusky, ed., *Social Stratification: Class, Race, and Gender in Sociological Perspective* (Boulder, CO: Westview, 1992).

Andrew Hacker, *Two Nations: Black and White, Separate, Hostile, Unequal,* updated edition (New York: Ballantine Books, 1995).

Charles E. Hurst, *Social Inequality: Forms, Causes, and Consequences* (Boston: Allyn and Bacon, 1992).

Vincent Jeffries and H. Edward Ransford, *Social Stratification: A Multiple Hierarchy Approach* (Boston: Allyn and Bacon, 1980).

Gerhard Lenski, *Power and Privilege: A Theory of Social Stratification* (New York: McGraw-Hill, 1966).

R. C. Lewontin, Steven Rose, and Leon J. Kamin, *Not in Our Genes: Biology, Ideology, and Human Nature* (New York: Pantheon, 1984).

Amartya Sen, *Inequality Reexamined* (Cambridge, MA: Harvard University Press, 1992).

Class

It was in autumn 1964, fresh from Harvard College, from a term at Oxford, and from the indulgence of three years as an expatriate and social dropout on the fringes of the literary life on the Left Bank of Paris, that I returned to the United States and chose, for reasons which I do not wholly understand, to find a job within a fourth-grade classroom of the Boston Public Schools. I had never read the works of Gunnar Myrdal, Michael Harrington, or Robert Coles. But it was in that year in Boston that I saw before my eyes a world of suffering, of hopelessness and fear, that I could never have imagined in the privileged and insulated decades of my childhood and schooling.

Up until 1964 I had been to Roxbury on very few occasions. Sometimes, on a Wednesday night, I had accompanied my father as we drove into the city to drop off the live-in maid who cleaned our house and cooked my meals and cared for me and for my sister six days out of seven. Thursday was the maid's day off. I used to wonder what she did, whether she had children and a household of her own, whether she suffered for the time in which she could not see them, how they could manage with no mother in their home. I knew that she was both a competent and gentle-hearted woman. She could clean and she could cook and she could offer love unstinted. I knew she couldn't read or write. That didn't seem to count. She did not need to read in order to perform the work of polishing the silverware and scrubbing kitchen floors.

When I asked her one day whether she had children, she replied that she had three. They lived in Roxbury with their grandmother. I worried about this sometimes, but not often. Not by the intention of my mother and my father, but by the enormous distance that divided my suburban life from anything that happened on that distant street of darkened houses where we dropped her off on Wednesday nights, I was inoculated against pangs of conscience. My curiosity about her children and about their lives was rapidly dissolved as I proceeded to evolve the plans for my career.

In 1964 I learned at last, and with a wave of shame and fear that turned before long into an unbounded and compensatory rage, that the children of our colored maid had been denied the childhood and happiness and care that had been given to me by their mother. I knew now that these children had been robbed of childhood. I had not robbed them: I had been recipient of stolen goods. What had been stolen from them seemed unspeakable: a crime, an evil past imagination.*

Introduction

The democratic ideology that "all men are created equal" has been a central value throughout U.S. history. We are often reminded by politicians, editorial writers, and teachers that ours is a society in which the equality of every person is highly valued. This prevailing ideology, however, does not mesh with reality. Slavery was once legal, and racial discrimination against Blacks was legal until the 1960s. Women were not permitted to vote until this century. Native Americans had their land taken from them and were then forced to locate on reservations. Japanese Americans were interned against their will during World War II. And, at a time (1994) when 120 people in the United States were billionaires, 37 million people were living below the official poverty line. Clearly, as George Orwell wrote in his classic, *Animal Farm,* "all . . . are equal but some are more equal than others" (1946:123).

The previous chapter considered some general principles and theories of social stratification. This chapter focuses on one hierarchy of stratification—the social class system, which is the ranking based primarily by economic resources. The chapter is divided into several parts, which describe (1) the dimensions of socioeconomic inequality, (2) the class structure in the United States, (3) the degree to which people can move from one class to another—social mobility, (4) the consequences of class position, and (5) poverty in the midst of plenty.

Dimensions of Inequality

There is a great deal of evidence that people in the United States rank differently from one another on a number of socioeconomic dimensions. Let us examine some of the documentation for the existence of these differences in the United States.

Wealth

Wealth is unquestionably maldistributed in the United States. There exists unbelievable wealth in the hands of a few and wretched poverty for millions. At the top are more than 120 billionaires, with the richest, Bill Gates, head of software giant Microsoft, worth an estimated $23 billion early in 1997.

The concentration of wealth is greatly skewed. The following are some facts:

■ The top 1 percent of wealth holders in 1989 controlled 39 percent of total household wealth (up from 34 percent in 1983). The share of wealth held by the bottom 80 percent of Americans, meanwhile *declined* from 19 percent in 1983 to 15 percent in 1989 (Wolff, 1995:7).

■ Considering just financial wealth, the richest 1 percent of households in 1989 owned 48 percent of the total, and the top 20 percent accounted for 94 percent of the total financial wealth (Wolff, 1995:10).

■ The number of households in 1992 with $1 million or more in investable assets was 3,200,000 (up from 834,000 in 1989) (Hacker, 1995:70).

■ Personal wealth is badly skewed by race. In 1989, the median White family in 1989 had twenty times the wealth of the median non-White family (up from eleven times the wealth in 1983). "More than one in three nonwhite households now have no positive wealth at all, in contrast to one in eight white households" (Wolff, 1995:2).

Income

The data on wealth always show more concentration than do income statistics, but the convergence of money among the few is still very dramatic when considering income. Consider the following facts:

■ In 1995, the median wage for men with four years of high school was $22,765. The bottom 20 percent of American households had incomes of $13,426 or less in income About 5.6 million workers earn the minimum wage. In 1990 there were 24.3 million year-round, full-time workers who had annual earnings of less than $12,195 (U.S. Census Bureau, 1992a:2). During his heyday, Michael Milken received more than $1.5 million *a day* in salary and commissions.

There is unbelievable wealth in the hands of a few people and wretched poverty for millions.

OF COURSE I DESERVE MORE MONEY... ...IT'S HARD WORK LAYING PEOPLE OFF ALL DAY.

EXECUTIVE PAY

DANZIGER

The Christian Science Monitor

Christian Science Monitor (*March 11, 1996*), p. 20.

- In 1960, the average chief executive officer (CEO) earned about as much as 41 factory workers. In 1992 that CEO made as much as 157 factory workers (Sklar, 1995a). The gap continues to widen. In 1995 the average compensation of CEOs (salary, bonus, and stock options) increased by 26.9 percent compared to the 2.8 percent increase in wages for the average worker (CNBC, 1996). This inequality gap is the highest in the industrialized world. In Japan the ratio is less than 25 to 1, in France and Germany the compensation ratio for CEOs and workers is less than 35 to 1.
- While benefits (pensions, medical) have been shrinking for most workers recently, top executives have seen theirs increase substantially (Schultz, 1993). Moreover, some 43 million Americans, many of whom work full-time, are not covered by any medical insurance.
- In 1994 the average income for physicians in private practice was $218,000, which was 8.3 times greater than the median earnings of U.S. workers (Hacker, 1995:72).
- Women workers make about 72 cents for every dollar men workers make.
- The median household income by race for 1994 was $35,126 for non-Hispanic Whites, $23,421 for Hispanics, and $21,027 for African Americans.

The data in Figure 10.1 show the gap between the rich and the poor and how income inequality is increasing in U.S. society. The top part of this figure shows the trend line in the Gini index, indicating an ever-higher level of income concentration for the wealthy from 1970 to 1994. The second part of this figure shows the data by income quintile that combine to form the Gini index. The difference in income between the top 20 percent and the bottom 20 percent is the greatest since the Census Bureau began gathering this information.

This relative gain in income by the upper 20 percent reflects the increased tax benefits received by the affluent from Congress and the administration since 1980 and the concurrent lowering of tax benefits to the middle class and the decrease in

FIGURE 10.1

Income Inequality in the United States

A. The Gini Index of Growing Inequality

Economists use the Gini scale to measure the distribution of income. The formula produces a scale that goes from 0 (where everyone earns the same amount) to 1 (one person earns all). Using this scale, inequality in the United States has grown steadily for a generation, and surged in the early 1990s.

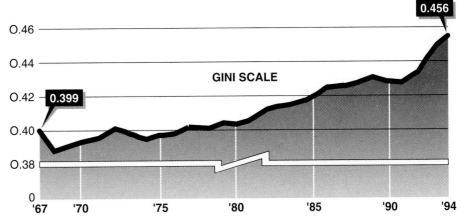

Source: Paul Overberg, "Digging for the Roots of Income Inequality," *USA Today* (September 23, 1996), p. 2B.

B. Share of Aggregate Household Income, by Quintile: 1968 to 1993

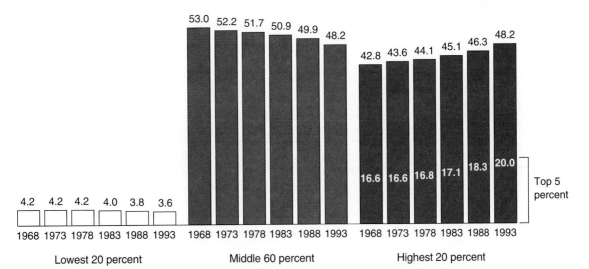

Source: U.S. Bureau of the Census, "Population Profile of the United States 1995," *Current Population Reports,* Series P23–189 (Washington, DC, U.S. Government Printing Office, 1995), p. 41.

welfare programs for the poor. Another important explanation for this increasing inequality gap is the changing job structure as the economy shifts from manufacturing to service and as U.S. jobs are exported, as described in Chapter 8.

Wealth and income disparities are great and growing. Since 1973 wages have fallen for 80 percent of the workforce, while the richest 20 percent have become richer by far. Lester Thurow, the esteemed economist, suggests that this widening gap may lead to trouble.

> These are unchartered waters for American democracy. Since accurate data have been kept, beginning in 1929, America has never experienced falling real wages for a majority of the work force while its per-capita GDP [Gross Domestic Product] was rising. In effect, we are conducting an enormous social and political experiment—something like putting a pressure cooker on the stove over a full flame and waiting to see how long it takes to explode. (Thurow, 1995:78)

Education

In the United States, people also vary considerably in educational attainment. The amount of formal education an individual achieves is a major determinant of her or his occupation, income, and prestige. Despite the standard belief by people in the United States in free mass education and the almost uniform requirement that persons complete at least eight years of formal schooling, real differences in educational attainment exist. About one in five adults age twenty-five and over have less than a high school education. See Table 10.1 for the 1993 data on educational attainment and race.

Perhaps the best indicator of inequality in education is the number of people in the United States who are illiterate or marginally illiterate. Jonathan Kozol summarizes these dismal data:

> Twenty-five million American adults cannot read the poison warnings on a can of pesticide, a letter from their child's teacher, or the front page of a daily paper. An additional 35 million read only at a level which is less than equal to the full survival needs of our society.
>
> Together, these 60 million people represent more than one-third of the entire adult population.

TABLE 10.1

Educational Attainment of Persons 25 Years Old and Over, by Race: 1993

RACE	4 YEARS OF HIGH SCHOOL	SOME COLLEGE	4 OR MORE YEARS OF COLLEGE
White	35.6%	23.3%	22.6%
Black	36.3	22.0	12.2
Hispanic	26.8	17.3	9.0

Source: Adapted from U.S. Bureau of the Census, "Population Profile of the United States 1995," *Current Population Reports,* Series P23–189 (Washington, DC: U.S. Government Printing Office, 1995), p. 19.

The largest numbers of illiterate adults are white, native-born Americans. In proportion to population, however, the figures are higher for blacks and Hispanics than for whites. Sixteen percent of white adults, 44 percent of blacks, and 56 percent of Hispanic citizens are functional or marginal illiterates. Figures for the younger generation of black adults are increasing. Forty-seven percent of all black seventeen-year-olds are functionally illiterate. . . .

Fifteen percent of recent graduates of urban high schools read at less than sixth-grade level. One million teenage children between twelve and seventeen cannot read above the third-grade level. Eighty-five percent of juveniles who come before the courts are functionally illiterate. Half the heads of households classified below the poverty line by federal standards cannot read an eighth-grade book. Over one-third of mothers who receive support from welfare are functionally illiterate. Of 8 million unemployed adults, 4 to 6 million lack the skills to be retrained for hi-tech jobs. (Kozol, 1985:4–5)

There is an obvious correspondence between being inadequately educated and receiving little or no income. The most recent data show that a household headed by a high school dropout had an annual income of $27,952, while a household headed by a high school graduate had an income of $41,078. If the head were a college graduate, annual income was $73,365, and if the head had a professional degree, the income soared to $122,956 (U.S. Census data cited in Burd, et al., 1996:A11). There is not only a generational correlation between these education and income but an intergenerational one as well. The children of the poor and uneducated tend not to do well in school and eventually drop out (regardless of ability), while the children of the educated well-to-do tend to continue in school (regardless of ability). Thus, the cycle of inequality is maintained.

Occupation

Another demonstration that persons diverge in status is that occupations vary systematically in prestige. The degree of prestige and difference accorded to occupations is variable. A justice of the Supreme Court obviously enjoys more prestige than a bartender. But society makes much more subtle prestige distinctions. There is a rather uniform tendency to rate physicians slightly higher than college professors, who in turn are somewhat higher in rank than dentists. Further down the prestige scale, mail carriers outrank carpenters, who in turn have higher prestige than do automobile mechanics.*

The culture provides a ready-made and well-understood ranking system. It provides a relatively uniform system based on several related factors: (1) the importance of the task performed (that is, how vital the consequences of the task are for the society), (2) the degree of authority and responsibility inherent in the job,

---

*C. C. North and Paul K. Hatt, the two sociologists who gathered these prestige rankings in 1947, found some degree of variation but a substantial agreement among a cross-section of adults in the United States (N = 3,000) (North and Hatt, 1947). This study was replicated in 1963 to ascertain if people had changed their ranking of occupations. The correlation of 0.99 between the two studies suggests that the rating of occupations has remained remarkably stable (Hodge, Siegel, and Rossi, 1964). Incidentally, sociologists have found a high correlation in the rating for occupations for a number of industrialized nations (Hodge, Treiman, and Rossi, 1966).

(3) the native intelligence required, (4) the knowledge and skills required, (5) the dignity of the job, and (6) the financial rewards of the occupation.

But society also presents us with warped images of occupations, which leads to the acceptance of stereotypes. The media, for example, through advertisements, television, and movie portrayals, evoke positive images for middle- and upper-class occupations and negative ones for lower-prestige occupations. Professional and business leaders are White, male, cultured, and physically attractive. They are decisive, intelligent, and authoritative. At the other end of the occupational spectrum workers are often portrayed as ethnic, bigoted, and ignorant.

Occupation, then, is a very important variable that sorts people into hierarchically arranged categories. It is highly correlated with income level, but the gender of the worker makes a tremendous difference. Regardless of the occupational category, women make considerably less, on average, than do men employed in the same category.

Social Classes

Social class is a complex concept that centers on the distribution of economic resources. That is, when a number of individuals occupy the same relative economic rank in the stratification system, they form a **social class.** A significant question is: Does economic ranking place people in an identifiable class to which they identify and share common interests with the other members or is the designation a fuzzy one? The dominant view is that there are no clear class boundaries, except perhaps those delineating the highest and lowest classes. A social class is not a homogeneous group, given the diversity within it, yet there is some degree of identification with other people in similar economic situations. Also, people have a sense of who is superior, equal, and inferior to them. This is evidenced in patterns of deference and feelings of comfort or uneasiness during interaction. Similarly, there tend to be commonalities in lifestyles and tastes (e.g., consumption patterns, childraising patterns, the role of women) among people in a similar economic position. But even though we can make fairly accurate generalizations about people in a social class, the heterogeneity within it precludes accurate predictions about each person included. In the words of Barbara Ehrenreich:

> Class is a notion that is inherently fuzzy at the edges. When we talk about class, we are making a generalization about large groups of people, and about how they live and make their livings. Since there are so many borderline situations, and since people do move up and down between classes, a description like middle class may mean very little when applied to a particular individual. But it should tell us something about the broad terrain of inequality, and about how people are clustered, very roughly, at different levels of comfort, status, and control over their lives. (Ehrenreich, 1989:13)

Sociologists agree that there are social classes and that money is a central criterion for classification, but they disagree on the meaning of social classes for people. For example, in contrast to the prevailing view that social classes are generally correlated with the society's income distribution and that their boundaries are inherently fuzzy, there is the opposing view that society is divided into conflicting classes with definite boundaries, each of which has a common interest. These two models of social class represent the views of the order model and the conflict model. Although this oversimplifies the debate, we examine these two theoretical ways to conceptualize social class. Let's examine these two positions and the resulting social-class structure that results from each approach (the following discussion is dependent on Wright, et al., 1982; Liazos, 1985:228–234; Vanneman and Cannon, 1987; Sanderson, 1988: 191–195; and Lucal, 1994).

The Order Model's Conception of Social Class

Order theorists use the terms *income, occupation,* and *education* as the fundamental indicators of social class, with *occupation* as central. Occupational placement determines income, interaction patterns, opportunity, and lifestyle. Lifestyle is the key dependent variable. Each social class is viewed as having its distinct culture. There are believed to be class-specific values, attitudes, and motives that distinguish its members from other classes. These orientations stem from income level and especially from occupational experiences (Collins, 1988:29). From this perspective, "*how* people get the money and *what* they do with it is as important (perhaps even more important than) as *how much* they have" (Liazos, 1985:230).

The typical class system from the order perspective has these classes, distributed in an income and status hierarchy.

1. *Upper-Upper Class.* Sometimes referred to as "the old rich," the members of this class are wealthy, and because they have held this wealth for several generations, they have a strong ingroup solidarity. They belong to exclusive clubs and attend equally exclusive boarding schools. Their children intermarry, and the members vacation together in posh, exclusive resorts around the world (Domhoff, 1970; Baltzell, 1958; Mills, 1959).

2. *Lower-Upper Class.* The wealth of the members is of relatively recent origin (hence, the term the *new rich*). The new rich differ from the old rich in prestige, but not necessarily in wealth. Great wealth alone does not ensure acceptance by the elite as a social equal. The new rich are not accepted because they differ from the old rich in behaviors and lifestyles. The new rich is composed of the self-made wealthy. These families have amassed fortunes typically through business ventures or because of special talent in music, sport, or other form of entertainment. Additionally, some professionals (doctors, lawyers) may become wealthy because of their practice and/or investments. Finally, a few persons may become very wealthy by working their way to the top executive positions in corporations, where high salaries and lucrative stock options are common.

3. *Upper-Middle Class.* The key distinguishing feature of this class is high-prestige (but not necessarily high-income) jobs that require considerable formal education and have a high degree of autonomy and responsibility. This stratum is composed largely of professional people, executives, and business people. They are self-made, having accomplished their relatively high status through personal education and occupational accomplishments.

4. *Lower-Middle Class.* These are white-collar workers (as opposed to manual workers) who work primarily in minor jobs in bureaucracies. They work, for example, as secretaries, clerks, salespeople, police officers, and teachers.

5. *Upper-Lower Class.* These people work at repetitive jobs with little autonomy that require no creativity. They are blue-collar workers who, typically, have no education beyond high school. They are severely blocked from upward mobility.

6. *Lower-Lower Class.* This class is composed of unskilled laborers whose formal education is often less than high school. The chronically unemployed are in this class. When they do work, it is for low wages, no fringe benefits, and no job security. Minority-group members—African Americans, Puerto Ricans, Mexican Americans, Native Americans—are disproportionately found in this category. These persons are looked down on by all others in the community. They live on the other side of the tracks. They are considered by other people to be undesirable as playmates, friends, organization members, or marriage partners. Lower-lowers are thought to have a culture of poverty—that is, their presumed traits of laziness, dependence, and immorality, which because they are opposite of good middle-class virtues, lock them into their inferiority.

The Conflict Model's Conception of Social Class

The conception of social class presented by the order theorists has important insights. As Liazos, a conflict theorist, has put it:

> Only a fool would deny that occupation, education, and the various "life-style" qualities (speech, dress, leisure activities, etc.) define a person's class. They do matter to people, and we do distinguish one person or family from another by the kind of work they do, where they went to school, and so on. (Liazos, 1985:230–231)

Conflict theorists, however, argue that order theorists understate the centrality of money in determining where people fall in the class system. "Where people live, how much education they receive, what they do to earn an income (or if they do not need to earn an income), who they associate with, and so forth, depend on how much money their families earn or have" (Liazos, 1985:231). Conflict theorists, in contrast to order theorists, focus on money and power, rather than on lifestyle. Again, turning to Liazos:

> In capitalist societies, the greatest class division is between the few who own and run corporations . . . and the rest of the people. This is not to say that all other people belong to one class; obviously they do not. But it is to say that the one million or so people who belong to the families that own, control, and profit by the largest corporations differ fundamentally from the rest of us. It is their *power and wealth* that essentially distinguish them from the rest of society, not their speech, dress, education, leisure activities, and so on. (Liazos, 1985:231)

Conflict theorists also differ from order theorists in how they view occupation as a criterion for social class. A social class, in this view, is not a cluster of similar occupations but, rather, a number of individuals who occupy a similar position within the social relations of economic production (Wright, et al., 1982). In other words, what is important about social classes is that they involve relationships of domination and subordination that are made possible by the systematic control of society's scarce resources. The key, then, is not the occupation itself but the control one has over one's own work, the work of others, decision making, and investments. People who own, manage, oppress, and control must be distinguished from those who are managed, oppressed and controlled (Eshleman, 1988:216).

Using these three criteria—money, relation to the means of production, and power—conflict theorists tend to distinguish five classes.

1. *Ruling Class.* The people in this class hold most of the wealth and power in society. The richest 1 percent own more wealth ($3.6 trillion in 1992) than the bottom 90 percent ($3.4 trillion). But the ruling class is smaller than the richest 1 percent. These are the few who control the corporations, banks, media, and politics. They are the very rich. According to Forbes (1996), there were 135 billionaires in 1996 (up from 96 in 1995). The top two—Bill Gates and Warren Buffett—had a combined fortune between them of $33.5 billion. The key is that the families and individuals in the ruling class own, control, govern, and rule the society. They control capital, markets, labor, and politics. In Marxist terms, the great wealth held by the ruling class is extracted from the labor of others.

2. *Professional-Managerial Class.* Four categories of persons are included in this class—managers, supervisors, professionals in business firms, and professionals outside business but whose mental work aids business.

   The most powerful managers are those near the top of the organizational charts who have broad decision-making powers and responsibilities. They have considerable power over the workers below them. In the words of Vanneman and Cannon:

   > As firms grew, an army of managers, professionals, and white-collar employees took over some of the managerial functions previously reserved for capitalists alone. These salaried officials work for owners of productive property, just as blue-collar workers do, but earn generous incomes and enjoy substantial prestige. And—what is crucial for a *class* analysis—the new middle class also shares in some of the *power* that capital has exercised over workers. (Vanneman and Cannon, 1987:53)

   There are also lower-level managers, forepersons, and other supervisors. They have less training than do the organizational managers, have limited authority, and are extensively controlled by top and middle managers. These people hold a contradictory class position. They have some control over others, which places them in this category, but their limited supervision of the routine work of others puts them close to the working class. The key for inclusion in this class, though, is that the role of supervisor places the individual with the interests of management in opposition to the working class (Vanneman and Cannon, 1987:55; see also Poulantzas, 1974:14). As Randall Collins has argued:

   > The more one gives orders, the more one identifies with the organizational ideals in whose name one justifies the orders, and the more one identifies with one's formal position, the more opposed they are to the interests of the working class. (Collins, 1988:31)

Another social category within this class includes professionals employed by business enterprises. These professionals (doctors, lawyers, engineers, accountants, inspectors) have obtained their position through educational attainment, expertise, and intellect. Unlike the ruling class, these professionals do not own the major means of production, but rather they work for the ruling class. They do not have supervisory authority, but they influence how workers are organized and treated within the organization. They are dominated by the ruling class, although this is mediated somewhat by the dependence of the elite on their specialized knowledge and expertise (for an extended discussion of this growing class, see Ehrenreich, 1989).

Finally, there are professionals who have substantial control over workers' lives but who are not part of business enterprises. Their mental labor exists outside the corporation but nonetheless their services control workers. Included in this category are social workers, who are responsible for ensuring that the unemployed and poor do not disrupt the status quo (Piven and Cloward, 1993). Educators serve as gatekeepers, sifting and sorting people for good and bad jobs, which gives them enormous power over workers and their children (Vanneman and Cannon, 1987:76). Doctors keep workers healthy, and psychologists provide help for troubled people and seek to bring deviants back into the mainstream where they can function normally. Vanneman and Cannon argue that these professionals outside business belong in the same social class as those professionals working directly for business.

> If [this class] is defined by the control it exerts over other people, then, it necessarily incorporates the social worker, teacher, and doctor as well as the first-line supervisor and plant manager. What the social worker, teacher, and doctor share with the engineer, accountant, and personnel officer is a specialization of mental labor: they all plan, design, and analyze, but their plans, designs, and analyses are largely executed by others. (Vanneman and Cannon, 1987:76)

3. *Small Business Owners.* The members of this class are entrepreneurs who own businesses that are not major corporations. They may employ no workers (thus, exploiting no labor power) or a relative few. The income and power over others by members of this class vary considerably.

4. *Working Class.* The members of this class are the workers in factories, restaurants, offices, and stores. They include both white-collar and blue-collar workers. White-collar workers are included because they, like blue-collar workers, do not have control over other workers or even over their own lives (Vanneman and Cannon, 1987:11). The distinguishing feature of this class is that they sell their labor power to capitalists and earn their income through wages. Their economic well-being depends on decisions made in corporate board rooms and by managers and supervisors. They are closely supervised by other people. They take orders. This is a crucial criterion for inclusion in the working class, because "the more one takes orders, the more one is alienated from organizational ideals" (Collins, 1988:31). Thus, they are clearly differentiated from classes whose members identify with the business firms for which they work.

5. *Poor.* These people work for minimum wages and/or are unemployed. They do society's dirty work for low wages. At the bottom in income, security, and authority, they are society's ultimate victims of oppression and domination.

Erik Olin Wright and his colleagues (1982) made an empirical investigation of the U.S. class structure using the conflict approach. Among their results are several interesting findings. First, it is incorrect to rank occupations, as order theorists do, because within the various occupational categories there are managers/supervisors *and* workers. In other words, workers in white-collar jobs can be divided into managers and workers (proletariat). So, too, in jobs for laborers, operatives, and unskilled services.

> There is a long tradition in sociology of arguing over whether or not lower white-collar jobs should be considered in the working-class or the "middle-class." Usually it is assumed in such debates that occupations as such can appropriately be grouped into classes, the issue being where a specific occupation ought to be located. . . . if classes are conceptualized in relational terms, this is not even the correct way to pose the problem. Instead, the empirical question is the extent of proletarianization within different occupational categories. (Wright, et al., 1982: 720)

Second, social class is closely related to gender and race. Wright and his associates found that women are more proletarianized, regardless of occupational category, than are men (54 percent occupying working-class locations compared with only 40 percent for men). Similarly, 64 percent of all Blacks are in the working class compared with only 44 percent of Whites.

> If we examine the combined race–sex–class distributions, we see that black women are the most proletarianized of all: 65 percent of black women in the labor force are in the working class, compared to 64 percent of black men, 52 percent for white women, and only 38 percent for white men. (Wright, et al., 1982:724)

Summary: Class from the Order and the Conflict Perspectives

Vanneman and Cannon have summarized the fundamental differences between the order and the conflict views of social class.

> In the [conflict] vision, class divides society into two conflicting camps that contend for control: workers and bosses, labor and capital, proletariat workers and bourgeoisie [middle class]; in this dichotomous image, classes are bounded, identifiable collectivities, each one having a common interest in the struggle over control of society. In the [order] vision, class sorts out positions in society along a many-runged ladder of economic success and social prestige; in this continuous image, classes are merely relative rankings along the ladder: upper class, lower class, upper-middle class, "the Toyota set," "the BMW set," "Brahmins," and the dregs "from the other side of the tracks." People are busy climbing up (or slipping down) these social class ladders, but there is no collective conflict organized around the control of society. (Vanneman and Cannon, 1987:39)

These radically different views on social class should not obscure the insights that both views provide for the understanding of this complex phenomenon. Occupation is critical to both, but for very different reasons. For the order theorist, occupations vary in how people evaluate them; some occupations are clearly superior to others in status. Thus, the perceptions of occupations within a population indicate clearly that there is a prestige hierarchy among them and the individuals identified with them.

The conflict theorist also focuses on occupations, but without reference to prestige. Where a person is located in the work process determines the degree of control that individual has over others and himself or herself. The key to determining class position is whether one gives orders or takes orders. Moreover, this placement determines one's fundamental interests, because one is either advantaged (living off the labor of others) or is disadvantaged (oppressed). Empirically, both of these views mesh with reality.

Second, order theorists focus on commonalities in lifestyles among individuals and families similar in education, income, and occupation. These varying lifestyles are real. There are differences in language use, tastes for music and art, interior decorating, dress, childrearing practices, and the like (see Fussell, 1983). Although real, the emphasis on lifestyle misses the essential point, according to conflict theorists. For them, lifestyle is not central to social class; giving or taking orders is. This is why there is disagreement on where, for example, to place lower-level white-collar workers, such as clerks and secretaries. Order theorists place them in the middle class because the prestige of their occupations is higher than those of blue-collar workers and because their work is mental rather than manual. Conflict theorists, on the other hand, place them with workers who take orders, that is, in the worker class.

Conflict theorists also point to two important implications of the emphasis on lifestyle. First, although culture is a dependent variable (that is, it is a consequence of occupation, income, and education), the culture of a social class is assumed to have a power over its members that tends to bind them to their social class (e.g., the culture of poverty is believed to keep the poor poor—see Chapters 7, 9, and 11). A second implication is the implicit assumption that these cultures are themselves ranked with the culture of the higher classes being the more valued. Conflict theorists have the opposite bias—they view the denigration of society's losers as blaming the victim. From this perspective, the higher the class, the more the members are guilty of oppressing and exploiting the labor of those below. In short, there is a strong tendency among conflict theorists to identify with the plight of underdogs and to label pejoratively the behaviors of topdogs.

Finally, each view of social class is useful for the understanding of social phenomena. The order model's understanding of inequality in terms of prestige and lifestyle differences has led to research that has found interesting patterns of behaviors by social location, which is one emphasis of sociology. Similarly, the focus of the order model has resulted in considerable research on mobility, mobility aspirations, and the like, which is helpful for the understanding of human motivation as well as the constraints on human behavior. The conflict model, on the other hand, examines inequality from differences in control—control over society, community, markets, labor, others, and oneself. The resulting class division is useful for understanding conflict in society—strikes, lockouts, political repression, social movements, and revolutions.

The Consequences of Social Class Position

Regardless of the theoretical position, there is no disagreement on the proposition that one's wealth is the determining factor in a number of crucial areas, including the chance to live and the chance to obtain those things (for example, possessions, education) that are highly valued in society. As discussed in Chapter 9, **life chances** refers to the chances throughout one's life cycle to live and to experience the good things in life. These chances are dependent almost exclusively on the economic circumstances of the family into which one is born. Gerth and Mills have contended that life chances refer to

> everything from the chance to stay alive during the first year after birth to the chance to view fine art, the chance to remain healthy and grow tall, and if sick to get well again quickly, the chance to avoid becoming a juvenile delinquent—and very crucially, the chance to complete an intermediary or higher educational grade. (Gerth and Mills, 1953:313)

Physical Health

Economic position has a great effect on how long one will live or in a crisis who will be the last to die. For instance, the official casualty lists of the trans-Atlantic luxury liner, the *Titanic,* which rammed an iceberg in 1912, listed 3 percent of the first-class female passengers as lost; 16 percent of the second-class female passengers drowned, and among the third-class females 45 percent were drowned (Lord, 1955:107). Apparently, even in a disaster, socioeconomic position makes a real difference—the higher the economic status of the individual, the greater the probability of survival.

The greater advantage toward longer life by the well-to-do is not limited to disasters such as the *Titanic.* A consistent research finding is that health and death are influenced greatly by social class.

Economic disadvantage is closely associated with health disadvantages. Put another way: "How people live, get sick, and die depends not only on their race and gender, but primarily on the class to which they belong" (Navarro, 1991:2). The poor are more likely than the affluent to suffer from certain forms of cancer (cancers of the lung, cervix, and esophagus), from hypertension, infant mortality, disabilities, and infectious diseases (especially influenza and tuberculosis). The affluent live longer, and when stricken with a disease they are more likely to survive than are the poor. For example, a study of 4,750 women with breast cancer found that those without insurance or on Medicaid were more likely to be diagnosed with cancer after it had progressed beyond a curable stage than were women with private insurance. "But even when it is detected in earlier, treatable stages, uninsured women are 66 percent more likely to die of the disease than women with private insurance. The increased risk for women on Medicaid is 40 percent" (reported in the *Wall Street Journal,* 1992a). Similarly, the American Cancer Society has reported that the cancer survival rate for people living below the poverty line is 10 to 15 percent below that of other people in the United States. Moreover, about 50 percent of the people who die of cancer because their illness was not diagnosed and treated early enough are poor.

The uninsured, of course, cannot afford the costs for physicians, dentists, and hospitals, so they often do without. Poor pregnant women (26 percent of women of childbearing age have no maternity coverage), as a result, often do not receive prenatal and postnatal health care. The consequences are a high maternal death rate (typically from hemorrhage and infection) and a relatively high infant mortality rate (of the twenty industrialized countries, the United States ranks eighteenth in infant mortality).

The common belief is that the poor are accountable for their health deficiencies. That is, their lack of education and knowledge may lead to poor health practices (diet, exercise, preventive health care). The essence of this argument is that the problems of ill health that beset the poor disproportionately are a consequence of their different lifestyle. This approach, however, ignores the fundamental realities of social class—that is, privilege in the social stratification system translates both directly and indirectly into better health in several major ways (Williams, 1990).

1. The privileged live in home, neighborhood, and work environments that are less stressful. The disadvantaged are more subject to the stresses (and resulting ill health) from high crime rates, financial insecurity, marital instability, death of loved ones, exposure to unhealthy work conditions, and exposure to pollution and toxic materials in their neighborhoods.

2. The children of privilege have healthier environments in the crucial first five years of life.

3. The privileged have better access to and make better use of the health care system. The fewer the economic resources, the less likely a person will receive preventive care and early treatment.

4. The privileged have health insurance to pay for a major portion of their physician, hospital, diagnostic tests, and pharmaceutical needs. Many people in the United States, however, cannot afford health insurance and/or their employers do not provide medical insurance, resulting in some 43 million uninsured people, many of whom are children (in 1994, 10 million children had no health insurance for the entire year) (Children's Defense Fund, 1996:16).

Family Instability

Research relating socioeconomic status to family discord and marital disruption has found an inverse relationship—the lower the status, the greater the proportion of divorce or desertion. An explanation for this relationship is that lower-class families experience greater economic and job insecurity. Given the tremendous emphasis in the United States on success and achievement, lower-class persons (particularly men) tend to define themselves and to be perceived by others in the society as a failure. Such a belief will, doubtless, hinder rather than help a marriage relationship.

The Draft

Involuntary conscription into the U.S. Army—the draft system—works to the disadvantage of the uneducated. In 1969, during the Vietnam War, only 10 percent of the men drafted were college men—yet over 40 percent of college-age men go to college. The Supreme Court has further helped the educated by ruling that a person can be a conscientious objector on a basis of either religion or philosophy. Young intellectuals can use their knowledge of history, philosophy, and even sociology to argue that they should not serve. The uneducated will not have the necessary knowledge or sharpened intellect to make such a case.

For those educated young men who end up in the armed services, there is a greater likelihood of their serving in noncombat supply and administrative jobs than for non-college-educated men. Persons who can type, do bookkeeping, or know computer programming will generally be selected to do jobs in which their skills can be used. Conversely, the nonskilled will generally end up in the most hazardous jobs. The chances for getting killed while in the service are greater, therefore, for the less educated than for the college educated (Zeitlin, Lutterman, and Russell, 1977; Baskir and Strauss, 1978; Useem, 1983; Feigelson, 1982).

When the draft is not used, as is the case at present, the personnel in the lower ranks of the military come disproportionately from the disadvantaged segments of society. This occurs because the military offers a job and stability for young persons who find little or no opportunity in the job market. This is a two-edged sword for the disadvantaged. On the one hand, it offers them training and job security, but on the other hand it offers a greater likelihood that they, rather than the privileged, will die or suffer injury during combat.

Justice

The administration of justice is unequal in the United States. Low-income persons are more likely to be arrested, to be found guilty, and to serve longer sentences for a given violation than are persons in the middle and upper classes.

Why is the system of justice unjust? The affluent can afford the services of the best lawyers for their defense, detectives to gather supporting evidence, and expert witnesses such as psychiatrists. The rich can afford to appeal the decision to a series of appellate courts. The poor, on the other hand, cannot afford bail and must await trial in jail, and they must rely on court-appointed lawyers, who are usually among the least experienced lawyers in the community and who often have heavy case loads. All the evidence points to the regrettable truth that a defendant's wealth makes a significant difference in the administration of justice.

A class bias held by most citizens, including arresting officers, prosecuting attorneys, judges, and jury members, affects the administration of justice. This bias is revealed in a set of assumptions about persons according to their socioeconomic status. The typical belief is that the affluent or the children of the affluent, if lawbreakers, are basically good people whose deviance is an aberration, a momentary act of immaturity. Thus, a warning will suffice or, if the crime is serious, a short sentence is presumed to cause enough humiliation to bring back their naturally conforming ways. Lawbreaking by the poor, on the other hand, is more troublesome and must be punished harshly, because these are essentially bad people and their deviance will persist if tolerated or mildly punished by the authorities.

Education

In general, life chances are dependent on wealth—they are purchased. The level of educational attainment (except for the children of the elite, where the best in life is a birthright) is the crucial determinant of one's chances of income.

Inequality of educational opportunity exists in all educational levels in many subtle and not-so-subtle ways. It occurs in the quality of education when schools are compared by district. The districts with a better tax base have superior facilities, better motivated teachers (because the districts can pay more), and better techniques than do the poorer districts. Within each school, regardless of the type of district, children are given standardized tests that have a middle-class bias. Armed with these data, children are placed in tracks according to ability. These tracks thus become discriminatory, because the lowest track is composed disproportionately of the lower socioeconomic category. These tracks are especially harmful in that they structure the expectations of the teacher.

Social Mobility

This section analyzes the degree of social mobility in society. This emphasis fits with the order model. It assumes that status (as opposed to class) differences are gradations, corresponding with occupation. Moreover, there is the assumption that a high degree of social mobility exists in U.S. society, with a growing middle mass of workers enjoying a high standard of living (Knottnerus, 1987).

Societies vary in the degree to which individuals may move up in status. Probably the most rigid stratification system ever devised was the **caste system** of India. In brief, this system (1) determines status by heredity, (2) allows marriage to occur only within one's status group (endogamy), (3) determines occupation by heredity, and (4) restricts interaction among the status groups. Even the Indian caste system, however, is not totally rigid, for some mobility has been allowed under certain conditions.

In contrast to this closed stratification system, the United States has a relatively open system. Social mobility is not only permitted, but it also is part of the U.S. value system that upward mobility is good and should be the goal of all people in the United States.

The United States, however, is not a totally open system. All U.S. children have the social rank of the parents while they are youths, which, in turn has a tremendous influence on whether the child can be mobile (either upward or downward).

Social mobility refers to an individual's movement within the class structure of society. **Vertical mobility** is movement upward or downward in social class. **Horizontal mobility** is the change from one position to another of about equal prestige. The shift in occupations from electrician to plumber is an example of horizontal mobility.

Social mobility occurs in two ways. **Intergenerational mobility** refers to vertical movement comparing a daughter with her mother or a son with his father. **Intragenerational mobility** is the vertical movement of the individual through his or her adult life.

There are societal factors that increase the likelihood of people's vertical mobility regardless of their individual efforts. The availability of cheap and fertile land with abundant resources gave many thousands of Americans in the nineteenth century opportunities for advancement no longer present. Similarly, the arrival of new immigrants to the United States from 1880 to 1920 provided a status boost for the people already here. Economic booms and depressions obviously affect individuals' economic success. Technological changes also can provide increased chances for success as well as diminish the possibilities for those trained in occupations now obsolete. Finally, the size of one's age cohort can limit or expand opportunities for success.

The most comprehensive study of intergenerational mobility was conducted by Peter Blau and Otis Dudley Duncan (1967). Some of their conclusions are that (1) few sons of white-collar workers become blue-collar workers, (2) most mobility moves are short in distance, (3) occupational inheritance is highest for sons of professionals (physicians, lawyers, professors), and (4) the opportunities for the sons of nonprofessionals to become professionals are very small. Another study, by the Carnegie Council on children, found that only one male in five exceeds his father's social status through individual effort and achievement (De Lone, 1979).

The commonly accepted belief of people in the United States that ours is a meritocratic society is largely a myth. Equality of opportunity does not exist because (1) employers may discriminate on the basis of race, sex, or ethnicity of their employees or prospective employees; (2) educational and job training opportunities are unequal; and (3) the family has great power to enhance or retard a child's aspirations, motivation, and cognitive skills.

Education and Social Mobility

The schools play a major part in both perpetuating the meritocratic myth and legitimizing it by giving and denying educational credentials on the basis of open and objective mechanisms that sift and sort on merit. The use of IQ tests and tracking, two common devices to segregate students by cognitive abilities, are highly suspect because they label children, resulting in a positive self-fulfilling prophecy for some children and a negative one for others. Moreover, the results of the tests and the placement of children in tracks because of the tests are biased toward middle- and upper-class experiences.

Educational attainment, especially receiving the college degree, is the most important predictor of success in the United States. But a college education is becoming more difficult to obtain for the less than affluent. Consider the following trends that diminish the chances for the poor to attend college (Burd, et al., 1996):

- Tuition has risen rapidly for years, while family incomes have stagnated. Tuition at private colleges has increased 90 percent since 1980, and at public institutions by 100 percent; yet in that same period, the median family income has increased by only 5 percent.
- Federal grant programs have failed to keep up with college costs. Pell Grants were instituted by the government to help students from poor families attend college. In 1980, a Pell Grant covered 82 percent of college costs at a public college or university; in 1995 it covered 34 percent.
- The majority (70 percent) government aid to students takes the form of loans. According to Thomas Mortenson, an expert on access to college, this inhibits the poor. "People from the lowest family incomes don't use loans to substitute for grants. These people don't view loans as vehicles to opportunity, but rather as obstacles to it" (cited in Burd, et al., 1996:A11).
- Institutional scholarships have shifted their emphasis from awards based on financial need to aid based on academic achievement.
- More and more four-year schools are raising admissions standards and limiting remediation programs that help those from disadvantaged school backgrounds to attend college and overcome their academic deficiencies.

■ Affirmative action programs are being challenged in both the political and judicial arenas. The political climate favors a restriction or elimination of affirmative action. If this occurs, then minority children, who are disproportionately poor, will be increasingly denied access to higher education. This trend is occurring at the very time that racial minorities are increasing in size.

In sum, money provides access to a higher education, which in turn increases one's life chances throughout life (see Figure 10.2).

Christopher Jencks and his associates provide the most methodologically sophisticated analysis of the determinants of upward mobility in their book *Who Gets Ahead?* (Jencks, 1979). Their findings, summarized, show the following as the most important factors leading to success.

1. Family background is the most important factor. Children coming from families in the top 20 percent in income will, as adults, have incomes of 150 to 186 percent of the national average, whereas those from the bottom 20 percent will earn 56 to 67 percent of the national average.

2. Educational attainment—especially graduating from college—is very important to later success. It is not so much what one learns in school but obtaining the credentials that counts. The probability of high educational attainment is closely tied to family background.

3. Scores from intelligence tests are by themselves poor predictors of economic success. Intelligence test scores are related to family background and educa-

FIGURE 10.2

Who Went to College in 1994 by Family Income

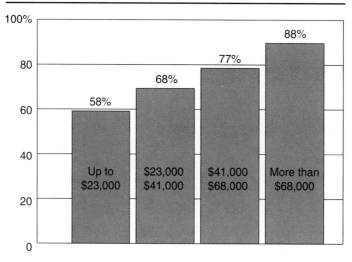

Source: Jasmine Stewart, "Who in 4 Family-Income Brackets Went to College in 1994," *The Chronicle of Higher Education* (June 14, 1996), p. A11.

tional attainment. The key remains the college degree. If people with a high IQ do not go to college, they will tend *not* to succeed economically.

4. Personality traits of high school students, more than grades and IQ, have an impact on economic success. No single trait emerges as the decisive determinant of economic success, but rather the combined effects of many different traits are found to be important. These are self-concept, industriousness (as rated by teachers), and the social skills or motivations that lead students to see themselves as leaders and to hold positions of leadership in high school.

Let's add another generalization to the list by Jencks. Not only are the financial, educational, and demographic assets of one's family important to success, but so, too, are *the assets of one's social environment*. As Fischer and his associates assert:

> The immediate neighborhood [affects] people's ways of life, whatever the family's own resources. . . . It is one thing to come from a low-income family but live in a pleasant suburb with parks, low crime, and quality schools, and another thing altogether to live in an inner-city neighborhood that lacks those supports. . . . The concentration of the disadvantaged in particular communities and particular schools undermines the fortunes of otherwise able youth. Schools in low-income and minority neighborhoods tend to lack resources and quality instruction. . . . In the local neighborhoods, similar effects occur. Low-income areas have fewer jobs, fewer resources, and poorer quality-services than do affluent ones. (Fischer, et al., 1996:83).

The picture drawn by Jencks and other experts on social mobility in the United States is of a relatively rigid society in which being born to the right family has a profound impact, especially on the probability of graduating from college. There are opportunities for advancement in society, but they are clustered among the already advantaged. If the stratification system were open with equality of opportunity, it would make sense that people, even the disadvantaged, would support it. The irony is that although the chances of the poor being successful are small, the poor tend to support the inequality generated by capitalism—truly a case of false consciousness. This irony becomes clearer as we see the consequences of inequality for individuals.

The New Downward Mobility and the Shrinking Middle Class

Throughout most of American history, children expected to do better economically than their parents, and many did. Upward mobility in every generation was a higher probability than downward mobility; but around 1973 the odds shifted.

> Sometime around 1973, the American dream stopped working. That's the year that the real (inflation-adjusted) hourly wage for nonsupervised workers—almost three-quarters of the workforce—peaked. Since then, it's fallen (with little interruption) almost 13 percent. (Henwood, 1992:195)

The median (exact middle, not average) annual income per worker in 1979 (in constant, inflation-adjusted dollars) was $25,896. In 1995, the median income was $24,700 a year ($1,126 less). In other words, over that sixteen years, those workers in the middle of the income distribution had suffered a *wage cut* of 4.6 percent.

Meanwhile, the income of those workers in the top one-third, in contrast, had incomes that *increased* by 7.9 percent. The richest 5 percent, by the way, had incomes that *expanded* by 29.1 percent (Cassidy, 1995).

Not only have wages declined since 1973, but unemployment and underemployment have become a greater threat since then as well. As corporations shut down their U.S. operations to move to other countries, merged with other business, used labor-saving technology, and downsized to expand profits, workers from the assembly-line to executive positions have lost work. If these workers found new work, often it was at lesser pay with fewer benefits, resulting, by definition, in downward social mobility.

The gap between the rich and the nonrich is wider now than at any time since the end of World War II (this is shown is Table 10.1). The top fifth of the people in the United States now earn more than the other four-fifths combined.

Tax policies have also exacerbated growing inequality in the United States. Between 1980 and 1990 there was a 16.1 percent increase in the tax burden for the poorest fifth;

> for the next fifth of households the tax increase was 6.0 percent. In sharp contrast, the richest fifth experienced a 5.5 percent *decrease* in their federal tax burden. Federal taxes *declined* 9.5 percent for the richest 5 percent and 14.4 percent for the richest 1 percent of U.S. households. And while the poorest fifth of households had a 5.2 decline in after-tax income between 1980 and 1990, the richest fifth, 5 percent, and 1 percent of U.S. households all claimed huge increases in after-tax income—32.5 percent, 50.6 percent, and 87.1 percent, respectively. (Timmer and Eitzen, 1993:4–5)

Thus, an increasing number of people in the United States have experienced declines in their purchasing power. Affording adequate health care, child care, mortgage payments, and the like has become increasingly problematic for people who once considered themselves middle class. Buying a new car, for example, is more expensive. At the end of 1994, the average cost of a new car exceeded $20,000 for the first time (Bennett, 1995). Twenty years earlier, the typical new car cost $4,400 (the equivalent of $12,800 after adjusting for inflation). Similarly, home ownership, the cornerstone of the American dream, is more costly now than two decades ago. As wages declined since 1973 the price of homes has increased much faster than inflation. So, too, with the cost of renting, at the very time those most likely to rent—young adults—saw their incomes *decrease* (Newman, 1993:34). While this problem is difficult for young White renters, it is much more so for those who face a less friendly labor market and housing discrimination.

> For minority families and single parents, the news has been worse: 98 percent of black and Hispanic families that rent could not buy a median-priced home; 97 percent of single women with children were in the same position. (Newman, 1993:38)

Two fundamental reasons explain why the current period is the first in American history in which the rate of downward mobility exceeds the rate of upward mobility. The first is demographic—the baby-boom generation, immigration, and the many women entering the work force have crowded the labor market. The unprecedented numbers competing for ever-scarcer jobs in the past fifteen years have depressed wages and family income.

Since 1973 downward mobility has exceeded upward mobility. The most important source of downward pressure is the structural transformation of the economy.

Although demography accounts for some of the problem, the second and more important source of downward pressure is the structural transformation of the economy (see Chapter 8). Computer chip technology has replaced workers. The massive shift away from traditional manufacturing to high technology and service industries has eliminated relatively high-wage jobs and created job opportunities in low-wage, part-time, and contingent jobs. As this shift has accelerated, the share of jobs providing a middle-class standard of living has shrunk. The moving of plants to low-wage regions of the country or to other countries further depresses wages. So, too, the foreign competition that produces goods that undersell U.S. products results in lower wages. Unions have acquiesced to these pressures by lowering their demands, making concessions, and even in some instances accepting a two-tiered wage scale in which the newly hired are paid considerably lower wages than workers hired earlier for the same work.

Poverty in the United States

What separates the poor from the nonpoor? In a continuum there is no absolute standard for wealth. The line separating the poor from the nonpoor is necessarily arbitrary. The Social Security Administration (SSA) sets the official poverty line based on what it considers the minimal amount of money required for a subsistence level of life. To determine the poverty line, the SSA computes the cost of a basic nutritionally adequate diet and multiplies that figure by three. This figure is based on a government research finding that poor people spend one-third of their income on food. Thereafter, the poverty level was readjusted annually by the Consumer Price Index to account for inflation. If we use this standard ($12,158 for a nonfarm family of three, $15,569 for a family of four) in 1995, 13.8 percent of the population

(36.4 million persons) were defined as living in poverty (the data on poverty in this section were taken from U.S. Bureau of the Census, 1996). (See Figure 10.3 for the poverty trend from 1959 to 1995.) Many were pleased in 1996 when it was reported that the poverty rate in 1995 declined to 13.8 percent from 14.5 percent. However, it is important to note the size of the poverty population. Michael Gartner (1996:13A) reports that 36.4 million (the poverty population) is "the equivalent of every man, woman, and child in the 25 largest cities in America" or seen another way, it is "the equivalent of every man, woman, and child in the District of Columbia and 23 states."

The following discussion considers the poor as people below this arbitrary line, realizing that it actually minimizes the extent of poverty in the United States. Schwarz and Volgy (1993), for example, argue that a new procedure is needed because the official definition of poverty has not kept up with ever-increasing costs for housing, medical costs, and taxes. If the government applied the formula to measure the cost of necessities (medical, utilities, and housing, not just food), the poverty line would be 50 percent higher and more than 60 million Americans would be counted as poor (see "Human Agency: Coping Strategies among the Poor").

Exact figures on the number of poor are difficult to determine. For one thing, the amount of money needed for subsistence varies drastically by locality. Compare, for example, the money needed for rent in New York City with that needed in rural

FIGURE 10.3

Poverty 1959–1995

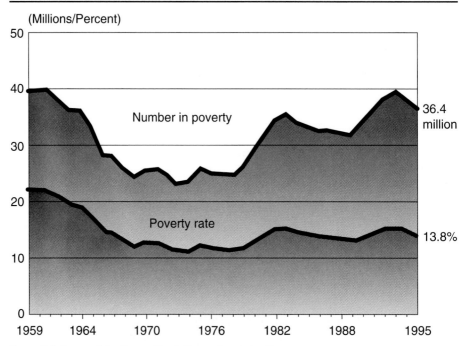

Source: U.S. Bureau of the Census, March Current Population Survey.

AGENCY

Coping Strategies among the Poor

The lot of poor people is difficult, to say the least. If the poor receive welfare, the benefits are insufficient to meet minimal needs of food, clothing, and shelter. Suitable housing in cities is especially difficult to obtain because rents are, typically, beyond the reach of the poor. Food, clothing, banking, and other purchases/services are more expensive in the inner cities than elsewhere. How do poor people deal with the lack of money to deal with exigencies of living?

Some do not do well at all. Some are forced to live in housing that is dangerous (exposure to the cold, lead, rats, and sewage; unsafe structures that defy city building codes). Some cannot even afford those dangerous places and must live on the streets or in homeless shelters. Some are malnourished because they cannot afford enough nutritious food. Many go without visits to doctors and dentists because the cost is beyond their means or the services are unavailable.

Other poor people do better through various coping strategies. Those with family or close friendship networks may share housing costs by doubling or tripling up. They may share child care to free parents to work. Families may go together to buy food in bulk at cheaper prices. And, they pool their resources in many other creative ways to manage the stresses and strains of poverty.

There are also a few organized networks that have emerged in various inner cities (St. Louis, Miami, Chicago, New York City, Cleveland, and Norfolk, Virginia). In the case of inner-city St. Louis, several thousand people are engaged in a barter economy where people short of cash can exchange their labor/expertise for that of others *without* using money. Individuals earn credit ("time dollars") by cleaning, painting, providing child care, delivery of goods, or repairing appliances, which can be exchanged for other services or even goods (food, clothing) that have been donated to the network. This plan has two major benefits: (1) It cushions the harshness of poverty by getting the goods and services to the people who need them; and (2) it creates a sense of community among the powerless, which may, ultimately, lead to power as collectively those in the network work together for common goals.

Sources: Peter T. Kilborn, "Build a Better Welfare System, and the World . . ." *Denver Post* (September 29, 1996):17A; Michael Hudson, *Merchants of Misery* (Monroe, ME: Common Courage Press, 1996); and Doug A. Timmer, D. Stanley Eitzen, and Kathryn D. Talley, *Paths to Homelessness: Extreme Poverty and the Urban Housing Crisis* (Boulder, CO: Westview, 1994).

Arkansas. Another difficulty is that the people most likely to be missed by the U.S. Census are the poor. They live in ghettos (where several families may be crowded into one apartment) or in rural areas, where some homes are inaccessible and where some workers follow the harvest from place to place and therefore have no permanent home. Transients of any kind may also be missed by the census.

The conclusion is inescapable that the proportion of the poor in the United States is underestimated, because the poor tend to be invisible, even to the government. This underestimate of the poor has important consequences, because U.S. Census data are the basis for political representation in Congress. These data are also used as the basis for instituting new governmental programs or abandoning old ones. Needless to say, an accurate count of the total population is necessary if the census is so used.

Despite these difficulties and the understanding of actual poverty by the government's poverty line, we do know some facts about the poor.

Racial Minorities

Income in the United States, as we have discussed, is maldistributed by race. Not surprisingly, then, 29.3 percent of all African Americans were poor in 1995, as were 30.3 percent of all Latinos, and 14.6 percent of all Asian Americans compared to only 8.5 percent of non-Hispanic Whites. Latinos replaced African Americans as the racial group with the highest poverty rate for the first time in 1994 (see Figure 10.4). Several facts regarding the Latino population should lead to an increase in this gap. First, Latinos tend to be much younger than Whites or Blacks generally, making them more likely to be newer to the work force and therefore among the lowest paid. Second, they tend to be concentrated in the lowest segment of the labor market, where pay is at or near the minimum wage regardless of longevity. Third, high unemployment is prominent in geographical areas heavily populated by Latinos. Fourth, Latinos are lagging behind Blacks in education. In 1995, only 57 percent of young Latinos had completed high school, as compared to 87 percent of young Black adults (Holmes, 1996). Also, Latinos are overrepresented among new immigrants, and the 1996 welfare legislation specifically denies immigrants federal supports for the first five years in this country. Finally, Latinos tend to have larger families than do Whites or Blacks, and Latino two-parent families are more likely than those in the other two racial groups to have just one wage earner.

Native Americans have about the same poverty rate as African Americans (Snipp, 1992). As with other racial categories, though, there is a wide variation among Native Americans, with some in the middle class, some poor, and some extremely poor. In the latter category are the 25 percent of Native Americans who live on reservations. Their poverty rates and unemployment tend to be very high, health problems rampant, and educational attainment comparatively low (Ropers,

FIGURE 10.4

Poverty Rates

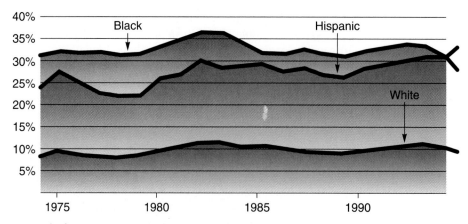

Percentage of population below poverty level, 1974–1994

Source: Clarifying Issues '96 (New York: Public Agenda, 1996), p. 39.

1991:49–50). On the Pine Ridge Reservation in South Dakota, for example, the poverty rate was 63.1 percent in 1991 (Kanamine, 1992).

Despite the overrepresentation of racial minorities among the poor, it is important to note that Whites have the highest numbers of people living below the poverty line. White poor, for example, outnumber the Black poor by more than two to one.

Women

Two out of three impoverished adults in the United States are women, a consequence of the prevailing institutional sexism in society that, with few exceptions, provides poor job and earnings opportunities for women. "Women working full time, year round, still earn only 72 cents for every dollar earned by men. They don't pay 72 cents on the dollar for rent, food, child care, or anything else" (Sklar, 1995b:21). This gender disparity, combined with the high frequency of marital disruption and the number of never-married women with children, has resulted in the high probability of women who head families being poor (in 1994, 34.6 percent of single-parent families headed by women were poor, compared to a poverty rate of only 6.1 percent for two-parent families).

This trend, termed the **feminization of poverty** (see Pearce, 1978; Ehrenreich and Stallard, 1982; Stallard, Ehrenreich, and Sklar, 1983), implies that the relatively large proportion of poor women is a new phenomenon in U.S. society. Thus, the term obscures the fact that women have always been more economically vulnerable than men, especially older women and women of color. But when women's poverty was mainly limited to these groups, their economic deprivation was mostly invisible. The plight of women's poverty became a visible problem when the numbers of White women in poverty increased rapidly in the past decade or so with ris-

Two out of three impoverished adults in the United States are women.

ing marital disruption. Even with the growing numbers of poor White women, the term *feminization of poverty* implies that all women are at risk when actually the probability of economic deprivation is much greater for certain categories of women. The issue, then, is not gender but class, race, and gender (Burnham, 1986).

Race and gender contribute independently to the poverty equation. "The black woman, with two strikes against her, is almost three times more likely to be poor as is a white woman. And an Hispanic woman is two and a half times more likely to be poor" (Shortridge, 1989:486).

Children

The nation's poverty rate was 13.8 percent in 1995, but the rate for children was 20.8 percent for those under age eighteen and 24.0 percent for those under six years of age. Of related children under age six living in families with a female house-holder, 63.7 percent were poor, compared to 12.3 percent of such young children in married-couple families. African American children (43.8 percent) and Latino children (41.5 percent) are far more likely than White children (16.9 percent) to live in poverty. "Despite the disproportionate burden of child poverty among minorities, however, the majority of America's poor children (9.3 million) are White" (Children's Defense Fund, 1996:2).

Especially noteworthy is that: "The United States has the highest youth poverty rate of any Western nation" (Males, 1994:18).

Elderly

Contrary to popular belief, the elderly as a category have a lower poverty rate (10.5 percent in 1995) than the general population (13.8 percent). In fact, there are four times as many children as elderly people living in poverty in the United States. This seeming anomaly is the result of government programs for the elderly being indexed for inflation, whereas many welfare programs targeted for the young were reduced or eliminated, especially since 1980. Two categories of the elderly are especially vulnerable to poverty—women and people living alone. Also, while the poverty rate for the elderly is relatively low, this disguises the fact that a large proportion of them are near-poor. That is, a higher proportion of elderly (7 percent) than nonelderly (4 percent) are concentrated just above the poverty line.

Place

Poverty is not randomly distributed geographically; it tends to cluster in certain places. Regionally, the area with highest poverty is the South, followed in order by the West, Midwest, and Northeast. The states with the highest poverty rates in 1995 were New Mexico (25.3 percent), Mississippi (23.5 percent), Alabama (20.1 percent), South Carolina (19.9 percent), and Louisiana (19.7 percent). Each of these states has a disproportionate number of racial minorities and has a higher rural population than urban population. The states with the lowest poverty rates were New Hampshire (5.3 percent), Alaska (7.1 percent), New Jersey (7.8 percent), Utah (8.4 percent), and Wisconsin (8.5 percent).

There are twenty-five counties in the United States with more than 45 percent of their people living below the poverty line, with two counties exceeding 60 percent (Shannon in South Dakota, where the Pine Ridge reservation is located, and Starr in Texas, which is predominantly Latino) (Kanamine, 1992).

In metropolitan areas the poverty rate is higher in the central cities (20.6 percent) than in suburban areas (9.1 percent). People living on farms have a higher rate of poverty than does the nonfarm population.

There are important differences between the rural and the urban poor. The rural poor have some advantages (low-cost housing, raising their own food) and many disadvantages (low-paid work, higher prices for most products, fewer social services, fewer welfare benefits) as compared with the urban poor (Maharidge, 1992). As a result, "the rural poor are more likely than the urban poor to be long-term poor" (O'Hare and Curry-White, 1992:6).

Poverty is greatest among those who do not have an established residence. People in this classification are typically the homeless and migrant workers. The homeless, estimated between half a million and 3 million, are those in extreme poverty—they are the poorest of the poor (see Timmer, Eitzen, and Talley, 1994). The other category, migrant workers, are believed to be about 3 million adults and children who are seasonal farm laborers working sporadically for low wages and no benefits. It is estimated that about 50 percent of all farm workers live below the official poverty line and this percentage has not changed since the 1960s (Cunningham, 1994). "The average migrant worker is a twenty-eight-year-old male, born in Mexico, who earns about $5,000 a year for twenty-five weeks of farm work. His life expectancy is forty-nine years" (Schlosser, 1995:82).

Finally, the United States, when compared to other major industrialized democracies, has more poverty, more severe poverty, and supports its poor people least. A study by the Joint Center for Political and Economic Studies found that

> the United States stands in ignominious isolation. Among industrialized countries, the United States has the highest incidence of poverty among the non-elderly and the widest distribution of poverty across all age and family groups. It is also the only western democracy that has failed to give a significant portion of its poor a measure of income security. (Cited in Albelda, 1991:20)

The Poor-Poor

The poor-poor are people living at or below half the poverty line (the following is taken from Whitman, 1990). About 5 percent of the people living in the United States live below *half* the poverty line. Some facts about these people, who are among the poorest of the poor, are:

- 44 percent are children under 18.
- 34 percent are African Americans and 17 percent are Latinos.
- Six of ten live in female-headed families.
- Only two of five are on welfare.

This category of the poor-poor has increased by almost 50 percent since 1979. This upsurge in the truly destitute occurred because: (1) Many of the poor-poor live in rural areas that have prospered less than other regions; (2) a decline in marriage (and a rise in divorce) resulted in a substantial increase in single mothers and unattached men; and (3) public assistance benefits, especially in the South, have steadily declined since 1980.

Myths About Poverty

What should be the government's role in caring for its less fortunate residents? Much of the debate on this important issue among politicians and citizens is based on erroneous assumptions and misperceptions.

Refusal to Work

To begin, we must recognize that half of the poor are not in the working ages. About 40 percent are under age 18 and another 10 percent are at least 65. Several facts belie the faulty assumption that poor people refuse to work. In 1994, nearly 6 million adults ages 18 to 64 worked at least half of the year yet were officially poor. Another 3 million poor adults worked less than 26 of the weeks in 1994. Poverty expert William P. O'Hare says:

> The existence of the working poor belies two common beliefs: (1) that people are poor because they do not, or will not, work and (2) that people who work will not be poor.
>
> The erosion of salaries, particularly in low-wage occupations, has pushed more working people into poverty over the past few decades. The share of workers earning below-poverty wages expanded from 24 percent in 1973 to 30 percent in 1995. (O'Hare, 1996:10)

The lot of the working poor is similar to that of the nonworking poor on some dimensions and worse on others (Newman, 1996). They do society's dirty work for low pay and no benefits. Like the poor, they live in substandard housing and their children go to underfinanced schools. They are poor but, unlike the nonworking poor, they are not eligible for many government supports such as subsidized housing, medical care, and food stamps.

Welfare Dependency

About three-fourths of the poor received some type of welfare in 1994 (Medicaid, food stamps), but only about 40 percent received cash welfare payments (O'Hare, 1996:11). As of 1996, welfare policies, however, changed, resulting in lower benefits (see "A Closer Look: The New Welfare Policy: A Critique").

Several facts demythologize the notion that welfare creates a cycle of dependency. First, the poverty population changes—that is, people move in and out of poverty every year. The average welfare recipient stays on welfare less than two years (Sklar, 1992:10). Only 12 percent of the poor remain poor for five or more consecutive years (O'Hare, 1996:11).

the Welfare Line

Z Magazine (*March 1994*), p 11.

Second, two out of three children whose parents received welfare do not receive them as adults.

Third, welfare is inadequate to meet the needs of the poor, falling far short. One study found that, on average, welfare mothers who do not receive housing subsidies (more than two-thirds do not) fell $519 short of meeting their monthly expenses with just the welfare benefits (Edin, 1995).

> Many poor families manage by cutting back on food, jeopardizing their health and the development of their children, or by living in substandard and sometimes dangerous housing. Some do without heat, electricity, telephone service, or plumbing for months or years. Many do without health insurance, health care, safe child care, or reliable transportation to take them to or from work. (Children's Defense Fund, cited in Sklar, 1992:10)

There is a fundamental misunderstanding by the U.S. public about where most governmental benefits are directed. We tend to assume that government monies and services go mostly to the poor (**welfare,** the receipt of financial aid and/or services from the government), when in fact the greatest government aid goes to the nonpoor ("**wealthfare,**" the receipt by the nonpoor of financial aid and/or services from the government). Most (about three-fourths) of the federal outlays for human resources go to the nonpoor, such as to all children in education programs and to most of the elderly through Social Security Retirement and Medicare. Some facts (Albelda and Folbre, 1996:18–19):

- In 1992 the federal government spent about $464 billion on entitlements that people receive regardless of their income level, such as Social Security, Medicare, and veteran's pensions. That is ten times greater than what was spent on Aid to Families with Dependent Children (AFDC) and Food Stamps that year.
- In 1994, 29 percent of families with incomes of at least $150,000 received government benefits averaging more than $16,000 through programs such as

A CLOSER LOOK

The New Welfare Policy: A Critique

During the Great Depression President Franklin Roosevelt's New Deal programs changed the fundamental relationship between the federal government and the needy. Among these programs were Social Security, Unemployment Insurance, and Aid to Families with Dependent Children (AFDC). In the 1960s the War on Poverty was initiated by President Lyndon Johnson to help poor families with programs such as Medicaid, Food Stamps, and Head Start.

During the 1980s, under Presidents Reagan and Bush, various poverty programs were gradually reduced. This erosion of welfare benefits accelerated with the election of President Clinton in 1992 and a Republican-controlled Congress in 1994. There was general agreement among the Republicans and Democrats that welfare needed to be changed dramatically. Their aim was not directed at programs for the elderly (Social Security and Medicare) nor at "wealthfare" for corporations and well-off individuals but rather at those programs for the weakest and neediest.

The rationale for dismantling the welfare state is that government efforts to reduce poverty actually cause poverty and other social problems. Welfare dependency, in this view, is the source of poverty, illegitimacy, laziness, crime, unemployment, and other social pathologies. If people were forced to go to work, there may be some hardships along the way, but this is the only way to make individuals moral and self-reliant.

Three of the major provisions of the resulting legislation were:

- *Devolution.* The new law decentralizes welfare policy through federal grants to state governments that are free (except for a few federal restrictions) to organize and run their own programs. State-run programs will likely have several problems: (1) the poor will generally receive less assistance than before; (2) the states will be uneven in their programs, some generous, some not (under the old plan, a family of four received $660 a month in New York but just $220 in Mississippi), some enlightened, some not; (3) some states may deliberately keep their benefits low to discourage poor people from settling there; (4) if the past is any guide, some states and localities will use their power to promote racial injustice; and (5) if a recession hits or there is a surge in poor families, the states, limited for the most part to their own resources, will provide less for the poor.

- *Time limits.* The new law states that welfare recipients must give up most benefits unless the

Social Security. Families with incomes of below $10,000, however, received benefits averaging less than $8,000.
- In 1992 the tax exemption for the value of employer-sponsored health insurance (that is, it is not counted as income and therefore not taxed) saved the nonpoor some $47 billion, while Medicaid spending (the government's health plan for the poor) in that year amounted to $27.5 billion.

The upside-down welfare system, with aid mainly helping the already affluent, is also accomplished by two hidden welfare systems. The first is through tax loopholes (called **tax expenditures**). Through these legal mechanisms the government officially permits certain individuals and corporations to pay lower taxes or no taxes at all. For illustration, one of the largest tax expenditure programs is the money that homeowners deduct from their taxes for real estate taxes and interest on their mort-

family head begins to work within two years. Also established was a lifetime time limit of 60 months (not necessarily consecutive) on receiving assistance. The problem with time limits is that people will be pushed off welfare *without* receiving help for child care, job training and jobs, as well as a minimum wage that would get the disadvantaged above the poverty line. Moreover, there are no federal plans to expand health care to low wage workers.

- *Ineligibility of legal immigrants.* Legal immigrants are denied most welfare benefits until they have been here five years. This is exceptionally problematic since these people are especially vulnerable to discrimination and by not knowing English and the American culture.

The 1996 welfare legislation embarks U.S. society on a huge social experiment. Will it work? Will society be safer or more dangerous? Will poverty be reduced when the pool of unskilled workers is expanded but there is no effort to create jobs for them? Will the lot of the children of the poor be improved or harmed? Evidence from other societies and sociological research suggests that the poor *and* society will be worse off. The number of people on the economic margins will rise. Reliable estimates show that this legislation will push over 3 million, including 1.1 million additional children, below the poverty line. Unemployment will surge, especially in inner-city neighborhoods where it was 30 to 50 percent *before* the welfare legislation. Homelessness will increase. Crime rates will swell. Public safety will become more problematic. The racial divide will widen. Civil unrest will intensify.

Contrary to what our politicians tell us, these grim predictions appear to be our future. They will be exacerbated even more as policymakers make further cutbacks in Medicaid, housing, legal aid, and other social services to the poor. The United States has the most meager safety net of any of the major industrialized countries. We have chosen to reduce that net even further. This decision takes us down a path where all of us, poor and nonpoor, are increasingly in peril.

Sources: William P. O'Hare, "A New Look at Poverty in America," *Population Bulletin* 51 (September 1996), pp. 3–5; Frances Fox Piven, "Welfare and the Transformation of Electoral Politics," *Dissent* 43 (Fall, 1996), pp. 61–67; Randy Albelda, "Farewell to Welfare," *Dollars and Sense,* No. 208 (November/December 1996), pp. 16–19; and D. Stanley Eitzen, "Is Dismantling the Welfare State the Solution to America's Social Problems?" *Vital Speeches of the Day* (June 15, 1996), pp. 532–536.

gages (mortgage interest is deductible on mortgages up to $1 million). In a telling irony, the government tax breaks to homeowners (over $60 billion in 1995) amount to a housing subsidy that is more than *five* times the Housing and Urban Development's budget for low-income housing. Put another way, while fewer than one-fifth of low-income Americans receive federal housing subsidies, "more than three-quarters of wealthy Americans, many living in mansions—get housing aid from Washington" (Dreier and Atlas, 1994:592).

The second hidden welfare system to the nonpoor is in the form of direct subsidies and credit to assist corporations, banks, agribusiness, defense industries, and the like. Some examples (taken from Goodgame, 1993; Nelson, 1994; Moberg, 1995):

- Business meals and entertainment are 80 percent deductible to businesses. "Tax deductible meals are virtually a federal food-stamp program for the benefit of the corporate class, since the average taxpayer enjoys no such ability to write off the cost of wining and dining" (Goodgame, 1993:36).

- Nearly half of all farm-aid programs go to farmers who earn more than $100,000 a year and who own assets worth more than $1 million. Moreover, scarce water from federal dams and irrigation projects, often worth $100 an acre-foot at market prices, sold to farmers for $7 to $25 an acre foot. If the irrigation water were sold at market rates, the government would receive $4.3 billion.
- Owners of businesses in oil, gas, and mining receive special tax breaks for depletion of mineral reserves and for the purchase of drilling and mining equipment. This saves them $1.7 billion annually. The Forest Service constructs about $140 worth of roads each year to subsidize timber companies logging on public lands.

These subsidy programs to the affluent and corporate interests amount to much more than welfare to the poor. The Cato Institute, a conservative think tank, argues that the government should cut subsidies to the wealthy by about $86 billion.

> By comparison, estimates from the Center on Budget and Policy Priorities find that total spending each year on social "welfare"—means-tested programs for recipients of Aid to Families with Dependent Children—comes to about $60 billion or less. (Moberg, 1995:25)

These subsidy programs to the non-poor transfer substantial sums primarily from the middle-class upward to large corporations and to individuals who own stock in them. Moreover, in times of budget-cutting, corporate welfare tends to be retained while that for the poor is cut. The Republican-controlled Congress acted this way in 1995:

> Republicans in Congress say balancing the federal budget is so important that the nation no longer can afford to spend $1.6 billion a year helping poor people pay their heating bills. Likewise, House Republicans say, the nation no longer can afford to spend $1.6 billion a year helping old and disabled poor people pay their rent; or $377 million on lawyers for poor people in legal trouble. . . . But both House and Senate budget plans agree that Americans still can afford to spend $1.4 billion a year subsidizing prices for big sugarcane farmers. It still can spend $2 billion a year helping high-tech companies build a space station. And oil companies still can keep a tax break to offset their "intangible" drilling expenses, which costs the Treasury about $1 billion a year. (Rankin, 1995:28A)

The Poor Get Special Advantages

The common belief is that the poor get a number of handouts for which other Americans have to work—food stamps, Medicaid, housing subsidies, and the like. As we have seen, these subsidies amount to much less than the more affluent receive, and recent legislation has reduced them more and more. Most significant, *the poor pay more than the nonpoor for many services.* This, along with low wages and paying a large proportion of their income for housing, explains why some have such difficulty getting out of poverty.

The urban poor find that their money does not go as far in the inner city. Food and commodities, for example, cost more since supermarkets, discount stores, outlet malls, and warehouse clubs have bypassed inner-city neighborhoods. Since many inner-city residents do not have transportation to get to the supermarkets and warehouse stores, they must buy from nearby stores, giving the store owners monopoly powers. As a result, the poor pay more. The New York City Department of Consumer Affairs found that groceries cost 8.8 percent more in poor neighborhoods than in middle-class areas. Similarly, a 1991 survey of Chicago found that the poor spent 18 percent more (see Timmer, Eitzen, and Talley, 1994:94–95).

Many companies, including some of the largest such as Citibank and American Express, provide financial services to approximately 60 million poor and near-poor who are shut out by banks and other conventional merchants. Thus, they provide a needed service but at an extremely high cost—230 percent interest from a rent-to-own company, 240 percent interest for a loan from a pawnbroker, 300 percent for a finance company loan, and as high as 2,000 percent for a quick "payday" loan from a check-cashing outlet (Hudson, 1996; Freedman, 1993:A1; Pascale, 1995; Berenson, 1996). A study by the National Association of Insurance Commissioners in 1994 concluded that poor people and minorities across the country have a harder time obtaining insurance and pay higher premiums than other customers (cited in Associated Press, 1994).

The conclusion is obvious: The poor pay more for commodities and services in absolute terms and they pay a much larger proportion of their incomes than the nonpoor for comparable items. Similarly, when the poor pay sales taxes on the items they purchase, the tax takes more of their resources than it does from the nonpoor, making it a **regressive tax.** Thus, efforts to move federal programs to the states will cost the poor more, since state and local taxes tend to be regressive (sales taxes), while federal taxation tends to be progressive.

Welfare Is a Black and Latino Program

The myth is that most welfare monies go primarily to African Americans and Latinos. While poverty rates are higher for Blacks and Hispanics than for other racial/ethnic groups, they do not make up the majority of the poor. Non-Hispanic Whites are the most numerous racial/ethnic groups (48 percent of the poor are White) among the poverty population, compared to 27 percent for African Americans and 22 percent of Latinos (O'Hare, 1996:11). Thus, Whites take the majority of the welfare budget. Barbara Ehrenreich states:

> . . . white folks have been gobbling up the welfare budget while blaming someone else. But it's worse than that. If we look at Social Security, which is another form of welfare, although it is often mistaken for an individual insurance program, then whites are the ones who are crowding the trough. We receive almost twice as much per capita, for an aggregate advantage to our race of $10 billion a year—much more than the $3.9 billion advantage African Americans gain from their disproportionate share of welfare. One sad reason: whites live an average of six years longer than African Americans, meaning that young black workers help subsidize a huge and growing "overclass" of white retirees. (Ehrenreich, 1991:84)

CHAPTER REVIEW

1. People in the United States vary greatly on a number of socioeconomic dimensions. Wealth and income are maldistributed. Educational attainment varies. Occupations differ greatly in prestige and pay.

2. Order theorists place individuals into social classes according to occupation. Each social class is composed of social equals who share a similar lifestyle. Each class-specific culture is assumed to have a power over its members.

3. Conflict theorists focus on money, relation to the means of production, and power as the determinants of class position. Crucial to this placement is not occupational prestige as the order theorists posit, but whether one gives orders or takes orders in the work process.

4. The consequences of one's socioeconomic status are best expressed in the concept of life chances, which refers to the chances to obtain the things highly valued in society. The data show that the higher one's economic position, the longer one's life, the healthier (physically and mentally) one will be, the more stable one's family, the less likely one will be drafted, the less likely one will be processed by the criminal justice system, and the higher one's educational attainment.

5. Societies vary in the degree to which individuals may move up in status. The most rigid societies are called *caste systems*. They are essentially closed hereditary groups. Class systems are more open, permitting vertical mobility.

6. Although the United States is a relatively open class system, the extent of intergenerational mobility (a son or daughter surpassing his or her parents) is limited.

7. The prime determinants of upward mobility appear to be (*a*) family background, (*b*) educational attainment, (*c*) graduation from college, and (*d*) personality traits.

8. In the past decade downward mobility has, for the first time in American history, exceeded upward mobility, resulting in a shrinking middle class. The two reasons for this shift are (*a*) the unprecedented numbers of baby boomers and women competing for scarce jobs, and (*b*) the structural transformation of the economy.

9. According to the government's arbitrary line, which minimizes the actual extent of poverty, in 1994, 14.5 percent of the U.S. population was officially poor. Disproportionately represented in the poor category are African Americans, Latinos, women, and children.

10. The poor are *not* poor because they refuse to work. Most adult poor either work at low wages, cannot find work, work part-time, are homemakers, are ill or disabled, or are in school.

11. Government assistance to the poor is *not* sufficient to eliminate their economic deprivation. Less than half of the poor actually receive any federal assistance. When compared with the nonpoor, their life chances are negative, with a higher incidence of health problems, malnutrition, social pathologies, and homelessness.

12. Most government assistance is targeted to the affluent rather than the poor. The nonpoor receive three-fourths of the federal monies allocated to human services. Tax expenditures and other subsidies provide enormous economic benefits to the already affluent, which further redistributes the nation's wealth upward.

13. The poor pay more than the nonpoor for services and commodities, which helps to trap them in poverty.

14. Contrary to popular belief, Whites receive more welfare than do African Americans and Latinos.

KEY TERMS

Social class
Life chances
Caste system
Social mobility
Vertical mobility

Horizontal mobility
Intergenerational mobility
Intragenerational mobility
Feminization of poverty
Welfare

Wealthfare
Tax expenditures
Regressive tax

STUDY QUESTIONS

1. What are the key differences in the conception of social class by order-model and conflict-model theorists?

2. What are the consequences of social-class position in terms of life chances?

3. What is the evidence that the gap between the haves and the have-nots is increasing in the United States?

4. To what extent is upward social mobility difficult for poor youth?

5. Which social categories are most likely to be poor? Referring to the discussion in Chapter 9, what are the fundamental reasons for the overrepresentation of these categories in the poor classification?

6. Write an essay entitled "The Poor Pay More."

FOR FURTHER READING

Randy Albelda, Nancy Folbre, and the Center for Popular Economics, *The War on the Poor: A Defense Manual* (New York: The New Press, 1996).

Children's Defense Fund, *The State of America's Children 1996* (Washington, DC: Children's Defense Fund, 1996).

Peter W. Cookson, Jr., and Caroline Hodges Persell, *Preparing for Power: America's Elite Boarding Schools* (New York: Basic Books, 1985).

Sheldon Danziger and Peter Gottschalk, *America Unequal* (Cambridge, MA: Harvard University Press, 1995).

Robert H. Frank and Philip J. Cook, *The Winner-Take-All Society* (New York: The Free Press, 1995).

Herbert J. Gans, *The War Against the Poor* (New York: Basic Books, 1995).

Irving B. Harris. *Children in Jeopardy: Can We Break the Cycle of Poverty?* (New Haven, CT: Yale University Press, 1996).

David L. Harvey, *Potter Addition: Poverty, Family, and Kinship in a Heartland Community* (New York: Aldine De Gruyter, 1993).

Michael Hudson, ed., *Merchants of Misery: How Corporate America Profits from Poverty* (Monroe, ME: Common Courage Press, 1996).

William A. Kelso, *Poverty and the Underclass: Changing Perceptions of the Poor in America* (New York: New York University Press, 1994).

Alex Kotlowitz, *There Are No Children Here: The Story of Two Boys Growing Up in the Other America* (New York: Doubleday/Anchor, 1991).

Jonathan Kozol, *Amazing Grace: The Lives of Children and the Conscience of a Nation* (New York: Crown, 1995).

Elliot Liebow, *Tell Them Who I Am: The Lives of Homeless Women* (New York: The Free Press, 1993).

Jay MacLeod, *Ain't No Makin' It: Aspirations and Attainment in a Low-Income Neighborhood,* revised edition (Boulder, CO: Westview, 1995).

Joel L. Nelson, *Post-Industrial Capitalism: Exploring Economic Inequality in America* (Thousand Oaks, CA: Sage, 1996).

Katherine S. Newman, *Declining Fortunes: The Withering of the American Dream* (New York: Basic Books, 1993).

Doug A. Timmer, D. Stanley Eitzen, and Kathryn D. Talley, *Paths to Homelessness: Extreme Poverty and the Urban Housing Crisis* (Boulder, CO: Westview, 1994).

Reeve Vanneman and Lynn Weber Cannon, *The American Perception of Class* (Philadelphia: Temple University Press, 1987).

Edward N. Wolff, *Top Heavy: A Study of the Increasing Inequality of Wealth in America* (New York: The Twentieth Century Fund Press, 1995).

Racial Inequality

In the last two decades of the twentieth century, social and economic inequalities based on race and ethnicity have reached a new urgency. The transition from a predominantly White society to a global society composed of diverse racial and ethnic minorities is exacerbating long-standing racial divisions. As racial and ethnic tensions around the world grow more intense, minorities in the United States still rank below Whites on every measure of socioeconomic status. These conditions are making race a central social and political issue of the 1990s.

Introduction

Different racial and ethnic groups are unequal in power, resources, prestige, or presumed worth. Why are some groups dominant and others subordinate? The basic reason is differential power—power derived from superior numbers, technology, weapons, property, or economic resources. The people holding superior power in a society—the **majority group**—establish a system of inequality by dominating less powerful groups, and this system of inequality is then maintained and perpetuated by power. The terms *majority* and *minority* describe the differences in power. The critical feature of the **minority group's** status is its inferior social position in which its interests are not effectively represented in the political, economic, and social institutions of the society. The term *dominant* may be used as a synonym for *majority* and *subordinate* as a synonym for *minority* (Yetman, 1991:11).

Like the class and gender hierarchies, racial and ethnic stratification is a basic feature of U.S. society. This stratification is built into society's policies and practices, which appear neutral but systematically deny equal access to power, prestige, and privilege. Normal arrangements provide privileges for Whites at the expense of Blacks, Hispanics, and other people of color.

Racial privilege, like class privilege, reaches far back into America's past. The racial hierarchy with White groups of European origin at the top and people of color at the bottom serves important functions for society and for certain categories of people. It ensures that some people are available to do society's dirty work at low wages. The racial hierarchy has positive consequences for the status quo: It enables the powerful to retain their control and their advantages. Racial stratification also offers better occupational opportunities, income, and education to White people. These advantages constitute racial privilege.

This chapter examines racial inequality from several vantage points. First, the characteristics of minority groups and racial and ethnic groups are presented. This is followed by brief profiles of four racial minority groups: African Americans, Latinos, Asian Americans, and Native Americans. We then examine explanations of racial inequality, followed by a look at its effect on Blacks and Hispanics in terms of income, jobs, education, and health. Finally, the chapter turns to contemporary trends in racial and ethnic relations.

The theme of the chapter is that contemporary differences between the races are the results of structural inequality. Forms of inequality have changed over time, but racial domination remains a persistent feature of U.S. society. Today, old forms of discrimination thrive alongside new, more subtle forms of inequality. Racial differences are created by social organization. The oppressed people are not the problem; the structure of society that distributes resources unequally is the problem. It is important to understand that minorities are not always passive victims of racial oppression. Their histories reveal struggles and resistance in the face of overwhelming odds. Nevertheless, racial discrimination continues to limit the opportunities of people of color.

Racial and Ethnic Minorities

Because majority–minority relations operate basically as a power relationship, conflict (or at least the potential for conflict) is always present. Overt conflict is most likely when the subordinate group attempts to alter the distribution of power. Size is not crucial in determining whether a group is the most powerful. A numerical minority may in fact have more political representation than the majority, as is the case in the Union of South Africa. Thus, the most important characteristic of a subordinate minority group is that it is dominated by a more powerful group.

Determining who is a minority is largely a matter of history, politics, and judgment—both social and political. All people in the United States are members of some minority group because no single ancestry group accounts for more than half of our population. Population characteristics other than race and ethnicity—such as age, gender, sexual orientation, or religious preference—are sometimes used to designate minority status. However, race and ethnicity are the characteristics used most often to define the minority and majority populations in contemporary U.S. society (O'Hare, 1992:5).

Racial distinctions are a way of classifying people with certain characteristics. Although racial categories operate as if they were real, there is no such thing as biological **race.** The crucial aspect of any racial category is that the characteristics that distinguish it are *socially defined* (Yetman, 1991:3). Racial classification in the United States is based on a Black/White dichotomy, that is, the construction of two opposing categories into which all people fit. Yet social definitions of race change over time and vary in different regions of the country. In the Southwest the divide has been between Anglos and Latinos; in parts of the West Coast it is between Asians and Whites (Rosenblum and Tavris, 1996:15). Today, our conceptions of racial categories are being dramatically transformed. Sociologists Michael Omi and Howard Winant (1994:55) call this **racial formation,** meaning that society is continually creating and transforming racial categories. Groups that were previously defined in terms of specific ethnic backgrounds (such as Mexican Americans and Japanese Americans) have become racialized as "Hispanics and Asian Americans." Even the U.S. Census Bureau, which measures race on the basis of self-identification, is now revising its racial categories for the 2000 census. A new classification system is needed to capture the growing complexity of self-identification in a multiracial society (Evinger, 1996:36) (See "Research Methods: Measuring Race and Ethnicity").

Although racial classification has been confounded by a Black/White dichotomy, common thought overlooks whiteness as a racial category. Most Whites do not think of themselves in racial terms because they are not people of color (McIntosh, 1992:79). Race is treated as something possessed by people of color and as something affecting *them,* whereas Whites are depicted "(usually implicitly) as having no race and as people whose lives are not affected by race" (Lucal, 1996:245–246). In this view whiteness is the normal or natural condition. It is racially unmarked (Frankenberg, 1993) and, therefore, something immune to

Research Methods

Measuring Race and Ethnicity

Many forms—whether used to register for school, apply for a mortgage, or respond to a consumer survey—ask individuals to identify their race or ethnic group. Some people consider this bothersome or even an invasion of privacy. But statistics on race/ethnicity are used to target consumer services, to measure relative health risks, and to track racial discrimination. Federal agencies collect race/ethnic data to comply with the 1964 Civil Rights Act, the 1965 Voting Rights Act, and other laws. But measuring race and ethnicity is surprisingly difficult. The system used by the Census Bureau and other government agencies was developed in 1977 by the Office of Management and Budget (OMB). They specify four racial categories (white, black, Asian/Pacific Islander, and American Indian/Alaska Native) and two ethnic categories (Hispanic and non-Hispanic). Ethnic identity is distinct from racial identity, so Hispanics may be of any race.

The distinction between race and ethnicity is often confusing. In the 1990 Census, for example, 10 million people reported themselves as "other race." Over 95 percent of these respondents were Hispanic.

Prompted by the racial diversity of recent immigrants, increases in interracial marriages and births, and evolving social attitudes, the federal government is reviewing its current racial and ethnic standards. Officials hope to have a new classification system designed and in place before the 2000 Census.

In developing new classifications, several questions arise:

- How many (and which) racial/ethnic groups should be measured?
- Should people be able to check more than one race or ethnic group?
- Should there be a biracial or multiracial category?
- Should race questions be combined with Hispanic-origin and ancestry questions into a single item?

- Which terms should be used to designate racial and ethnic groups (Latino or Hispanic? Black or African American?)

The Census Bureau, the Bureau of Labor Statistics, and the OMB have been working on these issues since 1993. Preliminary results from a 1995 test show the complexity and sensitivity of these questions. For example, roughly two-thirds of Hispanics told interviewers that they preferred to have "Hispanic origin" included as part of the racial question. But more people identified themselves as Hispanic when separate questions were asked rather than when Hispanic was one category in a combined race/ethnic question.

Cuban Americans were especially sensitive to the way in which these questions were asked. They were more likely than other Hispanics to select "white" over "Hispanic" when asked to choose between the two.

This poses a dilemma over how to word the race/ethnic question(s) for the 2000 Census. If the question is asked in a way that fewer Cubans, for example, identify themselves as Hispanic, the Hispanic share of the total population would be reduced. And since Cubans tend to have relatively higher incomes than other Hispanics, the proportion of poor people within the Hispanic population would increase.

OMB has published suggestions based on public comment for changing race/ethnic categories in the *Federal Register* (August 28, 1995). Further research to refine proposed categories and data collection procedures is also planned. Decisions regarding the treatment of race/ethnic categories in the 2000 Census will be made by mid-1997.

Source: Used with permission from Carol J. De Vita, "The United States at Mid-Decade," *Population Bulletin* 50(4) (March, 1996):18. (Population Reference Bureau, Washington, DC).

investigation. This is a false picture of race. In reality, the racial order shapes the lives of all people, even Whites who are advantaged by the system. Just as we must understand how different social classes exist in relation to each other, we must also use a relational model to see that definitions of all races are possible only in relation to other races. "Black" is meaningful only insofar as it is set apart from, and in contradistinction to, "White." This point is particularly obvious when people are referred to as "nonwhite" (a word that ignores the differences in experiences among people of color) (Lucal, 1996:246). Race should not be seen simply as a matter of two opposite categories of people but as a range of power relations among differently situated people.

Whereas race is used for socially marking groups based on presumed physical differences, **ethnicity** allows for a broader range of affiliation. Ethnic groups are distinctive on the basis of national origin, language, religion, and culture. The contemporary world is replete with examples of newly constructed ethnicities. In the United States, people began to affiliate along ethnic lines such as "Italian American" or "German American" much more frequently after the civil rights movement. In Europe, as the Western countries move toward economic and political integration, there is a proliferation of regional identification—people may no longer identify as Italian, but as Lombaridans, Sicilians, or Romans, as these regions lose economic resources to a larger entity—the European community (Wali, 1992:6). At the same time that the world is becoming a global community, it is torn by parochial hatreds dividing nations and regions into warring ethnic enclaves (Barber, 1992).

In the United States, race and ethnicity both serve to mark groups as different. Groups labeled as *races* by the wider society are bound together by their common social and economic conditions. As a result, they develop distinctive cultural or ethnic characteristics. Today, we often refer to them as **racial-ethnic groups** (or racially defined ethnic groups) (See and Wilson, 1988:224). The term *racial-ethnic* refers to groups that are socially subordinated and remain culturally distinct within U.S. society. It is meant to include: (1) the systematic discrimination of socially constructed racial groups, and (2) their distinctive cultural arrangements. Historically, the categories of African American, Latino, Asian American, and Native American were constructed as both racially and culturally distinct. Each group has a distinctive culture, shares a common heritage, and has developed a common identity within a larger society that subordinates it. The racial characteristics of these groups have become meaningful in a society that continues to change (Baca Zinn and Dill, 1994). Terms of reference are also changing, and the changes are contested both within groups as well as between them. For example, *Blacks* continue to debate the merits of the term *African American,* while *Latinos* disagree on the label *Hispanic.* In this chapter we use such interchangeable terms because they are currently used in both popular and scholarly discourse.

Differences among Racial and Ethnic Groups

Both race and ethnicity are historical bases for inequality, although they have differed in how they incorporated groups into society. Race was the social construction setting people of color apart from European immigrant groups (Takaki, 1993:10). Groups identified as races came into contact with the dominant majority through force, in work that was unfree, low in pay, status, and offered little opportunity for upward mobility. In contrast, European ethnics migrated to the United

States voluntarily, to enhance their status or to market their skills in a land of opportunity. They came with hope and sometimes with resources to provide a foundation for their upward mobility. Unlike racial groups, most had the option of returning if they found the conditions here unsatisfactory. The voluntary immigrants came to the United States and suffered discrimination in employment, housing, and other areas. Clashes among Germans, Irish, Italians, Poles, and other Europeans groups during the nineteenth and early twentieth centuries are well documented. But most European immigrants and their descendents—who accounted for four-fifths of the U.S. population in 1900—eventually achieved full participation in U.S. society (O'Hare, 1992:4). Because of their particular historical and social circumstances, Americans of European backgrounds today have the option of maintaining ethnic identities. Unlike people of color, who are defined racially, their "optional ethnicities" allow them to choose the aspects of being ethnic that appeal to them and discard those that do not (Waters, 1996).

While European ethnics have moved into the mainstream of society, racially defined peoples have remained in a subordinate status. Native Americans, African Americans, Latinos, and Asians have not been assimilated. Pervasive racial divisions and inequalities set them apart from others.

African Americans.   In 1995, African Americans (33 million) were nearly 13 percent of the population (U.S. Bureau of the Census, 1995a:3)—the largest and most visible minority group in the United States. Virtually all descend from people who were brought involuntarily to the United States before the slave trade ended in the nineteenth century. They entered the southern states to provide free labor to plantations, and as late as 1890, 90 percent of all Blacks lived in the South, 80 percent as rural dwellers. In the South, they endured harsh, violent, and arbitrary conditions under slavery, an institution that would have consequences for centuries to come. During the nineteenth century, the political storm over slavery almost destroyed the nation. Although Blacks left the South in large numbers after 1890, within northern cities they also encountered prejudice, discrimination, and an extreme level of segregation that exposed them to unusually high concentrations of poverty and other social problems (Massey, 1993:7; Takaki, 1993:7). African Americans have a distinctive history of slavery and racial subordination. Stating that someone is "Black" does more than indicate skin color or physical appearance; it implies a shared memory and a set of common experiences. The term *Black* denotes a meaningful social category that exists apart from the rubric used by statisticians to identify people of African ancestry (Massey, 1993:7).

Latinos.   As we saw in Chapter 8, the U.S. Latino population has doubled in the last twenty years and will soon become the nation's largest minority group. Already, Latinos are the second largest group of children in the country after Anglos (Jones, 1996:4). By mid-decade, Hispanics or Latinos numbered 27 million, 10 percent of the total U.S. population (De Vita, 1996:19). Sixty-four percent of all Hispanic Americans were Chicanos or Mexican Americans, 10 percent were Puerto Ricans, 4.7 percent were Cubans, 13.4 percent were Central American and South American, and 7 percent were "other Hispanic" (U.S. Bureau of the Census, 1995a:46).

The category "Hispanic" was created by federal statisticians to provide data on people of Mexican, Cuban, Puerto Rican, and other Hispanic origins in the United States. There is no precise definition of group membership, and Latinos do not agree among themselves on an appropriate group label. In theory, "Hispanics" include all those who trace their origins to a region originally colonized by Spain. The national origins are diverse, and so is the timing of their arrival in the United States. One group arrived largely in the period between 1960 and 1980; another has been migrating continually since around 1890; another obtained citizenship in 1989; another was forcibly annexed into the United States in 1848; and several groups have just begun migrating to the United States during the past few years.

As a result of these varied histories, Hispanics are found in many legal and social statuses—from fifth-generation to new immigrants, from affluent and well educated to poor and unschooled. Such diversity means that there is no "Hispanic" population in the sense that there is a Black population. Hispanics have no common history. They do not comprise a single, coherent community. Rather they are a disparate collection of national origin groups with heterogeneous experiences of settlement, immigration, political participation, and economic incorporation into the United States. Saying that someone is "Hispanic" or "Latino" reveals little about likely attitudes, behaviors, beliefs, race, religion, class, or legal situation in the United States (Massey, 1993).

Despite these differences, Latinos in the United States have a long history of oppression. For example, civil and property rights of Mexicans have been roughly violated. As Anglos moved into the southwestern states in the 1800s, they were largely dispossessed of power and property. As late as the 1940s, local ordinances in some Texas cities blocked Mexican Americans from owning real estate or voting. Also, Mexican Americans were required to attend segregated public schools in many jurisdictions before 1950 (O'Hare, 1992:5).

Asian Americans. Asian Americans are the fastest growing minority group in the country. At mid-decade, Asians accounted for 3 percent of the U.S. population. The nation's 7 million Asians exhibit great diversity and make up 42 percent of the nation's immigrants—as many as come from Latin American countries (Stone, 1991:11-A).

Like the Latino population, the Asian population in the United States is extremely diverse, giving rise to the term *Pan Asian*, which encompasses immigrants from Asian and Pacific Island countries and native-born citizens descended from those ethnic groups (Lott and Felt, 1991:6). Until recently, immigrants who arrived in the United States from Asian countries did not think of themselves as "Asians," or even as Chinese, Japanese, Korean, and so forth, but rather people from Toisan, Hoeping, or some other district in Guadong Province in China or from Hiroshima, Yamaguchi, or some other locale. It was not until the late 1960s, with the advent of the Asian American movement, that a Pan Asian consciousness was formed (Espiritu, 1996:51).

Today, the largest Asian American groups are Chinese (22.6 percent), Filipinos (19.3 percent), Japanese (11.2 percent), Vietnamese (8.4 percent), Korean (11 percent), and Asian Indian (11.2 percent). There also are Laotians, Kampucheans, Thais, Pakistanis, Indonesians, Hmongs, and Samoans.

The characteristics of Asians vary widely according to their national origins and time of entry in the United States. Most come from recent immigrant families, but many Asian Americans can trace their family's history in the United States more than 150 years. Much of this period was marked by anti-Asian laws and discrimination. The 1879 California Constitution barred the hiring of Chinese workers, and the federal Chinese Exclusion Act of 1882 halted the entry of most Chinese immigrants until 1943. Americans of Japanese ancestry were interned in camps during World War II by an executive order signed by President Franklin D. Roosevelt. Not until 1952 were Japanese immigrants granted the right to become naturalized U.S. citizens (O'Hare, 1992:5).

Whereas most of the pre-World War II Asian immigrants were peasants, the recent immigrants vary considerably by education and social class. On the one hand, many arrived as educated middle-class professionals with highly valued skills and some knowledge of English. Others, such as the Indochinese, arrived as uneducated, impoverished refugees. These differences are reflected in the differences in income and poverty level by ethnic category. Asian Americans taken together have higher average incomes than do other groups in the United States. Although a large segment of this population is financially well off, many are poor. Given this diversity in social classes among the immigrants, most Asian American leaders say the "model minority" label is misleading. Even the term *Asian American* masks great diversity.

Native Americans. Once thought to be destined for extinction, the Native American or American Indian population today is larger than it has been for centuries. Now at 1 percent of the total U.S. population (De Vita, 1996:19), Native Americans have more autonomy and are now more self-sufficient than at any time since the last century (Snipp, 1996:390). Nevertheless, the population remains one of the most destitute in society.

The tribes located in North America were and are extremely heterogeneous, with major differences in physical characteristics, language, and social organization. There were theocracies, democracies, and hereditary chiefdoms; matrilineal and patrilineal systems; hunters and farmers; nomads and villagers. In 1492, when Columbus landed at Watling's Island in the Bahamas, the North American continent was an area of astonishing ethnic and cultural diversity (Cook, 1981:118). Considerable debate exists as to the size of the total native population of the Western hemisphere at the time of Columbus' arrival. Anthropologist Russell Thornton (1996:44) estimates that there were approximately 75 million Native Americans in the Western hemisphere in 1492.

Native Americans, then, lived in a pluralistic world, with tribes of quite different cultures and social organizations. In contrast, the Europeans who settled in the New World were quite similar: They spoke some variant of Indo-European language; they had a common religious tradition—Christianity; and their political and social conventions were similar. They shared a belief in what they considered the international law of the right of discovery. This belief held that the European nation

Reprinted by permission of United Feature Syndicate.

first landing on and claiming the right to territory not formerly held by other Europeans had the exclusive authority to negotiate with the natives for the absolute ownership of the land. This ethnocentric notion was buttressed further by the Europeans' belief that they represented the highest level of civilization. They were convinced of their superiority to the natives of the New World, whom they considered to be not only infidels but also inferior beings.

The current political and economic status of American Indians is the result of the process by which they were incorporated into U.S. society. "This amounts to a long history of efforts aimed at subordinating an otherwise self-governing and self-sufficent people that eventually culminated in widespread economic dependency" (Snipp, 1996:290).

Important changes have occurred in the social and economic well-being of the Native American population from 1960 to the present. At the time of the 1970 Census, American Indians were the poorest group in the United States with incomes well below those of the Black population. By 1980, despite poverty rates on many Indian reservations, poverty among American Indians had declined and real incomes had risen to levels exceeding the real incomes of the Black population. By the standard of White Americans, Native Americans are not well educated, they are marginally attached to the labor force, and they do work that is not highly valued; and the consequences of these liabilities are poverty and economic hardship (cited in Sandefur, 1990:39). Economic conditions are particularly bad on many Indian reservations, where poverty can reach as high as 60 percent.

Despite the arrival of gambling facilities on reservations, which has enriched a handful of tribes, a third of the country's two million Native Americans live below the poverty line. On the reservations, half of all children under six live below the poverty line; one out of every five Indian homes lacks both a telephone and an indoor toilet (Biema, 1995:49).

Although Third-World conditions prevail on many reservations, a renaissance has occurred in American Indian communities. In cities, modern pan-Indian organizations have been successful in making the presence of American Indians known to the larger community and have mobilized to meet the needs of their people (Snipp, 1996:390). A college-educated Indian middle class has emerged, American Indian business ownership has increased, and some tribes are creating good jobs for their members (Fost, 1991:26).

Today, the combined population of the four racial minority groups accounts for just over one-fourth of the total U.S. population. New waves of immigration from non-European countries, high birth rates among these groups, and a relatively young age structure account for the rapid increase in minorities. By the middle of the twenty-first century, today's minorities will comprise nearly one-half (see Figure 11.1) of the U.S. population (O'Hare, 1992). African Americans, Latinos, Asian Americans, and Native Americans are different in many respects. Each group encounters different forms of exclusion. Nevertheless, as racial minorities they remain at the lowest rungs of society.

FIGURE 11.1

Percent of the Population, by Race and Hispanic Origin: 1990, 2000, 2025, and 2050 (Middle-series projections)

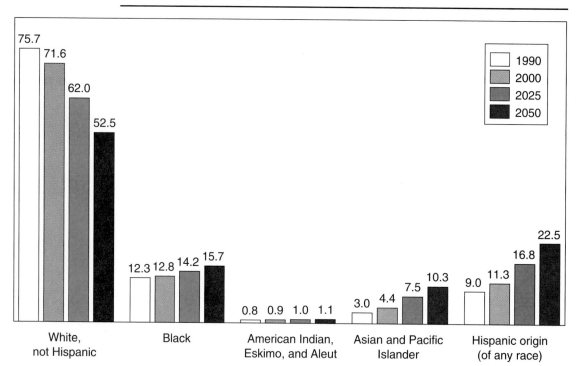

Source: U.S. Bureau of the Census. "Population Profile of the United States: 1995," Current Population Reports, Series P-23-189. Washington: U.S. Government Printing Office, p. 7.

Explanations of Racial and Ethnic Inequality

Why have some racial and ethnic groups been consistently disadvantaged throughout American history? Some ethnic groups, such as the Irish and the Jews, have experienced discrimination but moved up from the bottom economic rungs. But African Americans, Latinos, Asian Americans, and Native Americans have not been able to cast off their secondary status. Three types of theories have been used to explain why some groups are consistently singled out for discrimination: deficiency theories, bias theories, and structural discrimination theories. (The following discussion is based on Barrera, 1979:174–219.)

Deficiency Theories

A number of analysts have argued that some groups are inferior because they *are* inferior. That is, when compared with the majority, they are deficient in some important way. There are two varieties of **deficiency theory.**

Biological Deficiency.   This classical explanation for the inferiority of certain groups maintains that their inferiority is the result of flawed genetic—and, therefore, hereditary—traits. This is the position of Arthur Jensen and Richard Herrnstein (as we discuss in Chapter 9). *The Bell Curve* (Herrnstein and Murray, 1994) is the latest in a long series of works claiming that Blacks are mentally inferior to Whites and that genetic inferiority cannot be altered by environmental interventions (Gould, 1994). Despite the media attention given the work of these and other theorists, there is no definitive evidence for the thesis that racial groups differ in intelligence. Biological deficiency theories are generally not accepted in the scientific community (see the symposium on *The Bell Curve* in *Contemporary Sociology*, 1995).

Cultural Deficiency.   Many varieties of explanations for racial subordination center on cultural characteristics thought to be inherited from the past and handed down from generation to generation. Shortcomings rooted in characteristics of the groups themselves (including motivation, moral background, and behavior) are the reason some groups remain at the bottom economic rungs. Cultural-deficiency explanations argue that some flaw within the minority way of life is responsible for that minority group's secondary status.

From this perspective minorities are disadvantaged because of their own heritage and customs. Cultural deficiency provides the basis for the famous 1967 report of Daniel Patrick Moynihan. The report charged that the tangle of pathology within Black ghettos was rooted in the deterioration of the Negro family (U.S. Department of Labor, 1965). High rates of marital dissolution, female-headed households, out-of-wedlock births, welfare dependency, and the resulting family structure were explained as the residuals of slavery and discrimination, a complex web of pathological patterns passed down through successive generations. The Moynihan report was widely criticized for being a classic case of blaming the victim. It locates the cause of pathology within Blacks, not in the racially stratified society.

Culture-deficiency theorists ignore the external opportunity structures that affect groups in different ways. Some social scientists have always opposed cultural explanations. Nevertheless, this approach is present in both scholarship and popular thought. Today, much of the public discussion about race and poverty rests on false assumptions about the defective nature of minorities (Reed, 1990; di Leonardo, 1992). We return to this theme in the last section of this chapter.

Bias Theories

The deficiency theories just discussed blame the minorities for their plight. **Bias theories,** on the other hand, blame the members of the majority—in particular, they blame the prejudiced attitudes of majority members. Gunnar Myrdal, for example, argued in his classic, *An American Dilemma,* that prejudiced attitudes are the source of discriminatory actions, which keep minorities subordinate (Myrdal, 1944). The inferior status of minorities reinforces negative stereotypes that in turn justify the prejudice of the majority; the process is a vicious cycle that perpetuates the secondary status from generation to generation.

David Wellman made an extensive critique of bias theories and presented an alternative (Wellman, 1977). He challenged the notion that the attitudes of White Americans are the major cause of racism. The typical view is that Whites, particularly lower-class Whites, have hostile feelings toward and make faulty generalizations about minorities. Minorities are thus prejudged and misjudged by the majority, and the result is discrimination.

Prejudiced attitudes, however, do not explain the behaviors of unprejudiced Whites who defend the traditional arrangements that negatively affect minorities. Unbiased persons fight to preserve the status quo by favoring, for example, the seniority system in occupations, or they oppose affirmative action, quota systems, busing to achieve racial balance, and open enrollment in higher education. As Wellman has argued:

> The terms in which middle-class professionals defend traditional institutional arrangements are, strictly speaking, not examples of racial prejudice. They are neither overtly racial nor, given these people's *interests,* misrepresentations of facts. However, while the sentiments may not be prejudiced, they justify arrangements that in effect, if not in intent, maintain the status quo and thereby keep Blacks in subordinate positions. (Wellman, 1977:8)

Thus, to focus strictly on prejudice is to take too narrow a view. This view presents an inaccurate portrayal of racism because it concentrates only on the bigots and ignores the discriminating acts of those who are not prejudiced.

Moreover, according to Wellman, prejudice is not the cause of discrimination. Rather, it is the racial organization of society that is the cause of people's racial beliefs. The determining feature of majority–minority relations is not prejudice, but rather the superior position of the majority and the institutions that maintain this superiority. "The subordination of people of color is functional to the operation of American society as we know it and the color of one's skin is a primary determinant of people's position in the social structure" (Wellman, 1977:35). Thus, institutional and individual racism generate privilege for Whites. Discrimination provides the privileged with disproportionate advantages in the social, economic, and political spheres. Racist acts, in this view, are not only based on hatred, stereotyped conceptions, or prejudgment but also are rational responses to the struggle over scarce resources by individuals acting to preserve their own advantage.

Structural Discrimination Theories

Critics of the deficiency and bias theories argue that these explanations focus, incorrectly, on individuals. Both ignore the political/economic system that dominates and oppresses minorities. Parenti has criticized those who ignore the system as victim blamers. "Focusing on the poor and ignoring the system of power, privilege, and profit which makes them poor, is a little like blaming the corpse for the murder" (Parenti, 1978:24).

The alternative view is that racial inequality is not fundamentally a matter of what is in people's heads, not a matter of their *private* individual intentions, but rather a matter of *public* institutions and practices that create or perpetuate racism. **Structural discrimination theories** move away from thinking about "racism-in-the-head" toward understanding "racism-in-the-world" (Lichtenberg, 1992:5). These theories are based on racialized opportunity structures in the United States.

Institutional racism refers to the established, customary, and respected ways in which society operates to keep the minority in a subordinate position. For Carmichael and Hamilton (1967) there are two types of racism—individual and institutional. **Individual racism** consists of overt acts by individuals that harm other individuals or their property. This type of action is usually publicly decried and is probably on the decline in the United States. Institutional racism is more injurious than individual racism to more minority group members, but it is not recognized by the dominant-group members as racism. Carmichael and Hamilton illustrated the two types of racism as follows:

> When a black family moves into a home in a white neighborhood and is stoned, burned or routed out, they are victims of an overt act of individual racism which many people will condemn—at least in words. But it is institutional racism that keeps black people locked in dilapidated slum tenements, subject to the daily prey of exploitative slumlords, merchants, loan sharks, and discriminatory real estate agents. . . . Respectable individuals can absolve themselves from individual blame: *they* would never plant a bomb in a church: *they* would never stone a black family. But they continue to support political officials and institutions that would and do perpetuate institutionally racist policies. Thus *acts* of overt, individual racism may not typify the society, but institutional racism does. (Carmichael and Hamilton, 1967:4–5)

Some individuals and groups discriminate whether or not they are bigots. These individuals and groups operate within a social milieu that is also discriminatory. The social milieu includes laws, customs, religious beliefs, social stratification, the distribution of power, and the stable arrangements and practices through which things get done in society. These social arrangements and accepted ways of doing things may consciously or unconsciously disadvantage some social categories while benefiting others. The major sectors of society—the system of law and the administration of justice, the economic system, the formal educational structure, and health care—are all possible discriminators. Thus, the term *institutional discrimination* is a useful one. The institutions of society

> have great power to reward and penalize. They reward by providing career opportunities for some people and foreclosing them for others. They reward as well by the way social goods and services are distributed by deciding who receives training and skills, medical care, formal education, political influence, moral support and self-respect, productive employment, fair treatment by the law, decent housing, self-confidence, and the promise of a secure future for self and children. (Knowles and Prewitt, 1965:5)

To understand how discrimination works, we need to ask, How are things normally done in the society? Who gets preferential treatment under these normal arrangements? Who is automatically excluded because of these arrangements? The answers to these questions are not always easy because the arrangements are natural and the discrimination often unintentional or disguised. The task is especially difficult because the exact placement of responsibility is often impossible to pinpoint. Who is responsible for the low scores of ghetto children on standard IQ tests? Who is responsible for residential segregation? Who is responsible for the high unemployment rate of minority group members?

There are four basic themes of institutional discrimination (Benokraitis and Feagin, 1974). First is the importance of history in determining present conditions and affecting resistance to change. Historically, institutions defined and enforced norms and role relationships that were racially distinct. The U.S. nation was founded and its institutions established when Blacks were slaves, uneducated, and different culturally from the dominant Whites. From the beginning Blacks were considered inferior (the original Constitution, for example, counted a slave as three-fifths of a person). Religious beliefs buttressed this notion of the inferiority of Blacks and justified the differential allocation of privileges and sanctions in society. Laws, customs, and traditions usually continue to reinforce current thinking. Institutions have an inertial quality: once set in motion, they tend to continue on the same course. Thus, institutional racism is extremely difficult to change without a complete overhaul of society's institutions.

The second theme of institutional discrimination is that discrimination can occur *without* conscious bigotry. Everyday practices reinforce racial discrimination and deprivation. All it takes for institutional discrimination to continue is for employers to insist that prospective employees take aptitude or IQ tests that are based on middle-class experiences, or for decisions on who must be fired in times of financial exigency to be based on seniority, or for employers to stress educational requirements for hiring. These conditions, seemingly fair and neutral, are biased against minorities.

The system (customs, practices, expectations, laws, beliefs) works to deny equality to minority group members—most often without malicious intent. Even if "racism-in-the-head" disappeared, "racism-in-the-world" would not because it is the system that disadvantages (Lichtenberg, 1992). All that is needed for minorities to suffer is that the law continue to favor the owners of property over renters and debtors. All that is needed for job opportunities to remain unequal is for employers to hire people with the most conventional training and experience and to use machines when they seem more immediately economical than manual labor. All that is needed to ensure that poor children get an inferior education is to continue tracking, using class-biased tests, making education irrelevant in their work, rewarding children who conform to the teachers' middle-class concepts of the good student, and paying disproportionately less for their education (buildings, supplies, teachers, counselors) (Steinberg, n.d.:3). In other words, all that is needed to perpetuate discrimination in the United States is to pursue a policy of business as usual.

Institutional discrimination is also more invisible than individual discrimination. Institutional discrimination is more subtle and less intentional than individual acts of discrimination. As a result, establishing blame for this kind of discrimination is extremely difficult.

Finally, institutional discrimination is reinforced because institutions are interrelated. The exclusion of minorities from the upper levels of education, for example, is likely to affect their opportunities in other institutions (type of job, level of remuneration). Similarly, being poor means that your children will probably receive an inferior education, be propertyless, suffer from bad health, and be treated unjustly by the criminal justice system. These inequities are cumulative.

Institutional derogation occurs when minority groups and their members are made to seem inferior or to possess negative stereotypes through legitimate means by the powerful in society. The portrayal of minority group members in the media (movies, television, newspapers, and magazines) is often derogatory. A *USA Today* examination of prime-time network programming found that minorities are still shortchanged. Nearly two-thirds of prime-time television characters are male. Hispanics are virtually invisible. Although Blacks represent a realistic 13 percent of TV's players, they are stereotyped as oversexed and shiftless (Gable, 1993).

Why is the United States structured in racist ways? Different theories have been advanced to answer this question. A central issue in structural theories is the relationship between the economic organization of society and racial stratification. There is a long-standing debate in the sociology of race relations over the relative importance of race and class. Many scholars argue that modern race relations are produced by world capitalism. Using the labor of non-White peoples began as a means for White owners to accumulate profits. This perspective contends that capitalism as a system of class exploitation has shaped race and racism in the United States and the world (Bonacich, 1992b).

Other structural theories are based on the interplay between the U.S. economy and racially stratified labor systems. For example, **colonial theory** incorporates class and race to address the question of why some ethnic groups have overcome their disadvantaged status, whereas others have not. This issue is important, because it challenges the myth that the United States is a melting pot. Colonial theory argues that there are fundamental differences between the experiences of racial ethnics and European ethnics. Racial ethnics were colonized within the boundaries of the United States, but Europeans immigrated to this society. Internal colonialism determined the subordinate place of people of color within the dominant society, and it shaped their continuing experiences in this country. Using this framework, we can see that despite certain similarities (such as poverty and discrimination) the experiences of racial minorities contrasted sharply with those of European immigrants. These conditions make blending into the larger society a myth for people of color, because the colonial experiences trap them in a system of racial domination. The key ingredient in internal colonialism is that the racial control that began as the result of conquest is institutionalized in social, economic, and political spheres.

The colonial model assigns fundamental importance to the labor that people of color did when they were brought into the United States. European ethnics began work mostly in industry, or at least in industrial sectors of the economy, where they could move about as families or individuals in response to the needs of an industrializing economy. In contrast, Blacks and Chicanos were forced into certain types of work. Blauner has noted the consequences of preindustrial work:

> Like European overseas colonialism, America has used African, Asian, Mexican, and to a lesser degree Indian workers for the cheapest labor, concentrating people of color in the most unskilled jobs, the least advanced sectors of the economy and the most industrially backward regions of the nation. In an historical sense, people of color provided much of the hard labor (and the technical skills) that built up the agricultural base and the mineral-transport-communications infrastructure necessary for industrialization and modernization, whereas the Europeans worked primarily within the industrialized, modern sectors. The initial position of European ethnics, while low, was therefore strategic for movement up the economic and social pyramid. The placement of nonwhite groups, however, imposed barrier upon barrier on such mobility, freezing them for long periods of time in the least favorable segments of the economy. (Blauner, 1972:62)

Some contemporary theories point to race itself as a primary shaper of the social structure. For example, Omi and Winant's theory of racial formation proposes that the United States is organized along racial lines from top to bottom—a racial state, composed of institutions and policies to support and justify racial stratification (Omi and Winant, 1986).

Racial Stratification from the Order and the Conflict Perspectives

Order perspectives of race and ethnic relations have assumed that the United States is a land of opportunity and that all groups—ethnic and racial—would eventually assimilate or blend into the country's social melting pot. This was the experience of the European immigrants who came to the United States in the nineteenth and early twentieth centuries and were absorbed into the social mainstream within a few generations of arrival (O'Hare, 1992:42). Order theories accent patterns of inclusion, of the orderly integration and assimilation of racial and ethnic groups. The word **assimilate** comes from the Latin word *assimulare,* meaning "to make similar" (Feagin and Feagin, 1993:27). Order theories are primarily concerned with how minorities adapt to the core society. These theories see the situations of Blacks and non-Whites as similar to those of earlier White immigrants. Just as White ethnics made a place for themselves in the land of opportunity, so should racial minorities. With the proper attitudes, habits, and values, minorities could lift themselves up and succeed in the U.S. mainstream.

Conflict (or power-conflict theories) are critical of assimilation theories for ignoring structural factors that exclude racial minorities from full participation in U.S. society. Most conflict theories emphasize the deep-lying roots of racial and ethnic inequalities in the U.S. economy. Social organization, not group culture, keeps minorities stuck at the bottom rungs of society. Conflict theories argue that racial ethnics were never meant to assimilate. Racial stratification exists because certain segments of society benefit from it. Racial ethnics are located in the larger society in ways that prevent their assimilation. Minorities are stuck at the bottom because the U.S. economy does not provide equal opportunities for them. The melting pot does not apply to people of color. Differences between Whites and people of color produce conflict, not consensus, across race lines.

Neither the conflict nor the order model captures the complexity of today's multiracial society. Some immigrants seem to be following certain paths of European immigrants nearly a century ago, while others remain undereducated, underemployed, and in poverty (O'Hare, 1992:42). Today's dramatic population shifts will require sociologists to develop new theories for a changing world.

Discrimination against Blacks and Hispanics: Continuity and Change

The treatment of Blacks and Hispanics has been disgraceful throughout American history. Members of both categories have been denied equality in money, jobs, services, housing, and even the right to vote. Since World War II, however, under pressure from civil rights advocates, the government has led the way in breaking down these discriminatory practices. The 1960 civil rights movement overturned segregation laws, opened voting booths, created new job opportunities, and renewed hope for racial equality. In the past quarter century, many well-educated people of color have made considerable advances. For example, the Black middle class has expanded rapidly in the past two decades. A third of U.S. Blacks are now middle class. They have taken advantage of fair-housing legislation and moved to the suburbs looking for better schools, safer streets, better services (*The Economist,* 1993:17). Yet, having "made it" in the United States does not shield African Americans from discriminatory treatment. Joe R. Feagin and Melvin P. Sikes, who studied discrimination in public setting, found that middle-class Blacks were repeatedly denied service and treated with hostility in restaurants, hotels, and places of amusement (Feagin and Sikes, 1994). No matter how affluent or influential, a Black person cannot escape the stigma of being Black.

Even as successful African Americans have gotten richer, unsuccessful ones have been marginalized. As Roy Brooks puts it "deep class stratification within African American society is without a doubt the most significant development in the 'American dilemma' " since the civil rights movement of the 1960s (Brooks, 1990:xi, cited in Winant, 1994:62). As much as some things have changed, others have stayed the same. We are far from overcoming the legacy of the unique castelike segregation that distinguishes Blacks from all other groups (Harris and Bennett, 1995:145). A comprehensive four-year National Research Council study on the state of Black America during the past fifty years found a continuing gap in status between Blacks and Whites in the United States. The 1989 report revealed that on virtually every indicator of well-being—income and living standards, health and life expectancy, and residential opportunities, as well as political and social participation—Blacks remained substantially behind Whites (Jaynes and Williams, 1989).

Unequal treatment of minorities cannot be dismissed as wrongs committed in the past with no bearing on the present. African Americans at all class levels are still segregated in the United States. An important study by Douglas Massey and Nancy Denton documents high levels of segregation, isolation, and impoverishment (Massey and Denton, 1993). These sociologists make the case that Black/White segregation has not diminished. Middle-class Blacks tend to live in Black suburbs with weak tax bases and poor municipal services. Therefore, they are only marginally less segregated than poor Blacks.

Hispanics, too, fall well behind Whites on most indicators of status. Even though levels of well-being vary widely among Hispanic groups, they face common obstacles to becoming incorporated into the economic mainstream of society. The basic point of the next section is that inequalities faced by racial minorities reflect the routine operation of the political economy and the basic patterns of institutional discrimination.

Income

The average income for White families is greater than the average income for Black and Hispanic families. Such income disparities have remained unchanged over time. In 1994, the median income of Black families was $24,698, about 58 percent of the White median family income of $40,884. Hispanic median family income was $24,318, about 63 percent of the median income of White families (U.S. Bureau of the Census, 1994:7–10). Even though the median family income for Blacks is still below that of Hispanics, per-person income for Hispanics is actually lower because Hispanics tend to have larger families.

Poverty rates for all minority groups are higher than those of Whites. The percentage of Blacks, Hispanics, and Native Americans in poverty is about three times that of Whites. Even Asian Americans, who have a higher average income than Whites, are more likely to live in families with incomes below the poverty line (O'Hare, 1992:37). Although most poor people are White, Blacks remained disproportionately poor, followed by Hispanics and then Whites. In 1995, the poverty rate for Whites was 11.2 percent, compared with 29.3 for Blacks and 30.3 percent for Hispanics (U.S. Bureau of the Census, 1996). (See Table 11.1.) For Hispanics, these percentages are the highest number living in poverty since the Census Bureau began collecting figures on Hispanics in 1972. In recent years, the poverty rate of Hispanics has risen more rapidly than that of Whites or Blacks. However, poverty rates differ greatly among Hispanic groups. Among Puerto Ricans, poverty has hovered at a rate of 40 percent in the last several years. Recent evidence suggests that economic conditions in those areas where Hispanics are concentrated account for the difference in their well-being. Puerto Ricans are concentrated in major cities of the eastern end of the Snowbelt, where larger economic changes have affected unskilled workers (Aponte, 1991). Rising poverty rates coupled with

TABLE 11.1

Percent of People and Families in Poverty by Race and Ethnic Group, 1994

CHARACTERISTIC	ALL RACES	NON-HISPANIC WHITE	AFRICAN AMERICAN	ASIAN AMERICAN	HISPANIC
United States	14.5	9.5	30.5	14.6	30.7
Age					
Under 18	21.8	12.6	43.8	18.3	41.5
18–64	11.9	8.2	23.4	13.4	24.8
65+	11.7	9.6	27.4	13.0	22.6
Families*					
Married with children	8.3	5.5	11.4	13.4	23.9
Single parent, female	44.0	33.7	53.9	31.4	59.2
Regions					
Northeast	12.9	8.5	29.1	12.7	35.6
Midwest	13.0	9.9	35.4	11.9	23.9
South	16.1	9.9	30.1	13.9	30.1
West	15.3	9.2	25.3	15.8	30.5

*Percents based on family households with children.

Source: Used with permission from Carol J. De Vita, "The United States at Mid-Decade," in *Population Bulletin* 50 (4) (March, 1996):39. (Population Reference Bureau, Wahsington, DC).

growing numbers have made Latinos a larger component of the population in poverty in the nineties (Enchautegui, 1995:7).

The growing poverty rate among minority children is one the nation's most ominous problems (Harris and Bennett, 1995:196). In 1996, 16 percent of White children lived in poverty compared with 39 percent of Latino children and 46 percent of Black children (Jones, 1996:1). The situation is even worse in families headed by women. Over 65 percent of children living in African American or Latino families maintained by women alone were poor in 1992 (Folbre, 1995:3–13).

Black and Hispanic women maintaining families had lower labor-force-participation rates and higher unemployment rates than did White women maintaining families. These data give one explanation for the high incidence of poverty in families maintained by women. Thus, feminization of poverty is important in explaining some kinds of poverty, but it does not explain the persistent pattern of widening income inequality in minority families with a man and a woman present. A two-parent family is no guarantee against poverty for racial minorities to escape poverty. Many young children in a married couple home are in the lowest income tier—two in ten White children, three in ten Black children, and four in ten Hispanic children (Ahlburg and De Vita, 1992:38).

Many factors explain the difference in White and minority earnings. Racial ethnics are concentrated in the South and Southwest, where incomes are lower for everyone. Another part of the explanation is the differing age structure of minorities. They are younger, on average, than is the White population. A group with a higher proportion of young people of working age will have a lower average earning level, higher rates of unemployment, and lower rates of labor-force participation.

Looking at racial inequalities by age reveals another disturbing pattern. The degree of inequality increases after the teenage years. Racial disparities become greater in peak earning years. This suggests that another part of the explanation for racial inequalities in earnings lies in the lack of education and skill levels required to move out of poor-paying jobs. All of these explanations leave a substantial amount of inequality unexplained (Currie and Skolnick, 1988:151–155). Minorities at all levels of unemployment and education still earn less than do Whites due to current racial discrimination in the labor force, as we see in Chapter 13.

Education

In 1954, the Supreme Court outlawed segregation in the schools. Since then, more U.S. residents have completed high school and college. By 1995, when minorities made up one-third of public school students, they still had lower levels of educational completion that Whites. The American Council on Education recently reported that:

> Minority students' high school graduation rates are up somewhat, but the percentage of minority high school graduates entering college has declined. Though the absolute number of minority college graduates has increased slightly, it has not kept pace with population growth; thus the gap between white and minority college graduates is . . . wide. . . . (Zwerling, 1995:19)

Among young adults, Hispanics have the lowest educational attainment, while Whites and Asians have the highest. Sixty percent of Latinos ages twenty-five to forty-four had graduated from high school in 1992, compared with about 90 percent of Asians and non-Hispanic Whites (O'Hare, 1992:29). (See Figure 11.2.)

The minority education gap is the result of several factors, including language differences, malnutrition, drug abuse, teenage pregnancy, and lack of family support. Yet many of the problems have less to do with minority students themselves and more to do with what is occurring in society. Much of the segregation in the schools is due to the continuing segregation of residential patterns all over the country. Minority students attend schools with mostly minority students (Sidel, 1994:67). Interestingly, the greatest segregation of students no longer involves Black children. The most segregated group in the nation's public schools today is the rapidly increasing population of Hispanic students (Williams, 1994:28).

Several additional trends are creating problems for minority students. The general movement against increased taxes hurts public schools, especially the costly

FIGURE 11.2

Educational Attainment of Persons 25 Years Old and Over, by Sex, Race, and Hispanic Origin. 1993

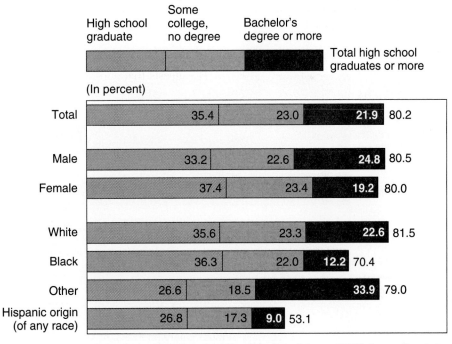

Source: U.S. Bureau of the Census. "Population Profile of the United States: 1995," Current Population Reports, Series P-23-189. Washington: U.S. Government Printing Office, p. 19.

programs for the disadvantaged (e.g., bilingual programs and Head Start). Inner-city schools, where minorities are concentrated and which are already understaffed and underfinanced, face even greater financial pressures because of the current trend to reduce federal programs to aid the disadvantaged.

In 1993 nine million students across the United States were enrolled in four-year colleges. Of these, 36.8 percent were White, 23.4 percent were African American, and 17.8 percent were Latinos. Although many colleges actively recruit students of color, many factors contribute to their having low retention rates (Celis, 1993:B6).

Yet, education, alone, is not the answer. Even with a college degree, African Americans and Latinos had far higher unemployment rates than their White counterparts in 1993 (Folbre, 1995:4–8). This is compounded by the reality that education does not pay equally. Minority members, regardless of their level of education, are underpaid compared with Whites of similar education. For example, Hispanic women with bachelor's degrees earned less on average in 1993 than White men with high school diplomas. African American women with bachelor's degrees earned just $600 per year more than White men with high school diplomas. (Outtz, 1995:68). (See Figure 11.3.)

FIGURE 11.3

Education Does Not Pay Equitably

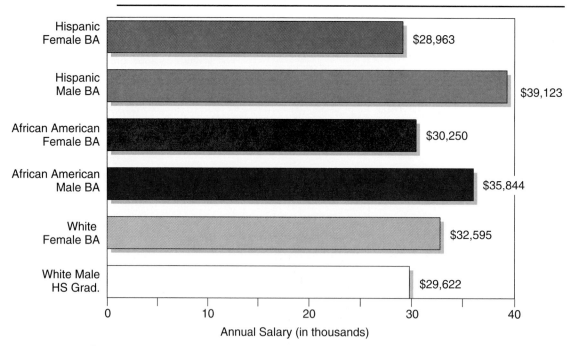

Source: Janice Hamilton Outtz, "Higher Education and the New Demographic Reality," in *Educational Record* 76, nos. 2, 3 (Spring/Summer, 1995):68.

Discrimination in the schools also creates problems for minority students. According to the National Coalition of Advocates for students, a child who is poor, Black, or Hispanic is much more likely to be physically disciplined, suspended, expelled, or made to repeat a grade—all practices shown to increase the likelihood that the child will drop out of school. A minority child is three times as likely as a White child to end up in vocational education or in classes for the mildly mentally retarded. In effect, minority children are being "pushed out" of schools.

Unemployment

Unemployment rates are particularly high among African Americans and Latinos. For the last three decades, unemployment rates among Black workers have been twice that of White workers with Latinos in between. But unemployment among Latinos is now almost as pervasive as among Blacks. In 1995, the unemployment rate for Latinos was 9.4 percent compared with 10 percent for African Americans and 4.8 percent for Whites (Thurm, 1995). Teenagers had an even harder time. The unemployment rate among Black youths was 36 percent; for Whites it was 16 percent (Folbre, 1995:4.7).

These government rates are misleading because they count as employed the almost six million people who work part-time because they cannot find full-time jobs, and they do not count as unemployed the discouraged former workers, numbering more than one million, who have given up their search for work.

Type of Employment

African Americans and Latinos have always been an important component of the U.S. labor force. But their job prospects are different from those of other people in the United States. Not only are minorities twice as likely as Whites to be unemployed, they are more likely to work in dead-end jobs. Those who do work are clustered in low-paying service or manufacturing jobs. About a quarter of all African Americans and a fifth of all Latinos work at the low end of the occupational ladder, in poorly paid service jobs (Folbre, 1995:4.9).

Although minorities are in the least rewarding jobs, and many face discrimination in hiring and promotion, there have been positive changes since 1960. The percentage of African Americans in managerial and professional occupations increased from 14 percent in 1980 to 17 percent in 1990. Their percentage in managerial–professional jobs rose slightly over the period for Latinos (from 12 to 13 percent) (O'Hare, 1992:33; Folbre, 1995:4.9). Despite these gains, however, a huge gap remains. As more minorities enter high status work, they are confronting new forms of job discrimination in the form of "job ceilings" that separate them from executive suites and board rooms (Higginbotham, 1994).

Economic restructuring of the U.S. economy is having devastating effects on minority employment patterns in communities across the country. The job crisis in minority communities is linked to the widening division in the U.S. economy and vanishing jobs for unskilled, poorly educated workers.

While employment status is declining in all regions, it is worse in areas of industrial decline; for Blacks the lowest employment rates are in the Midwest and Great Lakes region, that is, in the old industrial heartland. The labor market status of Whites has also been lowered in these areas, but the level of racial inequality has increased to new levels. In Swinton's words:

> In such cities as Detroit, Buffalo, Chicago, and Cleveland, the gap between the labor market position of blacks, especially black males, and whites probably exceeds the highest levels that ever existed in the most racist of the South's cities. (Swinton, 1987:68)

The new economy will be increasingly made up of people of color. According to the U.S. Department of Labor, one-third of the new entrants to the labor force by the year 2005 will be minorities (Edmondson, 1996). Minority access to higher-paying jobs must increase if this growing segment of the U.S. population is to have realistic life chances.

Health

The health of the U.S. population is distributed unevenly across race. Latinos are the most likely to be without health coverage. In 1993, 31 percent of Latinos, 20 percent of Black, and 14 percent of Whites lacked health insurance (U.S. Bureau of the Census, Population Profile, 1995a:37). Mexican Americans are especially vulnerable because most live in Southwestern states where jobs offer fewer benefits and public assistance is slim. In addition, many are immigrants concentrated in low-paying jobs. "Some are unfamiliar with the U.S. health care system, and a few are illegal immigrants who are afraid to seek medical assistance" (Folbre, 1995:7.12).

Racial discrimination affects health in other ways as well. **Environmental racism** is the disproportionate exposure of some racial groups to environmental toxic substances. Race is the strongest predictor of hazardous waste facilities in the country

One-third of the new entrants to the labor force by the year 2005 will be minorities.

even after adjustment for social class (Williams, 1996:409). On virtually every measure of health, African Americans and Latinos are disadvantaged, as revealed in the following facts:

- Whites live about six years longer than do Blacks (Williams, 1996:404).
- At all ages except for the very old, Blacks have higher death rates and a greater incidence of disease (*News Report,* 1989:4).
- Black babies are nearly twice as likely as White babies to die within their first year (O'Hare, et al., 1991:13).
- Inequalities exist in the kinds of medical care received by Blacks and Whites. A recent Harvard University study found that Blacks used clinics and emergency rooms more, had more difficulty getting to doctors, hospitals, and clinics, and were more likely than Whites to go to a different doctor than the one they saw at their last visit (Stevens, 1989:1).
- Minority children are less likely to have routine physicals—3.5 percent of White children, 4.2 percent of Black children, and 9.2 percent of Hispanic children have never had a physical (*USA Today,* March 3, 1989).

Contemporary Trends and Issues in U.S. Racial and Ethnic Relations

As population shifts alter the racial composition of the United States, race relations are being transformed. Three major trends are indicative of the growing social problems associated with racial inequality. They are growing racial strife, the economic polarization of minorities, and a national shift in U.S. racial policies. All these trends are occurring in a global context, closely associated with macro social forces at work around the world.

Growing Racial Strife

Together with racial impoverishment, the growing immigrant and minority presence is adding tensions in society. Here, and in countries around the world, racial diversity is marked by growing conflicts. Some cities are like racially divided societies where minorities seldom meet Whites as neighbors or as classmates in public schools (Harris and Bennett, 1995:158). Racial tensions often erupt in violence between Whites and minorities and among minorities themselves as individuals compete for a shrinking number of jobs and other opportunities. The 1992 Los Angeles riots exhibited rivalries between neighborhood groups and between Whites, Blacks, Latinos, and Koreans.

Racial violence is often associated with uncertain economic conditions. Lack of jobs, housing, and other resources can add to fear and minority scapegoating on the part of Whites. Despite evidence that immigrants actually strengthen the social fabric, immigration is becoming a scapegoat for social problems (see the myths about immigration in Chapter 8). In Florida and many parts of the West and Southwest, perceptions that Cubans, Mexicans, and other Hispanics are taking jobs from

Anglos have touched off racial tensions. Racial violence in the United States appears to be on the rise:

- *More bias crime.* In 1992, Klanwatch of the Southern Poverty Law Center documented a record number of bias-motivated murders and a sharp rise in the number and brutality of hate crimes. This made 1992 the deadliest and most violent year since Klanwatch began tracking hate crimes in 1979 (SPLC Report, 1996:12).
- *More White Supremacism.* White supremacist groups with such diverse elements as the Ku Klux Klan, Nazi-identified parties, and skinheads have expanded across the country (Langer, 1990). These groups are up 27 percent from a decade earlier (Mayfield, 1992).

A CLOSER LOOK

Relations on College Campuses

Both Black and White students face the task of developing their race and ethnic identities. Sociologists and psychologists note that at the time people leave home and begin to live independently from their parents, often ages eighteen to twenty-two, they report a heightened sense of racial and ethnic identity as they sort through how much of their beliefs and behaviors are idiosyncratic to their families and how much are shared with other people. It is not until one comes in close contact with many people who are different from oneself that individuals realize the ways in which their backgrounds may influence their individual personality. This involves coming into contact with people who are different in terms of their ethnicity, class, religion, region, and race. For White students, the ethnicity they claim is more often than not a symbolic one—with all of the voluntary, enjoyable, and intermittent characteristics I have described above.

Black students at the university are also developing identities through interactions with others who are different from them. Their identity development is more complicated than that of Whites because of the added element of racial discrimination and racism, along with the "ethnic" developments of finding others who share their background. Thus Black students have the positive attraction of being around other Black students who share some cultural elements, as well as the need to band together with other students in a reactive and oppositional way in the face of racist incidents on campus.

Colleges and universities across the country have been increasing diversity among their student bodies in the last few decades. This has led in many cases to strained relations among students from different racial and ethnic backgrounds. The 1980s and 1990s produced a great number of racial incidents and high racial tensions on campuses. While there were a number of racial incidents that were due to bigotry, unlawful behavior, and violent or vicious attacks, much of what happens among students on campuses involves a low level of tension and awkwardness in social interactions.

Many Black students experience racism personally for the first time on campus. The upper-middle-class students from White suburbs were often isolated enough that their presence was not threatening to racists in their high schools. Also, their class background was known by their residence and this may have prevented attacks being directed at them. Often Black students at the university who begin talking with other students and recognizing racial slights will remember incidents that happened to them earlier that they might not have thought were related to race.

Black college students across the country experience a sizable number of incidents that are clearly the result of racism. Many of the most blatant ones that occur between students are the result of drinking.

- *Black Church Arson.* Since January 1990, there have been 57 reported cases of arson or serious vandalism carried out in the South against Black churches, 36 of them in 1995–96 (Herman, 1996:38).
- *Maltreatment and Arrests.* Numerous reports testify to the widespread police practice of systematically stopping (and sometimes savagely beating) Black-driven and Latino-driven vehicles (Herman, 1996:38).

Recent headlines about racism on college campuses have surprised many people because educational institutions are formally integrated. Yet, we are witnessing a growing "balkanization" among students of different racial and ethnic backgrounds, and a parallel increase in racial conflict and tension (Winant, 1994:58). (See "A Closer Look: Relations on College Campuses.") Campus racism is widespread. From

Sometimes late at night, drunken groups of White students coming home from parties will yell slurs at single Black students on the street. The other types of incidents that happen include being singled out for special treatment by employees, such as being followed when shopping at the campus bookstore, or going to the art museum with your class and the guard stops you and asks for your I.D. Others involve impersonal encounters on the street—being called a nigger by a truck driver while crossing the street, or seeing old ladies clutch their pocketbooks and shake in terror as you pass them on the street. For the most part these incidents are not specific to the university environment, they are the types of incidents middle-class Blacks face every day throughout American society, and they have been documented by sociologists (Feagin, 1991).

In such a climate, however, with students experiencing these types of incidents and talking with each other about them, Black students do experience a tension and a feeling of being singled out. It is unfair that this is part of their college experience and not that of White students. Dealing with incidents like this, or the ever-present threat of such incidents, is an ongoing developmental task for Black students that takes energy, attention, and strength of character. It should be clearly understood that this is an asymmetry in the "college experience" for Black and White students. It is one of the unfair aspects of life that results from living in a society with ongoing racial prejudice and dis-

crimination. It is also very understandable that it makes some students angry at the unfairness of it all, even if there is no one to blame specifically. It is also very troubling because, while most Whites do not create these incidents, some do, and it is never clear until you know someone well whether they are the type of person who could do something like this. So one of the reactions of Black students to these incidents is to band together.

In some sense then, as Blauner (1992) has argued, you can see Black students coming together on campus as both an "ethnic" pull of wanting to be together to share common experiences and community, and a "racial" push of banding together defensively because of perceived rejection and tension from Whites. In this way the ethnic identities of Black students are in some sense similar to, say, Korean students wanting to be together to share experiences. And it is an ethnicity that is generally much stronger than, say, Italian Americans. But for Koreans who come together there is generally a definition of themselves as "different from" Whites. For Blacks reacting to exclusion, there is a tendency for the coming together to involve both being "different from" but also "opposed to" Whites.

Source: Mary C. Waters, "Optional Ethnicities: For Whites Only?" in *Origins and Destinies: Immigration, Race, and Ethnicity in America,* Silvia Pedraza and Ruben G. Rumbaut, (eds.) Belmont, CA: Wadsworth, pp. 450–451.

MIT to the University of California-Berkeley, and on campuses across the nation, racial attacks on Blacks, Hispanics, and Asians are revealing an extensive problem of intolerance. These problems are not isolated or unusual events. Instead, they reflect what is occurring in society (Sidel, 1994).

Economic Polarization in U.S. Inner Cities

The concept of a troubled underclass, locked in U.S. inner cities due to behavioral deficiencies, is commonly used to explain racial poverty. This view argues that cultural disorganization locks inner-city people in a cycle of poverty. What explains concentrated racial poverty? According to this reasoning, poor habits and attitudes along with broken families prevent minorities from taking advantage of the opportunities created by antidiscriminatory legislation. Like the older deficiency models, this explanation is in error on many counts. It relies too heavily on behavioral traits to explain poverty. It falls back on blaming the victim to explain patterns that are actually rooted in social structure. Economic changes in society have removed jobs and other opportunities from inner-city residents, and their families have been severely affected. This is a better explanation of persistent and concentrated poverty among Blacks.

This explanation is detailed in William J. Wilson's compelling book, *The Truly Disadvantaged* (1987). According to Wilson, social problems of the ghetto are due to transformations of the larger economy and the class structure of ghetto neighborhoods. The movement of middle-class Black professionals from the inner city has left behind a concentration of the most disadvantaged segments of the Black urban population. Wilson's new book, *When Work Disappears* (1996), argues that crime, family dissolution, and welfare are consequences of the disappearance of work.

Wilson (1987) provides evidence that jobs influence the likelihood of marriage among Blacks. He suggests that increasing male joblessness is a major underlying factor in the rise of Black single mothers and female-headed households. Wage discrimination also works against marriage. Wilson found that men with higher incomes are more likely to be married than are men with lower incomes. The underclass is largely the result of a long-term decline in the proportion of Black men, and particularly young Black men, who are in a position to support a family. These structural conditions make it necessary for many Black women to leave a marriage or to forego marriage altogether. Adaptations to structural conditions leave Black women disproportionately divorced and responsible for their children. The Black inner city is not destroying itself by its own behaviors and culture but is being destroyed by economic forces.

Changes in the U.S. economy in the last few decades have also hit Latinos hard because of their low educational attainment and their labor market positions. However, structural unemployment has a different effect on the many diverse Latino barrios across the nation (Moore and Pinderhughes, 1994). While the loss of jobs in Rustbelt cities has left many Puerto Ricans living in a bleak ghetto economy, Mexicans living in the Southwest, where low-paying jobs remain, have not suffered the same degree of economic dislocation. High rates of structural unemployment have led to poverty and female headship rates that are converging with, and in some cases higher than, the rates among Blacks. Despite high levels of poverty, Latino communities do not conform to the conventional portrait of the underclass.

A structural analysis of concentrated poverty does not deny that inner cities are beset with a disproportionate share of social problems. Crime, gangs, pollution, drugs, and inadequate housing are concentrated in these settings. But a structural analysis *does* focus on social conditions, not immoral peoples. A structural analysis examines how rising inequality and government policies of social abandonment keep minorities outside the social safety net.

Racial Policies at Century's End

The 1960s civil rights movement legalized race-specific remedies to end racial bias. Government policies based on race overturned segregation laws, opened voting booths, created new job opportunities, and brought hopes of racial justice for people of color. As long as it appeared that conditions were improving, government policies to end racial justice remained in place. (See "Human Agency: 25 Years Seeking Justice.")

But by the end of the 1980s, the United States had become a very different society from the one in which civil rights legislation was enacted. The restructuring of the economy brought new forms of economic dislocation to both Whites and minorities. And as racial minorities became an ever-larger share of the U.S. population, issues of racial identity and racial politics became increasingly important. Many Whites began to claim their racial identity and to feel uncomfortable with race-conscious policies in schools and the workplace. Politicians resorted to race-baiting strategies in their political campaigns. Racial tensions escalated, and debates about fairness of racial policies entered the political arena.

Ironically, just as the United States is becoming a multiracial society, we are witnessing a backlash against civil rights reforms. Despite continued racial discrimina-

Kirk Anderson.

AGENCY

HUMAN

25 Years Seeking Justice

Montgomery, Ala.—On July 6,1996, the Southern Poverty Law Center celebrates 25 years of achievements in the courtroom and in the classroom.

The Center, which began as a small civil rights law firm in 1971, is now internationally known for its legal victories against white supremacist groups, its sponsorship of the Civil Rights Memorial and its national tolerance education project.

Beginnings

In the late 1960s, the major legislative victories of the Civil Rights Movement had been won. In Montgomery, Ala., two white Southern lawyers who shared a commitment to racial equality were determined to exercise the new laws to their fullest potential.

In the face of opposition from city and state officials, Morris Dees and Joseph Levin pursued equal opportunities for minorities and the poor. By taking *pro bono* cases that few others had the time and resources to pursue, they helped implement the Civil Rights Act of 1964 and the Voting Rights Act of 1965. Some of their early lawsuits resulted in the desegregation of recreational facilities, the reapportionment of the Alabama legislature, the integration of the Alabama state troopers and the reform of state prison conditions.

Committed to continuing their efforts on behalf of minorities and the poor, Dees and Levin in 1971 formally incorporated the Southern Poverty Law Center and began seeking nationwide support for their work. They mailed out thousands of letters detailing the needs of their clients and received donations from committed activists all over the country. These donations enabled them to hire a staff of lawyers and to stretch the boundaries of their former practice. (In 1976, Joe Levin re-

signed as the Center's Legal Director to serve on newly elected President Jimmy Carter's transition team. In 1979 Levin returned to chair the SPLC Board of Directors, a position he continues to hold in 1996.)

During the 1970s and '80s, the Law Center's persistent courtroom challenges led to the end of practices that discriminated against women in the armed forces, the end of involuntary sterilization of women on welfare, the granting of monetary awards to textile workers with brown lung disease, and the development of comprehensive trial strategies for lawyers doing death penalty defense work.

Combating the Klan

In 1979, the resurgence of the Ku Klux Klan in the South brought back horrible reminders of the lynchings and bombings of the Civil Rights era. When Klansmen in Decatur, Ala., attacked a peaceful civil rights gathering on May 26, 1979, the Law Center brought its first civil suit against a major Klan organization, and in 1981 created a new department, Klanwatch, to monitor organized hate activity across the country.

In the mid-1980s, under the guidance of a new legal director, Richard Cohen, Center attorneys developed strategies to hold white supremacist leaders accountable for violence committed by their followers. Suing for monetary damages for victims of Klan violence, the Center was able to bankrupt several major Klan organizations and to draw national attention to the growing threat of white supremacist activity.

Law Center civil suits would eventually result in judgments against 37 individuals and seven major white supremacist organizations for their roles in hate crimes. Multimillion-dollar judgments against the

tion in all areas of public life, major retreats have been made in policies related to affirmative action, school desegregation, and voting rights. From state governments, to Congress, to the Supreme Court, new laws are removing social and legal supports for racial equality. A new political agenda denies the significance of race in determining life chances. Recent Supreme Court decisions treat racism as either a thing of the past,

United Klans of America and the neo-Nazi White Aryan Resistance effectively put those organizations out of business. Other suits halted harassment of Vietnamese fishermen in Texas by the Knights of the KKK and paramilitary training by the White Patriot Party in North Carolina.

As the white supremacist movement became more sophisticated—its members trained in the use of weapons and explosives and organized into secret cells—the data compiled by Klanwatch became even more important to law enforcement officials. By 1995, the *Intelligence Report,* a bimonthly newsletter published by Klanwatch, was read by law enforcement officers in more than 6,000 agencies nationwide. Research provided by Klanwatch led to criminal convictions in several cases.

In 1994, Klanwatch formed a special Militia Task Force to investigate white supremacist activity within the antigovernment militia movement.

After the bombing, the Center's Militia Task Force was able to supply investigators nationwide with critical information about the militia movement. In April 1996, Klanwatch will publish a comprehensive militia report, *False Patriots,* which traces the roots of paramilitary antigovernment activity.

Running Risks

Morris Dees and Joe Levin never expected that their work would be popular in the South.

When the Law Center began taking on the Klan in court, the threats of retaliation against the Center became real. The original Law Center offices were burned by Klansmen in 1983. Twice, plots to bomb the Center were narrowly thwarted—in 1985, White Patriot Party members were arrested in the process of stealing money to buy explosives; in 1995, suspected militia followers were caught in the process of manufacturing explosives.

Security at the Center was dramatically heightened following the bombing of the federal building in Oklahoma City, with the hope that stricter precautions and state-of-the art protection will deter attackers. Still, the threats continue.

The Next Generation

Center lawsuits were effective in weakening organized white supremacist activity, but random hate crime was still rising in the late 1980s, particularly among the nation's youth.

In 1991, the Center expanded its educational efforts when it launched a new multimillion-dollar project, Teaching Tolerance, to provide teachers with free, top-quality classroom materials on tolerance and diversity. The first issue of *Teaching Tolerance* magazine was published in January 1992, and, at the same time, a video-and-text teaching kit for secondary school students on the Civil Rights Movement was released. The award-winning magazine is now read by more than 150,000 teachers, and two Teaching Tolerance curriculum kits are in use in more than 50,000 schools.

That these programs will still be needed in years to come is beyond doubt. As the nation grows more diverse, the Center will continue to challenge and protect our nation's most cherished democratic ideals, both in the courtroom and in the classroom.

Source: Southern Poverty Law Center Report. "25 Years of Seeking Justice," (March, 1996) pp. 1–2.

or simply a question of personal prejudice, while expressing solicitude for the rights of Whites allegedly injured by official efforts to assist minorities (Foner, 1996:6). Minority scapegoating has become national policy in the United States. Welfare reform and other attacks on budgets serving the poor are further evidence of a return to a harsh racism of the past (Sidel, 1996; Herman, 1996).

CHAPTER REVIEW

1. Racial and ethnic stratification are basic features of U.S. society. These forms of inequality are built into normal practices, and they exclude people from full and equal participation in society's institutions. Racial and ethnic stratification exist because they benefit certain segments of society.

2. Race is a social category that serves as a basis for differential treatment. The concept of race is socially rather than biologically significant. Racial groups are set apart and singled out for unequal treatment.

3. An ethnic group is culturally distinct in race, religion, or national origin. The group has a distinctive culture. Some ethnic groups such as Jews, Poles, and Italians have distinguishing cultural characteristics that stem from religion and national origin. Because racial groups also have distinctive cultural characteristics, they are referred to as racial-ethnics.

4. Minority racial and ethnic groups are systematically disadvantaged by society's institutions. Both race and ethnicity are traditional bases for systems of inequality, although there are historical and contemporary differences in the societal placement of racial-ethnics and White-ethnics in this society.

5. Racial-ethnic groups are socially subordinated and remain culturally distinct within U.S. society. African Americans, Latinos, Asian Americans, and Native Americans are constructed as both racially and culturally distinct. Each group has a distinctive culture, shares a common history, and has developed a common identity within a larger society that subordinates them.

6. Deficiency theories maintain that minority groups are unequal because they lack some important feature common among the majority. These deficiencies may be biological (such as low intelligence), structural (such as weak family ties), or cultural (such as the culture of poverty).

7. Bias theories place the blame for inequality on the prejudiced attitudes of the members of the dominant group. These theories, however, do not explain the discriminatory acts of the unprejudiced, which are aimed at preserving privilege.

8. Structural theories argue that inequality is the result of the politico-economic system that dominates and oppresses minorities. There are four main features of institutional discrimination: (*a*) the forces of history shape present conditions; (*b*) discrimination can occur without conscious bigotry; (*c*) this type of discrimination is less visible than are individual acts of discrimination; and (*d*) discrimination is reinforced by the interrelationships among the institutions of society.

9. The assimilation model—that minorities will eventually become part of the mainstream once they give up their distinctive ethnicity and learn the skills required by society—does not apply to all minorities. Ongoing immigration within a changing racial order calls for new explanations of minority status.

10. Civil rights legislation improved the status of some racial ethnics, yet the overall position of Blacks and Hispanics relative to Whites has not improved. Large gaps remain in work, earnings, and education. Changing conditions in the economy have contributed to the persistent poverty in U.S. urban centers.

11. The racial demography of the United States is changing dramatically. Immigration and high birth rates among minorities are making this a multiracial, multicultural society. These trends are also creating new forms of racial segregation and racial conflict.

12. Public policy has shifted from race-conscious remedies to a color-blind climate that is dismantling historic civil rights reforms.

KEY TERMS

Majority group
Minority group
Race
Racial formation
Ethnicity

Racial-ethnic group
Deficiency theories
Bias theories
Structural discrimination theories
Institutional racism

Individual racism
Colonial theory
Assimilate
Environmental racism

STUDY QUESTIONS

1. What constitutes a minority group?

2. What is the key difference between deficiency theories and bias theories as they explain the existence of minorities?

3. Order theories argue that minorities should eventually assimilate. What does this mean, and why does the conflict perspective disagree with this assumption?

4. How does the social organization of society work to keep minorities subordinate?

5. What is meant by the changing demography of race? What are the anticipated consequences of this trend for schools, employment, incidents of violence, and life chances?

6. Is the persistent poverty of minorities a consequence of culture or structure?

FOR FURTHER READING

Margaret L. Andersen and Patricia Hill Collins, *Race, Class, and Gender: An Anthology,* 2nd ed. (Belmont, CA: Wadsworth Publishing Company, 1992).

Douglas S. Massey and Nancy Denton, *American Apartheid: Segregation and the Making of the Underclass* (Cambridge: Harvard University Press, 1993).

Joan W. Moore and Raquel Pinderhues, *In The Barrios: Latinos and The Underclass Debate* (New York: Russell Sage Foundation, 1994).

Rebecca Morales and Frank Bonilla, *Latinos in a Changing U.S. Economy* (Newbury Park, CA: Sage, 1993).

Michael Omi and Howard Winant, *Racial Formation in the United States,* 2nd ed. (New York: Routledge & Kegan Paul, 1994).

Silvia Pedraza and Ruben G. Rumbaut, eds., *Origins and Destinies: Immigration, Race, and Ethnicity in America* (Belmont, CA: Wadsworth, 1996).

Ruth Sidel, *Battling Bias* (New York: Viking Penguin, 1994).

C. Matthew Snipp, *American Indians: The First of This Land* (New York: Russell Sage Foundation, 1989).

Ronald Takaki, *A Different Mirror: A History of Multicultural America* (Boston: Little, Brown and Company, 1993).

David T. Wellman, *Portraits of White Racism* (Cambridge: Cambridge University Press, 1977).

William Julius Wilson, *When Work Disappears: The World of the New Urban Poor* (New York: Knopf, 1996).

Norman R. Yetman, ed., *Majority and Minority: The Dynamics of Racial and Ethnic Relations,* 5th ed. (Boston: Allyn and Bacon, 1991).

CHAPTER 12

Gender Inequality

Introduction

There is no nation where women and men are equals. Worldwide, women perform an estimated 60 percent of the work, yet they earn only 10 percent of the income and own only 10 percent of the land. Two-thirds of the world's illiterate are women. Despite massive political changes and economic progress in countries throughout the world, women continue to be the victims of abuse and discrimination. Even where women have made important strides in politics and the professions, women's overall progress remains uneven.

This chapter examines the patterns of behavior and social organization that make women unequal to men. The gender system organizes society in such a way that women and men are treated differently. From the macro level of the societal economy, through the institutions of society, to interpersonal relations, gender shapes activities, roles, and rewards. Gender is the patterning of difference and domination through distinctions between women and men (Acker, 1992:565). Virtually everything social is gendered. **Gendered** refers to distinguishing and differentially evaluating males and females.

Until recently, gender differentiation seemed natural. New research shows that gender is not natural at all but is socially constructed. Gender differences are a means of organizing the social world. Gender polarity refers to the fact that males and females are cast as opposites and placed into two mutually exclusive categories. This dichotomization is one of the central organizing principles of social life. In fact, the point of gender differentiation is "to justify the exploitation of an identifiable group—women" (Lorber, 1994:5).

Gender is not only about women. Men often think of themselves as "genderless," as if gender did not matter in the daily experience of their lives. However, their experiences throughout the life course and all social arenas are deeply gendered (Kimmel and Messner, 1995). In the aggregate, gender divisions make women unequal to men. But we cannot comprehend the gender system, nor women's and men's experiences, by looking at gender alone. Gender intersects with other characteristics such as race, class, and sexual orientation. As a result, different groups of men exhibit varying degrees of power, and different groups of women exhibit varying levels of inequality. Nevertheless, **gender polarity** denies both women and men the full range of human and social possibilities. The social inequalities created by gender differentiation are detrimental for society at large. This chapter examines **gender stratification** in U.S. society at both structural and interpersonal levels of social organization. Taking a **feminist approach** (one in support of women's equality), the theme of this chapter is that social rather than individual conditions are responsible for women's inequality.

The Differentiation and Ranking of Women and Men

Females and males are dichotomized and they are ranked. Gender stratification refers to the ranking of the sexes in such a way that women are unequal in power, resources, prestige, and presumed worth. Women's and men's roles are not the same throughout the world, but every society has certain ideas about what women and men should be like as well as ways of producing people who are much like these expectations.

To emphasize the point that gender is a socially constructed experience rather than a biological imperative, sociologists distinguish between *sex* and *gender.* **Sex** refers to one's biological identity as male or female. **Gender** is a learned identity—but as with race, it cannot be understood at the individual level alone (Andersen and Collins, 1995:327).

Scientist have competing explanations for gender differences. Biological models argue that innate biological differences between males and females program different social behaviors. Anthropological models look at masculinity and femininity cross-culturally, stressing the variations in women's and men's roles. Sociologists have tended to argue that gender differences are explained by differential learning (Kimmel and Messner, 1995:vx).

Is Gender Based on Biological or Social Differences?

We know that there are biological differences between the two sexes. The key question is whether these unlearned differences in the sexes contribute to the gender differences found in societies. To answer this question, let us first review the evidence for each position.

The Biological Bases for Gender Roles.   Males and females are different from the moment of conception. Chromosomal and hormonal differences make males and females physically different. Hormonal differences in the sexes are also significant. The male hormones (androgens) and female hormones (estrogens) direct the process of sex differentiation from about six weeks after conception throughout life. They make males taller, heavier, and more muscular. At puberty they trigger the production of secondary sexual characteristics. In males, these include body and facial hair, a deeper voice, broader shoulders, and a muscular body. In females, puberty brings pubic hair, menstruation, the ability to lactate, prominent breasts, and relatively broad hips. Actually, males and females have both sets of hormones. The relative proportion of androgens and estrogens gives a person masculine or feminine physical traits.

These hormonal differences may explain in part why males tend to be more active, aggressive, and dominant than females. Studies in animals provide some evidence for this assertion. Castrated rats and monkeys, deprived of the sex hormones created by the testes, have decreased levels of aggression. When testosterone is injected into these castrated males, their aggression levels increase (Quadagno, Briscoe, and Quadagno, 1977). However, critics of the biological model have argued that research on animals is irrelevant for human beings because of the importance of socialization and culture.

Biological differences that do exist between women and men are only averages, and they are often influenced by other factors. For example, although men are on the average larger than women, body size is influenced by diet and physical activity, which in turn may be influenced by culture, class, and race. The all-or-none categorizing of gender traits is misleading because there is considerable overlap in the distribution of traits possessed by women and men. Although most men are stronger than most women, some men are weaker than some women, and vice versa. And although males are on the average more aggressive than females, greater difference may be found among males than among males and females (Basow, 1996:81). Furthermore, gender is constantly changing. Femininity and masculinity do not bubble up into behavior codes from our genetic makeup. Instead, they are socially constructed, changing (1) from one culture to another, (2) within any one culture over time, (3) over the course of all women's and men's lives, and (4) between and among different groups of women and men, depending on class, race, ethnicity, and sexuality (Kimmel, 1992:166).

The Social Bases for Gender Roles.   Every society transforms biological females and males into socially interacting women and men. The cross-cultural evidence shows a wide variation of behaviors for the sexes. Table 12.1 provides some interesting cross-cultural data from 224 societies on the division of labor by sex. This table shows that for the majority of activities, societies are not uniform in their gendered division of labor. Even activities requiring strength, presumably a male trait, are not strictly apportioned to males. In fact, activities such as burden-bearing and water-carrying are done by females more than by males. Even an activity like house building is not exclusively male. Even though there is a wide variety in the social roles assigned to women and men, their roles "do not vary randomly" (O'Kelly, 1980:41). In most societies of the world, the domestic and familial is the world of women and that of the public and political is the world of men.

TABLE 12.1

Gender Allocation in Selected Technological Activities in 224 Societies

ACTIVITY	Number of Societies in Which the Activity Is Performed by:					
	MALES EXCLUSIVELY	MALES USUALLY	BOTH SEXES EQUALLY	FEMALES USUALLY	FEMALES EXCLUSIVELY	% MALE
Smelting of ores	37	0	0	0	0	100.0
Hunting	139	5	0	0	0	99.3
Boat building	84	3	3	0	1	96.6
Mining and quarrying	31	1	2	0	1	93.7
Land clearing	95	34	6	3	1	90.5
Fishing	83	45	8	5	2	86.7
Herding	54	24	14	3	3	82.4
House building	105	30	14	9	20	77.4
Generation of fire	40	6	16	4	20	62.3
Preparation of skins	39	4	2	5	31	54.6
Crop planting	27	35	33	26	20	54.4
Manufacture of leather products	35	3	2	5	29	53.2
Crop tending	22	23	24	30	32	44.6
Milking	15	2	8	2	21	43.8
Carrying	18	12	46	34	36	39.3
Loom weaving	24	0	6	8	50	32.5
Fuel gathering	25	12	12	23	94	27.2
Manufacture of clothing	16	4	11	13	78	22.4
Pottery making	14	5	6	6	74	21.1
Dairy production	4	0	0	0	24	14.3
Cooking	0	2	2	63	117	8.3
Preparation of vegetables	3	1	4	21	145	5.7

Source: Adapted from George P. Murdock and Caterina Provost, "Factors in the Division of Labor by Sex: A Cross-Cultural Analysis," *Ethnology* 12 (April, 1973):207. Reprinted by permission of the publisher.

Gender and Power

Gender is inseparable from power; it is defined by access to power. This means that gender relations are, among other things, about men's power over women. Everywhere we look—politics, corporate life, family life—men are *in power*. But men are not uniformly dominant. Some men have great power over other men. In fact, most men do not *feel* powerful; most feel powerless, trapped in stifling old roles and un-

able to implement the changes in their lives that they want (Kimmel, 1992:171). Yet male dominance through distinctions between women and men are integral to many social processes (Acker, 1992:565).

Male dominance refers to the beliefs, values, and cultural meanings that give higher value and prestige to masculinity than to femininity, that value men over women, and that institutionalize male control of socially valued resources. **Patriarchy** is the term used for forms of social organization in which men are dominant over women.

Patriarchy is intertwined with other inequalities to sort women and men differently. The interaction of race, class, and gender relations produces differences among women and differences among men. Some women derive benefits from their race and their class while they are simultaneously restricted by gender. Such women are subordinated by patriarchy, yet race and class intersect to create for them privileged opportunities and ways of living. Similarly, manhood is defined in opposition to subordinated men (Baca Zinn, et al., 1997). Men are encouraged to behave in "masculine" fashion to prove that they are not gay (Connell, 1992). In defining masculinity as the negation of homosexuality, *compulsory heterosexuality* is

Femininity and masculinity are socially constructed and change along with other norms of behavior.

an important component of the gender system. **Compulsory heterosexuality** imposes negative sanctions on those who are homosexual or bisexual. This system of sexuality shapes the gender order by discouraging attachment with members of the same sex. This enforces the dichotomy of "opposite" sexes. Sexuality is also a form of inequality in its own right because it systematically grants privileges to those in heterosexual relationships. Like race, class, and gender, sexual identities are socially constructed categories. **Sexuality** is a way of organizing the social world based on sexual identity and a key linking process in the matrix of domination structured along the lines of race, class, and gender (Messner, 1996:223). (See "A Closer Look: Lesbians, Gays, and Other 'Queers' in the Matrix of Domination.")

Another important issue in the study of gender has been whether male dominance is universal, found in all societies across time and space. Many scholars once adopted this position, claiming that all societies exhibit some forms of patri-

A CLOSER LOOK

Lesbians, Gays, and Other "Queers" in the Matrix of Domination

If I told you that sexuality, like gender, race, and class, is an organizing principle of society, you might actually think about it for awhile. Then if I told you I'm a lesbian, you might say, "This is bunk. You just want special treatment so you can get a larger piece of the American pie." And I would smile and say, "Sexuality is an *equal* piece of the pie; a point that many people refute. The very fact that you question my motives based on my sexuality illustrates how the experiences and thoughts of lesbians, gays, and other 'queers' are dismissed and subordinated by a dominant heterosexual society." So you want me to prove to you that sexuality deserves equal status? Okay, I will.

Several forms of stratification organize social life. They create hierarchies which offer different opportunities to different people. Race, class, and gender are socially and economically structured inequalities. They have three main characteristics (Baca Zinn and Eitzen, 1996). First, they are hierarchies of stratification, or structured inequalities. *Structured* refers to socially patterned stratifications. This means that inequalities are based on social, not biological, factors. Second, structured inequalities socially locate groups of people differently so that some have greater (or less) access to wealth, power, and privilege. Based on their distinctive social locations, people have different life

chances and experiences. Finally, this leads to relations of power and domination. Because structural inequalities allocate resources on an unequal basis, people with wealth, power, and privilege dominate those with limited access to those resources.

As a lesbian, it is easy for me to see how sexuality fits the definition of an organizing principle. Sexuality is a socially patterned hierarchical system. My sexuality has been manipulated to differentiate me as inferior to heterosexual women. The social interpretation that one sexuality is more "moral" or "natural" is based on this hierarchical system. Furthermore, there are no privileges associated with being nonheterosexual. Lesbians and gays have no legal support to secure a job, a home, or a family. Finding a neighborhood where people approve of our existence is next to impossible. We don't even have the privilege to love who we chose without facing social and economic consequences.

In terms of wealth, if we are "out" to our coworkers, we risk losing our jobs. Thus, by virtue of who we are we have precarious access to wealth through work. And what kind of power do we have? Being denied legal and financial power makes access to any other power nearly impossible. Of course we do have the collective power to resist.

archy in marriage and family forms, in division of labor, and in society at large (Ortner, 1974; Rosaldo, 1974). More recently, however, scholars have challenged the universality of patriarchy by producing cases that serve as counterexamples (Shapiro, 1981). Today, the thinking in anthropology tends to follow the latter course. Sexual differentiation, it seems, is found in all societies, but it does not always indicate low female status (Rogers, 1978). Gender stratification, male dominance, and female subordination are not constants. Just as these conditions vary as they interact with other inequalities in any given society, they also vary from society to society.

It is important to keep in mind that although women may be subordinate, they are not always passive victims of patriarchy. Like other oppressed groups, they have created various survival strategies and have often engaged in political struggles to end discrimination.

But sexuality is a system based on relations of power and domination. Society is organized along heterosexual lines. If you are emotionally and physically intimate with someone of the other sex, then you are rewarded by having access to the legal, emotional, and material goods of society. Heterosexuals have created social institutions to support their own existence. They oppress those who diverge from their mythical "norm."

While this is all clear to me, many feminists see sexuality as coming from the rib of gender and not as its own hierarchy of stratification. I agree that sexuality and gender share a very special relationship. One link between these two social forces involves notions of femininity and masculinity. These are both gendered concepts, ones which if adhered to or disregarded, place people's sexuality in privileged or socially challenged positions. For example, women who cut their hair short, don't shave their legs, don't wear make-up, or who deny men sexual access are not real "women." Similarly, men who are "effeminate" or don't prove their masculinity through sexual relations with women are not "real" men. In fact, these women and men are seen as both genderly and sexually "queer." These prescribed gender roles are socially constructed to keep heterosexual men in power and allow them both gender and sexual control over certain women and men.

The special relationship between gender and sexuality blurs their boundaries, making them hard to discern from one another. Despite this complexity, ignoring their distinctions and subsuming one under the other is misguided. It is crucial to understand sexual oppression separate from gender oppression. I am both a woman and a lesbian. I experience the sexism most women feel in the United States. But when homophobic people know that I am a lesbian, that's a whole different oppression. A good example is motherhood. A heterosexual woman who decides *not* to have children goes against *gender* norms. But a lesbian who decides to *have* children goes against *sexuality* norms (Lewin, 1993). In this case, the lesbian is actually following socially prescribed *gender* norms. Gender and sexuality are clearly enmeshed, but they are different.

Obscuring sexuality through gender invalidates people's lives. It makes them invisible and gives a distorted view of the social world. If sociologists and feminists want to understand what Patricia Hill Collins (1990) calls the matrix of domination, we must see sexuality as a social system in its own right and not hide it under the guise of gender.

Source: Nancy J. Mezey, 1997. Department of Sociology, Michigan State University. This was written expressly for the eighth edition of *In Conflict and Order.*

Gender Stratification from the Order and the Conflict Perspectives

The Order Perspective

From the order perspective, biology, history, and the needs of society combine to separate men and women into distinctive roles. Biologically, men are stronger, and women bear and nurse children. These facts have meant that men have tended to be the providers, while women have naturally dealt with childrearing and family nurturance.

The necessity for women to nurse their infants and stay near home meant that for most of human history they have done the domestic chores while men were free to hunt and leave the village for extended periods. Thus, a whole set of customs and traditions supporting men as the providers and women as the nurturers established the expectations for future generations of men and women.

Although modern technology has freed women from the necessity of staying at home and has allowed them to work at jobs formerly requiring great strength, the order theorists believe that the traditional division of labor is beneficial for society as a whole. The clear-cut expectations for each sex fulfill many needs for individuals and provide order. The traditional roles for men and women—for example, women as housekeepers and rearers of children and men as breadwinners—promote stable families and an efficient system of specialized roles, with boys and girls trained throughout their youth to take their natural places in society.

Talcott Parsons, a major order theorist, has argued that with industrialization, the family and the role of women as nurturers and caretakers have become more important than ever. The husband in the competitive world outside the home needs a place of affection. As women take on the "expressive" roles of providing affection and emotional support within the family, men perform "instrumental" roles outside the family that provide economic support. Not only is this division of labor practical, but it is also necessary because it assures that the important societal tasks are accomplished (Parsons, Bales, et al., 1955:3–9).

The Conflict Perspective

A different view of gender emerges from the conflict perspective. Conflict theorists are critical of the order model because it neglects what is most important about gender roles—that they are unequal in power, resources, and prestige. According to the conflict view, gender roles are not neutral ways of meeting societies' needs but are part of the larger system of power and domination.

There are several conflict models of gender stratification. All emphasize male control and domination of both women and valued resources. For example, Randall Collins has traced gender stratification in simple societies as well as in those that are more complex. In simple societies, men dominate by virtue of sheer strength. As societies become more developed, male domination takes the form of control of valued economic resources. Women use their femininity to acquire resources through marriage, but they become subordinated in the process (Collins, 1972, 1975).

Most conflict theories explain gender stratification as an outcome of how women and men are tied to the economic structure of society (Nielson, 1990:215). This idea originated in the work of Friedrich Engels and Karl Marx, who viewed marriage as a means of enforcing male power. As societies moved beyond subsistence stages and private property developed, men instituted the monogamous family in order to pass on wealth to their biological children.

Gender stratification theories say women's economic role in society is a primary determinant of their overall status (Dunn, 1996:60). They point out that women's roles of mother and wife, although vital to the well-being of society, are devalued and also deny women access to highly valued resources. They point out that gender stratification is greater where women's work is directed inward to the family and men's work is directed outward to trade and the marketplace. The domestic and public spheres of activity are associated with different amounts of property, power, and prestige. Women's reproductive roles and their responsibilities for domestic labor limit their association with the resources that are highly valued (Rosaldo, 1980). Men are freed from these responsibilities. Their economic obligations in the public sphere assure them control of highly valued resources and give rise to male privilege.

In capitalist societies the domestic–public split is even more significant, because highly valued goods and services are exchanged in the public, not the domestic, sphere. Women's domestic labor, although important for survival, ranks low in prestige and power because it does not produce exchangeable commodities (Sacks, 1974). Because of the connections between the class relations of production (*capitalism*) and the hierarchical gender relations of its society (*patriarchy*) (Eisenstein, 1979), the United States is a capitalist patriarchy where male supremacy keeps women in subordinate roles at work and in the home.

The Implications of the Order and the Conflict Perspectives

A point should be made about the implications of the conflict and the order perspectives. Each position, with its emphasis on different factors, calls for a different approach to the study of gender. One consequence of the focus on gender roles by the order model has been to treat gender inequality as a problem of roles. Outmoded masculine and feminine roles are thought to be responsible for keeping women from achieving their full potential. This interpretation is inadequate because it ignores the ways in which women's roles are based on and reproduce relations of power.

The difference between the order and the conflict models lies in whether the individual or the society is the primary unit of analysis. The **gender-roles approach** emphasizes characteristics that individuals acquire during the course of socialization, such as independent or dependent behaviors and ways of relating. The **structural approach** emphasizes factors that are external to individuals, such as the social structures and concrete settings that are themselves gendered, that shape gendered interaction, and that locate and reward women and men differently. These approaches differ in how they view the sexes, in how they explain the causes and effects of sexism, and in the solutions they suggest for the elimination of inequality. Both the individual and the structural approaches are necessary for a complete understanding of sexism. This chapter places primary emphasis on social structure as the cause of inequality. Sociologists have moved from studying gender as individual attributes to the study of gendered institutions. As Joan Acker explains, "the term **'gendered institutions'** means that gender is present in the processes, practices, images, and ideologies, and distributions of power in the various sectors of social life. Taken more or less as functioning wholes, the institutional structures of the United States and other societies are organized along lines of gender" (Acker, 1992:567). Although gender roles are learned by individuals and produce differences in the personalities, behaviors, and motivations of women and men, gender stratification essentially is maintained by societal forces.

Learning Gender

The most complex, demanding, and all-involving role that a member of society must learn to play is that of female or male. "Casting" for one's gender role

> takes place immediately at birth, after a quick biological inspection; and the role of "female" or "male" is assigned. It is an assignment that will last one's entire lifetime and affect virtually everything one ever does. A large part of the next 20 years or so will be spent gradually learning and perfecting one's assigned sex role; slowly memorizing what a "young lady" should do and should not do, how a "little man" should react in each of a million frightening situations—practicing, practicing, playing house, playing cowboys, practicing—and often crying in confusion and frustration at the baffling and seemingly endless task. (David and Brannon, 1980:117)

From infancy through early childhood and beyond, children learn what is expected of boys and girls, and they learn to behave according to those expectations.

The characteristics associated with traditional gender roles are those valued by the dominant society. Keep in mind that the gender is not the same in all classes and races. However, most research on gender socialization reflects primarily the experience of White middle-class persons—those who are most often the research subjects of these studies. How gender is learned depends of a variety of social conditions affecting the socialization practices of girls and boys. Still, society molds boys and girls along different lines.

The Child at Home

Girls and boys are perceived and treated differently from the moment of birth. Parents describe newborn daughters as tiny, soft, and delicate, and sons as strong and alert (Richardson, 1981:48), and they interact differently with newborn daughters and sons. In comparing the lives of young girls with those of young boys, we find a critical difference: girls are treated more protectively and subjected to more restrictions and controls; boys receive greater achievement demands and higher expectations. Girl infants are talked to more. Girls are the objects of more physical contact such as holding, rocking, caressing, and kissing (Lewis, 1972). We also know that fathers, especially working-class fathers, are more concerned than mothers about their young children engaging in behaviors considered inappropriate for their sex.

Research comparing the influence that mothers, fathers, and peers in rewarding and punishing gendered behavior in three- and five-year-old children found that fathers provided the strongest pressures for gender-specific behaviors (Langlois and Downs, 1980). In addition, fathers used different techniques with daughters and sons. They rewarded their daughters and gave them positive feedback for gendered behavior. With their sons they used more negative feedback and punished them for gender-inappropriate behavior. Mothers were more likely to reinforce behavior of both boys and girls with rewards and positive feedback. Peers, in contrast, were more likely to use punishment on both sexes. The researchers concluded that the combined pattern of the three socializing agents provides a finely tuned system in which fathers, mothers, and peers each make a unique contribution in reinforcing gendered behavior (Langlois and Downs, 1980).

In addition to the parents' active role in reinforcing society's gender demands, a subtler message is emitted from picture books for preschool children. A classic sociological study of eighteen award-winning children's books from 1967 to 1971 found the following characteristics (Weitzman, et al., 1972):

- Females were virtually invisible. The ratio of male pictures to female pictures was 11:1. The ratio of male to female animals was 95:1.
- The activities of boys and girls varied greatly. Boys were active in outdoor activities, while girls were passive and most often found indoors. The activity of the girls typically was that of some service for boys.
- Adult men and women (role models) were very different. Men led, women followed. Females were passive and males active. Not one woman in these books had a job or profession; they were always mothers and wives.

Since the 1960s, there have been improvements in how girls and women are portrayed. Females are no longer invisible, they are as likely as males to be included in the books, and they have begun to move outside the home if not into the labor market. In many respects, however, female storybook characters remain consistent with traditional culture. An update of the classic Weitzman study found that no behavior was shared by a majority of the females, whereas all males were portrayed as independent and active. Girls expressed no career goals, and there were no adult female role models to provide any ambition. The researchers found that only one woman in the entire 1980s collection of twenty-four books had an occupation outside of the home, and she worked "as a waitress at the Blue Tile Diner" (Williams, et al., 1987:155). Today, female characters are more likely to be depicted using household artifacts, whereas men use non-domestic objects (summarized in Andersen, 1997:39).

Two books by the same author best illustrate how children's books are biased toward traditional occupational roles apportioned by sex. The first book, *What Boys Can Be,* lists fourteen occupations: fireman, baseball player, bus driver, policeman, cowboy, doctor, sailor, pilot, clown, zoo manager, farmer, actor, astronaut, and president (Walley, n.d.). The book *What Girls Can Be* also lists fourteen occupations: nurse, stewardess, ballerina, candyshop owner, model, actress, secretary, artist, nursery school teacher, singer, dress designer, bride, housewife, and mother (Walley, n.d.).

Even the television show *Sesame Street* is sexist! Although it is one of the best shows on television for small children, and the adult characters of the show are balanced, the puppet stars of the show are gendered. Bert, Ernie, and most of the major animal characters are male. The female puppets always play children while the male puppets play adult parts (Heiman and Bookspan, 1992:30).

Differences can be found even where gender roles are changing and socialization is becoming more flexible or androgynous. **Androgyny** refers to the integration of traditional feminine and masculine characteristics. Jeanne Brooks-Gunn at the Educational Testing Service in Princeton, New Jersey, conducted a study of masculine, feminine, and androgynous mothers. The androgynous mothers were self-reliant as well as tender, affectionate as well as assertive. Although they encouraged nurturing and independent behavior in their daughters, they did not promote nurturing in their sons. One can thus speculate that in the next generation, some females will be androgynous but that men will still be socialized in the traditional way (Shreve, 1984:43). Research by Jacqueline Eccles has found that parents uphold sex stereotypes more in the 1980s than they did in the 1970s, when she began her research (cited in Keegan, 1989:26).

The Child at Play

Children teach each other to behave according to cultural expectations. Same-sex peers exert a profound influence on how gender is learned. In a classic study of children's play groups, Janet Lever discovered how children's play groups stress particular social skills and capabilities for boys and others for girls. Her research among fifth graders, most of whom were White and middle class, found that boys, more than girls, (1) played outdoors, (2) played in larger groups, (3) played in age-heterogeneous groups, (4) were less likely to play in games dominated by the opposite sex, (5) played more competitive games, and (6) played in games that lasted longer (Lever, 1976).

Barrie Thorne's study of gender play in multiracial school settings (1993) found that boys control more space, more often violate girls' activities, and treat girls as contaminating. According to Thorne, these common ritualized interactions reflect larger structures of male dominance. In reality, the fun and games of everyday school children are *power play,* a complex social process involving both gender separation and togetherness and changing with age, ethnicity, race, class, and social context. Thorne shifts the focus from individuals to social relations in her analysis of how children create and recreate gender in their daily interactions:

> The social construction of gender is an active and ongoing process. . . . Gender categories, gender identities, gender divisions, gender-based groups, gender meanings—all are produced actively and collaboratively, in everyday life. When kids maneuver to form

same-gender groups on the playground or organize a kickball game as "boys-against-the-girls," they produce a sense of gender as dichotomy and opposition. And when girls and boys work cooperatively on a classroom project, they actively undermine a sense of gender as opposition. This emphasis on action and activity, and on everyday social interactions that are sometimes contradictory, provides an antidote to the view of children as passively socialized. Gender is not something one passively "is" or "has". . . . (Thorne, 1993:4–5)

Toys play a major part in gender socialization. Toys entertain children; they also teach particular skills and encourage children to explore through play a variety of roles they may occupy as adults. Today, most toys for sale are gender-linked. Toys for boys tend to encourage exploration, manipulation, invention, construction, competition, and aggression. In contrast, girls' toys typically rate high on manipulability, creativity, nurturance, and attractiveness. Playing with gendered toys may be related to the development of differential cognitive skills and social skills in girls and boys (Renzetti and Curan, 1995:94–95).

Dichotomous gender experiences may be more characteristic among White middle-class children than among children of other races. An important study on Black adolescent girls by Joyce Ladner has shown that Black girls develop in a more independent fashion (Ladner, 1971). Other research has also found that among African Americans, both girls and boys are expected to be nurturant and expressive emotionally as well as independent, confident, and assertive (McAdoo, 1988; Stack, 1990).

Formal Education

In 1972, Congress outlawed sex discrimination in public schools though Title IX of the Educational Amendments Act. But girls and boys in the United States are still not receiving the same education. A major report by the American Association of University Women (AAUW) (1992) offers compelling evidence that 20 years after the passage of Title IX, discrimination remains pervasive. Whether one looks at achievement scores, curriculum design, or teacher–student interaction, schools shortchange girls. Let us examine the following areas: course offerings, textbooks, teacher–student interactions, sports, female role models, and counseling.

Curriculum.   Schools are charged with the responsibility of equipping students to study subjects (e.g., reading, writing, mathematics, and history) known collectively as the formal curriculum. But schools also teach students particular social, political, and economic values that constitute the so-called hidden curriculum operating alongside the more formal one. Both formal and informal curricula are powerful shapers of gender (Renzetti and Curan, 1995:105). The AAUW Report offers the following findings (taken from the AAUW Report Executive Summary, 1992):

- Differences between girls and boys in math achievement are small and declining. Yet, in high school, girls are still less likely than boys to take the most advanced courses and to be in the top-scoring math groups.
- The gender gap in science, however, is not decreasing and may, in fact, be increasing. One-fourth of boys take physics in high school, in contrast to 15 percent of girls.

■ The *evaded curriculum* is a term coined in the AAUW report to refer to matters central to the lives of students that are touched on only briefly, if at all, in most schools. Students receive inadequate education on sexuality, teen pregnancy, the AIDS crisis, and the increase of sexually transmitted diseases among adolescents.

Textbooks.   The content of textbooks transmits messages to readers about society, about children, and about what adults are supposed to do. For this reason, individuals and groups concerned about gender bias in schools have looked carefully at how males and females are portrayed in textbooks assigned to students. Their findings provide a consistent message: textbooks commonly used in U.S. schools are both overtly and covertly sexist. Sexism has become a recent concern of publishers, and a number have created guidelines for creating positive sexual and racial images in educational materials.

Despite these efforts, the AAUW study reports that the contributions of girls and women are still marginalized or ignored in many textbooks used in our nation's schools (1992). Regardless of the subject—English, history, reading, science— minorities and women continue to be underrepresented. When women are mentioned, it is usually in terms of traditional feminine roles, such as for nursing, Florence Nightingale; for sewing, Betsy Ross; and Dolley Madison and Jackie Kennedy Onassis for being married to famous men (Renzetti and Curan, 1995:117).

Teacher–Student Interactions.   Even when girls and boys are in the same classrooms, they are educated differently. Girls receive significantly less attention from classroom teachers than do boys. A large body of research indicates that teachers give more classroom attention and more esteem-building encouragement to boys.

In one study conducted by Myra and David Sadker, boys in elementary and middle school called out answers eight times more often than girls. When boys called out, teachers listened. But when girls called out, they were told to "raise your hand if you want to speak" (cited in AAUW Report, 1992). Even when boys do not volunteer, teachers are more likely to encourage them to give an answer or an opinion than they are to encourage girls (Sadker and Sadker, 1994).

Teachers are now being advised to encourage cooperative cross-sex learning, to monitor their own (teacher) behavior, to be sure that they reward male and female students equally, and actively familiarize students with gender atypical roles by assigning them specific duties as leaders, recording secretary, and so on (Lockheed, 1985, cited in Giele, 1988).

The Reinforcement of Gender in School Sports.   Sports in U.S. high schools and colleges have historically been almost exclusively a male preserve (this section is dependent on Eitzen and Sage, 1997). The truth of this observation is clearly evident if one compares by sex the number of participants, facilities, support of school administrations, and financial support.

Such disparities have been based on the traditional assumptions that competitive sport is basically a masculine activity and that the proper roles of girls and women are as spectators and cheerleaders. What is the impact on a society that encourages its boys and young men to participate in sports while expecting its girls and young women to be spectators and cheerleaders? Sports reinforce societal expectations for males and females. Males are to be dominant and aggressive—the doers—while females are expected to be passive supporters of men, attaining status through the efforts of their menfolk.

An important consequence of this traditional view is that approximately one-half of the population was denied access to all that sport has to offer (physical conditioning, enjoyment, teamwork, goal attainment, ego enhancement, social status, and competitiveness). School administrators, school boards, and citizens of local communities have long assumed that sports participation has general educational value. If so, then girls and women should also be allowed to receive the benefits.

In 1972 passage of Title IX of the Educational Amendments Act required that schools receiving federal funds must provide equal opportunities for males and females. Despite considerable opposition by school administrators, athletic directors, and school boards, major changes have occurred over time because of this federal legislation. More monies were spent on womens' sports; better facilities and equipment were provided; and women were gradually accepted as athletes. The most significant result was an increase in female participation. The number of high school girls participating in interscholastic sports increased from 300,000 in 1971 to 2.2 million in 1995. By 1995, 39 percent of all high school participants were female, and the number of sports available to them was more than twice the number available in 1970. Similar growth patterns occurred in colleges and universities.

On the positive side, budgets for women's sports improved dramatically, from less than 1 percent of the men's budgets in 1970 at the college level to approximately 35 percent of the men's budgets in 1995. On the negative side, budgets for women's sports will stay at about the same level because football is so expensive and it is exempt from the equation. Thus, womens' sports remain and will remain unequal to men's sports. This inequality is reinforced by unequal media attention, the scheduling of games (men's games are always the featured games), and the increasing lack of women in positions of power. One ironic consequence of Title IX has been that as opportunities for female athletes increased and programs expanded, many of the coaching and administration positions formerly held by women are being filled by men. In the early 1970s most coaches of women's intercollegiate teams were women. By the late 1980s, however, the majority were men. This trend is also true at the high school level. Also, whereas women's athletic associations at the high school and college levels were once controlled by women, they have now been subsumed under male-dominated organizations. Thus, females who aspire to coaching and athletic administration have fewer opportunities; girls and women see fewer women as role models in such positions and inequality is reinforced as women are dominated by males in positions of power. Thus, even with federal legislation mandating gender equality, male dominance is maintained.

Female Role Models in Education. The jobs held by men and women in the schools support traditional gender roles. The pattern is the familiar one found in hospitals, business offices, and throughout the occupational world: women occupy the bottom rungs, and men are in the prestigious and decision-making positions.

Women make up a large percentage of the nation's classroom teachers but a much smaller percentage of school district superintendents. In 1995 women comprised 83 percent of all elementary school teachers, more than half of all secondary school teachers (51 percent), and 41 percent of all school administrators (U.S. Bureau of the Census, 1995:411).

As the level of education increases, the proportion of women teachers declines. In 1995, 19 years after the Office of Civil Rights issued guidelines spelling out the obligations of colleges and universities in the development of affirmative action programs, women represented only 31 percent of full-time faculty. Furthermore, they remained overwhelmingly in the lower faculty ranks, where faculty are much less likely to hold tenure. In 1995, women comprised 16 percent of full professors, 31 percent of associate professors, 44 percent of assistant professors, and 47 percent of instructors/lecturers (*Academe*, 1995:15) Women make up only 16 percent of all college presidents, more than half of them at private institutions. Of the 453 women college presidents in 1995, 15 percent were women of color. In 1995, there were 39 African American women college presidents. Other minority women college presidents included 14 Latinas, 7 American Indians, and 2 Asians (*Monthly Forum on Women in Higher Education,* 1995:9).

Counseling. A fundamental task of school guidance personnel is to aid students in their choice of a career. The guidance that students receive on career choice tends to be biased. High school guidance counselors may channel male and female students into different (i.e., gender stereotyped) fields and activities. There is evidence that gender stereotyping is common among counselors and that they often steer females away from certain college preparatory courses, especially in mathematics and the sciences (Renzetti and Curran, 1995:124).

In the past, aptitude tests have themselves been sex-biased, listing occupations as either female or male. Despite changes in testing, counselors may inadvertently channel students into gendered choices.

Socialization as Blaming the Victim

The discussion so far shows clearly the many ways in which gender differences are learned. Thus, socialization appears useful for explaining the situation of women. However, the socialization perspective on sexism can be misused in such a way that it blames women themselves for sex inequality. A critique of the socialization perspective by Elaine Enarson and Linda Peterson contends that, when used uncritically, socialization diverts attention from the oppression imposed by the dynamics of contemporary social structure:

> Misuse of the concept of socialization plays directly into the Blaming the Victim ideology; by focusing on the victim, responsibility for "the woman problem" rests not in the social system with its sex-structured distribution of inequality, but in socialized sex differences and sex roles. (Peterson and Enarson, 1974:8)

Not only is the cause of the problem displaced, the solutions are also:

> Rather than directing efforts toward radical social change, the solution seems to be to change women themselves, perhaps through exhortation ("If we want to be liberated,

we'll have to act more aggressive . . . ") or, for example, changing children's literature and mothers' child rearing practice. (Peterson and Enarson, 1974:8)

This issue raises a critical question: If the socialization perspective is limited and perhaps biased, what is a better way of analyzing gender inequality? To answer this question, let us look at how male dominance affects our society.

The Reinforcement of Male Dominance

Male dominance is both a socializing and a structural force. It exists at all levels of society, from the interpersonal interactions of women and men, to the institutional structures of the United States and other societies. Social institutions have been developed by men, are currently dominated by men, and symbolically interpreted from the standpoint of men (Acker, 1992:567). This section describes the interpersonal and institutional reinforcement of gender inequality.

Language

Language perpetuates male dominance by ignoring, trivializing, and sexualizing women. Use of the pronoun *he* when the sex of the person is unspecified and of the generic term *mankind* to refer to humanity in general are obvious examples of how the English language ignores women. Common sayings like "that's women's work" (as opposed to "that's men's work!"), jokes about women drivers, phrases like "women and children first," or "wine, women, and song" are trivializing. Women, more than men, are commonly referred to in terms that have sexual connotations. Terms referring to men ("studs," "jocks") that do have sexual meanings imply power and success, whereas terms applied to women ("broads," "dogs," "chicks") imply promiscuity or being dominated. In fact, the term *promiscuous* is usually applied only to women, although its literal meaning applies to either sex (Richmond-Abbott, 1992:93). Terms such as *dogs* and *chicks* tell us a great deal about how women are regarded by society.

Interpersonal Behavior

Day-to-day interaction between women and men perpetuates male dominance. Gender differences in conversational patterns reflect differences in power.

According to sociolinguist Deborah Tannen (1990), women and men have different styles of communication and different communication goals. Women and men speak different "genderlects." Like cultural dialects, these differences sometimes lead to miscommunication and misunderstanding based on how girls and boys learn to use language differently in their sex-separate peer groups:

Typically, a girl has a best friend with whom she sits and talks, frequently telling secrets. It's the telling of secrets, the fact and the way that they talk to each other, that makes them best friends. For boys, activities are central: Their best friends are the ones they do things with. Boys also tend to play in larger groups that are hierarchical. High-status boys give orders and push low-status boys around. So boys are expected to use language to seize center stage: by exhibiting their skill, displaying their knowledge, and challenging and resisting challenges. (Tannen, 1991:B3)

Research has found that in conversations, men are more direct, interrupt more, and talk more, notwithstanding the stereotype that women are more talkative. Men also have greater control over what is discussed (Parlee, 1979). Another indication of women's lack of power lies in the work they do to keep conversations going. Fishman (1978) studied male–female conversations and found that women work harder in conversations, even though they have less control over the subject matter.

Male dominance is also sustained by various forms of nonverbal communication. Men take up more space than do women and also touch women without permission more than women touch men. Women, on the other hand, engage in more eye contact, smile more, and generally exhibit behavior associated with low status. These behaviors show how gender is continually being created in various kinds of social interaction that occur between women and men. Candace West and Don Zimmerman call this "doing gender" (1987). It involves a complex of socially guided interactional activities that cast certain behaviors as expressions of masculinity and femininity. Doing gender takes place in specific social settings and legitimates gender inequality.

Mass Communications Media

Much of the information we receive about the world around us comes not from direct experience but from the mass media of communication (newspapers, magazines, television, and radio). Although media are often blamed for the problems of modern society, they are not monolithic and do not present us with a simple message. Nevertheless, the portrayal of women in society is distorted. Furthermore, the mass media are controlled by organizations in which men hold the visible, high-status positions and women hold lower status jobs (Sapiro, 1994:209–294).

In the print media, women's influence has not matched their larger presence in the field. At U.S. newspapers, one-third of the work force is female, but women hold only 15 percent of the executive positions. In magazines women's portrayal has become less monolithic since the 1908s. With the rise of feminism, many magazines devoted attention to women's achievements. Alongside these new magazines for the new woman, many "ladies' " magazines continue to define the lives of women in terms of men—husbands or lovers. Women are 52 percent of the population, but you would not know it by reading most newspapers or watching network news. A 1992 study found that women are still underrepresented in newsrooms. In radio, women were 29 percent of the work force, in television women were 25 percent, in wire services 26 percent, in daily newspapers 34 percent, and in news magazines 46 percent (*USA Today*, 1993b:11A).

Studies have continually demonstrated that highly stereotyped behavior characterizes both children's and adult programming as well as commercials. Male role models are provided in greater numbers than are female, with the exception of daytime soap operas, in which men and women are equally represented. Prime-time television is distorted. Although men represent 49 percent of the U.S. population, they represent 63 percent of prime-time television characters. And while women represent 52 percent of the population, they represent only 37 percent of prime-time television characters (Gable, 1993:D3). Such imbalance has also been found with respect to occupations of men and women. Males are represented as occupying a disproportionately high percentage of the work force, a greater diversity of occupations, and higher-status jobs.

Images of women on television have improved in recent years. Working women have enjoyed a positive decade on entertainment television. A report by The National Commission on Working Women has found increasing diversity of characters portraying working women as television's most significant improvement in the past decade. In many serials, women do play strong and intelligent roles, but in just as many shows, men are still the major characters and women are cast as glamorous objects, scheming villains, or servants. And for every contemporary show that includes positive images of women, there are numerous other shows in which women are sidekicks to men, sexual objects, or helpless imbeciles (Andersen, 1997:55).

Television commercials have long presented the sexes in stereotyped ways. Women appear less frequently in ads than men, are much more likely to be seen in the home rather than in work settings, and are much more likely to be in ads for food, home, and beauty/clothing products (Benocratis and Feagin, 1995:27). In the past decade, however, the potential buying power of working women has caused the advertising industry to modify women's image. Working women have become targets of advertising campaigns. But most advertising aimed at women with jobs sends the message that they should be superwomen, managing multiple roles of wife, mother, career woman, and be glamorous as well. Such multifarious expectations are not imposed on men. A cologne advertisement illustrates well the new expectations placed on employed women. Appealing to the "24-hour woman," the advertisement suggested that she "bring home the bacon, fry it up in a pan, and never let him forget he's a man." Under the guise of liberation, advertisers contribute to gender inequality by reinforcing the notion that domestic labor, child rearing, and pleasing men are women's responsibilities.

The advertising aimed at the so-called new woman places additional stresses on women and at the same time upholds male privilege. Television commercials that show women breezing in from their jobs to sort the laundry or pop dinner in the oven reinforce the notion that it is all right for a woman to pursue a career as long as she can still handle the housework.

Religion

The customs, beliefs, and behaviors that discriminate against women are reinforced by organized religion. Despite important differences in religious doctrines, there are common views about gender. Limiting discussion to the Judeo–Christian heritage, let us examine some teachings from the Old and New Testaments regarding the place of women. The Old Testament established male supremacy in a number of ways. God is believed to be a male. Women were obviously meant to be second to males because Eve was created from Adam's rib. According to the Scriptures, only a male could divorce a spouse. A woman who was not a virgin at marriage could be stoned to death. Girls could be purchased for marriage. Employers were enjoined to pay women only three-fifths the wages of men: "If a male from 20 to 60 years of age, the equivalent is 50 shekels of silver by the sanctuary weight; if it is a female, the equivalent is 30 shekels" (*Leviticus* 27:4). As Gilman notes:

> The Old Testament devotes inordinate space to the listing of long lines of male descent to the point where it would seem that for centuries women "begat" nothing but male offspring. Although there are heroines in the Old Testament—Judith, Esther and the like—it's clear that they functioned like the heroines of Greek drama and later of French: as counterweights in the imaginations of certain sensitive men to the degraded position of women in actual life. The true spirit of the tradition was unabashedly revealed in the prayer men recited every day in the synagogue: "Blessed art Thou, O Lord . . . for not making me a woman." (Gilman, 1971:51)

The New Testament continued the tradition of male dominance. Jesus was a male. He was the son of a male God, not of Mary, who remained a virgin. All the disciples were male. The great leader of the early church, the Apostle Paul, was especially adamant in arguing for the primacy of the male over the female. According to Paul, "the husband is supreme over his wife," "woman was created for man's sake," and "women should not teach nor usurp authority over the man, but to be silent."

Contemporary religious thought reflects this heritage. Some conservative denominations severely limit or even forbid women from any decision making. Women have been disproportionately absent from positions of authority over larger, affluent congregations and in denominational leadership (Nesbitt, 1996:183).

There are, however, some indications of change. Recently, the National Council of Churches called for elimination of sexist language and the use of "inclusive language" in the Revised Standard Version of the Bible. Terms such as *man, mankind, brothers, sons, churchmen,* and *laymen* would be replaced by neutral terms that include reference to female gender.

Across the United States, women are struggling for equal rights and status. The revolution for equality within organized religions has been met with resistance at every level. In 1995, only 11 percent of the clergy were women despite a near doubling of female seminary enrollment since 1980 (Briggs, 1995:2-A). Yet women have made some notable gains, opening doors previously closed to them within their churches. Today most Protestant religions ordain women into the ministry, giving them the same rights as their male counterparts to preach the word and administer the sacraments. Ten to twenty percent of all Protestant clergy are female (Simon, et al., 1993:115). Since the first female rabbi was ordained in 1972, their numbers have grown to approximately 4 percent of an estimated 3,500 rabbis in the United States (Simon, et al., 1993). Within the Black church, African American women have also made progress. Some notable firsts were the election in 1984 of Rev. Leontine T. C. Kelly as bishop by the United Methodist Church, and in 1989, the Most Rev. Barbara Harris was also made the first woman bishop within the Episcopal church (*Ebony*, 1995:94). Due to continued pressure by women of the Catholic faith, and a predicted shortage of male priests, even the Catholic church has been pressured into softening its position on women's participation. Today Catholic women are involved in all administrative activities and most ministerial functions except exercising the sacramental power of celebrating mass and hearing confession (Henley, 1994). Thus, despite the continued oppression of organized religion, many women are making advances in established churches and leaving their mark on the ministerial profession.

The Law

That the law has been discriminatory against women is beyond dispute. One need only to recall that women were specifically denied the right to vote prior to the passage of the Nineteenth Amendment. Less well known, but very important, was the 1824 Mississippi Supreme Court decision upholding the right of husbands to beat their wives (the U.S. Supreme Court finally prohibited this practice in 1891). Another interesting case that shows the bias of the legal system is *Minor* v. *Happerset* (1874). The Supreme Court ruled that the "equal protection" clause of the Fourteenth Amendment did not apply to women. Another ruling by the Supreme Court, at the time of the early feminist Susan B. Anthony, said that women were entitled to counsel, but that it must be male counsel.

During the past three decades, legal reforms and public policy changes have attempted to place women and men on more equal footing. Some laws that focus on employment include the 1963 Equal Pay Act, Title VII of the 1964 Civil Rights Act, and the 1978 Pregnancy Discrimination Act. The 1974 Educational Amendments Act calls for gender equality in education. Other reforms have provided the framework for important institutional changes. For example, sexist discrimination in the granting of credit has been ruled illegal, and discrimination against pregnant women in the work force is now prohibited by the law. Affirmative action has remedied some kinds of gender discrimination in employment, sexist discrimination in housing is prohibited, and the differential requirements by gender as traditionally practiced by the airline industry have been eliminated. The force of these new laws, however, depends on their enforcement as well as on the interpretation of the courts when they are disputed.

Legal discrimination remains in a number of areas. There are still hundreds of sections of the U.S. legal code and of state laws that are riddled with sex bias or sex-based terminology in conflict with the ideal of equal rights for women (Benokraitis and Feagin, 1995:24). State laws vary considerably concerning property ownership by spouses, welfare benefits, and the legal status of homemakers.

Many legal reforms are threatened by recent Supreme Court decisions in the areas of abortion and affirmative action. In 1989 and 1992, the Supreme Court narrowed its 1973 landmark *Roe* v. *Wade* decision that had established the right to abortion. *Roe* v. *Wade* was considered a major breakthrough for women, giving them the ultimate right to control their bodies. The 1989 and 1992 decisions make it easier for the states to restrict women's reproductive freedoms at any stage of pregnancy, including the first three months. These decisions threw the future of abortion rights in limbo. By moving abortion battleground to state legislatures, the Supreme Court has withdrawn the rights it granted in 1973. The present assault by the Supreme Court on affirmative action poses new threats to women's equality.

Politics

Women's political participation has always been different from that of men. Women received the right to vote in 1920, when the Nineteenth Amendment was ratified.

Although women make up a very small percentage of officeholders, 1992 was a turning point for women in politics. Controversies such as Anita Hill's harassment allegations, the abortion rights battle, and the lack of representation at all levels of politics propelled women into the political arena. 1992 ushered into Congress the biggest influx of women (and minorities) in history. The 1996 elections increased the number of women in our national legislature. Today, nine U.S. Senators are women and fifty-one women are in the House of Representatives. The growing presence of women in public office is placing family issues at the top of the domestic policy agenda. At the same time, many current legislative actions that reduce or eliminate federal programs have a direct impact on women and their children.

The gender gap in our nation's capital remains scandalous. In the less visible work force of professional staff employees, women hold 60 percent of the jobs, but they are nowhere equal to men. Congress has two classes of personal staff employees; highly paid men who hold most of the power and lower-paid women who tend to be relegated to clerical and support staff. Many answer the phones and write letters to constituents, invisible labor that is crucial to their boss's re-election. A recent study of congressional staff workers conducted by Gannett News Service found:

- House members pay women about 22 percent less than men.
- Senate members pay women about 24 percent less than men.
- The pay gap exists for female workers no matter who they work for: male or female; Republican or Democrat; Black, White, or Hispanic; newcomer or veteran (Brogan, 1994).

This discrimination is legal because Congress exempts itself from federal sex-discrimination laws that it passes for the rest of the nation!

Compared to other industrialized nations the United States ranks low in terms of granting women access to political leadership. Many nations have larger percentages of women lawmakers in their top legislative bodies. The United States has just over 10 percent of women lawmakers in the U.S. Congress. Countries with high percentages of women are: Finland, 39 percent; Norway, 36 percent; Sweden, 34 percent; Cuba, 23 percent; Austria, 21 percent; and China, 21 percent (Baumann, 1994:8A). In the 200-year history of the United States, there has never been a woman president or vice-president. Before 1993, there was only one female justice of the Supreme Court.

Voting studies of national elections since 1980 demonstrate that women often vote differently from men. The gender gap refers to measurable differences in the way women and men vote and view political issues. This gap continues today.

Structured Gender Inequality

In this section of the chapter, we focus on the contemporary workplace because it is a key arena for inequality. The workplace maintains inequality by concentrating women and men in different settings, assigning them different duties, and rewarding them unequally (Reskin and Padavic, 1994:31). Women's economic roles are linked to their status in both the public sector and the family.

Occupational Distribution

The shifting economy discussed in Chapter 8 has changed both women's and men's employment rates. Increasingly it is viewed as "normal" for adult women and men, regardless of parental status, to be employed (Bianchi, 1995:110). Yet, men's labor-force participation rates have decreased slightly while women's have increased dramatically. By 1994, 75 percent of all men were in the labor force compared with 58 percent of all women. Today, women make up nearly half of the work force. African American women have had a long history of high work-force participation rates, and these rates increased only modestly after World War II. Much greater rates of increase have occurred among White and Latina women. In 1994, 58 percent of African American women and White women and 53 percent of Hispanic women were in the labor force (U.S. Department of Labor, 1995). (See Table 12.2)

Today's working woman may be any age. She may be any race. She may be a nurse or a secretary or a factory worker or a department store clerk or a public school teacher. Or she may be—though it is much less likely—a physician or the president of a corporation or the head of a school system. Hers may be the familiar face seen daily behind the counter at the neighborhood coffee shop, or she may work virtually unseen, mopping floors at midnight in an empty office building. The typical woman worker is a wage earner in clerical, service, manufacturing, and some technical jobs that pay poorly and give her little possibility for advancement or control over her work.

Massive economic changes have shifted the gender distribution of many occupations. Since 1980, women have taken 80 percent of the new jobs created in the economy. But the overall degree of gender segregation has not changed much since 1900. Women and men are still concentrated in different occupations (Herz and Wootton, 1996:56). **Gender segregation** refers to the pattern whereby women and men are situated in different jobs throughout the labor force (Andersen, 1997:114). The economy's growing demand for workers in service and clerical jobs has been met by women who continue to work in gender-segregated jobs. By the early 1990s the six most prevalent occupations for women were, in order of magnitude, secretaries, school teachers (excluding those teaching in colleges and universities), semi-skilled machine operators, managers and administrators, retail and personal sales workers, and bookkeepers and accounting clerks (U.S. Department of Labor, Women's Bureau, 1993:6–7). The explosion of services in the new economy would appear to benefit women. But most of the newly created jobs are in the low-wage sectors of the work force with limited opportunities for advancement.

Media reports of women's gains in traditionally men's jobs are often misleading. For example, in blue-collar fields gains look dramatic at first glance, with the number of women in blue-collar jobs rising by 80 percent in the 1970s. But the increase was so high because women had been virtually excluded from these occupations until then. Women's entry into skilled blue-collar work such as construction and

TABLE 12.2

Employed Women by Occupation, Race, and Hispanic Origin, 1994 (percent distribution)**

OCCUPATION	TOTAL	WHITE	BLACK	HISPANIC ORIGIN
Total employed women (in thousands)	56,610	47,738	6,595	4,258
Total percentage*	100.0	100.0	100.0	100.0
Managerial and professional specialty	28.7	29.8	21.3	16.7
Executive, administrative, & managerial	12.4	12.9	8.7	8.3
Professional specialty	16.3	16.9	12.6	8.4
Technical, sales, & administrative support	42.4	43.1	38.4	39.1
Technicians and related support	3.6	3.6	3.4	2.5
Sales occupations	12.8	13.4	9.6	12.4
Administrative support, including clerical	26.0	26.2	25.4	24.2
Service occupations	17.8	16.6	25.7	25.6
Private household	1.4	1.3	2.0	5.1
Protective service	0.7	0.6	1.4	0.5
Service, except prvt. household & protective	15.7	14.8	22.3	20.1
Precision production, craft, and repair	2.2	2.1	2.6	3.4
Operators, fabricators, and laborers	7.7	7.0	11.6	13.3
Machine operators, assemblers, & inspectors	5.2	4.7	8.2	9.9
Transport & material moving occupations	0.9	0.8	1.2	0.8
Handlers, equip. cleaners, helpers, & laborers	1.6	1.5	2.3	2.6
Farming, forestry, and fishing	1.2	1.4	0.3	1.9

*Percentages may not add to 100 because of rounding.

**Bureau of Labor Statistics 1994b.

Source: Diane E. Herz and Barbara H. Wooton, "Women in the Workforce: An Overview," in *The American Woman, 1996–97.* Cynthia Costello and Barbara Kivimae Krimgold, eds. New York: W. W. Norton and Company, p. 59.

auto-making was limited by the very slow growth in those jobs (Amott, 1993:76). In 1995, only 3 percent of mechanics, 1.8 percent of construction workers, and 0.5 percent of auto mechanics were women (U.S. Bureau of the Census, 1995:413). However, some women made inroads into historically mens' jobs in the highly paid primary sector. The years 1970 to 1990 found more women in the fields of law, medicine, journalism, and higher education. Today, women fill one-third of all management positions (up from 19 percent in 1972). Despite recent progress in the prestige professions, there are fewer women in these jobs than men. In 1995, only 23 percent of lawyers, 22 percent of doctors, and 43 percent of university or college teachers were women (U.S. Bureau of Labor, 1995). Although women have made inroads in the high-paying and high-prestige professions, White women were

The economy's growing demand for workers in service and clerical jobs has been met by women who continue to work in gender segregated jobs.

the major beneficiaries of the new opportunities. There has been an occupational "trickle down" effect, as White women improved the occupational status by moving into male-dominated professions such as law and medicine, while African American women moved into the *female-dominated* jobs, such as social work and teaching, vacated by White women. There is some evidence that the improvement for White women was related to federal civil rights legislation, particularly the requirement that firms receiving federal contracts comply with affirmative action guidelines (Amott, 1993:76).

As the economy is being transformed from its traditional manufacturing base to a base in service and high technology, particular categories of men and women are affected differently. In general, men have been most affected by the loss of industrial jobs while more women are employed in service jobs. However, economic restructuring has caused all women to lose ground in secondary-sector manufacturing jobs, such as machine operators and laborers. Latinas have been especially hard hit (Amott, 1993:76).

Earning Discrimination

Although women's labor-force participation rates have risen, the gap between women's and men's earnings has remained relatively constant for three decades. Women workers do not approach earnings parity with men even when they work in similar occupations and have the same levels of education. Over the last decade, the earning gap narrowed and was the most important "gender news" of the 1980s. Current estimates suggest that women earn about 72 percent of the wage rate of men (Bianchi, 1995:110; Dunn, 1996:60). In 1980, women earned 59 percent of what men earned. This means that women's overall pay relative to men's has increased by about a penny a year in the past ten years (Woller, 1991:4B).

The earning gap persists for several reasons:

- Women are concentrated in lower-paying occupations.
- Women enter the labor force at different and lower-paying levels than do men.
- Women as a group have less education and experience than do men; therefore, they are paid less than men.
- Women tend to work less overtime than do men.

These conditions explain only part of the earning gap between women and men. They do not explain why women workers earn substantially less than do men workers with the same number of years of education and with the same work histories, skills, and work experience. Several studies have found that if women were men with the same credentials, they would earn substantially more. For example, researchers at the University of Michigan examined the income gap to determine whether it can be explained by differences in job qualifications of men and women. They found that women's and men's credentials explained some differences, but that experience accounted for only about one-third of the wage gap. The largest part of the wage gap is caused by institutional sex discrimination in the labor market that blocks women's access to the better-paying jobs through hiring or promotion or simply paying women less than men in any job (*ISR Newsletter* 1982; Dunn, 1996).

Differential earning can be found even within occupational classification. Fully employed women, when compared with fully employed men, are consistently underpaid by thousands of dollars when equal in type of occupation.

Intersections of Gender, Race, and Work

Gender inequality in the workplace is intertwined with racial inequality. There are important racial differences in the occupational concentration of women and men (see Table 12.3). Women of color illustrate the combined effects of gender and race in the workplace. They are at the bottom of the work hierarchy, concentrated in jobs that are low paying and have few fringe benefits, poor working conditions, high turnover, and little chance of advancement. Latinas, for example, are concentrated in service jobs such as housekeeping and kitchen work. Both Black women and Latinas are more likely than their White counterparts to work in service occupations or as machine operators or laborers. A much larger share of White women (30 percent) than Black women (21 percent) or Latinas (17 percent) hold managerial and professional specialty jobs (Herz and Wooton, 1996:58–59).

Segregation by race and gender has enormous consequences for women's earnings. Although men earn more than women in almost every occupation, those occupations populated by women workers are the lowest paid of all. Furthermore, the higher the concentration of women in a given occupational category, the worse the pay (Dill, Cannon, and Vanneman, 1987). In 1994, White men who worked full-

TABLE 12.3

Occupations with the Highest Concentration by Race/Gender, 1995

WORKERS	OCCUPATIONS
Hispanic men	Surveyor's helpers, plasterers, farm workers, agricultural nursery workers
Hispanic women	Graders and agricultural workers, housekeepers, inspectors of agricultural products, child care workers (private household)
African American men	Longshore equipment operators, inspectors of agricultural products, baggage porters and bell hops, garbage collectors, barbers
African American women	Cooks (private households), housekeepers, winding and twisting machine operators, nursing aides
White men	Mining engineers, agricultural engineers, supervisors carpenters and related workers, supervisors plumbers, pipe and steam fitters
White women	Dental hygienists, stenographers, secretaries, dental assistants, speech therapists

Source: Unpublished data from U.S. Department of Labor Bureau of Labor Statistics, *Employment and Earnings* 42, no. 1 (1995). Prepared by Darcel Smith, Department of Sociology, Michigan State University.

time earned the most of any group, followed by White women and Black men. Black women and Hispanic men and women had the lowest earnings (Herz and Wooton, 1996:67) (see Table 12.4).

Pay Equity

Women's low earnings create serious problems for women themselves, for their families, and for their children. Increasingly, families rely on the wages of both spouses, and many working women are the sole providers of their families. Given these trends, it is essential that women be able to earn as much as men for work of comparable value.

The Equal Pay Act passed in 1963 prohibits private employers from paying women less than men for the same work. But this federal law does not require equal pay for work that is *comparable* but not exactly *equal.* For example, to be a secretary (usually a woman) requires as much education and takes as much responsibility as being a carpenter (usually a man), but the secretarial job is paid far less (Folbre, 1995). The law does not view such differences as discrimination. In the early 1980s a number of state and local governments began addressing the pay gap issue by instituting pay-equity policies in the public sector. **Pay equity** policies are designed to bring the pay levels of women in closer alignment with those of men. Because pay equity calls for jobs of comparable value to be paid the same, it is also

TABLE 12.4

Median Weekly Earnings of Full-Time Wage-and-Salary Workers, by Sex, Race, Hispanic Origin, and Educational Attainment, 1994 (in current dollars)*

RACE, HISPANIC ORIGIN, AND SEX	TOTAL	Educational Attainment		
		LESS THAN A HIGH SCHOOL DIPLOMA	HIGH SCHOOL DIPLOMA, NO COLLEGE	BACHELOR'S DEGREE OR HIGHER
Total	467	292	493	708
Men	522	315	572	798
Women	399	248	416	613
White	484	296	507	725
Men	547	318	590	821
Women	408	251	424	619
Black	371	278	389	599
Men	400	305	419	630
Women	346	239	362	574
Hispanic origin	324	260	400	613
Men	343	276	432	671
Women	305	225	357	561

*Bureau of Labor Statistics 1994b.

Source: Diane E. Herz and Barbara H. Wooton, "Women in the Workforce: An Overview," in *The American Woman, 1996–97.* Cynthia Costello and Barbara Kivimae Krimgold, eds. New York: W. W. Norton and Company, p. 68.

called *comparable worth* (Hacker, 1986; Sociologists for Women in Society, 1986). Since 1980, 20 states implemented pay-equity programs that reduced the gender wage gap. Minnesota, Oregon, and Washington were among the most successful (Folbre, 1995:3.7). These are important gains. Unfortunately, pay-equity struggles have not retained their momentum in the nineties. The notion that those doing "women's work" should be compensated as well as those doing traditionally men's jobs has been hard to sell in an uncertain economy.

How Workplace Inequality Operates

Common explanations for women's low status in the workplace rest on individual characteristics. Women's socialization, their low aspirations, and their greater commitments to family than to work are said to place them differently. But sociological research shows that the gendered nature of work itself treats women and men differently. Let us examine the organization of the labor force that assigns better jobs and greater rewards to men and positions of less responsibility with lower earnings to women.

The labor market is divided into two separate segments, with different characteristics, different roles, and different rewards. The primary segment is charac-

Reprinted by permission of Grimmy, Inc.

LOOK GUYS...WHY DON'T WE JUST SAY THAT ALL MEN ARE CREATED EQUAL...AND LET THE LITTLE LADIES LOOK OUT FOR THEMSELVES?

ized by stability, high wages, promotion ladders, opportunities for advancement, good working conditions, and provisions for job security. The secondary market is characterized by low wages, fewer or no promotion ladders, poor working conditions, and little provision for job security. Women's work tends to fall in the secondary segment. For example, clerical work, the largest single occupation for women, has many of the characteristics associated with the secondary segment.

Structural conditions produce gender differences. A classic study by Rosabeth Moss Kanter, *Men and Women of the Corporation* (1977), found that workplace conditions shape behavior. Virtually all of the differences between women and men were a function of the opportunities they face. People in low-mobility or blocked situations (regardless of their sex) tend to limit their aspirations, seek satisfactions in activities outside work, dream of escape, and create sociable peer groups in which interpersonal relationships take over other aspects of work. Kanter argued that "when women seem to be less motivated or committed, it is probably because their jobs carry less opportunity" (Kanter, 1977:159). The jobs held by most women workers tend to be associated with shorter chains of opportunity. What has been considered typical women's behavior can be explained by structural position.

Other processes block women's advancement. In the white-collar work force, the well-documented phenomenon of women going just so far—and no further—in their occupations and professions is called the **glass ceiling.** This refers to the invisible barriers that limit women's mobility despite their motivation and capacity for positions of power and prestige (Lorber, 1994:227). The movement of women into highly skilled blue-collar work has been limited by the steady decline of manufacturing jobs (see Chapter 8). Those who do enter blue-collar work often confront blatant resistance from men co-workers. (See "Diversity: Changing Gender Relations in Skilled Trade Work"). Even the movement of women into male jobs

Diversity

Changing Gender Relations in Skilled Trade Work

Women have found it difficult to enter and succeed in blue-collar occupations. Their on-the-job experiences do not mirror those of white-collar women workers. Using evidence from a study of skilled trade women in a Michigan auto factory, this panel discusses two forms of male resistance to women's presence in the trades; stereotyping women and withholding training.

Female skilled trade apprentices often find themselves struggling against negative stereotypes of women. They have to overcome male suspicion that they won't be smart enough, able to do the physical work, or willing to get dirty. Female apprentices' attitudes and commitment are tested in ways not required of male apprentices. Mary, a Black electrician, describes what happened to her when she first went on the trades. "My foreman assigned me to work with a (male) journeyman* who did hard, robust jobs that were dirty and nasty to see if I would last. I was assigned to work with him for a year, which was far longer than any male apprentice." The work female journeymen do is generally monitored and scrutinized more closely than their male counterparts. Glenda, a White diemaker, claims "you're really in the limelight because you're a woman. If you make a mistake, it's going to be talked about like crazy, but a man could make the same mistake and it wouldn't mean much; they wouldn't talk about it. . . . Most of these guys think women can't handle this work and they're waiting for you to fail. And they're watching for you to fail. So through your apprenticeship you felt like you were trying to prove yourself all the time, and it is a lot of pressure." Negative stereotypes and double standards disadvantage female apprentices and female journeymen, because they create extra pressure for them to continually work hard in order to overcome them.

Receiving adequate on-the-job training is crucial for apprentices to be successful and work safely. However, many of the women who went on the trades, especially in the mid-1970s and early 1980s, found many male journeymen reluctant to train them. Greg, a White machine repairman, states: "A significant number of men would rather not be bothered with (training) women." Sue, a White tinsmith, told how one male journeyman flatly refused to train her by stating "I ain't workin with no fuckin peehole." Carol says of her apprenticeship in welder repair: "I got a specialty in holding the flashlight." Refusing to properly train a female apprentice is an effective way to put her apprenticeship in jeopardy. The long-term effect of inadequate training is that when these women receive their journeyman's card, they are less knowledgeable and confident than their male counterparts.

These women have found effective ways to counter male resistance to their presence in the trades. Some described their effort to establish a personal support network of male and female journeymen willing to give them advice and assistance when they need it. Others protect themselves by keeping a daily journal of events at work. Most women claim they feel forced to be more confrontational in an effort to get their training needs met, and their ideas heard. Still others, seasoned female journeymen, go out of their way to help new female apprentices.

While still a "man's world," the factory is slowly becoming a less hostile environment for women. Male resentment has diminished. This is due in large part to three factors. Female journeymen, especially those with twenty or more years of seniority, have established themselves in the trades and proven themselves capable workers. Affirmative Action policies and anti-discriminatory and sexual harassment legislation have also helped women obtain and keep their apprenticeships. Finally, many of the lower-seniority male journeymen are generally more accepting of women's presence in the trades. Part of the reason for this is that many of them have trained and worked with women. Still, if asked, most of the women interviewed would probably agree with Flo's assessment of her experience as a tinsmith: "Being in skilled trades is a lot like being Ginger Rogers; she did everything Fred Astaire did but she did it backwards and while wearing high-heels."

Source: Darcel Smith, 1997. Department of Sociology, Michigan State University. This was written expressly for the eighth edition of *In Conflict and Order.*

*The term journeyman refers to both male and female journeypersons.

does not always bring about integration. Sociologists Barbara Reskin and Patricia Roos (1990) studied eleven once male-dominated fields that had become integrated between 1979 and 1988: book editing, pharmacy, public relations, bank management, systems analysis, insurance sales, real estate sales, insurance adjusting and examining, bartending, baking, and typesetting and composition. Reskin and Roos found that women gained entry into these fields only *after* earnings and upward mobility in each of these fields declined; that is, salaries had gone down, prestige had diminished, or work had become more like "women's work" (Kroeger, 1994:50). Furthermore in each of these occupations women specialized in lower status specialties, in different and less-desirable work settings, and in lower-paid industries. Reskin and Roos call this process *ghettoization*. Some occupations changed their sex-typing completely, while some became resegregated by race as well as gender (Reskin and Roos, 1990; Amott, 1993:80).

Many fields that have opened up to women are taking on new forms of stratification. For example, they are composed of prestige jobs and a new category of more routinized jobs that are professional in name only. Carter and Carter (1981) have shown that women are concentrated in the new, more routinized sectors of professional employment, but the upper tier of relatively autonomous work continues to be male-dominated, with only token increases in female employment.

Changes in the organization of three professions—medicine, college teaching, and law—have degraded women's work. In medicine, the growth of hospital-based practice has paralleled women's admission to the profession. Women doctors are

G. Olliver.

more likely than men to be found in hospital-based practice, which provides less autonomy than the more traditional office practice. In college and university teaching, demand is greatest in two-year colleges, where heavy teaching responsibilities leave little time or energy for writing and publishing—the keys to academic career advancement. And in law, women's advancement to prestigious positions is being eroded by the growth of the legal clinic, where much legal work is routinized.

Despite women's important inroads into the professions, the occupations to which they have gained access in recent years no longer have the same meaning in terms of economic or social status that they once possessed.

Many of the old discriminatory patterns are difficult to change. In the professions, for example, sponsor-protégé systems and informal interactions among colleagues limit women's mobility. Cynthia Epstein's classic work pointed to the importance of sponsorship in training personnel and ensuring leadership continuity. Women are less likely to be acceptable as protégés. Furthermore, their sex status limits or excludes their involvement in the buddy system or the old-boy network (Epstein, 1970). These informal interactions create alliances that can further chances for social mobility, but they are systematically blocked for women.

Women and Men in Families

Women's status in the family parallels their status in other social institutions. The gender-structured family assigns maintenance work (work with no identifiable product) to women. In the role of wife and mother, a woman earns no money for her household chores of cleaning, cooking, and caring for the needs of the household members. Like most women throughout the world, U.S. women spend as much or more time working than men when unpaid housework is taken into account (see Figure 12.1).

Today, men are doing more shopping and housework, but only because women are making them change. In reality, men cannot move fast enough to meet women's expectations (Crispell, 1992). Although many wife–husband relationships are becoming more equal, men continue to exercise greater power within the family (see Chapter 15).

The Costs and Consequences of Sexism

Who Benefits?

Clearly, gender inequality enters all aspects of social life in the United States. This inequality is profitable to certain segments of the economy, and it also gives privileges to individual men.

Capitalists derive extra profits from paying women less than men. Women's segregation in low-paying jobs produces higher profits for certain economic sectors; namely, those where most of the labor force is female. Women who lack the eco-

FIGURE 12.1

Burning More Midnight Oil
Developed countries where women work more than two hours longer per week than men. Work includes both housework and economic activity.*

Men   Women

Work hours per week

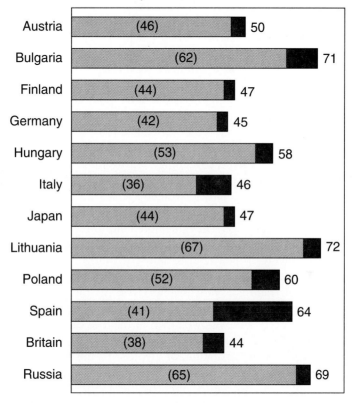

	Men	Women
Austria	(46)	50
Bulgaria	(62)	71
Finland	(44)	47
Germany	(42)	45
Hungary	(53)	58
Italy	(36)	46
Japan	(44)	47
Lithuania	(67)	72
Poland	(52)	60
Spain	(41)	64
Britain	(38)	44
Russia	(65)	69

* United Nations, 1984, '92

Source: George Moffit. "Report Card on Women," *Christian Science Monitor* (Wednesday, Sept. 6, 1995) p. 11.

nomic support of husbands and who are in the wage-labor force on only a temporary basis have always been a source of easily exploitable labor. These women provide a significant proportion of the marginal labor force capitalists need to draw on during upswings in the business cycle and to release during downswings (Edwards, Reich, and Weisskopf, 1978:333).

Gender inequality is suited to the needs of the economy in other ways as well. Capitalism involves not only the accumulation of capital but also the maintenance of labor power. This means that the workers must be physically and emotionally maintained. Women maintain the workers through the unpaid work they do inside the home. This keeps capitalism going, and it also provides privileges for individual men, all at women's expense.

The Social and Individual Costs

Gender inequality benefits certain segments of society. Nevertheless, society at large and women and men as individuals pay a high price for inequality. Sexism diminishes the quality of life for all people. Our society is deprived of half of its resources when women are denied full and equal participation in its institutions. If women are systematically kept from jobs requiring leadership, creativity, and productivity, the economy will obviously suffer. The pool of talent consisting of half the population will continue to be underutilized and underproductive.

Sexism also produces suffering for millions of people. We have seen that individual women pay for economic discrimination. Their children pay as well. Women and children are swelling the ranks of the poor at great cost to society. The "feminization of poverty" refers to the growing proportion of poor women and their children. This poverty trend is the consequence of a sexist society in which women earn less than what men earn and almost always end up with the children after a divorce.

Many women pay a psychological price for sexism. The devaluation of women by society can create identity problems, low self-esteem, and a general sense of worthlessness, particularly as women age.

Given the occupational patterns of our society, men generally gain in prestige and power as they age. They therefore tend to retain or even enhance their attractiveness to women. The reverse, however, is not the case. The result is that widowed or divorced men tend to remarry younger women. Widowed or divorced women either remain single or marry older men. Consequently, although the male–female ratio is approximately 1:1 in the forty-five to sixty-four age bracket, there are three times as many single, divorced, and widowed women as there are single, divorced, and widowed men in that age category. Women who worked inside the home for husbands and children can become displaced homemakers through the death, separation, or divorce of a husband.

Sexism also denies men the potential for full human development. Gender segregation denies employment opportunities to men who wish to enter such fields as nursing, grade-school teaching, or secretarial work. Eradication of sexism would benefit such males. It would benefit all males who have been forced into stereotypic male behavioral modes. In learning to be men, boys express their masculinity through physical courage, toughness, competitiveness, and aggression. Expressions typically associated with femininity, such as gentleness, expressiveness, and responsiveness, are seen as undesirable for males. In rigidly adhering to gender expectations, males pay a price for their masculinity. As Pleck has put it:

> The conventional expectations of what it means to be a man are difficult to live up to for all but the lucky few and lead to unnecessary self-deprivation in the rest when they do not measure up. Even for those who do, there is a price: they may be forced, for example, to inhibit the expression of many emotions. (Pleck, 1981:69)

Male inexpressiveness can hinder communication between husbands and wives, between fathers and children; it has been labeled a tragedy of U.S. society (Balswick and Peck, 1971). Certainly, it is a tragedy for the man himself, crippled by an inability to show the best part of a human being—his warm and tender feelings for other people (Balswick and Collier, 1976:59).

Ideally, men and women should be able to integrate traditionally feminine and traditionally masculine traits. Such **androgyny** would permit all people to be either rational or emotional, either assertive or yielding, depending on what is appropriate to the situation.

Fighting the System

Feminist Movements in the United States

Gender inequality in this society has led to feminist social movements. Three stages of feminism have been aimed at overcoming sex discrimination. The first stage grew out of the abolition movement of the 1830s. Working to abolish slavery, women found that they could not function as equals with their male abolitionist friends, and they became convinced that women's freedom was as important as freedom from slavery. In July 1848 the first convention in history devoted to issues of women's position and rights was held at Seneca Falls, New York. Participants in the Seneca Falls convention approved a declaration of independence, asserting that men and women are created equal, and that they are endowed with certain inalienable rights.

During the Civil War feminists for the most part turned their attention to the emancipation of Blacks. After the war and the ratification of the Thirteenth Amendment abolishing slavery, feminists were divided between those seeking far-ranging economic, religious, and social reforms and those seeking voting rights for women. The second stage of feminism gave priority to women's suffrage. The women's suffrage amendment, introduced into every session of Congress from 1878 on, was ratified on August 26, 1920, nearly three-quarters of a century after the demand for women's suffrage had been made at the Seneca Falls convention. From 1920 until the 1960s feminism was dormant. "So much energy had been expended in achieving the right to vote that the woman's movement virtually collapsed from exhaustion" (Hole and Levine, 1979:554).

Feminism was reawakened in the 1960s. Social movements aimed at inequalities gave rise to an important branch of contemporary feminism. The civil rights movement and other protest movements of the 1960s spread the ideology of equality. But like the early feminists, women involved in political protest movements found that male dominance characterized even movements seeking social equality. Discovering injustice in freedom movements, they broadened their protest to such far-reaching concerns as health care, family life, and relationships between the sexes.

Another strand of contemporary feminism emerged among professional women who discovered sex discrimination in earnings and advancement. Formal organizations, such as the National Organization of Women, evolved, seeking legislation to overcome sex discrimination (Freeman, 1979).

These two branches of contemporary feminism gave rise to a feminist consciousness among millions of U.S. women. As a consequence, during the 1960s and early 1970s many changes occurred in the roles of women and men. However, periods of recession, high unemployment, and inflation in the late 1970s fed a backlash against feminism. The contemporary women's movement may be the

HUMAN AGENCY

Women Creating Social Change at Century's End

What can we do to solve the problems stemming from gender and its intersecting inequalities? According to Teresa Amott, the answer lies in the nature of structural transformation itself. When old institutions are changing, there are new opportunities for experimentation, for changing ideologies and for political and cultural realignments. Today, at the grassroots level, there are hundreds of thousands of groups working for progressive change, seeking to restructure the economy, the household, and the state for democratic and participatory ends.

Some groups are organizing in ways that bring together new constituencies, often constituencies that the conservative movement is attempting to pit against one another. For instance, workers in different countries have begun to come together to address common issues and to resist business's attempt to divide and conquer. These new international coalitions alert one another to potential plant movements, support one another's strikes, and share information on job safety and environmental issues.

To counter the conservative division of "taxpayer against recipient," new coalitions protesting budget cutbacks have united community members and state workers, such as human services providers and their clients, teachers and their students. These new groups, many of them led by women defending programs that

benefit themselves and their children, have also turned their attention to the tax side of government budgets, identifying progressive tax proposals and linking them with the need to maintain public services.

Another aspect of grassroots organizing against the effects of economic crisis radically alters the inner workings of older institutions, such as labor unions, or practices, such as wage determination. To organize women, people of color, and immigrants, unions have developed creative tactics, often reminiscent of the civil rights movement, such as sit-ins, demonstrations, use of the media, and direct appeals to consumers of goods and services. The new union movement addresses family and worklife issues, job safety issues, and the relationship between the community and the workplace by providing childcare centers, as well as classes in adult literacy and English as a second language. Rather than permit the underground economy to grow and exploit ever more women and immigrants, unions are attempting to organize sweatshops from the border towns of Mexico to the garment shops of New York and Los Angeles. New organizing drives in hotels and restaurants, universities, and the public sector are democratic, inviting all workers to participate in decision-making and in collective bargaining.

The comparable worth movement has challenged traditional practices of wage determination, in which

first in U.S. history to face the opposition of an organized antifeminist social movement. From the mid-1970s a coalition of groups calling themselves profamily and prolife emerged. These groups, drawn from right-wing political organizations and religious organizations, oppose feminist gains in reproductive, family, and antidiscrimination policies. Political, legal, and media opposition to feminism continues to undermine women's equality (Faludi, 1991). Nevertheless, there are hundreds of thousands of groups across the country working for social change and women's rights. (See "Human Agency: Women Creating Social Change at Century's End.")

the history of race- and sex-typing of jobs continues to drag down women's wages and those of people of color. Pay equity plans, developed as a result of pressure from unions, women's advocacy groups, and people of color, force state and local governments and private employers to scrutinize their pay scales for race and sex bias. In the process, value judgments that place equipment over people, and financial management over human services, can be addressed and reversed.

Other forms of organizing develop and support entirely new institutions that address human needs in radically different ways. Bargaining with private employers and with city and state governments, unmarried heterosexual couples and gay and lesbian couples are demanding coverage under health and pension plans equal to that provided to married couples. New forms of employment, such as worker ownership, are challenging capital's right to create and define jobs. Some worker-owned firms have been created to save jobs when a business is on the brink of bankruptcy or its owners no longer wish to operate it. Others are entirely new efforts, redesigning working conditions in a way that meets the needs of both the workers and the larger community.

What do all these efforts have in common? They create collective possibilities for analyzing the causes of the crisis and overturning existing relationships of exploitation and domination. They bring people together across lines of race, ethnicity, gender, and sexual orientation in ways that include those the conservatives have scapegoated and that therefore reject the politics of division. They are democratic to their core, involving people at the grassroots in the decisions that affect their lives.

In each of these areas, described above and elsewhere in this book, women have taken the lead. Creative strategies have been developed by women of color, poor women, lesbians, and disabled women. Perhaps this is because these women have been so severely affected by the crisis, forced to assume new burdens of work and responsibility but deprived of safety nets and guarantees. Perhaps, caught in the crisis, women have been able to see it more clearly than those whose privileges have insulated them from its worst effects. And finally, perhaps it is the very diversity of women's experiences that has given them a vision of alternative possibilities that is richer, more pluralistic, and more democratic. At this moment of crisis, when the old framework is dead, women are giving birth to the new.

Source: Adapted from Teresa Amott, *Women and the U.S. Economy Today,* New York: Monthly Review Press (1993):139–141. Copyright © 1993 by Teresa Amott. Reprinted by permission of Monthly Review Foundation.

CHAPTER REVIEW

1. United States society, like other societies, ranks and rewards women and men unequally.

2. Gender differentiation is not natural but is, instead, socially constructed. Although gender divisions make women unequal to men, different groups of men exhibit varying degrees of power, and different groups of women exhibit varying levels of inequality.

3. Men as well as women are gendered beings.

4. Gender works with the inequalities of race, class, and sexuality to produce different experiences for all women and men.

5. Conflict and order perspectives provide different explanations of the origin and persistence of the gender system. Order theorists emphasize division of labor and social integration; conflict theorists emphasize the economic structure of society in producing women's inequality.

6. Many sociologists have viewed gender inequality as the consequences of behavior learned by individual women and men. More recently sociologists have moved from studying gender as individual attributes to the study of gendered institutions.

7. Gender inequality is reinforced through language, interpersonal behavior, mass communication, religion, the law, and politics.

8. The segregation of women in a few gendered occupations contrasts with that of men, who are distributed throughout the occupational hierarchy; and

women, even with the same amount of education and when doing the same work, earn less than men in all occupations.

9. Gender segregation is the basic source of gender inequality in the labor force. Work opportunities for women tend to concentrate in a secondary market that has few advancement opportunities, fewer job benefits, and lower pay.

10. The combined effects of gender and racial segregation in the labor force keep women of color at the bottom of the work hierarchy where working conditions are harsh and earnings are low.

11. The position of women in families parallels their status in the labor force. Their responsibility for domestic maintenance and child care frees individual men from such duties and supports the capitalist economy.

12. Gender inequality deprives society of the potential contributions of half of its members, creates poverty among families headed by women, and limits the capacities of all women and men.

13. Feminist movements aimed at eliminating inequality have created significant changes at all levels of society, but because inequalities are deeply embedded in the social structure, women's equality will require a fundamental transformation of U.S. society.

KEY TERMS

Gendered
Gender polarity
Gender stratification
Feminist approach
Sex
Gender

Male dominance
Patriarchy
Compulsory heterosexuality
Sexuality
Gender-roles approach
Structural approach

Gendered institutions
Androgyny
Gender segregation
Pay equity
Glass ceiling

STUDY QUESTIONS

1. In explaining gender inequality, order theorists emphasize the gender-roles approach whereas conflict theorists focus on structural factors. Compare and assess these two approaches.

2. What are the individual and institutional mechanisms that reinforce gender inequality in society?

3. The incomes of men and women differ significantly. Why?

4. How do women officeholders make a difference?

5. Have recent Supreme Court decisions increased or reduced gender inequality?

6. Who benefits from gender inequality?

FOR FURTHER READING

Teresa Amott, *Caught in the Crisis: Women and the U.S. Economy Today* (New York: Monthly Review Press, 1993).

Margaret L. Andersen, *Thinking about Women,* 4th ed. (Boston: Allyn and Bacon, 1997).

Maxine Baca Zinn, Pierrette Hondagneu-Sotelo, and Michael A. Messner, eds. *Through the Prism of Difference: A Sex and Gender Reader* (Boston: Allyn and Bacon, 1997).

Michael S. Kimmel and Michael A. Messner, *Men's Lives,* 3rd ed. (Boston: Allyn and Bacon, 1995).

Judith Lorber, *Paradoxes of Gender* (New Haven: Yale University Press, 1994).

Barbara Reskin and Irene Padavic, *Women and Men at Work* (Thousand Oaks, CA: Pine Forge Press, 1994).

Barrie Thorne, *Gender Play, Girls and Boys in School* (New Brunswick, NJ: Rutgers University Press, 1993).

PART FOUR

The Economy

T he following excerpt is from an essay by Bernard Sanders of Vermont, the only Independent in the U.S. House of Representatives:

One of the major economic crises facing our nation is that not only are ten million workers unemployed and six million under employed—but the wages of those who are employed are in significant decline. Twenty years ago, the United States led the world in the wages and benefits we provided our workers. Today, we're in 12th place and declining. We must reverse that trend.

It should not be acceptable to President Clinton and the U.S. Congress that the average weekly earnings of production workers have declined by more than 15 percent since 1973, and that we have lost millions of decent paying manufacturing jobs in the last dozen years. It should not be acceptable that there has been a major increase in the percentage of Americans working at low wage jobs, and that the minimum wage today has 26 percent less purchasing power than it had in 1970. It should not be acceptable that Americans work longer hours and enjoy less paid vacation time than almost any other industrialized country, or that we are the only major nation without a national health care system. (Sanders, 1993:17)

Introduction

The next five chapters of this book describe the fundamental institutions of society. As noted in Chapter 2, **institutions** are social arrangements that channel behavior in prescribed ways in the important areas of social life. They are interrelated sets of normative elements—norms, values, and role expectations—that the people making up the society have devised and passed on to succeeding generations in order to provide solutions to society's perpetually unfinished business.

The institutions of society—family, education, religion, polity, and economy—are interrelated. But even though there are reciprocal effects among the institutions, the economy and the polity are the core institutions. The way society is organized to produce and distribute goods and services and the way power is organized are the crucial determinants of the way the other institutions are organized. We begin, then, with a chapter on the economy, followed by a chapter on the polity. The remaining three chapters focus on the supporting institutions of the family, education, and religion. Each of these institutions is strongly affected by the form of the economy and power arrangements in the contemporary United States.

The task of this chapter is to describe the economy of the United States. Four areas are emphasized: the domination of huge corporations, the maldistribution of wealth, the social organization of work, and the current economic crises. We start, though, with a brief description of the two fundamental ways societies can organize their economic activities.

Capitalism and Socialism

Industrialized societies organize their economic activities according to one of two fundamental forms: capitalism and socialism. Although no society has a purely capitalist or socialist economy, the ideal types provide opposite extremes on a scale that helps us measure the U.S. economy more accurately.

Capitalism

Three conditions must be present for pure **capitalism** to exist—private ownership of the means of production, personal profit, and competition. These necessary conditions constitute the underlying principles of a pure capitalist system. The first is private ownership of the means of production. Individuals own not only private possessions but, most important, also the capital necessary to produce and distribute goods and services. In a purely capitalist society, there would be no public ownership of any potentially profitable activity.

The pursuit of maximum profit, the second essential ingredient principle, implies that individuals are free to maximize their personal gains. Most important, the proponents of capitalism argue that this profit-seeking by individuals has positive consequences for the society. Thus, seeking individual gain through personal profit is considered morally acceptable and socially desirable.

Competition, the third ingredient, is the mechanism for determining what is produced and at what price. The market forces of supply and demand will ensure that capitalists will produce the goods and services wanted by the public, that the goods will be high in quality, and that they will be sold at the lowest possible price. Moreover, competition is the mechanism that keeps individual profit seeking in check. Potential abuses such as fraud, faulty products, and exorbitant prices are negated by the existence of competitors, who will soon take business away from those who violate good business judgment. So, too, economic inefficiency is minimized as market forces cause the inept to fail and the efficient to succeed.

These three principles—private property, personal profit, and competition—require a fourth condition if true capitalism is to work: a government policy of **laissez-faire**, allowing the marketplace to operate unhindered. Any government intervention in the marketplace will, argue capitalists, distort the economy by negatively affecting incentives and freedom of individual choice. If left unhindered by government, the profit motive, private ownership, and competition will achieve the greatest good for the greatest number in the form of individual self-fulfillment and the general material progress of society.

Socialism

Socialism is an economic system in which the means of production are owned by the people for their collective benefit. The five principles of socialism are democratism, egalitarianism, community, public ownership of the means of production, and planning for common purposes. True socialism must be democratic. Representatives of a socialist state must be answerable and responsive to the wishes of the public they serve. Thus, it is a fallacy to equate true socialism with the politico-economic systems of the former Soviet Union, the People's Republic of China, or Cuba. These societies are socialistic in most respects; that is, their material benefits are more evenly distributed than those in the United States. But their economies and governments are controlled by a single political party in an inflexible and authoritarian manner. Although these countries claim to have democratic elections, in fact the citizens have no electoral choice but to rubber-stamp the candidates of the ruling party. The people are denied civil liberties and freedoms that should be the hallmark of a socialist society. In a pure socialist society democratic relations must operate throughout the social structure: in government, at work, at school, and in the community.

The second principle of socialism is egalitarianism: equality of opportunity for the self-fulfillment of all; equality rather than hierarchy in decision making; and equality in sharing the benefits of society. For some socialists the goal is absolute equality. For most, though, equality means a limit to inequality, with some acceptable disparities in living standards. This more realistic goal of socialism requires a fundamental commitment to achieving a rough parity by leveling out gross inequities in income, property, and opportunities. The key is a leveling of advantages so that all citizens receive the necessities (food, clothing, shelter, medical care, decent wages, sick pay, and retirement benefits).

The third feature of socialism is community, which is the "idea that social relations should be characterized by cooperation and a sense of collective belonging rather than by conflict and competition" (Miller, 1991:406).

The fourth characteristic of socialism is the public ownership of the means of production. The people own the basic industries, financial institutions, utilities, transportation, and communication companies. The goal is serving the public, not making profit.

The fifth principle of socialism is planning. The society must direct social activities to meet common goals. This means that socialists oppose the heart of capitalism, which is to let individuals and corporations acting in their own interests in the marketplace determine overall outcomes. For socialists, these uncoordinated activities invite chaos and, while possibly helping some in the society, will do damage to others. Thus, a purely socialist economy requires societal planning to provide, at the least possible individual and collective cost, the best conditions to meet the material needs of its citizens. Planning also aims to achieve societal goals such as protecting the environment, combating pollution, saving natural resources, and developing new technologies. Public policy is decided through the rational assessment of the needs of society and of how the economy might best be organized to achieve them. In this situation the economy must be regulated by the government, which acts as the agent of the people. The government sets prices and wages; important industries are run at a loss if necessary. Dislocations such as surpluses or shortages or unemployment are minimized by central planning. The goal is to run the economy for the good of the society.

The Corporation-Dominated Economy

The U.S. economy has always been based on the principles of capitalism; however, the present economy is far removed from a free enterprise system. The major discrepancy between the ideal system and the real is that the U.S. economy is no longer based on competition among more or less equal private capitalists. It is now dominated by huge corporations that, contrary to classical economic theory, control demand rather than respond to the demands of the market. However well the economic system might once have worked, the increasing size and power of corporations disrupt it. This development calls into question the appropriate economic form for a modern post-industrial society. We examine the consequences of concentrated economic power domestically and internationally, for they create many important social problems. The second contradiction of U.S. economic life is the existence of what has been called corporate socialism: the dependence of corporations on governmental largesse, contracts, and regulation of the market for profit. We examine these developments in turn.

Monopolistic Capitalism

Karl Marx, more than 120 years ago, when bigness was the exception, predicted that capitalism was doomed by several inherent contradictions that would produce a class of people bent on destroying it. The most significant of these contradictions for our purposes is the inevitability of monopolies.* Marx hypothesized that free enterprise would result in some firms becoming bigger and bigger as they eliminate their opposition or absorb smaller competing firms. The ultimate result of this process is the existence of a monopoly in each of the various sectors of the economy. Monopolies, of course, are antithetical to the free enterprise system be-

---

*Marx prophesied that capitalism carried the seeds of its own destruction. In addition to resulting in monopolies, capitalism (1) encourages crises—inflation, slumps, gluts, depressions—because the lack of centralized planning will mean the overproduction of some goods and the underproduction of others; (2) encourages mass production for expansion and profits, but in so doing a social class, the proletariat (working class), is created that has the goal of equalizing the distribution of profits; (3) demands the introduction of labor-saving machinery, which forces unemployment and a more hostile proletariat; and (4) will control the state, the effect of which is that the state will pass laws favoring the wealthy, thereby incurring the further wrath of the proletariat. All these factors increase the probability of the proletariat building class consciousness, which is the condition necessary before class conflict and the ushering in of a new economic system (Marx, 1967).

Big corporations dominate the U.S. economy. Less than 1 percent of all corporations produce over 80 percent of the private sector output.

cause they, not supply and demand, determine the price and the quality of the product.

For the most part, the evidence in U.S. society upholds Marx's prediction. Less than 1 percent of all corporations produce over 80 percent of the private sector output (Parenti, 1995:10). Most sectors of the economy are dominated by few corporations. Instead of one corporation controlling an industry, the typical situation is domination by a small number of firms. When four or fewer firms supply 50 percent or more of a particular market, a **shared monopoly** results, which performs much as a monopoly or cartel would. Most economists agree that above this level of concentration—a four-firm ratio of 50 percent—the economic costs of a shared monopoly are manifest (e.g., higher prices by 25 percent). Government data show that a number of industries are highly concentrated (e.g., each of the following industries has four or fewer firms controlling at least 60 percent): light bulbs, breakfast cereals, turbines/generators, aluminum, cigarettes, beer, chocolate/cocoa, photography equipment, guided missiles, and roasted coffee.

This trend toward ever-greater concentration among the largest U.S. business concerns has accelerated because of two activities—mergers and interlocking directorates.

Megamergers. Every year thousands of mergers and leveraged buyouts occur. For example, in 1995 nearly 9,000 mergers and acquisitions, worth a record $460 billion, occurred.

This trend toward megamergers has at least five negative consequences: (1) it increases the centralization of capital, which reduces competition and raises prices for consumers; (2) it increases the power of the huge corporations over workers, unions, and governments; (3) it diminishes the number of jobs; (4) it increases corporate debt (currently, U.S. corporations spend about half their earnings on interest payments); and (5) it is nonproductive. Elaborating on this last point, mergers and takeovers do not create new plants, products, or jobs. Rather, they create profits for lawyers, accountants, brokers, bankers, and big investors (Hightower, 1987:25).

Defenders of a free and competitive enterprise system should attack the existence of monopolies and shared monopolies as un-American. There should be strong support of governmental efforts to break up the largest and most powerful corporations.

Interlocking Directorates. Another mechanism for the ever-greater concentration of the size and power of the largest corporations is **interlocking directorates,** the linkage between corporations that results when an individual serves on the board of directors of two companies (a **direct interlock**) or when two companies each have a director on the board of a third company (an **indirect interlock**). Such arrangements have great potential to benefit the interlocked companies by reducing competition through the sharing of information and the coordination of policies. As a Senate report has put it:

> Personal interlocks between business leaders may lead to a concentration of economic or fiscal control in a few hands. There is in this the danger of a business elite, an ingrown group impervious to outside forces, intolerant of dissent, and protective of the status quo, charting the direction of production and investment in one of several industries. (U.S. Senate, 1978:6)

In 1914 passage of the Clayton Act made it illegal for a person to serve simultaneously on the corporate boards of two companies that were in direct competition with each other. Financial institutions and indirect interlocks, however, were exempt. Moreover, the government has had difficulty in determining what constitutes "direct competition." The result is that despite the prohibition, interlocking directorates are widespread. For example, there is a direct interlock between AT&T and Citicorp, linking a customer of financial services and a lending institution. Indirect interlocks, even among competitors, are commonplace. IBM and AT&T, for example, are competitors in telecommunications equipment and services, yet in 1976 they were indirectly linked through common memberships on the boards of twenty-two other companies.

Interlocking directorates proliferate throughout U.S. industry. When directors are linked directly or indirectly, there is the potential for cohesiveness, common action, and unified power. Clearly, the principles of capitalism are compromised when this phenomenon occurs.

Multinational Corporations

The thesis of the previous section is that there is a trend for corporations to increase in size, resulting, eventually, in huge enterprises that join with other large companies to form effective monopolies. This process of economic concentration provides the largest companies with enormous economic and political power. Another trend—the globalization of the largest U.S. corporations—makes their power all the greater. This fact of international economic life has very important implications for social problems, both domestically and abroad.

There has been a tendency of late for U.S. corporations to increase their foreign investments sharply. Why are U.S. corporations shifting more and more of their total assets outside of the United States? The obvious answer is that the rate of profit tends to be higher abroad. Resources necessary for manufacture and production tend to be cheaper in many other nations, and labor costs are substantially lower. Wages in general are much lower than in the United States, and unions are nonexistent.

The consequences of this shift in production from the United States to outside this country are significant. Most important is the drying up of many semi- and unskilled jobs. The effects of the increased unemployment are twofold: increased welfare costs and increased discontent among those in the working class. (This problem of domestic job losses through overseas capital investments was discussed in Chapter 8.)

The problems of domestic unemployment exacerbated by foreign investment are the problems of lost revenues through taxes and a negative balance of payments. Tax revenues are lost because corporations can escape domestic taxes by having goods produced overseas and by undervaluing exports and overvaluing imports. Indirectly, taxes are also lost by increased unemployment. The balance of payments problem (i.e., more money flowing out of the country than arriving) is aggravated by the flow of investment money overseas, the reduced domestic production, and the purchase of goods produced in foreign countries.

Another result of the twin processes of concentration and internationalization of corporations is the enormous power wielded by the gigantic multinational corporation. In essence, the largest corporations control the world economy. Their decisions to build or not to build, where to relocate a plant, and to start a new product or to scrap an old one have tremendous impacts on the lives of ordinary citizens in the countries they operate from and invest in.

In their desire to tap low-wage workers, the multinational corporations have tended to locate in poor countries. On the surface this would appear to have positive consequences for these nations (e.g., by providing a higher standard of living and access to modern technology). Unfortunately, this has not been the case. One reason is that the profits generated in these countries tend to be expatriated back to the United States in the form of dividends. Second, global companies do not have a great impact in easing the unemployment of the poor nations because they use advanced technology whenever feasible, and this reduces the demand for jobs. Third, the multinational companies tend to exploit the natural resources of the poor countries.

Finally, multinational corporations tend to meddle in the internal affairs of other nations in order to protect their investments and maximize profits. These activities include attempts to overthrow governments considered unfriendly to corporate interests, and the payment of millions in bribes and political contributions to reactionary governments and conservative leaders in various countries (Simon and Eitzen, 1993:8–9).

Capitalism and Inequality

Inequality is endemic to capitalism. In the competition for profits there are winners and losers. We have seen how corporate wealth is concentrated through shared monopolies and interlocking directorates. Let's begin by reviewing the degree to which corporate wealth is concentrated.

Concentration of Corporate Wealth

Wealth in the business community is centralized in a relatively few corporations, and this concentration is increasing. In 1994 the total amount of revenues of the 500 largest corporations was equivalent to 63 percent of the gross domestic product (GDP) (*Z Magazine,* 1995:5). The following examples reveal just how concentrated wealth is among the major U.S. corporations:

- Less than 1 percent of all corporations account for over 80 percent of the total output of the private sector (Parenti, 1995:10). Similarly less than 1 percent of corporations control two-thirds of the corporate assets of the United States (Parenti, 1988:11).
- Forty-nine of the largest banks hold a controlling interest in the 500 largest corporations (Parenti, 1995:10). Of the 15,000 commercial U.S. banks, the largest 50 hold more than one-third of all assets.
- One percent of all food corporations control 80 percent of all the industry's assets and about 90 percent of the profits. Six U.S.-based multinational corporations ship 90 percent of the grain in the world market (Parenti, 1995:12).

Concentration of Private Wealth

Capitalism generates inequality. Wealth is concentrated not only in the largest corporations but also among individuals and families. Some examples: William Gates, co-founder of Microsoft, is worth $18 billion; Michael Eisner, Walt Disney chief executive officer, had compensation of $14.8 million in 1995 plus stock options worth $317.9 million; Roberto Goizueta, Coca Cola CEO, received compensation of $13.09 million in pay plus a 1 million share stock option grant worth $25.6 million in 1995; Steven Spielberg, movie producer, made $120 million in 1995; and Michael Jordan, basketball star, signed a $30 million contract to play in 1996–97, which adds to his endorsement income in excess of $30 million annually.

A few families are fabulously wealthy and colossal in corporate magnitude. Michael Parenti describes the holdings of the DuPonts and the Rockefellers:

> The DuPonts control ten corporations, each worth billions of dollars, including General Motors, Coca Cola, and United Brands, along with many smaller firms. . . . They own about forty manorial estates and private museums in Delaware alone, and have set up thirty-one tax-exempt foundations. . . .

Another powerful family enterprise, that of the Rockefellers, extends into just about every industry in every state of the Union and every nation in the non-socialist world. The Rockefellers control five of the twelve largest oil companies and four of the largest banks in the world. (Parenti, 1995:13)

Concentration of Want and Misery

The inequality generated by a capitalist economy has a dark side. Summarizing the 1994 data on poverty in the United States (found in Chapter 10), 13.8 percent of the population (36.4 million people) were below the poverty line. According to the National Council on Economic Opportunity, another 30 million were on the edge of poverty. The data indicate that the poor are concentrated among certain social categories, especially people of color and families headed by women.

Again, summarizing from earlier chapters, research strongly substantiates how the life chances of the poor are jeopardized by their lack of resources. The fewer the resources available, the greater are the possibilities for any of the following to occur:

- Premature births and babies born mentally retarded because of prenatal mal-nourishment;
- Below average life expectancy;
- Disproportionate death from tuberculosis, influenza, pneumonia; from cancer of the stomach, lung, bronchus, and trachea; and from accidents;
- Impaired health because of differences in diet, sanitary facilities, shelter, and medical care;
- More frequent and longer periods of illness;
- An arrest, conviction, and serving of a longer sentence for a given violation;
- A lower-than-average level of educational attainment;
- Spouse and child abuse, divorce, and desertion.

Thus, the economic position of a family has very telling consequences on the probability of good health, educational attainment, justice, and a stable marriage.

Work in U.S. Society

Work is central to the human experience. Societies are organized to allocate work in order to produce the goods and services needed by the society and its members for sustenance, clothing, shelter, defense, and even luxury. Work provides individuals with their social identity, economic resources, and social location. Work dominates their time and is a primary source of life's meaning because it constitutes their contributions to other people.

The world of work also has a dark side, however. The structure of work is a major source of social problems. Work is alienating for many people. The organization of work sometimes exploits, does harm to workers, and often dehumanizes them. The distribution of work and how it is rewarded are major sources of inequality in society. This section focuses on the social problems generated by the social organization of work.

The Problems of Work

Work is a universal human activity. People everywhere engage in physical and mental activities that enhance the physical and social survival of themselves and others. Although people universally must work to meet their material needs, the way work is structured varies by society. Let's examine problems that emanate from the way work is structured in U.S. society.

The Control of Workers.   With the advent of the Industrial Revolution more and more families left agrarian life, moved to cities, and worked in factories. Work in these factories was sometimes difficult, often tedious, and usually boring. There was always the threat of lowered productivity and worker unrest under these adverse conditions. The factory owners and their managers used several tactics to counteract these potential problems and especially to maintain high productivity—scientific management, hierarchical control, technical control, and extortion.

   Scientific management (called *Taylorization,* after its founder, Frederick Taylor) came to the fore in U.S. industry around 1900. The emphasis was on breaking down work into very specialized tasks, the standardization of tools and procedures, and the speeding up of repetitive work. These efforts to increase worker efficiency and therefore to increase profits meant that workers developed a very limited range of skills. Instead of a wide knowledge of building cars or furniture, their knowledge was severely curtailed. This specialization had the effect of making the workers highly susceptible to automation and to being easily replaced by cheaper workers. But this scientific management approach also had a contradictory effect. In its attempt to increase efficiency by having workers do ever more compartmentalized tasks, it increased the repetition, boredom, and meaninglessness of work—hence, the strong tendency for workers to become alienated and restless. Consider the description by George Ritzer:

> [The assembly line is clearly] a dehumanizing setting in which to work. Human beings, equipped with a wide array of skills and abilities, are asked to perform a limited number of highly simplified tasks over and over. Instead of expressing their human abilities on the job, people are forced to deny their humanity to act as robots. People cannot express themselves in their work. (Ritzer, 1996:26)

   Closely related to scientific management is the use of bureaucracy to control workers. Work settings, whether in factories, offices, or corporations, are organized into bureaucratized hierarchies. In this hierarchy of authority (chain of command) each position in the chain gives orders to those below, taking responsibility for their actions and following orders from above. The hierarchical arrangement controls workers by holding out the possibility of advancement, with more prestigious job titles, higher wages, and greater benefits as one moves up the ladder. Those who hope to be upwardly mobile in the organization must become obedient rule-followers who do not question authority.

Similarly, work organized along an assembly line permits maximum control over workers. "Workers must do certain tasks at specific points during the production process. It is immediately obvious when a worker fails to perform the required tasks" (Ritzer, 1996:25–26).

Workers are also controlled by management's use of technology to monitor and supervise them. Some businesses use lie detectors to assess worker loyalty. Psychological tests and drug tests are used to screen applicants for work. Telephone taps have been used to determine whether workers use company time for personal use. Closed-circuit television, two-way mirrors, and other devices have been used by management to determine whether workers are using their time most productively. The most common contemporary technology for worker control is the computer. The computer can count keystrokes, time phone calls, monitor frequency of errors, assess overall employee performance, and even issue warnings when the employee falls short of the ideal.

A final management tool to control workers is extortion. If workers become too militant in their demands for higher wages, safe working conditions, or benefits, management can threaten them with reprisals. In the past owners threatened to hire cheaper labor (new immigrants, for example) or to use force to end a strike. Today, the most common and successful management tool is the threat to move the plant to a nonunion state (or even outside the United States if the union does not reduce its demands) or to replace the workers with robots or other forms of automation.

Alienation.   **Alienation** refers to the separation of human beings from each other, from themselves, and from the products they create. In capitalism, according to Karl Marx, worker alienation occurs because the workers do not have any control over their labor, because they are manipulated by managers, because they tend to work in large, impersonal settings, and because they work at specialized tasks. Under these circumstances workers use only a fraction of their talents and have no pride in their own creativity and in the final product. Thus, we see that worker alienation is linked with unfulfilled personal satisfaction. As Blauner has described it,

> Alienation exists when workers are unable to control their immediate work processes, to develop a sense of purpose and function which connects their jobs to the overall organization of production, to belong to integrated industrial communities, and when they fail to become involved in the activity of work as a mode of personal self-expression. (Blauner, 1964:5)

Put another way, this time by philosopher Albert Camus: "Without work all life goes rotten. But when work is soulless, life stifles and dies" (quoted in Levitan and Johnson, 1982:63).

In the absence of satisfaction and personal fulfillment, work becomes meaningless. When this meaninglessness is coupled with management's efforts to control workers, the repetitious nature of the work, and the requirement of punching a time clock, many workers feel a profound resentment. This resentment may lead workers to join together in a union or other collective group to improve their working conditions. For many workers, though, the alienation remains at a personal level and is manifested by higher worker dissatisfaction, absenteeism, disruption in the workplace, and alcohol or other drug abuse on the job.

Alienation is not limited to manual workers. The work of white-collar workers such as salesclerks, secretaries, file clerks, bank tellers, and keypunchers is mostly routine, repetitive, boring, and unchallenging. These workers, like assembly line workers, follow orders, do limited tasks, and have little sense of accomplishment.

Studs Terkel, in introducing his book *Working,* summarized the personal impact of alienating work:

> This book, being about work, is, by its very nature, about violence—to the spirit as well as to the body. It is about ulcers as well as accidents, about shouting matches as well as fistfights, about nervous breakdowns as well as kicking the dog around. It is, above all (or beneath all), about daily humiliations. To survive the day is triumph enough for the walking wounded among the great many of us.
>
> It is about a search, too, for daily meaning as well as daily bread, for recognition as well as for cash, for astonishment rather than torpor; in short, for a sort of life rather than a Monday through Friday sort of dying. Perhaps immortality, too, is part of the quest. To be remembered was the wish, spoken and unspoken, of the heroes and heroines of this book.
>
> For the many, there is a hardly concealed discontent. The blue-collar blues is no more bitterly sung than the white-collar moan. "I'm a machine," says the spotwelder. "I'm caged," says the steelworker. "A monkey can do what I do," says the receptionist. "I'm less than a farm implement," says the migrant worker. "I'm an object," says the high-fashion model. Blue collar and white call upon the identical phrase: "I'm a robot." (Terkel, 1975:xiii–xiv)

Dangerous Working Conditions.   In a capitalist economy workers represent a cost to profit-seeking corporations. The lower that management can keep labor costs, the greater will be their profits. Historically, low labor costs meant that workers received low wages, had inferior or nonexistent fringe benefits such as health care, and worked in unhealthy conditions. Mines and factories were often extremely unsafe. The labor movement early in this century gathered momentum because of the abuse experienced by workers.

After a long and sometimes violent struggle the unions were successful in raising the wages for workers, adding fringe benefits, and making the conditions of work safer. But the owners were slow to change; and worker safety was, and continues to be, one of the most difficult areas. Many owners of mills, mines, and factories continue to consider the safety of their workers a low-priority item, presumably because of the high cost.

According to the Labor Department, approximately 10,000 workers are killed each year in industrial accidents and 70,000 are permanently disabled (reported in *Multinational Monitor,* 1991:5). Most significant, "30 percent of industrial accidents are caused by illegal safety violations" (*Multinational Monitor,* 1990:6).

The extent of job-induced illnesses is much more difficult than the number of job-related accidents to determine exactly, primarily because for some diseases it takes many years of exposure to affect the skin, lungs, blood chemistry, nervous system, or various organs. Jeffrey Reiman's estimate (which he considers conservative), after reviewing the evidence, is that annually there are 150,000 job-related serious illnesses and 25,000 deaths from occupational diseases (Reiman, 1995:73).

Significant occupational dangers still exist. The dangers today are invisible contaminants such as nuclear radiation, chemical compounds, coal tars, dust, and asbestos fibers in the air. These dangers from invisible contaminants are increasing because the production of synthetic chemicals has increased so dramatically. The following examples describe the specific risks of continued exposure to dangerous chemicals in certain industries:

- Workers in the dyestuffs industry (working with aromatic hydrocarbons) have about thirty times the risk of the general population of dying from bladder cancer.
- About 10 percent of coal miners suffer from black lung, caused by years of breathing coal dust in areas with inadequate ventilation.
- Migrant farm workers have a life expectancy thirty years below the national average. This low rate is a consequence of living in poverty or near-poverty and, most significant, of the exposure to herbicides and pesticides sprayed on the fields where they work.
- Workers in the semiconductor industry face special dangers from exposure to acids, gases, and solvents used in chip manufacturing.
- Pregnant operators of video display terminals have disproportionate numbers of miscarriages or babies with birth defects, apparently from exposure to nonionizing radiation.

The record of industry has often been one of ignoring the scientific data, or of stalling through court actions, or claims that jobs will be lost because of the cost to clean up the factories or mills, resulting in higher prices to consumers. Most important, some companies have not informed workers of the dangers. This discussion raises some critical questions: Should profits supersede human life? Are owners guilty of murder if their decisions to minimize plant safety result in industrial deaths? Who is a greater threat, the thug in the streets or the executives in the suites? Jeffrey Reiman answers these questions:

> Is a person who kills another in a bar brawl a greater threat to society than a business executive who refuses to cut into his profits to make his plant a safe place to work? By any measure of death and suffering the latter is by far a greater danger than the former. Because he wishes his workers no harm, because he is only indirectly responsible for death and disability while pursuing legitimate economic goals, his acts are not called "crimes." Once we free our imagination from the blinders of the one-on-one model of crime, can there be any doubt that the criminal justice system does not protect us from the gravest threats to life and limb? It seeks to protect us when danger comes from a young-lower-class male in the inner city. When a threat comes from an upper-class business executive in an office, the criminal justice system looks the other way. (Reiman, 1995:76–77)

Sweatshops. A **sweatshop** is a substandard work environment where workers are paid less than the minimum wage, not paid overtime premiums, and other labor laws are violated. Although sweatshops occur in various types of manufacturing, they occur most frequently in the garment industry. There are 20,000 small garment makers in the United States that supply half of the country's clothing which is not imported. Many of these enterprises are sweatshops, violating health and safety regulations, sometimes paying less than a dollar an hour, sometimes enslaving their employees. In one notorious case in 1995 federal agents raided a garment sweatshop in El Monte (a suburb of Los Angeles):

Many of the small U.S. garment makers are sweatshops, violating health and safety regulations, paying less than the minimum wage, and sometimes enslaving their employees.

Like many immigrants from poor countries, the 66 Thai immigrants that the inspectors liberated had come in pursuit of the good life. Soon after arriving in Los Angeles, however, they found themselves locked in a barbed-wire-encircled labor camp and forced to work seven days a week in shifts that, during some rush periods, extended as long as 20 hours a day.

Some of these workers—all but six of whom were women—had been imprisoned for five years. For 70 cents an hour, they produced garments than ended up in retail stores such as Hecht's, the Gap and Montgomery Ward. They spent their meager wages at an on-site company store. Attempts to escape were repressed with beatings and threats of rape. [Labor Secretary Robert Reich said] "It's the worst case of slavery in America's recent history . . . ." (Rizvi, 1995:6)

The government estimates that more than half of the garment shops in San Francisco violate labor laws, as do more than 3,000 apparel sweatshops with 50,000 workers in New York City (Echaveste and Nussbaum, 1994). Garment sweatshops are also common in Los Angeles, El Paso, and Seattle. The workers in these places make clothes for such brands as Levi Strauss, Esprit, Casual Corner, the Limited, and the Gap (Rizvi, 1995) and for such merchandisers as J. C. Penney, Sears, and Wal-Mart (Headden, 1993). The workers, mostly Latina and Asian immigrant women, are paid much below the minimum wage, receive no benefits, and work in crowded, unsafe, and stifling conditions. For a hopeful sign of what happens when sweatshop workers organize, see "Human Agency: Sweatshop Workers Organize and Win."

Unions and Their Decline. Historically, labor unions have been extremely important in changing management–labor relations. Joining together, workers challenged owners to increase wages, add benefits, provide worker security, and promote safety in the work place. Through the use of strikes, work slowdowns, public relations, and political lobbying, working conditions improved and union members, for the most part, prospered. The labor movement in the United States has fought for Social Security, Medicare, Medicaid, FHA mortgages, student loans, and increasing the

AGENCY

HUMAN

Sweatshop Workers Organize and Win

The sweatshop is back with a vengeance. From maquiladoras in Mexico and Central America to a slave-labor factory in El Monte, California, poor young women trapped in desperate conditions are making designer clothes for upscale consumers.

Because subcontractors—not the clothing manufacturers themselves—employ these workers, the industry has managed to fend off traditional organizing efforts. But a recent victory demonstrates the value of using strategies that go beyond usual labor-organizing practice.

The Asian Immigrant Women's Association (AIWA) announced in April that it had reached a settlement with millionaire fashion designer Jessica McClintock. AIWA had been mobilizing community pressure for three years to win justice for a dozen women who lost their jobs while making clothing for McClintock, Inc. An Oakland, California, garment subcontractor for Mc-Clintock called Lucky Sewing Company declared bankruptcy in 1992, leaving its workers unpaid. Lucky owed the women more than $10,000 in back wages.

AIWA launched the Garment Workers Justice Campaign against McClintock, arguing that it had a moral responsibility to reimburse the workers even though the company was not legally liable for Lucky Sewing's financial problems. AIWA conducted a creative, multi-faceted campaign in cities across the country, which included several full-page ads in *The New York Times* portraying McClintock as a heartless Marie Antoinette saying to the starving workers, LET THEM EAT LACE.

McClintock is a purveyor of frilly prom dresses and other "romantic" clothing, an image that does not fit well with pictures of sweatshops filled with underpaid women workers.

The settlement with McClintock includes back wages for the laid-off workers, a garment-workers' education fund and scholarships, an outreach campaign to inform garment workers of their rights, and a toll-free hot-line in English and Cantonese that can be used to report illegal wages and working conditions. The break in the campaign came last fall when the Department of Labor published a list of "fair labor fashion trendsetters"—corporations notable for their commitment to upholding worker protections. McClintock. Inc., was listed. AIWA contacted the Department of Labor, notifying them of the Garment Workers Justice Campaign and the glaring contradiction between McClintock's verbal commitment to worker protections and the company's use of sweatshop labor. Faced with the prospect of removal from the list, McClintock gave in.

"The clothing manufacturers are vulnerable," says Charlie Kernaghan of the National Labor Committee. "They've gotten fat and lazy, and with the right strategy we can beat them, even though we can't match their resources."

Source: John Anner, "Sweatshop Workers Organize and Win," *The Progressive* 60 (June 1996), p. 15. Reprinted by permission from *The Progressive,* 409 East Main Street, Madison, WI.

minimum wage. In the past unions were a powerful force for economic security and social justice. But that was forty years ago, when unions were strong. In the mid-1950s, 35 percent of all workers belonged to unions, 80 to 90 percent in major industries such as auto, steel, and coal mining. This percentage slipped to 28 percent in the mid-1970s. Now it is only 15 percent of the entire workforce, and a mere 11 percent in private industry (Sweeney, 1996). With such small and dwindling numbers, labor unions are in danger of becoming irrelevant.

The reasons for the decline in union membership (and clout) are several. First, there was a direct assault against unions by Republican presidents Reagan and Bush. Both of these administrations were unsympathetic with strikes and sometimes used federal leverage to weaken them. Similarly, their appointees to the post of Secretary of Labor and the National Labor Relations Board (NLRB) were probusiness rather than prolabor. Long delays in decision making at the NLRB and their anti-union rulings have resulted in management sometimes firing pro-union workers with impunity. In effect, the NLRB from 1981 on reversed its previous policies of protecting worker rights (Novak, 1991).

Second, public opinion has turned against unions because some of them are undemocratic, scandal-ridden, and too zealous in their demands. Public opinion has also turned against organized labor because of a probusiness, procapitalist bias that increased during the era of supply-side economics that dominated the Reagan and Bush administrations and much of Congress during that time. That bias, although muted a bit, continued during the Clinton administration.

A major reason for the decline of union strength is the transformation of the economy (discussed in Chapter 8). Manufacturing jobs, which are in decline, have historically been pro-union while service jobs, which are increasing, have been typically nonunionized. Many businesses, faced with stiff competition from low-wage economies, have insisted on reducing wages and/or worker benefits or said they would go bankrupt or move overseas themselves. The increased use of microchip technology threatens jobs with increased automation in the factory (robots to replace assembly-line workers) and in the office (computers to displace typists and file clerks). Similarly, the advent of computers, modems, and fax machines has increased the number of workers who work at home, as temporaries, and part-time. These workers are the least likely to join unions.

These forces have given the strong advantage to management. This trend has several negative consequences. First, faced with the threat of plants closing or moving to nonunion localities or to low-wage nations, unions have chosen, typically, to give back many of the gains they made during the 1960s and 1970s. Thus, workers have lost real wages and benefits.

A second consequence of union decline is that the work place may be less safe.

> Some of the most injury-prone industries, like food processing and textiles, have clustered in right-to-work [i.e., nonunion] states across the South, where labor organizers get the kind of welcome that used to greet Freedom Riders. (Lacayo, 1991:29)

A major consequence of union decline is the further dwindling of the middle class. In the words of Albert Shanker, president of the American Federation of Teachers, the union movement took a lot of workers who were relatively unskilled and turned them into middle class people who educated their children and supported the United States economy. Now, we've got businesses turning their employees into third-world workers. (Shanker, 1992:E9)

Implied in this statement is a related consequence: if businesses turn their employees into third-world workers, then they will not be able to purchase enough goods and services to encourage economic growth and societal-wide prosperity. As Norman Birnbaum has said, "nations with strong unions and social contracts have the highest living standards" (Birnbaum, 1992:319).

Another consequence is a weakened voice and political power for working people.

Today, we need unions to raise money and raise hell as much as to raise wages. In politics, business is outspending labor 3 to 1, has captured the votes of Washington and sets the agenda for national debate—a debate that pits the far right against the moderate right and ignores everyone else. . . . Democracy doesn't work unless everyone has a say. Today, it's out of whack. (Gartner, 1995:11A)

A final consequence points to a possible contradiction—the precipitous decline in unions may actually lead to labor's regeneration. As the unions decline, with workers poorly compensated and ever fearful of losing their jobs, with management becoming more arrogant and demanding, the situation may get bad enough that there will be a turnaround—a surge in union membership and worker militancy. There was some indication in 1996, with a change to a more militant union leadership, that the unions were poised for a turnaround. If, indeed, the unions became stronger, this would lead not only to a stronger collective voice in the work arena but also in the nation's politics. Those nations with strong unionized labor (e.g., Canada, Germany, Sweden) have a social democratic conception of society, which means universal health care, progressive income taxes, and more equitable government programs.

Of course, the above scenario may not occur. Unions may continue to decline in size and influence; the pay and benefits to workers may continue to erode; and workers will be fragmented rather than united (see Salvatore, 1992).

Discrimination in the Workplace: The Perpetuation of Inequality. Women and minorities have long been the objects of discrimination in U.S. industry. Currently (and we have progressed mightily), approximately fifty thousand charges of discrimination by organizations are filed annually with the U.S. Equal Opportunity Commission. The charges now and in the past have centered on hiring policies, seniority rights, restricted job placement, limited opportunities for advancement, and lower pay for equal work. A number of court suits (and those settled out of court) illustrate that discriminatory policies have been common among such major corporations as AT&T, General Motors, and Northwest Airlines and in such industries as banking and steel.

There are two mechanisms operating in the U.S. economy that perpetuate inequalities in the job market by social class, race, and gender—the segmented labor market and capitalist patriarchy.

Segmented Labor Market.   The capitalist economy is divided into two separate sectors that have different characteristics, different roles, and different rewards for laborers within each. This organization of the economy is called the **segmented labor market,** or the **dual labor market.** The primary sector is composed of large, bureaucratic organizations with relatively stable production and sales. Jobs within this sector require developed skills, are relatively well paid, occur in good working conditions, and are stable. Within this sector there are two types of jobs. The first type, those in the upper tier, are high-status professional and managerial jobs. The pay is very good for the highly educated persons in these jobs. They have a high degree of personal autonomy, and the jobs offer variety, creativity, and initiative. Upward mobility is likely for those who are successful. The second type, the lower-tier jobs within the primary sector, are held by working-class persons. The jobs are either white-collar clerical or blue-collar skilled and semiskilled. The jobs are repetitive, and mobility is limited. The jobs are relatively secure because of unionization, although they are much more vulnerable than those in the upper tier. When times are difficult, these workers tend to be laid off rather than terminated.

The secondary economic sector is composed of marginal firms in which product demand is unstable. Jobs within this sector are characterized by poor working conditions, low wages, few opportunities for advancement, and little job security. Little education or skill is required to perform these tasks. Workers beginning in the secondary sector tend to get locked in because they lack the skills required in the primary sector and they usually have unstable work histories. A common interpretation of this problem is that secondary-sector workers are in these dead-end jobs because of their pathology—poor work history, lack of skills, and lack of motivation. Such an explanation, however, blames the victim. Poor work histories tend to be the result of unemployment caused by the production of marginal products and the lack of job security. Similarly, these workers have few, if any, incentives to learn new skills or to stay for long periods with an employer because of the structural impediments to upward mobility. And unlike workers in the primary sector, workers in the secondary sector are more likely to experience harsh and capricious work discipline from supervisors, primarily because there are no unions.

The significance of this dual labor market is threefold. First, placement in one of these segments corresponds with social class, which tends to be perpetuated from generation to generation. Second, employment in the secondary sector is often so inadequately paid that many full-time workers live in poverty, as noted in Chapter 6. And third, the existence of a dual labor market reinforces racial, ethnic, and gender divisions in the labor force. White males, while found in both segments, tend to predominate in the upper tier of the primary sector. White females tend to be clerks in the lower tier of the primary sector, and White ethnics tend to be clerks in the lower tier of the primary sector. Males and females of color are found disproportionately in the secondary sector. These findings explain why unemployment rates for Blacks and Hispanics are consistently much higher than the rate for Whites (see Figure 13.1). They explain the persistent wage differences found by race and gender.

These findings also explain the vast overrepresentation of people of color and women living in poverty. Referring to women, Ehrenreich and Stallard have argued that occupational segregation makes a crucial difference:

FIGURE 13.1

Unemployment Rates by Race

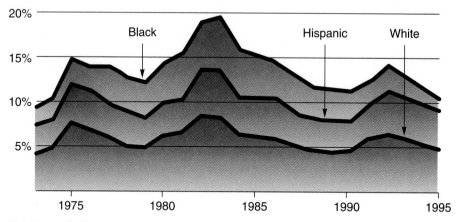

Percentage of population that is unemployed, 1973–1995*

*U.S. Bureau of Labor Statistics
Source: Clarifying Issues '96 (New York: Public Agenda, 1996), p. 39.

For women, employment is not necessarily an antidote to poverty. The jobs that are available to us are part of the problem. The list is familiar—clerical work, sales, light manufacturing, and the catchall category, "service work," which includes nurse's aides and grade-school teachers, waitresses, and welfare caseworkers. Only 20 out of 420 listed occupations account for 80 percent of employed women, and it is this occupational segregation that accounts for women's low average earnings. In general, "women's work" not only pays less than men's but is less inflation proof. . . . The extreme occupational segregation of women in our society makes for a crucial difference between women's poverty and men's. For men, poverty is often a consequence of unemployment, and is curable by getting a job. But for women, concentrated in the low-wage stratum of the work force, a job may not be a solution to poverty. According to the National Advisory Council on Economic Opportunities, "poverty among hundreds of thousands of women already working underlines the failure of the 'job' solution." (Ehrenreich and Stallard, 1982:220)

Similarly, people of color are doubly disadvantaged. As Baron observes,

the combination of racial [disadvantage] with the primary–secondary segmentation compounds the immobility, low wages, and poor working conditions of the large number of black workers [and we would add Hispanics, Native Americans, and others of color] who participate in the secondary labor market. On the whole they are considerably worse off than the white poor and the near poor who work in the secondary sector. (Baron, 1975:205)

Capitalist Patriarchy.   Closely tied to segmented labor markets is the phenomenon of **capitalist patriarchy.** Although male supremacy (patriarchy) existed before

Kirk Anderson.

capitalism and is found in noncapitalist societies today, a strong relationship between the two helps explain the present oppression of women in U.S. society (Eisenstein, 1979). The concept refers to male dominance in work-related roles. This dominance is reflected in two ways—males tend to make the rules and enforce them and males receive unequal (i.e., greater) rewards.

Current gender inequality results from a long history of patriarchal social relations where men have consciously kept women in subordinate roles at work and in the home. Men as workers consistently have acted in their own interests to retain power and to keep women either out of their occupations or in subordinate and poorly paid work roles. Historically, through their unions, males insisted that the higher-status and better-paying jobs be exclusively male. They lobbied legislatures to pass legislation supportive of male exclusiveness in occupations and in opposition to such equalization measures as minimum wages for women. Also, the male unions prevented women from gaining the skills that would lead them to equal-paying jobs. The National Typographical Union in 1854, for example, insisted not only that women be refused jobs as compositors but also that they not be taught the skills necessary to be a compositor (Hartmann, 1976).

Throughout U.S. history capitalists have used gender inequality in the workplace to their advantage. Women were hired because they would work for less money than men, which made men all the more fearful of women in the workplace. Capitalists even used the threat of hiring lower-paid women to take the place of higher-paid men to keep the wages of both sexes down and to lessen labor militancy.

In contemporary U.S. society capitalism and patriarchy interact to oppress women. Males and females are accorded different, and unequal, positions in religious, government, school, work, and family activities. Looking only at work, women and men do different work both in the family and in the labor force. This division of labor between the sexes preserves the differential power, privilege, and prestige of men (see Chapter 9).

Unemployment

The Bureau of Labor Statistics supplies the official unemployment statistics. The official unemployment rate in the United States since 1980 has ranged from a high of 9 percent in 1982–83 to a low of 4.8 percent in 1988. In February 1996 the rate was 5.5 percent. These rates are misleading because they understate, dramatically, the actual amount of unemployment. Not included in the data are the 60 million or so people who are not in the labor force because they are in school, disabled, retired, homemakers, or not seeking work.

The data are distorted by undercounting the unemployed in two ways. First, persons who have not actively sought work in the four weeks prior to being interviewed are not counted in the unemployed category. Typically, there are more than 1 million such **discouraged workers,** most of whom were once employed in the secondary sector of the segmented labor force. Women comprise about two-thirds of these discouraged workers, and racial minorities represent about 30 percent. The rationale of the Bureau of Labor Statistics for excluding dispirited workers is that the function of the statistic is to chart fluctuations in the conditions of the active labor force, not to provide a complete portrait of the jobless. Regardless of the reasoning, the official data of the government, by undercounting joblessness, diminish the perceived severity of unemployment and therefore reduce the zeal to do anything about the problem. The extent to which the public perceives unemployment as a problem is further lessened by the counting as employed anyone who had worked for as little as an hour for pay in the week before being interviewed. Thus, people who subsist on odd jobs, temporary work, or minimal part-time work are counted as fully employed by the government.

Even the decidedly understated government figures on unemployment reveal that there are many millions of people who want to work but do not. See "A Closer Look: The Real Un(der) Employment Rate" for a truer picture of unemployment, and the huge surplus of labor in the United States.

According to Levitan and Johnson, since World War II

> the demand for labor has failed to keep pace with the supply of job seekers. No doubt, some portion of this unemployment is inevitable in a democratic society, as both employers and workers freely choose to accept or reject work situations. Yet the bulk of unemployment is neither frictional nor voluntary. Due to whatever combination of structural barriers and governmental policies, the economy, though it has continued to expand, has failed to generate sufficient numbers of jobs in the aggregate or to produce a reasonable match between the skills of unemployed workers and the emerging demands of labor. (Levitan and Johnson, 1982:55)

Ironically, there are those who favor having a certain proportion of the population unemployed. English reports that

> economists generally consider 6 to 6.5 percent to be the nation's long-term, underlying jobless rate, below which it is difficult to reduce unemployment without causing inflationary pressures. It is also the level at which every person who can be reasonably expected to hold a job has one, and only those with little education, training or work skills are jobless. (English, 1984:56)

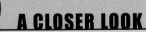

A CLOSER LOOK

The Real Un(der)employment Rate

If you believe the Clinton administration, unemployment has practically disappeared as a problem. But while the official rate is now around 5.5% (still well above what we used to think of as full employment), this figure omits millions of people who want full-time jobs but can't find them. If all these people were included, the rate would rise above 12%—presenting a far more dismal picture of job prospects in the United States.

The two main categories omitted from the unemployment statistics are:

- Everyone who wants a job but has not looked for one during the past month, due to discouragement or other difficulties.

- Everyone who has a part-time job but wants full-time work.

The true underemployment rate was a whopping 17.3% in 1992, perhaps explaining George Bush's loss to Bill Clinton in the presidential race. And although the true rate today is more than what Clinton claims, it may be low enough compared to recent years to reward him with reelection.

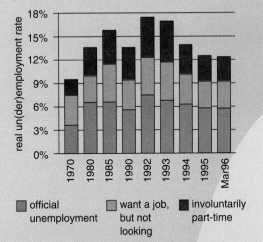

Sources: Monthly Labor Review, Employment & Earnings, both by Bureau of Labor Statistics, U.S. Department of Labor. (See also "The Real Un(der)employment Rate," *D&S,* May/June 1995).

Source: Marc Breslow, "The Real Un(der)employment Rate," *Dollars and Sense* No. 207 (September/October 1996), p. 51.

Not only is unemployment commonly believed to be functional for society by reducing inflationary pressures, but it is also kept relatively high by capitalists because high unemployment deflates wages and therefore increases profits. When there are unemployed people willing to work, workers will not make inordinate demands for higher wages for fear that they will be replaced by cheaper labor. Thus, even unionized labor becomes relatively docile when unemployment is high. The Feagins have summarized the capitalist argument:

> The . . . unemployed are essential to the operation of the capitalist system because they put downward pressure on wages and provide a reserve labor force that can be drawn back into employment when profit and investment conditions require it. Not only the officially unemployed, but also other groups make up this reserve labor force: discouraged workers, part-time workers, newly arrived immigrant laborers, and housewives who might enter the market in the future. (Feagin and Feagin, 1994:91–92)

This **reserve army of the unemployed** is disproportionately comprised of people of color. In February 1996, for example, when the official unemployment rate was 5.5 percent, the unemployment rate for Whites was 4.9 percent; Latinos, 9.7 percent; and Blacks, 10.3 percent. These proportions by race tend to be relatively constant whether the overall unemployment rate is high or low, whether the economy is in a boom or a slump. Thus, the labor market assigns people of color disproportionately not only to the low-paying jobs but also to jobs that are the most unstable, precisely the situation of the secondary sector in the segmented labor market.

An important consequence of the reserve army of the unemployed being composed primarily of racial minorities is that it inflames racial antipathies against them by people who hold unstable jobs. These job holders perceive their enemy as the people below them who will work for lower wages, rather than the capitalists who make decisions to downsize their workers, move their operations overseas, oppose unions, and resist full employment and adequate wages for all people.

In summary, the problems associated with work in U.S. society are structural in origin. The source is not in unmotivated or unwilling workers. To understand the work setting in our society, we must understand the nature of capitalism, where profit rather than the human consequences guides managerial decisions. And in looking at unemployment, we must recognize that the economy fails to produce enough jobs with living wages and adequate benefits for the workers to maintain a middle-class lifestyle. Finally, in examining this labor market, we must understand that the economy is undergoing a profound transformation (Chapter 8). The next few generations will be caught in the nexus between one stage and another, and many will suffer because of the dislocations. So, too, will a society that refuses to plan but, rather, lets the marketplace dictate the choices of economic firms.

Capitalism in Crisis

The Negative Consequences of Private Profitability over Social Need

We have written elsewhere (Eitzen and Baca Zinn, 1997) that the major social problems in the United States are in large measure the result of the form of the economy. This is illustrated by the role of capitalists as they seek profit in the climate engendered by the economic transformation just discussed. Entrepreneurs, as they seek to maximize profit, shut down plants, reduce work forces, replace workers with machines, or threaten to move operations overseas to force workers to accept lower wages and benefits. They also continue to pollute the environment and fight government attempts to enforce worker and consumer safety. These entrepreneurs, corporate boards of directors, and corporate executives have no allegiance to consumers, workers, or the communities in which their operations are located. Their ultimate loyalty is to the bottom line. Parenti describes this fundamental logic of capitalism and capitalists:

Capitalism's purpose is not to create jobs; in fact, capitalists are constantly devising ways of eliminating jobs in order to cut labor costs. Nor is its purpose to build communities, for capitalists will build or destroy communities as investment opportunities dictate. Nor is capitalism dedicated to protecting the family or traditional life, for no system in human history has been more relentless in battering down ancient practices and destroying both rural and urban homegrown cultures. Nor is capitalism intent upon protecting the environment on behalf of generations yet to come; for corporations will treat the environment like a septic tank in order to cut production costs and maximize profits without regard for future generations or for the generation enduring it all today. Nor can we say that capitalists are committed to economic efficiency as such, since they regularly pass on their hidden diseconomies to the public in the form of overproduction, overpricing, pollution, unemployment, population dislocation, harmful products, and personal injury. And as the military budget shows, they actively court waste and duplication if it brings fatter contracts and bigger profits.

Capitalism has no loyalty to anything but its own process of capital accumulation, no loyalty to anything but itself. Nor could it be otherwise if one wished to survive as a capitalist; for the first law of the market is to make a profit off other people's labor or go out of business. Private profitability rather than social need is the determining condition of capital investment. (Parenti, 1986:1–2)

Can society continue to allow capitalists the freedom to make investment decisions unfettered by the concerns of society? Can corporations pollute the environment and produce waste with impunity? Should businesses be allowed to shut down a plant without sufficient warning and compensation to the affected workers and communities? Should taxes be levied on robots with the monies spent on job retraining of workers displaced by them? As the next chapter shows, the close relationship between economic power and political power appears to preclude government curbs on the abuses created by capitalists. And the rationale provided by many people for the lack of governmental control of business will likely be that capitalism is not the problem but really the solution to society's problems—if allowed to operate without restraints.

Declining Wages, Jobs, Consumerism, and Profits

According to Karl Marx, one of the contradictions of capitalism that will bring its downfall is the **"falling rate of profit."** This refers to the propensity of employers to maximize profits by reducing labor expenses. This is accomplished by using labor-saving machines and by paying the minimum in wages and benefits. The result of this capitalist rationale, argued Marx, would actually be to reduce profits because the workers would be less and less able to purchase products. Some industrialists, such as Henry Ford, recognized this problem. "Mass production," Ford said, "requires mass consumption, which means higher wages" (cited in Harrington, 1986:13). The logic, more commonly held by capitalists, though, is to increase profits by keeping wages low. This, as seen in this chapter, is evidenced by the purchase of new microelectronic technology to replace workers, the movement of production sites from relative high wage areas to low wage ones such as in the southern U.S. or to foreign countries, and the hiring of part-time or temporary workers in order to escape paying benefits.

The result is that the purchasing power of labor is declining. The following facts from a study by Lawrence Mishel and Jared Bernstein for the Economic Policy Institute (reported in Lawlor, 1993b) show this decline:

- Since 1979, the median hourly wage for males has dropped by 16 percent. Women's wages increased in this period by 2 percent, but they trail men by $2.38 an hour ($10.92 for men and $8.54 for women).
- Only 46 percent of the 1.9 million jobs created during the 1991–1993 recovery were nontemporary, private-sector jobs. Nearly 28 percent of the new jobs were in the temporary-help industry. Another 26 percent of the new jobs were part-time, and three-fourths of these were taken by workers who would prefer a full-time job.
- Wages for white-collar and college-educated workers have fallen since 1987.

These are indicators of personal and family economic decline. The middle-class is smaller. More and more workers receive substandard wages, substandard pensions, and substandard fringe benefits. The result is a reduction in lifestyle. For families on the economic margin, purchases will be limited to necessities. As more and more people in the United States are adversely affected, the sale of consumer goods and services will decline. This means that corporate profits will suffer, causing further efforts by management to reduce expenses. Thus, one possible future scenario is that of an economic downward spiral. The way out, to repeat Henry Ford's admonition, is to encourage mass consumption through higher wages.

The prospect for higher wage jobs, however, is bleak as corporations downsize, the defense industry is reduced, and U.S. corporations and U.S. workers compete with even lower wage economies elsewhere.

The Lack of Economic Planning

The capitalist philosophy dating back to Adam Smith is that the government should stay out of economic affairs. According to this view, the marketplace will force businesses to make the decisions that will best benefit them and, indirectly, the citizenry. Yet when the government does receive valuable information with which it could make decisions to avert future crises, the strong tendency in the United States is to remain aloof.

Ironically, the government is involved in central planning in the areas of space exploration and defense. As one commentator has said:

> The U.S. launched Mariner 10 on Nov. 3, 1973, and it flew to Venus and then to Mercury, which it circled for a total of a billion miles. It performed magnificently and sent back photographs. That took years of planning. But planning for a thing like that is one thing. Social planning and foreseeing energy shortages before they happen, that is different, and to some, slightly sinister. (TRB, 1975:2)

The issue of central planning revolves around whether the society is able and willing to respond to present *and* future social problems. Is a capitalist society capable of meeting the problems of poverty, unemployment, social neglect, population growth, energy shortages, environmental damage, and monopoly? Robert Heilbroner, a distinguished economist, has argued that we will not prepare for the

problems of the future: "The outlook is for what we may call 'convulsive change'—change forced upon us by external events rather than by conscious choice, by catastrophe rather than by calculation" (Heilbroner, 1974:132).

The lack of central planning points to the undemocratic nature of U.S. society. It is commonly believed that the people, through their economic choices, actually govern business decisions. While this is partially true, it ignores the manipulation of the public by business interests through advertising and other hypes. Neither the public nor its elected representatives are involved in the economic decisions of the giant corporations—and these decisions often have dire consequences domestically and internationally. As Andrew Hacker has argued:

> The power to make investment decisions is concentrated in a few hands, and it is this power which will decide what kind of a nation America will be. Instead of government planning there is boardroom planning that is accountable to no outside agency; and these plans set the order of priorities on national growth, technological innovation, and ultimately, the values and behavior of human beings. Investment decisions are sweeping in their ramifications—no one is unaffected by their consequences. Yet this is an area where neither the public nor its government is able to participate. (Hacker, 1970:52)

The lack of central planning is also a result of the resistance of powerful interest groups in society. Short-term goals such as employment for labor groups or profit for corporations lead special interests to block government efforts to meet future needs. Thus, the power of the economic dominants in society has the effect of superseding the interests of the nation, as shown in the next chapter.

CHAPTER REVIEW

1. Economic activity involves the production and distribution of goods and services.

2. There are two fundamental ways society can organize its economic activities—capitalism and socialism.

3. Capitalism in its pure form involves (*a*) the private ownership of the means of production, (*b*) the pursuit of personal profit, (*c*) competition, and (*d*) a government policy of allowing the marketplace to function unhindered.

4. Socialism in its pure form involves (*a*) democracy throughout the social structure; (*b*) equality—equality of opportunity, equality rather than hierarchy in making decisions, and equality in sharing the benefits of society; and (*c*) efficiency in providing the best conditions to meet the material needs of the citizens.

5. Marx's prediction that capitalism will result in an economy dominated by monopolies has been fulfilled in the United States. But rather than a single corporation dominating a sector of the economy, the United States is characterized by the existence of *shared monopolies*—where four or fewer corporations supply 50 percent or more of a particular market.

6. Economic power is concentrated in a few major corporations and banks. This concentration has been accomplished primarily through mergers and interlocking directorates.

7. The power of the largest corporations in the United States is increased by their international activities. Multinational corporations have important consequences: (*a*) decline in domestic jobs; (*b*) crippling of the power of unions; (*c*) hurting the government through lost revenues in taxes and a negative balance of payments; (*d*) increased power of corporations over the world economy and world events; and (*e*) exploitation of workers and natural resources in Third World countries.

8. Inequality is endemic to capitalism. Corporate wealth and private wealth are highly concentrated. Poverty, too, is concentrated disproportionately among people of color and in households headed by women.

9. Societies are organized to allocate work in order to produce the goods and services required for survival. The way work is organized generates important social problems.

10. Owners and managers of firms and factories control workers in several ways: (*a*) through scientific

management, (*b*) through bureaucracy, (*c*) by monitoring worker behavior, and (*d*) through extortion.

11. Blue-collar and white-collar workers in bureaucracies and factories are susceptible to alienation, which is the separation of human beings from each other, from themselves, and from the products they create. Specialized work in impersonal settings leads to dissatisfaction and meaninglessness.

12. A primary goal of business firms in a capitalist society is to reduce costs and thus increase profits. One way to reduce costs is not to provide adequately for worker safety.

13. Labor unions have declined in numbers and power. This has resulted in lower real wages and benefits, less safe work conditions, and a declining middle class.

14. Another work-related problem is discrimination, in which women and minorities have long received unfair treatment in jobs, pay, and opportunities for advancement. Two features of the U.S. economy promote these inequities: (*a*) the segmented labor market and (*b*) capitalist patriarchy.

15. The official government data on unemployment hide the actual amount by undercounting the unemployed in two ways: (*a*) people not actively seeking work (discouraged workers) are not counted; and (*b*) people who work at part-time jobs are counted as fully employed.

16. Unemployment has positive consequences for some people. Having a certain portion unemployed tends to keep inflation in check, according to some economists. Also, unemployment benefits capitalists by keeping wages down.

17. U.S. capitalism is facing three crises: (*a*) the primacy of profit over human considerations; (*b*) the propensity of corporate managers to increase profitability by reducing the workforce and lowering wages, which means that ultimately profits will fall because workers will be forced to reduce their purchases; and (*c*) the lack of central planning to solve current problems and anticipate future ones.

18. Two facts about institutions of society are especially important: (*a*) although they are interrelated, the economy is the most dominant and shapes each of the other institutions; and (*b*) the particular way that an institution is organized is at once a source of stability and a source of problems.

KEY TERMS

Institutions
Capitalism
Laissez-faire
Socialism
Shared monopoly
Interlocking directorate

Direct interlock
Indirect interlock
Scientific management
  ("Taylorization")
Alienation
Sweatshop

Segmented labor market
Capitalist patriarchy
Discouraged workers
Reserve army of the unemployed
Falling rate of profit

STUDY QUESTIONS

1. What are the mechanisms within the U.S. economy that work against the capitalist ideal of free enterprise?

2. Why is inequality endemic to capitalism? Is this good?

3. A major assumption of conflict theorists is that capitalism is a primary source for many social problems. Parenti's critique of capitalism (in the section entitled "The Negative Consequences of Private Profitability over Social Need") is an example of this approach. Do you agree or disagree? Why?

4. Given the conditions of the "structural transformation of the economy" (Chapter 8), should the government become more involved in the economy (violating "laissez-faire") with policies to alleviate current problems and central planning to lessen or eliminate future problems?

FOR FURTHER READING

Teresa Amott, *Caught in the Crisis: Women and the U.S. Economy Today* (New York: Monthly Review Press, 1993).

Carol J. Auster, *The Sociology of Work* (Thousand Oaks, CA: Pine Forge Press, 1996).

Dissent. "Labor's Future in the United States," *Dissent 39* (Winter 1992): special issue.

Peter F. Drucker, *Post-Capitalist Society* (New York: HarperCollins,1993).

Kathleen Gerson, *No Man's Land: Men's Changing Commitments to Family and Work* (New York: Basic Books, 1993).

Jacqueline Jones. *Labor of Love, Labor of Sorrow: Black Women, Work, and the Family from Slavery to the Present* (New York: Basic Books, 1985).

Paul Kennedy, *Preparing for the Twenty-First Century* (New York: Random House, 1993).

James O'Connor, *The Fiscal Crisis of the State* (New York: St. Martin's Press, 1973).

Wallace C. Peterson, *Silent Depression: The Fate of the American Dream* (New York: Norton, 1994).

Jeremy Rifkin, *The End of Work: The Decline of the Global Labor Force and the Dawn of the Post-Market Era* (New York: Jeremy P. Tarcher/Putnam, 1995).

George Ritzer, *The McDonaldization of Society: An Investigation into the Changing Character of Contemporary Social Life,* rev. ed. (Newbury Park, CA: Pine Forge Press, 1996).

Juliet B. Schor, *The Overworked American* (New York: Basic Books, 1991).

John J. Sweeney, *America Needs a Raise: Fighting for Economic Security and Social Justice* (Boston: Houghton Mifflin, 1996).

William Julius Wilson, *When Work Disappears: The World of the New Urban Poor* (New York: Alfred A. Knopf, 1996).

Michael D. Yates, *Longer Hours, Fewer Jobs: Employment & Unemployment in the United States* (New York: Monthly Review Press, 1994).

Mary Zey, *Banking on Fraud: Drexel, Junk Bonds, and Buyouts* (Hawthorne, NY: Aldine de Gruyter, 1993).

CHAPTER 14

Power and Politics

I n Washington, DC, there are about 20,000 lawyers, association executives, public relations experts, and technical workers who are lobbyists. This makes "lobbying the fourth largest business in the nation's capital, after government, printing, and tourism" (Rukeyser and Cooney, 1991:141). These lobbyists work on behalf of interest groups to influence legislators and regulatory agencies. Lobbyists' tactics include supplying information, doing favors, providing entertainment, giving campaign contributions, flooding Congress with telegrams, and furnishing transportation.

The phenomenon of lobbying can be interpreted in two opposite ways—*each of which illustrates a fundamental view of the distribution of power for the whole society.* The first view is that lobbying is the essence of democracy, as each competing pressure group presents its best case to the decision makers. These officials, faced with these countervailing forces, tend to compromise and make decisions most beneficial to the public. In contrast, other people view lobbying as another instance of the privileged few consistently getting their way. Interest groups are not equal in power. Some have enormous power and are not challenged by effective opposition. For example, the American Petroleum Institute has a staff of 350 people and an annual lobbying budget of $50 million. Also, the U.S. Chamber of Commerce has a $20 million budget and represents 89,500 corporations and 2,500 local communities. These and other business-oriented lobbies are extremely well organized and financed. Their opposition is negligible. Clearly, from this perspective, power in Washington is centralized and represents the powerful few.

The compelling questions of this chapter are, Who are the real power wielders in U.S. society? Is it an elite, or are the people sovereign? The location and exercise of power are difficult to determine, especially in a large and complex society such as the United States. Decisions are necessarily made by a few people, but in a democracy these few are to be representatives of the masses and therefore subject to their influence. But what of nonrepresentatives who aid in shaping policy? What about the pressure on the decision makers by powerful groups? What about those pressures on the decision makers that are so diffuse that the leaders may not even know who is applying the pressure?

Models of the National Power Structure

There are two basic views of the power structure—the **elitist model** and the **pluralist model of power.** The elitist view of power is that there is a pyramid of power. Those persons at the apex control the rest of the pyramid. The pluralists, on the other hand, see power as dispersed rather than concentrated. Power is broadly distributed among a number of organizations, special interests, and the voters. This chapter examines different elitist and pluralist conceptions of power in the United States. As each is surveyed, the fundamental questions are, How does a particular model mesh with the facts of our contemporary society? Does the model portray things as they are or as they should be?

Pluralist Models

Pluralism I: Representative Democracy.   Many people in the United States accept the notion promoted in high school civics books that the country is a "government of the people, by the people, for the people." **Democracy** is the form of government in which the people have the ultimate power. The will of the majority prevails, there is equality before the law, and decisions are made to maximize the common good. In a complex society of more than 265 million persons, the people cannot make all decisions; they must elect representatives to make most decisions. So, decision making is concentrated at the top, but it is to be controlled by the people who elect the decision makers. This model is shown in Figure 14.1. (See "A Closer Look: Structural Barriers to Democracy.")

FIGURE 14.1

Representative Democracy

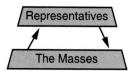

The most important component of a democratic model is that the representatives, because they are elected by the people, are responsive to the wishes of the people. This model, however, does not conform to reality. The United States is undemocratic in many important ways. The people, although they do vote for their representatives every few years, are really quite powerless. For example, who makes the really important decisions about war and peace, economic policies, and foreign policy? The people certainly do not. The record shows that many times the people have been deceived when the object was to conceal clandestine illegal operations, mistakes, undemocratic practices, and the like. These illicit activities have been carried out by Democratic and Republican presidents alike.

Not only have the people in the United States been misinformed at times, but the basic democratic tenet that the public be informed has also been defied on occasion. On the one hand, Congress has shown its contempt for the electorate by the use of secret meetings. The executive branch, too, has acted in secret. Recent presidents have gone months without holding a press conference, have used executive privilege to keep presidential advisors from testifying before congressional committees, and have refused to debate opponents in election campaigns.

Many persons who are appointed rather than elected wield tremendous power. Technical experts, for example, evaluate extremely complicated issues; they can virtually dictate to the president and Congress what is needed for defense, shoring up the economy, or winning friends abroad because they are the experts. The coterie of advisors may convince the president to act in particular ways. The members appointed to the regulatory agencies have tremendous power to shape various aspects of the economy.

Perhaps one of the most undemocratic features (at least in its consequences) of the U.S. political system is a result of how campaigns are financed. Political campaigns are expensive, with money needed to pay for staff, direct-mail operations, phone banks, polling, computers, consultants, and media advertising. The campaigns for Congress and president cost about $1.5 billion overall, including monies from the federal government (each major presidential candidate received about $70 million in public funds), individuals, political parties, and political action committees (PACs). The average cost of a winning U.S. House seat in 1994 was $516,000. For winning a senate seat it was $4.5 million, up from $610,000 in 1976. In 1994, Michael Huffington's unsuccessful bid for the Senate seat in California cost about $28 million. The winner, Diane Feinstein, spent $16 million—in the most expensive Senate race in history.

These expensive campaigns are funded by the candidates' personal wealth (this was the primary source, for example, of Huffington's campaign treasury), individual contributions, and (in the case of congressional candidates) money donated from special-interest groups through PACs. In 1974 PACs gave $12.4 million to congressional candidates; in 1992 PACs gave $189 million.

The increasingly higher sums given to congressional candidates have led some cynics to comment that we have "The Best Congress Money Can Buy" (Stern, 1988). PACs are formed to represent interests such as labor unions, doctors, realtors, auto dealers, teachers, and corporations. Each PAC may give up to $5,000 to any candidate in a primary and another $5,000 in a general election. As *U.S. News & World*

A CLOSER LOOK

Structural Barriers to Democracy

In 1994 Republicans running for Congress pledged a "Contract With America." They won majorities in each house of Congress and claimed a mandate for the conservative "Contract." But did they have a mandate? Only 38 percent of the electorate voted in 1994, and only 52 percent of that three-eighths, or 19.8 percent of the public, voted for the Republicans. Those who voted were disproportionately White, relatively affluent, and suburban. What about the poor and the near poor, racial minorities, blue-collar laborers, and city dwellers who chose not to vote? Why did they not vote? What is the source of their alienation? Is the problem with these apathetic people or is it with the system? Let's look at the systemic sources that block democracy in the United States.

The two-party system that has emerged (it is not part of the Constitution) is a major impediment to democracy. Corporations, special interests, and wealthy individuals sponsor both parties. Since candidates from minor parties rarely win, they do not receive their monetary support, which fulfills the prophecy. They also remain minor parties because the government subsidizes the two major parties in two ways: First, the Republican and Democratic Parties receive $12.4 million each from the federal government to fund their nominating conventions. Second, political parties receive federal matching campaign funds based on their presumed viability. Thus, in 1996 the presidential candidates of the

major parties each received $62 million; Ross Perot of the Reform Party, however, was only eligible to receive $32 million because he received 19 percent of the vote in the 1992 presidential race. On the surface this "matching funds" approach seems fair, but in practice it keeps the strong parties strong and the weak parties weak.

The bias toward the two-party system was revealed again when a "bi-partisan" commission ruled that Ross Perot could not participate in the 1996 presidential debates. He could not take part, they argued, because he had no chance of winning. Of course, not being part of the debates makes that prophecy a certainty. The commission, by the way, was composed of members selected from the Republican and Democratic Parties!

Another obstacle to third parties is that they cannot break the two-party control at every level of government. Even if the candidate of a third party were successful in winning the presidency, he or she would have difficulty in governing because both houses of Congress would be controlled by one or the other of the major parties. Moreover, since the two major parties control both houses of Congress (chairing committees, majorities on committees and in Congress), independents (there is only one currently in the House, Bernie Sanders of Vermont) have no power.

A major problem lies with the winner-take-all system. A state with 30 percent Latino population may

Report editorialized, "PACs of every ilk have a way of contributing their allowed $5,000 chunks to candidates who either have voted 'right' or had better do so shortly" (Stone, 1978:112). (See "A Closer Look: Mischievous Myths about Money in Politics" on the imbalance in campaign financing.)

In addition to PACs, there are three other legal ways for individuals and special interests to funnel money to the candidate or political party of their choice. First, each individual can give up to $1,000 to a candidate. A common tactic is for the executives of a corporation to "bundle" their $1,000 contributions so that a sizable gift is given to a political candidate. The corporation can reimburse these executives for their contributions with Christmas bonuses. A second legal way is to not have any Latino representation in Congress because a White majority in each Congressional district voted for the White candidate. Similarly, a city may have a seven-member city council elected at large by majority vote. The usual result is that not one council member represents a poor section of the city. The method used to elect the president, the Electoral College, decrees that the candidate winning a plurality of votes in that state receives *all* of the electoral votes allocated to the state. The consequence is that all votes for other candidates are wasted.

> To understand the problem, consider what happened in Alabama in the 1992 election. George Bush won the state handily with 47.9 percent of the vote, claiming all nine of its electoral votes. But exit polls indicated that 91 percent of African-American voters in Alabama—who make up roughly two-ninths of the state's electorate—voted for Bill Clinton. Despite this overwhelming level of support, Clinton, with only 30 percent of the White vote, didn't secure a single electoral vote in Alabama. African-American voters might just as well have stayed home. (Hoffman, 1996:15)

Both parties seek the largest number of voters by appealing to those who are most likely to vote (upper-middle class, White, fiscal conservatives from the suburbs). Both parties push for middle-class tax cuts, "family values," and a tougher stance on crime. But this leaves out many who find each of the two major parties irrelevant to their interests. Neither party, for example, has a plan to revitalize the cities, desegregate housing, and provide affordable housing for the working poor. Neither the Republicans nor the Democrats has been willing "or professed to see the necessity to mount an attack on the economic trends that had created the inner-city ghetto and that also were keeping many Whites and non-ghetto Blacks in poverty and hopelessness" (Wicker, 1996:12). Neither party has pressed hard for further racial gains or for the enforcement of what has been accomplished. In short, many if not most of the nation's eligible voters are electorally homeless (Hightower, 1996).

The U.S. system is in sharp contrast to the multinational party systems found in the European democracies, where religious minorities, racial groups, the working class, and other special interests form viable political parties. The result is that citizens can find a political party with an agenda compatible to their interests. As a consequence, voter turnout in Canada and Europe ranges between 80 and 90 percent, compared to the 50 percent in U.S. presidential elections.

contribute through what is called "soft money." Here, any amount can be given by individuals, corporations, unions, and other organizations to political parties at the national, state, and local levels, or to other private organizations that are technically independent of the candidates. These gifts are not covered by the federal election laws and thus are unlimited. This loophole was used by wealthy persons to contribute $263 million in 1996, up from $87 million in 1992 (Eisner, 1997). The *New York Times* called this major loophole in the financing of presidential campaigns "sewer money" (Clymer, 1992:A16).

The third method to raise money is through contributions to a "foundation" sponsored by a candidate. Robert Dole, for example, set up "The Better America

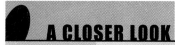

Mischievous Myths about Money in Politics

The key to real campaign finance reform is an accurate perception of the problem. Here are [two] of the most common money-in-politics myths that serve to obscure our vision—myths still accepted by many journalists, pundits and even reformers. . . .

The "Balance" Myth: "The 'special interests' all balance each other out."

- *Fact:* Combining PAC and large individual contributions for the 1991–1992 elections (the latest for which individual contribution data is available), business out-gave labor by a factor of 7-to-1.

- *Fact:* During the 1992 elections, polluting industries out-contributed all environmental groups combined by more than 10-to-1, and the weapons industry out-contributed peace and disarmament groups 20-to-1.

- *Fact:* Of the 1,100 PACs that gave $20,000 or more to Congress during the 1994 elections, none represented poor people, toxics victims, unemployed workers, or small banking depositors and borrowers.

The "Participation" Myth: "Making campaign contributions is one of the primary ways that Americans participate in our democracy."

- *Fact:* Of the 250 million people who live in the United States, fewer than 900,000, or one-third of 1 percent, gave direct individual contributions of $200 or more to congressional candidates in 1991–92—yet such contributions comprised well over half of the total amount given by individuals.

- *Fact:* The residents of one zip-code area— 10021—on New York City's Upper East Side contributed more money to Congress during the 1994 elections than did all the residents of each of 24 states.

- *Fact:* People in the United States with family incomes above $75,000 are over 100 times more likely to contribute to candidates than those with family incomes below $15,000.

The "No Cost" Myth: "Our system of privately-financed elections doesn't cost taxpayers any money."

- *Fact:* Tobacco interests plied members of Congress with $792,000 in campaign contributions during the first six months of 1995 alone. Then, in July of 1995, they persuaded Congress to reject a bill that would have ended $50 million in federal support for growing tobacco.

- *Fact:* Weapons contractor PACs gave Congress $7.5 million during 1993–1994. Then, in 1995, Congress approved a defense budget that exceeded the Pentagon's request by $7 billion.

- *Fact:* The enormity of the savings and loan collapse of the late 1980s is closely linked to the influence of private campaign contributions. It is estimated that during the 30-to-40-year period of the S&L bailout, the total cost will come to $300 billion, or $3,000 on average for every taxpayer.

Source: Excerpted from Ellen Miller and Randy Kekhler, "Mischievous Myths about Money in Politics," *Dollars & Sense,* No. 206 (July/August 1996), pp. 22–23.

Foundation," which raised $5 million in the first six months of 1995 for his presidential bid. Through this loophole, donors can give *unlimited* contributions to a candidate with their identities hidden from the public record.

What do the contributors of large sums receive for their donations? Obviously, they have access to the politician, perhaps even influence. It is difficult to prove conclusively that receiving campaign contributions from a special interest buys a vote, but there is some indirect evidence that such contributors do gain advantage:

- PACs often give to candidates who run unopposed.
- Some PACs give money to both sides in an election. Other PACs contribute after the election to the candidate they opposed but who won anyway.
- Some corporations work both sides of the street by giving "soft money" to both parties.
- PACs overwhelmingly support incumbents. By giving to the incumbent, the giver is almost assured of giving to the winner.
- PAC money disproportionately goes to the most powerful members of the House and Senate (those in leadership roles).

Money presents a fundamental obstacle to democracy because only the interests of the wealthy tend to be served. It takes money—and lots of it—to be a successful politician. The candidate must either be rich or be willing to accept contributions from other people. In either case, the political leaders will be part of or beholden to the wealthy.

Closely related to the financing of campaigns is the process by which political candidates are nominated. Being wealthy or having access to wealth is essential for victory because of the enormous cost. This means that the candidates tend to represent a limited constituency—the wealthy.

The two-party system also works to limit choices among candidates to a rather narrow range. Each party is financed by the special interests—especially business.

When all of these direct and indirect gifts (donations provided directly to candidates or through numerous political action committees of specific corporations and general business organizations) are combined, the power elite can be seen to provide the great

Copyright © Carol A. Simpson 1995, Z Magazine, October 1996, p. 49

The important question is: Do these elected officials represent the interests of the people or the narrow interests of their contributors?

bulk of the financial support to both parties at the national level, far outspending the unions and middle status liberals within the Democrats, and the melange of physicians, dentists, engineers, real-estate operators and other white-collar conservatives within the right wing of the Republican Party. (Domhoff, 1979:148)

Affluent individuals and the largest corporations influence candidate selection by giving financial aid to those sympathetic with their views and withholding support from those who differ. The parties, then, are constrained to choose candidates with views congruent with the monied interest.

Pluralism II: Veto Groups. Although some groups have more power than others and some individuals have more power than others, the power structure in the United States is viewed according to the "veto groups" model as a plurality of interest groups (Riesman, 1950:213–217). Each interest group (for example, the military, labor, business, farmers, education, medicine, law, veterans, the aged, African Americans, and consumers) is primarily concerned with protecting its own interests. The group that primarily exercises power varies with the issue at stake. There is a balance of power, since each veto group mobilizes to prevent the others from actions threatening its interests. Thus, these groups tend to neutralize each other.

The masses are sought as an ally (rather than dominated, as is the case in the various elitist models) by the interest groups in their attempts to exert power over issues in their jurisdiction. Figure 14.2 shows the relationship between the various levels in this model.

This pluralist model assumes that there are a number of sectors of power. The most powerful persons in each sector are usually wealthy—probably upper class. But the pluralist view is that the upper class is not a unified group—there is considerable disagreement within the upper-class category because of differing interests. Power is not concentrated, but is viewed as a shifting coalition depending on the issue. The basic difference between pluralists and elitists is on the question of

FIGURE 14.2

Veto-Groups Model

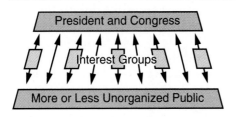

whether there is a basic unity or disagreement among the powerful from different sectors (basically, those who are wealthy enough to be upper class).

Several criticisms of this pluralistic model stem from the knowledge that it, like the other pluralistic model (for representative democracy), is an idealized conception of the distribution of power—as such, it does not conform with reality and is subject to question on several grounds. First, is the power structure so amorphous that power shifts constantly from one power source to another? Second, are the interest groups so equal in power that they neutralize each other? The special bias of this view is that it does not give attention to the power differentials among the various interest groups. It is absurd to claim that the power of big business is neutralized by the countervailing power of farmers. A more probable occurrence is that there is a hierarchy of power among these veto groups.

A final criticism is that the leaders in each sector come disproportionately from the upper economic stratum. If this assertion is correct, the possibility of a power elite that transcends narrow interest groups is present, since they may know each other, tend to intermarry, and have similar economic interests (as we discuss later in this chapter).

The pluralist models are not altogether faulty. A number of possible power centers often compete for advantage. Shifting coalitions are possible. There are instances when elected officials are responsive to public opinion. However, it seems to us that most of the evidence supports an elitist view, although each of the three types described below also has its faults.

Elitist Models

The elitist views of societal power are usually structured quite similarly to the views of Karl Marx. For Marx, economics was the basis for the stratification system (that is, unequal distribution of rewards, including power). The economic elite, because of its ownership and control of the economy, exerts tremendous influence on government policies and actions and is, therefore, a ruling class. The elite manipulate the masses through religion, nationalism, control of the media, and control of the visible governmental leaders (Marx and Engels, 1947:39). Marxists agree that the state serves the interests of the capitalist class. They disagree on how this is accomplished. One position is called the **instrumentalist view** (the following is from Marger, 1987:42–44). Here, the ruling class rules by controlling political officials and institutions through money and influence. Research shows, for example, the connections (social backgrounds) between top corporate and political decision makers. The state is seen as functioning "in terms of the instrumental exercise of power by people in strategic positions, either directly through the manipulation of state policies or indirectly through the exercise of pressure on the state" (Gold, Lo, and Wright, 1975:34). In effect, then, the government is an active instrument of the ruling class used to accomplish its goals.

The second way Marxists see the ruling class is the **structuralist view.** From this perspective, the linkage between the economic elite and the political elite is not important. Rather, the ruling class gets its way because "the structure of political and economic institutions in capitalist society makes it imperative that the state serve those interests regardless of whether big businessmen directly or indirectly take part in state affairs" (Marger, 1987:43). From this perspective, then, the system is viewed as biased in favor of the elite without their active manipulation.

Power Elite I: The Thesis of C. Wright Mills.   C. Wright Mills's view of the U.S. structure of power posits that the key persons in three sectors—the corporate rich, the executive branch of the government, and the military—combine to form a **power elite** that makes all important decisions (Mills, 1956).

The elite is a small group of persons who routinely interact together. They also, as Mills assumed, have similar interests and goals. The elite is the power elite because the members have key institutional positions—that is, they command great authority and resources in specific and important sectors, and each sector is dependent on the other sectors.

There are three levels in Mills's pyramid of power. The uppermost is the power elite—composed of the leaders of three sectors. Mills implied that of the three, the corporate rich are perhaps the most powerful (first among equals). The middle level of power is comprised of local opinion leaders, the legislative branch of government, and the plurality of interest groups. These bodies, according to Mills, do the bidding of the power elite. The third level is the powerless mass of unorganized people who are controlled from above. They are exploited economically and politically. The three levels of power are depicted in Figure 14.3.

Mills (who was writing in the 1950s) believed that the power elite was a relatively new phenomenon resulting from a number of historical and social forces that have enlarged and centralized the facilities of power, making the decisions of small groups much more consequential than in any other age (Mills, 1968).

The two important and related factors giving rise to the recent emergence of the power elite are that the means of power and violence (1) are now infinitely greater than they were in the past, and (2) are also increasingly centralized. The decisions of a few people become ultimately crucial when they have the power to activate a system that has the capability of destroying hundreds of cities within minutes. Transportation, communication, the economy, and the instruments of warfare are examples of several areas that have become centralized—making a power elite possible. The federal government taxes, regulates, and passes laws so that the lives of almost all people in the United States are affected.

This same bureaucratic process is evident in the military, where decisions are more and more centralized. The Pentagon, which oversees the largest and most ex-

FIGURE 14.3

Mills's Pyramid of Power

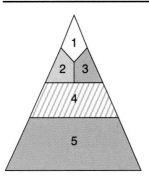

(Legend: 1, corporate rich; 2, executive branch; 3, military leaders; 4, leaders of interest groups, legislative branch, local opinion leaders; 5, unorganized masses.)

pensive feature of the government, is a relatively new phenomenon. The economy in the United States was once composed of many, many small productive units that were more or less autonomous. But over time the number of semiautonomous economic units has dwindled through mergers, interlocking directorates, and chain stores, putting the financial squeeze on the small businessperson. The result is that the economy has become dominated by less than 200 giant corporations.

The tremendous advances in transportation and communication have made it much more likely that the persons holding key positions in the political, economic, and military hierarchies can be in contact with each other if they wish to do so. If, as Mills assumed, they have similar interests, then they must be in contact so that their activities can be coordinated to the best mutual advantage.

The key decision makers also have instruments to influence the masses, such as television, public relations firms, and techniques of propaganda that are unsurpassed in the history of humankind. Hence, if there is a power elite and they want to manipulate the masses to accept their decisions, they have the instruments of mass persuasion at their disposal.

Mills also contended that the importance of institutions has shifted. Whereas the family and religion were once the most important U.S. institutions, they (along with education) have become subordinate to the three power institutions of the economy, polity, and military—thus making the leaders of these three domains the power elite. Mills said, "families and churches and schools adapt to modern life; governments and armies and corporations shape it; and, as they do so, they turn these lesser institutions into means for their ends" (Mills, 1968:267). For example, religious institutions supply chaplains to the armed forces, where they increase the effectiveness of the combat units by raising morale. Schools train persons for their places in the giant corporations. Fathers and sons are sometimes taken from their homes to fight and die for their country. And, Mills said, the symbols of these lesser institutions are used to legitimate the decisions of the power elite who dominate the powerful institutions.

A most important impetus for the formation of the power elite was World War II. United States participation in a war worldwide in scope and where the possibility of defeat was very real meant, among other things, that a reorganization of various sectors had to be accomplished. The national government, particularly the executive department, had to be granted dictatorial powers so that the war could be conducted. Decisions had to be made quickly and in secret, two qualities not compatible with a democracy. The nation's corporations had to be mobilized for war. They made huge profits. Finally, the military became very prominent in decision making. Their expertise was essential to the making of wartime strategy.

Following World War II, the United States was faced with another threat, the spread of communism. This meant, in effect, that the executive department, the corporations, and the military did not shift back to their peacetime ways. The military remained in the decision-making process, the corporations remained dependent on lucrative defense contracts, and the executive branch continued to exercise its autonomous or at least semiautonomous powers.

All these factors, according to Mills, ensured that the domains of the polity, economy, and military were enlarged and centralized. Decisions made in each of these domains became increasingly crucial to all citizens, but particularly to the leaders of the other key domains. The result had to be a linkage between the key persons in each domain. It was in their interests to cooperate. Because each sector affected the others, the persons at the top of each hierarchy had to interact with the leaders from the other sectors, so that the actions and decisions would benefit all. Thus, they have come to form a triangle of power, an interlocking directorate of persons in the three key domains making coordinated decisions—a power elite.

An important ingredient in Mills's view is that the elite is a self-conscious cohesive unit. This unity is based on three factors: psychological similarity, social interaction, and coinciding interests.

1. *Psychological similarity.* The institutional positions men and women occupy throughout their lifetimes determine the values they will hold. For example, career military men hold certain values by virtue of being socialized into the military subculture. The famous quote that "What's good for General Motors is good for the country" by Secretary of Defense (under President Eisenhower) Charles Wilson is also indicative of this probability. Thus, for Mills, the psychology of these leaders is largely shaped by the values they develop in their institutional roles. Additionally, the psychological similarity among the members of the elite is derived from their similar social origins and style of life.

2. *Social interaction.* Mills stated that the ruling elite are involved in a set of overlapping groups and intricately connected cliques.

> The people of the higher circles may also be conceived as members of a top social stratum, as a set of groups whose members know one another, see one another socially and at business, and so, in making decisions, take one another into account. The elite, according to this conception, feel themselves to be, and are felt by others to be, the inner circle of "the upper social classes." They form a more or less compact social and psychological entity; they have become self-conscious members of a social class. People are either accepted into this class or they are not, and there is a qualitative split, rather than merely a numerical scale, separating them from those who are not elite. They are more

or less aware of themselves as a social class and they behave toward one another differently from the way they do toward members of other classes. They accept one another, understand one another, marry one another, tend to work and to think if not together at least alike. (Mills, 1956:11)

3. *Coinciding interests.* A third unifying condition hypothesized by Mills is the existence of similar interests among the elite. The interest of the elite is, among other things, maintenance of the capitalist system with themselves at the top. Additionally, the government needs adequate defense systems, to which the military agree and that the corporations gladly sell for a profit. The huge corporations have large holdings in foreign countries. They therefore expect the government to make policy decisions that will be beneficial (profitable) for these U.S. interests. These similar interests result in a unity and a need for planning and coordination of their efforts. Because each sector affects the other, the persons at the top of each hierarchy must interact with leaders of the other sectors so that their actions will benefit all. Top decisions, Mills argued, thus become coordinated decisions.

Much of Mills's argument seems to fit with the realities of U.S. politics. Certainly those at the top of the key sectors wield enormous power. Some elements in Mills's thesis, however, are not consistent with the facts. First, Mills believed that the three subelites that comprise the power elite are more or less equal, with the corporate rich probably having the most power. The equality of these groups is not proved. Certainly, with the dismantling of the Soviet empire the power of the military elite has diminished. Military leaders are influential only in their advisory capacities and their ability to convince the executive branch and Congress. What looks like military power is often actually the power of the corporations and/or the executive branch carried out in military terms. In the view of many observers (especially Domhoff, as we see in the next section), the business leaders comprise the real power elite. Even though this is debatable, the fact is that they surpass the military in power, and because the executive branch is composed of ex-businesspeople, the logical conclusion is that business interests prevail in that sector as well.

Conflict occurs among the three sectors. There is often bitter disagreement between corporations and the government, between the military and the executive branch, and between the military and some elements in the business community. How is this conflict to be explained if, as Mills contended, the power elite is a group that acts in concert, with joint efforts planned and coordinated to accomplish the agreed-on goals? A good deal of empirical evidence shows that the heads of the three major sectors do *not* comprise a group.

Mills relegates a number of powerful (or potentially powerful) forces to the middle ranges of power. What about the power of pressure groups that represent interests other than business or the military? Certainly, organized labor, farmers, professional organizations such as the American Medical Association, and consumers exert power over particular issues. Sometimes business interests even lose. How is this to be explained?

Finally, is Congress only in the middle level of the power structure? In Mills's view, Congress is a rubber stamp for the interests of business, the executive branch, and the military. Congress is apparently not composed of puppets for these interests, although the laws most often seem to favor these interests. But Congress does have its mavericks, and some of these persons, by virtue of seniority, exert tremendous power (for either the blockage or passage of legislation). Should not the key congressional leaders be included in the power elite? The problem is that they often have interests that do not coincide with those of the presumed elite.

Power Elite II: Domhoff's "Governing Class" Theory.   In the view of Mills, power is concentrated in a relatively small, cohesive elite; G. William Domhoff's model of power is more broadly based in a "governing class." Domhoff (1983) defined this **governing class** as the uppermost social group (approximately 0.5 percent of the population), which owns a disproportionate amount of the country's wealth and contributes a disproportionate number of its members to the controlling institutions and key decision-making groups of the country. This status group is composed mainly of rich businesspeople and their families, many of whom are, according to Domhoff's convincing evidence, closely knit through stock ownership, trust funds, intermarriages, private schools, exclusive social clubs, exclusive summer resorts, and corporation boards.

The governing class in Domhoff's analysis controls the executive branch of the federal government, the major corporations, the mass media, foundations, universities, and the important councils for domestic and foreign affairs (for example, the Council on Foreign Relations, Committee for Economic Development, National Security Council, National Industrial Conference Board, and the Twentieth Century Fund). If they can control the executive branch, this governing class can probably also control the very important regulatory agencies, the federal judiciary, the military, the Central Intelligence Agency, and the Federal Bureau of Investigation.

The governing class has greater influence (but not control) than any other group on Congress and on state and local governments. These parts of the formal power structure are not directly controlled by the governing class in Domhoff's analysis, but because he claims that such a class controls the executive and judicial branches, the Congress is effectively blocked by two of the three divisions of government. Thus, U.S. foreign and domestic policies are initiated, planned, and carried out by members and organizations of a power elite that serves the interests of an upper class of rich business people. Decisions are made that are considered appropriate for the interests of the United States—a strong economy, an adequate defense, and social stability. While perhaps beneficial to all people in the country, policies designed to accomplish these goals especially favor the rich. Consequently, U.S. corporations overseas are protected, foreign trade agreements are made that benefit U.S. corporations, and the tax structure benefits corporations or the very wealthy (by means of allowances for oil depletion, for capital gains and capital losses, for depreciation of equipment, and for other business expenses).

Domhoff has demonstrated in detail the manner in which the governing class interacts (which we examined in Chapter 10). Once he established the interlocking ties brought about by common interests and through interaction, he cited circumstances that show the impact of individuals and subgroups within the elite on the decision-making structure of the United States. To mention a few:

- Control of presidential nominations through the financing of political campaigns: The evidence is clear that unless candidates have large financial reserves or the backing of wealthy persons, they cannot hope to develop a national following or compete in party primaries.

- Control of both major political parties: Even though the Democratic Party is usually considered the party of the common person, Domhoff shows that it, like the Republican Party, is controlled by aristocrats (Parenti, 1995; this is documented well in Greider, 1992).

- Almost total staffing of important appointive governmental positions (cabinet members, members of regulatory agencies, judges, diplomats, and presidential advisors): These appointees are either members of the upper class or persons who have held positions in the major corporations, and are thereby persons who accord with the wishes of the upper class.

As a result of the circumstances above (and others), all the important foreign and domestic decisions are seen as made by the governing class. Domhoff's view of the power structure is reconstructed graphically in Figure 14.4.

In many ways, Domhoff's model of the U.S. power structure was a refinement of the one posited earlier by Mills. Domhoff's assessment of the power structure was similar to Mills's in that they both (1) view the power structure as a single pyramid, (2) see the corporate rich as the most powerful interest group, (3) relegate Congress to a relatively minor role and place the executive branch in an important role in the decision-making process, and (4) view the masses as being dominated by powerful forces rather than having much grass-roots power.

FIGURE 14.4

Domhoff's View of the Structure of Power

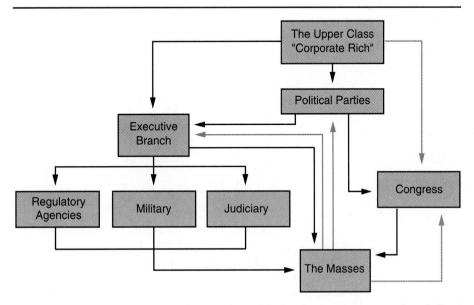

(Legend: black line, control; color line, influence.) This model is based on our interpretation of Domhoff and is therefore subject to minor errors in emphasis.

The major difference between the views of Mills and Domhoff is that Domhoff has asserted the complete ascendancy of the upper class to the apex of power. The executive branch is controlled by upper-class businesspeople, industrialists, and financiers rather than the two groups being more or less equal partners in the power elite, as Mills saw it. Moreover, the placement of the military in the pyramid of power is quite different. Mills saw the military as part of the alliance of the troika, whereas Domhoff saw the military as having much less power and being dominated by the corporate rich through the executive branch.

Domhoff's view of power is quite persuasive, but there are also several criticisms. First, much of Domhoff's proof is in the form of listing the upper-class pedigrees of presidential advisors, cabinet members, ambassadors, regulatory agency members, and so on. Even though persons in these positions are disproportionately from upper-class backgrounds (as evidenced by their attendance at prestige schools,

By permission of Johnny Hart and Creators Syndicate, Inc.

their membership in exclusive social clubs, and their placement in the various social registries), we are given no proof that these persons actually promote the interests of the corporate rich. This is an assumption by Domhoff that appears
reasonable, but it is an oversimplification. There is always the possibility of wealthy
persons' making decisions on bases other than economics, such as religious or
moral altruism or civil rights or human rights. Thus, Domhoff's assumption is one
of Marxian economic determinism, and as such is subject to the criticism of oversimplification of a complex process. Even though an economic motive of some kind
may explain a great deal of social behavior, its operation with other prestige factors
may be very complex, and it will not explain all of human behavior.

Although Domhoff had denied his belief in an upper-class conspiracy, his books
strongly suggest that he does hold this view, at least implicitly. The upper class is
shown to get its way either by force or fraud. His chapter on social legislation
showed, for example, that workmen's compensation, Social Security, and collective
bargaining were accomplished not by pressure from working people, but because
the upper class felt it was in their long-range economic interest to pass such seemingly socialistic legislation. Domhoff, therefore, viewed the efforts of the upper class
(assuming that they indeed form an elite) as only self-seeking, never as altruistic.
Moreover, the power of labor and other pressure groups in the forming of social legislation was virtually ignored (Domhoff, 1970).

Power Elite III: Parenti's "Bias of the System" Theory. We commonly think of the
machinery of government as a beneficial force promoting the common good. The
government can be organized for the benefit of the majority, but it is not always
neutral. The state regulates; it stifles opposition; it makes and enforces the law; it
funnels information; it makes war on enemies (foreign and domestic); and its policies determine how resources are apportioned. And in all of these areas, the government is generally biased toward policies that benefit the wealthy, especially the
business community (this section is taken from Parenti, 1978, 1995).

Power in the United States is concentrated among the people who control the
government and the largest corporations. This assertion is based on the assumption
that power is not an attribute of individuals but rather of social organizations. The
elite in U.S. society is composed of persons who occupy the power roles in society.
The great political decisions are made by the president, the president's advisors,
cabinet members, the members of regulatory agencies, the Federal Reserve Board,
key members of Congress, and the Supreme Court. The individuals in these government command posts have the authority to make war, raise or lower interest
rates, levy taxes, dam rivers, and institute or withhold national health insurance.

Once economic activity was the result of many decisions made by individual
entrepreneurs and the heads of small businesses. Now, a handful of companies have
virtual control over the marketplace. The decisions by the boards of directors and
the management personnel of these huge corporations determine employment and
production, consumption patterns, wages and prices, the extent of foreign trade,
and the rate at which natural resources are depleted, for example.

The few thousand persons who comprise this power elite tend to come from backgrounds of privilege and wealth. It would be a mistake, however, to equate personal
wealth with power. Great power is manifested only through decision making in the

very large corporations or in government. We have seen that this elite exercises great power. Decisions are made by the powerful, and these decisions tend to benefit the wealthy disproportionately. But the power elite is not organized and conspiratorial.

The interests of the powerful (and the wealthy) are served, nevertheless, because of the way society is organized. This bias occurs in three ways—by their influence over elected and appointed governmental officials at all levels, through systemic imperatives, and through the ideological control of the masses.

As discussed in an earlier section, the wealthy are able to receive favorable treatment by actually occupying positions of power or by having direct influence over those who do. The laws, court decisions, and administrative decisions tend to give them the advantage.

More subtly, the power elite can get its way without actually being mobilized at all. The choices of decision makers are often limited by various **systemic imperatives;** that is, the institutions of society are patterned to produce prearranged results regardless of the personalities of the decision makers. In other words, there is a bias that pressures the government to do certain things and not to do other things. Inevitably, this bias favors the status quo, allowing people with power to continue to exercise it. No change is easier than change. The current political and economic systems have worked and generally are not subject to questions, let alone change. In this way, the laws, customs, and institutions of society resist change. Thus, the propertied and the wealthy benefit, while the propertyless and the poor remain disadvantaged. As Parenti has argued:

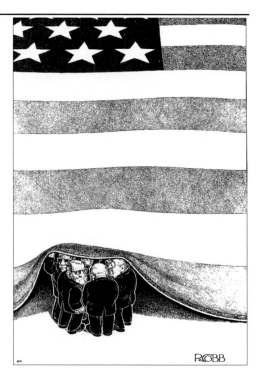

The law does not exist as an abstraction. It gathers shape and substance from a context of power, within a real-life social structure. Like other institutions, the legal system is class-bound. The question is not whether the law should or should not be neutral, for as a product of its society, it cannot be neutral in purpose or effect. (Parenti, 1978:188)

In addition to the inertia of institutions, there are other systemic imperatives that benefit the power elite and the wealthy. One such imperative is for the government to strive to provide an adequate defense against our enemies, which stifles any external threat to the status quo. Thus, Congress, the president, and the general public tend to support large appropriations for defense, which, in turn, provide extraordinary profit to many corporations. In addition, the government will protect U.S. multinational companies in their overseas operations, so that they enjoy a healthy and profitable business climate. Domestic government policy also is shaped by the systemic imperative for stability. The government promotes domestic tranquility by squelching dissidence.

Power is the ability to get what one wants from someone else. This can be achieved by force or by getting that someone to think and believe in accordance with your interests. "The ability to control the definition of interests is the ability to define the agenda of issues, a capacity tantamount to winning battles without having to fight them" (Parenti, 1978:41). United States schools, churches, and families possess this power. The schools, for instance, consciously teach youth that capitalism is the only correct economic system. This indoctrination to conservative values achieves a consensus among the citizenry concerning the status quo. In other words, each of us comes to accept the present arrangements in society because they seem to be the only options that make sense. Thus, there is a general agreement on what is right and wrong. In sum, the dominance of the wealthy is legitimized. "The interests of an economically dominant class never stand naked. They are enshrouded in the flag, fortified by the law, protected by the police,

G. Olliver.

nurtured by the media, taught by the schools, and blessed by the church" (Parenti, 1978:84).

Finally, the belief in democracy works to the advantage of the power elite, as Parenti has noted in the following passage:

> As now constituted, elections serve as a great asset in consolidating the existing social order by propagating the appearances of popular rule. History demonstrates that the people might be moved to overthrow a tyrant who shows himself provocatively indifferent to their woes, but they are far less inclined to make war upon a state, even one dominated by the propertied class, if it preserves what Madison called "the spirit and form of popular government." Elections legitimate the rule of the propertied class by investing it with the moral authority of popular consent. By the magic of the ballot, class dominance becomes "democratic" governance. (Parenti, 1978:201)

The Consequences of Concentrated Power

The way power is concentrated in the United States raises this question: Who benefits? At times most everyone does, but for the most part, the decisions made tend to benefit the wealthy. Whenever the interests of the wealthy clash with those of other groups or even of the majority, the interests of the wealthy are served. As examples, examine carefully how the president and Congress deal with the problems of energy shortages, inflation, or deflation. Who is asked to make the sacrifices? When cuts are made in the budget, where do the cuts occur? When the Congress considers tax reform, after the roar of rhetoric recedes, which groups benefit by the new legislation or by the laws that are left alone? When a corporation is found guilty of fraud, violation of antitrust laws, or bribery, what are the penalties? How do they compare with the penalties for crimes committed by poor individuals such as welfare chiselers, and thieves? When there is an oil spill or other ecological disaster caused by huge enterprise, what are the penalties? Who pays for the cleanup and the restoration of nature? The answers to these questions are obvious—the wealthy benefit at the expense of the less well-to-do. In short, the government is an institution made up of people—the rich and powerful or their agents—who seek to maintain their advantageous positions in society.

The bias of the system today is nothing new. Since the nation's founding, the government's policy has primarily favored the needs of the wealthy. The Founding Fathers were upper-class holders of wealth. The Constitution they wrote gave the power to people like themselves—property owners. This bias continued throughout the nineteenth century as bankers, railroad entrepreneurs, and manufacturers joined the landed gentry to make the power elite.

The shift from local business to large-scale manufacturing during the last half of the nineteenth century saw a concomitant increase in governmental activity in the economy. Business was protected from competition by protective tariffs, public subsidies, price regulation, patents, and trademarks. Throughout that century when there was unrest by troubled miners, farmers, and laborers, the government inevitably took the side of the strong against the weak. The militia and federal troops were used to crush the railroad strikes. Antitrust laws, which were not used to stop the monopolistic practices of business, were invoked against labor unions. President Cleveland's attorney general, Richard Olney, a millionaire owner of railroad stocks,

> used antitrust laws, court injunctions, mass arrests, labor spies, federal troops against workers and their unions. From the local sheriff and magistrate to the President and the Supreme Court, the forces of "law and order" were utilized to suppress unions. Statutes declared to be unworkable against the well known monopolistic and collusive practices of business were now effectively invoked against "labor conspiracies." (Parenti, 1995:65)

During this time approximately one billion acres of land in the public domain (almost one-half the present size of the United States) were given to private individuals and corporations. The railroads in particular were given huge tracts of land as a subsidy. These lands were and continue to be very rich in timber and natural resources. This active intervention of the government in the nation's economy during the nineteenth century was almost solely on the behalf of business. Parenti notes, "The government remained laissez-faire in regard to the needs of the common people, giving little attention to poverty, unemployment, unsafe working conditions, child labor, and the spoliation of natural resources" (Parenti, 1995:66).

The early twentieth century was a time of great governmental activity in the economy, which gave the appearance of restraining big business. However, the actual result of federal regulation of business was to increase the power of the largest corporations. The Interstate Commerce Commission, for instance, helped the railroads by establishing common rates to replace ruinous competition (Huntington, 1965). The federal regulations in meat packing, drugs, banking, and mining weeded out the weaker cost-cutting competitors, leaving a few to control the markets at higher prices and higher profits (Renshaw, 1968). Even the actions of that great trust-buster, Teddy Roosevelt, were largely ceremonial. His major legislative proposals reflected the desires of corporate interests. Like other presidents before and since, he enjoyed close relations with big businessmen and invited them into his administration (Parenti, 1995:67–68).

World War I intensified the governmental bias on behalf of business. Industry was converted to war production. Corporate interests became more actively involved in the councils of government. Governmental actions clearly favored business in labor disputes. The police and military were used against rebellious workers because strikes were treated as efforts to weaken the war effort and therefore were treasonous.

The New Deal is typically assumed to be a time when the needs of those impoverished by the Great Depression were paramount in government policies. But the central dedication of the Franklin Roosevelt administration was to *business recovery* rather than to *social reform* (Parenti, 1980:74). Business was subsidized by credits, price supports, bank guarantees, and stimulation of the housing industry, for example. Welfare programs were instituted to prevent widespread starvation, but even these humanitarian programs also worked to the benefit of the big business community. The government provided jobs, minimum wages, unemployment compensation, and retirement benefits, which obviously aided those in dire economic straits. But these programs were actually promoted by the business community because of benefits to them. The government and business favored social programs at this time not because millions of people were in misery but because violent political and social unrest posed a real threat.

Two social scientists, Piven and Cloward, after a historical assessment of government welfare programs, have determined that the government institutes massive aid to the poor *only* when the poor constitute a threat (Piven and Cloward, 1993). When large numbers of people are suddenly barred from their traditional occupations, the legitimacy of the system itself may be questioned. Crime, riots, looting, and social movements bent on changing the existing social, political, and economic arrangements become more widespread. Under this threat, the government initiates or expands relief programs in order to diffuse the social unrest. During the Great Depression, Piven and Cloward contend, the government remained aloof from the needs of the unemployed until there was a surge of political disorder. Added proof for Piven and Cloward's thesis is the contraction or even abolishment of public assistance programs when stability is restored. Perhaps this theory explains how African Americans have gradually attained their constitutional rights (see "Human Agency: The Use of the Courts to Achieve Racial Equality").

The historical trend for government to favor business over less powerful interests continues in current public policy. Let us look at some examples.

Subsidies to Big Business

There is a general principle that applies to the government's relationship to big business—business can conduct its affairs either undisturbed by or encouraged by government, whichever is of greater benefit to the business community. The following are some illustrative cases in which governmental decisions benefited business:

- In 1979 the Chrysler Corporation, after sustaining losses of $207 million in the previous year, appealed to the government and received $1.5 billion in loan guarantees. The government's aid to Chrysler is typical—if the company is big enough. Earlier in the 1970s, Penn Central received $125 million when it faced bankruptcy, and the government guaranteed Lockheed $250 million in new bank loans. In other celebrated cases the banking industry and certain large banks have received large sums of government aid. In 1983 the International Monetary Fund was bailed out with $8 billion in federal monies to offset the bad debts incurred by U.S. bank loans to Third World nations. Also, in 1984, when Continental Bank of Illinois was on the brink of bankruptcy, the federal government put together a $7.5 billion rescue package (Parenti, 1995:77–78).
- In 1987 the government bailed out two Texas financial concerns—$970 million to Houston's First City Bancorporation and $1.3 billion to Vernon Savings. This bailout of savings and loans was only the beginning, as Congress in 1989 approved an administration package that will cost an estimated $500 billion over ten years for aid to about 500 of these failing enterprises (Sherrill, 1990).
- State and local governments provide businesses with a variety of subsidies such as low-interest loans, tax-free financing, subsidized employee training, and tax breaks to entice them to locate or stay in their jurisdictions. In 1991 these handouts by the states to corporations amounted to $16 billion (Grochot, 1992).

■ Quotas are placed on imports of beef, wheat, oil, and other products to protect the profits of U.S. industry.

■ A number of major U.S. corporations such as DuPont, General Motors, Ford, Exxon, and ITT owned factories in enemy countries during World War II. These factories made products for the Axis war effort. "After the war, rather than being prosecuted for trading with the enemy, ITT collected $27 million from the U.S. government for war damages inflicted on its German plants by Allied bombings. GM and Ford subsidiaries built the bulk of Nazi Germany's heavy trucks which served as 'the backbone of the German Army transportation system.' GM collected more than $33 million in compensation for damages to its war plants in enemy territories. Ford and other multinational corporations collected lesser sums." (Snell, 1974:14–16; see also Di Baggio, 1976; Borkin, 1978; Higham, 1983)

■ The federal government directly subsidizes the shipping industry, railroads, airlines, and exporters of iron, steel, textiles, paper, and other products.

■ From 1965 to 1967 several major petroleum companies leased acreage in Alaska for oil exploration, paying $12 million for leases worth at least $2 billion. In another oil lease auction, the companies paid the government $900 million for lands that were expected to be worth some $50 billion within a decade (Parenti, 1983:93).

■ The government develops new technologies at public expense and then turns them over to private corporations for their profit. This transfer occurs routinely with nuclear energy, synthetics, space communications, and mineral exploration. For example, taxpayers spent $20 billion to develop the satellite communications system, which was later put under the control of AT&T (in 1982). Similarly, in 1982, two major corporations built a synthetic fuel plant, with the government paying 98 percent of the $4.5 billion cost (Parenti, 1988:83–84). A variation of this government subsidy to business occurs with universities as the linkage. Universities are permitted to sell to companies exclusive licenses on discoveries made under a company's sponsorship. "This adds up to a fat public subsidy for private business. In 1988, the federal government allocated approximately $7 billion to universities for research and development. That same year, corporations bought control of many of the fruits of that research for a puny $750 million" (Bourke, 1989:495). In another example, the National Cancer Institute developed a cancer drug, Taxol, after decades of research. The Institute in 1991 gave Bristol-Myers Squibb the exclusive right to sell Taxol. It is estimated that between 1993 and 1998 Bristol-Myers Squibb will sell $3.3 billion of Taxol (Bliefuss, 1995a).

■ Two decisions in 1994 and 1995 by Congress and the president—NAFTA and GATT—helped multinational corporations by simplifying investments where wages are lowest, reducing taxes, and reducing safety, consumer, and environmental protections (Parenti, 1995:80).

Perhaps the best illustration of how business benefits from government policies is the fact that corporations pay a much smaller percentage of their income as taxes than do individuals. They legally escape much of the tax burden through a number of loopholes (e.g., investment tax credit, accelerated depreciation, and

AGENCY

HUMAN

The Use of the Courts to Achieve Racial Equality

In his widely acclaimed study *In the Matter of Color,* A. Leon Higginbotham dates the beginning of the inextricable link between race and the law with the colonial period. As early as the 1670s, statutes in Virginia and Maryland codified slavery into a system of permanent bondage for Africans and their descendants. These laws, moreover, become the basis for similar legislation throughout British North America.

Meanwhile, from Massachusetts to South Carolina, African peoples used the same laws to petition for freedom and rights. The case of *Quock Walker* vs. *Jennison* (1781), for example, is widely viewed as cementing the abolition of slavery in Massachusetts in 1783. Walker sued Jennison, charging assault and battery. Jennison responded that Walker was his property and not his neighbor, and, as property, he could be punished. A jury disagreed.

The Bill of Rights, however, introduced new ambiguities and opportunities, which were exacerbated by the retreat from the ennobling principles of the Declaration of Independence and the American Revolution. As David Brion Davis sketched in *The Problem of Slavery in the Age of Revolution,* the Constitution's framers evinced considerable ambivalence about the presence of slaves and the practice of slavery. Few could say they had never engaged in the "execrable commerce." Fewer yet believed Africans their equals. Consequently, scores of African-Americans found themselves in legal limbo as they traversed the nation as free or enslaved people.

Did the right to petition the government for redress of grievances include them? Could they comfortably assume that the 4th Amendment, which protected all citizens from unlawful search and seizure, safeguarded them from slave catchers and bounty hunters? Contemporaries and scholars agree: They could not be so assured. Instead, the question of citizenship and unlawful search and seizure awaited the Supreme Court's landmark ruling in *Scott* vs. *Sandford* (1857).

The *Dred Scott* decision momentarily settled the question of citizenship. Writing for the majority, U.S. Supreme Court Chief Justice Roger B. Taney concluded that African-Americans could be citizens of individual states but not the U.S. Although poorly reasoned and badly researched, the opinion proved politically expedient—temporarily protecting Southern and some Northern interests by limiting what it meant to be free and black in our republic. If blacks were not citizens of the U.S., they had no right to petition the court for redress, no right to claim benefit from the Bill of Rights.

Fortunately, the Bill of Rights proved a living document, open to new interpretations, new protections. Following the Civil War, the country eliminated the ambiguities of the previous century by amending the Constitution once again. The new statutes of liberty—the 13th, 14th and 15th Amendments—expanded upon the rights and privileges articulated in the Bill of Rights.

The 13th Amendment abolished slavery, putting into the Constitution language stricken from the Declaration of Independence and excluded from the Constitution altogether. The 14th Amendment determined the grounds for citizenship, ensured equal protection and due process, and, among other things, endowed Congress with the powers to enforce the laws. And the 15th Amendment granted male citizens of all races the right to vote. But to the chagrin of many, African-Americans had to remain ever vigilant lest their civil rights be eroded.

The retreat from equal protection came early and definitively. Between 1876 and 1896, a series of Supreme Court rulings severely narrowed the Bill of Rights and the post-Civil War amendments. The first substantive

capital gains). Some corporations are able to escape paying taxes altogether—even when they are profitable—because of these tax subsidies.

The proportion of federal revenues coming from corporate taxes has dropped dramatically from 50 percent in 1945 to 8 percent in 1994. The resultant revenue loss was

hint of the new social order came in *The Slaughter-House Cases* (1873). A divided Supreme Court distinguished between the rights of a federal and a state citizen by greatly restricting the former. Three years later, in *United States* vs. *Cruishank,* the court addressed the barbarous murder of 100 blacks in Colfax, La., and overturned a lower court ruling and found that the defendants had not violated the 1st, 2nd and 14th Amendments. The line of judicial reasoning culminated in the 1896 *Plessy* decision, which legalized the doctrine of separate but equal.

Over the course of the next century, new challenges and new opportunities to refer to the Bill of Rights arose. African-Americans, in their dogged determination to fulfill the dream of equality, helped expand the meaning of the law—the Bill of Rights.

Perhaps the most heralded and surprising example dates from the '30s. In 1931, nine black youths hopped a train and had a chance encounter with a smaller group of whites. To the later surprise of the nine blacks, two in the other party were females. When confronted by law officials and questioned about their presence on the train, the women alleged the most heinous of all interracial crimes had occurred: the rape of white women by black men. The black youths were charged and convicted.

The drama that unfolded became known nationally and internationally as the *Scottsboro* boys case. And, as Dan Carter noted in his classic study *Scottsboro,* the case changed both the nation and the Southern social landscape.

How the case changed the Southern social landscape is another story; how it changed the nation had a direct bearing on the Bill of Rights. The 6th Amendment guaranteed all citizens a speedy trial before an "impartial jury of the state and district wherein the crime shall have been committed." It also assured all the assistance of competent counsel for their defense.

The defendants in the *Scottsboro* boys case charged that they were denied competent counsel and an impartial jury. During the hastily concluded initial trial, which lasted six days and resulted in the death penalty for all nine, the court-sanctioned attorneys lacked the time, the will and the skills to defend. Moreover, African Americans in that part of Alabama had been systematically excluded from the jury rolls. In *Powell* vs. *Alabama* (1932), the Supreme Court upheld the right of the accused to counsel. Because the 6th Amendment granted protection to defendants in federal trials, the court turned to the equal-protection clause of the 14th Amendment, which offered protection at both the state and federal levels.

Three years later, in *Norris* vs. *Alabama,* the U.S. Supreme Court ruled that the exclusion of blacks from juries violated the 14th Amendment.

The men who authored the original Bill of Rights recognized what it ignored as well as what it covered. Since that time we have struggled to improve on their enduring genius. That they were imperfect is beyond dispute. Nonetheless, their undeniable concern for democratic values—despite their skirting the issue of slavery—enabled others to modify or amend their work.

Most importantly, the ideals that fueled the writings of the Bill of Rights also inspired African Americans to struggle for two centuries to keep the Bill of Rights a living document. In the process, blacks helped the nation examine the importance of freedom of speech, freedom of assembly, freedom of the press, due process and justifiable bail and punishment.

Source: Earl Lewis, "African-Americans and the Bill of Rights," *In These Times* (December 18–24, 1991), pp. 12–13. Reprinted from *In These Times,* a weekly newspaper published in Chicago.

made up for by an increase in taxes on middle- and working-class earnings and greater government borrowing. In 1983, a working mother with three children and a salary of $10,500 paid more federal taxes than Boeing, General Electric, Du Pont, Texaco, Mobil, and AT & T combined. These companies paid nothing, though they enjoyed combined profits of $13.7 billion. (Parenti, 1995:81; see Greider, 1992)

In 1994 Congress passed NAFTA, which helped multinational corporations but was opposed by unions because it would depress wages and reduce jobs in the United States.

Foreign Policy for Corporate Benefit

The operant principle here is that "foreign policy seems to be carried on in the light of the needs of the munitions makers, the Pentagon, the CIA, and the multinational corporations" (Hutchins, 1976:4). Several examples make this point. First, military goods are sold overseas for the profit of the arms merchants. Sometimes arms are sold to both sides in a potential conflict, the argument being that if we did not sell them the arms, then other nations would, so we might as well make the profits.

The government has supported foreign governments that are supportive of U.S. multinational companies regardless of how tyrannical these governments might be. The Reza Shah's government in Iran, Chiang's regime in China, Chung Hee Park's dictatorship in South Korea, and Ferdinand Marcos's rule in the Philippines are four examples of this tendency.

The U.S. government has directly intervened in the domestic affairs of foreign governments to protect U.S. corporate interests. In Latin America, for example, the United States has intervened militarily since 1950 in Guatemala, the Dominican Republic, Chile, Uruguay, Nicaragua, Grenada, and Panama. As Parenti has characterized it:

> Sometimes the sword has rushed in to protect the dollar, and sometimes the dollar has rushed in to enjoy the advantages won by the sword. To make the world safe for capitalism, the United States government has embarked on a global counterrevolutionary

strategy, suppressing insurgent peasant and worker movements throughout Asia, Africa, and Latin America. But the interests of the corporate elites never stand naked; rather they are wrapped in the flag and coated with patriotic appearances. (Parenti, 1988:94)*

The Powerless Pay the Burden

Robert Hutchins, in his critique of U.S. governmental policy, characterized the basic principle guiding internal affairs in this way: "Domestic policy is conducted according to one infallible rule: the costs and burdens of whatever is done must be borne by those least able to bear them" (Hutchins, 1976:4). Let us review several examples of this statement.

When threatened by war the government institutes a military draft. A careful analysis of the draft reveals that it is really a tax on the poor. During the height of the Vietnam War, for instance, only 10 percent of men in college were drafted, although 40 percent of draft-age men were in college. Even for those educated young men who ended up in the armed services, there was a greater likelihood of their serving in noncombat jobs than for the non-college-educated. Thus, the chances for getting killed while in the service were about three times greater for the less educated than for the college educated (Zeitlin, Lutterman, and Russell, 1977; Baskir and Strauss, 1978). Even more blatant was the practice that occurred legally during the Civil War. The law at that time allowed the affluent who were drafted to hire someone to take their place in the service.

The poor, being powerless, can be made to absorb the costs of societal changes. In the nineteenth century the poor did the back-breaking work that built the railroads and the cities. Today they are the ones pushed out of their homes by gentrification, urban renewal, and the building of expressways, parks, and stadia (e.g., what occurred in Atlanta with the preparation for the 1996 Olympics).

The government's attempts to solve economic problems generally obey the principle that the poor must bear the burden. A common solution for runaway inflation, for example, is to increase the amount of unemployment. Of course the poor, especially minorities (whose rate of unemployment is consistently twice the rate for Whites), are the ones who make the sacrifice for the economy. This solution, aside from being socially cruel, is economically ineffective because it ignores the real sources of inflation—excessive military spending, excessive profits by energy companies (foreign and domestic), and administered prices set by shared monopolies, which, contrary to classical economic theory, do not decline during economic downturns (Harrington, 1979).

More fundamentally a certain level of unemployment is maintained continuously, not just during economic downturns. Genuine full employment for all job seekers is a myth. But why, if all political candidates extol the work ethic and it is declared national policy to have full employment? Economist Robert Lekachman (1979) has argued that it is no accident that we tolerate millions of unemployed persons. The reason is that a moderate unemployment rate is beneficial to the affluent.

Among these benefits are that (1) people are willing to work at humble tasks for low wages, (2) the children of the middle and upper classes avoid the draft as the unemployed join the volunteer army, (3) the unions are less demanding, (4) workers are less likely to demand costly safety equipment, (5) corporations do not have to pay their share of taxes because local and state governments give them concessions to lure them to their area, and (6) the existing wide differentials between White males and the various powerless categories such as females, Latinos, and African Americans are retained.

Trickle-Down Solutions

Periodically the government is faced with the problem of finding a way to stimulate the economy during an economic downturn. One solution is to spend federal monies through unemployment insurance, government jobs, and housing subsidies. In this way the funds go directly to the people most hurt by shortages, unemployment, inadequate housing, and the like. Opponents of such plans advocate that the subsidies should go directly to business, which would help the economy by encouraging companies to hire more workers, add to their inventories, and build new plants. Subsidizing business in this way, the advocates argue, benefits everyone. In effect, proponents argue, because the government provides direct benefits to businesses and investors, the economic benefits indirectly trickle down to all.

There are at least two reasons government officials tend to opt for these trickle-down solutions. First, because they tend to come from the business class, government officials believe in the conservative ideology that says what is good for business is good for the United States. The second reason for the probusiness choice is that government officials are more likely to hear arguments from the powerful. Because the weak, by definition, are not organized, their voice is not heard or, if heard, not taken seriously in decision-making circles.

Although the government most often opts for trickle-down solutions, such plans are not very effective in fulfilling the promise that benefits will trickle down to the poor. The higher corporate profits generated by tax credits and other tax incentives do not necessarily mean that companies will increase wages or hire more workers. What is more likely is that corporations will increase dividends to the stockholders, which further exacerbates the existing problem of the maldistribution of resources. Job creation is also not guaranteed because companies may use their newly acquired wealth to purchase labor-saving devices. If so, then the government programs will actually have widened the gulf between the haves and the have-nots.

In summary, this view of power argues that the power of wealthy individuals and the largest corporations is translated into public policy that disproportionately benefits the power elite. Throughout U.S. history there has been a bias that pervades government and its policies. This bias is perhaps best seen in the aphorism once enunciated by President Calvin Coolidge and repeated by contemporary presidents: "The business of America is business."

Conclusion

Power is unequally distributed in all social organizations. In our examination of the structure of power at the societal level, two basic views were presented—the pluralist and the elitist. The former is consistent with the world view of order theorists, while the latter is congruent with the way conflict theorists perceive reality (see Table 14.1).

One glaring weakness of many pluralists and elitists is that they are not objective. Their writings tend often to be polemics because so much effort is spent attempting to prove what they believe is the nature of the power structure. The evidence is presented to ensure the absolute negation of the opposite stance. This points to a fundamental research problem. Are the data reliable? Are our observations distorted by bias? Sociologists or political scientists are forced in the study of power to rely on either the perceptions of other people (who are presumed to be knowledgeable) or on their own observations, which are distorted by not being present during all aspects of the decision-making process. Unfortunately, one's perceptions are also affected by one's model (conflict or order). Ideological concerns often cause either faulty perceptions or a rigidity of thought that automatically rejects conflicting evidence.

The task for sociologists is to determine the real distribution of power with our ideological distortion. Given these problems with objectivity, we must ask (1) What is the power structure really like? (2) What facts are consonant with the pluralist model and what facts fit the elitist model?

TABLE 14.1

Assumptions of the Order and the Conflict Models about Politics

ORDER MODEL	CONFLICT MODEL
1. People in positions of power occupy bureaucratic roles necessary for the rational accomplishment of society's objectives.	1. People in positions of power are motivated largely by their own selfish interests.
2. The state works for the benefit of all. Laws reflect the customs of society and ensure order, stability, and justice—in short, the common good.	2. The state exists for the benefit of the ruling class (law, police, and courts protect the interests of the wealthy).
3. Pluralism: (1) competing interest groups; (2) majority rule; (3) power is diffused.	3. Power is concentrated (power elite).

CHAPTER REVIEW

1. In answering the question of who the real power wielders are in U.S. society, there are two contrasting answers from pluralists and elitists.

2. The representative democracy version of pluralism emphasizes that the people have the ultimate power. The people elect representatives who are responsive to the people's wishes. This version ignores the many instances in which the people have been deliberately misled by their leaders, secrecy, and the undemocratic manner in which election campaigns are funded.

3. The veto-groups version of pluralism recognizes the existence of a number of organizations and special-interest groups that vie for power. There is a balance of power, however, with no one sector getting its way. The groups tend to neutralize each other, resulting in compromise. Critics of this view of power argue that it is an idealized version that ignores reality. The interest groups are not equal in power. Power does not shift from issue to issue. Also, at the apex of each of the competing groups are members of the upper class, suggesting the possibility of a power elite.

4. Marxists assert that there is a ruling class. There are two variations on this theme. The instrumentalist view is that the ruling class (capitalists) does not govern (i.e., hold office) but that they rule by controlling political officials and institutions. The structuralist view is that the state serves the interests of the capitalist class because whoever holds government office will make decisions that promote stability and a healthy business climate—both of which enhance the interests of the capitalist class.

5. In C. Wright Mills's view of power, there is a power elite composed of the top people in the executive branch of the federal government, the military, and the corporate sector. Although these persons represent different interests, they tend to perceive the world in a like manner because of their similar social class backgrounds and similar role expectations, because they interact socially, because their children go to the same schools and intermarry, and because they share similar interests. There is considerable evidence for the linkages among these three sectors. There are some problems with this view, however. The equality of these three groups is not a fact. There is conflict among the three sectors. There are other sectors of power that are ignored.

6. In G. William Domhoff's view of power, there is a governing class—the uppermost social class. The very rich control the nation's assets, control the corporations, are overrepresented in the key decision-making groups in society, and through contributions and activities control both major political parties. The major criticism of this view is that while the people in key positions tend to have upper-class pedigrees, there is no evidence that these people actually promote the interests of the corporate rich.

7. Michael Parenti's bias of the system view is another elitist theory. The powerful in society (those who control the government and the largest corporations) tend to come from backgrounds of privilege and wealth. Their decisions tend to benefit the wealthy disproportionately, but the power elite is not organized and conspiratorial. The interests of the wealthy are served, nevertheless, by the way society is organized. This bias occurs by their influence over elected and appointed officials, systemic imperatives, and through the ideological control of the masses.

8. The pluralist model of power is congruent with the order model: (*a*) people in powerful positions work for the accomplishment of society's objectives; (*b*) the state works for the benefit of all; and (*c*) power is diffused through competing interest groups.

9. The elitist model of power fits with the conflict model: (*a*) people in powerful positions are motivated largely by selfish interests; (*b*) the state exists for the benefit of the ruling class; and (*c*) power is concentrated in a power elite.

KEY TERMS

Elitist model of power	Instrumentalist view	Governing class
Pluralist model of power	Structuralist view	Systemic imperatives
Democracy	Power elite	Power

STUDY QUESTIONS

1. How does the way political campaigns are financed have undemocratic consequences?

2. What is your reaction to the "Closer Look" panel on the structural impediments to democracy in the United States? Is the United States a democracy (consider also your response to the first study question here)? Elaborate.

3. Classify Mills, Domhoff, and Parenti as either instrumentalists or structuralists. Justify your placement of each.

4. Summarize the three variations of the conflict view of politics by Mills, Domhoff, and Parenti. Which variation most closely approximates politics in contemporary United States? Why? Or, alternatively, is each variation incorrect? If so, why?

5. How have government decisions tended to increase the gap between the haves and the have-nots?

FOR FURTHER READING

Paul A. Baran and Paul M. Sweezy, *Monopoly Capital* (New York: Monthly Review Press, 1968).

Donald Barlett and James B. Steele, *America: What Went Wrong?* (Kansas City: Andrews and McMeel, 1992).

Lois Bryson, *Welfare and the State: Who Benefits?* (St. Martin's Press, 1992).

Dan Clawson, Alan Neustadtl, and Denise Scott, *Money Talks: Corporate PACs and Political Influence* (New York: Basic Books, 1992).

G. William Domhoff, *The Power Elite and the State: How Policy Is Made in America* (New York: Walter de Gruyter, Inc., 1990).

William Greider, *Who Will Tell the People: The Betrayal of American Democracy* (New York: Simon & Schuster, 1992).

C. Wright Mills, *The Power Elite* (New York: Oxford University Press, 1956).

Michael Parenti, *Power and the Powerless* (New York: St. Martin's Press, 1978).

Michael Parenti, *Land of Idols: Political Mythology in America* (New York: St. Martin's Press, 1994).

Michael Parenti, *Democracy for the Few,* 6th ed. (New York: St. Martin's Press, 1995).

Kevin Phillips, *Boiling Point: Democrats, Republicans, and the Decline of Middle-Class Prosperity* (New York: Random House, 1993).

Frances Fox Piven and Richard A. Cloward, *Regulating the Poor: The Functions of Public Welfare,* updated edition (New York: Vintage Books, 1993).

Howard Zinn, *A People's History of the United States* (New York: Harper and Row, 1980).

CHAPTER 15

Families

Families are far different from what they used to be. They are more diverse, they include more alternative forms of household arrangements, and they are more easily fractured. Family members spend less time together, and parents have less influence over their children to name a few differences from earlier times. Many find these changes threatening. They yearn for a time when families were more stable, when fathers were providers and mothers stayed home as homemakers and nurturers.

Family changes occurring in the last few decades have led some social analysts to conclude that the family is in serious trouble; that we have lost our **family values,** and that family collapse is responsible for our worst social problems. In the media and on the campaign trail, we hear that family patterns of the late twentieth century are symptoms of decline and decay. This view of the world is flawed in two fundamental respects. First, it reverses the relationship between family and society by treating families as the building blocks of society. Second, it ignores the structural reasons for family breakdown and the profound changes occurring throughout the world. Even in very different societies, families and households are undergoing similar shifts as a result of global economic changes. (See "Other Societies: Families in Upheaval Worldwide.")

This chapter examines the family as a social institution and relates families to society as a whole. Families in the United States are diverse, with regional, social class, religious, racial, and ethnic differences; nonetheless, distinct patterns can be found in family life. The theme of the chapter is that families are not isolated units free from outside constraints but that social forces outside the family affect life inside families.

The Mythical U.S. Family

There are a number of myths about families. These beliefs are bound up with nostalgia, selective perception, and cultural values concerning what is correct, typical, and true about families. The following beliefs, based on folk wisdom, religious beliefs, and common attitudes, are rarely challenged except by social scientists and family scholars:

Other Societies Other Ways

Families in Upheaval Worldwide

Around the world, in rich and poor countries alike, the structure of family life is undergoing profound changes, a new analysis of research from numerous countries has concluded.

"The idea that the family is a stable and cohesive unit in which father serves as economic provider and mother serves as emotional care giver is a myth," said Judith Bruce, an author of the study. "The reality is that trends like unwed motherhood, rising divorce rates, smaller households and the feminization of poverty are not unique to America, but are occurring worldwide."

The report, "Families in Focus," was released by the Population Council, an international nonprofit group based in New York that studies reproductive health. It analyzed a variety of demographic and household studies from dozens of countries around the world.

Among the major findings:

- Whether because of abandonment, separation, divorce or death of a spouse, marriages are dissolving with increasing frequency. In many developed countries, divorce rates doubled between 1970 and 1990, and in less-developed countries, about a quarter of first marriages end by the time women are in their 40s.

- Parents in their prime working years face growing burdens caring for children, who need to be supported through more years of education, and for their own parents, who are living longer.

- Unwed motherhood is increasingly common virtually everywhere, reaching as many as a third of all births in Northern Europe, for example.

- Children in single-parent households—usually families with only a mother present—are much more likely to be poor than those who live with two parents, largely because of the loss of support from the fathers.

- Even in households where fathers are present, mothers are carrying increasing economic responsibility for children.

The idea that families are changing in similar ways, even in very different cultures, should bring about new thinking on social policy, experts say, and in particular on the role government should play in supporting families.

The Population Council report says women around the world tend to work longer hours than men, at home and on the job.

In studies of 17 less-developed countries, women's work hours exceeded men's by 30 percent. Data from 12 industrialized countries found that formally employed women worked about 20 percent longer hours than employed men.

Women's economic contributions also are becoming increasingly important.

In Ghana, the report said, a third of households with children are maintained primarily by women.

1. *The myth of a stable and harmonious family of the past.* The common assumption is that families of the past were better than families of the present. They are believed to have been more stable, better adjusted, and happier. However, family historians have found that there is no golden age of the family. There have always been desertion by spouses, illegitimate children, and certainly spouse and child abuse. Divorce rates were lower, but this does not mean that love was stronger in the past. Many women died earlier from pregnancy complications, which kept divorce rates lower, and meant that many children were raised by single parents or stepparents, just as now. Divorces were relatively uncommon also because of strong

In the Philippines, women were found to contribute about a third of households' cash income, but 55 percent of household support if the economic value of their activities at home, such as gathering wood or growing food, is included.

In the United States, a Louis Harris survey released earlier this month found that nearly half of employed married women contribute half or more of their family's income.

While the reason for entering the work force may vary from country to country, women everywhere are finding that to give their children an adequate life, they must earn more money, said Ms. Bruce, one of the report's authors.

"In traditional Bangladesh, it may be because the husband was much older and died while the children were still young," she said. "In sub-Saharan Africa, a woman might have a baby prematurely and have no strong connection with the father, or she might have a husband who goes on to another polygamous marriage and supports the children of that union."

"In Asia," she added, "the husband may have migrated for better economic opportunities and stopped sending money after a year or two. And everywhere, parents are finding that there are fewer jobs that pay enough to support a family."

Even among rural people in less-developed countries, Ms. Bruce said, the need for a cash income is becoming more pressing.

"Parents all over the world have an increasing awareness that their children will need literacy and numeracy," Ms. Bruce said. "That means that instead of having their 6 year old working with them in the fields, they have to pay for school fees, uniforms, transportation and supplies."

The fact that many developing countries have cut their spending for public education as part of their debt-reduction plans creates further pressure on families, she said.

One apparent exception to the general trends is Japan, where single-parent households and unwed motherhood have remained relatively rare.

The Population Council report, written by Ms. Bruce, Cynthia B. Lloyd and Ann Leonard, found that while most countries have extensive data on women as mothers, there has been little research on men as fathers.

But studies have found that although fathers' income usually exceeds mothers' income, women usually contribute a larger proportion of their earnings to their household, while men keep more for their personal use.

Collecting child support is also difficult. Among divorced fathers, three-quarters in Japan, almost two-thirds in Argentina, half in Malaysia and two-fifths in the United States do not pay child support, the report said.

Source: Tamar Lewin, "Families in Upheaval Worldwide," *International Herald Tribune* (May 31, 1995) pp. 1, 9. Copyright © *New York Times*, 1995.

religious prohibitions and community norms against divorce. As a result, many "empty" marriages continued without love and happiness to bind them.

Historian Stephanie Coontz (1992) has reexamined our deepest assumptions about the history of the family. Her book *The Way We Never Were* explodes the myth that family life has recently "gone bad." The reality of past family life was quite different from the stereotype. Desertion by spouses, the presence of illegitimate children, and other conditions that are considered modern problems existed in the past. Part of the family nostalgia holds that there were three generations living under one roof or in close proximity. This image of the three-generational family is also false. Few examples of this "classical family of western nostalgia" (Goode, 1984:43) have been found by family historians.

2. *The myth of the family as a "haven in a heartless world"* (Lasch, 1977). This is the positive image of the family as a place of intimacy, love, and trust where individuals escape the competition and dehumanizing forces in modern society. Of course, love, intimacy, and trust are the glue for many families, but this glorification of private life tends to mask the ugly side of some families, where emotional and physical aggression are commonplace, and where competition between spouses and among children sometimes destroys relationships. This myth ignores the harsh effects of economic conditions (e.g., poverty or near-poverty, unemployment and underemployment, downward mobility or the threat of downward mobility). It ignores the social inequalities (racism, sexism, ageism, homophobia) that prevent certain kinds of people from experiencing the good things in life. And the idealized family view masks the inevitable problems that arise in intimate settings (tensions, anger, and even violence in some instances).

3. *The myth of the monolithic family form.* We get a consistent image of what the American family is supposed to look like from our politicians, from our ministers and priests, from children's literature, and from television. This faulty image is of a middle-class, monogamous, father-at-work, father-in-control, mother- and children-at-home family living in a one family house. This model, however, accounts for only about 7 percent of today's families.

4. *The myth of an undifferentiated family experience.* We assume that all family members experience family life in the same way. This image hides the diversity within families. The family is a gendered institution. Women and men experience marriage differently. There are gender differences in decision making, in household division of labor, and in forms of intimacy and sexuality. Similarly, divorce affects them differently. Remarriage patterns differ by gender, as well. Girls and boys experience their childhoods differently, as there are different expectations, different rules, and different punishments according to gender.

5. *The myth of family breakdown as the cause of social problems.* The family-values rhetoric common today argues that all family arrangements *different* from the two-parent, father-working, children-at-home model are the sources of social problems. Fatherless families, or women working outside the home, are said to be the reasons for poverty, violence, drug addiction, and crime. Divorce, and unwed mothers, in this view are damaging children, destroying families, and tearing apart the fabric of society.

Families in Contemporary U.S. Society

The Family in Capitalism

Family history in the United States is closely related to economic development. Industrialization moved the center of production from the domestic family unit to the workplace. Families became private domestic retreats set off from the rest of society. Men went off to earn a wage in factories and offices, while women remained in the home to nurture their children. From the rise of the industrial economy until World War II, capitalism operated within a simple framework. Employers assumed that most families included one main breadwinner—a male—and one adult working at home directing domestic work—a female; in short, jobs with wives. As a result, many men received the income intended to support a family (Albelda, 1992:7).

The emergence of the private family with a breadwinner father and a homemaker mother pattern was important, but economic conditions precluded this pattern for many families. As the nation's economy industrialized, wave after wave of immigrants filled the industrial labor force. Through working for wages, entire families became an integral part of society. Immigrant families did not separate themselves into privatized units. Instead, they used extended family ties to adjust in the new society. Families were crucial in assisting their newly arrived kin and other members of their ethnic groups to adapt to the new society. Many immigrants came to the United States in family groupings, or they sent for families once they were established in cities. Kin assisted in locating jobs and housing, and they provided other forms of support. Contrary to the typical portrayal of immigrants, their transplanted kinship and ethnic bonds did not disintegrate, but rather were maintained and regenerated in the new society (Vecoli, 1964; Early, 1983).

The developing capitalist economy did not provide equal opportunities for all people. Racial/ethnic people did not have the opportunity to become part of the industrial labor force. Instead, they labored in nonindustrial sectors of the economy. This often required family arrangements that were different from those in the dominant society.

The breadwinner–homemaker pattern never applied to immigrants and racial minorities because they were denied the opportunities to earn a family wage. So, many married women took jobs to make ends meet. Some women took in boarders or did piecework; some worked as maids in middle-class and upper-class homes; and some became wage workers in sweatshops, department stores, and offices. For these families the support of the community and extended family members was crucial (Albelda, 1992:7).

Families have always varied with social conditions. What many uphold as the legitimate family is a product of social structure. From the original settlement of the American colonies through the mid-twentieth century, families of European descent often received economic and social supports to establish and maintain families. Following World War II, the G. I. Bill, the National Defense Education Act, the expansion of the Federal Housing Authority and Veterans Administration loan subsidy programs, and government funding of new highways provided the means through which middle-class Whites were able to achieve the stable suburban family lives that became the ideal against which other families were judged (Coontz, 1992). These kinds of supports have rarely been available for people of color, and until quite recently were actively denied them through various forms of housing and job discrimination. A careful reading of family history makes it clear that family patterns are the result of far more than group-specific culture, individual values, or morality (Dill, Baca Zinn, and Patton, 1993).

What we think of as "the family" is an ideal. It implies a private retreat set apart from society. This image masks the real relationship between families and the larger society. A better way of understanding how families are related to other social institutions is to distinguish between families and households. A **family** is a construct of meanings and relationships; a **household** is a residential and economic unit (Osmond and Thorne, 1993:607; Rapp, 1982). To put it another way, "family" designates the way things *should be,* while "household" refers to the manner in which women, men, and children *actually* come together in domestic units (Fernandez-Kelly and Garcia, 1990: 141). A good example of the importance of distinguishing between family and household is the restructuring of family obligations and household composition after divorce (Ferree, 1991:107).

Stratification and Family Life

In previous chapters, we examined growing inequalities in the distribution of resources and rewards. These stratification hierarchies—class, race, and gender—are changing and reshuffling families and individuals. In this section, we examine the effects of social class on families in the United States.

Families are embedded in a class hierarchy that is "pulling apart" to shrink the middle class while more families join the ranks of the rich or the poor (Usdansky, 1992). This movement creates great differences in family living and no longer guarantees that children's placement in the class system will follow that of their parents. Still, a family's location in the class system is the single most important determinant of family life.

Social and economic forces produce different family configurations. Households in different parts of the class structure have different connections with opportunity structures and different ways of acquiring the necessities of life. They do so through inheritance, salaries, wages, welfare, or various involvements with the hidden economy, the illegal economy, or the irregular economy. Families with more secure resources conform more closely to the nuclear family ideal of self-support. In a stratified society, family structures differ because households vary systematically in their ability to hook into, accumulate, and transmit wealth, wages, or welfare (Rapp, 1982). This variation is closely related to the connections that households and families have with other social institutions. The social networks or relationships outside the family—at work, school, church, voluntary associations—are the social forces that shape class and racial differences in family life.

The middle-class family form is the one most idealized in our society. This form, composed of mother, father, and children in a self-supporting, free-standing

Kirk Anderson.

unit, has long been most characteristic of middle-class and upper-middle class families. Middle-class families of the nineties are quite different from the employed-father and homemaker-mother model that evolved with industrialization. Today, many families can sustain their class status only through the economic contributions of employed wives. Here, households are based on stable and secure resources provided by the occupations of adult women and men. Family "autonomy" is shaped by supportive forces in the larger society. When exceptional economic resources are called for, nonfamilial institutions usually are available in the form of better medical coverage, expense accounts, and credit at banks (Rapp, 1982:181).

These links with nonfamily institutions are precisely the ones that distinguish life in middle-class families from families in other economic groups. The strongest links are with the occupations of middle-class family members, especially those of the husband-father. Occupational roles greatly affect family roles and the quality of family life (Schneider and Smith, 1973). Occupations are part of the larger opportunity structure of society: Occupations that are highly valued and carry high-income rewards are unevenly distributed. The amount of the paycheck determines how well a given household can acquire resources for survival and perhaps for luxury. (See Table 15.1 for a breakdown of median income by race and type of family in 1994.) The job or occupation that is the source of the paycheck connects families with the opportunity structure in different ways.

In the working class, material resources depend on wages acquired in exchange for labor. When such hourly wages are insufficient or unstable, individuals in households must pool their resources with other people in the larger family network. The pooling of resources may involve exchanging baby sitting, sharing meals, or lending money. Pooling represents an attempt to cope with the tenuous

TABLE 15.1

Median Income by Race and Family, 1994

All Races

Married-couple families	$44,959
Wife in labor force	53,309
Male householder, no wife present	27,251
Female householder, no husband present	18,236

White

Married-couple families	$45,474
Wife in labor force	53,977
Male householder, no wife present	29,460
Female householder, no husband present	20,795

Black

Married-couple families	$40,432
Wife in labor force	47,235
Male householder, no wife present	20,977
Female householder, no husband present	13,943

Hispanic

Married-couple families	$29,621
Wife in labor force	38,559
Male householder, no wife present	21,787
Female householder, no husband present	12,117

Source: "Income, Poverty, and Valuation of Noncash Benefits: 1994, "Current Population Reports Consumer Income, Series P60-189" (Feb. 1996), U.S. Dept. of Commerce and Statistics Administration, Bureau of the Census, pp. 7–10.

nature of connections between households and opportunity structures of society, and it requires that the boundaries of "the family" be expanded. This is one reason that the idealized nuclear family is impossible for many people to sustain. At the lower levels of the class hierarchy, people lack the material resource to form autonomous households.

The fluctuating boundaries of these families do not make them unstable. Instead, this family flexibility is a way of sustaining the limited resources that result from their place in the class hierarchy. Even the Black single-parent family, which has sometimes been criticized as being disorganized or even pathological, is often embedded in a network of sharing and support. Latino families also exhibit strong and persistent kinship bonds that provide socioeconomic and emotional support. In fact, most racial/ethnic families are characterized by the presence of extended kinship and networks of support spread across multiple households. Looking at how these families are influenced by larger social forces allows us to see that variation in family organization is a way of adapting to a society where racial stratification shapes family resources and family structures (Baca Zinn, 1990).

Most important, the differences in family boundaries arise from different kinds of linkages with institutions that are *consequences* of class position, not causes of that position. Lacking economic resources to purchase services from specialists outside the family, poor people turn to relatives and exchange these services. This family network then becomes a crucial institution in both the working class and the lower class.

Middle-class families with husbands (and perhaps wives) in careers have both economic resources and built-in ties with supportive institutions such as banks, credit unions, medical facilities, and voluntary associations. These ties are intrinsic to some occupations and to middle-class neighborhoods. They are structurally determined. Such institutional linkages strengthen the autonomy of middle-class families. Yet the middle-class is shrinking, and many middle-class families are without middle-class incomes because of changes in the larger economy. Changes in family structure have also contributed to the lowering of family income. High divorce rates, for example, create many more family units with lower incomes.

Turning to the upper class, we find that family boundaries are more open than are those of the middle class, even though class boundaries are quite closed. Among the elite, family constitutes not only a nuclear family but also the extended family. The elite have multiple households (Rapp, 1982:182). Their day-to-day life exists within the larger context of a network of relatives (Dyer, 1979:209).

The institutional linkages of the elite are national in scope. Families in various sections of the country are connected by such institutions as boarding schools, exclusive colleges, exclusive clubs, and fashionable vacation resorts. In this way the elite remains intact, and the marriage market is restricted to a small (but national) market (Blumberg and Paul, 1975:69).

Family life of the elite is privileged in every sense, as Stein, Richman, and Hannon report:

> Wealthy families can afford an elaborate support structure to take care of the details of everyday life. Persons can be hired to cook and prepare meals and do laundry and to care for the children. (Stein, Richman, and Hannon, 1977:9)

The vast economic holdings of these families allow them a high degree of control over the rewards and resources of society. They enjoy freedoms and choices not available to other families in society. These families maintain privileged access to **life chances** and lifestyles.

Kinship ties, obligations, and interests are more extended in classes at the two extremes than they are in the middle (McKinley, 1964:22). In the upper extreme and toward the lower end of the class structure, kinship networks serve decisively different functions. At both extremes they are institutions of resource management. The kin-based family form of the elite serves to preserve inherited wealth. It is intricately tied to other national institutions that control the wealth of society. The kin-based family form of the working and lower classes is a primary institution through which individuals participate in social life as they pool and exchange their limited resources to ensure survival. It is influenced by society's institutions, but it remains separate from them.

Structural Transformation and Family Life

In Chapter 8, we discussed the structural transformation of the economy. Given the magnitude of the economic transformation, we should not be surprised that families and individuals are profoundly affected by the global shifts now occurring.

As U.S. companies move production overseas, use new technology to replace workers, and engage in megamergers, jobs are lost and wages decline. Declining industries are those that historically proved high-earning positions for men. On the other hand, the new growth in the U.S. economy has been precisely in the sectors that are major employers of women. As the need for certain kinds of labor diminishes, more and more working-class and middle-class families are the victims of economic dislocations. Families are affected when their resources are reduced, when they face economic and social marginalization, and when family members are unemployed or underemployed. The modern economic system undermines "family values" (Thurow, 1995:A-11). (This section is adapted from Baca Zinn and Eitzen, 1996:103–105.)

Economic changes have affected white-collar workers and managers as well. What does **downward mobility** mean for families? Katherine Newman describes the experience of the downwardly mobile middle class:

> They once "had it made" in American society, filling slots from affluent blue-collar jobs to professional and managerial occupations. They have job skills, education, and decades of steady work experience. Many are, or were, homeowners. Their marriages were (at least initially) intact. As a group they savored the American dream. They found a place higher up the ladder in this society and then, inexplicably, found their grip loosening and their status sliding. Some downwardly mobile middle-class families end up in poverty, but many do not. Usually they come to rest at a standard of living above the poverty level but far below the affluence they enjoyed in the past. They must, therefore, contend not only with financial hardship but with the psychological, social, and practical consequences of "falling from grace, of losing their proper place" in the world. (Newman, 1988:8)

The personal consequences of "falling from grace" involve stigma, embarrassment, and guilt for those affected. Downward mobility is devastating in U.S. society not only because of the loss in economic resources but also because self-worth is so closely connected to occupation. People in the United States tend to interpret loss of occupational status as the fault of the downwardly mobile.

Downward mobility also occurs within the stable working class whose links with resource-granting opportunity structures have always been tenuous. Many downwardly mobile families find successful coping strategies to deal with their adverse situations. Some families develop a tighter bond to meet their common problems. Others find support from families in similar situations or from their personal kin networks. For many families, however, downward mobility adds tensions that make family life especially difficult. Family members experience stress, marital tension, and depression. Newman has suggested that these conditions are normal, given the persistent tensions generated by downward mobility. Many families experience some degree of these pathologies and yet somehow endure. But some families disintegrate under these pressures, with serious problems of physical brutality, incapacitating alcoholism, desertion, and even suicide (Newman, 1988: 134–140).

Although families throughout the social structure are changing as a result of macroeconomic forces, the changes are most profound among the working class. Blue-collar workers have been hardest hit by the economic transformation. Their jobs have been eliminated by the millions because of new technologies and competition from other lower-wage (much lower) economies. They have disproportionately been fired or periodically laid off. Sometimes their places of work have shut down entirely and moved to other societies. Their unions have lost strength (in numbers and clout). And their wages have declined.

The changing forms of the family are a major consequence of the economic transformation. In 1950 some 60 percent of U.S. households fit this pattern: an intact nuclear household composed of a male breadwinner, his full-time homemaker wife, and their dependent children. Sociologist Judith Stacey (1990, 1991) calls this type of family the **modern family.** But this model for the family was disrupted by deindustrialization and the changes in women's work roles. Stacey found that working-class families, especially the women in them, created innovative ways to cope with economic uncertainty and domestic upheavals. In effect these women were and are the pioneers of emergent family forms. Stacey calls these new family forms **postmodern** because they do not fit the criteria for a "modern" family. Now there

The so-called "modern family" has been replaced by a variety of family forms, each with its unique coping strategies.

are divorce-extended families that include ex-spouses and their lovers, children, and friends. Households now expand and contract as adult children leave and then return home only to leave again. The vast majority of these postmodern families have dual earners. Many now involve husbands in greater child care and domestic work than in earlier times. Kin networks have expanded to meet economic pressures. Parents now deal with their children's cohabitation, single and unwed parenthood, and divorce. The result is that only 7 percent of households now conform to the "modern" family form. According to Stacey:

> No longer is there a single culturally dominant family pattern, like the modern one, to which the majority of Americans conform and most of the rest aspire. Instead, Americans today have crafted a multiplicity of family and household arrangements that we inhabit uneasily and reconstitute frequently in response to changing personal and occupational circumstances. (Stacey, 1991:19)

These "postmodern" family forms are new to working-class and middle-class families as they adjust to the structural transformation, *but they are not new to the poor.* The economic deprivation faced by the poor has always forced the poor to adapt in similar ways: single-parent families, relying on kin networks, sharing household costs, and multiple wage-earners among family members.

The Changing Composition of Households and Families

Households are defined by the Census Bureau as taking one of three general forms: family, **nonfamily**, and **single-person households.** First, family households consist of two or more persons living together who are related through marriage, birth, or adoption. The most common family household is a married couple with or without children in the home. A single parent with one or more children also comprises a family household. Nonfamily households consist of two or more unrelated individuals who share living quarters. They can be nonmarried couples, of the same or opposite sex. Single-person households are individuals who live alone in their own separate residential units.

Over the years, U.S. households have changed in several important ways. Average household size fell from 3.14 members in 1970 to 2.76 members in 1980 to 2.63 members in 1990. This decline is due to more single-parent families, childless married couples, and people living alone (Waldrop and Exter, 1991:35). Household size has not decreased since 1990. By the year 2000, households made up of married couples will increase only slightly in number, while other types of households will increase dramatically. Fewer households will have children present. Even today most "families" do not have children. In 1994, barely half of U.S. families had one or more children present in the home (U.S. Bureau of the Census, "Population Profile of the United States," 1995a:22). Figure 15.1 highlights the significant changes in the nation's households during the past twenty years. No one household arrangement is typical. Instead, a very diverse world of households, families, and individual life histories is emerging. Such diversity has meant great economic inequality across households. "Some of the new, nontraditional families, such as dual-earner couples, are doing very well; others, such as single-mother families, are doing poorly" (McLanahan and Casper, 1995:2).

FIGURE 15.1

Household Composition: 1970 to 1994 (In percent)

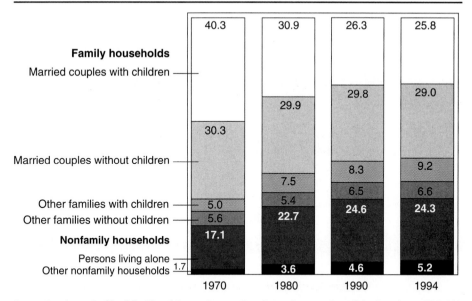

Source: *Population Profile of the United States,* Current Population Reports, Special Studies, Series P23–189 (July, 1995), p. 22.

Families headed by women account for a growing proportion of American families over the last two decades. In 1970, female-headed families were 10 percent of all families. Divorce, separation, and premarital births have *doubled* the proportion of single-parent households in the past twenty years. By 1993, 17 percent of all family households were headed by women. (See Figure 15.2, "One- and Two-Parent Families, by Race.")

The rise in single-parent households is one of the main factors contributing to the growing proportion of children raised in poverty. Between 1973 and 1994 the percentage of U.S. children living in poverty expanded from 14 percent to 22 percent. Families headed by a single parent run a high risk of being poor because they lack the economic resources of dual-earner families. Furthermore, single-parent households are usually headed by women. The earnings gap found in all occupations makes female-headed households especially vulnerable. (Table 15.1 depicts the low median income of female householders when compared to husband–wife families.) In 1994, the poverty rate for female-headed families with children was 44 percent, compared with 8.3 percent for married couple families with children (O'Hare, 1996:19–21). This growing class of families "already encompassing one-quarter of all young children in the United States, has profound implications not only for the future of the nation's poor families but for the society as a whole: its economy, productivity, and the well-being and character of its people" (Bronfenbrenner, et al., 1996:93).

FIGURE 15.2

One- and Two-Parent Families, by Race
Family groups with children under 18, 1993*

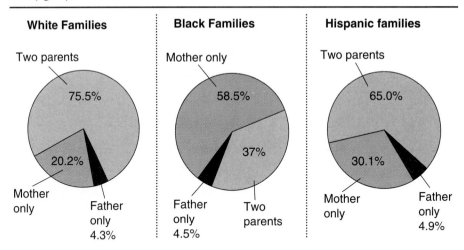

White Families

Two parents
75.5%

Mother only
20.2%

Father only
4.3%

Black Families

Mother only
58.5%

37%

Father only
4.5%

Two parents

Hispanic families

Two parents
65.0%

Mother only
30.1%

Father only
4.9%

*U.S. Census Bureau

Source: Clarifying Issues '96 (New York: Public Agenda), p. 38.

Changing Family Roles

Marriage

Marriage is still very much the norm, with about 90 percent of the population eventually marrying. However, the married adult population has grown much slower than the unmarried adult population. Currently, married persons represent a smaller proportion of adults. In 1992 61 percent of all adults were married, compared with 72 percent in 1970 (U.S. Bureau of the Census, 1992d:v). The decline in marriage has many causes, including new social conditions and lessened social pressures. The declining marriage rate is also partly a function of people marrying later. In 1960, the median age at first marriage was 22.8 years for men and 20.3 years for women. This contrasts with the 1994 statistics of 26.7 years for men and 24.5 years for women (U.S. Bureau of the Census, "Population Profile," 1995a:24). Racial groups differ considerably with respect to marital patterns. Today, White women are the most likely to be married, Black women the least likely, and Hispanic women are in between (McLanahan and Casper, 1995:13).

The continuing decline in marriage rates makes it likely that one in four Black women never will marry and one in ten White or Hispanic women will not marry

(Usdansky, 1992). Economic hardships and demographic trends create different marriage patterns among people of color and Whites. William J. Wilson (1987) has argued that much of the decline in marriage rates in the inner city can be traced to the dearth of African American men capable of supporting families.

Each marriage is the creation of a new social unit. The two members of this social unit—in which the interaction is intense and the feelings intimate—do not, strange as it may seem, always share the same interpretation and reap the same rewards from their shared life. Because marriage is gendered, women and men are assigned different activities that are unequally ranked. This difference is the foundation on which marriage rests. The gender system structures women's and men's life differently. One of the most useful ways of understanding this is Jessie Bernard's concept of "his" and "her" marriages. Bernard's classic work (1972) on marriage revealed that every marital union actually contains two marriages, which do not always coincide.

A fundamental irony about marriage is that single men resist it while single women long for it, yet men benefit much more from marriage than do women. There is strong evidence that while married people are in better physical and emotional health than are nonmarried, husbands benefit more than wives (Gove, Style, and Hughes, 1990; Ross, Mirowski, and Goldstein, 1991). Marriage protects men from death more than it does women (Litwack and Messeri, 1989). It protects their physical health more than it does women's (Bird and Fremont, 1989), and it gives them better psychological well-being (Gove, 1984). Husbands, in general, receive more social support in commitment and caring from their spouses than they return.

In general, women are more attracted to marriage than are men, but once in it they get less out of it than do men. The adverse effects of marriage are strongest for women whose only roles are of wife and mother. The research shows that employed women are physically healthier than are nonemployed women (Waldron and Jacobs, 1988). They have less depression, anxiety, and other forms of psychological distress than do exclusive homemakers (Gove, 1984). However, employed wives perform certain duties that overload their days and create stress. Both housewives and employed wives pay more and gain less in marriage.

Why are the effects of marriage so different for women and men? According to Bernard and other social scientists, this can be explained by the legal, social, and personal changes that take place in women's lives when they become wives. Women are disadvantaged by the dependency, the secondary status, and the uneven responsibilities that marriage brings with it. According to sociologist Arlie Hochschild, traditional gender ideologies lead women to identify with home and family, whereas men identify with work and career (Hochschild, 1989:15). Wives and husbands, even though they live in the same physical space, experience differently the social world of the family.

Roles themselves, as well as how wives and husbands feel about them, can create a vast gulf between spouses. As they go about their separate activities, they may find they have less and less to talk about. This is especially true in blue-collar families, where roles are traditionally segregated. Lack of economic resources makes it difficult for wives and husbands to go out by themselves, and so they spend time with relatives in sex-segregated activities (the men watch a ball game on television while the women prepare meals and watch over children). Leisure time spent in the home includes little real interaction. The following excerpt from Lillian Rubin's classic study of blue-collar families illustrates the separateness of wives and husbands:

> Frank comes home from work; now it's about five, because he's been working overtime every night. We eat right away, right after he comes home. Then, I don't know. The kids play a while before bed, watch t.v., you know, stuff like that. Then, I don't know . . . maybe watch more t.v. or something like that. I don't know what else—nothing, I guess. We just sit, that's all. The husband: I come home at five and we have supper right away. Then, I sit down with coffee and a beer and watch t.v. After that, if I'm working on a project I do that for a while. If not, I just watch t.v. (Rubin, 1973:124)

The quality of marital relationships is strongly influenced by class position. The three positive attributes most frequently mentioned by working-class women in Rubin's study were "He's a steady worker, he doesn't drink, he doesn't hit me" (Rubin, 1973:93). Not one woman in the professional middle-class families mentioned these qualities when answering the same question. They tended to focus on such issues as intimacy, sharing, and communication, and, while expressed in subtle ways, on the comforts, status, and prestige their husbands' occupations afford. E. E. LeMasters (1974:48) comments that one never hears expressions such as "wonderful" or "terrific"—these are simply not part of their marital vocabulary. Instead, they refer to their husbands as being "considerate" or "thoughtful" or "good to me and the children."

Gender differences make communication in intimate relations sometimes difficult (Tannen, 1990). Many frictions arise because boys and girls grow up in what are essentially different cultures. The result is that talk between women and men is cross-gender communication, leading at times to misunderstanding and friction. Deborah Tannen, a sociolinguist, argues that men in conversations seek to dominate, while women seek to connect. Thus, Tannen analyzes a situation with her husband:

> My husband was simply engaging the world in a way that many men do: as an individual in a hierarchical social order in which he was either one-up or one-down. In this world, conversations are negotiations in which people try to achieve and maintain the upper hand if they can, and protect themselves from others' attempts to put them down and push them around. Life, then, is a contest, a struggle to preserve independence and avoid failure. I, on the other hand, was approaching the world as many women do: as an individual in a network of connections. In this world, conversations are negotiations for closeness in which people try to seek and give confirmation and support, and to reach consensus. They try to protect themselves from others' attempts to push them away. Life, then, is a community, a struggle to preserve intimacy and avoid isolation. Though there are hierarchies in this world, too, they are hierarchies more of friendship than of power and accomplishment. Women are also concerned with achieving status and avoiding failure, but these are not the goals they are *focused* on all the time, and they tend to pursue them in the guise of connection. And men are also concerned with achieving involvement and avoiding isolation, but they are not *focused* on these goals, and they tend to pursue them in the guise of opposition. (Tannen, 1990:24–25)

Even though marriages in this society differ in many ways, husbands in all social classes and racial categories generally have greater power than do wives. **Marital power** is the ability to control the spouse and to influence or control family decisions and activities. Important sources of marital power are the resources each spouse brings to the relationship. The most important resource is economic. This resource involves not only income but also status and prestige based on success in the occupational world. Husbands, typically, are the main provider in families; only about 20 percent of two-spouse families have wives as the primary source of income (Conant, 1986). Because of their relative economic clout, husbands have greater power in marriage than do wives. It is important to note, though, that employed wives, even when they make less money than their husbands, have increased say in decision making, have less traditional gender-role ideologies, and have more egalitarian family roles than do nonemployed wives (Beckman and Houser, 1979). This relationship between income and power in marriage is buttressed by the study of more than 7,000 couples by Blumstein and Schwartz (1983:53–59). They found that in three-fourths of the couples the amount of money one partner earns relative to the other establishes relative power in the relationship.

Patriarchal or *traditional* are terms frequently applied to working-class families, and *democratic* or *egalitarian* are terms applied to middle-class families. Many studies have shown that not all working-class or middle-class families conform to these descriptions. In fact, it can be argued that the power advantage of middle-class husbands is greater than that of working-class husbands simply because they possess the resources and the status that can be translated into power. The stereotype of the egalitarian middle-class marriage persists partly because the middle class has a more egalitarian *ideology*. However, the ideology and the actual distribution of power are at odds. As William Goode has observed:

> Lower-class men concede fewer rights ideologically than their women in fact obtain, and the more educated men are more likely to concede more rights ideologically than they in fact grant. (Goode, 1963:21)

Middle-class husbands actually have several sources of power that working-class husbands do not have. Male dominance is legitimated by patriarchy in the larger society. Furthermore, material and professional resources justify control of family decisions and activities. This means that middle-class men can "accept the doctrine of equality without having to live it" (Gillespie, 1972:134).

In sum, husbands tend to have more marital power than do wives. Husbands tend to be the main providers and, by virtue of their gender, age, education, skills, and physical stature, they are advantaged in the marital relationship. Although women tend to have less power, changes are reducing the impact of men's authority in contemporary marriages. More and more wives are in the labor force, which makes them less dependent economically on their husbands and in which they are developing communication and other assertive skills. Second, although clearly in a minority, more and more wives are outperforming their husbands in the occupational world in income and prestige, which gives them power. And third, gender norms are changing in society. Many couples are developing relationships based on egalitarian principles and shared decision making.

Divorce and Remarriage

Even though most people in the United States marry, all marriages do not last forever; some eventually are dissolved. In 1992, 11 percent of all adults age fifteen years and over who had ever been married were currently divorced compared with 4 percent in 1970 (U.S. Bureau of the Census, 1992d:vii). Recent divorce rates show that the chances of a first marriage in the United States ending in divorce are about one in two. One expert (Bumpass, 1990) argues that if current levels persist, 60 percent of recent marriages will end in divorce. The U.S. divorce rate is the world's highest—more than triple the Japanese rate and at least double the divorce rates in the other major industrial democracies except England. (See Table 15.2.)

Many politicians, ministers, editorial writers, and other people have shown great concern over the current high rates of marital dissolution in the United States. Although the present divorce rate is historically near its peak, it is important to recognize that the rate has been rising since at least 1860. Divorce and marital separation are not evenly distributed through the population but vary according to social and economic characteristics. The following are some generalizations about divorce in the United States:

1. Half of all divorces occur during the first seven years of marriage.
2. The younger the age at marriage of the partners, the greater the likelihood of divorce. Martin and Bumpass (1989) conclude that age at first marriage is the

TABLE 15.2

**Divorce Rates
(per Thousand Existing Marriages)
for the Major Industrial Democracies: 1990**

COUNTRY	RATE
United States	21.2
United Kingdom	12.9
Canada	12.9
Sweden	11.7
France	8.5
West Germany	8.3
Japan	5.4
Italy	1.1

Source: House Select Committee on Children, Youth, and Families, reported in *USA Today* (July 9, 1991), p. 1. Copyright 1991 USA Today. Reprinted with permission.

strongest predictor of divorce in the first five years of marriage. "Men and women who are under the age of 20 when they first marry are two to three times more likely to divorce than their counterparts who first marry in their 20s" (Price and McKenry, 1988:17).

3. The lower the income, the greater is the likelihood of divorce. According to the U.S. Bureau of the Census, poor two-parent families are twice as likely to dissolve as are two-parent families not in poverty. Thus, poverty is a major factor contributing to the breakup of families (Pear, 1993:A6).

4. The higher the education for males, the lower the incidence of divorce. In contrast to males, a more complicated pattern is found for women. The highest rate of divorce is found among the least educated women, followed by those with postgraduate degrees. The lowest rates were found for those women with high school and college educations.

5. The divorce patterns for Blacks and Hispanics differ significantly from those of Whites. Data from 1960 through 1992 show African American divorce rates are twice as great as those of Whites and Hispanics (U.S. Bureau of the Census, 1992d:viii).

6. About four out of every five of those persons who obtain a divorce will remarry, with men more likely than women to do so. Some of the many reasons for the increased divorce rate include increased independence (social and financial) of women; economic restructuring that eliminates many jobs for men and makes women's employment necessary; women's inequality; greater tolerance of divorce by religious groups; and reform of divorce laws, especially the adoption of no-fault divorce in many states (that is, one spouse no longer has to prove that the other was at fault in order to obtain a divorce).

Despite changes in public attitudes toward divorce, many social critics persist in seeing family break-up as a main cause of social problems. This is creating a national discussion about divorce reform. Eighteen states are currently exploring legislation to "toughen up" divorce, including a two-tiered system which would make ending marriages in which minor children are involved harder to obtain than those for childless marriages. Although some blame no-fault divorce for the increases in divorce, this ignores the fact that dissolution rates had been increasing before and continued to increase after no-fault was introduced (Kitson, 1996; *U.S. News and World Report,* 1996).

Like marriage, divorce is gendered, resulting in unfair treatment of women and children. Ex-husbands have some major advantages over their ex-wives. They are almost always much better off financially. Typically, they were the major economic producers for their families, and after the separation their incomes stay disproportionately with them. A ten-year study in California, for example, found that men after divorce were much better off than were women (Weitzman, 1985; Peterson, 1996; Weitzman, 1996).

Divorce does not mean a permanent withdrawal from the marriage arena. The United States has the highest remarriage rate in the world (Coleman and Ganog, 1991:193). Most divorced persons remarry—five of six divorced men and three of four divorced women remarry after a divorce. As a result, in 1990 more than one million marriages (46 percent of marriages in the United States that year) were remarriages for one or both partners. The probability of remarriage is affected by four important variables: age, socioeconomic status, race, and religion.

Age is significant for women but not for men. The older a woman at the time of divorce, the lower her chances of remarrying. A greater percentage of men than women remarry, and men are more likely than women to marry soon after divorce. Divorced women who seek remarriage are disadvantaged over men, because the size of the pool of potential male spouses is small. One reason for this shortage in available men is the shorter life expectancy for men than for women. The second and more important reason for this imbalance is the propensity for men to remarry younger women. In a gendered society, men generally gain in property, prestige, and power as they age. Therefore, they tend to retain or even enhance their attractiveness to women as they age. These differences in the attraction patterns by sex and age result in a great imbalance in eligible marriage partners, as most men marry younger women, and women must therefore marry older men.

The race of the divorced who remarry is a significant factor, with Blacks taking longer to remarry, if they do at all. Divorced White women wait an average of 26.5 months to remarry; Hispanic women, 29.9 months; Black women, 38.3 months (Dunn, 1991). Put another way, "although three-quarters of separating white women are likely to remarry, less than half of separating black women are likely to do so" (Bumpass, Sweet, and Martin, 1990:753).

Remarriage may solve the economic problems of single-parent families by adding a male income. It may also relieve the many burdens of running a household alone. Remarriage also frequently involves blending together two families into one, a process complicated by the absence of clear-cut ground rules for how to accomplish the merger. Families formed by remarriages can become quite complex, with children from the spouses' previous marriages and/or from the new marriage, along with numerous sets of grandparents, step-grandparents, and other kin and quasi-kin (Cherlin and Furstenburg, 1983:8).

The Worlds of Work and Family

Changes in families are closely related to changes in the workplace. The institutions of the economy and the family are linked together in many ways. The economy provides jobs with varying amounts of social status and economic resources for the family and in this way sets limits on its standard of living. The family supplies skilled workers to the economy. Jobs impose different constraints on families, such as the amount of time spent working and the scheduling of work, which determine the amount of time workers can spend with their families. In addition, work has psychological costs and benefits that influence family interaction. Extensive research on work and family in recent years has given us new information on how these "greedy institutions" operate. We know that most working women and men are experiencing a "time famine" for their families and that family and personal time is more prized than at any other time in history.

The most fundamental change affecting U.S. families is the increase in mothers' employment. Women's labor-force participation has been going up since the beginning of the twentieth century. In the early part of the century, the increase occurred primarily among young unmarried women. After 1940 married women began entering the labor force in greater numbers and, after 1960, married mothers with children at home followed suit. In the early 1950s, only about 30 percent of married mothers with school-aged children worked outside the home. By 1990, the number had risen to over 73 percent. In just four short decades, a behavior that once described only a minority of mothers now fits a large majority of mothers, and this was true of mothers of all marital statuses (McLanahan and Casper, 1995:12–13). (See Figure 15.3.) Nearly 70 percent of children age six have a mother who works outside of the home.

Families with two working parents or a single parent who works are the dominant family patterns. One out of every five families is headed by a single woman who works. The new standard, however, is the two *working-parent* family (Hulbert, 1993:27). Employed mothers in two-earner families contribute about 40 percent of household income, while fathers contribute about 67 percent (Gallinsky and Bond, 1996:87). The rise in employed mothers has introduced new tensions between work and family. A national survey of working parents (*The National Study of the Changing Workforce*) conducted in the early nineties found that employed mothers are more dissatisfied with their work and family lives than employed fathers. By their self-reports, employed mothers are more stressed, coping less effectively in their lives, more burned out by their jobs, less satisfied with their marital relations, and less satisfied with themselves as parents. Furthermore, the survey found that mothers "assume

FIGURE 15.3

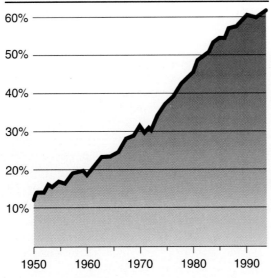

Percentage of Married Working Women with Children Under 6, 1950–1994*

*Bureau of Labor Statistics

Source: Clarifying Issues '96 (New York: Public Agenda), p. 27.

more family responsibilities than do men. Among wage-and-salary workers with children, women and men agree that the lion's share of the responsibility for maintaining the household belongs to women" (Gallinsky and Bond, 1996:80).

This gendered and uneven relationship of work and family or "the **work-family role system**" (Pleck, 1977) reinforces traditional division of labor in both work and family. Although more and more wives share the provider role, husbands do not often share the family labor. For wives, this produces a second work shift. In her study of working families, sociologist Arlie Hochschild found enormous conflicts between work and family. (See "Research Methods: Researching Families.") Women were much more deeply torn between the demands of work and family than were their husbands. The additional hours that working women put on the **second shift** of housework, she calculated, add up to an extra month of work each year. Even though social class is important in determining how the household labor gets done (more affluent families can afford to purchase more labor-saving services), Hochschild has found that social class, race/ethnicity, and personality give limited clues about who does and does not share the second shift. Gender is paramount. This finding is repeated in study after study.

Child care, one of the most fundamental problems for children of employed parents, remains unsolved. In general, U.S. society is unresponsive to the needs of working parents. The traditional organization of work—an inflexible eight-hour workday—makes it difficult for parents to cope with family problems or with the conflicting schedules of family members. Many European countries have some form of flexitime arrangement in which workers can meet their family and work obligations; but in the United States only about one in six employees has such an opportunity. Similarly, several European countries provide for paid leaves (for a specified number of days) to care for a sick child and for paternity leave for fathers as well.

Until the passage of the Family and Medical Leave Act in 1993, the United States lacked any policy that would help families function well in contemporary so-

Although more and more wives share the provider role, husbands do not often share the family labor.

Research Methods

Researching Families: How Sociologist Arlie Hochschild Interviewed Couples about the Demands of Work and Family

With my research associates Anne Machung and Elaine Kaplan, I interviewed fifty couples very intensively, and I observed in a dozen homes. We first began interviewing artisans, students, and professionals in Berkeley, California, in the late 1970s. This was at the height of the women's movement, and many of these couples were earnestly and self-consciously struggling to modernize the ground rules of their marriages. Enjoying flexible job schedules and intense cultural support to do so, many succeeded. Since their circumstances were unusual they became our "comparison group" as we sought other couples more typical of mainstream America. In 1980 we located more typical couples by sending a questionnaire on work and family life to every thirteenth name—from top to bottom—of the personnel roster of a large, urban manufacturing company. At the end of the questionnaire, we asked members of working couples raising children under six and working full time jobs if they would be willing to talk to us in greater depth. Interviewed from 1980 through 1988, these couples, their neighbors and friends, their children's teachers, daycare workers and baby-sitters, form the heart of this book. . . .

We also talked with other men and women who were not part of two-job couples; divorced parents who were war-weary veterans of two-job marriages, and traditional couples, to see how much of the strain we were seeing was unique to two-job couples.

I also watched daily life in a dozen homes during a weekday evening, during the week-end, and during the months that followed, when I was invited on outings, to dinner, or just to talk. I found myself waiting on the front doorstep as weary parents and hungry children tumbled out of the family car. I shopped with them, visited friends, watched television, ate with them, walked through parks, and came along when they dropped their children at daycare, often staying on at the baby-sitter's house after parents waved good-bye. In their homes, I sat on the living-room floor and drew pictures and played house with the children. I watched as parents gave them baths, read bedtime stories, and said good night. Most couples tried to bring me into the family scene, inviting me to eat with them and talk. I responded if they spoke to me, from time to time asked questions, but I rarely initiated conversations. I tried to become as unobtrusive as a family dog. Often I would base myself in the living room, quietly taking notes. Sometimes I would follow a wife upstairs or down, accompany a child on her way out to "help Dad" fix the car, or watch television with the other watchers. Sometimes I would break out of my peculiar role to join in the jokes they often made about acting like the "model" two-job couple. Or perhaps the joking was a subtle part of my role, to put them at ease so they could act more naturally. For a period of two to five years, I phoned or visited these couples to keep in touch even as I moved on to study the daily lives of other working couples—black, Chicano, white, from every social class and walk of life.

I asked who did how much of a wide variety of household tasks. I asked who cooks? Vacuums? Makes the beds? Sews? Cares for plants? Sends Christmas or Hanukkah cards? I also asked: Who washes the car? Repairs household appliances? Does the taxes? Tends the yard? I asked who did most household planning, who noticed such things as when a child's fingernails need clipping, cared more how the house looked or about the change in a child's mood.

Source: Arlie Hochschild with Anne Machung, *The Second Shift.* New York: Viking Penguin, 1989, pp. 4–6.

ciety. The new family and medical leave law requires employers of fifty or more people to provide twelve weeks of unpaid leave to any worker who has a medical emergency or needs to care for an adopted or newborn child or a seriously ill child, spouse, or parent.

Children and Adolescents

Family changes have profoundly affected children. During the last two decades, youth in the United States experienced the most rapid deterioration in economic and social conditions since the Depression. In the last twenty years, child and young poverty rose by 60 percent. Youth are, by far, our poorest age group. One in four is impoverished, twice the rate among other groups. Although this society purports to value children, the United States ranks first in child poverty. Welfare reform and other social disinvestment policies will increase the ranks of poor children (Males, 1993:18; Males, 1996).

Child poverty is clearly linked to the changes in family structure discussed in this chapter. A child's likelihood of experiencing poverty during the formative years is partially determined by the type of family he or she lives in. The rise is often linked to the surge in families headed by single women. However, the rise in mother-only families is but one factor contributing to higher poverty rates. Poverty has also increased significantly for young families with children. Young parents, whether living alone or as married couples, are especially vulnerable to poverty because they are likely to have less job experience than older workers. Because they have less job experience than older workers, they are often the first to lose their jobs during economic downturns (O'Hare, 1996:19–20).

Family changes affect children and adolescents in other ways as well. Most children are now raised in families where mothers and fathers work away from home. Two important implications of this are: (1) that children now spend less time with their parents and more time with other adult caregivers; and (2) the rise in latchkey children. These factors can combine to loosen the bond between parents and their children as their interaction decreases. Eleven million preschool children whose mothers work spend their days in child care supervised by adults other than their parents (Labich, 1991). Fifteen million U.S. children are growing up without fathers, a rate twice that of a generation ago (Davidson, 1990). Family interaction has decreased. Intact families eat fewer meals together than was true in the past, and fewer engage in family activities. Watching television, often in separate parts of the house, has diminished the number and quality of conversations among family members. So too have video games, personal computers, and personal stereos with headsets. The results for some people are attenuated family relationships and adverse outcomes for infants, children, and adolescents (Hamburg, 1993). Other parents and children manage well even with these deficits in interaction time.

A number of work-related factors affect parents and their interactions with children (the following is adapted from Baca Zinn and Eitzen, 1993a:318). When both parents work, preschool children will be cared for by someone other than the parents. Once the child is of school age, the school (that is, teachers, policies, and curriculum) becomes an important socialization agent, sometimes in opposition to the wishes of the parents. Peers become increasingly important to youth, especially in adolescence, and they often have a profound influence on their values and behaviors.

Religious ideology can become salient, and again this may not always be congruent with the ideology of parents (as evidenced by the attempts by parents to deprogram children they feel have been brainwashed by religious cults). Media's depictions of violence, sexual mores, recreational drugs, alternative lifestyles, and social issues such as abortion, war, evolution, and capital punishment may persuade or provide justifications for some youth to choose ways different from their parents. The most crucial outside variable, however, is social class (Bronfenbrenner, et al., 1996:123). The amount of economic resources available to a family and the degree of esteem the family members receive from others outside the family are of ultimate importance to the child's well-being, self-concept, and opportunities.

Most basically, social-class position provides for the child's life chances. The greater the family's economic resources, the better the chance to live past infancy, to be in good health, to receive a good education, to have a satisfying job, to avoid being labeled a criminal, to avoid death in war, and to live the good life. Negatively, this means that millions of the nation's children are denied these advantages because they were born to parents who were unemployed, underemployed, stuck in the lower tier of the segmented labor market, disabled, victims of institutional racism or sexism, divorced or separated, or otherwise disadvantaged.

Significantly, the family's resources and educational achievements affect how children perceive themselves. These ascribed characteristics (along with race/ethnicity and gender) place children in the perceptions of others, which in turn give children an understanding of their worth. If they have favored characteristics, they are likely to gain nourishment from the social power and esteem that come from high social position. But the children of the poor and minorities find they are devalued by persons outside the immediate family and kin network, which can have a profound effect on their psyches and behavior regardless of the efforts of their parents (Kagan, 1977:35).

About 13 percent of the total population is between the ages of thirteen and nineteen years. This is a very significant category in U.S. society, for several reasons. First, teenagers are a strong economic force. For example, they account for a sizable proportion of CD and tape sales and constitute an important movie audience. Collectively, they spend an enormous amount of money on clothes and toiletries. As they shift from fad to fad, fortunes are made and lost in the clothing and entertainment industries.

The rise of a service economy has produced a new demand for service workers. This trend has recently begun to capture the attention of family researchers. By the 1980s, three out of four high school seniors were working an average of eighteen hours a week and bringing home more than $200 a month. Their earnings went mostly to discretionary items such as cars, stereos, clothing, concert tickets, and drugs. Researchers at the University of Michigan found that less than 11 percent of high school seniors save all or most of their earnings for long-term purposes. This has created for many a "premature" affluence, an unrealistic level of discretionary income that is impossible to maintain at college unless they have extravagant parents (Woodward, 1990:57).

The stage of adolescence in U.S. society is a period of stress and strain for many teens. The most important reason is that it is an age of transition from one social status to another. There is no clear line of demarcation between adolescence and adulthood. Are people considered adult when they can get a full-time job, when they are physically capable of producing children, or when they can be drafted for military service? Conversely, are they still adolescents when they continue to live at home with their parents as more than one-fifth of 25 year olds did in 1995 (Mogelesky,

1996)? There is no clear distinction between adolescence and childhood. Unlike pre-modern societies which have rites of passage serving to identify the individual as a child or an adult, adulthood in U.S. society is unclear. Surely much of the acting out by adolescents in the United States can be at least partially explained by these status ambiguities.

The Aged

The population of the United States is increasingly older:

- In colonial times, the median age was 16. In 1900, it was 23. By 1990, it had risen to 33 years, twice that of 1800. By 2020, the median age is expected to be 38 rising to 39 in 2030 (Treas and Torrecilha, 1995:49).
- In 1900, the average life expectancy was 49 years of age. In 1990, it was 75.6 years. As the population has grown older, the older population has grown, too. The 1870 Census of Population reported about one million people aged 65 and over out of a total population of 39 million. The 1990 Census of Population counted over 31 million older people out of 249 million. So many Americans are old that the membership of the American Association of Retired Persons (AARP) exceeds that of all religious bodies except the Roman Catholic Church (Treas and Torrecilha, 1995:49–50).

There are several important implications in the trend toward an increasingly elderly population in the United States. First, this trend means that an ever-larger number of people are moving into a devalued, stigmatized, and oppressed social category. To be old in U.S. society is to be considered unnecessary because one is a nonproducer in a society that values productivity. This newly acquired devalued status by an individual often has negative consequences for self-esteem and may lead to depression, withdrawal from social relationships, and confusion over role expectations.

A second ramification of the aging trend involves the financial burden on the old and the nonold. Typically, when people retire from work, they must lower their expenditures because their Social Security and other pension benefits are significantly less than were their wages. Many elderly persons and couples must now live in near-poverty or poverty conditions. Widows are especially disadvantaged because of a bias in the Social Security system—a widow receives 82.5 percent of her deceased husband's benefits. The marginal financial status of the elderly is alleviated sometimes by their children, who supplement their parents' income with contributions or who invite the parents to move in with them. In either case, the family is affected by the lowering of discretionary income or by the disruption of family patterns through the intrusion of new members in the home.

Most significant, the increasing numbers of elderly will place a tremendous burden on the younger generation to finance their retirement. This is the result of a major shift in the dependency ratio—the number of workers compared with the number of Social Security recipients. In 1960 this ratio was 5 to 1, but it will drop to 2 to 1 by the year 2035. This demographic fact increases the financial burden progressively onto the workers, which may have either of two consequences. On the one hand, the ever-higher taxes on workers to finance Social Security will reduce the workers' level of affluence and increase their hostility toward the aged. On the other, political agitation by workers may reduce their taxes and the benefits to the elderly, further lowering the incomes of the elderly and increasing their ill will toward the young.

An ever-aging population has a third consequence: it affects marital relationships in several fundamental ways. An obvious result is that the longer people live, the greater the likelihood that marriage will end in divorce or separation. Several generations ago the average marriage ended with the death of one spouse (usually the wife because of complications during childbirth) after only twenty years of marriage or so. Now, the average couple could live twenty to thirty years after the last child leaves home. Obviously, with couples increasing their potential living time together from twenty to fifty years, the potential for marital conflict and an eventual rift is enhanced.

Marital relationships are also affected by women outliving men by an average of seven years. This means not only that there are five times as many widows as widowers but also that elderly women will have fewer chances than elderly men to remarry.

Another consequence of the graying of the country also has an impact on the family—the longer life expectancy has made grandparents a regular part of children's growing up (Cherlin and Furstenberg, 1994). The four-generation family is now relatively commonplace as more than one-half of all persons sixty-five and over have great-grandchildren (Shanas, 1980). The elderly today tend to live apart from their children, although there are strong ties with them, frequent interaction, and help in times of difficulty.

Violence in Families

The family has two faces. On the positive side, it is a haven from an uncaring, impersonal world, a place where love and security prevail. The family members love each other, care for each other, and accept each other under all circumstances. However, there is another side to the family. The presence of tension and discord can be found in all families at various phases in the family life cycle. The intensity that characterizes intimate relationships can give way to conflict. Some families resolve the inevitable tensions that arise in the course of daily living, but in other families conflict gives way to violence.

Although the family is based on love among its members, the way it is organized encourages conflict. The family, like all other social organizations, is a power system; that is, power is unequally distributed between parents and children and between spouses. Parents have authority over their children. They feel they have the right to punish children in order to shape them in the ways they consider important. It is essential to see violence in the broader social context of power relations. A feminist perspective views violence as a symptom of a greater problem—that is, a systematic set of gendered structures that produce violence against women

(Breines and Gordon, 1983). Gender differences may not present a problem in some homes, but for many couples these problems can become a constant source of stress.

Unlike most organizations in which activities and interests are relatively narrow, the family encompasses almost everything. Thus, there are more "events" over which a dispute can develop. Closely related to this phenomenon, there is a vast amount of time during each day when family members can interact. This lengthy interaction increases the probability of disagreements, irritations, violations of privacy, and the like, which increase the risk of violence.

Family privacy is another characteristic that enhances the likelihood of violence. The rule in our society that the home is private has two negative consequences. First, it insulates the family members from the protection that society could provide if a family member gets too abusive. And second, the rule of privacy often prevents the victims of abuse from seeking outside help.

Violence in the family presents the ultimate paradox—the physical abuse of loved ones in the most intimate of social relationships. The bonds between wife and husband, parent and child, and adult child and parent are based on love, yet for many people these bonds represent a trap in which they are victims of unspeakable abuses.

Although it is impossible to know the extent of battering that takes place in families, the problem these forms of violence represent is not trivial. The threat of violence in intimate relationships exists for all couples and for parents and children. For people who do not cope well, the result is the abuse by the strong of the weak. But violence in the family is not only a problem of family units. It represents an indictment of society, its institutions, and the cultural norms that support violence.

The Modern Family from the Order and the Conflict Perspectives

From the order perspective, biology and social needs combine to produce a nuclear family that is well-suited to modern society. This arrangement separates men and women into distinctive roles. Biologically, men are stronger and women bear and nurse children. These facts have meant that men have been the providers, and women have "naturally" dealt with child-rearing and family nurturance. With industrialization, the family with women as nurturers and caretakers became more important than ever before. This situation created stable families and an efficient role system, with boys and girls trained throughout their youth to take their places in society. This image of the family became the dominant sociological framework in the 1950s and 1960s. It was based on a single-family type—more statistically prevalent in the 1950s than today, but by no means the only family form even then—and generalized to the family. Talcott Parsons and Robert Bales, et al. (1955), defined the family as a particular set of people (a married couple and their children) filling two central functions (socialization of children and emotional support) with a fixed division of labor (a stay-at-home, nurturing mother and a breadwinning father). This then became known as "the normal family" (Boss and Thorne,

1989:79). According to this view, the family operates most effectively when a division of labor is present in the nuclear family. Women fill the "expressive" or emotional roles of providing affection and support, while men fill the "instrumental" roles that provide economic support by working outside of the family.

In the order perspective, families provide a haven from the harsh outside world of work and the marketplace. The nuclear family is the bedrock of society in an achievement-oriented world. The family fits with other social institutions and contributes to social order.

The argument that changes in the family are destroying the country's social fabric is an outgrowth of the order perspective. "Family values" is a way of distinguishing the two-parent family from all other family arrangements. This ignores the invisible social forces that create diverse families.

From the conflict perspective, the family is a product of social structure. Different family arrangements emerge out of social and economic conditions. At the macro level, the family is a vital part of the capitalist economy because it produces both workers and consumers to keep the economy going. The family is one of the primary mechanisms for perpetuating social inequality. Wealth is locked up in elite families and then passed down through intergenerational inheritance. This limits the resources and opportunities of those who are lower in the socioeconomic hierarchy. As we have seen, families pass on their advantages and disadvantages to their offspring. While this transmission of social-class position promotes stability in society—which the order theorists cherish—it also promotes inequality based on *ascribed status*.

The family serves the requirements of capitalism in another way—by idealizing the realm of the personal. This serves the economy through heightened consumerism, and it also supports the interests of the dominant class by promoting false consciousness. The family is one of the primary socialization agents of youth, and as such it promotes the status quo by transmitting the culture of society. Children are taught to accept the inequalities of society as natural, and they are taught to accept the political and economic systems without question.

The family, from the conflict perspective, is not the haven posited by the order theorists. Family relations are not simply matters of love and agreement, but political arrangements as well. What is thought to be a private relationship of love is really a social relationship of power. At the micro level, conflict is generated by (1) female resistance to male domination and (2) the demands of work and economic hardships that work against intimacy and companionship between spouses. Thus, the modern family is not a tranquil institution, but one fraught with potential and actual conflict.

Conflict theorists argue that the nuclear family has positive consequences for capitalism, but can be negative for individuals (Zaretsky, 1976). The economic system benefits when employers are able to move individuals from place to place without great disruption. The economy is served when employers do not have to worry about satisfying the emotional needs of workers. Finally, the system benefits when the family is isolated and therefore cannot affect society.

This system has negative consequences for individuals, the conflict theorists maintain, because the family has sole responsibility for maintaining a private refuge from an impersonal society and for providing personal fulfillment, and is thus structured to fail. The demands are too great. The family, alone, cannot provide for all the emotional needs of its members, although its members try to fulfill these needs through consumerism, leisure, and family fun. Conflict theorists argue that society should be restructured so that personal fulfillment is met not only in the family but also in the community, at work, and in the other institutions of society.

Families of the Future

We have examined a number of trends that characterize contemporary families. Many of these trends have important implications for the future of families. Some of the most important are:

- The majority of married couples have both spouses in the work force.
- The majority of mothers with preschool children are in the work force.
- There are more families without children at home than there are with children at home.
- One out of every five children is born to an unwed mother.
- Over 60 percent of children will spend some time in a single-parent household before they are eighteen.
- Without national policy changes, children in single-parent households will face diminished life chances as rates of child poverty rise.
- More and more married couples are separated geographically on a semipermanent basis, not because of incompatibility but because their careers require working in separate locations.
- At least half of all the marriages begun in the 1980s and after will end in divorce.
- Most divorced persons remarry, expanding kin networks for their children.
- One out of twenty households headed by a couple is a co-habitating household. Thirty percent of these households include at least one child.
- Alternative household forms, including heterosexual and homosexual unions, will continue to redefine traditional and legal definitions of kinship and family. (See "Diversity: Why Family Issues Matter for Lesbians and Gays.")

These differing patterns lead to the conclusion that variation is typical rather than that there is a typical U.S. family. Most significant, at the personal level most of us have been and will be participants in a variety of family forms as we move through the life cycle. This is not only the case for individuals but also for individual families, for they, too, will change forms as members enter and leave and work situations change.

Mutually supportive and loving relationships are possible in any family form. In fact, intimate relationships may be enhanced as a particular nontraditional form suits the unique personal, social, and economic needs of its members.

As we move toward the new century, many different family arrangements will exist together with traditional family forms and in this way will contribute to the diversity and flexibility of the family.

Diversity

Why Family Issues Matter for Lesbians and Gays

What is a family? According to opinion polls, a majority of Americans understand family as a group of people who love one another and take care of each other in good times and bad.

What is a family? In the hands of the radical Christian Right, it has become a symbol and a weapon. A symbol of an imagined past when everything was just fine. A weapon that divides people into categories of good or bad, moral or immoral, productive citizen or irresponsible parasite. The allegedly "pro-family" rhetoric of the radical right is deeply homophobic and antifeminist, and exploits historically powerful racist stereotypes.

What is a family? For lesbians and gay men, family has become the frontier issue in our struggle for freedom, justice, and respect. Everywhere we look, family issues are surfacing—in the courts, in state legislatures, in workplaces, in the schools, in communities of faith, in the activities of our community centers and other organizations. Sometimes, picking up a copy of a gay newspaper, nothing but family issues of one sort or another seem to fill its pages.

It wasn't always so. When I was first coming out in the late sixties, as a college student influenced by the hippie counterculture and the first wave of radical feminist theory, "family" was something I could do without. It seemed that my only choices were to have a family, which meant my family of origin, or to be gay, which meant exile and escape from the constrictions of a heterosexist institution.

So why does family seem so important to us in the 1990s? Is the concern for family simply a defensive, reactive move on our part, a knee-jerk response to the "traditional family values" rhetoric of the Radical Christian Right? Or does the rise of family issues tell us something about how we have changed and what we want?

I think it's the latter. There are good reasons growing out of the history of our movement and communities that have pushed family issues to the front burner.

One has to do with growing diversity of the public face of our movement and our community organizations. Lesbians, for instance, have often taken the lead in campaigns involving custody, adoption, and our right to be parents. Lesbians and gays of color have spoken and written passionately of the importance of strong, extended family ties for the survival of their home communities in the face of racism, and of their unwillingness to have to choose between family ties or their sexual identity. As gays and lesbians in smaller communities come out of the closet and organize for change, family is something just around the corner, not something to escape from.

Family issues challenge homophobia in new and important ways. One of the most destructive and persistent stereotypes used to perpetuate hatred against us and keep us isolated and separated is the claim that we are a danger to children. The gay man who molests children, or the lesbian teacher who corrupts her students, have been common cultural myths. As more and more parents come out of the closet and assert their right to keep their children, as more and more of us choose to have children even after coming out, we force the issue of queers and children in proactive ways.

Parents are becoming front-line activists in institutions that reach into the lives of most Americans. Take public schools, for instance. As the children of openly gay or lesbian parents make their way through the public schools, these parents have to confront the insidious effects of homophobia in compelling ways. Will the schools, through their curriculum, be teaching these children to hate their parents? Will these children be the targets of ridicule, ostracism, and harassment? What must parents do to protect the integrity of their family relationships and to keep their children from harm? The actions they take—whether at parent-teacher conferences, at PTA meetings, or in one-on-one conversations with parents of their children's friends, is the stuff of permanent grassroots social change.

Family issues matter. Whether it be the public rituals we create to celebrate our committed relationships or our decisions to have children in our lives, the articulation of a lesbian and gay "family politics" has the power to move our freedom struggle forward.

Source: John D'Emilio, "Commentary: What is a Family?" *Sociologists' Lesbian and Gay Caucus Newsletter* (Summer, 1996), pp. 3–4.

CHAPTER REVIEW

1. The family is one of the most idealized and mythologized of all of society's institutions. New sociological research has given us a better understanding of the U.S. family in the past and present.

2. Families are embedded in class and race hierarchies. This gives them different connections with institutions that can provide resources for family support. It also creates variation in household and family structure. Class and race are important determinants of the quality of family life.

3. The changing nature of work has a direct impact on the family in several significant ways: (*a*) as the need for skilled labor has diminished, many blue-collar families have experienced unemployment or underemployment; (*b*) having both spouses work outside the home has become an economic necessity for many families; and (*c*) some forms of work have moved into the home with mixed consequences for women.

4. About one-fourth of all households with children are single-parent families; more than one-half of all Black families, one-third of Hispanic families, and one-fifth of White families are in this category. In 90 percent of the cases these families are headed by women. Single-parent families have a number of unique problems, the most prominent one being a lack of economic resources.

5. Twenty-two percent of all children in the United States live in poverty.

6. Although work and family are interdependent, husbands give priority to jobs over families, and employed wives give priority to families over their jobs. Gender inequality in the larger society reinforces the gendered family. Women and men experience the family in different ways, and men benefit more than women from family arrangements.

7. The family is not a tranquil institution, but one fraught with potential and actual conflict. Families are a major setting for violence in this society.

8. The divorce rate in U.S. society is the highest in the world. The reasons for this high rate are poverty, increased social and financial independence of women, increased affluence, greater tolerance of divorce by religious groups, passage of no-fault divorce laws, and a change toward leniency in the public attitude toward divorce.

9. Adolescence is a difficult time in U.S. society for many young people and their parents. The fundamental reason for this is that adolescents are in a transitional stage between childhood and adulthood, with no clear distinction to indicate when adulthood is reached.

10. The aged also experience ambivalence because they are in a transitional stage between work and death. Moreover, they are the objects of discrimination in a youth-oriented society.

11. Order theorists view the family as a source of stability for individuals and society. The traditional division of labor by sex contributes to social order.

12. Conflict theorists argue that the traditional family supports the economy but is detrimental to individuals. The family is a major source of false consciousness and the primary agent by which the system of social stratification is perpetuated.

13. A number of trends indicate that the United States will continue to change; for example, the high divorce rate, the rising number of childless marriages, and the fact that the fastest-growing family type is the female-headed household.

KEY TERMS

Family values

Family

Household

Life chances

Downward mobility

Modern family

Postmodern family

Nonfamily household

Single-person household

Marital power

Work-family role system

Second shift

STUDY QUESTIONS

1. What are the myths about U.S. families?
2. What is the relationship between the economy and family patterns?
3. Explain the statement: Families are embedded in class and race hierarchies. What are the consequences of this fact for family life?
4. Explain how family and work are interconnected.
5. What are the consequences for families of an aging population?
6. Contrast the differing views of families by order and conflict theorists.

FOR FURTHER READING

Dennis A. Ahlburg and Carol J. De Vita, *New Realities of the American Family* (Washington, DC: Population Reference Bureau. August, 1992.)

Maxine Baca Zinn and D. Stanley Eitzen, *Diversity in Families,* 4th ed. (New York: Harper Collins, 1996).

Stephanie Coontz, *The Way We Never Were: American Families and the Nostalgia Trap* (New York: Basic Books, 1992).

Arlie Hochschild, *The Second Shift* (New York: Viking, 1989).

Demi Kurz, *For Richer, For Poorer: Mothers Confront Divorce* (New York: Routledge, 1995).

Sara McLanahan and Gary Sandefur, *Growing Up With a Single Parent: What Hurts, What Helps* (Cambridge: Harvard University Press, 1994).

Lillian Breslow Rubin, *Families on the Fault Line: America's Working Class Speaks about the Family, the Economy, Race, and Ethnicity* (New York: Basic Books, 1994).

Judith Stacey, *Brave New Families* (New York: Basic Books, 1994).

Ronald L. Taylor, *Minority Families in the United States: A Multicultural Perspective* (Englewood Cliffs, NJ: Prentice-Hall, 1994).

Barrie Thorne, with Marilyn Yalom, *Rethinking the Family: Some Feminist Questions,* 2nd ed. (Boston: Northeastern University Press, 1992).

CHAPTER 16

Education

On an average morning in Chicago, about 5,700 children in 190 classrooms come to school only to find they have no teacher. Victimized by endemic funding shortages, the system can't afford sufficient substitutes to take the place of missing teachers. . . .

The odds these [mostly] black kids in Chicago face are only slightly worse than those faced by low-income children all over America. Children like these will be the parents of the [future]. Many of them will be unable to earn a living and fulfill the obligations of adults; they will see their families disintegrate, their children lost to drugs and destitution. When we later condemn them for "parental failings," as we inevitably will do, we may be forced to stop and remember how we also failed them in the first years of their lives.

It is commonplace that a society reveals its reverence or contempt for history by the respect or disregard that it displays for older people. The way we treat our children tells us something of the future we envision. The willingness of the nation to relegate so many of these poorly housed and poorly fed and poorly educated children to the role of outcasts in a rich society is going to come back to haunt us.*

Introduction

This chapter is divided into four sections. The first describes the characteristics of U.S. education. The second focuses on how corporate society reproduces itself through education—in particular, how the schools socialize youth in accordance with their class position and point them toward factory, bureaucratic, or leadership roles in the economy. The third section describes the current role of education in perpetuating inequality in society. The final section summarizes the chapter by looking at education from the order and the conflict perspectives.

The Characteristics of U.S. Education

Education as a Conserving Force

The formal system of education in U.S. society (and in all societies) is conservative, since the avowed function of the schools is to teach newcomers the attitudes, values, roles, specialties, and training necessary to the maintenance of society. In other words, the special task of the schools is to preserve the culture, not to transform it. Thus, the schools indoctrinate their pupils in the culturally prescribed ways. Children are taught to be patriotic. They learn the myths, the superiority of their nation's heritage, who are the heroes and who are the villains. Jules Henry has put it this way:

> Since education is always against some things and for others, it bears the burden of the cultural obsessions. While the Old Testament extols without cease the glory of the One God, it speaks with equal emphasis against the gods of the Philistines; while the children of the Dakota Indians learned loyalty to their own tribe, they learned to hate the Crow; and while our children are taught to love American democracy, they are taught contempt for the totalitarian regimes. (Henry, 1963:285–286)

There is always an explicit or implicit assumption in U.S. schools that the American way is the only really right way. When this assumption is violated on the primary and secondary school level by the rare teacher who asks students to consider the viability of world government, or who proposes a class on the life and teachings of Karl Marx or about world religions, then strong enough pressures usually occur from within the school (administrators, school board) or from without (parents, the American Legion, Daughters of the American Revolution) to quell the disturbance. As a consequence, creativity and a questioning attitude are curtailed in school, as Parenti points out forcefully:

> Among the institutions . . . our educational system looms as one of the more influential purveyors of dominant values. From the earliest school years, children are taught

to compete individually rather than work cooperatively for common goals and mutual benefit. Grade-school students are fed stories of their nation's exploits that might be more valued for their inspirational nationalism than for their historical accuracy. Students are instructed to believe in America's global virtue and moral superiority and to fear and to hold a rather uncritical view of American politico-economic institutions. One nationwide survey of 12,000 children (grades two to eight) found that most youngsters believe "the government and its representatives are wise, benevolent and infallible, that whatever the government does is for the best."

The study found that teachers concentrate on the formal aspects of representative government and accord scant attention to the influences that wealthy, powerful groups exercise over political life. Teachers in primary and secondary schools who wish to introduce radical critiques of American politico-economic institutions do so often at the risk of jeopardizing their careers. High school students who attempt to sponsor unpopular speakers and explore controversial views in student newspapers have frequently been overruled by administrators and threatened with disciplinary action.

School texts at the elementary, high-school, and even college levels seldom give more than passing mention to the history of labor struggle and the corporate exploitation of working people at home and abroad. Almost nothing is said of the struggles of Native Americans, indentured servants, small farmers, and Latino, Asian, and European immigrant labor. The history of resistance to slavery, racism, and U.S. expansionist wars is largely untaught in American schools at any level. (Parenti, 1995:35)*

Mass Education

People in the United States have a basic faith in education. This faith is based on the assumption that a democratic society requires an educated citizenry so that individuals can participate in the decisions of public policy. It is for this reason that they not only provide education for all citizens, but also compel children to go at least to the eighth grade or until age sixteen (although this varies somewhat from state to state).

Surely all children should be compelled to attend school, since it should be for their own good. After all, the greater the educational attainment, the greater the likelihood of larger economic rewards and upward social mobility. However, to compel a child to attend school for six hours a day, five days a week, forty weeks a year, for at least ten years, is quite a demand. The result is that many students are in school for the wrong reason. The motivation is compulsion, not interest in acquiring skills or curiosity about their world. This involuntary feature of U.S. schools is unfortunate because so many school problems are related to the lack of student interest.

As a result of the goal of and commitment to mass education, an increasing proportion of persons have received a formal education. In 1940, for example, 38 percent of the people in the United States aged twenty-five to twenty-nine years had completed high school. This proportion increased to 74 percent in 1970 and 86 percent in 1990 (U.S. Bureau of the Census, 1991c:4).

Local Control of Education

Although the state and federal governments finance and control education in part, the bulk of the money and control for education comes from local communities. There is a general fear of centralization of education—into a statewide educational system or, even worse, federal control. Local school boards (and the communities themselves) jealously guard their autonomy. Because, as it is commonly argued, local people know best the special needs of their children, local boards control allocation of monies, curricular content, and the rules for running the schools, as well as the hiring and firing of personnel.

There are several problems with this emphasis on local control. First, tax money from the local area traditionally finances the schools. Whether the tax base is strong or weak has a pronounced effect on the quality of education received (a point we return to later in this chapter). Second, local taxes are almost the only outlet for a taxpayers' revolt. Dissatisfaction with high taxes (federal, state, and local) on income, property, and purchases is often expressed at the local level in defeated school bonds and school tax levies. A current population trend increases the likelihood of the defeat of school issues—families with school-age children declined from 46.3 percent of the U.S. population in 1950 to 34.6 percent in 1990 (M. J. Barrett, 1993). Third, because the democratic ideal requires that schools be locally controlled, the ruling body (school board) should represent all segments of that community. Typically, however, the composition of school boards has overrepresented the business and professional sectors and overwhelmingly underrepresented blue-collar workers and various minority groups. The result is a governing body that is typically conservative in outlook and unresponsive to the wishes of people unlike themselves.

Fourth, local control of education may mean that the religious views of the majority (or at least, the majority of the school board) may intrude in public education. An explicit goal of the Christian Coalition, a conservative religious organization founded by Pat Robertson (see Chapter 17), is to win control of local school boards. Their agenda opposes globalism, restricts sex education to the promotion of "family values," promotes the teaching of biblical creationism in science classes, school prayer, and censors books that denigrate Christian values (favorite targets are, for example, *The Catcher in the Rye* by J. D. Salinger and John Steinbeck's *Grapes of Wrath*).

One organization of the Religious Right, Citizens for Excellence in Education, sees schools as a battleground on which "to confront the world and its abominable sins of homosexuality/lesbianism, witchcraft, necromancy, promiscuous sex for children, and atheistic socialism" (quoted in Galst, 1994:58).

A final problem with local control is the lack of curriculum standardization across the nation's 15,367 school districts and fifty states.

> Unlike virtually every other industrialized country, the United States has no national curriculum and no agency that services the development of classroom materials. *Each of the nation's 15,367 school districts is a kingdom unto itself*—with the power to decide what its students will be taught. [emphasis added] (Kantrowitz and Wingert, 1992:59)

Arguing for a common curriculum, Albert Shanker, the president of the American Federation of Teachers, states:

> A common curriculum means that there is agreement about what students ought to know and be able to do and, often, about the age and grade at which they should be able to accomplish these goals. . . . In most countries with a common curriculum, linkage of curriculum, assessment and teacher education is tight. . . . In the U.S., we have no such agreement about curriculum—and there is little connection between what students are supposed to learn, the knowledge on which they are assessed, and we expect our teachers to know. (Shanker,1991:E7)

The lack of a common curriculum has at least two negative consequences. First, there is a wide variation in the preparation of students. Second, there are large numbers of children moving from district to district who find the requirements of their new schools different, sometimes very different, from their previous schools. A 1994 Government Accounting Office report stated that one in six of the nation's third-graders has attended three schools since the first grade. The rate is higher in urban areas and especially among low-income families (Holmstrom, 1996).

The Competitive Nature of U.S. Education

Not surprisingly, schools in a highly competitive society are competitive. Competition extends to virtually all school activities. The compositions of athletic teams, cheerleading squads, pompom squads, debate teams, choruses, drill teams, bands, and dramatic play casts are almost always determined by competition among classmates. Grading in courses, too, is often based on the comparison of individuals (grading on a curve) rather than on measurement against a standard. To relieve boredom in the classroom, teachers often invent competitive games such as spelling baseball or hangman. In all these cases, the individual learns at least two lessons: (1) your classmates are enemies, for if they succeed, they do so at your expense, and (2) fear of failure is the great motivator, not intellectual curiosity or love of knowledge.

The Sifting and Sorting Function of Schools

Schools play a considerable part in choosing the youth who come to occupy the higher-status positions in society. Conversely, school performance also sorts out those who will occupy the lower rungs in the occupational prestige ladder. Education is, therefore, a selection process. The sorting is done with respect to two different criteria: a child's ability and his or her social class background. Although the goal of education is to select on ability alone, ascribed social status (the status of one's family, race, and religion) has a pronounced effect on the degree of success in the educational system. The school is analogous to a conveyor belt, with people of all social classes getting on at the same time but leaving the belt in accordance with social class—the lower the class, the shorter the ride (see "Diversity: Cooling Out the Failures").

Diversity

Cooling Out the Failures

Although our schools can be a golden avenue of opportunity for those who succeed in them, they are also the arena in which many confront failure that condemns them to the more subservient positions in our society. How are those who "fail" handled so they do not become bitter revolutionaries intent on overthrowing the system that so brutally used them?

"Cooling out" is the process of adjusting victims to their loss. When someone has lost something that is valuable to him, it leads to intense frustration. This frustration and its accompanying anger are dangerous to society because they can be directed against the social system if the social system is identified as being responsible for the loss. But our educational system is insidiously effective, and many who fail within it (perhaps most), never even need to be cooled out. They learn early in grade school that they are stupid and that higher education is meant for others. They suffer miserably in school as they continue to be confronted year after year with more evidence of their failure, and they can hardly wait until they turn sixteen so they can leave for greener pastures. Such persons are relieved to end their educational miseries and need no cooling out.

For those who do need to be cooled out, however, a variety of techniques is used. The primary one makes use of the ideology of individualism. To socialize students into major cultural values means to teach them more values than conformity and competition. . . . Two other major values students consistently confront in our educational system are the ideologies of individualism and equal opportunity. They are taught that people make their own way to the top in a land of equal opportunity. Those who make it do so because of their own abilities, while those who do not make it do so because of a lack of ability or drive on their own part. They consequently learn to blame themselves for failure, rather than the system. It was not the educational system that was at fault, for it was freely offered. But it was the fault of the individual who failed to make proper use of that which society offered him. Individualism provides amazing stabilization for the maintenance of our social system, for it results in the system

going unquestioned as the blame is put squarely on the individual who was himself conned by the system.

If this technique of cooling out fails to work, as it does only in a minority of cases, other techniques are put into effect. Counselors and teachers may point out to the person that he is really "better suited" for other tasks in life. He may be told that he will "be happier" doing something else. He might be "gradually disengaged" from the educational system, perhaps be directed to alternate sources of education, such as vocational training.

The individual may also be encouraged to blame his lack of success on tough luck, fate, and bad breaks. In one way or another, as he is cooled out, he is directed away from questioning the educational system itself, much less its relationship to maintaining the present class system and his subservient position within it. . . .

Finally, the malcontent-failure has the example before him of those from similar social class circumstances as his own who did "make it." This becomes incontrovertible evidence that the fault does lie with himself and not the system, for if they could make it, so could he. This evidence of those who "made it" is a powerful cooling out device, as it directly removes any accusatory finger that might point to the educational social systems.

Having our educational system set up in such a way that some lower class youngsters do manage to be successful and are able to enter upper middle class positions serves as a pressure valve for our social system. In the final analysis, it may well be this pressure valve which has prevented revolutions in our country—as the most able, the most persistent, and the most conforming are able to rise above their social class circumstances. And in such instances, the educational system is pointed to with pride as representing the gateway to golden opportunity, freely open to all.

Source: James M. Henslin, Linda K. Henslin, and Steven D. Keiser, "Schooling for Social Stability: Education in the Corporate Society," in *Social Problems in American Society.* James M. Henslin and Larry T. Reynolds, eds., 2nd ed. (Boston: Allyn and Bacon, 1976):311–312. Reprinted by permission of the publisher.

The Preoccupation with Order and Control

Most administrators and teachers share a fundamental assumption that school is a collective experience requiring subordination of individual needs to those of the school. U.S. schools are characterized, then, by constraints on individual freedom. The school day is regimented by the dictates of the clock. Activities begin and cease on a timetable, not in accordance with the degree of interest shown or whether students have mastered the subject. Another indicator of order is the preoccupation with discipline (that is, absence of unwarranted noise and movement, and concern with the following of orders).

In their quest for order, schools also demand conformity in clothing and hair styles. Dress codes are infamous for their constraints on the freedom to dress as one pleases. School athletic teams also restrict freedom, and these restrictions are condoned by the school authorities. Conformity is also demanded in what to read, where to set the margins on the computer or typewriter, and how to give the answers the teacher wants.

The many rules and regulations found in schools meet a number of expressed and implicit goals. The school authorities' belief in order is one reason for this dedication to rules: teachers are rated not on their ability to get pupils to learn but rather on the degree to which their classroom is quiet and orderly. The community also wants order. An excerpt from a famous (or infamous) book entitled *The Student as Nigger* dramatizes the demands for order in U.S. schools.

> [Students] haven't gone through twelve years of public school for nothing. They've learned one thing and perhaps only one thing during those twelve years. They've for-

Schools are preoccupied with order and control. To what degree is this emphasis appropriate? Does it also stifle creativity and learning?

gotten their algebra. They've grown to fear and resent literature. They write like they've been lobotomized. But Jesus, can they follow orders! . . . Students don't ask that orders make sense. They give up expecting things to make sense long before they leave elementary school. Things are true because the teacher says they're true. At a very early age we all learn to accept "two truths," as did certain medieval churchmen. Outside of class, things are true to your tongue, your fingers, your stomach, your heart. Inside class things are true by reason of authority. And that's just fine because you don't care anyway. Miss Wiedemeyer tells you a noun is a person, place or thing. So let it be. You don't give a rat's ass; she doesn't give a rat's ass. The important thing is to please her. Back in kindergarten, you found out that teachers only love children who stand in nice straight lines. And that's where it's been at ever since. (Farber, 1970:92)

The paradoxes listed below indicate the many profound dilemmas in U.S. education. They set the foundation for the remaining sections of this chapter, which deal with the crises facing education and with some alternative modes.

- Formal education encourages creativity but curbs the truly creative individual from being too disruptive to society.
- Formal education encourages the open mind but teaches dogma.
- Formal education has the goal of turning out mature students but does not give them the freedom essential to foster maturity.
- Formal education pays lip service to meeting individual needs of the students but in actuality encourages conformity at every turn.
- Formal education has the goal of allowing all students to reach their potential, yet it fosters kinds of competition that continually cause some people to be labeled as failures.
- Formal education is designed to allow people of the greatest talent to reach the top, but it systematically benefits certain categories of people regardless of their talent: the middle- and upper-class students who are White.

The Political Economy of Education in Corporate Society

People in the United States want to believe that their society is a meritocratic one in which the most intelligent and talented people rise to the top. Because public schools are free and available to everyone, individuals can go as high as their ability and drive will take them. In this view education is the great equalizer, providing opportunities for everyone to develop his or her full potential. This section and the next argue that this belief is a myth. The truth is that schools reinforce inequality in society (this section is taken from Bowles, 1977; Bowles and Gintis, 1973; Spring, 1972; and Carnoy, 1975). This belief, besides being a myth, has an especially negative outcome: it tends to blame or credit individuals for their level of failure or success without considering the aspects of the social structure that impel or impede their progress (another instance of blaming the victim). Thus, it results in praise of the system and condemnation of individuals who are defined as losers.

The Role of Education in Corporate Society

The schools perform several vital functions for the maintenance of the prevailing social, political, and economic order. Education, along with the institutions of the family and religion, has a primary responsibility for socializing newcomers to the society. A second function of education is the shaping of personalities so that they are in basic congruence with the demands of the society. In other words, one goal of the educational system of any society is to produce people with desired personality traits (such as competitiveness, altruism, bravery, conformity, or industriousness, depending on the culture and organization of the society). A third function is preparing individuals for their adult roles. In U.S. society this means preparing individuals for the specialized roles of a highly complex division of labor. It also means preparing youngsters for life in a rapidly changing world.

Social Class Biases of the Educational System

Through their curricula, testing, bureaucratic control, and emphasis on competition, the schools reflect the social-class structure of society by processing youth to fit into economic slots quite similar to those of their parents. As the educational system rapidly expanded during the nineteenth and early twentieth centuries, a system of class stratification emerged within the schools (Katz, 1968). As the high schools opened to youth of all social classes, the older curriculum, which provided a standard education for all, was supplanted by the progressive notion that school should be tailored to meet the individual needs of each child. Even though this makes obvious sense, the effects of the new curriculum tended to provide vocational school tracks for children of working-class families and preparation for college for children of professionals. Such a division was not blatant, because objective tests were used to decide the program for each child. Though seemingly fair, these tests were biased. The IQ test, for example, is clearly biased to reward children who have had middle-class experiences (Kagan, 1973). Thus, they unfairly legitimate a hierarchical division of labor by separating individuals into different curricula, with different expectations, which in turn then fulfill the prophecy of the original test scores. Moreover, they serve to reconcile people to their eventual placement in the economic system (Bowles and Gintis, 1976:74).

The amount of schooling one has is directly correlated with economic success in society. Thus, schools act as society's gatekeepers. But how the schools work biases the outcome, as we have seen. Two rules-of-the-school games serve to buttress this further. The first rule is that

> excellence in schooling should be rewarded. Given the capacity of the upper class to define excellence in terms on which upper class children tend to excel (for example, scholastic achievement), adherence to this principle yields inegalitarian outcomes (for example, unequal access to higher education) while maintaining the appearance of fair treatment. Thus the principle of rewarding excellence serves to legitimize the unequal consequences of schooling by associating success with competence. At the same time, the institution of objectively administered tests of performance serves to allow a limited amount of upward mobility among exceptional children of the lower class, thus

providing further legitimation of the operations of the social system by giving some credence to the myth of widespread mobility. (Bowles, 1977:148)

The second rule of the game is the principle that elementary and secondary schooling should be financed largely from local revenues. This principle is supported on the seemingly logical grounds that the local people know what is best for their children. The effect, however, is to perpetuate educational inequalities. The next section catalogs the reasons for this perpetuation and the many other ways in which education reinforces inequality.

Education and Inequality

Education is presumed by many people to be the great equalizer in U.S. society—the process by which the disadvantaged get their chance to be upwardly mobile. The data in Figure 16.1 show, for example, that the higher the educational attainment, the higher the income. But these data do not in any way demonstrate equality of opportunity through education. They show clearly that Blacks and Hispanics with the same educational attainment as Whites receive lower economic rewards.

FIGURE 16.1

Income of Full-Time Workers, by Race

Median income of full-time workers by level of education, 1994*

	High school graduates			College graduates		
WHITE	$21,370			$37,700		
BLACK		$16,690			$31,150	
HISPANIC			$17,890			$31,880

☐ WHITE   ■ BLACK   ■ HISPANIC

*U.S. Census Bureau

Source: Clarifying Issues '96 (New York: Public Agenda), p. 38.

These differences by race reflect discrimination in society, not just in schools. This section examines how the schools help perpetuate class and race inequities.

As we have seen, a fundamental function of the schools is to "sift and sort" their products. Those who succeed in school will occupy the higher-status positions in society. Conversely, school performance also sorts out those who will occupy the lower rungs in the occupational ladder.

Education is therefore a selection process. The sorting is done with respect to two different criteria: the child's ability and his or her social class background. Although the goal of education is to select on ability alone, ascribed social status (the status of one's family, race, ethnicity, and religion) has a pronounced effect on the degree of an individual's success in the educational system.

To document this assertion and analyze its consequences, this section examines how the schools help perpetuate class and race inequities.

The Relation between School Success and Socioeconomic Status

The evidence that educational performance is linked to socioeconomic background is clear and irrefutable. The advantages of the children of the relatively affluent over those of the poor are enormous, as seen in the following illustration from a study by the Carnegie Council on Children:

> Jimmy is a second grader. He pays attention in school, and enjoys it. School records show he is reading slightly above grade level and has a slightly better than average I.Q. Bobby is a second grader in a school across town. He also . . . enjoys school and his test scores are quite similar to Jimmy's. Bobby is a safe bet to enter college (more than four times as likely as Jimmy) and a good bet to complete it—at least twelve times as likely as Jimmy.
>
> Bobby will probably have at least four years more schooling than Jimmy. He is twenty-seven times as likely as Jimmy to land a job which by his late forties will pay him an income in the top tenth of all incomes. Jimmy has one chance in eight of earning a median income.
>
> These odds are the arithmetic of inequality in America. . . . Bobby is the son of a successful lawyer whose annual salary . . . puts him well within the top 10 percent of the United States income distribution. . . . Jimmy's father, who did not complete high school, works from time to time as a messenger and a custodial assistant. His earnings . . . put him in the bottom 10 percent. (Kempton, 1979:8–9)

The research of Bowles and Gintis also makes the point that socioeconomic background determines how much education one receives. They found that people in the lowest 10 percent in socioeconomic background *with the same average IQ scores* as those in the highest 10 percent will receive an average of 4.9 fewer years of education (Bowles and Gintis, 1976:31).

Christopher Jencks and his associates have added to the work of Bowles and Gintis (Jencks, et al., 1979). Among their findings is that educational attainment, especially graduation from college, is very important to later success; but it is not so much what one learns in school as the obtaining of the credentials that counts.

Most important, the probability of high educational attainment is closely tied to family background.

Inequality in education occurs also along racial lines (which are closely related to socioeconomic status). In 1991, for example, 79.9 percent of adult Whites were at least high school graduates compared with 66.7 percent of African American adults, and 51.3 percent of Latino adults. The racial disparity increases with greater educational attainment: 22.2 percent of White adults have four or more years of college, compared with 11.5 percent of African Americans and 9.7 percent of Latinos (Kominski and Adams, 1993:14).

The Coleman report, an analysis of all third-, sixth-, ninth-, and twelfth-grade pupils in 4,000 schools, noted that Whites surpass Blacks in various achievement areas and that the gaps increase the longer they remain in school (Coleman, et al., 1966). Clearly, the school is to blame, for in no instance is the initial gap narrowed. Moreover, the increasing gaps are *understated,* because there is a greater tendency for the people of lowest aptitude among the minority groups to drop out of school.

William Ryan has summarized the situation as follows:

> The school is better prepared for the middle-class child than for the lower-class child. Indeed, we could be tempted to say further that the school experience is tailored for, and stacked in favor of, the middle-class child. The cause-and-effect relationship between the lack of skills and experiences found among lower-class children and the conditions of lower-class life has yet to be delineated. So far, explanations of this relationship have been, at best, sketchy, and have been based on casual observation. We know poor and middle-class children exhibit certain differences in styles of talking and thinking, but we do not know yet why or how these differences occur.
>
> We do know, however, that these differences—really differences in *style* rather than ability—are not handicaps or disabilities (unlike barriers to learning such as poor vision, mild brain damage, emotional disturbance or orthopedic handicap). They do represent inadequate *preparation* for the reality of the modern urban school. They are, in no sense, cultural or intellectual defects. (Ryan, 1976:35–36)*

How is the educational system stacked in favor of middle- and upper-class children and against children from the lowest classes?** At least four interrelated factors explain why the education system tends to reinforce the socioeconomic status differentials in the United States: finances, curriculum, segregation, and personnel.

Finances. Though not a guarantee of educational equality, if schools spent approximately the same amount of money per pupil, this would be a significant step

---

*Reprinted by permission of the publisher.

We have phrased the question to focus on the system, not on the victims, contrary to the typical response, which is to focus on the **cultural deprivation of the poor. That approach attacks the home and culture of poor people. It assumes that these people perform inadequately because they are handicapped by their culture. Observers cannot, however, make the value judgment that a culture is deprived. They can note only that their milieu does not prepare children to perform in schools geared for the middle class. In other words, children of the poor and/or minority groups are not nonverbal—they are very verbal, but not necessarily in the language of the middle class.

toward meeting that goal. This has not been accomplished nationwide, because wealthier states are able to pay much more per-pupil than are poorer states. In 1990, for example, the top five states in per-pupil spending were New Jersey ($8,439), New York ($8,094), Connecticut ($7,934), Alaska ($7,252), and Rhode Island ($6,523). The five states with the lowest per pupil spending were Utah ($2,733), Idaho ($3,037), Mississippi ($3,151), Arkansas ($3,272), and South Dakota ($3,312) (U.S. Bureau of the Census, 1991c:149). Because the federal government provides only about 6 percent of the money for public schools, equalization from state to state is impossible as long as the states vary in wealth and commitment to public education.

The disparities in per-pupil expenditures within a given state are also great, largely because of the tradition of funding public schools through local property taxes. This procedure is discriminatory because rich school districts can spend more money than poor ones on each student, and at a *lower* taxing rate. Thus, suburban students are more advantaged than are students from the inner city (see "Diversity: Inequality and Education of the Urban Poor"); districts with business enterprises are favored over agricultural districts; and districts blessed with natural resources are better able to provide for their children than are districts with few resources.

Texas has the greatest disparity in spending for each pupil by district. The spending averages $11,801 per pupil for the 5 percent in the richest districts, compared to an average of $3,190 for the poorest 5 percent (Verhovek, 1993). Examined another way, the 150,000 students living in the poorest districts of Texas

The disparities in per-pupil expenditures within a given state are great, largely because of the tradition of funding public schools through local property taxes.

Diversity

Inequality and Education of the Urban Poor

Poor children live in a societal context that seriously disadvantages them. Because of unhealthy living conditions (exposure to toxic chemicals, pollution, and inadequate diets and housing), and lack of immunizations and no health insurance, they are at high risk for infant mortality, infectious diseases, and even brain damage.

Only about one in four eligible children is able to participate in Head Start, even though this program has been shown to increase school success and improve eventual employability (Schorr, 1988). This program is underfunded because it receives a relatively low priority by the federal government.

School funding is based on the wealth of local districts. This places urban schools at a disadvantage, compared to their suburban neighbors. The cities are disproportionately the home of the poor and the near-poor, who pay little taxes and require many services. The cities have a disproportionate number of tax-free institutions such as churches, colleges, hospitals, and art museums. Cities must pay a relatively large part of their limited tax revenues on police matters (because of a relatively high rate of street crime in inner cities) and fire department costs (due to the unusual number of fires because of substandard wiring, dilapidated housing, and abandoned warehouses).

Ironically, the tax treatment of property taxes for schooling promotes inequality in education. Consider the argument by Jonathan Kozol:

> Because the property tax is counted as a tax deduction by the federal government, home-owners in a wealthy suburb get back a substantial portion of the money that they spend to fund their children's schools—effectively, a federal subsidy for an unequal education. Home-owners in poor districts get this subsidy as well, but, because their total tax is less, the subsidy is less. The mortgage interest that home-owners pay is also treated as a tax deduction—in effect, a second, federal subsidy. These subsidies, as I have termed them, are considerably larger than most people understand. In 1984, for instance, property-tax deductions granted by the federal government were $9 billion. An additional $23 billion in mortgage-interest deductions were provided by home-owners: a total of some $32 billion. Federal grants to local schools, in contrast, totaled only $7 billion, and only part of this was earmarked for low-income districts. Federal policy, in this respect, increases the existing gulf between the richest and the poorest schools. (Kozol, 1991:55)

Added to these inequities is the actual amount spent per pupil, comparing rich school districts with poor school districts. Kozol presents some examples (1991: 236–237):

- In 1989, Chicago spent $5,265 per student compared to $9,371 in Niles Township High School.

- In 1989, the Princeton district in New Jersey spent $7,725 per pupil while the Camden district spent $3,538.

- In 1987, New York City spent $5,585 compared to $11,372 in Manhasset, $11,325 in Jerico, and $11,265 in Great Neck.

Actually, these gaps are wider than they appear because the poorer urban schools spend a smaller proportion of their budget on instruction than do the suburban schools. This is because dilapidated schools require more maintenance and higher fuel costs than do newer, fuel-efficient buildings. The result is the poor urban children enter school with a disadvantage, and the unequally financed schooling they receive compounds that disadvantage. The system, in effect, condemns these children to unequal lives.

receive educations costing half of their 150,000 wealthiest counterparts (Wise and Gendler, 1989).

The U.S. Supreme Court in *San Antonio v. Rodriquez* (1973) ruled that even though there were unequal expenditures in Texas, these disparities did not violate the Constitution. In effect, the Court ruled that this was a matter for the individual states to decide and that equal access to education is not a fundamental right under the Constitution. Moreover, the Court ruled that property-tax collection was a permissible way to fund schools even if it led to great spending disparities.

Since the *San Antonio v. Rodriquez* decision at least thirty states have been challenged in state courts over their unequal financing of schools, with the systems in thirteen states judged unconstitutional. Various schemes have been proposed to meet with the objections of the courts, but inequities remain even in these more progressive states (see Table 16.1 for the disparity between two school districts in Massachusetts).

If the equalization of finances were accomplished, it would have significant consequences.

> It equalizes the capacity of poor districts to secure the services of a sufficient number of teachers, even to bid for the services of highly qualified teachers. It permits schools from poor districts to exercise the same choice—Shall we offer Latin or Russian? Shall we buy computers or microscopes?—that schools from wealthy districts now enjoy. It ensures, to the extent that is possible, that educational opportunity is independent of the wealth of one's parents and neighbors.
>
> Improving education for children in poor school districts would benefit them and the nation. A future physicist is as easily born in Jersey City as in Princeton, a future pianist in Edgewood as in Alamo Heights. But it is not only potential luminaries that are lost; it is part of an entire generation of citizens whose potential contributions are stunted by the inadequacy of the education they are provided. School finance reform cannot solve all of the problems of education, but it can equalize the opportunities that the state provides. To continue to distribute better education to children in rich districts

TABLE 16.1

A Tale of Two Cities—The Massachusetts Supreme Court Recently Invalidated Wide Disparities in Local Education Spending

WELLESLEY		LOWELL
3,057	Total enrollment	14,098
$1,042,000	Value of assessed taxable property, per student	$208,000
$11.45	Property-tax rate (per $1,000 assessed value)	$17.72
$6,797	Revenue per student raised from local property taxes	$1,803
$46,985	Average teacher salary	$31,987
82%	Percentage of teachers with master's degrees	47%
191	Number of students per guidance counselor	252
$171	Library spending per student (FY '92)	$3.50

Figures for Wellesley and Lowell, Mass., school districts FY '93 unless noted.

Source: "A Tale of Two Cities," *U.S. News & World Report* (Aug. 2, 1993): 45.

INNER CITY STUDENTS

OUTER RING SUBURBAN STUDENTS

SEPARATE BUT EQUAL

Kirk Anderson.

and worse education to children in poor districts is only to exacerbate the inequalities that children bring to school. To equalize educational opportunity is to redress some of the accidents of birth. (Wise and Gendler, 1989:37)

But the states (with the exception of Hawaii) have decided that property taxes will supply about half of the funds for local education. Thus, the structure (the financing of schools) creates inequality by class and race:

> Given the grossly unequal distribution of property in the U.S. and the intense segregation of communities by race and class, it's inevitable that schools heavily dependent on property taxes will be unequal. In fact . . . the reliance on property taxes functions as a sorting mechanism for class and race privilege, and allows pockets of "elite schooling" to exist within the public system. (Karp, 1995:27)

For a comparison of U.S. expenditures on education with those of other industrialized nations, see "Other Societies: U.S. Expenditures on Education."

Family Economic Resources. The College Board reported that the average combined SAT scores for youth from families whose annual income was at least $70,000 was 997, compared to an average score of 768 for youth from families whose incomes were less than $10,000 (reported in *Harper's Magazine,* 1992:13). What is the explanation for this difference of 229 points on the SATs? Among the reasons are the benefits that come from economic privilege. Poor parents, most without health insurance, are unable to afford prenatal care, which increases the risk of babies born at low birthweight, a condition that may lead to learning disabilities. As these poor children age, they are less likely to receive adequate nutrition, decent medical care, and a safe and secure environment. These deficiencies increase the probability of poor children being less alert, less curious, and less able to interact effectively with their environment than are healthy children.

Poor children are more likely than the children of the affluent to attend schools with poor resources, which, as we have seen, means that they are less likely to receive an enriched educational experience. Similarly, most poor young people live in communities where

> opportunities to apply academic skills and build new ones are either not available or not accessible. The lack of community resources is especially destructive during the summer months, the time when children doing least well in school (a group that is disproportionately poor) slide backward the farthest. Recent research shows that most of the learning gap between poor and nonpoor children is due to this summer learning loss. (Children's Defense Fund, 1990:74)

Children from poor families cannot afford private early development programs, which prepare children for school. They can be in Head Start, but these government programs only have the funding for 40 percent of those eligible.

Poor teens are more likely than their more affluent peers to fall behind in school. Among sixteen-year-olds who have lived at least half of their lives below the poverty line, 40 percent have repeated at least one grade, a rate twice as great as for those whose families had never lived in poverty (Children's Defense Fund, 1990:69).

The level of affluence also affects how long children will stay in school, because schools, even public schools, are costly. There are school fees (many school districts, for example, charge fees for participation in music, athletics, and drama), supplies, meals, transportation, and other costs of education. These financial demands pressure youngsters from poorer families to drop out of school prematurely to go to work. The children from the middle and upper classes, not constrained by financial difficulties, tend to stay in school longer, which means better jobs and pay in the long run. Because minorites are overrepresented among the poor, their school dropout rate is disproportionate to that of Whites—in 1993 the dropout rate for Latinos was 27.5 percent, 11.6 percent for African Americans, and 7.9 percent for Whites (U.S. Department of Education, reported in Puente and Sanchez, 1995).

> These children [dropouts]—most of them poor, black or Hispanic—are America's educational underclass. While middle-class kids enjoy gleaming laboratories and computers, these children struggle in an educational Third World where supplies are shoddy, teachers are baffled by a barrage of different languages, and discrimination handicaps even the brightest and most willing child. From this classroom ghetto, it's a short journey to the world of adults trapped in joblessness and poverty. (Horn, 1987:66)

Other Societies Other Ways

U.S. Expenditures on Education

Does the United States spend more on education than other industrialized countries? That's what a couple of presidents and secretaries of education have gone around the country telling us. And that's why no one was surprised when President Bush proposed to reform America's schools without serious increase in education spending. If we already pour money into our schools and get lousy results, more money is obviously not the answer. The trouble is, this picture of America as the educational big spender is a myth. I'm not saying that just spending more on education will solve all our problems, but we're kidding ourselves if we think our investment in education is extremely generous.

Last year, the Economic Policy Institute, a liberal think tank, reported that 13 other industrialized countries invest more public dollars in education, in proportion to their economy, than the U.S. Critics in the U.S. Department of Education and elsewhere attacked this finding because it was based on only one measure of expenditure. According to the critics, other measures, like per-capita or per-student expenditures, would present a quite different picture. But a recent study by the American Federation of Teachers applies all the measures critics called for and finds that, no matter what measures you use, public spending for education is lower in the United States than in a number of other industrialized countries.

In "International Comparison of Public Spending on Education," economist F. Howard Nelson looks at the income (gross domestic product, or GDP) devoted to education, at per-capita expenditures, per-pupil expenditures, pupil-teacher ratios and teacher salaries and finds that the United States lags behind a number of other industrialized countries in every comparison. And this, despite the fact that we have the world's highest standard of living and enroll the most students.

Here are some of Nelson's findings: the majority are based on 1987 figures, the most recent available:

- The United States spent 3.7 percent of its GDP on elementary and secondary school education. This put us 11th among the 15 nations. Denmark, the top-ranking nation, spent 5.5 percent; Canada spent 4.5 percent.

- We ranked 9th in public spending for higher education even though we have the highest postsecondary enrollment rate in the world—double that of any other country except for Canada.

- Our per-capita public expenditure on education was $860. Four other countries spent more, among them Canada, which spent $1,153 per capita.

- United States per-pupil expenditure of $3,398 was 6th among the 15 nations.

- Our classrooms are among the most crowded of the countries studied. The pupil-teacher

The affluent also give their children educational advantages, such as home computers, travel experiences abroad and throughout the United States, visits to zoos and libraries, and various cultural activities. Another advantage available to the affluent is the hiring of tutors to help children having difficulty in school or to transform already good students into outstanding ones. And, they may also send them to specialized tutorials such as computer schools.

Consider FutureKids, the world's largest computer-school chain for children. The program, which costs up to $25 an hour, goes where the money is. There are 25 franchises in Los Angeles, but none in the inner city. (*Christian Science Monitor,* 1994:1)

ratio in the United States was 19 children for every teacher; the 15-country average was 16.

- United States teachers do not earn as much as their counterparts in other countries. Average pay in the 1980s consistently ranked in the bottom third of the nations studied. Also U.S. teachers make less in relation to the salary of the average worker than teachers in any other country surveyed, except for Sweden. It's no wonder we have a hard time recruiting teachers from the upper half of college graduating classes.

In short, the argument that the United States is the world's biggest spender on education has no basis. Does that mean we need to spend more? Not necessarily, but if we look at the discrepancy between what we hope to do—and how much we plan to pay for it—I think the answer is obvious.

Most people agree that it's essential for our country's economic and political health to achieve the national education goals set by President Bush and the nation's governors; it's a top national priority. But how will we reach the goal of making sure that "by the year 2000, all children in America will start school ready to learn"—without spending more money? And if we meet that goal, where will we find the resources to make the U.S. students first in math and science by the year 2000? Or to make sure that every adult American is literate?

How will we carry out the ambitious program to restructure U.S. education that President Bush presented a few weeks ago without spending more money? How will we set up a national examination system and fund 535 dazzlingly innovative schools? People say that creativity and will are necessary, and they are. But the president's proposals are going to require money, too; and there's no way that private initiatives will be able to supply what we'll need.

It's time for us to stop thinking about education as something in which we already invest too large a percentage of our resources. Instead, we should be thinking in terms of what we must invest to turn our schools around. People say that we are in tough economic times and that spending money is no guarantee of success. Both are true, but when it comes to top national priorities, we usually ignore arguments like these and spend the money. That's how we built the weapons and the military establishment that won the war in the Persian Gulf. And we didn't ask how much was barely enough to do the job—maybe that's why we did it so well. What's wrong with trying this approach in reforming our schools?

Source: Albert Shanker, "U.S. Expenditures on Education: The Myth of the Big Spender Debunked," *The New York Times* (May 5, 1991), p. E7. Reprinted with permission.

The well-to-do also have the option of sending their children to private schools (about 12 percent of U.S. children attend these schools). Parents send their children to private schools for many reasons. Some do so for religious reasons. Some choose them because private schools, unlike public schools, are selective in whom they let in, so parents can ensure that their children will interact with children similar to theirs in race (some private schools were expressly created so that White children could avoid attending integrated public schools) and social class. Similarly, private schools are much more likely than are public schools to get rid of troublesome students (those with behavioral problems and low achievers), thereby providing an educational environment more conducive to achievement. A final reason for attending private schools is that the most elite private schools provide a demanding education *and* entree to the most elite colleges and universities, which, in turn, lead to placement in top positions in the professional and corporate occupational worlds.

Obtaining a college degree is a most important avenue to later success (the annual rate of return on the cost of a college degree is about 11 percent for life) (Farrell, 1996). One's family finances are directly related to whether one attends college and, if so, what type.

These high costs, which continue to rise (see Figure 16.2), coupled with declining scholarship monies, preclude college attendance not only for the able poor but also increasingly for children of the working- and lower-middle classes. The ability to pay for college reinforces the class system in two ways. The lack of money shuts out the possibility of college for some students. For those who do attend college, money stratifies. The poorest, even those who are talented, are most likely to attend community colleges, which are the least expensive; they emphasize technical careers and are therefore limiting in terms of later success (about 45 percent of the nation's college students attended community colleges). Students with greater resources are likely to attend public universities. Finally, those with the greatest financial backing are the most likely to attend elite and prestigious private schools, where the annual cost in 1996 was around $30,000. It is important to note that, al-

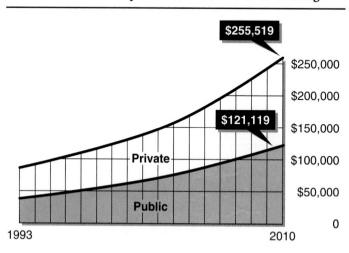

FIGURE 16.2

How Costs Will Rise: Projected Costs[1] for Four Years of College

1 – including tuition, room and board, transportation, books and other expenses; prices 7% annual increases

Source: USA Today (August 9, 1993):D1. Copyright 1993, *USA Today.* Reprinted with permission.

though ability is an important variable, it is money—not ability—that places college students in this stratified system. For example, "some less qualified students from upper-class families are able to attend elite universities because of admission programs that favor the children of alumni and the children of big contributors to the university's fund-raising campaigns" (Coleman and Cressey, 1990:103).

Minorities and Higher Education.   Because racial minorities are much more likely than Whites to be poor or near-poor, they are underrepresented in college education. The following facts make this point.

First, even though more minorities are attending college than ever, they continue to be underrepresented in higher education. They also have higher dropout rates in college.

As reported by the American Council on Education, in 1990, 39.4 percent of White eighteen- to twenty-four-year-old high school graduates were in college, compared to 33 percent of Blacks and 29 percent of Latinos (reported in Kelly, 1992:1D). The proportion of Black and Latino men in college is especially low (Scarpitti and Andersen, 1992:581).

Second, racial minorities are more likely than Whites to attend community colleges and schools that are less well funded (Ramirez, 1992). Third, the minority students who attend college are less likely than Whites to graduate, and if they do graduate, it takes them longer.

Fourth, the disproportionately low number of college degrees earned by minorities is reflected in the relatively low number of students who attend and grad-

FIGURE 16.3

Recipients of Doctorates from U.S. Universities by Gender and Race*

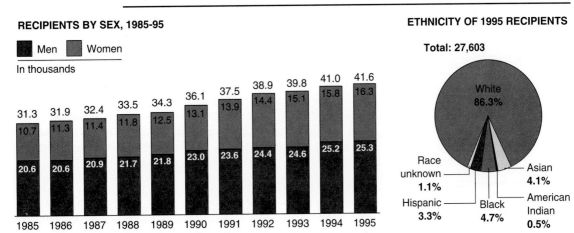

Note: Details may not add to totals because of rounding.

Figures cover only U.S. citizens.

*"Summary Report 1995," National Research Council
Source: Lora Thompson Powell, "Who Got Doctorates from U.S. Universities," *Chronicle of Higher Education* (June 14, 1996), p. A25. Reprinted with permission of the National Academy of Sciences, Washington, DC.

uate from graduate school (see Figure 16.3 for the data on doctorates by gender and race). This, of course, results in a low proportion of minority professionals in the near future. The problem can be seen in the current racial composition of full-time faculty in higher education: White (88.5 percent), African American (4.5 percent), Latino (2.0 percent), Asian American (4.7 percent), and Native American (0.3 percent) (Mullins, 1992).

Curriculum.   United States schools are essentially middle or upper class. The written and spoken language in the schools, for example, is expected to be middle class. For children of the poor, however, English (at least middle-class English) may be a second language. English is clearly a second language for many Hispanic youngsters, making their scores on tests and success in U.S. schools especially problematic. Standardized tests often ask the student to determine how objects are similar. For those students whose first language is Spanish, this presents a problem. "Spanish, which separates words into masculine and feminine categories, tends to emphasize the differences between objects. This interferes with tasks that require the subject to describe how objects are similar" (Philippus, 1989:59). The schools, in general, have failed to recognize the special needs of these and other bilingual students, which results in their overall poor student performance.

In these and other matters, the curriculum of the schools does not accommodate the special needs of the poor. To the contrary, the schools assume that the language and behaviors of the poor are not only alien but also wrong—things to be changed. This assumption denigrates the ways of the poor and leads to loss of ego strength (a trait already in short supply for the poor in a middle-class world).

The curriculum also is not very germane to the poor child's world. What is the relevance of conjugating a verb when you are hungry? What is the relevance of being able to trace the path of how a bill becomes law when your family and neighbors are powerless? Irrelevancy for the poor is also seen in the traditional children's primers, which picture middle-class surroundings and well-behaved blond children. There is little effort at any educational level to incorporate the experience of slum children in relation to realistic life situations of any kind. Schools also have a way of ignoring real-life problems and controversial issues. Schools are irrelevant if they disregard topics such as race relations, poverty, and the distribution of community power.

The typical teaching methods, placement tests, and curricula are inappropriate to children from poor families. This factor, along with the others mentioned earlier, results in failure for a large proportion of these youngsters. They perceive themselves (as do others in the system) as incompetents. As Silberman has put it:

> Students are not likely to develop self-respect if they are unable to master the reading, verbal, and computational skills that the schools are trying to teach. Children must have a sense of competence if they are to regard themselves as people of worth; the failure that minority-group children, in particular, experience from the beginning can only reinforce the sense of worthlessness that the dominant culture conveys in an almost infinite variety of ways, and so feed the self-hatred that prejudice and discrimination produce. Chronic failure makes self-discipline equally hard to come by; it is

these children's failure to learn that produces the behavior problems of the slum school . . . and not the behavior problems that produce the failure to learn. (Silberman, 1970:67)

Silberman's discussion of the problems of minority-group children can be broadened to include all poor children (who are, after all, also a minority group). The poor of all races experience prejudice and discrimination. They quickly learn that they are considered misfits by the middle class (teacher, administrator, citizen).

Segregation

United States schools tend to be segregated by race and social class, both by neighborhood and, within schools, by ability grouping. Schools are based in neighborhoods that tend to be relatively homogeneous by socioeconomic status. Racial and economic segregation is especially prevalent at the elementary-school level, carrying over to a lesser degree in the secondary schools. Colleges and universities, as we have seen, are peopled by a middle- and upper-class clientele. Thus, at every level, children tend to attend a school with others like themselves in socioeconomic status and race. In terms of race, during the 1991–92 school year, two-thirds of African American students and almost three-fourths of Latino students attended schools that were predominantly minority (slightly more than one-third of each group attended schools that were at least 90 percent minority) (Kelly, 1994). This

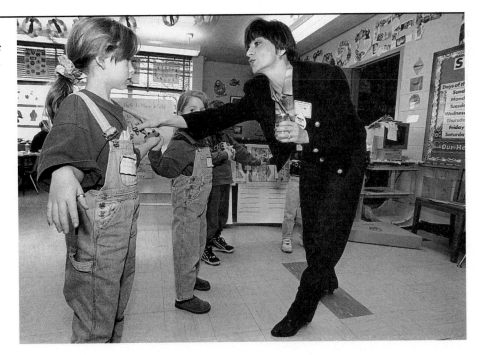

U.S. schools tend to be segregated by race and social class, both by neighborhood and, within schools, by ability grouping.

segregation by race and social class results, typically, in unequal resources, because affluent districts provide more than poor districts do for their pupils. Moreover, within districts, the schools labeled *lower class* tend to get a disproportionately smaller slice of the economic pie than do middle-class schools.

Tracking and Teachers' Expectations

In 1956 the Supreme Court declared segregated schools unconstitutional. As we have seen, many schools remain at least partially segregated by social class and race because schools draw students from residential areas that are more or less homogeneous by class and race. Segregation is reinforced further by the tracking system within the schools. **Tracking** (also known as ability grouping) sorts students into different groups or classes according to their perceived intellectual ability. The decision is based on grades and teachers' judgments but primarily through standardized tests. The result is that children from poor families and from ethnic minorities are overrepresented in the slow track, while children from advantaged backgrounds are disproportionately in the middle and upper tracks. The rationale for tracking is that it provides a better fit between the needs and capabilities of the student and the demands and opportunities of the curriculum. Slower students do not retard the progress of brighter ones, and teachers can adapt their teaching more efficiently to the level of the class if the students are relatively homogeneous in ability. The special problems of the different ability groups, from gifted to retarded, can be dealt with more easily when groups of students share the same or similar problems. The arguments are persuasive. It is estimated that 80 percent of United States secondary schools and 60 percent of elementary schools use some form of ability grouping (Mansnerus, 1992).

Although these benefits may be real, tracking is open to serious criticisms. First, students in lower tracks are discouraged from producing up to their potential. They tend to be given repetitive and unchallenging tasks. Students labeled as *low-ability* tend to get a curriculum empty of ideas (Rachlin, 1989). They are given low-level work that increases the gap between them and the higher tracks. Rather than seeing the remedial track as a way to get students up to speed, many "teachers see themselves as weeders, getting rid of the kids who can't make it, rather than nurturers trying to make all grow to their potential" (Rachlin, 1989:52).

Second, students in the upper track develop feelings of superiority, whereas those in the lower track tend to define themselves as inferior. As early as the second grade students know where they stand on the smart-or-dumb continuum, and this profoundly affects their self-esteem. These psychological wounds can have devastating effects.

Third, the low-track students are tracked to fail. The negative labels, low teacher expectations, poor education resources (the highest track is much more likely to have access to computers, for example), and the fact that teachers typically do not want to teach these classes (there is a subtle labeling among teachers regarding who gets to teach what level), all lead to a high probability of failure among students assigned to the lowest track. Given all of these negatives, it is not surprising that students who are discipline problems or who eventually drop out come disproportionately from the low track.

Fourth, the tracking system is closely linked to the stratification system—that is, students from low-income families are disproportionately placed in the lowest track, resulting in a reinforcement of the social class structure. Data from a nationwide study of 14,000 eighth-grade students in English classes reveal that this is true (see Table 16.2). Thus, U.S. schools deny equality of educational opportunity, which is contrary to the ideal of the school system as open and democratic.

Finally, and most telling, recent research calls into serious question whether tracking has educational value. Research at the Johns Hopkins University found, for example, that "given the same curriculum in elementary and middle-grade schools, there is no difference in achievement between advanced students in a tracked school and students in the top third of a class made up of students with varying abilities" (cited in Rachlin, 1989:52). The Carnegie Corporation in a report assessing the state of middle-grade schools advocated "abolishing tracking on the grounds that it discriminates against minorities, psychologically wounds those labeled slow, and doesn't work" (cited in Rachlin, 1989:51).

The tracking system appears not to accomplish its educational goals, but it is powerful in its negative effects. There are four principal reasons this system stunts the success of students who are negatively labeled.

Stigma.   Assignment to a lower track carries a strong **stigma** (a label of social disgrace). Such students are labeled as intellectual inferiors. Their self-esteem wanes

TABLE 16.2

Ability Grouping by Race and Class (From a National Study of 14,000 Eighth-Grade Students in English Classes)

CATEGORY	Percent in			
	HIGH ABILITY	MIDDLE ABILITY	LOW ABILITY	MIXED
Race/ethnicity:				
Asian	40%	37%	16%	7%
White	32	40	14	15
Hispanic	18	42	29	12
Black	15	38	34	13
Native American	9	44	35	13
Socioeconomic status:				
Top one-fourth	39	39	14	8
Bottom one-fourth	13	36	37	14

Source: U.S. Department of Education, National Center for Educational Statistics, National Education Longitudinal Study of 1988, Washington, DC: U.S. Government Printing Office (1990).

as they see how other people perceive them and behave toward them. Thus, individuals assigned to a track other than college prep perceive themselves as second class, as unworthy, stupid, and in the way. Clearly, assignment to a low track is destructive to a student's self-concept.

The Self-Fulfilling Prophecy.   This effect is closely related to stigma. If placed in the college-prep track, students are likely to receive better instruction, have access to better facilities, and be pushed more nearly to their capacity than are those assigned to other tracks. The reason is clear: the teachers and administration *expect* great things from the one group and lesser things from the other. Moreover, these expectations are fulfilled. Those in the higher track do better, and those in the lower track do not. These behaviors justify the greater expenditures of time, faculties, and experimental curricula for those in the higher track—thus perpetuating what Merton has called a "reign of error" (Merton, 1957:421–436).

An example comes from a controversial study by Rosenthal and Jacobson. Although this study has been criticized for a number of methodological shortcomings, the findings are consistent with theories of interpersonal influence and with the labeling view of deviant behavior. In the spring of 1964, all students in an elementary school in San Francisco were given an IQ test. The following fall the teachers were given the names of children identified by the test as potential academic spurters, and five of these were assigned to each classroom. The spurters were chosen by means of a table of random numbers. The only difference between the experimental group (those labeled as spurters) and the control group (the rest of the class) was in the imaginations of the teachers. At the end of the year all the children were again tested, and the children from whom the teachers expected greater intellectual gains showed such gains (in IQ and grades). Moreover, they were rated by their teachers as being more curious, interesting, happy, and more likely to succeed than the children in the control group (Rosenthal and Jacobson, 1968).

The implications of this example are clear. Teachers' expectations have a profound effect on students' performance. When students are overrated, they tend to overproduce; when they are underrated, they underachieve. The tracking system is a labeling process that affects the expectations of teachers (and fellow students and parents). The limits of these expectations are crucial in the educational process. Yet the self-fulfilling prophecy can work in a positive direction if teachers have an unshakable conviction that their students *can* learn. Concomitant with this belief, teachers should hold *themselves,* not the students, accountable if the latter should fail (Silberman, 1970:98). Used in this manner, the self-fulfilling prophecy can work to the benefit of *all* students.

Future Payoff.   School is perceived as relevant for students going to college. Grades are a means of qualifying for college. For the non-college-bound student, however, school and grades are much less important for entry into a job. At most they need a high school diploma, and grades really do not matter as long as one does not flunk out. Thus, non-college-bound students often develop negative attitudes toward school, grades, and teachers. These attitudes for students in the lower tracks are summed up by sociologist Arthur Stinchcombe:

Rebellious behavior is largely a reaction to the school itself and to its promises, not a failure of the family or community. High school students can be motivated to conform by paying them in the realistic coin of future advantage. Except perhaps for pathological cases, any student can be motivated to conform if the school can realistically promise something valuable to him as a reward for working hard. But for a large part of the population, especially the adolescent who will enter the male working class or the female candidates for early marriage, the school has nothing to offer. . . . In order to secure conformity from students, a high school must articulate academic work with careers of students. (Quoted in Schafer, Olexa, and Polk, 1972:49)

As we have seen, being on the lower track has negative consequences. These students are more rebellious both in school and out and do not participate as much in school activities. Finally, what is being taught is often not relevant to their world. Thus, we are led to conclude that many of these students tend to feel that they are not only second-class citizens but perhaps even pariahs (outcasts). What other interpretation is plausible in a system that disadvantages them, shuns them, and makes demands of them that are irrelevant?

The Student Subculture. The reasons given above suggest that a natural reaction of persons in the lower track would be to band together in a subculture that is antagonistic toward school. This subculture would quite naturally develop its own system of rewards, since those of the school are inaccessible.

These factors (stigma, negative self-fulfilling prophecy, low future payoff, and a contrary student subculture) show how the tracking system is at least partly responsible for students in the lower tracks tending to be low achievers, unmotivated, uninvolved in school activities, and more prone to break school rules and drop out of school. To segregate students either by ability or by future plans is detrimental to the students labeled as inferior. Tracking is a barrier to equal educational opportunity for lower-income and other minority students who are disproportionately assigned to the lowest track. It is an elitist system that for the most part takes the children of the elite and educates them to take the elite positions in society. Conversely, children of the nonelite are trained to recapitulate the experiences of their parents. In a presumably democratic system that prides itself on providing avenues of upward social mobility, such a system borders on immorality (Oakes, 1985).

The conclusion is inescapable: inequality in the educational system causes many people to fail in U.S. schools. This phenomenon is the fault of the schools, not of the children who fail. To focus on these victims is to divert attention from the inadequacies of the schools. The blame needs to be shifted.

We are dealing, it would seem, not so much with culturally deprived children as with culturally depriving schools. And the task to be accomplished is not to revise, and amend, and repair deficient children but to alter and transform the atmosphere and operations of the schools to which we commit these children. Only by changing the nature of the educational experience can we change its product. (Ryan, 1976:60)*

*Reprinted by permission of the publisher.

Education from the Order and the Conflict Perspectives

From the order perspective, schools are of crucial importance in maintaining social integration. They are a vital link between the individual and society, deliberately indoctrinating youth with the values of society and teaching the skills necessary to fit into society. Most important, the schools sift and sort children so that they will find and accept their appropriate niche in the societal division of labor.

The conflict perspective emphasizes that the educational system reinforces the existing inequalities in society by giving the advantaged the much greater probability of success (in grades, in achievement tests, in IQ tests, in getting an advanced education; all of which translate into economic and social success outside school). Conflict adherents also object to the **hidden curriculum** in schools—that is, learning to follow orders, to be quiet, to please persons in authority regardless of the situation. In short, students learn to fit in, to conform. This may be functional for society and for students who will act out their lives in large bureaucracies, but it is not conducive to personal integrity and to acting out against situations that ought to be changed.

CHAPTER REVIEW

1. The U.S. system of education is characterized by (*a*) conservatism—the preservation of culture, roles, values, and training necessary for the maintenance of society; (*b*) belief in mass education; (*c*) local control; (*d*) competition; (*e*) reinforcement of the stratification system; and (*f*) preoccupation with order and control.

2. The belief that U.S. society is meritocratic, with the most intelligent and talented at the top, is a myth. Education, instead of being the great equalizer, reinforces social inequality.

3. Schools perform four functions that maintain the prevailing social, political, and economic order: (*a*) socializing the young; (*b*) shaping personality traits to conform with the demands of the culture; (*c*) preparing youngsters for adult roles; and (*d*) providing employers with a disciplined and skilled labor force.

4. The curricula, testing, bureaucratic control, and emphasis on competition in schools reflect the social-class structure of society by processing youth to fit into economic slots similar to those of their parents.

5. The schools are structured to aid in the perpetuation of social and economic differences in three ways: (*a*) by being financed principally through property taxes; (*b*) by providing curricula that are irrelevant to the poor; and (*c*) by tracking according to presumed level of ability.

6. The tracking system is closely correlated with social class; students from low-income families are disproportionately placed in the lowest track. Tracking thwarts the equality of educational opportunity for the poor by generating four effects: (*a*) stigma, which lowers self-esteem; (*b*) self-fulfilling prophecy; (*c*) a perception of school as having no future payoff; and (*d*) a negative student subculture.

KEY TERMS

Cultural deprivation

Tracking

Stigma

Hidden curriculum

STUDY QUESTIONS

1. Formal education reinforces the status quo. Should it? Must it? Should there be some point in the educational process when schools promote a critical assessment of society? If so, when?

2. What is meant by the political economy of education?

3. How does the formal system of education reinforce the social stratification system in society?

4. Contrast the order and the conflict perspectives on formal education.

FOR FURTHER READING

Naadya Aisenberg and Mona Harrington, *Women of Academe: Outsiders in the Sacred Grove* (Amherst: University of Massachusetts Press, 1988).

Peter W. Cookson, Jr., and Caroline Hodges Persell, *Preparing for Power: America's Elite Boarding Schools* (New York: Basic Books, 1985).

Jonathan Kozol, *Savage Inequalities: Children in America's Schools* (New York: Crown, 1991).

Daniel U. Levline and Robert J. Havighurst, *Society and Education*, 8th ed. (Boston: Allyn and Bacon, 1992).

William Noble, *Bookbanning in America* (Middlebury, VT: Paul S. Eriksson Publisher, 1990).

Myra Sadker and David Sadker, *Failing at Fairness: How America's Schools Cheat Girls* (New York: Scribner, 1994).

U.S. Department of Education, National Center for Education Statistics, *Urban Schools: The Challenge of Location and Poverty*, NCES 96–184 (Washington, DC: U.S. Government Printing Office, 1996).

Anne Wheelock, *Crossing the Tracks: How "Untracking" Can Save America's Schools* (New York: The New Press, 1992).

CHAPTER 17

Religion

The following excerpt is from a sermon by Robert H. Meneilly, senior pastor of the Village Presbyterian Church, Prairie Village, Kansas:

Religion can be the greatest thing on earth or the worst. It can be the greatest healing therapy in society, or the greatest hazard to a society's health. It can be a democratic republic's greatest good or its worst threat.

Look at the hot spots of the earth and you see religious extremists lighting the fuses—whether in Northern Ireland, Israel, Bosnia, or California. Religious extremists are breeding all kinds of "culture wars." Religion can breed all kinds of harassment, bigotry, prejudice, intolerance and deception.

Religion is peculiar. When it is not in earnest, it doesn't hurt anyone, but it doesn't do any good either. When it is in earnest, it is a most powerful force for good or evil. . . . We Christians must face up to the fact that our Christianity has propagated, in the name of Jesus, devilish acts, bloody wars, awful persecutions, hate crimes and political chaos. . . . (Meneilly, 1993:E15)

Introduction

Sociologists are interested in studying religion for two fundamental reasons. First, religion is a ubiquitous phenomenon that has a tremendous impact on human behavior. In the words of sociologist Meridith McGuire:

> Religion is one of the most powerful, deeply felt, and influential forces in human society. It has shaped people's relationships with each other, influencing family, community, economic, and political life. . . . Religious values influence their actions, and religious meanings help them interpret their experiences. (McGuire, 1992:3)

Second, sociologists study religion because of its influence on society and society's impact on religion. Religion is part of a large social system, affected by and affecting the other institutions of the society—that is, patterns of the family, the economy, education, and the polity. Because religious trends may be responses to fundamental changes in society, and some religious ideas may constrain social behaviors in a narrowly prescribed manner, the understanding of any society is incomplete unless one comprehends the religion of that society.

But, what is religion? The variety of activities and belief systems that have fallen under this rubric is almost infinite. There are some elements essential to religion, however, that allow us to distinguish it from other phenomena (taken from Nottingham, 1954:1–11). A starting point is that religion is a social construction, that is, it is created by people and is a part of culture. It is an integrated set of ideas by which a group attempts to explain the meaning of life and death. Religion is also a normative system, defining immorality and sin as well as morality and righteousness. Let us amplify some of these statements further.

- Religion deals with the ultimate of human concerns—the meaning of life and death. It provides answers as to the individual's place in society and in the universe.
- There is an emphasis on human conduct. There are prescriptions for what one ought to do as well as the consequences for one's misconduct.
- There is a distinction between the sacred and the secular. Some objects and entities are believed to have supernatural powers and are therefore treated with respect, reverence, and awe. What is sacred and what is not is a matter of belief. The range of items believed to be sacred is limitless. They may be objects (idols, altars, or amulets), animals or animal totems, parts of the natural world (sun, moon, mountains, volcanos, or rivers), transcendental beings (gods, angels, devils), or persons (living or dead, such as prophets, messiahs, or saints) (see "A Closer Look: Holy Tortilla").
- Because the sacred is held in awe, there are beliefs (theologies, cosmologies) to express and reinforce proper attitudes among believers about the sacred. The set of beliefs attempts to explain the meaning of life. McGuire says: "Religion shapes what the adherent *knows* about the world. This cosmic knowledge organizes the individual's perceptions of the world and serves as a basis for action" (McGuire, 1992:16).

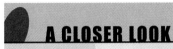

A CLOSER LOOK

Holy Tortilla

Lake Arthur, N.M.—The woman crawled on her knees from the railroad tracks in this tiny southern New Mexico town down the dirt road to the house of Maria and Eduardo Rubio.

She came in to worship, then crawled out beyond the tracks and disappeared.

The Rubios were not surprised. They have accepted that the Lord works in mysterious ways. And so have the 10,190 pilgrims who since Oct. 5, 1977, have made their way to the modest Rubio home in the middle of southeastern New Mexico's beanfields.

Mrs. Rubio was making lunch for her husband, a farmhand, on that October afternoon. That's when the face of Jesus appeared on a tortilla frying in her skillet.

She called her sister to witness the "miracle," and awakened Eduardo, who was taking a nap.

"She was crying," recalled Blanca Rubio, 21, one of the family's six children. "He told her to go to the church and the priest blessed it." Word of the event spread. The Rubios erected a wall in their living room to separate the television and the couch from a shrine to the holy object. A family from a town about 50 miles away donated a specially built altar topped by a hollow square about 10 inches deep.

Inside that square rests a spray of lavender and white plastic flowers, which Mrs. Rubio changes occasionally, a wad of cotton simulating a cloud, and the tortilla. In a square-inch of burn marks on it, some see the profile of a long-haired man with a likeness to some depictions of Jesus.

On the wall above the altar, and beside a velvet painting of a weeping Jesus, are a string of *milagros*—small metal emblems depicting arms, legs, hearts, eyes and other ailing body parts believers want hung for healing near the tortilla.

Sometimes it works, Mrs. Rubio said in Spanish. "A lady about 55 years old came here a couple of years ago in a wheelchair. She was paralyzed and promised to walk here all the way from Artesia once a year if she was cured.

"She was, and made her first walk last year," Mrs. Rubio claimed.

The oil refineries of Artesia are about 11 miles south of Lake Arthur.

Each weekend, someone prays for a sick relative or expresses gratitude for a recovery at the shrine of the tortilla. "Just yesterday, a neighbor's son pulled out of a coma, and she came by to offer thanks," said Mrs. Rubio.

More than a hundred letters have come to Lake Arthur, a few from as far as Europe, asking the Rubios' prayers to remedy a hundred kinds of suffering.

Source: Steve Chawkins, "Holy Tortilla: Burden or Blessing?" *Rocky Mountain News* (June 6, 1982):10. Reprinted from the *Rocky Mountain News*, Denver.

- **Ritual** consists of symbolic actions (e.g., processions, sacraments, candles, chanting, singing) that reinforce the collective remembering of the group's shared meanings. Ritual, then, evokes shared understandings among the believers (awe, reverence, ecstasy, fear), which lead to group unity.
- An essential ingredient of religion is the existence of a community of believers. There must be a social group that shares a set of beliefs and practices, moral values, and a sense of community (a unique identity). Again, turning to McGuire, "Coming together with fellow believers reminds members of what they collectively believe and value. It can also impart a sense of empowerment to accomplish their religious and everyday goals" (McGuire, 1992:20).

One important consequence of a group of persons having the same religious heritage and beliefs is unity. All believers, whether of high or low status, young or old, are united through the sharing of religious beliefs. Thus, religion, through the holding of common values to be cherished, sins to be avoided, rules to be followed, and symbols to be revered, integrates. Group unity is also accomplished through the universal feeling that God or the gods look on this particular group with special favor (the ethnocentric notion that "God is on our side"). An example of this is found in a verse of the national anthem of Great Britain:

> O lord our God, arise
> Scatter our enemies
> And make them fall.
> Confound their politics,
> Frustrate their knavish tricks,
> On thee our hopes, we fix,
> God save us all.

Another consequence of religion is that it constrains the behavior of the community of believers, thus providing a social control function. This is accomplished in two ways. First, there are explicit rules to obey that if violated are punished. Second, in the process of socialization, children internalize the religious beliefs and rules. In other words, they each develop a conscience, which keeps them in line through guilt and fear.

A final consequence of religion is the legitimation of social structures that have profane origins (Berger, 1967b:343–344). There is a strong tendency for religious beliefs to become intertwined with secular beliefs, thereby providing religious blessings to the values and institutions of society.

> As recently as twenty years ago, clergy in the Dutch Reformed Church of South Africa still used the Bible (Genesis 9:18–27; Joshua 9:21–27) to defend apartheid, arguing that Blacks were considered the children of Ham and therefore destined to be the "hewers of wood and the drawers of water." (Parenti, 1994:121)

Similarly, in United States society the church has endorsed a number of secular activities. The Puritan Church of the early settlers condoned witch hunts. The defeat of the Native Americans was justified by most Christian groups on the grounds that the Indians were heathens and in need of Christianity. Finally, most religious denominations sought Biblical rationalizations for slavery (van den Berghe, 1967:82).

The same religious bases that promote group integration also divide. Religious groups tend to emphasize separateness and superiority, thereby defining others as inferior (infidels, heathens, heretics, or nonbelievers). This occurs because each religious group tends to feel it has the way (and perhaps the only way) to achieve salvation or reach nirvana or whatever the goal.

Religious differences accentuate the differences among societies, denominations, and even within local churches. Because religious groups have feelings of superiority, there may be conflict brought about by discrimination, competition for converts, or feelings of hatred. Also, because religious ideas tend to be strongly held, groups may split rather than compromise. Liberals and fundamentalists, even within the same religion, denomination, or local church, will, doubtless, disagree on numerous issues. A common result, of course, is division.

A major divisive characteristic of religion is its tendency, through established churches, to accept the acts of the state. Within the church, there have always been people who spoke out against the church's cohabitation with the secular. This ability of the church to rationalize the activities of the state no matter how onerous has split many churches and denominations. The slavery issue, for example, split Baptists into American Baptists and Southern Baptists.

Conflict itself can occur between religious groups (with the sanction of each religion). Recent world history gives bloody evidence of this occurrence (for example, Muslims versus Hindus in India and Pakistan; Muslims versus Jews in the Middle East; Catholics versus Protestants in Northern Ireland; Catholics, Eastern Orthodox, and Muslims fighting each other in Bosnia-Herzegovina). Religious conflict has also occurred within the United States at various times. Confrontations between Catholics and Protestants, between warring sects of Muslims (Black Muslims versus Sunni Muslims), as well as between Protestants and Jews, have been fairly commonplace. Clearly, religious values are reason enough for individuals and groups to clash.

Classical Sociology's Differing Interpretations of Religion

The great classical sociologists—Emile Durkheim (1858–1917), Karl Marx (1818–1883), and Max Weber (1864–1920)—wrote perceptively about religion. From different perspectives and asking different questions, each theorist adds to our sociological understanding of the differing consequences of religion on society and its members.

Religion from the Order Perspective of Emile Durkheim

Durkheim, the French sociologist, wrote *The Elementary Forms of Religious Life* in 1912 (1965). This classic work explored the question of why religion is universal in human societies. He reasoned that religion must help to maintain society. Durkheim studied the religion of the Australian aborigines to understand the possible role of religion in societal survival.

Durkheim found that each aborigine clan had its own totem, an object it considered sacred. The totem—a kangaroo, lizard, tree, river, or rock formation—was sacred because the clan believed that it symbolized the unique qualities of the clan. Two of Durkheim's interpretations are important in this regard. First, people bestow the notion of the sacred onto something, rather than that object being intrinsically sacred. Second, what the group worships is really society itself. Thus, people create religion.* Because the members of a society share religious beliefs, they are a moral community and as such the solidarity of the society is enhanced.

The society is held together by religious rituals and festivals in which the group's values and beliefs are reaffirmed. Each new generation is socialized to accept these beliefs, ensuring consensus on what is right and wrong. Religion, then, whether it be among the pre-industrial Australian aborigines, the Muslims of the Middle East, the Buddhists of Asia, or the Christians of North America, serves the same functions of promoting order and unity. In short, as people meet together to affirm common beliefs and values, they are bound together in a moral community.

Religion from the Conflict Perspective of Karl Marx

Whereas Durkheim interpreted the unity achieved through religion as positive, Marx viewed it as negative. Religion inhibits societal change by making existing social arrangements seem right and inevitable. The dominant form of economics in society, the type of government, the law, and other social creations are given religious sanction. Thus, the system remains stable, which the order theorists see as good, when it perhaps should be transformed to meet the needs of all of the people.

Religion promotes the status quo in other ways. The powerless are taught to accept religious beliefs that are against their own interests. The Hindus, for example, believe that it is the person's duty to accept his or her caste. Failure to do so will result in being reincarnated to a lower caste or even as an animal. Christianity proclaims that the poor should accept their lot in this life for they will be rewarded. As the Bible says, "the meek shall inherit the earth." This says, in effect, do not assert yourself, accept oppression, and good things will happen. From this perspective, oppression and poverty are reinterpreted by religion to be a special form of righteousness. Thus, religion is the ultimate tool to promote false consciousness.

Max Weber's View of Religion and Social Change

Max Weber disagreed fundamentally with Marx's notions that (1) religion impeded social change by being an **opiate of the masses** and by encouraging the oppressed to accept their lot and (2) economic considerations superseded ideology. Weber's classic, *The Protestant Ethic and the Spirit of Capitalism* (1958, first published in 1904), refuted Marx on both grounds. Weber demonstrated that the religious beliefs of John Calvin (1509–1564) were instrumental to the rise of capitalism in Europe. The Calvinist doctrine of predestination was the key. Because God, by

---

*This raises an important question: Do we create God or is there a supernatural force somewhere that human beings grope to find? Durkheim is correct in stating that religion is a social product. This universal response, however, does not prove or disprove the existence of God(s). Sociologists as individuals may have strong religious beliefs, but as sociologists they focus on the complex relationship between religion and society.

definition, knows everything, God knows who will go to heaven (the elect) and who will be condemned to hell *even before they are born.* This view was disconcerting to believers because it meant that one's future was locked in (predestined). Calvinists dealt with their anxiety by emphasizing economic success as the indicator to themselves and others of being one of God's elect. The rationale for this emphasis was that surely God would reward the chosen in this life as well as in the afterlife. This belief led Calvinists to work very hard, to live frugally, to accumulate savings, and to invest those savings in more land, equipment, and labor. Thus, the particular religious beliefs of the Calvinists were conducive to the development of capitalism in Europe and later among the colonies in America. Religious ideology, in this case, led to economic change.

Some Distinctive Features of U.S. Religion

Civil Religion

One feature of U.S. religion, traditionally, has been the separation of church and state (established by the First Amendment to the Constitution). This is both a consequence and the cause of the religious diversity found in the United States. There is a relationship between religion and the state in the United States, but it differs from the usual conception of one dominant church that is inseparable from the state. In many respects, "God and Country" are conceived by most people as one. This has been labeled the civil religion of the United States (Bellah, 1967).

Civil religion in the United States is seemingly antithetical to the constitutional demand for separation of church and state. The paradox is that on the one hand the government sanctions God (the Pledge of Allegiance has the phrase "one nation, under God"; the phrase "In God We Trust" is stamped on all money; every presidential inaugural address except Washington's second has mentioned God; and present-day presidents have regularly scheduled prayer breakfasts), while at the same time declaring it illegal to have prayer and/or religious instruction in the public schools. The basis for the paradox is that the civil religion is not a specific creed. It is a set of beliefs, symbols, and rituals that is broad enough for all citizens to accept. The God of the civil religion is all things to all people. One thing is certain—politicians, if they want to be successful, must show some semblance of piety by occasionally invoking the blessings of this nondenominational, nonsectarian God.

Several central themes of the civil religion are important for understanding U.S. society. First, there is the belief that God has a special destiny for the United States. This implies that God is actively involved in history and, most important, that the country has a holy mission to carry out God's will on earth. John F. Kennedy phrased this message well in the conclusion to his inauguration address: "With a good conscience our only sure reward, with history the final judge of our deeds, let

One thing is certain—politicians, if they want to be successful, must show some semblance of piety by invoking the blessings of the nondenominational, nonsectarian God of civil religion.

us go forth to lead the land we love, asking His blessing and His help, but knowing that here on earth God's work must truly be our own" (quoted in Bellah, 1967:1–2). This belief has been the source of self-righteousness in foreign relations. It has allowed people to subdue the pagan Indians, win the frontier, follow a policy of manifest destiny, and defeat fascism and communism. President Reagan, for example, exhorted people in the United States to understand that Communism was evil and that God wanted us to be strong. Thus, he invoked Scripture to justify a strong defense:

> I found myself wanting to remind you of what Jesus said in Luke 14:31: "Oh, what king, when he sets out to make [war]—or meet another king in battle will not first sit down and take counsel whether he is strong enough with 10,000 men to encounter the one coming against him with 20,000. Or else, while the other is still far away, sends a delegation and asks the terms of peace." I don't think the Lord that blessed this country, as no other county has ever been blessed, intends for us to have to someday negotiate because of our weakness. (quoted in Piernard and Linder, 1988:280)

Similarly, President Bush argued that God was on our side in the Persian Gulf war.

> During the 1992 presidential campaign, Bush cited Jesus Christ as the moral force behind his military interventionism, claiming that during the Persian Gulf war "America, as Christ ordained" was "a light unto the world." (Parenti, 1992:43)

A second aspect of the civil religion is maintenance of the status quo. The God of civil religion is more closely allied to law and order than to changing the system. Thus, civil religion tends strongly toward uncritical endorsement of U.S. values and the system of stratification. Order and unity are the traditional ways of God, not change and dissent. Thus, public policy tends to receive religious sanction.

At the same time, however, the civil religion enjoins people in the United States to stand up for certain principles—freedom, individualism, equal opportunity. Consequently, there are occasions when current governmental policy or the policy of some group is criticized because it does not measure up to certain ideals. The civil religion of the United States, then, accomplishes both the **priestly** (acceptance of what is) and the **prophetic** (challenging the existing system) **roles of religion,** with emphasis, however, on the former.

The Variety of Religious Belief

Some societies are unified by religion. All persons in those societies believe the same religious ideas, worship the same deities, obey the same moral commandments, and identify strongly with each other. Superficially, through its civil religion, the United States appears to be homogeneous along religious lines. A 1990 survey of 113,000 people nationwide found that 86.5 percent of the people in 1990 were Christian; 3.7 belonged to non-Christian faiths; 7.5 percent had no religion; and 2.3 percent refused to participate in the survey (reported in Goldman, 1991). It is important to note, that while Christians are the clear majority in the United States, there are also 6 million Jews, 5 million Muslims, and millions of other non-Christians, including Buddhists and Hindus (see "Diversity: Islam in the United States").

The range of attitudes and beliefs among U.S. Christians is fantastically wide. Among Roman Catholics, for example, there are radical priests, nuns, and parish-

Diversity

Islam in the United States

Islam has about 1 billion followers worldwide, second only to Christianity (the following is taken from Stone, 1994; El-Badry, 1994; Herrmann, 1994; and Sontag, 1993). Muslims believe in one god, Allah, as their creator and the sustainer of the universe. The founder of Islam was Mohammed, an Arab born in Mecca about 570 who is believed to be Allah's messenger. Their scripture, the Koran, is a recording of divine revelation as revealed by the prophet Mohammed. Observant Muslims perform five key duties (the Five Pillars of Islam): accepting no god but Allah and Mohammed as his prophet, prayer five times a day, fasting during the ninth month in the Islamic lunar year, giving to charity, and making a pilgrimage to Mecca at least once in a lifetime.

There are about 5 million Muslims in the United States, outnumbering Episcopalians and Presbyterians. About 1 million Muslims live in California, 800,000 in New York, and 420,000 in Illinois (300,000 in Chicago). Early in the next century, Muslims in this country will likely surpass Jews in number, making them the second largest religion. Their growth in the United States is evidenced by the tenfold growth in the number of Islamic houses of worship (mosques) since 1960—from 104 to 1,100 in 1993.

American Muslims do not comprise a monolithic group. More than half came as immigrants, from many different countries (24 percent from the nations of South Asia—India, Pakistan, Bangladesh, and Sri Lanka; 12 percent from the Middle East; 6 percent from Africa; others come from Iran, Turkey, Southeast Asia, and Eastern Europe). Of those U.S.-born converts to Islam, 42 percent are African Americans. Although most Muslims are conservative on social issues (opposing abortion, premarital sex, homosexuality, divorce, alcohol use, and dancing), there are differences in beliefs and levels of activism. For example, although Muslim women are encouraged to dress modestly, their clothing varies from head scarfs and floor-length dresses to fashions not unlike that of other U.S. women. Only 10 percent of U.S. Muslims practice Islam's five pillars. Like any other religious group, Muslims have different sects within; there are Sunnis and Shiites (they differ on who are descendants of Mohammed); there are about 20,000 who belong to Louis Farrakhan's Nation of Islam.

Their religion differs from Christianity, they are typically people of color, and they are stereotyped as religious and political zealots. Therefore, Muslims in the United States are often objects of discrimination, hostility, and hate crimes. During the Gulf War, for example, hate crimes (arsons, bombings, physical assaults) against Arab-Americans surged. Before and after the Gulf War, FBI agents surveilled business and community leaders of Arab descent. Immediately after the bombing of the federal building in Oklahoma City, there were rumors that this was the work of Muslim terrorists. In short, Muslims are marginalized. As Ghazi Khankan, president of the National Council on Islamic Affairs, has put it: "To demonize, to dehumanize my people, my way of life, my religion is unfair, un-American and undemocratic" (quoted in Sontag, 1993:19).

---

ioners who disobey the instructions of bishops, cardinals, and even the Pope. At the same time, however, there are Catholics who rigidly adhere to all the rules set down by the church authorities. The range within Protestantism is even greater. Many Protestants believe that the Bible is to be taken literally, word for word; for others, the Bible is purely allegorical. Some religious groups have so much faith in the healing power of religion that their members refuse to see physicians under any circumstances. Within Protestantism are Amish, Hutterites, Quakers, high-church Episcopalians, Pentecostal Holiness groups, Congregationalists, and even snake handlers.

Religious Organization

Church and Sect.   Very broadly, U.S. religious organizations can be divided according to their secular commitments into two categories—churches and sects (Troeltsch, 1931). Religious groups have a choice—to reject and withdraw from the secular society, or to accommodate to it. The basis for a decision to reject the social environment is maintenance of spiritual and ethical purity. Such a choice, by definition, entails withdrawal from the world, thereby consciously avoiding any chance to change it. The opposite choice—accommodation—requires compromise and the loss of distinctive ideals, but it also means that the groups can influence the larger society. The accommodation or resistance to the secular world is the fundamental difference between a church and a sect.

The **church,** as an ideal type, has the following attributes:

- The tendency to compromise with the larger society and its values and institutions.
- Membership tends to occur by being born to parents who belong. Membership, moreover, takes place through infant baptism, which implies that all members are saved.
- A hierarchy of authority, with those at the top being trained for their vocation.
- Acceptance of a diversity of beliefs, because the membership is large, and for many the scriptures are interpreted metaphorically rather than literally. There is a tolerance of the popular vices.

A **sect** in its perfect form is exactly opposite a church in every way.

- There is a fundamental withdrawal from and rejection of the world. A sect is a moral community separate from and in many ways hostile toward the secular world (see Scanzoni, 1980).
- Membership is only through a conversion experience. Membership is therefore voluntary and limited to adults. Hence, adult baptism is the only accepted form of baptism.
- Organization is informal and unstructured. Ministers are untrained. They became ministers by being called from the group.
- The belief system is rigid. The Bible is the source, and it is interpreted literally. The goal of the membership is spiritual purity as found in the early Christian Church.
- There are rigid ethical requirements restraining the members from the popular vices of drinking, smoking, card playing, dancing, and cursing.

The church–sect dichotomy does not exhaust all the possibilities. Some religious groups would fit somewhere in between—as institutionalized sects. These groups (for example, Mormons, Disciples of Christ, and Southern Baptists) incorporate features of both a church (trained leadership, some accommodation to the larger society) with the sectlike attributes of adult baptism and an unwillingness to compromise on some theological questions.

For our purposes, however, the church–sect dichotomy, while oversimplifying the situation, is useful in two ways: to depict a form of social change, and to show why certain categories of persons are attracted to one type and not the other.

The church–sect dichotomy illustrates an important sociological phenomenon—the process of organization deflects away from the original goal of the group. A group may form to pursue a goal such as religious purity, but in so doing it creates a new organization, which means that some of the group's energies will be spent in organizational maintenance. Consequently, a sect may form with the explicit intention of eliminating a hierarchy and a codification of beliefs. Patterns of behavior emerge, however, as certain practices are found to be more effective. In particular, the selection of ministers tends to become routinized, and a system of religious instruction for children is developed so that they will learn the catechism in the proper sequence.

Sects, then, tend to become churches. This is illustrated by the type of leader found in each. Often a sect is formed by a charismatic person and his or her followers. This person is followed because he or she is believed to possess extraordinary qualities of leadership, saintliness, gifts of prophecy, or ability to heal.

What happens to such an organization when this leadership is gone? The organization is faced with a crisis of succession. Groups typically find ways to pass on the **charisma** (the extraordinary attributes) of the original leader. This process is called the **routinization of charisma** (whereby an organization attempts to transmit the charisma of the former leader to a new one). This is done by (1) selection of the successor by the original charismatic leader, (2) designation of a successor by the group closest to the original leader ("disciples"), (3) hereditary transmission, or (4) transmission of charisma by ritual ("laying on of hands") (Weber, 1947:358–366). In this last instance there is the recognition of a **charisma of office**—that is, whoever holds the position possesses charisma. When this occurs, the organizational machinery is advanced enough to move the group away from its sectlike qualities toward a church. The important sociological point here is that organizations seldom remain the same. The simple tends to become complex. But the process does not stop at complexity; as the original goal of the sect (religious purity with the necessity of separation from the world) is superseded when the organization gets larger and more bureaucratic, some persons will become dissatisfied enough to break away and form a new sect. Thus, the process tends to be cyclical.

Increased bureaucratization (and subsequent splintering) is characteristic of modern urban society. This leads us to a final consideration relative to the church–sect dichotomy—the motivation to join sects. At the risk of oversimplification, two important features of sects help explain why some categories of persons are especially prone to join sects rather than churches. The first is that a sect (more so than a church) may provide a total world of meaning and social identity, and a close circle of persons to whom members can turn when troubled. The sect provides precisely those things missing in the lives of many urban dwellers. They find meaning in a meaningless world. They find friends in a sea of strangers. They find stability in a setting that is rapidly undergoing change. Thus, the alienated are especially attracted to sects. So, too, are new migrants to the city. In the city, they are confronted with a variety of new and difficult problems—industrialized work, work insecurity, loss of kinship ties, and disruption of other primary-group ties. The sects, unlike the established city churches, appeal to such persons by their form of worship, emphasis on individual attention, and lack of formal organization (Yinger, 1961:21–25).

A second variable affecting attraction to a sect or church is social class. Generally, low-status persons tend to be attracted to sects rather than to churches because religious status is substituted for social status (or as the Bible puts it, "and the last shall be first"). It makes sense for persons of low social or economic status to reject this world and the religious bodies that accommodate to it. Such persons would be especially attracted to a religious group that rejects this world and assures its followers that in the next world true believers—those who are religiously pure—will have the highest status. The sect represents to its followers a reaction against or escape from the dominant religious and economic systems in society. It is a protest against the failure of established churches to meet the needs of marginal groups (Pope, 1942:140). The sect, moreover, rejects the social class as irrelevant and, in fact, as a system of rewards that is in exact reverse order from God's will.*

Churches, on the other hand, attract the middle and upper classes. Since these persons are successful, they obviously would not turn to a religious organization that rejects their world. As Max Weber has said:

> Other things being equal, classes with high social and economic privilege will scarcely be prone to evolve the ideas of salvation. Rather, they assign to religion the primary function of legitimizing their own life pattern and situation in this world. (Weber, 1963:107)

Both the sect and the church, consequently, have well-developed theodicies (Berger, 1967a). A **theodicy** is a religious legitimation for a situation that otherwise might cause guilt or anger (such as defeat in a war or the existence of poverty among affluence). Sects tend to have a theodicy of suffering—that is, a religious explanation for their lack of power and privilege. Churches must explain the inequalities of society, too, but their emphasis is on legitimation of possessing power and privilege. This tendency to develop theodicies has the important social function of preserving the status quo. Churches convince their adherents that all is well, that one should accept one's fate as God-given. This makes people's situations less intolerable and the possibility of revolution remote—the suffering know they will be rewarded, while the guilt of the well-off is assuaged. Consequently, there is no reason to change the system.

Cult. A **cult** is a new religion with practices and teachings at odds with the dominant culture and religion. In other words, a cult rejects society and established religions. Typically, the members of a cult give extreme devotion to a charismatic leader who requires much of them (their material goods, their work, a demanding lifestyle, and a total, intense commitment). A cult differs from a sect in one fundamental way. A sect is a religious group that leaves an established church to recapture what it considers the essence of their religious tradition. A cult, on the other hand, represents religious innovation, a new religious expression.

---

*It is incorrect to say, however, that all lower-class persons who are alienated will join religious sects in order to attack the establishment. Their estrangement may lead them to join other kinds of social movements (e.g., labor or political) or toward social isolation.

We tend to think of cults and their followers as bizarre. They are because, by definition, they differ from the rest of us; they reject society and claim to have religious experiences that are alien to most of us. Most of these groups ultimately fail. The message fades; the predictions misfire; the charismatic leader dies and his or her replacement disappoints. But while we tend to think of these groups as weird and transitory, we should remember that many of the major religious groups of today, including Christianity, Mormonism, Islam, and Judaism, began as cults.

Class, Race, Gender, Sexuality, and Religion

The Relationship between Socioeconomic Status and Religion

The dominant religion in the United States, Christianity, stresses the equality of all people in the sight of God. All persons, regardless of socioeconomic status, are welcomed in Christianity. We might expect, therefore, that the distribution of members by socioeconomic status within any denomination would be randomly distributed. We might also assume that the organization of any local congregation would ignore status distinctions. Although these two assumptions seem to have surface validity, the empirical situation refutes them.

We have seen that sects and churches tend to have a social-class bias—the lower the socioeconomic status, the greater the probability of belonging to a sect. There also seems to be a ranking of denominations in terms of the socioeconomic status of their members. Although there is always a range of the social classes within any one denomination, there is a modal status that characterizes each. The reasons for this are varied: the proportion of members living in rural or urban areas, which immigrant groups brought the religion to the colonies or United States and during what historical period, and the appeal of the religious experience (ritual, evangelism, close personal ties, salvation, legitimation of the social system, or attacks on the establishment). This last point is especially important because "life conditions affect men's religious propensities, and life conditions are significantly correlated with the facts of stratification in all societies" (O'Dea, 1966:60).

There is a relationship between socioeconomic status, educational attainment, and denominational affiliation. Judaism has the highest proportion of high-education and high-income members, followed in order by Episcopalian, Presbyterian, Methodist, Lutheran, Catholic, and Baptist. This is an oversimplification, however, since each denomination includes persons of high, middle, and lower status.

Local churches, even more so than denominations, tend to be homogeneous in socioeconomic status. This is partly the result of residential patterns—that is, neighborhoods are relatively homogeneous by socioeconomic status, and the local churches are attended mostly by persons living nearby. Another reason, and perhaps just as important, is the tendency for persons to want to belong to organizations composed of persons like themselves. They do not want to feel out of place, so they are attracted to churches where the members have the same lifestyle (for example, speech patterns, clothing tastes, and educational backgrounds). The result, then, is that persons belonging to a particular denomination will often seek out the local congregation in the city where they feel most comfortable.

There is some range, however, in every local church. Probably no one congregation is comprised totally of persons from exactly the same status niche. Although the status differentials may be minimal within a local congregation, they are evidently important to the parishioners. The rule is that the higher the socioeconomic status of the member, the greater his or her influence in the running of the local church. There is greater likelihood that such persons will be elected or appointed to office (elder, deacon, trustee, Sunday school superintendent) and that their opinions will carry greater weight than persons of lower social status. This may be partly a function of the disproportionately large financial contributions by the more well-to-do, but the important point here is that the secular world intrudes in the organization of each local congregation. The common indicators of religious involvement—church membership, attendance at church services, and participation in the church's activities—demonstrate a relationship to socioeconomic status. On each of these measures, persons of high status are more involved than those of low status. Unfortunately, these are not very good measures of religiosity, although often assumed to be. The problem is that upper-class persons are much more likely to join and actively participate in all sorts of organizations. The joining of churches and attending services are the manifestations of a more general phenomenon—the tendency for middle- and upper-class persons to be joiners, while lower-class individuals tend to isolate themselves from all types of organizations. The spuriousness of the relationship between socioeconomic status and religiosity is more clearly seen when we analyze the importance of religion to persons of varying socioeconomic circumstances, as well as differences in religious beliefs and the degree to which church activities are secular by social class.

William J. Goode, after comparing white-collar church members with working-class church members, found that while the former were more likely to belong to and participate in formal activities of the church, the latter were actually more religious.

> They participate less in formal church activities, but their religious activity does not appear to be nearly so secularized. It is more specifically religious in character. This is indicated by the fact that on a number of other religious dimensions, dimensions not dependent on extraneous nonreligious variables, individuals of manual-status levels appear to display a considerably higher level of religious response. This is true particularly of psychological variables, such as religious "salience," the greater feeling that the church and religion are great forces in the lives of respondents. It is also true for "religiosity" as measured by a higher level of religious concern, and for religious "involvement," the extent to which the individual is psychologically dependent on some sort of specifically religious association in his life. (Goode, 1966:111)

There is evidence for the "secularization of religion" by social class. Polling data reveals that the more education and income, the less likely to find religion important and to hold traditional religious beliefs. Table 17.1 shows this tendency regarding beliefs about heaven, hell, and the Devil.

In summary, there is a rather complex relationship between socioeconomic status and religion. Although the relatively poor and uneducated are more likely to be indifferent to religion than are the better educated and financially well-off, those who are religious tend to make religion a more integral part of their lives than do better-off persons. They go to church more for religious than secular reasons. They believe much more strongly than do the well-to-do in the fundamental beliefs as expressed in the Bible. Thus, we have the paradox that on many objective measures of religious involvement—church attendance and participation in formal church activities—middle- and upper-status people exceed those of less status, whereas if importance of religion in the lives of the individual is considered, the poor who go to church outstrip their more economically favored brethren.

Religion and Race: The Case of African Americans

As with other social phenomena, race and religion separate people. As noted earlier, historically most White churches in the United States chose to ignore or actively support racial segregation. The issue of the legitimacy of slavery divided some White congregations and denominations. For example, the Southern Baptist Convention was a denomination conceived out of support for slavery. In 1995, 150

TABLE 17.1

Belief in Heaven, Hell, the Devil by Income and Education

	HEAVEN		HELL		THE DEVIL		
	YES	NO	YES	NO	BELIEVE	NOT SURE	DON'T BELIEVE
Income							
$75,000 & over	80%	19%	65%	34%	58%	6%	36%
$50,000 to 74,999	86%	13%	72%	27%	61%	7%	32%
$30,000 to 49,999	89%	9%	77%	21%	70%	8%	22%
$20,000 to 29,999	92%	7%	77%	21%	67%	10%	22%
Under $20,000	92%	6%	71%	25%	66%	6%	26%
Education							
College postgrad.	75%	21%	58%	39%	45%	14%	40%
College graduate	80%	16%	65%	33%	54%	10%	35%
Some college	90%	9%	75%	23%	67%	8%	24%
No college	94%	5%	76%	20%	70%	6%	23%

Source: The Gallup Poll Monthly, No. 352 (January 1995):16. Reprinted by permission.

years after taking that pro-slavery stand, the Southern Baptists Convention passed a resolution confessing to a sin of historic proportion: "We lament and repudiate historic acts of evil such as slavery from which we continue to reap a bitter harvest" (quoted in Sheler, 1995:10). Similarly, Pope John Paul II apologized for the church's complicity in the African slave trade. Also, of historic importance to Blacks everywhere, the Dutch Reformed Church in 1991 formally apologized to Black South Africans for having provided religious justification for apartheid. While these sweeping apologies are important symbolically, we should note that they were slow in coming. It took the Southern Baptists, for example, 150 years—and a full 30 years after the height of the civil rights struggle—to finally admit to their support of racism.

Local churches are among the most segregated organizations. They tend to be exclusively of one race or predominantly White or Black. Some observers have suggested, for example, that the most segregated hour left in the United States is 11 o'clock on Sunday morning.

This segregation by race is the consequence of a number of factors: a reflection of residential segregation patterns, past and present discrimination, and denominational loyalty (Jaynes and Williams, 1989:92). Most significant for African Americans is that their local churches are one of the few organizations over which they have control. Moreover, these historic Black churches have been not only the foci of their religion but also key components of the Black community's social life, the sources for helping those in need, and centers for Black political activities. Significantly, the leaders of the civil rights movement in the 1960s were almost exclusively African American clergy. These Black churches have been targets of arson by White racists (over 100 burned from 1990 to mid-1996) precisely because they are so important socially and politically to their Black communities. According to C. Eric Lincoln, this present-day expression of racism carries on the tradition of White supremacist violence that has been common since the beginning of Black churches in this country (Lincoln, 1996).

Religion and Gender

The three dominant religions in the United States—Christianity, Judaism, and Islam—have been patriarchal. Each worships a male God, recognizes only males as prophets, and has historically given men the highest religious leadership roles. Significantly, their belief systems have been used to legitimize female subordination to males (see "Diversity: Religion and Patriarchy").

These religions began in historical times and places where women were clearly subservient to men in all aspects of society. However, this patriarchal tradition continues. Women are formally denied the role of pastor, minister, priest, or rabbi in the Missouri Synod Lutheran Church, the Greek Orthodox Church, the Church of Latter Day Saints, the Catholic Church, the Southern Baptist Church, and Orthodox Judaism. Pope John Paul II, for example, stated in 1995 that the Roman Catholic Church's ban on women priests is "founded on the written Word of God and that it is to be held always, everywhere and by all" (quoted by Religion News Service, 1995). In other denominations there have been bitter fights over this matter, with

Diversity

Religion and Patriarchy

The great religions and their leaders have consistently taught that women were secondary to men. Consider the following examples of this thought, which supported men as God's chosen leaders:

- One hundred women are not worth a single testicle.
  Confucius (551–479 BC)

- In childhood a woman must be subject to her father; in youth to her husband; when her husband is dead, to her sons. A woman must never be free of subjugation.
  The Hindu Code of Manu (circa 100 AD)

- If . . . the tokens of virginity are not found in the young woman, then they shall bring out the young woman to the door of her father's house, and the men of the city shall stone her to death with stones because she has wrought folly . . . so you shall purge the evil from the midst of you.
  Deuteronomy 22:20–21 (Old Testament)

- Blessed art thou, O Lord our God and King of the Universe, that thou didst not create me a woman.
  Daily prayer (ancient and contemporary) of the Orthodox Jewish male

- Let a woman learn in silence with all submissiveness. I permit no woman to teach or to have authority over men; she is to keep silent.
  I Timothy 2:11–15 (New Testament)

- Men are superior to women.
  The Koran (circa 650 AD)

- Women should remain at home, sit still, keep house, and bear and bring up children . . .
  Martin Luther (1438–1546)

- Woman in her greatest perfection was made to serve and obey man, not rule and command him.
  John Knox (1505–1572)

Given these pronouncements we should not be surprised that women traditionally have not held positions of spiritual leadership within organized religion. But these statements were made long ago at historical times when women were clearly subservient to men in all aspects of society.

Serious questions remain: Will congregations accept women clergy in the same way they do men? Will women clergy be called to lead the largest and most prestigious congregations? Will the hierarchy in the various denominations promote women to the highest offices? And, will some religious groups continue to deny women the clergy role?

Source: The quotations were taken from a list compiled by Meg Bowman, "Why We Burn: Sexism Exorcised," The Humanist 43 (November/December 1983):28–29.

some dissidents breaking away to form separate organizations when women were allowed to become ministers. The majority of Protestant denominations now have women in the ministry, as do Reformed and Conservative Judaism. Clearly, though, women clergy are not only underrepresented but have not kept up with the gains by women in other professions—women now account for 25 percent of lawyers and 21 percent of physicians, *but only 11 percent of clergy.* Moreover, women clergy with the same training as men clergy were much less likely to be senior pastors, thereby receiving, on average $5,000 less in annual salary and benefits than their male peers (Briggs, 1995).

Religion and Sexuality

The Judeo–Christian tradition considers homosexual behavior a heinous sin. The Old Testament approves of sexual intercourse only within marriage and for the purpose of procreation. The New Testament continued this tradition. The Apostle Paul, for example, wrote in *Corinthians* that homosexuals would never inherit the kingdom of God.

Contemporary Christian churches and denominations have varied in their response to homosexuality. For conservatives there is no issue—homosexuality is a sin. The Reverend Jerry Falwell, fundamentalist preacher and founder of the Moral Majority, for example, called the outbreak of AIDS among homosexuals a "form of judgment of God upon a society" (cited in Crooks and Baur, 1987:312). The fundamentalists also try to affect public and corporate policy regarding their values. The Southern Baptist Convention in 1996, for instance, threatened to boycott the Walt Disney Corporation because Disney provides the same health care benefits for the live-in mates of gay employees as it does for the spouses of straight workers.

In the more liberal denominations and churches, the issue has often been divisive, with some resisting doctrinal change while others seek the acceptance of homosexuals, the recognition of loving unions outside of marriage, and even the ordination of gay and lesbian clergy.

Religious Trends

Religion in U.S. society is a paradox. On the one hand, religion seems to be losing its vitality. The data show that in the past forty years or so there has been a downward trend, a leveling off, and most recently a decrease in regular church attendance (see Table 17.2). There are several trends within these data. First, the attendance by Protestants during this period has remained about the same, while the percentage of Catholics attending church at least once a week has fallen dramatically. The data also show that the percentage of young adults attending church regularly has fallen, and that the largest denominations—Episcopal, Methodist, and Presbyterian—are declining in both attendance and membership.

On the other hand, however, there are indications that people in the United States are just as religious as ever, and in some areas there is even dramatic growth. Bill Moyers argues that there is a current surge in the search for an understanding of core principles of belief.

> We shouldn't be surprised by all this stirring. It's a confusing time, marked by social and moral ambivalence and, for many, economic insecurity. People yearn for spiritual certainty and collective self-confidence. (Moyers, 1996:4)

Americans have consistently and overwhelmingly believed in God, with survey findings that about nine out of ten adults in the United States believes in God or a

TABLE 17.2

Percentage Attending Church during Average Week (1954–1994)							
1954	46	1964	45	1974	40	1984	40
1955	49	1965	44	1975	40	1985	42
1956	46	1966	44	1976	41	1986	40
1957	47	1967	43	1977	41	1987	40
1958	49	1968	43	1978	41	1988	42
1959	47	1969	42	1979	40	1989	43
1960	47	1970	42	1980	40	1991	43
1961	47	1971	40	1981	41	1992	43
1962	46	1972	40	1982	41	1993	41
1963	46	1973	40	1983	40	1994	38

Source: The Gallup Poll Monthly, No. 353 (February 1995):19. Reprinted by permission.

universal spirit. Martin E. Marty, a religion scholar from the University of Chicago, reflecting on these data, said that it is

> astonishing that in a high-tech, highly affluent nation, we have 90 percent who identify themselves as religious. If such a poll were done in Western Europe, the ancestral home of many Americans, you would run at least a third or lower on every indicator. (quoted in Goldman, 1991:E3)

Contrary to the experience of the mainline churches, some religious groups are growing rapidly in members and interest. The fastest growing in percentage gain is the Mormon Church. More significant because of their growing numbers nationwide and their political leverage are the evangelical denominations and sects. In this section we highlight three major trends of U.S. religion: (1) the decline of the mainline churches, (2) the rise of the evangelicals, and (3) the new political activism of the evangelicals and the decline of religious pluralism. Because social conditions have led to these shifts, the focus is on the societal conditions that have given impetus to these trends.

Decline of the Mainline Denominations

Together, the mainline denominations of the United Church of Christ (which includes most Congregationalists), Presbyterians, Episcopalians, American Baptists, United Methodists, Evangelical Lutherans, and the Disciples of Christ (Christian) suffered membership losses of 6.1 million from 1965 to 1992, a time when the U.S. population rose by more than 50 million (Woodward, 1993). At the same time, the Mormons, African American Protestant groups, and the conservative evangelical groups increased membership substantially.

The reasons for the decline in the mainline denominations are not altogether clear, but the following appear plausible. These denominations have lost their vitality as they have become more and more churchlike (and have moved away from the qualities characterizing sects). The beliefs within these churches have become so pluralistic that to many people the faith seems watered down. Many churchgoers want authority, but they too often receive only more ambiguity. The mainline churches also have lost members because of a preoccupation with political and social issues at the expense of an emphasis on an old-fashioned faith and biblical teachings for personal growth.

Because other parts of society emphasize rationality, efficiency, and bureaucracy, many persons seek a religion that will emphasize feelings and fellowship. However, the mainline churches, for the most part, are just as impersonal and ossified as the other bureaucracies in society.

The Catholic Church has been especially vulnerable to losses in attendance. In this case, the rigidity of the Catholic hierarchy is partly responsible. The Church has taken strong stances against contraception, abortion, gender equality, homosexuality, and divorce. Many Catholics feel that the Church authorities are out of step with contemporary life. The Catholic and some other traditional churches have also lost credence with some people for their refusal to accept women in leadership roles. This patriarchal emphasis by some churches, however, is a positive attraction for some individuals, as we discuss later.

An interesting recent development has been the defection of many Latino Catholics for evangelical Protestant denominations. Surveys indicate that approximately 20 percent of Latino Americans identify themselves as Protestant, with about 60,000 joining Protestant denominations each year. There are several reasons for this shift away from traditional membership patterns. First, the emotional power of the evangelicals appeals to many Whites and Latinos alike. Second, Latino Catholics often find linguistic and cultural barriers in the Church. Only 2 percent of Catholic priests (fewer than 2,000), for example, are Latino. Meanwhile, the Southern Baptists, to name just one evangelical denomination, has 2,300 Latino pastors and 500 more in seminary training. Finally, critics charge that Latino Americans suffer various forms of discrimination within the U.S. Catholic Church. These charges include the failure of the Church hierarchy to encourage religious vocations among Latino Americans, a hesitancy to elevate Latino priests to higher posts, and a reluctance to accept rituals meaningful to Latinos, such as devotions to the Virgin of Guadelupe.

Rise of Christian Fundamentalism

Beginning in the late 1960s there has been a rise in Christian fundamentalism. Although there are variations among fundamentalists, there is a set of beliefs they tend to share.

> Most simply put, [Christian fundamentalism] refers to the world view of people who think that the Bible is the inerrant word of God and who have accepted Jesus Christ as their Lord and Savior. But [it] goes beyond acceptance of such fundamentals of the faith.

It involves at least the idea that the Bible and a person's relationship with Jesus provide answers to most personal and social problems—the biblically based world view is in principle all-encompassing. Fundamentalists are especially concerned about upholding a tradition, about maintaining the true faith in a defensive reaction against a perceived threat. On the basis of the fundamentals of faith and morality, they also wish to bring the wider culture back to its religious roots, to restore the Christian character of American society: the tenets of the faith are presumed to have implications for social change. (Lechner, 1989:51)

There are two categories of fundamentalists—evangelicals and pentecostals. Evangelicals emphasize a personal relationship with Jesus, public declaration of their faith, and spreading the faith to nonbelievers. Pentecostals share these beliefs with fundamentalists and also emphasize the active presence of the Holy Spirit in their lives and church services. Their church services are very emotional (crying, laughing, shouting, applauding, moving about) with special emotional experiences involving faith healing and "speaking in tongues."

Both of these strands of religious fundamentalism are growing rapidly in the United States. This growth caught many religious observers and sociologists by surprise because they assumed that modernizing societies undergo processes that tend to make religion increasingly irrelevant to the affairs of society (Lechner, 1989). What, then, are the reasons for this unforeseen rise?

The most obvious reason the fundamentalists are increasing in number is their great emphasis on converting other people to their faith. They stress this activity because Christ commanded "Go ye into all the world and preach the gospel to every creature."

Second, fundamentalist congregations emphasize community. The people are friendly, accepting, and caring in a world that for many people is unfriendly, unaccepting, and uncaring. Thus, the fundamentalists tend to provide for many people the ingredients they find missing in the mainline churches and in the other impersonal bureaucracies of which they are a part.

Third, the fundamentalists offer the truth. They believe intensely that they are right and other people are wrong. In a society characterized by rapid change and a plurality of ideas and choices, many people seek authority, a foundation to provide consistency and constancy in their lives. The fundamentalists provide a rigid set of beliefs based on the infallibility of the Bible as the word of God.

A fourth appeal of the fundamentalists is their insistence that society has made wrong choices and that we must go back to laws and customs based on biblical truths. Thus, fundamentalism offers not only a critique of modern society but also an action program based on its set of absolute beliefs.

Fifth, the evangelicals appeal directly to youth and young adults. The approach to people is warm rather than aloof (parishioners and clergy are more apt to hug). The buildings, lighting, staging, and music are contemporary. Compare evangelical music, for example, with that found in mainline churches. Instead of hymns and organ music, there is music of praise, music with a beat with guitars and drums.

Sixth, some of these churches have become huge (the Willow Creek Community Church of suburban Chicago has 27,000 people attend six services on an average Sunday). There are about 400 of these **megachurches** (with at least 2,000 in

There are about 400 megachurches in the United States. Their growth is a result of combining religious fundamentalism with entertainment, providing services, and specialized ministries for targeted groups.

attendance each week). Their growth is fueled by entertaining church services (fast-paced, scripted productions, with high energy music, dramatic skits, and sermons with real-life applications), providing a number of services during the week (e.g., child care, aerobics, weight rooms, saunas, movies, gardening, and crafts) as well as specialized ministries for targeted groups (elderly, newly divorced, parents of teenagers, Vietnamese immigrants, compulsive eaters) (Niebuhr, 1995).

Finally, the fundamentalists have increased their popularity through an emphasis on modern marketing techniques (e.g., direct mail advertising, radio, and television). This type of ministry, which is particularly effective in reaching the disabled and the elderly, began with the advent of radio in the 1920s and expanded greatly with the growth of television in the 1950s and 1960s, cable television in the late 1970s, and satellite transmission in the 1980s.

The Electronic Church

Religious television, which is almost exclusively fundamentalist in doctrine (Robert Schuller, whose message is personal growth, optimism, self-esteem, and achievement, is the only major exception), has had an enormous impact in the number of people affected and the amounts of money generated (Hadden and Shupe, 1988). In 1989, for example, 336 television stations and 1,485 radio stations in the United States were owned by religious organizations (Applebome, 1989).

At its peak the television ministry reached an estimated 4.4 million people daily. In sharp contrast, scholars estimate that Jesus, in his lifetime, preached to no more than 30,000 persons. The success of this electronic church has been enhanced by the use of sophisticated methods, such as professional production of programs, showmanship, computerized mailing lists, and personalized letters written by computers. The successful televangelists have combined the communication technologies used in entertainment, business, and politics to reach and manipulate their audiences with the greatest effectiveness.

The electronic church began faltering in 1987 after a series of publicized scandals involving Jim Bakker (convicted in 1989 of defrauding his followers of $3.7 million, as well as confessing to sexual improprieties), Jimmy Swaggart (who confessed to hiring prostitutes to pose for him), and the outrageous claims of Oral Roberts (e.g., claiming that if he did not receive $8 million by the first of the month God would "call him home"). As a result, the television ministries of Rex Humbard and Jim Bakker are gone. After Jimmy Swaggart's second incident with a prostitute (1991), his television ministry, which in 1987 had reached 3.6 million viewers a day and brought in more than $50 million a year, was over. The television ministry of Jerry Falwell has been scaled back; and that of Oral Roberts has shrunk from 1.1 million households in 183 markets to 536,000 households in 122 markets (Shipp, 1991).

While some televangelists have fallen in popularity, others continue to thrive. These are, most notably, Robert Schuller, James Dobson, and Pat Robertson. James Dobson mixes religion and social issues in his half-hour program "Focus on the Family," which reaches 5 million Americans daily. His programs generate $100 million a year from contributions and "suggested donations" for some 6,000 items (books, magazines, tapes). Robertson bought a television station in 1960 for $37,000 and renamed the station the Christian Broadcasting Network. Today Robertson's "700 Club," a twice-daily religious broadcast, is seen on 300 television stations in 70 countries. Moreover, his financial empire was churning out annual revenues of $140 million ($90 million in contributions) (Cohen, 1995).

Contemporary Christianity and Politics

Religious organizations are sometimes organized for political action. The National Council of Churches, for example, tends to take liberal political positions on social issues, while the Christian Coalition supports far-right causes and candidates. Political concerns tend to unite fundamentalist churches, while the membership of many mainline churches is split on political issues.

The Religious Right

Fundamentalists and evangelicals believe that they live in a society that is suffering from a moral breakdown. The family is no longer stable, with many people working outside the home and a high divorce rate. Crime is rampant. The public schools give away condoms but will not allow Bible study. The media promote sexual promiscuity, violence, and drug use. Abortion is legal. Gays and lesbians openly espouse what the Religious Right considers a sinful lifestyle. Thus, they fight for practices consistent with their Biblical view of the Christian family and the Christian society. The political beliefs that emanate from this view are described by sociologist Sara Diamond:

> [The political beliefs of the Christian Right have a] consistent yet contradictory pattern. That is that the right, typically, these are generalizations, supports state institutions or government institutions or government action when the role that's being played is what I call an "enforcer" role. So the right, for example, has historically supported U.S. military intervention all over the world, until fairly recently; supports, under the rubric of "law and order," very tough law enforcement, draconian measures, even, draconian police power, even violations of people's civil liberties. Also, the right typically supports what they call a "traditional morality," a religiously-derived code of behavior and therefore supports a very strong role for the state in regulating, if not outlawing abortion, access to contraception, sex education; and wants the government to maintain sodomy laws.
>
> At the same time the right is anti-government, rhetorically, at least, when it comes to the state's role as distributor of wealth and power. The right does not want the government to be active in terms of anti-poverty programs, spreading the wealth more equitably

Z Magazine (*September 1993*), p. 19.

throughout society via the tax structure, or through funding various welfare programs. (Diamond, in Barsamian, 1996:36–37)

Leading the charge by the religious right nationally is Reverend Pat Robertson, who founded the Christian Coalition in 1989. By 1995 this organization had 1.7 million members (their stated goal is 10 million by 2000), and an annual budget of more than $21 million. The goal of the Christian Coalition is to have evangelicals elected at the local, state, and national levels so that public policies can be changed to conform with their Bible-based agenda. This includes taking over the Republican Party at each of these levels, a goal that has been reached in eighteen states, while wielding substantial influence in about a dozen others (Parry, 1995). The organization provides a manual and leadership schools to teach members how to organize and win campaigns. They advise their candidates to conceal their ultimate purposes until elected because if their conservatism were known (e.g., changing school curricula to include creationism), they likely would not get elected (L. I. Barrett, 1993). They also organize cadres of church-based workers as volunteers to disseminate political information to people most likely to be compatible with their religious and political views. Also, the Christian Coalition actively works to defeat candidates who they feel hold what they believe to be antibiblical positions. In the 1996 election, the Christian Coalition distributed 45 million voter guides in 120,000 churches and contacted about five million voters in person or by phone (Feinsilber, 1996).

The Religious Right is a social movement with a network of leaders and organizations. In addition to Robertson's Christian Coalition (and its director, Ralph Reed), there are James Dobson's "Focus on the Family," Beverly LaHaye's "Concerned Women of America" (which promotes traditional roles for women), Donald Wildmon's "American Family Association" (which opposes pornography), Robert Simond's "Citizens for Excellence in Education," Phyllis Schlafly's "The Eagle Forum," and Gary Bauer's "Family Research Council."

The Role of Mainline Churches: Comfort or Challenge?

The political activism among the fundamentalists is different from that found in the mainline churches. The difference is that whereas fundamentalist congregations are relatively homogeneous in religious and political ideologies, the mainline congregations are much more pluralistic. This pluralism places the clergy in a precarious position, a dilemma brought about by the two contradictory roles (analogous to order and conflict approaches to the social order) of the church—to comfort the afflicted and to afflict the comforted (or to comfort and to challenge). The comforting role is one of aiding individuals in surmounting trials and tribulations of sickness, the death of loved ones, financial woes, and social interaction with family, neighbors, colleagues, or enemies. The church aids by such means as pastoral counseling and collecting and distributing food and clothing to the needy. Another way the church comforts the afflicted is through providing a rationale for suffering (*theodicy*), the consequence of which is sanctification of the status quo.

Three related criticisms of the comforting function are immediately apparent. First, some would say that the church (and the clergy) have allowed this function to supersede the other role of challenger. Second, if the church would do more challenging and less comforting, evils such as poverty would be reduced. By helping people to accept an imperfect society, the church preserves the status quo—that is, the injustice and inequality that caused the problems in the first place. In this way, religion is an opiate of the masses because it convinces them to accept an unjust situation rather than working to change it from below. Third, the comfortable will not feel guilty, thereby preventing them from working to change the system from above.

The other function of the church—to challenge—is the injunction to be an agent of social protest and social reform. The church, through its pronouncements and leadership, seeks to lead in the fight to right the inequities of the society. A fundamental problem is in winning the support of the members. Change is almost by definition controversial, because some persons benefit under the existing social arrangements. When the church takes a stand against racial segregation, abortion, war, or the abuses of business or labor, some members will become alienated. They may withdraw their financial support or even leave the church. The church, of course, has a commitment to its members. Because it cannot afford to lose its membership, the church may compromise its principles. Such an action, however, may make other members angry at the church because of its hypocrisy. Consequently, the church is in the unenviable position of trying to maintain a precarious balance between compromise and purity.

Of course, the clergy vary in their interpretation of the role of the church. They are truly people in conflict. There are conflicting expectations of the clergy from all sides (resulting in *role conflict*). The church hierarchy expects the clergy to behave in a particular way (consider the rules issued by the Catholic hierarchy, such as celibacy and absolute obedience to authority). Most parishioners favor the comforting role. They want counsel in times of personal crisis. If poor, they want to be assured that they will be rewarded later, and if rich, they want their holding of wealth and power legitimized.

Although they are a minority in most congregations, some parishioners wish the clergy to take stands on controversial issues and work for social change. This wish puts their clergy in a bind because to take a public stand on controversial issues is divisive.

A final source of the clergy's role conflict arises from their own definition of the role. These various expectations, and the resulting role conflict of the clergy, amount to one reason they may drop out. Another is that if they take a stand (or do not), they may automatically alienate a segment of the parish and perhaps the church hierarchy. They may, consequently, be forced to resign.

Clergy who do not resign may solve their dilemma by being noncontroversial. This non-boat-rocking stance is all too familiar and results in another problem—irrelevancy. By not talking about social problems, one, in fact, legitimates the status quo. Hence, the inequities of the society continue, because the moral force of the churches is mainly quiet.

Not all clergy are content with the emphasis on comfort. As noted in the previous section, increasing numbers of clergy have become politically active on the moral issues of abortion, homosexuality, and pornography. Typically, though, this view of morality ignores the social problems of inequalities and injustices. Other clergy are not content to let the church continue to perpetuate injustice by not speaking and acting out. They are committed to a socially relevant church, one that seeks social solutions to social problems.

A recent trend appears to be a resurgence in religious activism on social issues, not only by religious fundamentalist groups opposed to such things as sex education in the schools, gay rights, and abortion, but also by the leadership in the mainline churches. The leaders in almost every mainline religious organization have gone on record as opposing the government's budget cuts to the disadvantaged, U.S. military aid to dictatorships, and the arms race. For example, the bishops of the Roman Catholic Church in the United States have formally challenged the fundamental assumptions and strategies of the U.S. defense system. Justifying this new wave of social concern by the church, the late Joseph Bernardin, the Archbishop of Chicago, said:

> Some people say we shouldn't talk politics and that we should address ourselves to truly religious issues. Well, it's not as simple as all that. It's our responsibility to address the moral dimension of the social issues we face. These issues, of course, do have a political dimension as well as a moral dimension. I don't deny that, but that doesn't mean we're not permitted to talk about them. But our perspective must always be from the moral or ethical dimension. I reject out of hand that we have taken a leftward swing. What we are trying to do is focus on the teaching of the Gospel as we understand it, and to apply that teaching to the various social issues of the day. Our central theme is our respect for God's gift of life, our insistence that the human person has inherent value and dignity. (Quoted in *Time*, 1982:77; see also National Conference of Catholic Bishops, 1986)

But political stands from the general leadership of a denomination are viewed quite differently than political activism by local ministers or priests. When local ministers or priests speak out, participate in marches, work for integrated housing, and demonstrate against excessive militarism, many of their parishioners become upset. As a result, the socially active clergy often become the objects of discrimination by their parishioners. Another consequence is that the laity trust their clergy less and less. As behavior in one area is questioned (e.g., social activism), church members are likely to withdraw confidence in others as well. Finally, churches have divided on this issue. Some want social action instead of just pious talk. Others want to preserve the status quo. The hypocrisy found in many churches forces splits, the formation of underground churches, or total rejection of Christianity as the source of social action. Other members may leave because they feel that the church has wandered too far from the beliefs on which the faith was founded. This dilemma accelerates the current dropout problem among mainline churches—by parishioners and clergy alike. The problem seems to be that for the most part those who drop out are the social activists who leave the church with a residue of comforters. If this is the case, the future of the church is bleak unless there is a reversal and prophets of social action ascend—an unlikely possibility, given the propensity of most parishioners for the message of comfort over the message of challenge. Meanwhile, the political message and action from the religious right unite and energize its clergy and followers.

Religion from the Order and the Conflict Perspectives

As usual, order and conflict theorists view this social phenomenon—religion—very differently. Also, as usual, the unity and diversity found within this institution suggest that both models of society are partially correct.

Adherents of the order model emphasize the solidarity functions of religion. Religion helps individuals through times of stress, and it benefits society by binding people together through a common set of beliefs, reaffirmed through regularly scheduled ceremonial rituals.

Conflict theorists acknowledge that religion may unify in small societies, but in diverse societies religious differences divide. Religious conflict occurs commonly at all levels, however, from intersocietal religious warfare to schisms in local congregations. From the conflict perspective, religious unity within a society, if it does occur, has negative consequences. Such unity is used to legitimate the interests of the powerful (for example, slavery, racial segregation, conquest of pagans, and war). Similarly, the interests of the powerful are served if the poor believe that they will be rewarded in the next life. Such a theodicy prevents revolutions by the oppressed and serves, as Marx suggested, as "an opiate of the masses."

CHAPTER REVIEW

1. Religion is socially created and has a tremendous impact on society. It is an integrated set of beliefs by which a group attempts to explain the meaning of life and death. Religion defines immorality and sin as well as morality and righteousness.

2. The consequences of religion are unity among the believers, conformity in behavior, and the legitimation of social structures. Religion also divides. It separates believers from nonbelievers, denominations, religions, and even the members of local religious groups.

3. Emile Durkheim, an order theorist, explored the question of why religion is universal. He reasoned that what any group worships is really society itself. The society is held together by religious rituals and festivals in which the group's values and beliefs are reaffirmed.

4. Karl Marx, a conflict theorist, saw religion as inhibiting social change by making existing social arrangements seem right and inevitable. Religion further promotes the status quo by teaching the faithful to accept their condition—thus religion is the ultimate tool to promote false consciousness.

5. Max Weber, contrary to Marx, saw religious ideology as the catalyst for economic change. He demonstrated this with his analysis of the relationship between Calvinist ideology (predestination) and the rise of capitalism.

6. Civil religion is the belief that "God and Country" are one. God is believed to have a special destiny for the United States. Order and unity are thus given religious sanction.

7. Although most people in the United States identify with Christianity, there is a wide variety of religious belief in U.S. society.

8. United States religious organizations can be divided according to their secular commitment into two categories. A *church* tends to compromise with the larger society, tolerates popular vices, and accepts a diversity of beliefs. A *sect,* in sharp contrast, rejects the world. It is a moral community with rigid ethical requirements and a narrow belief system.

9. A *theodicy* is a religious legitimation for a situation that otherwise might cause guilt or anger. Sects tend to have a theodicy of suffering, explaining their lack of power and privilege. Churches have theodicies that legitimate the possession of power and privilege.

10. A *cult* is a religious group that rejects the society and religions of the mainstream. It provides a new religious expression that some are willing to follow completely. A cult differs from a sect in one fundamental way. A sect results from a breakoff from an existing religious organization. The members do not seek a new religion but rather to recapture the true faith. Cults, on the other hand, represent a new religion. Most cults fail, but a few have become major religions.

11. There is a relationship between socioeconomic status (SES) and religion: (*a*) the lower the SES, the greater the probability of belonging to a sect; (*b*) there is a relationship between SES and denominational affiliation (e.g., the lower the SES, the more likely to be Baptist, the higher the SES, the more likely to be Episcopalian); (*c*) the higher the SES of the member, the greater his or her involvement and influence in the local church.

12. Religious groups hold beliefs or behave in ways that support the racial, gender, and sexuality norms of society.

13. One trend is the decline in the mainline denominations. These churches are often bureaucratic and impersonal. Their beliefs are pluralistic. The Catholic Church is losing members because its stands against contraception and divorce are out of tune with contemporary life.

14. Another trend is the rise of Christian fundamentalism. The two categories of fundamentalists are evangelicals and pentecostals. They are alike except that pentecostal congregations are more emotional—personally experiencing the Holy Spirit. Fundamentalists are growing (while the mainline churches are declining) because they (*a*) emphasize evangelism;

(*b*) tend to be friendly, accepting, and caring communities; (*c*) have the truth based on the infallibility of the Bible; (*d*) offer a critique of modern society and a prescription for its change back to a God-centered society; and (*e*) use modern marketing techniques and radio and television.

15. The electronic church is almost exclusively fundamentalist in religious doctrine. This form of outreach has been enormously successful in raising money and meeting the needs of many followers. Although scandals among some of the televangelists in 1987 had adverse effects on this movement, the setbacks appear to be temporary.

16. The contemporary mainline Christian churches are faced with a basic dilemma brought about by their two contradictory roles—to comfort the afflicted and to afflict the comforted. The comforting function is criticized because it focuses on helping the individual but ignores the problems of society. The challenging function—the injunction to be an agent of social protest and social reform—is criticized because it is divisive, alienating some members who disagree with the position taken. The evidence is clear that the majority of clergy are opting for the comforting function over the challenging function.

17. The order model emphasizes the solidarity functions of religion, which they interpret as good.

18. From the conflict perspective, religious beliefs have negative consequences because they sanctify the status quo. That is, religion legitimates the interests of the powerful while also justifying the existence of inequality. Thus, revolutionary activity by the oppressed is suppressed by religion because it serves, as Marx suggested, as "an opiate of the masses."

KEY TERMS

Ritual	Church	Theodicy
Opiate of the masses	Sect	Cult
Civil religion	Charisma	Megachurches
Priestly role of religion	Routinization of charisma	
Prophetic role of religion	Charisma of office	

STUDY QUESTIONS

1. What are the social consequences for a community of believers?

2. Explain the contradiction that religion is both a source of stability and a source of conflict.

3. Contrast the views of religion by Durkheim, Marx, and Weber.

4. Is religion generally supportive of existing class and gender hierarchies? Give evidence to support your position.

5. Explain the contrast in growth patterns by the mainline denominations and the more fundamentalist denominations.

FOR FURTHER READING

Dick Anthony and Thomas Robbins, *In Gods We Trust: New Patterns of Religious Pluralism in America,* 2nd ed. (New Brunswick, NJ: Transaction, 1990).

Chris Bull and John Gallagher, *Perfect Enemies: The Religious Right, the Gay Movement, and the Politics of the 1990s.* (New York: Crown, 1996).

Carol P. Christ and Judith Plaskow (eds.), *Womanspirit: A Feminist Reader in Religion* (San Francisco: Harper, 1992).

Harvey Cox, *Fire From Heaven: The Rise of Pentecostal Spirituality and the Reshaping of Religion in the Twenty-First Century* (Reading, MA: Addison-Wesley, 1995).

Sara Diamond, *Spiritual Warfare: The Politics of the Christian Right* (Boston: South End Press, 1989).

Jeffrey K. Hadden and Anson Shupe, *Televangelism: Power and Politics on God's Frontier* (New York: Henry Holt and Company, 1988).

Michael Harrington, *The Politics at God's Funeral: The Spiritual Crisis of Western Civilization* (New York: Penguin Books, 1983).

Meredith B. McGuire, *Religion: The Social Context,* 3rd ed. (Belmont, CA: Wadsworth, 1992).

National Conference of Catholic Bishops, *Economic Justice for All: Pastoral Letter on Catholic Social Teaching and the U.S. Economy* (Washington, DC: United States Catholic Conference, Inc., 1986).

Richard V. Pierard and Robert D. Linder, *Civil Religion and the Presidency* (Grand Rapids, MI: Zondervan Publishing House, 1988).

Thomas Robbins and Dick Anthony, *In Gods We Trust: New Patterns of Religious Pluralism in America* (New Brunswick, NJ: Transaction, 1989).

Wade Clark Roof, *A Generation of Seekers: The Spiritual Journeys of the Baby Boom Generation* (San Francisco: Harper San Francisco, 1993).

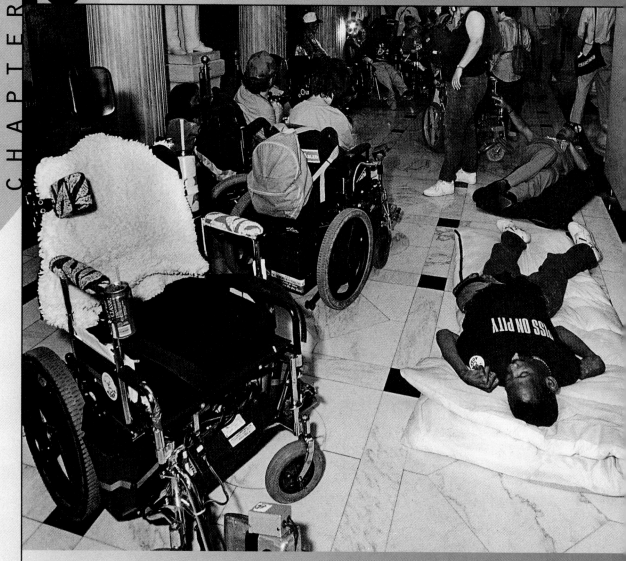

Human Agency: Individuals and Groups in Society Changing Social Structures

The Sociological Paradox: Social Structure and Agency

Sociology is the study of things social. This book, with its emphasis on the societal level, emphasizes the social context and the social forces that so strongly impact human behavior. As Peter Berger says (as quoted in Chapter 1):

> Society not only controls our movements, but shapes our identity, our thoughts and our emotions. The structures of society become the structures of our own consciousness. Society does not stop at the surface of our skins. Society penetrates us as much as it envelops us. (Berger, 1963:121).

This **deterministic** view is too strong, however. While society *constrains* what we do, it does not *determine* what we do (Giddens, 1991:863). While society and its structures are powerful, the members of society are not totally controlled. We are not passive actors. We can take control of the conditions of our own lives. Human beings cope with, adapt to, and change social structures to meet their needs. Individuals, acting alone or with others, can shape, resist, challenge, and sometimes change the social institutions that impinge on them. These actions constitute **human agency.** This chapter focuses on the macro dimensions of agency—i.e., those collective actions that change and overcome societal constraints.

The paradox of sociology—the power of society over its members/the power of social actors to change society—has several important meanings and implications (see Chapters 1 and 2). Foremost, society is not a rigid, static entity composed of robots. People in interaction are the architects of society in an ongoing project. That is, society is created, sustained, and changed by people.

Second, the social forms that people create often take on a sacred quality—the sanctity of tradition—that constrains behavior in socially prescribed ways. The sociological insight is, to restate the previous point, that what many consider sacred and therefore unchangeable, is a social construction and can, therefore, be reconstructed.

A third implication is that since social structures are created and sustained by people, they are imperfect. There are positive *and* negative consequences of the way people have organized. Many are content with the status quo because they benefit from it. Others accept it even though they are disadvantaged by it. But, there are also those who seek change to improve it or, perhaps, to change it completely. They are the agents of change.

In sum, the essence of agency is that individuals through collective action are capable of changing the structure of society and even the course of history. But while agency is important, we should not forget the power of the structures that subordinate people, making change difficult or, at times, impossible.

This chapter is divided into two major parts. The first is conceptual, considering social movements, the collective and organized efforts of human actors to change society. This section describes the types of social movements and the conditions under which they succeed or fail. The second part is illustrative, providing two case studies of agency—the civil rights movement and the movement to bring gender equity to sport.

Social Movements

Individuals seeking to change social life in some way are limited in what they can accomplish by themselves. We need to join with others who share our goals, if we are to have any hope of success. Kenneth Kammeyer, George Ritzer, and Norman Yetman show the importance of social movements if we are to be effective agents of change.

> As individuals, we are limited in our ability to make the societal changes we would like. There are massive social forces that make change difficult; these forces include the government, large and powerful organizations, and the prevailing values, norms, and attitudes. As individuals going to a voting booth, we have minimal power. As individuals protesting to officials, we have minimal power. As individuals standing against the tide of public opinion, we have little hope of exerting influence. As individuals confronting a corporate structure, we are doomed to frustration and failure. But if we combine with others who share our convictions, organize ourselves, and map out a course of action, we may be able to bring about numerous and significant changes in the social order. Through participation in a social movement, we can break through the social constraints that overwhelm us as individuals. (Kammeyer, Ritzer, and Yetman, 1997:632–633)

Individual actors seeking change typically join with others for greater power to become part of a social movement. A **social movement** is a collective attempt to promote or resist change. These movements arise when people are sufficiently discontented that they will work for a better system. Hence, social movements are inherently political because they seek to affect public policy. A social movement is a goal-directed effort by a substantial number of people. It is an enduring organization with leaders, a division of labor, an ideology, a blueprint for collective action, and a set of roles and norms for the members (see Blumer, 1951; Smelser, 1962).

Although money and organizational skills are important, ideology is the key to a movement's success. The ideology provides the goal and the rationale for action, binds diverse members together in a common cause, and submerges individuals to the movement. An **ideology** is a set of ideas that explains reality, provides guidelines for behavior, and expresses the interests of a group. An ideology may be elaborate, such as Christianity, Marxism, or capitalism. Such an ideology provides a consistent framework from which to act and believe on a number of issues. Or the ideology may be narrowly aimed at one side or the other on issues such as animal rights, abortion, protection of the environment, capital punishment, gun control, gay rights, nuclear energy, universal health insurance, pay equity, and welfare. For each of these issues, groups on either side have an ideology that explains their position, provides the goal, brings members together, and offers a compelling argument used to recruit new members.

Types of Social Movements

Three types of social movements are political in nature: resistance movements, which are organized to prevent changes; reform movements, which seek to alter a specific part of society; and revolutionary movements, which seek radical changes.

One type of social movement is explicitly organized to resist change. These **resistance movements** are organized to resist change, or they are reactionary in that they seek to reverse changes that have already occurred and restore "traditional values."

Because periods of rapid change foster resistance movements, there are numerous contemporary examples of this phenomenon. There are current efforts to stop the trend toward the use of nuclear power for energy. People have organized to stop the damming of rivers or the logging of forests because they want to protect the environment. The move to make the Equal Rights Amendment part of the Constitution was met with considerable organized resistance, even from women. Antiabortion groups have formed to reverse legislation and judicial acts that make abortion legal or easy to obtain. Evangelicals in a number of communities have organized to pressure school boards to reverse schools' policies they consider opposite to Christian principles. As examples, they oppose the teaching of evolution and seek to have the schools also teach creationism. They want prayer in the schools. They oppose the teaching of sex education and, most certainly, the distribution of condoms. They resist courses in the curriculum that promote international cooperation.

Reform movements seek to alter a specific part of society. These movements commonly focus on a single issue, such as women's rights, gay liberation, or the environment. Typically, there is an aggrieved group such as women, African Americans, Native Americans, homosexuals, the differentially abled, farmers, or workers that focuses its strategy on changing the laws and customs to improve its situation (see "A Closer Look: Winning Civil Rights for People with Disabilities"). At various times in U.S. history oppressed groups have organized successful drives to change the system to provide more equity. The civil rights movement of the 1950s and 1960s provides an example.

The third type of social movement—the **revolutionary movement**—seeks radical changes. Such movements go beyond reform by seeking to replace the existing social institutions with new ones that conform to a radically different vision of society. For example, throughout Eastern Europe, new nations have been created out of the Soviet Union and its satellites. These nations, newly independent, are adopting new forms of government and new economies that are drastically different from what they had in the last fifty years. These changes will dramatically change all areas of social life.

The Life Course of Social Movements

Social movements move through predictable stages. For a movement to begin it must attract members. Usually there is some societal condition—institutional racism, institutional sexism, economic depression, war, immigration wave, the passage of a controversial law or court decision, technological change—that threatens or harms some segment of society. This causes social unrest, but it is unfocused.

The second stage of a movement is when grievances become focused. A leader or leaders emerge who use ideology and **charisma** (extraordinary personal attributes) to define the central problem(s) they face, and to challenge and inspire followers to join in a common quest to change society for the better. Sometimes there are individuals whose acts of personal courage, such as provoking the powerful, getting jailed, injured, or killed, serve to coalesce the previously unfocused. This is especially important in an age of instant communication, where public attention is centered on the charismatic leader's message and personal valor, the heroism of martyrs, the repressive acts by authorities, the terrorism of those opposing the movement, and the continuing inequities in society on which the movement is centered. This is a critical stage where those in similar situations realize that others share their feelings of discontent, anger, or injustice, and that together they can make a difference. They begin to acquire a collective identity and a sense of common purpose. It is a time of excitement over the possibilities for collectively bringing about needed social change.

The third phase involves moving toward organization. Resources (money, equipment, and members) are mobilized. A formal organizational structure is developed with rules, policies, and procedures to be followed. Power is centralized and levels of organization are delineated. Strategies are formed to confront the authorities, attract new members, and to keep the older members energized. Alliances may be formed with other groups with similar goals (allowing them to share

A CLOSER LOOK

Winning Civil Rights for People with Disabilities

In 1989 Congress passed historic legislation to protect the civil rights of people with disabilities. This bill, the Americans with Disabilities Act, extends to people with disabilities the same protections against discrimination that were given African Americans and women in the 1960s and 1970s.

There are 43 million people in the United States with disabilities, defined as anyone with a physical or mental impairment that "substantially limits" everyday living. In other words, this category includes a wide range of people, such as people with mental retardation, paraplegics, the blind, those with cerebral palsy, and those with AIDS. Before this legislation, people with disabilities faced discrimination in jobs, social situations, and transportation. The new law prohibits stores, hotels, restaurants, and theaters from denying access to persons with disabilities. Employers can no longer reject qualified workers just because they are disabled. Moreover, employers must modify the workplace to make it accessible to their workers with disabilities. Public buildings under construction or undergoing remodeling must be made accessible to wheelchair users under the new legislation. So, too, must public transportation vehicles be equipped with lifts to accommodate wheelchair users. Finally, telephone companies must now have operators who can take messages typed by deaf persons on a Telecommunications Device for the Deaf and then relay it orally to a hearing person on another phone.

People with disabilities are one of the last minority groups to win their civil rights. They were behind racial minorities and women because they did not mobilize a vast movement with highly visible protests. They also lacked a charismatic leader, as had Blacks with Martin Luther King, Jr., and women with Betty Friedan. Nevertheless, they achieved some early victories with a 1973 law that protected people with disabilities from discrimination by institutions receiving federal funding (similar to Title IX legislation prohibiting discrimination against women in education) and 1975 legislation that ensured access to schools to all children with disabilities.

The sweeping 1989 victory for people with disabilities was won despite the contrary efforts of many in the business community who argued that the provisions were too costly to businesses. Success was achieved over this considerable opposition through a number of means. Foremost, people with disabilities have developed a common identity (class consciousness) through a shared outrage at the discrimination they experience. Now, instead of feelings of isolation, feelings of a common bond and empowerment have emerged among the disabled. Even though more people with disabilities now receive an education (a result of greater access fostered by the 1973 and 1975 federal laws), they continue to face severe discrimination in the job market.

The resulting frustration has led many people to become active in the disabilities movement. Some of these people joined advocacy groups; others joined together to use tactics of civil disobedience, such as disrupting public transportation or blocking access to city hall, in order to make their plight more visible. In one celebrated case, the students at Gallaudet University, a college for the deaf, protested the selection of a hearing president in 1988. They refused to go to classes and occupied the administration building, eventually forcing the newly appointed president to resign and the governing board to appoint the university's first deaf president. The 1989 victory was also fueled by increased numbers of people with disabilities, including the aged, who had become disabled with blindness, deafness, arthritis, and the like (it is estimated that the number of elderly Americans with at least one disability increased from 5 million in 1984 to 6.2 million in 1990) and people with AIDS. With the realization that about one-fifth of Americans have disabilities, politicians have found it difficult to vote against them. As a cohesive group, people with disabilities have considerable potential political clout. Their growing sense of a shared condition and common identity has made their voting as a bloc on certain issues more likely than ever. The result has been, finally, legislation guaranteeing their civil rights.

Sources: The content of this essay has been taken from a number of sources, especially, Joseph P. Shapiro, "Liberation Day for the Disabled," *U.S. News & World Report* (September 18, 1989): 20–24; Jason De Parle, "Realizing the Rights of the Disabled," *The New York Times* (December 17, 1989), Section 4, pp. 1, 5; and Mary Johnson, "Disabled Americans Push for Access," *The Progressive* 55 (August 1991): 21–23.

Successful social movements require a leader with extraordinary personal attributes (charisma), to define the central problems they face, and to challenge and inspire followers to join in a common quest to change society for the better.

computerized mailing lists of likely contributors or new members, and the like). In short, this is a bureaucratization (or formalization) stage where a once-unfocused number of people now have become an organization. Where once leadership was charismatic, it is now composed of administrators and managers (this is called the **routinization of charisma**).

The final stage occurs if the movement is successful. If so, the movement becomes integrated into society. The goals of the movement have been accomplished. This is the stage of **institutionalization.** While this is the goal of the social movement, this stage has its dangers. A common danger is **goal displacement.** This occurs when the goal of maintaining the formal structure of the movement's organization supersedes the original goals of the social movement. Another threat involves power struggles within the movement, which divert effort from the common goal. Finally, and related to the last point, success can lead to the leadership elite using its power to keep power and the extraordinary status and rewards that come with that power. In effect, then, "organizational success and its consequences can corrupt the original goals of the movement" (Hess, Markson, and Stein, 1993:596).

◤Agency: Social Change from the Bottom Up

Often the people lead and the leaders of government and business follow. Harlan Cleveland has stated that:

> The tidal waves of social change of our lifetimes—environmental sensitivity, civil rights for all races, the enhanced status of women, recognition of the rights of consumers and small investors—were not generated by the established leaders in government, busi-

ness, labor, religion, or higher education. They boiled up from people (and new leaders) who had not previously been heard from. (Cleveland, 1992:16)

This section provides two case studies where the efforts of seemingly powerless individuals and groups changed powerful social structures. The first case involves the centuries-long struggles by African Americans to obtain the civil rights due all citizens. The second case study is of the specific situation where recent actions by individuals and groups have brought significant changes moving toward gender equity within athletics.

The Civil Rights Movement

Many believe that the civil rights movement began when Rosa Parks was arrested for not giving up her seat to a White on a bus in Montgomery, Alabama in 1955, and a successful bus boycott followed. The civil rights movement is not the result of one event but the "inevitable outcome of centuries of mistreatment of black people by white people and their governments" (Powledge, 1991:xi). Or, as Vincent Harding puts it, the movement is long and continuous,

> flowing like a river, sometimes powerful, tumultuous, and roiling with life; at other times meandering and turgid. . . . The river of black struggle is people, but it is also the hope, the movement, the transformative power that humans create and that create them, us, and makes them, us, new persons. So we black people are the river; the river is us. The river is in us, created by us, flowing out of us, surrounding us, re-creating us and this entire nation. (Harding, 1981:xix)

Africans were brought to this country as slaves and as slaves they were exploited, demeaned, and kept powerless (this section is taken in part from Zinn, 1980; Harding, 1981; Powledge, 1991; and Berry, 1994). The laws and the customs permitted the oppression of the slaves.

> Beginning in Virginia at the end of the 1630s, laws establishing lifelong African slavery were instituted. They were followed by laws prohibiting black–white intermarriage, laws against the ownership of property by Africans, laws denying blacks all basic political rights. . . . In addition, there were laws against the education of Africans, laws against the assembling of Africans, laws against the ownership of weapons by Africans, laws perpetuating the slavery of their parents to African children, laws forbidding Africans to raise their hands against whites even in self-defense. . . . [The laws] outlawed many rituals connected with African religious practices, including dancing and the use of drums. In many places they also banned African languages. Thus they attempted to shut black people out from both cultures, to make them wholly dependent neuters. (Harding, 1981:27)

Despite the oppressive control of Blacks and the severe punishments for their violations of the laws and customs, many African men and women struggled against the domination of White power. Some engaged in individual acts of rebellion. Some ran away, heading North. At times Black fugitives formed small guerrilla bands, creating bases from which to harass neighboring plantations and places to which others might flee. These fugitives (known as outlyers) were very significant to the oppressed. Their existence meant that the apparently total institution of slavery was not all-encompassing. Most important, "the outlyers represented a hidden, submerged black power that the masters could not break. They were a radical presence, challenging blacks and whites alike" (Harding, 1981:40). For those who remained in bondage, some chose to resist, using such tactics as refusing to learn how to use a tool without breaking it, work slowdowns, persistent noncooperation, arson, and even poisoning.

Around 1800 Blacks constituted about 20 percent of the U.S. population. Of the one million, 900,000 were held in legal slavery. In that year Gabriel Prosser and forty other slaves were executed for daring to revolt against their masters. This insurrection and the punishment ushered in a period of some thirty-five years of intensified slave rebellions. Also efforts to escape escalated, as the chances for success increased with the Underground Railroad, a network of Blacks and Whites who smuggled thousands of slaves to the North. And, among the slaves who stayed behind, agency took many forms such as keeping African traditions, fighting to keep family ties, community solidarity, and creating their own rituals that recognized marriage and parenthood. Summarizing the pre-Civil War situation for Blacks, historian Vincent Harding states:

> [The slave community] was not a community caught in the flatness of despair. It was not a community without hope. It lived with brutality, but did not become brutish. Often it was treated inhumanely, but it clung to its humanity. There was too much in the river [Harding's metaphor of the cumulative effects of the Black struggle] which suggested other possibilities, announced new comings, and hurled restless movements against the dam of white oppression. Always, under the surface of slavery, the river of black struggle flowed with, and was created by, a black community that moved actively in search of freedom, integrity, and home—a community that could not be dehumanized. (Harding, 1981:74)

After the Civil War, the Emancipation Proclamation, and the passage of the Thirteenth, Fourteenth, and Fifteenth Amendments to the Constitution, Blacks were freed from slavery and given certain rights. But while they were technically free, they remained oppressed. One form of oppression—slavery—was lifted, only to be replaced by other modes of oppression—economic slavery by low-wage jobs and sharecropping arrangements with landowners, and being treated as inferiors by Whites. In the 1880s the average wage of Black farm workers in the South was about fifty cents a day. They were usually paid in "orders," not money, which could only be used at a store controlled by the landowner. The sharecropper had to borrow from the store to get the seed to plant the crop.

> When everything was added up at the end of the year he was in debt, so his crop was constantly owed to someone, and he was tied to the land, with the records kept by the planter and storekeeper so that the Negroes are swindled and kept forever in debt. (Zinn, 1980:204)

Despite these roadblocks, there was more freedom than before, and many Blacks found ways to reinforce their liberty such as hunting with guns, driving carriages, meeting with other Blacks in public places, forming political unions, changing their names, asserting their rights to Whites, and omitting the long-standing and deeply understood signs of inferior status.

> One of the most significant movements toward the definition of freedom came as black families all over the South made a momentous decision to withdraw their women from the full-time agricultural labor force. In many cases children moved out of the role of full-time field hands as well. Everywhere in slavery's former domain, black families were openly declaring the autonomy they had fought so hard to develop and maintain under the old regime; they were establishing their right to decide who should work and how. Now mothers and wives were often free to give more attention to their own families and work; children could attend the schools now being created at great cost by blacks and their white allies. (Harding, 1981:282)

White violence toward Blacks escalated in response to the behavioral changes of the former slaves. The Ku Klux Klan and local vigilante groups used raids, lynchings, beatings, and burnings to intimidate Blacks. The courts were much more likely to send Blacks to prison than Whites. And in the penitentiary system of the South, there were beatings, chain-gangs, and forced labor as contractors purchased their labor cheaply.

The Black Codes were laws passed by Southern states and local governments to keep Blacks "in their place." These codes were intended to keep Blacks from achieving equality, to control Blacks, and to keep Blacks bound to jobs and land controlled by Whites. Although the laws varied from state to state and city to city, the patterns were essentially the same. There were restrictions against land ownership or rental by Blacks. There were vagrancy laws insisting that Blacks have lawful employment. In South Carolina, for example, a vagrant could be sentenced to a year of hard labor and be hired out to an individual. The laws created harsh penalties against Black workers who broke contracts with landowners or other employers. Other laws placed severe restrictions on the kinds of work that Blacks could do. In effect these laws meant that Blacks were subjected to many special punishments that did not apply to Whites.

> The patterns were clear: in almost every situation having to do with black–white relationships, freedom of movement, freedom of choice in jobs, a personal sense of independence, and control over their own families, the Black Codes were the slave codes revived . . . . (Harding, 1981:314)

Moving to the early 20th century, a rigid system of segregation emerged in the South, where interaction between the races as equals was denied. These "Jim Crow" laws (supported by an 1896 U.S. Supreme Court decision—*Plessy v. Ferguson,* which justified the principle of "separate but equal") meant that all public facilities in the South such as restaurants, restrooms, schools, and public transportation could be segregated. Nevertheless, African Americans often banded together to fight injustice, share resources, and maintain control over their lives. The National Association for the Advancement of Colored People (NAACP) was founded in 1909, and the National Urban League began a year later. Both fought for civil rights in public opinion and in the courts, but with little success until after World War II.

The military was segregated during World War II, although defense industries were prohibited from discrimination based on racial differences (by executive order of President Roosevelt). Toward the conclusion of the war, the Black press and a few Whites in the media pushed for integration, arguing that since Blacks had fought in the war for the principles of equality, freedom, and democracy, they should have the same rights.

Shortly after World War II, the NAACP challenged the concept of separate but equal schooling in the courts. This effort was rewarded in 1954 when the Supreme Court ruled in *Brown v. Board of Education of Topeka, Kansas,* that "separate educational facilities are inherently unequal." This ruling was resisted in the South by the Ku Klux Klan, White Citizens Councils, mayors, school boards, and governors.

In addition to this momentous court decision, two events in the next year galvanized Blacks into a mass movement that ultimately changed race relations in the United States. The first incident was the lynching of Emmitt Till in Mississippi. Till, a fourteen-year-old Black from Chicago, was visiting relatives. To show off to his cousins, he violated the unwritten code of conduct for Blacks in the rural South by making a "smart" remark to a White woman. The woman's husband and brother-in-law kidnapped Till from his uncle's house. Later young Till's mutilated body was found in a river. In court, Till's uncle identified the two men who took his nephew from his house (the first time in Southern history that a Black man accused Whites of a felony crime in court). Despite this heroic act, the all-White jury found Till's murderers not guilty (they later admitted, with pride, that they had killed him).

The second case involved the jailing of a Black woman, Rosa Parks, in Montgomery, Alabama, for not giving her seat on a bus to a White man as was the custom fortified by the law. As a result of this courageous act, the Black community in Montgomery mobilized to bring down the segregated public busing system. A leader emerged, a young local minister, Martin Luther King, Jr., who inspired Blacks to use nonviolent resistance to overthrow their oppressors and their unfair laws and practices. The Blacks boycotted the transportation system for 381 days, walking to work or using a car pooling network. The city eventually abolished segregation in public transportation—a clear case of agency, as the powerless successfully changed an unfair system.

Under the leadership of Reverend King, Blacks and White sympathizers mobilized to desegregate other public facilities. There were sit-ins in restaurants, waiting rooms, and churches, and wade-ins at public beaches. Economic boycotts were organized. Court cases were initiated. Brave students became the first Blacks to integrate schools. And, there were protest marches to publicize grievances. These efforts were violently resisted by Whites. King and others were jailed. Demonstrators were abused verbally and physically. There were lynchings, the most infamous being the murder by Klansmen of three civil rights workers in Mississippi. Birmingham Police Commissioner "Bull" Conner ordered the police to disperse protesters with fire hoses, clubs, and police dogs, an event watched by millions on television. There were also drive-by shootings and other forms of intimidation to keep Blacks from registering to vote.

King's reform movement was bent on tearing down the segregationist norms and values and substituting new ones. To a limited, but nonetheless significant extent, the movement succeeded. Schools were desegregated with the help of federal troops. The 1964 Civil Rights Bill banned discrimination in public facilities, education, employment, and in any agency receiving government funds. The 1965 Voting Rights Act prohibited the use of literacy and similar tests to screen voting applicants and allowed federal examiners to monitor elections.

But the civil rights movement has not achieved equality. As noted in various parts of this text, considerable residential segregation occurs in the North and the South, many schools remain racially segregated, Blacks have less spent on their education than Whites, Black unemployment is twice that of Whites, wages are considerably less for Blacks, the poverty rate for Blacks is triple that of Whites, racial discrimination continues in receiving loans, and the economic position of Black women is far worse than that of White women.

In short, while civil rights battles have been won, the war for equality is still being fought in legislatures, in the courts, in school districts, and in neighborhoods. As before, individuals and groups are taking agency seriously, working to change institutional racism in all its forms.

Gender Equity in Sports

In the last century or so women have made several significant advances. The courts have ruled that women are not the property of the husbands. Women now own property. Women vote. Women serve on juries. Women are now elected to public office. In each case, women fought against a patriarchal social order where it just seemed "natural" for men to have the power to win these rights (Kuttner, 1996). The battles for gender equity are ongoing, especially regarding equal employment and promotion opportunities, and the acceptance of women in leadership roles (religion, government, education, corporations). One of the most recent, interesting, and successful battles for gender equity has occurred in sports, the case study described here.

Historically, sport has been a male preserve (this section is dependent on a number of sources: Eitzen and Sage, 1997:Ch. 14; Malec, 1997; and Coakley, 1994: Ch. 9). When women did participate, they were ignored by fans and the media, trivialized (given team nicknames such as the "Wildkittens" or the "Teddy Bears") (Eitzen and Baca Zinn, 1989), or demeaned for being "masculine" or lesbians. Thus, sport was (and is) an institution that contributed to and perpetuated male dominance in society (Hall, 1985).

With a few exceptions, U.S. sport in the early 1970s was for men and boys. Only one in 27 high school girls participated in sport, compared to one in three now. At that time, *Sports Illustrated* writers Bill Gilbert and Nancy Williamson said:

> There may be worse (more socially serious) forms of prejudice in the United States, but there is no sharper example of discrimination today than that which operates against girls and women who take part in competitive sports, wish to take part, or might wish to if society did not scorn such endeavors. (Gilbert and Williamson, 1973:90)

Compare this statement with the situation now. United States women were celebrated in the 1996 Olympic Games for the successes (team gold medals in gymnastics, basketball, softball, and dominance in swimming and track and field). Women professionals in tennis and golf are on television and highly rewarded for victories. New professional leagues for women are springing up in basketball, volleyball, and other sports. At the collegiate level, schools field women's teams in an average of 7.5 sports, and the successful teams, especially in basketball, are given strong fan and media support (women's collegiate basketball attracted 3.6 million fans in 1994–95, which is triple the attendance of 1985). In high schools the number of female participants in competitive sports has risen from 294,000 in 1971 to 2,240,000 in 1995. Youth sports now have girls' teams, and some have boys and girls playing on the same teams, in sharp contrast to a generation ago when many youth sports programs had formal policies excluding girls from any participation.

These important changes were *not* initiated by the powerful—by the federal government, state governments, the National Collegiate Athletic Association, the various state high school associations, local school boards, Little League Baseball, or other youth sports organizations. The changes came about because of a wider social movement for women's rights and the acts of individual parents, athletes, and groups who challenged patriarchal tradition, laws, and the policies of various athletic and school organizations. As a result of their acts of agency, sport has been changed so that "the next generation of sportswomen will likely find equality in athletics so ordinary and natural that they could forget where it came from" (Kuttner, 1996:5).

The l960s and early l970s was a time of societal upheaval. Rebellion was ubiquitous. The powerless (e.g., racial minorities, welfare mothers, gays and lesbians) challenged discriminatory laws and practices. Students confronted school administrations about their archaic and paternalistic practices. Young people contested the government's war in Southeast Asia. Rather than be drafted to serve in a war they did not believe in, some young men fled to Canada and others chose jail. Youth defied traditions and the materialistic ways of their parents and the older generation. In this time of insurgence, insubordination, defiance, and reforms, the women's movement took root. Actually, women had fought for equality for a hundred years

Women's sports programs have made tremendous progress since 1970. These changes were not initiated by the powerful but came about because of a wider social movement for women's rights and the acts of individual parents, athletes, and groups who challenged patriarchal tradition, laws, and the policies of various athletic and school organizations.

or more, but in the 1960s the movement gained many followers and significant momentum. There were intellectual strands such as Betty Friedan's *The Feminine Mystique* (1963), which argued for an all-out effort to remove the obstructions that had restricted women's access to equal opportunities in society. Feminist intellectuals argued also that girls and women are enhanced as human beings when they are given the opportunities to become competent intellectually and physically. The women's movement also redefined occupational and family roles for women, providing them with increased time and resources for other pursuits.

Organizations emerged, such as the National Organization of Women (NOW), with branches throughout the United States. This organization was instrumental in promoting progress in women's sports in two major ways. First, it asked local organizations to gather information about the differences for boys and girls and men and women in local schools and community programs (number of teams, participants, budgets, equipment, and facilities). This provided a national data base for proposed legislation and court cases as well as information for each participating community so that strong arguments for equity could be made before school boards or the courts. Indirectly, this survey was important because local women learned about the inequities of their communities firsthand and thus were likely candidates for more activist responses later.

The second contribution of NOW was its lobbying effort for national legislation to correct gender inequities. Armed with national data, women as individuals and as members of women's groups applied pressure on political representatives. After two years of intense lobbying, the Congress passed Title IX of the Educational Amendments of 1972. This act declared, "No person in the United States shall, on the basis of sex, be excluded from participation in, be denied the benefits of, or be subjected to discrimination under any educational program or activity receiving federal financial assistance."

Title IX was resisted vigorously by the male establishment in athletic organizations and schools as being too radical, impractical, and burdensome. As a result, enforcement in the early years was sporadic at best. There was a setback in 1984 when the Supreme Court in *Grove City v. Bell* ruled that Title IX did not apply to school athletic programs because they did not receive federal monies directly (even though the schools did). Congress made Title IX stronger in 1988 with the passage of the Civil Rights Restoration Act (over President Reagan's veto), which mandated equal opportunity to all programs in any organization receiving federal money. Most significant, the U.S. Supreme Court ruled that schools could sue schools for financial damages if the schools had intentionally violated Title IX.

Court cases have been used throughout the struggle for gender equity in sports. Regarding youth sports, in 1973 the Little League Baseball's ban against participation by girls was challenged and overturned in several lawsuits by individual parents. As a result, the various youth sports have permitted female participation.

At the high school level, lawsuits have been brought by girls and their parents against school districts or state high school regulatory bodies. Typically these cases involve one of three situations: (1) a girl wishing to participate on a boys' team because her school did not provide a girls' team (the courts generally ruled in favor of the girl in these cases); (2) a girl wanting to be on a boys' team even though her school provided a girls' team (the courts generally ruled against her in this type of case because equal opportunity had not been denied her); and (3) girls wanting a team because neither a boys' team or a girls' team exists in a particular sport. As an example of this last situation, Nebraska settled four class-action lawsuits in 1996, agreeing that high schools must provide girls' softball, with facilities and equipment equal to boys' baseball.

Gender inequity in intercollegiate athletics has been challenged officially in two ways (Eitzen and Sage, 1997:294–296). Between 1972, when Title IX became law, and 1992, for example, over one thousand complaints were filed on behalf of women with the Department of Education's Office of Civil Rights. In addition, dozens of lawsuits have been filed against colleges and universities because of gender inequity. For example, in 1992 Colorado State University dropped several sports, including the women's softball team, because of budgetary constraints. Nine members of the softball team filed suit against CSU, claiming the university violated Title IX. The Colorado Supreme Court ruled that CSU had to reinstate women's softball. In another case, the California chapter of NOW filed a sex-discrimination lawsuit against the California State University system in 1993, claiming that only 30 percent of its participants in sports are women and that women's sports receive less than 25 percent of the athletics budget. Within a year, the California State University system agreed to increase significantly its athletics opportunities and finances for women. In 1994 a U.S. district court, reacting to a suit brought by women athletes at Brown University, ordered that the school reinstate women's gymnastic and volleyball teams and provide "equal treatment" to women's athletics.

Aside from the courts, there are other challenges by women to the male-dominated system of athletics. Some women athletes compete with men in the traditional male sports of football and wrestling (across the country, in high schools, over a hundred girls in football and several hundred girls on wrestling teams). There are a few women coaches of men's teams. There are also women athletic directors (even a few at NCAA Division I-A schools). There are some women sportswriters. There have been a few women umpires and referees. In each instance, these women invaded a male domain and, as a result, they have often encountered hostility, disrespect, and various uncooperative actions from males. But by crossing traditional gender boundaries, these pioneers are extremely important players in this struggle for gender equity.

The past twenty-five years have seen dramatic changes in sports opportunities for women and girls. Participation is way up. Public interest in women's sports is growing rapidly. The number of sports for girls and women offered by schools has risen dramatically. Budgets, resources, and facilities are enormously better. Gender equality in sport, however, is still a goal, not a reality. For example, while a slight majority of college students are women, women only receive 35 percent of the athletic scholarship money that is distributed. Men's football is the culprit since it has been allowed to be exempt from the accounting. In 1993, eighty-five Division I-A schools spent an average of $4 billion on men's football alone, while spending an average of $1.8 million on *all* women's sports (Weistart, 1996:193). A second area of concern is the *decrease,* since Title IX, in the proportion of women's teams with women in leadership positions (coach, administrator) at both the high school and college levels. Third, media attention is not equal. The argument by television networks and newspapers is that they give the public what they want, and the public wants male sports. This, of course, is a self-fulfilling prophecy. Fourth, opportunities in sports careers (professional sports, sports journalism, athletic trainers, referees) for women still lag behind the opportunities and rewards for men. Fifth, women athletes, especially those involved in sports requiring strength and aggression, continue to battle stereotypes, because they do not conform to the dominant cultural definitions of femininity.

So, despite dramatic and positive changes, sport is still a battleground for those wishing to achieve gender equity. Continued acts of agency, collectively and individually, are required if the positive trend is to stay on track.

Conclusion

This book is an introduction to sociology. The primary purpose was to make you more perceptive and more analytical regarding things social. Our hope is that you will build on this knowledge in a lifelong quest to understand society and your place in it.

The theme of this last chapter is the importance of human beings in constructing and reconstructing society. This has two important implications for each of us. First, we do not have to be passive actors who accept society's institutional imperatives as inevitable. To the contrary, we can be actively engaged in social life, working for the improvement or even radical change of faulty social structures. Second, the personal is political. While there are broad political struggles within society that involve us, politics also occurs at the micro level. Issues of social justice may be present in our work situations, at church and other organizations to which we belong, in our neighborhoods, in our families, and in our personal relationships. We can promote social justice in these situations or thwart it. In all cases, our actions have political implications.

At the macro level, the most important struggles involve the overturning of existing structures of exploitation and domination (Amott, 1993). These include collective efforts to bring about universal programs for greater equality such as universal health care, pensions, equal opportunity education, and expanding and upgrading the societal infrastructure (highways, bridges, water supply, airports, mass transit). New family forms require programs such as paid parental leave and a national system of dependent care. The changing economy requires management–labor cooperation to increase productivity while providing fair wages and protecting job security, job safety, job training, and collective bargaining rights. Issues of social justice involve progressive taxation (the more money made, the higher proportion paid in taxes), pay equity, and programs to guard against race, gender, and sexuality biases in employment, housing, and lending practices.

In sum, society's structural arrangements are not inevitable. Individuals converging across lines of race, ethnicity, gender, and sexual orientation can work at the grassroots level organizing opposition, educating the public, demonstrating to promote a cause, electing allied candidates, using the courts, or employing other tactics to transform society. Human beings are agents of change if they choose to be. The choice is ours.

Frances Fox Piven, the eminent social scientist, in writing about the need for social change to solve our current social problems, says:

> No one has ever successfully predicted the movements when ordinary people find their footing, discover new capacities for solidarity and power and new visions of the possible. Still, the development of American democracy depended on the perennial emergence of popular revolt in the past, and it does once again. (Piven, 1996:67)

CHAPTER REVIEW

1. The sociological paradox is that while society has power over its members, social actors have the power to change society. This means that: (*a*) society is not a rigid entity, composed of robots; (*b*) what people consider sacred, and therefore unchangeable, is a social construction that can be reconstructed; and (*c*) since social structures are created they are imperfect, always in need of reform or transformation.

2. A social movement is a collective attempt to promote or resist change.

3. There are three types of social movements: (*a*) resistance movements, which are organized to resist change or to reverse changes that have occurred; (*b*) reform movements, which seek to alter a specific part of society; and (*c*) revolutionary movements, which go beyond reform by seeking the transformation of the entire society.

4. Social movements move through predictable stages. Initially, a number of people share feelings of discontent or anger over some societal condition. The second stage is where the grievances of these people become more focused. A leader emerges who defines the goals, identifies the enemies, and challenges and inspires followers to work together for positive change. The followers are further galvanized as their target is provoked and the powerful attack them. Stage three involves organization, with formal rules, policies, procedures, and tactics. Alliances are formed with similar groups for mutual advantage. When the goals of the movement are accepted by society, the movement has arrived at the final stage, institutionalization.

5. The point of social movements and individual acts of agency is that institutional changes tend to come, not from the leaders of government and business, but rather boiled up from the people.

6. The civil rights movement did not begin in the 1960s, but rather from the time Blacks arrived here as slaves. Moreover, the civil rights movement is not the result of a single event. It carries the cumulative effects of centuries of mistreatment of Blacks by Whites and White governments.

7. Despite the oppressive control of Blacks, many of them exhibited agency by individual acts of rebellion, work slowdowns, and running away to join with others in bands that harassed Whites. Others fought the slave codes by promoting community solidarity, fighting to keep family ties, and creating their own rituals that recognized marriage and parenthood. After the Civil War, Blacks remained oppressed by low wages and sharecropping arrangements. Black Codes, laws that were biased against Blacks, were passed to keep Blacks from achieving equality. Similarly, in the early 20th century, Jim Crow laws enforced rigid segregation. Again, in the face of these indignities, Blacks engaged in various forms of agency.

8. The civil rights movement came together in the 1950s, with the passage of the Supreme Court decision desegregating the schools, the outrage of the lynching of Emmitt Till, and the Montgomery bus boycott. Sit-ins were organized. Economic boycotts against White businesses were initiated. Grievances were taken to court. The movement was partially successful, as the segregationist laws and practices were abolished. Racial equality has not yet been achieved, however, as measured by wages, employment opportunities, unemployment rates, poverty rates, desegregated neighborhoods, and differences in money spent on education.

9. Before 1970 U.S. sport was almost exclusively for men and boys. However, as a consequence of court cases; individual acts of courage by women pioneers in sport as athletes, coaches, administrators, and referees; and the efforts of women's organizations, dramatic moves toward gender equity in sports have been accomplished. Archaic rules by athletic organizations prohibiting girls from competition were overturned.

Legislation, most prominently Title IX, was passed which gave impetus to greater participation by girls and women in school sports. And, rulings by the courts have given women greater equity in this previously male preserve. Full gender equity, however, has not yet been reached.

10. Society's structural arrangements are not inevitable. Individuals acting alone or with others in grassroots organizations can be agents of change.

KEY TERMS

Determinism
Agency
Social movement
Ideology

Resistance movements
Reform movements
Revolutionary movements
Charisma

Routinization of charisma
Institutionalization
Goal displacement

STUDY QUESTIONS

1. What is the fundamental sociological paradox?

2. Provide contemporary (United States and worldwide) examples of the three types of social movements.

3. Using the case study of the civil rights movement (beginning with Rosa Parks), show how that movement has gone through the various stages of social movements.

4. What are the implications of this chapter's thesis—that human beings construct and reconstruct society?

FOR FURTHER READING

Barry D. Adam, *The Rise of a Gay and Lesbian Movement* (Boston: Twayne, 1987).

Teresa Amott, *Caught in the Crisis: Women and the U.S. Economy Today* (New York: Monthly Review Press, 1993).

Herbert Blumer, "Collective Behavior," in Alfred M. Lee, ed., *Principles of Sociology*, 2nd ed. (New York: Barnes and Noble, 1955), pp. 165–198.

Taylor Branch, *Parting the Waters: America in the King Years 1954–63* (New York: Simon and Schuster Touchstone, 1988).

Robert A. Goldberg, *Grassroots Resistance: Social Movements in Twentieth Century America* (Belmont, CA: Wadsworth, 1991).

John C. Hammerback, Richard J. Jensen, and Jose Angel Gutierrez, *A War of Words: Chicano Protest in the 1960s and 1970s* (Westport, CT: Greenwood Press, 1985).

Vincent Harding, *There Is a River: The Black Struggle for Freedom in America* (New York: Harcourt Brace Jovanovich, 1981).

Fred Powledge, *Free at Last? The Civil Rights Movement and the People Who Made It* (Boston: Little, Brown, 1991).

Joseph P. Shapiro, *No Pity: People with Disabilities Forging a New Civil Rights Movement* (New York: Times Books/Random House, 1993).

Howard Zinn, *A People's History of the United States* (New York: Harper & Row, 1980).

GLOSSARY

Accommodation. Acceptance of one's position in a situation without struggle.

Achieved status. A position in a social organization attained through personal effort.

Age cohort Individuals from the same generation and thus affected by similar societal events such as an economic depression or war.

Ageism. Discrimination against the elderly.

Aggregate. A collection of individuals who happen to be at the same place at the same time.

Alienation. An individual's feeling of separation from the surrounding society.

Altruistic suicide. The sacrificing of one's life for the good of the group.

Androgyny. Having the characteristics of both males and females.

Anomic suicide. Durkheim's term anomie indicates a social condition characterized by the absence of norms or conflicting norms. At the individual level, the person is not sure what the norms are, which leads to a relatively high probability of suicide.

Anticipatory socialization. Learning and acting out the beliefs, norms, and values of a group before joining it.

Argot. The specialized or secret language peculiar to a group.

Ascribed status. Social position based on such factors as age, race, and family over which the individual has no control.

Assimilation. The process by which individuals or groups voluntarily or involuntarily adopt the culture of another group, losing their original identity.

Baby boom. A term referring to a fifteen-year period in U.S. history following World War II in which an extraordinary number of babies were born.

Bias theory. An explanation that blames the prejudiced attitudes of majority members for the secondary status of the minority.

Blaming the victim. The belief that some individuals are poor, criminals, or school dropouts because they have a flaw within them.

Bourgeoisie. Marx's term for the class of persons that owns the means of production in a capitalist society.

Bureaucracy. A system of administration that is characterized by specialized roles, explicit rules, and a hierarchy of authority.

Bureaucratization. The trend toward greater use of the bureaucratic mode of organization and administration within society.

Capital flight. The investment choices that involve the movement of corporate monies from one investment to another (e.g., investments in other countries, plant relocation, and mergers).

Capitalism. The economic system based on private ownership of property, guided by the seeking of maximum profits.

Capitalist patriarchy. A condition of capitalism in which male supremacy keeps women in subordinate roles at work and in the home.

Case study. The research strategy that involves the detailed and thorough analysis of a single event, community, or organization.

Caste system. The closed system of social stratification. Membership is fixed at birth and is permanent.

Caveat emptor. The Latin phrase that means "let the buyer beware."

Charisma. The extraordinary attributes of an individual that enable the possessor to lead and inspire without the legal authority to do so.

Charisma of office. Instead of charisma based on personal attributes, in some organizations, the holder of a particular position is believed to possess charisma.

Church. The highly organized, bureaucratic form of religious organization that accommodates itself to the larger society.

Civil religion. The set of religious beliefs, rituals, and symbols outside the church that legitimates the status quo.

Class. Ranking in a stratification system based on economic resources.

Class consciousness. Karl Marx's term that refers to the recognition by persons in a similar economic situation of a common interest.

Class segregation. Barriers that restrict social interaction to the members of a particular social class.

Cloning. The artificial production of genetically identical offspring.

Cohabitation. The practice of two people living together as a couple without being married.

Colonial theory. A structural explanation of minority subordination that rests on use of power by the dominant group to oppress a racial minority group.

Commune. A small, voluntary community characterized by cooperation and a common ideology.

Compulsory heterosexuality. The system of sexuality that imposes negative sanctions on those who are homosexual or bisexual.

Conflict model, perspective. A view of society that posits conflict as a normal feature of social life, influencing the distribution of power and the direction and magnitude of social change.

Consensus. Widely held agreement on the norms and values of society.

Conspicuous consumption. The purchase and obvious display of material goods to impress other people with one's wealth and assumed status.

Constraint. The state of being controlled by some force.

Contingent employment. This employment arrangement refers to employees who work for an employer as "temporaries" or as "independent contractors."

Control group. A group of subjects in an experiment who are not exposed to the independent variable but are similar in all other respects to the group exposed to the independent variable.

Cooptation. The process by which representatives of a potentially destabilizing subgroup are incorporated into the leadership or management level of an organization to avert problems.

Corporate crime. The illegal and/or socially harmful behaviors that result from the deliberate decisions of corporate executives in accordance with corporate goals.

Correlation. The degree of relationship between two variables.

Counterculture. A subculture that fundamentally opposes the dominant culture.

Crime. An act that is prohibited by the law.

Cult. A religion with practices and teachings at odds with the dominant culture and religion.

Cultural deficiency theories. Explanations that argue that some flaw in a social group's way of life is responsible for its secondary status.

Cultural deprivation. An ethnocentric term implying that the culture of another group is not only deficient but also inferior.

Cultural relativity. The belief that customs of another society must be viewed and evaluated by their standards, not by an outsider's.

Cultural tyranny. The belief that the socialization process forces narrow behavioral and attitudinal traits on persons.

Culture. The knowledge that the members of a social organization share.

Culture of poverty. The view that the poor are qualitatively different in values and lifestyles from the rest of society and that these cultural differences explain continued poverty.

Deferred gratification. The willingness to sacrifice in the present for expected future rewards.

Deficiency theories. Explanations that view the secondary status of minorities as the result of their own behaviors and cultural traits.

Deflation. The part of the economic cycle when the amount of money in circulation is down, resulting in low prices and unemployment.

Deindustrialization. The widespread, systematic diversion of capital (finance, plant, and equipment) from investment in the nation's basic industries into service and knowledge sectors of the economy or overseas.

Democracy. The form of government in which the citizens participate in government, characterized by competition for office, public officials being responsive to public opinion, and the citizenry having access to reliable information on which to make their electoral choices.

Demography. The scientific study of the size, composition, and changes in human populations.

Dependent variable. A variable that is influenced by the effect of another variable (the independent variable).

Deprogramming. The process in which persons believed to have been brainwashed by cults are abducted and retrained against their will.

Derogation. Discrimination in the form of words that put a minority down.

Determinism. The belief that human behavior is controlled by some force, whether genetic, economic, or political. Taken to the extreme, deterministic theories leave no room for human beings to adapt to and change social structures to meet their needs.

Deviance. Behavior that violates the expectations of society.

Dialectic. The clash between conflicting ideas and forces.

Differential association. The theory that a person becomes deviant because of an excess of definitions favorable to the violation of societal expectations over definitions supporting the norms and values.

Direct interlock. A type of interlocking directorate in which an individual serves on the board of directors of two companies.

Direct social control. Direct intervention by the agents of society to control the behavior of individuals and groups.

Discouraged workers. People who have not actively sought work for four weeks. They are not counted as unemployed by the Bureau of Labor Statistics.

Discrimination. To act toward a person or group with partiality, typically because they belong to a minority.

Division of labor. The specialization of economic roles resulting in an interdependent and efficient system.

Dual-career marriage. A marriage in which a husband and wife are both employed outside the home.

Dysfunction. A consequence that is disruptive for the stability and cohesion of the social organization.

Economy. The institution that ensures the maintenance of society by producing and distributing the necessary goods and services.

Egalitarianism. Fundamental belief in equality.

Ego. According to Freud, the conscious, rational part of the self.

Egoistic suicide. Durkheim's finding that persons lacking ties to social groups are more susceptible to suicide than are those with strong group attachments.

Elitist model of power. The assumption that power is concentrated in a few rather than dispersed (the pluralist view).

Environmental racism. The disproportionate exposure of some racial group to toxic substances.

Epistemology. The philosophical position that all reality is socially constructed.

Ethnic group. A social group with a common culture distinct from the culture of the majority because of race, religion, or national origin.

Ethnicity. A term referring to shared cultural heritage.

Ethnocentrism. The universal tendency to deprecate the ways of persons from other societies as wrong, old-fashioned, or immoral and to think of the ways of one's own group as superior (as the only right way).

Ethnomethodology. The subdiscipline in sociology that studies the everyday living practices of people to discover the underlying bases for social behavior.

Eugenics. The attempt to improve the human race through the control of hereditary factors.

Experimental group. A group of subjects in an experiment who are exposed to the independent variable, in contrast to the control group, which is not.

Falling rate of profit. One of the contradictions of capitalism argued by Karl Marx. This refers to the propensity of employers to maximize profits by reducing labor expenses (technology and paying lowest possible wages). The result of this capitalist rationale, argued Marx, would actually be to reduce profits because the workers would be less and less able to purchase products.

False consciousness. In Marxian theory, the idea that the oppressed may hold beliefs damaging to their interests.

Family. A particular societal arrangement whereby persons related by ancestry, marriage, or adoption live together, form an economic unit, and raise children.

Family values. The conservative term supporting the heterosexual two-parent family. The implication is that all other family arrangements are the source of social problems.

Feminist approach. An approach based on support for women's equality.

Feminization of poverty. A reference to the relatively large number of female-headed households living in poverty.

Feral children. Children reputedly raised by animals; they have the characteristics of their peers (animals) rather than of human beings.

Fertility rate. The frequency of actual births in a population.

Folkways. Relatively unimportant rules that if violated are not severely punished.

Function. Any consequence of a social arrangement that contributes to the overall stability of the system.

Functional integration. Unity among divergent elements of society resulting from specialized divisions of labor.

Functionalism (the order perspective). The theoretical perspective that emphasizes the order, harmony, and stability of social systems.

Gender. Refers to the cultural and social definition of feminine and masculine. Differs from *sex,* which is the biological fact of femaleness or maleness.

Gendered. Behavior patterned as feminine or masculine.

Gender roles' (approach to sexual inequality). The understanding of gender differences that emphasize the characteristics that individuals learn in the socialization process.

Gender segregation. The location of women and men in different job categories throughout the work force.

Gender stratification. The differential ranking and rewarding of women's and men's roles.

Generalized other. Mead's concept that refers to the internalization of the expectations of the society.

Genetic engineering. The scientific effort to manipulate DNA molecules in plants and animals.

Glass ceiling. Invisible barriers that limit women's mobility in organizations.

Glossolalia. The emotional religious experience involving the incoherent "speaking in tongues."

Goal displacement. When the original goals of an organization are displaced by the goals of maintaining the organization.

Governing class. Domhoff's model of power that posits that the very wealthy in society contribute a disproportionate number of people to the controlling institutions and key decision-making groups.

Group. A collection of people (two or more) who, because of sustained interaction, have evolved a common culture.

Hedonism. The pursuit of pleasure and self-indulgence.

Hidden curriculum. That part of the school experience that has nothing to do with formal subjects but refers to the behaviors that schools expect of children (obedience to authority, remaining quiet and orderly, etc.).

Hierarchy. The arrangement of people or objects in order of importance.

Home-based work. Women working for pay in their homes.

Horizontal mobility. Changes in occupations or other situations without moving from one social class to another.

Household. A residential unit of unrelated individuals who pool resources and perform common tasks of production and consumption.

Human agency. When individuals, acting alone or with others, shape, resist, challenge, and sometimes change the social institutions that impinge on them.

Id. Freud's term for the collection of urges and drives persons have for pleasure and aggression.

Ideal type. An abstraction constructed to show how some phenomenon would be characterized in its pure form.

Ideological social control. The efforts by social organizations to control members by controlling their minds. Societies accomplish this, typically, through the socialization process.

Ideology. A set of ideas that explains reality, provides guidelines for behavior, and expresses the interests of a group.

Independent variable. A variable that affects another variable (the dependent variable).

Indirect interlock. A type of interlocking directorate in which two companies each have a director on the board of a third company.

Individual racism. Overt acts by individuals of one race to harm a member or members of another race.

Inflation. The situation when too much money purchases too few goods, resulting in rising prices.

Institutions. Social arrangements that channel behavior in prescribed ways in the important areas of societal life.

Institutional derogation. When the normal arrangements of society act to reinforce the negative stereotypes of minority groups.

Institutional discrimination. When the social arrangements and accepted ways of doing things in society disadvantage some social category.

Institutionalization of a social movement. When a movement's beliefs are accepted by the larger society and its goals achieved.

Institutional process. The concept designating the forces that resist change, which emanate from the assumed human need for certainty and stability.

Institutional racism. When the social arrangements and accepted ways of doing things in society disadvantage a racial group.

Institutional sexism. When the social arrangements and accepted ways of doing things in society disadvantage females.

Institutional violence. When the normal workings of the society do harm to a social category.

Instrumental process. The search for technological solutions to human problems as an impetus for change.

Instrumental view of power. A view held by some Marxists that the ruling class controls political institutions through money and influence. Other Marxists accept the structuralist view of power.

Interest group. A group of like-minded persons who organize to influence public policy.

Intergenerational mobility. The difference in social class position between (typically) a son and his father.

Interlocking directorate. The linkage between corporations that results when an individual serves on the board of directors of two companies (a direct interlock) or when two companies each have a director on the board of a third company (an indirect interlock).

Internalization. In the process of socialization society's demands become part of the individual, acting to control his or her behavior.

Intragenerational mobility. The movement by an individual from one social class to another.

"Iron cage" of rationality. This refers to the dehumanizing aspects of bureaucracy. Max Weber saw bureaucracies as cages with people trapped in them, denied of their basic humanity.

Labeling theory (societal reactions). The explanation of deviant behavior that stresses the importance of the society in defining what is illegal and in assigning a deviant status to particular individuals, which in turn dominates their identities and behaviors.

Laissez-faire. The government policy of allowing the marketplace to operate unhindered.

Latent consequence, function. An unintended consequence of a social arrangement or social action.

Life chances. Weber's term that refers to the chances throughout one's life cycle to live and experience the good things in life.

Looking-glass self. Cooley's concept that refers to the importance of how other people influence the way we see ourselves.

McDonalization. George Ritzer's term for the process by which the principles of fast-food restaurants are coming to dominate more and more sectors of American society as well as the rest of the world.

Machismo (macho). An exaggerated masculinity, evidenced by male dominance, posturing, physical daring, and an exploitative attitude toward women.

Macro level. The large-scale structures and processes of society, including the institutions and the system of stratification.

Majority group. The social category in society holding superordinate power and who successfully impose their will on less-powerful groups (minority groups).

Male chauvinism. Exaggerated beliefs about the superiority of the male and the resulting discrimination.

Male dominance. This refers to the beliefs, values, and cultural meanings that give higher value and prestige to masculinity than to femininity, and that institutionalize male control of socially valued resources.

Manifest consequence, function. An intended consequence of a social arrangement or social action.

Marginality. The condition resulting from taking part in two distinct ways of life without belonging fully to either.

Marital power. The ability to control the spouse and to influence or control family decisions and activities.

Material technology. Refers to the technical knowledge needed to use and make things.

Matriarchal family. A family structure in which the mother is dominant.

Matrix of domination. The intersections of the hierarchies of class, race, and gender in which each of us exists.

Megachurch. A trend among evangelicals is toward very large churches. Their growth is fueled by entertaining church services, the provision of services, and specialized ministries for targeted groups.

Meritocracy. A system of stratification in which rank is based purely on achievement.

Micro level. The social organization and processes of small-scale social groups.

Military-industrial complex. The term that refers to the direct and indirect relationships between the military establishment (the Pentagon) and the corporations.

Minority group. A social category composed of persons who differ from the majority, are relatively powerless, and are the objects of discrimination.

Modal personality type. A distinct type of personality considered to be characteristic of the members of a particular society.

Model. The mental image a scientist has of the structure of society. This influences what the scientists look for, what they see, and how phenomena are explained.

Modern family. The nuclear family that emerged in response to the requirements of an urban, industrial society. It consisted of an intact nuclear household unit with a male breadwinner, his full-time homemaker wife, and their dependent children.

Monogamy. The form of marriage in which an individual may not be married to more than one person at a time.

Monopolistic capitalism. The form of capitalism prevalent in the contemporary United States, where a few large corporations control the key industries, destroying competition and the market mechanisms that would ordinarily keep prices low and help consumers.

Monopoly. When a single firm dominates an industry.

Mores. Important norms, the violation of which results in severe punishment.

Mortality rate. The frequency of actual deaths in a population.

Multinational corporation. A corporation that operates in more than one country.

Myth of peaceful progress. The incorrect belief that throughout U.S. history disadvantaged groups have gained their share of power, prosperity, and respectability without violence.

Myth of separate worlds. The belief that work and family roles operate independently of each other.

New immigration. Unlike previous waves of immigration where the immigrants were primarily White and European, the latest wave of immigration is composed primarily of people of color (from Latin America and Asia).

New poor. The poor who are displaced by new technologies or whose jobs have moved away to the suburbs, to other regions of the country, or out of the country.

Nominalist position. A philosophical position that a group is nothing more than the sum of its parts.

Nomos. Literally, meaningful order. The opposite of anomie.

Nonfamily household. Persons who live alone or with unrelated individuals.

Norms. This part of culture refers to rules that specify appropriate and inappropriate behavior (in other words, the shared expectations for behavior).

Nuclear family. A kinship unit composed of husband, wife, and children.

Nuptiality. The proportion of married persons.

Ontology. The philosophical position that accepts the reality of things because their nature cannot be denied.

Opiate of the masses. Marx's term for religion's affect on the masses. In this view religion inhibits societal change by making existing social arrangements seem right and inevitable. The dominant form of economics in society, the type of government, the law, and other social creations are given religious sanction.

Order model, perspective. The conception of society as a social system characterized by cohesion, consensus, cooperation, reciprocity, stability, and persistence.

Paradigm. The basic assumptions a scientist has of the structure of society (see Model).

Participant observation. A method in which researchers engage in the activities of the people they are observing.

Participatory socialization. The mode of socialization in which parents encourage their children to explore, experiment, and question.

Patriarchal family. A family structure in which the father is dominant.

Patriarchy. A form of social organization in which males dominate females.

Pay equity. Policies designed to bring the pay levels of women in closer alignment with those of men. Also called *comparable worth*.

Peer group. Friends usually of the same age and socioeconomic status.

Peter Principle. The view that most people in an organization will be promoted until they eventually reach their level of incompetence.

Pluralism. A situation in which different groups live in mutual respect but retain their racial, religious, or ethnic identities.

Pluralist model of power. The diffuse distribution of power among various groups and interests.

Political crime. Either crime against the state (the order model's view) or crime by the state (the conflict model's view).

Polity. The societal institution especially concerned with maintaining order.

Population implosion. The trend for people to live in ever-denser localities (the movement of people from rural areas to the urban regions).

Positivism. The scientific model for understanding reality.

Postmodern family. Judith Stacey's term for the multiplicity of family and household arrangements that has emerged as a result of a number of social factors, such as women in the labor force, divorce, remarriage, and cohabitation arrangements.

Poverty. A standard of living below the minimum needed for the maintenance of adequate diet, health, and shelter.

Power. The ability to get what one wants from someone else.

Power elite. Mills's term for the coalition of the top echelon of the military, the executive branch of the federal government, and business.

Prestige. The respect of an individual or social category as a result of his or her social status.

Priestly role of religion. One role of the church and the clergy is to comfort individuals, helping them through difficult times. The church also celebrates the various important stages in life (birth, marriage, death). This role is conservative since it does not challenge the system.

Primary deviance. The original illegal act preceding the successful application of the deviant label.

Primary groups. Small groups characterized by intimate, face-to-face interaction.

Privilege. This refers to the distribution of goods and services, situations, and experiences that are highly valued and beneficial.

Progressive tax. A tax rate that escalates with the amount of income.

Proletariat. Marx's term for the industrial workers in a capitalistic society.

Prophetic role of religion. One function of the church is to challenge the existing system, leading the fight to right the inequities of society.

Protestant ethic (Puritan work ethic). The religious beliefs, traced back to Martin Luther and John Calvin, that emphasize hard work and continual striving in order to prove that one is saved by material success.

Psychosurgery. A form of brain surgery used to change the behavior of the patient.

Pygmalion effect. Students placed in a track are treated by teachers in a way that ensures that the prophecy is fulfilled.

Race; racial group. A group socially defined on the basis of a presumed common genetic heritage resulting in distinguishing physical characteristics.

Racial-ethnic group. Groups labeled as races by the wider society and bound together by their common social and economic conditions resulting in distinctive cultural and ethnic characteristics.

Racial formation. The socio-historical processes by which races are continually being shaped and transformed.

Racism. The domination and discrimination of one racial group by the majority.

Radical nonintervention. Schur's term referring to the strategy of leaving juvenile delinquents alone as much as possible rather than processing (and labeling) them through the criminal justice system.

Random sample. The selection of a subset from a population so that every person has an equal chance of being selected.

Realist position. The philosophical position that a group is more than the sum of its parts (referring to the emergence of culture and mechanisms of social control that affect the behavior of members regardless of their personalities).

Recidivism. Reinvolvement in crime.

Reference group. A group to which one would like to belong and toward which one therefore orients his or her behavior.

Reform movement. A social movement that seeks to alter a specific part of society.

Regressive tax. A tax rate that remains the same for all persons, rich or poor. The result is that poor persons pay a larger proportion of their wealth than do affluent persons.

Reliability. The degree to which a study yields similar results when repeated.

Religion. The social institution that encompasses beliefs and practices regarding the sacred.

Repressive socialization. The mode of socialization in which parents demand rigid conformity in their children, enforced by physical punishment.

Reserve army of the unemployed. Unemployed people who want to work. Their presence tends to depress the wages of workers and keeps those workers from making demands on employers for fear of being replaced.

Resistance movement. The organized attempt to reinforce the traditional system by preventing change.

Revolutionary movement. The collective attempt to bring about a radical transformation of society.

Rites of passage. The ritual whereby the society recognizes the adult status of a young member.

Ritual. This consists of symbolic actions that reinforce the collective remembering of the group's shared meanings.

Role. The behavioral expectations and requirements attached to a position in a social organization.

Role performance (role behavior). The actual behavior of persons occupying particular positions in a social organization.

Routinization of charisma. The process by which an organization attempts to transmit the special attributes of the former leader to a new one. This is done by various means, for example, laying on of hands and the old leader choosing a successor.

Sacred. That which inspires awe because of its believed supernatural qualities.

Sample. A representative part of a population.

Sanctions. Social rewards or punishments for approved or disapproved behavior.

Secondary deviance. Deviant behavior that is a consequence of the successful application of the deviant label.

Secondary groups. Large, impersonal, and formally organized groups.

Second shift. The term referring to women's responsibilities for housework, child care, and home management that she must do in addition to her labor in the workforce.

Sect. A religious organization, in contrast to a church, that tends to be dogmatic, fundamentalistic, and in opposition to the world.

Secular. Of or pertaining to the world; the opposite of sacred.

Segmented labor market. The capitalist economy is divided into two distinct sectors, one where production and working conditions are relatively stable and secure; the other is composed of marginal firms where working conditions, wages, and job security are low.

Segregation. The separation of one group from another.

Self. George Herbert Mead's term for an individual's personality.

Self-esteem. The opinion of oneself.

Self-fulfilling prophecy. An event that occurs because it was predicted. The prophecy is confirmed because people alter their behavior to conform to the prediction.

Sex-gender system. A system of stratification that ranks and rewards gender roles unequally.

Sexism. The individual actions and institutional arrangements that discriminate against women.

Sex role. The learned patterns of behavior expected of males and females by society.

Sexuality. A way of organizing the social world based on sexual identity.

Sexual stratification. A hierarchical arrangement based on gender.

Shared monopoly. When four or fewer companies control 50 percent or more of an industry.

Sibling. A brother or sister.

Significant others. Mead's term referring to those persons most important in the determining of a child's behavior.

Social class. A number of persons who occupy the same relative economic rank in the stratification system.

Social control. The regulation of human behavior in any social group.

Social construction of reality. The process by which individuals learn how to define reality from other people in interaction and by learning the culture.

Social Darwinism. The belief that the principle of the survival of the fittest applies to human societies, especially the system of stratification.

Social determinism. The assumption that human behavior is explained exclusively by social factors.

Social differentiation. The process of categorizing persons by some personal attribute.

Social facts. Durkheim's term referring to those forces outside individuals that constrain them in their behaviors.

Social group. Two or more people who identify with each other and who share a distinctive set of relationships.

Social inequality. The ranking of persons by wealth, family background, race, ethnicity, or sex.

Social interaction. When individuals act toward or respond to each other.

Socialism. The economic system in which the means of production are owned by the people for their collective benefit.

Socialization. The process of learning the culture.

Socialization agents. Those individuals, groups, and institutions responsible for transmitting the culture of society to newcomers.

Social location. One's position in society based on family background, race, socioeconomic status, religion, and other relevant social characteristics.

Social mobility. The movement by an individual from one social class or status group to another.

Social movement. A collective attempt to promote or resist change.

Social organization. The order of a social group as evidenced by the positions, roles, norms, and other constraints that control behavior and ensure predictability.

Social problem. There are two types of social problems: (1) societally induced conditions that cause psychic and material suffering for any segment of the population; and (2) acts and conditions that violate the norms and values of society.

Social relationship. When two or more persons engage in enduring social interaction.

Social stratification. When people are ranked in a hierarchy that differentiates them as superior or inferior.

Social structure. The patterned and recurrent relationships among people and parts in a social organization.

Social system. A differentiated group whose parts are interrelated in an orderly arrangement, bounded in geographical space or membership.

Social technology. The knowledge necessary to establish, maintain, and operate the technical aspects of social organization.

Society. The largest social organization to which individuals owe their allegiance. The entity is located geographically, has a common culture, and is relatively self-sufficient.

Socioeconomic status (SES). The measure of social status that takes into account several prestige factors, such as income, education, and occupation.

Sociological theory. A set of ideas that explains a range of human behavior and a variety of social and societal events.

Sociology. The scholarly discipline concerned with the systematic study of social organizations.

Stagflation. The contemporary economic phenomenon that combines the problems of inflation and deflation—high prices, high unemployment, wage-price spiral, and a profits squeeze.

Status. A socially defined position in a social organization.

Status anguish. A fundamental concern with the contradictions in the individual's status set.

Status group. Persons of similar status. They view each other as social equals.

Status inconsistency. The situation in which a person ranks high on one status dimension and low on another.

Status withdrawal. The loss of status that occurs with downward mobility.

Stereotype. An exaggerated generalization about some social category.

Stigma. A label of social disgrace.

Structural approach to sexual inequality. The understanding of gender differences resulting from factors external to individuals.

Structural transformation of the economy. The shift to a new era evidenced by the move from a manufacturing to a service/information economy with microchip

technology, the global economy, and the rapid movement of capital.

Structuralist view of power. A Marxian interpretation arguing that the ruling class gets its way because the political and economic institutions are biased in its favor. Other Marxists hold the instrumental view of power.

Structural discrimination theories. Explanations that focus on the institutionalized patterns of discrimination as the sources of the secondary status of minorities.

Structured social inequality. Refers to the patterns of superiority and inferiority, the distribution of rewards, and the belief systems that reinforce the inequities of society.

Subculture. A relatively cohesive cultural system that varies in form and substance from the dominant culture.

Subsidy. Financial aid in the form of tax breaks or gifts granted by the government to an individual or commercial enterprise.

Suburb. A community adjacent to a city.

Sunrise industries. Industries characterized by increased output and employment.

Sunset industries. Industries declining in both output and employment.

Superego. Freud's term that refers to the internalization of society's morals within the self.

Survey research. The research technique that selects a sample of people from a larger population in order to learn how they think, feel, or act.

Sweatshop. A substandard work environment where workers are paid less than the minimum wage, not paid overtime premiums, and other labor laws are violated.

Symbol. A thing that represents something else, such as a word, gesture, or physical object (cross, flag).

Synthesis. The blending of the parts into a new form.

Systemic imperatives. The economic and social constraints on the decision makers in an organization, which promote the status quo.

Tax expenditures. These are legal tax loopholes that permit certain individuals and corporations to pay lower taxes or no taxes at all.

Technology. The application of science to meet the needs of society.

Theodicy. The religious legitimation for a situation that might otherwise cause guilt or anger (such as defeat in a war or the existence of poverty among affluence).

Tracking. A practice of schools of grouping children according to their scores on IQ and other tests.

Transcience. Toffler's term that refers to the rapid turnover in things, places, and people characteristic of a technological society.

Underemployment. Being employed at a job below one's level of training and expertise.

Undocumented immigrant. Immigrants who have entered the United States illegally.

Urbanism. The ways in which city life characteristically affects how people feel, think, and interact with one another.

Urbanization. The trend referring to the movement of people from rural to urban areas.

Urban region (megalopolis, conurbation, strip city). The extensive urban area that results when two or more large cities grow together until they are contiguous.

Validity. The degree to which a scientific study measures what it attempts to measure.

Value neutrality. The attempt by scientists to be absolutely free of bias in their research.

Values. The shared criteria used in evaluating objects, ideas, acts, feelings, or events as to their relative desirability, merit, or correctness.

Variable. An attitude, behavior, or condition that can vary in magnitude from case to case (the opposite of a constant).

Vertical mobility. The movement upward or downward in social class.

Voluntary association. Organizations that people join because they approve of their goals.

Wealthfare. Receipt by the affluent of financial aid and/or services from the government.

Welfare. Receipt of financial aid and/or services from the government.

White flight. Whites leaving the central cities for the suburbs to avoid interaction with Blacks, especially the busing of children.

Work-family role system. Traditional uneven division of labor in which men's work role takes priority over the family role, and women, even those who work outside the home, are to give priority to the family role.

REFERENCES

Academe. 1995. *Bulletin of the American Association of University Professors* 81 (March/April).

Acker, Joan. 1973. "Women and Stratification: A Case of Intellectual Sexism," *American Journal of Sociology* 78 (January):936–945.

———. 1978. "Issues in the Sociological Study of Women's Work," in *Women Working,* Ann H. Stromberg and Shirley Harkess (eds.). Palo Alto, CA: Mayfield, pp. 134–161.

———. 1980. "Women and Stratification: A Review of the Recent Literature," *Contemporary Sociology* 9 (Winter).

———. 1992. "Gendered Institutions: From Sex Roles to Gendered Institutions," *Contemporary Sociology* 21 (September):565–568.

Ahlburg, Dennis A., and Carol J. De Vita. 1992. "New Realities of the American Family," *Population Bulletin* 47 (August):entire issue.

Albelda, Randy. 1991. "Left in the Dust: U.S. Trails Other Nations in Support for Poor," *Dollars & Sense* 172 (December):20–21.

———. 1992. "Whose Values, Which Families?" *Dollars & Sense* 182 (December):6–9.

———. 1996. "Farewell to Welfare," *Dollars & Sense* 208 (November/December):16–19.

———. and Nancy Folbre. 1996. *The War on the Poor: A Defense Manual.* New York: The New Press.

American Association of University Women. 1992. "How Schools Shortchange Girls," executive summary, the *AAUW Report,* The American Association of University Women Educational Foundation.

American Psychological Association. 1993. *Violence & Youth.* Washington, DC: American Psychological Association.

Amott, Teresa. 1993. *Caught in the Crisis: Women and the U.S. Economy Today.* New York: Monthly Review Press.

Andersen, Margaret L. 1983. *Thinking about Women: Sociological and Feminist Perspectives.* New York: Macmillan.

———. 1992. *Thinking about Women,* 3rd ed. New York: Macmillan.

———. 1997. Thinking about Women, 4th ed. Boston: Allyn and Bacon.

———, and Patricia Hill Collins (eds.). 1992. *Race, Class, and Gender: An Anthology.* Belmont, CA: Wadsworth.

———, and Patricia Hill Collins (eds.). 1995. *Race, Class, and Gender: An Anthology,* 2nd ed. Belmont, CA: Wadsworth.

Anderson, Jack. 1983. "Plans to Test Adolescents Smack of 1984," *Rocky Mountain News* (October 13):106.

Aponte, Robert. 1991. "Urban Hispanic Poverty: Disaggregations and Explanations," *Social Problems* 38 (4):516–528.

Applebome, Peter. 1989. "Scandals Aside, TV Preachers Thrive," *New York Times* (October 8):12.

Asch, Solomon E. 1958. "Effects of Group Pressure upon the Modification and Distortion of Judgments," in *Readings in Social Psychology,* 3rd ed., Eleanor E. Maccoby, Theodore M. Newcomb, and Eugene L. Hartley (eds.). New York: Holt, Rinehart and Winston.

Associated Press. 1976. "Jungle Boy Remains More Like Monkey" (May 15).

———. 1989. "Lobotomies Proposed for Criminals" (June 22).

———. 1994. "Study: Poor, Minorities Pay More for Insurance" (December 23).

Baca Zinn, Maxine. 1983. "Familism among Chicanos: A Theoretical Review," *Humboldt Journal of Social Relations* 10 (Spring):224–238.

———. 1990. "Family, Feminism and Race in America," *Gender and Society* 14 (March): 62–86.

————, and Bonnie Thornton Dill. 1994. "Difference and Domination," in *Women of Color in U.S. Society,* Maxine Baca Zinn and Bonnie Thornton Dill (eds.). Philadelphia: Temple University Press, pp. 3–12.

————. 1996. "Theorizing Difference from Multicultural Feminism," *Feminist Studies* 22 (Summer): 1–11.

————, and D. Stanley Eitzen. 1993a. *Diversity in Families,* 3rd ed. New York: HarperCollins.

————, and D. Stanley Eitzen. 1993b. "The Demographic Transformation and the Sociological Enterprise." *The American Sociologist* 24 (Summer):5–12.

————, and D. Stanley Eitzen. 1996. *Diversity in Families,* 4th ed. New York: HarperCollins.

————, Pierrette Hondagneu-Sotelo, and Michael A. Messner. 1997. "Sex and Gender Through the Prism of Difference," in *Through the Prism of Difference: A Sex and Gender Reader,* Maxine Baca Zinn, Pierrette Hondagneu-Sotelo, and Michael A. Messner (eds.). Boston: Allyn and Bacon.

Balswick, Jack, and Charles Peck. 1971. "The Inexpressive Male: A Tragedy of American Society," *Family Coordinator* 20:363–368.

————, with James Lincoln Collier. 1976. "Why Husbands Can't Say 'I Love You,'" in *The Forty-Nine Percent Majority,* Deborah S. David and Robert Brannon (eds.). Reading, MA: Addison-Wesley.

Baltzell, E. Digby. 1958. *Philadelphia Gentlemen: The Making of a National Upper Class.* New York: Free Press.

Banfield, Edward C. 1974. *The Unheavenly City Revisited.* Boston: Little, Brown.

Barber, Benjamin R. 1992. "Jihad *vs.* McWorld," *The Atlantic Monthly* 269 (March):53–63.

Barker, Eugene C. 1965. *Mexico and Texas, 1821–1835.* New York: Russell and Russell.

Barkley, Daniel. 1995. "Immigration." *Z Magazine* 8 (January):9–10.

Barlett, Donald L., and James B. Steele. 1992. *America: What Went Wrong?* Kansas City: Andrews and McMeel.

Barnet, Richard J. 1994. "Just Undo It: Nike's Exploited Workers," *New York Times* (February 13):F11.

Barnouw, Victor. 1979. *Culture and Personality,* 3rd ed. Homewood, IL: Dorsey.

Baron, Harold M. 1975. "Racial Domination in Advanced Capitalism," in *Labor Market Segmentation,* Richard C. Edwards, et al. (eds.). Lexington, MA: D.C. Heath.

Barrera, Mario. 1979. *Race and Class in the Southwest: A Theory of Racial Inequality.* Notre Dame, IN: University of Notre Dame Press.

Barrett, Laurence I. 1993. "Fighting for God and the Right Wing," *Time* (September 13):58–60.

Barrett, Michael J. 1993. "The Newest Minority," *The Atlantic* 272 (July):22–25.

Barringer, Felicity. 1992. "As American as Apple Pie, Dim Sum or Burritos," *New York Times* (May 31):Section 4, p. 2.

Barsamian, David. 1996. "Politics of the Christian Right: An Interview with Sara Diamond," *Z Magazine* 9 (June):36–41.

Baskir, Laurence M., and William A. Strauss. 1978. *The Draft, The War, and the Vietnam Generation.* New York: Knopf.

Basow, Susan. 1996. "Gender Stereotypes and Roles," in *The Meaning of Difference,* Karen E. Rosenblum and Toni-Michelle Travis (eds.). New York: McGraw-Hill, pp. 81–96.

Baum, Martha. 1972. "Love, Marriage, and the Division of Labor," in *Family, Marriage, and the Struggle of the Sexes,* Hans Peter Dreitzel (ed.). New York: Macmillan.

Bauman, Zygmunt. 1990. *Thinking Sociologically.* Cambridge, MA: Basil Blackwell.

Baumann, Marty. 1994. "Progress Mixed for World's Women," *USA Today* (June 21):A8.

Beauvoir, Simone de. 1970. *The Second Sex.* H. M. Parshley, trans. New York: Bantam.

Beck, Joan. 1995. "Preschool Can Help Close the Poverty Gap," *Denver Post* (January 19):B7.

Becker, Howard S. 1963. *The Outsiders: Studies in the Sociology of Deviance.* New York: Free Press.

————. 1967. "Whose Side Are We On?" *Social Problems* 14 (Winter):239–247.

Beckman, L. J., and B. B. Houser. 1979. "The More You Have, The More You Do: The Relationship Between Wife's Employment, Sex-Role Attitudes and Household Behavior," *Psychology of Women Quarterly* 4 (Winter): 160–174.

Begus, Sarah. 1984. "Votes for Women," *The Women's Review of Books* 2 (October):3.

Bellah, Robert N. 1967. "Civil Religion in America," *Daedalus* 96 (Winter):1–21.

Benett, Jeanne, and Selwyn Jones. 1993. "Labor Force Occupation," *Current Population Reports,* P23–185 (May):24–25.

Bennett, James. 1995. "Soaring New Car Prices: Will They Ever Stop?" *Denver Post* (January 29):G3.

Benokraitis, Nijole, and Joe R. Feagin. 1974. "Institutional Racism: A Review and Critical Assessment of the Literature," Paper presented at the American Sociological Association, Montreal (August).

———— and Joe R. Feagin. 1995. *Modern Sexism,* 2nd ed. Englewood Cliffs, NJ: Prentice-Hall.

Berardo, Felix. 1968. "Widowhood Status in the United States," *The Family Coordinator* 17 (July):191–203.

Berenson, Alex. 1996. "Quickie Lenders Popular," *Denver Post* (July 4):C1.

Berg, Ivar (ed.). 1981. *Sociological Perspectives on Labor Markets.* New York: Academic Press.

Berger, Peter L. 1963. *Invitation to Sociology: A Humanistic Perspective.* Garden City, NY: Doubleday Anchor Books.

————. 1967a. *The Sacred Canopy.* New York: Doubleday.

————. 1967b. "Religious Institutions," in *Sociology,* Neil J. Smelser (ed.). New York: John Wiley.

————. 1975. "Religion and World Construction," in *Life as Theatre,* Dennis Brissett and Charles Edgley (eds.). Chicago: Aldine.

————, and Hansfried Kellner. 1975. "Marriage and the Construction of Reality," in *Life as Theatre,* Dennis Brissett and Charles Edgley (eds.). Chicago: Aldine.

————, and Thomas Luckman. 1967. *The Social Construction of Reality.* Garden City, NY: Doubleday.

Bernard, Jessie. 1972. *The Future of Marriage.* New York: Bantam.

Bernay, Elayn, 1978. "Affirmative Inaction and Other Facts, Trends, Tactics for Academic Life," *Ms.* (November).

Bernstein, Aaron. 1996. "Is America Becoming More of a Class Society?" *Business Week* (February 26):86–91.

Berry, Mary Frances. 1994. *Black Resistance; White Law,* rev. ed. New York: Penguin Books.

Bianchi, Suzanne M. 1995. "Changing Economic Roles of Women and Men," in *State of the Union: America in the 1990s,* Vol. 1, Reynolds Farley (ed.). New York: Russell Sage, pp. 107–154.

Biema, David. 1993. "When White Makes Right," *Time* (August 9):40–42.

————. 1995. "Bury My Heart in Committee," *Time* (September 18):48–51.

Bierstedt, Robert. 1974. *The Social Order,* 4th ed. New York: McGraw-Hill.

Bird, Chloe, and Allen Fremont. 1989. "Gender, Social Roles, and Health," Paper presented at the American Sociological Association, San Francisco (August).

Birdwhistell, Ray L. 1980. "The Idealized Model of the American Family," in *Marriage and the Family in a Changing Society,* James M. Henslin (ed.). New York: Free Press.

Birnbaum, Norman. 1992. "One Cheer for Clinton," *The Nation* (September 28):318–320.

Blau, Francine D. 1979. "Women in the Labor Force: An Overview," in *Woman: A Feminist Perspective,* 2nd ed., Jo Freeman (ed.). Palo Alto, CA: Mayfield.

————, and Carol L. Jusenius. 1976. "Economists' Approaches to Sex Segregation in the Labor Market," in *Women and the Workplace,* Martha Blaxall and Barbara Regan (eds.). Chicago: University of Chicago Press.

Blau, Peter M., and Otis Dudley Duncan. 1967. *The American Occupational Structure.* New York: John Wiley.

————, and Marshall W. Meyer. 1971. *Bureaucracy in Modern Society,* 2nd ed. New York: Random House.

————, and W. Richard Scott. 1962. *Formal Organizations: A Comparative Approach.* San Francisco: Chandler.

Blauner, Robert. 1964. *Alienation and Freedom.* Chicago: University of Chicago Press.

————. 1972. *Racial Oppression in America.* New York: Harper & Row.

————. 1992. "Talking Past Each Other: Black and White Languages of Race," *American Prospect* (Summer):55–64.

Bleifuss, Joel. 1995a. "Cancer Politics," *In These Times* (May 1):12–13.

————. 1995b. "House of Cards," *In These Times* (December 25):12–14.

Blood, Robert O., and Donald Wolfe. 1960. *Husbands and Wives.* New York: Free Press.

Blumberg, Paul M., and P. W. Paul. 1975. "Continuities and Discontinuities in Upper-Class Marriage," *Journal of Marriage and Family* 37 (February).

Blumer, Herbert, 1951. "Collective Behavior," in *New Outline of the Principles of Sociology,* Alfred McClung Lee (ed). New York: Barnes and Noble, pp. 167–222.

Blumstein, Philip, and Pepper Schwartz. 1983. *American Couples: Money, Work, Sex.* New York: William Morrow.

Bonacich, Edna. 1976. "Advanced Capitalism and Black/White Relations in the United States: A Split Labor Market Interpretation," *American Sociological Review* 41:34–51.

————. 1992a. "Class and Race," *Encyclopedia of Sociology,* Vol. 1. New York: Macmillan, pp. 204–208.

————. 1992b. "Inequality in America: The Failure of the American System for People of Color," in *Race, Class, and Gender,* Margaret L. Andersen, and Patricia Hill Collins (eds.). Belmont, CA: Wadsworth, pp. 96–109.

Boocock, Sarane S. 1975. "Is U.S. Becoming Less Child Oriented?" *National Observer* (February 22):12.

Borkin, Joseph. 1978. *The Crime and Punishment of I. G. Farben.* New York: Free Press.

Boss, Pauline, and Barrie Thorne. 1989. "Family Sociology and Family Therapy: A Feminist Linkage," in *Women in Families,* Monica McGadrick, Carol M. Anderson, and Froma Walsh (eds.). New York: W. W. Norton, pp. 78–89.

Bourke, Jaron. 1989. "Mergermania," *The Nation* (October 30):495.

Bowles, Samuel. 1977. "Unequal Education and the Reproduction of the Social Division of Labor," in *Power and Ideology in Education,* Jerome Karabel and A. H. Halsey (eds.). New York: Oxford University Press, pp. 137–153.

———, and Herbert Gintis. 1973. "I.Q. and the U.S. Class Structure," *Social Policy* 3 (January/February):65–96.

———, and Herbert Gintis. 1976. *Schooling in Capitalist America.* New York: Basic Books.

Brackman, Harold, and Steven P. Erie. 1986. "The Future of the Gender Gap," *Social Policy* 16 (Winter):5–11.

Branigin, William. 1997. "U.S. Border Tactic Failing," *Denver Post* (February 8):1A, 15A.

Branscombe, Art. 1982. "Court Upholds School Finance Law," *The Denver Post* (May 25):A1–8.

Bradsher, Keith. 1995. "Widest Gap in Income? Research Points to the U.S.," *New York Times* (October 27):D2.

Breines, Wini, and Linda Gordon. 1983. "The New Scholarship on Family Violence," *Signs* 8 (Spring):490–531.

Briggs, David. 1995. "Women's Gains Fall Short in Pulpit," *Denver Post* (May 5):A2.

Brogan, Pamela. 1994. "Gender Pay Gap Runs Deep in Congress, Study Finds," *Denver Post* (February 26):A17.

Bronfenbrenner, Urie, Peter McClelland, Elaine Wethington, Phyllis Moen, and Stephen J. Ceci. 1996. *The State of Americans.* New York: The Free Press.

Bronowski, J. 1978. *The Common Sense of Science.* Cambridge, MA: Harvard University Press.

Brooks, James. 1993. "Slavery on Rise in Brazil, as Debt Chains Workers," *New York Times* (May 23):3.

Brouillette, John R., and Ronny E. Turner. 1992. "Creating the Sociological Imagination on the First Day of Class: The Social Construction of Deviance," *Teaching Sociology* 20 (October):276–279.

Brown, Dee. 1971. *Bury My Heart at Wounded Knee.* New York: Holt, Rinehart and Winston.

Buchanan, Patrick. 1994. "Is U.S. Culturally Superior?" *Denver Post* (May 19):B7.

Budiansky, Stephen. 1996. "The Spirit of Capitalism," *U.S. News & World Report* (March 18):12–13.

Bukovinsky, Janet. 1982. "A Wife Is Abused Every 18 Seconds, FBI Says," *Rocky Mountain News* (March 9):38, 42.

Bull, Chris, and John Gallagher. 1996. *Perfect Enemies: The Religious Right, the Gay Movement, and the Politics of the 1990s.* New York: Crown.

Bumpass, Larry L. 1990. "What's Happening to the Family? Interactions between Demographic and Institutional Change," *Demography* 27 (November):483–498.

———, and Ronald R. Rindfuss. 1979. "Children's Experience of Marital Disruption," *American Journal of Sociology* 85 (July):49–65.

———. James A. Sweet, and Teresa Castro Martin. 1990. "Changing Patterns of Remarriage," *Journal of Marriage and the Family* 52 (August):747–756.

Burd, Stephen, Patrick Healy, Kit Lively, and Christopher Shea. 1996. "The Widening Gap in Higher Education," *The Chronicle of Higher Education* (June 14):A10-A12.

Burke, Meredith. 1995. "Mexican Immigrants Shape California's Fertility, Future," *Population Today* 23 (September):4–5.

Burnham, Linda. 1986. "Has Poverty Been Feminized in Black America?" in *For Crying Out Loud: Women and Poverty in the U.S.,* Rochelle Lefkowitz and Ann Withorn (eds.). New York: Pilgrim, pp. 69–83.

Business Week. 1989. "Hispanics, a Nation within a Nation" (September 25):144–145.

CNBC. 1996. "Business News" (April 8).

Cabib, Amalia. 1981. "Indians of the Americas: Refugees in Their Own Land," *Intercom* 9 (June):3.

Campbell, Frances A., and Craig T. Ramey. 1994. "Effects of Early Intervention on Intellectual and Academic Achievement: A Follow-Up Study of Children from Low-Income Families," *Child Development* 65 (April):684–698.

Cannon, Lynne Weber, and Stella Warren. 1983. "Feminization of Poverty," *Newsletter.* Memphis: Center for Research on Women (April):2–3.

Caplan, Nathan, and Stephen D. Nelson. 1973. "On Being Useful: The Nature and Consequences of Psychological Research on Social Problems," *American Psychologist* 28 (March):199–211.

Carmichael, Stokely, and Charles V. Hamilton. 1967. *Black Power: The Politics of Liberation in America.* New York: Random House.

Carnegie Foundation Report. 1981. Cited in "Hispanics Make Their Move," *U.S. News & World Report* (August 24):64.

Carnoy, Martin (ed.). 1975. *Schooling in a Corporate Society: The Political Economy of Education in America,* 2nd ed. New York: David McKay.

Carroll, John B. (ed.). 1956. *Language, Thought, and Reality: Selected Writings of Benjamin Lee Whorf.* Cambridge, MA: MIT Press.

Carter, Michael J., and Susan Boslego Carter. 1981. "Women Get a Ticket to Ride after the Gravy Train Has Left the Station," *Feminist Studies* 7:477–504.

Carville, James. 1996. *We're Right, They're Wrong: A Handbook for Spirited Progressives.* New York: Random House.

Cassidy, John. 1995. "Who Killed the Middle Class?" *The New Yorker* (October 16):113–123.

Castro, Janice. 1993. "The Disposable Workers," *Time* (March 29):43–47.

Cauchon, Dennis. 1993. "Balanced Justice? Sentences for Crack Called Racist," *USA Today* (May 26):A1–2.

Celis, William. 1993. "Colleges Battle Culture and Poverty to Swell Hispanic Enrollments," *New York Times* (February 23):B6.

The Center on Social Welfare and Law. 1996. "Welfare Myths: Fact or Fiction?" Washington, DC: The Center on Social Welfare and Law.

Chafetz, Janet Saltzman. 1974. *Masculine/Feminine or Human?* Itasca, IL: F. E. Peacock.

Chambliss, William J. 1969. *Crime and the Legal Process.* New York: McGraw-Hill.

———. 1973. "The Saints and the Roughnecks," *Society* 11 (November-December):24–31.

———. 1974. *Functional and Conflict Theories of Crime.* Module 17. New York: MSS Modular Publications.

———. 1976. "Functional and Conflict Theories of Crime: The Heritage of Emile Durkheim and Karl Marx," in *Whose Law, What Order? A Conflict Approach to Criminology,* William J. Chambliss and Milton Mankoff (eds.). New York: John Wiley.

Chavira, Ricardo. 1991. "Browns vs. Blacks," *Time* (July 29):14–16.

Cherlin, Andrew, and Frank F. Furstenburg, Jr. 1983. "The American Family in the Year 2000," *The Futurist* 17 (June).

——— and Frank F. Furstenberg, Jr. 1994. "The Modernization of Grandparenthood," in *Family in Transition,* Arlene S. Skolnick and Jerome H. Skolnick (eds.). New York: HarperCollins, pp. 104–111.

Children's Defense Fund. 1990. *The Adolescent and Young Adult Fact Book.* Washington, DC: Children's Defense Fund.

———. 1996. *The State of America's Children Yearbook 1996.* Washington, DC: Children's Defense Fund.

Christensen, Kathleen. 1988. *Women and Home-Based Work.* New York: Henry Holt.

Christian Science Monitor. 1994. "Will Computers in Schools Make the Poor Poorer?" (February 25):1.

Cleveland, Harlan. 1992. "The Age of People Power," *The Futurist* 26 (January/February):14–18.

Clymer, Adam. 1992. "Spending in Congressional Races Is Up in a Topsy-Turvy Year," *New York Times* (August 9):16.

Coakley, Jay J. 1994. *Sport in Society: Issues and Controversies,* 5th ed. St. Louis: Times Mirror/Mosby.

Cohen, Albert K. 1955. *Delinquent Boys: The Culture of the Gang.* Glencoe, IL: Free Press.

———. 1966. *Deviance and Control.* Englewood Cliffs, NJ: Prentice-Hall.

Cole, David. 1994. "Five Myths About Immigration," *The Nation* (October 17):410–412.

Cohen, Gary. 1995. "On God's Green Earth," *U.S. News & World Report* (April 24):31–32.

Cole, Stephen. 1975. *The Sociological Orientation: An Introduction to Sociology.* Chicago: Rand McNally.

Coleman, James S. et al. 1966. *Equality of Educational Opportunity.* Washington, DC: Government Printing Office.

Coleman, James William, and Donald R. Cressey. 1990. *Social Problems,* 4th ed. New York: Harper and Row.

Coleman, Marilyn, and Lawrence H. Ganong. 1991. "Remarriage and Stepfamily Research in the 1980s: Increased Interest in an Old Family Form," in *Contemporary Families: Looking Forward, Looking Back,* Alan Booth (ed.). Minneapolis: National Council on Family Relations, pp. 192–207.

Collins, Patricia Hill. 1990. *Black Feminist Thought.* Cambridge, MA: Unwin Hyman.

Collins, Randall. 1972. "A Conflict Theory of Sexual Stratification," in *Family, Marriage and the Struggle of the Sexes,* Hans Peter Dreitzel (ed.). New York: Macmillan.

———. 1975. *Conflict Sociology.* New York: Academic Press.

———. 1988. "Women and Men in the Class Structure," *Journal of Family Issues* 9 (March):27–50.

————. 1992. *Sociological Insight: An Introduction to Non-Obvious Sociology,* 2nd ed. New York: Oxford University Press.

Comer, Lee. 1978. "Women and Class, the Question of Women and Class," *Women's Studies International Quarterly* 1:165–173.

Conant, Jennet. 1986. "The New Pocketbook Issue," *Newsweek* (December 1):72.

Connell, Robert W. 1992. "A Very Straight Gay: Masculinity, Homosexual Experience, and the Dynamics of Gender," *American Sociological Review* 57:735–751.

Contemporary Sociology. 1995. "Symposium: The Bell Curve." Vol. 24 (March):149–161.

Cook, James. 1981. "The American Indian through Five Centuries," *Forbes* (November 9).

Cooley, Charles Horton. 1964. *Human Nature and the Social Order.* New York: Schocken.

Coontz, Stephanie. 1992. *The Way We Never Were.* New York: Basic Books.

Coser, Lewis. 1966. *The Functions of Social Conflict.* New York: Free Press.

Crispell, Diane. 1992. "The Brave New World of Men," *American Demographics* 14 (January):38–43.

Crooks, Robert, and Kakrla Baur. 1987. *Our Sexuality,* 3rd ed. Menlo Park, CA: Benjamin Cummings.

Cunningham, Shea. 1994. "Farm Workers in the '90s," *Food First Action Alert* 16 (Fall):1–4.

Currie, Elliott, and Jerome H. Skolnick. 1988. *America's Problems: Social Issues and Public Policy,* 2nd ed. Boston: Little, Brown.

Curtis, Richard. 1986. "Household and Family in Theory and Inequality," *American Sociological Review* 51 (April):168–183.

Cutler, James E. 1905. *Lynch-Law: An Investigation into the History of Lynching in the United States.* New York: Longmans, Green.

Cuzzort, R. P. 1969. *Humanity and Modern Sociological Thought.* New York: Holt, Rinehart and Winston.

————. 1989. *Using Social Thought: The Nuclear Issue and Other Concerns.* Mountain View, CA: Mayfield.

Dahl, Robert. 1961. *Who Governs?* New Haven, CT: Yale University Press.

Dahrendorf, Ralf. 1959. *Class and Class Conflict in Industrial Society.* Stanford, CA: Stanford University Press.

————. 1968. "Out of Utopia: Toward a Reorientation of Sociological Analysis," *American Journal of Sociology* 64 (September).

David, Deborah S., and Robert Brannon. 1980. "The Male Sex Role," in *Family in Transition,* 3rd ed., Arlene S. Skolnick and Jerome H. Skolnick (eds.). Boston: Little, Brown.

Davidson, Nicholas. 1990. "Life without Father: America's Greatest Social Catastrophe," *Policy Review,* No. 51 (Winter):40–44.

Davies, James A. 1966. "Structural Balance, Mechanical Solidarity, and Interpersonal Relations," in *Sociological Theories in Progress I,* Joseph Berger, Morris Zelditch, Jr., and Bo Anderson (eds.). Boston: Houghton Mifflin.

Davis, Kingsley. 1940. "Extreme Social Isolation of a Child," *American Journal of Sociology* 45 (January): 554–564.

————. 1948. *Human Society.* New York: Macmillan.

————, and Wilbert E. Moore. 1945. "Some Principles of Stratification," *American Sociological Review* 10 (April):242–249.

Davis, Nanette J. 1975. *Sociological Constructions of Deviance Perspectives and Issues in the Field.* Dubuque, IA: Wm. C. Brown.

Deckard, Barbara Sinclair. 1983. *The Women's Movement,* 3rd ed. New York: Harper and Row.

Defreitas, Gregory. 1994. "Fear of Foreigners: Immigrants as Scapegoats for Domestic Woes," *Dollars & Sense* 191 (January/February):8–9,33.

Degler, Carl. 1980. *At Odds: Women and the Family in America from the Revolution to the Present.* New York: Oxford University Press.

De Lone, Richard H. 1979. *Small Futures: Children, Inequality, and the Limits of Liberal Reform.* New York: Carnegie Council on Children. Cited in Patricia McCormack, "Economic Gap between Classes," *Rocky Mountain News* (August 22):66.

Demos, John. 1977. "The American Family of Past Time," in *Family in Transition,* 2nd ed., Arlene S. Skolnick and Jerome H. Skolnick (eds.). Boston: Little, Brown.

Dentler, Robert A., and Kai T. Erickson. 1959. "The Functions of Deviance in Groups," *Social Problems* 7 (Fall):98–107.

De Vita, Carol J. 1996. "The United States at Mid-Decade," *Population Bulletin* 50 (March):entire issue.

Di Baggio, Thomas. 1976. "The Unholy Alliance," *Penthouse* (May):74–91.

Dibble, Ursula, and Murray S. Straus. 1980. "Some Social Structure Determinants of Inconsistency between Attitudes and Behavior: The Case of Family Violence," *Journal of Marriage and Family* 42 (February).

di Leonardo, Micaela. 1992. "Boyz on the Hood," *The Nation* (August 17–24):178–186.

Dill, Bonnie Thornton, Maxine Baca Zinn, and Sandra Patton. 1993. "Feminism, Race, and the Politics of Family Values," *Report from the Institute for Philosophy and Public Policy,* University of Maryland, Vol. 13 (Fall).

————, Lynn Weber Cannon, and Reeve Vanneman. 1987. "Race, Gender, and Occupational Segregation," in *Pay Equity: An Issue of Race, Ethnicity, and Sex.* Washington, DC: National Committee on Pay Equity.

Domhoff, G. William. 1970. *The Higher Circles: The Governing Class in America.* New York: Random House.

————. 1979. *The Powers That Be: Processes of Ruling Class Domination in America.* New York: Random House.

————. 1983. *Who Rules America Now?* Englewood Cliffs, NJ: Prentice-Hall.

Donner, Frank. 1971. "The Theory and Practice of American Political Intelligence," *New York Review of Books* 16 (April 22):27–39.

Doyle, Jack, and Paul T. Schindler. 1974. "The Incoherent Society," Paper presented at the American Sociological Association, Montreal (August 25–29).

Dreier, Peter, and John Atlas. 1992. "The Scandal of Mansion Subsidies," *Dissent* 39 (Winter):93–94.

————, and John Atlas. 1994. "Reforming the Mansion Subsidy." *The Nation* (May 2):592–595.

Drucker, Peter F. 1993. *The Post-Capitalist Society.* New York: HarperCollins.

————. 1994. "The Age of Social Transformation," *Atlantic Monthly* 274 (November):53–80.

Duncan, Greg J. 1984. *Years of Poverty, Years of Plenty: The Changing Economic Fortunes of American Workers and Families.* Ann Arbor: Institute of Social Research.

Dunn, Dana. 1996. "Gender and Earnings," in *Women and Work: A Handbook,* Paula J. Dubeck and Kathryn Borman (eds.). New York: Garland Publishing, pp. 61–63.

Dunn, William. 1991. " 'I Do' Is Repeat Refrain for Half of Newlyweds," *USA Today* (February 15):1A.

Durkheim, Emile. 1951. *Suicide,* reprinted ed. Glencoe, IL: Free Press.

————. 1958. *The Rules of Sociological Method,* 8th ed., Sarah A. Solovay and John H. Mueller, trans. Glencoe, IL: Free Press.

————. 1960. *The Division of Labor in Society,* George Simpson, trans. New York: Free Press.

————. 1965. *The Elementary Forms of Religious Life,* Joseph Ward Swain, trans. New York: Macmillan.

Dyer, Everett D. 1979. *The American Family: Variety and Change.* New York: McGraw-Hill.

Early, Frances H. 1983. "The French-Canadian Family Economy and Standard of Living in Lowell, Massachusetts, 1870," in *The American Family in Social Historical Perspective,* 3rd ed., Michael Gordon (ed.). New York: St. Martin's, pp. 482–503.

Ebony. 1995. "Amazing Grace: 50 Years of the Black Church," Vol. 50 (April):87–96.

Echaveste, Maria, and Karen Nussbaum. 1994. "96 Cents an Hour: The Sweatshop is Reborn," *New York Times* (March 6):F13.

The Economist. 1993. "The Other America" (July 10): 17–18.

Edgley, Charles, and Ronny E. Turner. 1975. "Masks and Social Relations," *Humboldt Journal of Social Relations* 3 (Fall-Winter).

————. 1991. "The Boomlet's Still Booming," *American Demographics* 13 (June):8–10.

Edin, Kathryn J. 1995. "The Myths of Dependence and Self-Sufficiency: Women, Welfare, and Low-Wage Work," *Focus* 17 (Fall-Winter):1–9.

Edmondson, Brad. 1996. "Work Slowdown," *American Demographics* 18 (March):4–7.

Edwards, Richard C., Michael Reich, and Thomas E. Weisskopf. 1978. "Sexism," in *The Capitalist System,* 2nd ed. Englewood Cliffs, NJ: Prentice-Hall.

Ehrenreich, Barbara. 1986. "Two, Three, Many Husbands," *Mother Jones* (July-August):8.

————. 1989. *Fear of Falling: The Inner Life of the Middle Class.* New York: Pantheon.

————. 1991. "Welfare: A White Secret," *Time* (December 16):84.

————, and Karin Stallard. 1982. "The Nouveau Poor," *Ms.* (August).

Eisenstein, Zillah. 1979. "Developing a Theory of Capitalist Patriarchy and Socialist Feminism," in *Capitalist Patriarchy and the Case for Socialist Feminism,* Zillah R. Eisenstein (ed.). New York: Monthly Review Press, pp. 5–40.

————. 1982. "The Sexual Politics of the New Right: Understanding the 'Crisis of Liberalism' for the 1980's," *Signs* 7 (Spring):567–588.

Eisner, Alan. 1997. "Republicans Won '96 Race for Funds by $217 Million," *Rocky Mountain News* (January 11):34A.

Eitzen, D. Stanley. 1996. "Is Dismantling the Welfare State the Solution to America's Social Problems?" *Vital Speeches of the Day* (June 15):532–536.

————. Forthcoming. "Social Control and Sport," in *Handbook of Sport and Society,* Eric Dunning and Jay J. Coakley (eds.). London: Sage, Ltd.

————, and Maxine Baca Zinn. 1989. "The Forces Reshaping America," in *The Reshaping of America,* D. Stanley Eitzen and Maxine Baca Zinn (eds.). Englewood Cliffs, NJ: Prentice-Hall, pp. 1–13.

————, and Maxine Baca Zinn. 1989. "The De-Athleticization of Women: The Naming and Gender Marking of Collegiate Sport Teams," *Sociology of Sport Journal* 6 (December):362–370.

————, and Maxine Baca Zinn. 1997. *Social Problems,* 7th ed. Boston: Allyn and Bacon.

————, and George H. Sage. 1997. *The Sociology of North American Sport,* 6th ed. Madison, WI: Brown & Benchmark.

Ekman, Paul, Wallace V. Friesen, and John Bear. 1984. "The International Language of Gestures," *Psychology Today* 18 (May):64–69.

El-Badry, Samia. 1994. "Understanding Islam in America," *American Demographics* 16 (January):10–11.

Elliott, Michael. 1994/1995. "Forward to the Past," *Newsweek* (December 26/January 2):130–133.

Enchautegui, Maria E. 1995. *Policy Implications of Latino Poverty.* Washington, DC: The Urban Institute.

English, Carry W. 1984. "From High Unemployment to a Labor Shortage," *U.S. News & World Report* (September 17):56.

Epstein, Cynthia Fuchs. 1970. *Woman's Place.* Berkeley: University of California Press.

Erickson, Kai T. 1966. *Wayward Puritans: A Study in the Sociology of Deviance.* New York: John Wiley.

Eshleman, J. Ross. 1988. *The Family,* 5th ed. Boston: Allyn and Bacon.

Espiritu, Yen Le. 1996. "Asian American Panethnicity," in *The Meaning of Difference,* Karen E. Rosenblum and Toni-Michelle Travis (eds.). New York: McGraw-Hill, pp. 51–61.

Evinger, Suzanne. 1996. "How to Record Race," *American Demographics* 18 (May):36–41.

Faludi, Susan. 1991. *Backlash: The Undeclared War Against Women.* New York: Crown.

Farber, Jerry. 1970. *The Student as Nigger.* New York: Pocket Books.

Farberman, Harvey, and Erich Goode. 1973. *Social Reality.* Englewood Cliffs, NJ: Prentice-Hall.

Farrell, Christopher. 1996. "The New Math of Higher Education," *Business Week* (March 18):39.

Feagin, Joe R. 1986. *Social Problems,* 2nd ed. Englewood Cliffs, NJ: Prentice-Hall.

————. 1991. "The Continuing Significance of Race: Antiblack Discrimination in Public Places," *American Sociological Review* 56.

————, and Clairece Booher Feagin. 1993. *Racial and Ethnic Relations.* Englewood Cliffs, NJ: Prentice-Hall.

————, and Clairece Booher Feagin. 1994. *Social Problems: A Critical Power-Conflict Perspective,* 4th ed. Englewood Cliffs, NJ: Prentice-Hall.

————, and Melvin P. Sikes. 1994. *Living with Racism: The Black Middle-Class Experience.* Boston: Beacon Press.

Feigelson, Jeremy. 1982. "Our Next War: Who Will Fight It?" *Civil Rights Quarterly* 14 (Spring):16–21.

Feinsilber, Mike. 1996. "Christian Coalition Mobilizes," *Denver Post* (October 23):21A.

Fernandez-Kelly, Maria Patricia, and Anna M. Garcia. 1990. "Power Surrendered, Power Restored: The Politics of Work and Family among Hispanic Garment Workers in California and Florida," in *Women, Politics, and Change,* Louise A. Tilly and Patricia M. Gurin (eds.). New York: Russell Sage, pp. 130–149.

Ferree, Myra Marx. 1991. "Feminism and Family Research," in *Contemporary Families: Looking Forward, Looking Back,* Alan Booth (ed.). Minneapolis: National Council on Family Relations, pp. 103–121.

Festinger, Leon, Henry W. Riecken, Jr., and Stanley Schachter. 1956. *When Prophecy Fails.* Minneapolis: University of Minnesota Press.

Fischer, Claude S., Michael Hout, Martin Sanchez Jankowski, Samuel R. Lucas, Ann Swidler, and Kim Voss. 1996. *Inequality by Design: Cracking the Bell Curve Myth.* Princeton, NJ: Princeton University Press.

Fishman, Pamela M. 1978. "Interaction: The Work Women Do," *Social Problems* 25 (April):397–406.

FitzGerald, Francis. 1979. *America Revised: History Schoolbooks in the Twentieth Century.* Boston: Atlantic/Little, Brown.

Flora, Cornelia Butler. 1979. "Changes in Women's Status in Women's Magazine Fiction," *Social Problems* 26 (June):558–569.

Folbre, Nancy. 1995. *The New Field Guide to the U.S. Economy.* New York: The New Press.

Foner, Eric. 1996. "Plessy Is Not Passe," *The Nation* (June 3):6.

Forbes. 1992. "Made in America" (July 20):161.

————. 1994. "Made in America" (July 18):154–155.

————. 1995. "The Richest 400 People in America" (October 16).

————. 1996. "The 400 Wealthiest Americans" (October 14).

Fost, Dan. 1991. "American Indians in the Nineties," *American Demographics* 13 (December):26–34.

Frankenberg, Ruth. 1993. *The Social Construction of Whiteness: White Women, Race Matters.* Minneapolis: University of Minnesota Press.

Franklin, Deborah. 1989. "What a Child Is Given," *New York Times Magazine* (September 3):36–41, 49.

Freedman, Alelx M. 1993. "Peddling Dreams: A Marketing Giant Uses Its Sales Prowess to Profit from Poverty," *Wall Street Journal* (September 22):A1-A12.

Freeman, Jo. 1979. "The Women's Liberation Movement: Its Origins, Organizations, Activities, and Ideas," in *Women: A Feminist Perspective,* 2nd ed., Jo Freeman (ed.). Palo Alto, CA: Mayfield, pp. 557–574.

Freud, Sigmund. 1946. *Civilization and Its Discontents.* Joan Riviére, trans. London: Hogarth Press.

Frey, William H. 1991. "Are Two Americas Emerging?" *Population Today* 19 (October):6–8.

Friedan, Betty. 1963. *The Feminine Mystique.* New York: W. W. Norton.

Fulwood, Sam III. 1993. "Out-of-Wedlock Births Soar in U.S., Study Says," *Denver Post* (July 14):20A.

Fussell, Paul. 1983. *Class.* New York: Ballantine.

Gable, Donna. 1993. "Series Shortchange Working-Class and Minority Americans," *USA Today* (August 30):3D.

Gallinsky, Ellen, and James T. Bond. 1996. "Work and Family: The Experiences of Mothers and Fathers in the U.S. Workforce," in *The American Woman, 1996–97,* Cynthia Costello and Barbara Kivimae Krimgold (eds.). New York: W. W. Norton, pp. 79–103.

The Gallup Poll Monthly. 1995. "Belief in Heaven, Hell, The Devil," 352 (January):15–16.

Gallup Report. 1989. "Poverty" (August):4.

Galst, Liz. 1994. "The Right Fight," *Mother Jones* 19 (March/April):58–59.

Gans, Herbert J. 1962. *The Urban Villagers.* New York: Free Press.

————. 1971. "The Uses of Power: The Poor Pay All," *Social Policy* 2 (July-August): 20–24.

————. 1979. *Deciding What's News.* New York: Pantheon.

Gardner, Robert W., Bryant Robey, and Peter C. Smith. 1985. "Asian Americans: Growth, Change, and Diversity," *Population Bulletin* 40 (October):entire issue.

Garfinkel, Harold. 1967. *Studies in Ethnomethodology.* Englewood Cliffs, NJ: Prentice-Hall.

Gartner, Michael. 1995. "Unions Can Still Speak for the Little Guy," *USA Today* (June 20):A11.

————. 1996. "Poverty Rate Nothing to Crow About," *USA Today* (October 1):A13.

Gelles, Richard J. 1977. "No Place to Go: The Social Dynamics of Marital Violence," in *Battered Women,* Marina Roy (ed.). New York: Van Nostrand.

————. 1979. "The Myth of Battered Husbands," *Ms.* 8 (October):65–66a, 71–74.

Gentry, Curt. 1991. *J. Edgar Hoover: The Man and His Secrets.* New York: W. W. Norton.

Gerrard, Nathan L. 1968. "The Serpent Handling Religions of West Virginia," *Trans-action* 5 (May).

Gerth, Hans, and C. Wright Mills, 1953. *Character and Social Structure: The Psychology of Social Institutions.* New York: Harcourt, Brace, and World.

Gibbs, Jack P. 1966. "Conceptions of Deviant Behavior: The Old and the New," *Pacific Sociological Review* 9 (Spring):9–14.

Giddens, Anthony. 1991. *Introduction to Sociology.* New York: W. W. Norton.

Giele, Janet Z. 1988. "Gender and the Sex Rolls," in *Handbook of Sociology,* Neil J. Smelser (ed.). Newbury Park, CA: Sage, pp. 291–323.

Gilbert, Bil, and Nancy Williamson. 1973. "Sport Is Unfair to Women," *Sports Illustrated* (May 28).

Gillespie, Dair. 1972. "Who Has the Power? The Marital Struggle," in *Family, Marriage, and the Struggle of the Sexes,* Hans Peter Dreitzel (ed.). New York: Macmillan, pp. 105–157.

Gillmor, Dan, and Steven K. Doig. 1992. "Segregation Forever?" *American Demographics* 14 (January):48–51.

Gilman, Richard. 1971. "Where Did It All Go Wrong?" *Life* (August 13).

Glazer, Nona. 1977. "Introduction, Part Two," in *Woman in a Man-Made World,* 2nd ed., Nona Glazer and Helen Youngelson Waehrer (eds.). Chicago: Rand McNally.

Glenn, Evelyn Nakano, and Roslyn L. Feldberg. 1979. "Clerical Work: The Female Occupation," in *Women: A Feminist Perspective,* 2nd ed., Jo Freeman (ed.). Palo Alto, CA: Mayfield.

Goffman, Erving. 1959. *The Presentation of Self in Everyday Life*. Garden City, NY: Doubleday.

———. 1979. *Gender Advertisements*. New York: Harper/Colophon. Gold, Allan R. 1989. "The Struggle to Make Do without Health Insurance," *New York Times* (July 30):1, 11.

Gold, David A., Clarence Y. H. Lo, and Erik Olin Wright. 1975. "Recent Developments in Marxist Theories of the Capitalist State," *Monthly Review* 27 (October):29–45.

Goldman, Ari L. 1991. "Portrait of Religion in U.S. Holds Dozens of Surprises," *New York Times* (April 10):E3.

Goldsen, Rose K. 1977. *The Show and Tell Machine: How Television Works and Works You Over.* New York: Delta.

Goode, Erich. 1966. "Social Class and Church Participation," *American Journal of Sociology* 72 (July).

Goode, William J. 1963. *World Revolution and Family Patterns.* New York: Free Press.

———. 1976. "Family Disorganization," in *Contemporary Social Problems*, 4th ed., Robert K. Merton and Robert Nisbet (eds.). New York: Harcourt, Brace Jovanovich.

———. 1984. "Idealization of the Recent Past: The United States," in *Family in Transition,* 4th ed., Arlene S. Skolnick and Jerome H. Skolnick (eds). Boston: Little, Brown, pp. 43–53.

Goodgame, Dan. 1993. "Welfare for the Well-Off," *Time* (February 22):36–38.

Gould, Stephen Jay. 1994. "Curveball," *The New Yorker* (November 28):139–149.

Gouldner, Alvin W. 1962. "Anti-Minotaur: The Myth of Value-Free Sociology," *Social Problems* 9 (Winter).

Gove, Walter R. 1984. "Gender Differences in Mental and Physical Health: The Effects of Fixed Roles and Nurturant Roles," *Social Science and Medicine* 19: 77–84.

———, Carolyn Briggs Style, and Michael Hughes. 1990. "The Effect of Marriage on the Well-Being of Adults," *Journal of Family Issues* 11 (March):4–35.

Graff, E. J. 1996. "Retying the Knot," *The Nation* (June 24):12.

Graham, Hugh Davis, and Ted Robert Gurr. 1969. *The History of Violence in America.* New York: Bantam Books.

Greenfeld, Lawrence A. 1991. "Capital Punishment 1990," *Bureau of Justice Statistics Bulletin* (September). Washington, DC: U.S. Department of Justice.

Greenwald, John. 1996. "Deadbeat and Upbeat," *Time* (July 8):42.

Greider, William. 1992. *Who Will Tell the People: The Betrayal of American Democracy.* New York: Simon & Schuster.

Grochot, J. C., Sr. 1992. "Wealth-Fare Cheaters," *In These Times* (January 15–21):24.

Gutman, Herbert G. 1976. *The Black Family in Slavery and Freedom, 1750–1925.* New York: Pantheon.

Gwynne, S. C. 1988. "Are You Better Off?" *Time* (October 10):28–32.

Hacker, Andrew. 1970. *The End of the American Era.* New York: Atheneum.

———. 1986. "Women at Work," *New York Review of Books* 33 (August 14):26–32.

———. 1995. "Who They Are," *New York Times Magazine* (November 19):70–71.

Hadden, Jeffrey K., and Anson Shupe. 1988. *Televangelism: Power and Politics on God's Frontier.* New York: Henry Holt.

Hall, M. Ann. 1985. "Knowledge and Gender: Epistemological Questions in the Social Analysis of Sport," *Sociology of Sport Journal* 2:25–42.

Hamburg, David A. 1993. "The American Family Transformed," *Society* 31 (January/February):60–69.

Harding, Vincent. 1981. *There Is a River: The Black Struggle for Freedom in America.* New York: Harcourt, Brace Jovanovich.

Hareven, Tamara K. 1976. "Modernization and Family History," *Signs* 2:190–206.

———. 1976. "Women and Men: Changing Roles," in *Women and Men: Changing Roles, Relationships and Perceptions,* Libby A. Carter, Anne Firor Scott, and Wendy Martyna (eds.). Aspen, CO: Aspen Institute for Humanistic Studies.

Harper's Magazine. 1992. "Harper's Index" (April):13.

———. 1993. "Harper's Index" (June):11.

Harrington, Michael. 1963. *The Other America: Poverty in the United States.* Baltimore: Penguin.

———. 1979. "Social Retreat and Economic Stagnation," *Dissent* 26 (Spring):131–134.

———. 1984. *The New American Poverty.* New York: Holt, Rinehart, and Winston.

———. 1985. *Taking Sides: The Education of a Militant Mind.* New York: Holt, Rinehart and Winston.

———. 1986. *The Next Left.* New York: Henry Holt.

Harris, Irving B. 1996. *Children in Jeopardy: Can We Break the Cycle of Poverty?* New Haven, CT: Yale University Press.

Harris, Marvin. 1975. *Cows, Pigs, Wars, and Witches: The Riddles of Culture.* New York: Random House.

————. 1978. "India's Sacred Cows," *Human Nature* 1 (February).

Harrison, Bennett. 1990. "The Wrong Signals," *Technology Review* (January):65.

Harris, Roderick J., and Claudette Bennett. 1995. "Racial and Ethnic Diversity," in *The State of the Union: America in the l990s*, Vol. 2: "Social Trends," Reynolds Farley (ed.). New York: Russell Sage, pp. 141–210.

Hartjen, Clayton A. 1974. *Crime and Criminalization*. New York: Praeger.

Hartmann, Heidi I. 1976. "Capitalism, Patriarchy, and Job Segregation by Sex," *Signs* 1 (Spring): 137–169.

Headden, Susan. 1993. "Made in the U.S.A.," *U.S. News & World Report* (November 22):48–55.

Heer, David. 1996. *Immigration in America's Future: Social Science Findings and the Policy Debate*. Boulder, CO: Westview Press.

Heilbroner, Robert L. 1974. *An Inquiry into the Human Prospect*. New York: W. W. Norton.

Heiman, Diane, and Phyllis Bookspan. 1992. "Word on the Street: Bias There, Too," *Rocky Mountain News* (July 28):30.

Henley, Nancy M. 1977. *Body Politics: Power, Sex, and Nonverbal Communication*. Englewood Cliffs, NJ: Prentice-Hall.

Henley, Robert J. 1994. "The Role of Women in Catholic Parish Life," *American* 171 (September):6–7.

Henneberger, Melinda, and Michael Marriott. 1993. "For Some, Youthful Courting Has Become a Game of Abuse," *New York Times* (July 11):A1, A14.

Henry, Jules. 1963. *Culture against Man*. New York: Random House Vintage.

Henry, William A. III. 1990. "Beyond the Melting Pot," *Time* (April 9):28–35.

Henwood, Doug. 1992. "American Dream: It's Not Working," *Christianity and Crisis* (June 8):195–197.

Herman, Edward S. 1994. "The New Racist Onslaught," *Z Magazine* 7 (December):24–26.

————. 1995. "Immiserating Growth: The First World," *Z Magazine* 8 (January):44–48.

————. 1996. "America the Meritocracy," *Z Magazine* 9 (July/August):34–39.

Hermann, Andrew. 1994. "Muslims Plan Census to Chart Growth Here," *Chicago Sun-Times* (February 12):4.

Herrnstein, Richard. 1971. "I.Q.," *The Atlantic* 228 (September):43–64.

————. 1973. *I.Q. in the Meritocracy*. Boston: Little, Brown.

————, and Charles Murray. 1994. *The Bell Curve: Intelligence and Class Structure in American Life*. New York: The Free Press.

Herz, Diane E., and Barbara H. Wootton. 1996. "Women in the Workforce: An Overview," in *The American Woman, 1996–1997*, Cynthia Costello and Barbara Kivimae Krimgold (eds.). New York: W. W. Norton, pp. 44–78.

Hess, Beth B., Elizabeth W. Markson, and Peter J. Stein. 1993. *Sociology*, 4th ed. New York: Macmillan.

Higginbotham, Elizabeth. 1994. "Black Professional Women: Job Ceilings and Employment Sectors," in *Women of Color in U.S. Society*, Maxine Baca Zinn and Bonnie Thornton Dill (eds.). Philadelphia: Temple University Press, pp. 113–131.

Higham, Charles. 1983. *Trading with the Enemy*. New York: Dell.

Hightower, Jim. 1987. "Where Greed, Unofficially Blessed by Reagan, Has Led," *New York Times* (June 21):25.

————. 1996. "Homeless Electorate," *Dollars & Sense* 206 (July/August):7.

Hines, Colin, and Tim Lang. 1994. "Times for a New Protectionism," *Multinational Monitor* 15 (October):26–28.

Hirschi, Travis. 1969. *Causes of Delinquency*. Berkeley: University of California Press.

Hoch, Paul. 1972. *Rip Off the Big Game*. New York: Doubleday.

Hochschild, Arlie. 1989. *The Second Shift*. New York: Viking.

Hodge, Robert W., Paul M. Seigel, and Peter H. Rossi. 1964. "Occupational Prestige in the United States, 1925–63," *American Journal of Sociology* 70 (November):286–302.

————, Donald J. Treiman, and Peter H. Rossi. 1966. "A Comparative Study of Occupational Prestige," in *Class, Status, and Power*, 2nd ed., Reinhard Bendix and S. M. Lipset (eds.). New York: Free Press, pp. 309–321.

Hoffman, Matthew. 1996. "Electoral College Dropouts," *The Nation* (June 17):15–16.

Hole, Judith, and Ellen Levine. 1979. "The First Feminists," in *Women: A Feminist Perspective*, Jo Freeman (ed.). Palo Alto, CA: Mayfield.

Hollingshead, August B., and Frederick C. Redlich. 1958. *Social Class and Mental Illness*. New York: John Wiley.

Holmes, Steven A. 1996. "For Hispanic Poor, No Silver Lining," *New York Times* (October 13):E5.

Holmstrom, David. 1996. "Mobile Kids Daunt Urban Schools," *Christian Science Monitor* (March 26):1,13.

Homans, George. 1964. "Bringing Men Back In," *American Sociological Review* 29 (December):809–818.

Horn, Miriam. 1987. "The Burgeoning Educational Underclass," *U.S. News & World Report* (May 18):66–67.

Horne, Gerald. 1992–93. "Race Backwards: Genes, Violence, Race, and Genocide," *Covert Action* (Winter):29–35.

Horton, John. 1966. "Order and Conflict Theories of Social Problems as Competing Ideologies," *American Journal of Sociology* 71 (May):701–713.

Huaco, George A. 1966. "The Functionalist Theory of Stratification: Two Decades of Controversy," *Inquiry* 9 (Autumn):215–240.

Hudson, Michael. 1996. "Cashing in on Poverty," *The Nation* (May 20):11–14.

Hulbert, Ann. 1993. "Home Repairs," *New Republic* 209 (August):26–32.

Hull, Jon D. 1995. "The State of the Union," *Time* (January 30):53–75.

Hunter, Floyd. 1953. *Community Power Structure.* Chapel Hill: University of North Carolina Press.

Huntington, Samuel P. 1965. "The Marasmus of the ICC," in *Bureaucratic Power in National Politics,* Francis Rourke (ed.). Boston: Little, Brown, pp. 73–86.

Hutchins, Robert M. 1976. "Is Democracy Possible?" *Center Magazine* 9 (January-February):2–6.

Hymnowitz, Carol, and Timothy D. Schellhardt. 1986. "The Glass Ceiling," *The Wall Street Journal* (March 24):1, 4.

Iglitzen, Lynn B. 1972. *Violent Conflict in American Society.* San Francisco: Chandler.

ISR Newsletter. 1982. "Why Do Women Earn Less?" Institute for Social Research, The University of Michigan (Spring/Summer).

Jackson, Robert L. 1982. "Tax-Cheating Loss," *The Denver Post* (March 18):A1–7.

Janzen, David. 1974. "Love 'em and Leave'em Alone," *The Mennonite* (June 11):390.

Jaynes, Gerald David, and Robin M. Williams, Jr. 1989. *A Common Destiny: Blacks and American Society.* Washington, DC: National Academy Press.

Jeffries, Vincent, and H. Edward Ransford. 1980. *Social Stratification: A Multiple Hierarchy Approach.* Boston: Allyn and Bacon.

Jencks, Christopher, et al. 1979. *Who Gets Ahead? The Determinants of Economic Success in America.* New York: Basic Books.

Jensen, Arthur R. 1969. "How Much Can We Boost IQ and Scholastic Achievement?" *Harvard Educational Review* 39 (Winter):1–123.

———. 1980. *Bias in Mental Testing.* New York: Free Press.

Jones, Barry. 1982. *Sleepers Awake! Technology and the Future of Work.* Melbourne: Oxford University Press.

———. 1990. *Sleepers, Awake! Technology and the Future of Work,* New Edition. Melbourne: Oxford University Press.

Jones, J. H. 1981. *Bad Blood.* New York: Free Press.

Jones, Rachel L. 1996. "Hispanic Children Biggest Minority," *Denver Post* (July 2):A1-A11.

Kagan, Jerome. 1973. "What Is Intelligence?" *Social Policy* 4 (July-August):88–94.

———. 1977. "The Child in the Family," *Daedalus* 106 (Spring):33–56.

Kammeyer, Kenneth C. W., George Ritzer, and Norman R. Yetman. 1997. *Sociology,* 7th ed. Boston: Allyn and Bacon.

Kanamine, Linda. 1992. "Amid Crushing Poverty, Glimmers of Hope," *USA Today* (November 30):A7.

Kanter, Rosabeth Moss. 1977. *Men and Women of the Corporation.* New York: Basic Books.

Kantrowitz, Barbara, and Pat Wingert. 1992. "One Nation, One Curriculum?" *Newsweek* (April 6):59–60.

Karp, Stan. 1995. "Money, Schools, and Courts," *Z Magazine* 8 (December):25–29.

Katz, Michael B. 1968. *The Irony of Early School Reform: Educational Innovation in Mid-Nineteenth Century Massachusetts.* Cambridge, MA: Harvard University Press.

Katzenstein, Mary Fainsod. 1984. "Feminism and the Meaning of the Vote," *Signs* 10 (Autumn):4–26.

Katz-Fishman, Wanda. 1990. "Higher Education in Crisis: The American Dream Denied," *Society for the Study of Social Problems Newsletter* 21 (Fall):22–23.

Keegan, Patricia, 1989. "Playing Favorites," *New York Times Magazine* (August 6):A26.

Keller, Helen. 1954. *The Story of My Life.* Garden City, NY: Doubleday.

Kelly, Dennis. 1992. "Minorities Make Gains on Campuses," *USA Today* (January 20):1D.

———. 1994. "The Breakdown for Minorities," *USA Today* (February 16):D4.

Kempton, Murray. 1979. "Arithmetic of Inequality," *The Progressive* 43 (November):8–9.

Kennedy, Paul. 1993. *Preparing for the Twenty-First Century.* New York: Random House.

Kerbo, Harold R. 1983. *Social Stratification and Inequality: Class Conflict in the United States.* New York: McGraw-Hill.

Kesey, Ken. 1962. *One Flew over the Cuckoo's Nest.* New York: Signet Books.

Kimmel, Michael. 1992. "Reading Men, Masculinity, and Publishing," *Contemporary Sociology* 21 (March):162–171.

——— and Michael A. Messner. 1995. *Men's Lives,* 3rd ed. Boston: Allyn and Bacon.

Kitano, Harry H. L., and Roger Daniels. 1988. *Asian Americans: Emerging Minorities.* Englewood Cliffs, NJ: Prentice-Hall.

Kitson, Gay. 1996. "Chair's Notes," *Family Forum: Newsletter of the American Sociological Association Family Section* (Summer):1–2.

Kluckhohn, Clyde, and D. Leighton. 1946. *The Navaho.* Cambridge, MA: Harvard University Press.

Knottnerus, J. David. 1987. "Status Attainment Research and Its Image of Society," *American Sociological Review* 52 (February):113–121.

Knowles, Louis L., and Kenneth Prewitt (eds.). 1965. *Institutional Racism in America.* Englewood Cliffs, NJ: Prentice-Hall.

Kominski, Robert, and Andrea Adams. 1993. "Educational Attainment," *Current Population Reports,* Special Studies P23–185 (May):14–15.

Kopkind, Andrew. 1993. "The Gay Moment," *The Nation* (May 3):577, 590–602.

Kozol, Jonathan. 1985. *Illiterate America.* New York: New American Library.

———. 1991. *Savage Inequalities: Children in America's Schools.* New York: Crown.

Kramer, R. C. 1982. "Corporate Crime," in *White Collar and Economic Crime,* P. Wickman and T. Dailey (eds.). New York: Lexington, pp. 75–94.

Kroeger, Brook. 1994. "The Road Less Rewarded," *Working Woman* (July):50–55.

Kuttner, Robert. 1996. "Fair Play for Female Athletes," *Washington Post National Weekly Edition* (August 26-September 1):5.

Labich, Kenneth. 1991. "Can Your Career Hurt Your Kids?" *Fortune* (May 20):38–56.

Lacayo, Richard. 1991. "Death on the Shop Floor," *Time* (September 16):28–29.

Ladner, Joyce A. 1971. *Tomorrow's Tomorrow.* New York: Doubleday.

Langer, Elinor. 1990. "The American Neo-Nazi Movement Today," *The Nation* (July 16–23):82–107.

Langlois, Judith H., and A. Chris Downs. 1980. "Mothers, Fathers, and Peers as Socialization Agents of Sex-Typed Play Behaviors in Young Children," *Child Development* 57:1237–1247.

Lasch, Christopher. 1977. *Haven in a Heartless World.* New York: Basic Books.

Lawlor, Julia. 1993. "More Jobs, But Not Good Ones," *USA Today* (September 7):4B.

Lechner, Frank J. 1989. "Fundamentalism Revisited," *Society* 26 (January/February):51–59.

Lekachman, Robert. 1979. "The Specter of Full Employment," in *Crisis in American Institutions,* 4th ed., Jerome H. Skolnick and Elliott Currie (eds.). Boston: Little, Brown, pp. 50–58.

LeMasters, E. E. 1974. *Parents in Modern America: A Sociological Analysis,* rev. ed. Homewood, IL: Dorsey.

Lemert, Edwin M. 1951. *Social Pathology: A Systematic Approach to the Theory of Sociopathic Behavior.* New York: McGraw-Hill.

———. 1967. *Human Deviance, Social Problems and Social Control.* Englewood Cliffs, NJ: Prentice-Hall.

Lenski, Gerhard E. 1966. *Power and Privilege: A Theory of Social Stratification.* New York: McGraw-Hill.

———. 1970. *Human Societies: A Macrolevel Introduction to Sociology.* New York: McGraw-Hill.

Lever, Janet. 1976. "Sex Differences in the Games Children Play," *Social Problems* 23 (April): 478–487.

Levitan, Sar A., and Clifford M. Johnson. 1982. *Second Thoughts on Work.* Kalamazoo, MI: W. E. Upjohn Institute for Employment Research.

———, Richard S. Belous, and Frank Gallo. 1988. *What's Happening to the American Family?* rev. ed. Baltimore: Johns Hopkins University Press.

Lewin, Ellen. 1993. *Lesbian Mothers: Accounts of Gender in American Culture.* Ithaca, NY: Cornell University Press.

Lewis, Michael. 1972. "There's No Unisex in the Nursery," *Psychology Today* 5 (May):54–57.

Liazos, Alexander. 1972. "The Poverty of the Sociology of Deviance: Nuts, Sluts, and Preverts," *Social Problems* 20 (Summer):103–120.

———. 1985. *Sociology: A Liberating Perspective.*Boston: Allyn and Bacon.

Lichtenberg, Judith. 1992. "Racism in the Head, Racism in the World," *Report from the Institute for Philosophy and Public Policy,* University of Maryland, Vol. 12 (Spring/Summer):3–5.

Liebow, Elliot. 1967. *Tally's Corner.* Boston: Little, Brown.

————. 1993. *Tell Them Who I Am: The Lives of Homeless Women.* New York: The Free Press.

Lincoln, C. Eric. 1996. *Coming Through the Fire: Surviving Race and Place in America.* Durham, NC: Duke University Press.

Lipman-Blumen, Jean. 1984. *Gender Roles and Power.* Englewood Cliffs, NJ: Prentice-Hall.

Litwack, Eugene, and Peter Messeri. 1989. "Organizational Theory, Social Supports, and Mortality Rates," *American Sociological Review* 54:49–66.

Lockheed, Marlaine. 1985. "Sex Equity in the Classroom Organization and Climate," in *Handbook for Achieving Sex Equity Through Education,* Susan S. Klein (ed.). Baltimore: Johns Hopkins University Press, pp. 189–217.

Loeb, Penny, Dorian Friedman, and Mary C. Lord. 1993. "To Make a Nation," *U.S. News & World Report* (October 4):47–54.

Lorber, Judith. 1994. *Paradoxes of Gender.* New Haven: Yale University Press.

Lord, Walter. 1955. *A Night to Remember.* New York: Henry Holt.

Lott, Juanita Tamayo, and Judy C. Felt. 1991. "Studying the Pan Asian Community," *Population Today* 19 (April 1):6–8.

Lucal, Betsy. 1994. "Class Stratification in Introductory Textbooks: Relational or Distributional Models?" *Teaching Sociology* 22 (April):139–150.

————. 1996. "Oppression and Privilege: Toward a Relational Conceptualization of Race," *Teaching Sociology* 24 (July):245–255.

Luker, Kristin. 1991. "Dubious Conceptions: The Controversy over Teen Pregnancy," *The American Prospect* 5 (Spring):73–83.

McAdoo, John. 1988. "Changing Perspectives on the Role of the Black Father," in *Fatherhood Today, Men's Changing Role in the Family,* P. Bronstein and C. P. Cowan (eds.). New York: John Wiley, pp. 79–92.

McCaghy, Charles H. 1976. *Deviant Behavior: Crime, Conflict, and Interest Groups.* New York: Macmillan.

McCarthy, Sarah J. 1979. "Why Johnny Can't Disobey," *The Humanist* (September-October).

McGee, Reece. 1975. *Points of Departure: Basic Concepts in Sociology,* 2nd ed. Hinsdale, IL: Dryden Press.

McGuire, Meredith B. 1992. *Religion: The Social Context.* Belmont, CA: Wadsworth.

McGuire, Stryker, and Andrew Murr. 1993. "California in the Rearview Mirror," *Newsweek* (July 19):24–25.

McIntosh, Peggy. 1992. "White Privilege and Male Privilege," in *Race, Class, and Gender,* Margaret L. Andersen and Patricia Hill Collins (eds.). Belmont, CA: Wadsworth, pp. 70–81.

McKinley, Donald Gilbert. 1964. *Social Class and Family Life.* Glencoe, IL: Free Press.

McLanahan, Sara, and Lynne Casper. 1995. "Growing Diversity and Inequality in the American Family," in *State of the Union, America in the 1990s,* Vol. 2: "Social Trends," Reynolds Farley (ed.). New York: Russell Sage, pp. 1–45.

McWhirter, Norris, and Ross McWhirter. 1972. *Guinness Book of World Records,* 11th ed. New York: Sterling.

Macewan, Arthur. 1994. "Markets Unbound: The Heavy Price of Globalization." *Dollars & Sense* 195 (September/October):8–9, 35–37.

Maharidge, Dale. 1992. "And the Rural Poor Get Poorer," *The Nation* (January 6–13):10–12.

Malec, Michael A. 1997. "Gender Equity in Athletics," in *Perspectives on Current Social Problems,* Gregg Lee Carter (ed.). Boston: Allyn and Bacon, pp. 209–218.

Males, Mike. 1993. "Infantile Arguments," *In These Times* (August 9):18–20.

————. 1994. "The Real Generational Gap," *In These Times* (February 7):18–19.

————. 1996. *The Scapegoat Generation: America's War on Adolescents.* Monroe, ME: Common Courage Press.

Mandel, Michael J., and Christopher Farrell. 1992. "The Immigrants," *Business Week* (July 13):114–122.

————, and Christopher Farrell. 1993. "The Price of Open Arms: Aliens Are Straining Budgets and Tolerance," *Business Week* (June 21):32–35.

Mansnerus, Laura. 1992. "Should Tracking Be Derailed?" *New York Times* (November 1):E14–E16.

Manuel, Herschel. 1934. "The Mexican Population of Texas," *Southwestern Social Science Quarterly* 15 (June):29–51.

Marger, Martin N. 1987. *Elites and Masses: An Introduction to Political Sociology,* 2nd ed. Belmont, CA: Wadsworth.

Martin, Philip, and Elizabeth Midgley. 1994. "Immigration to the United States: Journey to an Uncertain Destination," *Population Bulletin* 49 (September):entire issue.

Martin, Philip, and Jonas Widgren. 1996. "International Migration: A Global Challenge," *Population Bulletin* 51 (April):entire issue.

Martin, Teresa Castro, and Larry L. Bumpass. 1989. "Recent Trends in Marital Disruption," *Demography* 26:37–51.

Marx, Karl. 1967. *Capital: A Critique of Political Economy,* Vol. 1. New York: International Publishers.

————, and Friedrich Engels. 1947. *The German Ideology.* New York: International Publishers.

————. 1959. *Marx and Engels: Basic Writing on Politics and Philosophy,* Lewis S. Feuer (ed.). Garden City, NY: Anchor Books.

Maschinot, Beth. 1995. "Behind the Curve," *In These Times* (February 6):31–34.

Massey, Douglas S. 1993. "Latino Poverty Research: An Agenda for the 1990s," *Items,* The Social Science Research Council, Vol. 47 (March):7–11.

————, and Nancy Denton. 1993. *American Apartheid: Segregation and the Making of the Underclass.* Cambridge, MA: Harvard University Press.

Matza, David. 1964a. "Position and Behavior Patterns of Youth," in *Handbook of Modern Sociology,* Robert E. L. Faris (ed.). Chicago: Rand McNally.

————. 1964b. *Delinquency and Drift.* New York: John Wiley.

Mayfield, Marc. 1991. "Hate Groups Increase—As Do Their Crimes," *USA Today* (February 20):A3.

Mead, George Herbert. 1934. *Mind, Self, and Society.* Chicago: University of Chicago Press.

Meadow, James B. 1993. "Office Espionage," *Rocky Mountain News* (August 26):C7-C8.

Meddis, Sam Vincent. 1993. "Is the Drug War Racist? Disparities Suggest the Answer Is Yes," *USA Today* (July 23):A1–2.

Meisler, Stanley. 1993. "Large Migrant Shifts Put More Cities Under Stress," *Denver Post* (July 7):3A.

Meneilly, Robert H. 1993. "Government Is Not God's Work," *New York Times* (August 29):15E.

Merton, Robert K. 1957. *Social Theory and Social Structure,* 2nd ed. Glencoe, IL: Free Press.

Messner, Michael A. 1996. "Studying Up on Sex," *Sociology of Sport Journal* 13:221–237.

Mewshaw, Michael. 1976. "Irrational Behavior or Evangelical Zeal?" *Chronicle of Higher Education* (October 18):32.

Meyer, Michael. 1992. "Los Angeles 2010: A Latino Subcontinent," *Newsweek* (November 9):32–33.

Michels, Robert. 1966. *Political Parties,* Eden Paul and Cedar Paul, trans. New York: Free Press.

Miller, David. 1991. "A Vision of Market Socialism," *Dissent* 38 (Summer):406–414.

Miller, Ellen, and Randy Kehler. 1996. "Mischievous Myths about Money in Politics." *Dollars & Sense* 206 (July/August):22–23.

Miller, Walter B. 1958. "Lower Class Culture as a Generating Milieu of Gang Delinquency," *Journal of Social Issues* 14 (No. 3):5–19.

Mills, C. Wright. 1956. *The Power Elite.* New York: Oxford University Press.

————. 1959. *The Power Elite.* Fair Lawn, NJ: Oxford University Press.

————. 1968. "The Power Elite," in *Reader in Political Sociology,* Frank Lindenfeld (ed.). New York: Funk & Wagnalls, pp. 263–276.

Mills, Nicolaus. 1996. "Lifeboat Ethics and Immigration Fears." *Dissent* 43 (Winter):37–44.

Moberg, David. 1991. "Cutting Corporate Aid." *In These Times* (April 17):24–25.

————. 1992. "Decline and Inequality After the Great U-Turn," *In These Times* (May 27):7, 22.

————. 1995. "Reviving the Public Sector," *In These Times* (October 16):22–24.

Mogelesky, Marcia. 1996. "The Rocky Road to Adulthood," *American Demographics* 18 (May):26–35.

Monthly Forum for Women in Higher Education. 1995. "Women College Presidents," *Monthly Forum for Women in Higher Education* 1 (December):9.

Moore, Joan. 1976. *Mexican Americans.* Englewood Cliffs, NJ: Prentice-Hall.

————. 1981. "Minorities in the American Class System," *Daedalus* 110 (Spring).

————. 1990. "Is There a Hispanic Underclass?" *Social Science Quarterly* 70 (June):266–284.

————, et al. 1978. *Homeboys: Gangs, Drugs, and Prison in the Barrios of Los Angeles.* Philadelphia: Temple University Press.

———— and Raquel Pinderhughes (eds.). 1994. *In the Barrios: Latinos and the Underclass Debate.* New York: Russell Sage.

Moore, Wilbert E. 1969. "Social Structure and Behavior," in *The Handbook of Social Psychology,* 2nd ed., Vol. IV, Gardner Lindzey and Elliot Aronson (eds.). Reading, MA: Addison-Wesley.

Morales, Rebecca, and Frank Bonilla. 1993. *Latinos in a Changing U.S. Economy.* Newbury Park, CA: Sage.

Moskos, Charles C., Jr. 1975. "The American Combat Soldier in Vietnam," *The Journal of Social Issues* 31 (Fall):25–37.

Mother Jones. 1996. "Corporate Welfare Poster Boys," *Mother Jones* 60 (June):15.

Mott, Paul E. 1965. *The Organization of Society.* Englewood Cliffs, NJ: Prentice-Hall.

Moyers, Bill. 1996. "America's Religious Mosaic," *USA Weekend* (October 11):4–5.

Mullins, Marcy E. 1992. "How Minority Groups Are Faring," *USA Today* (January 20):11A.

Multinational Monitor. 1990. "Criminal Business," 11 (June):6.

———. 1991. "Fight for the Living," 12 (April):5.

Mulvaney, Jim. 1993. "Skinhead Founder Sorry Now," *Denver Post* (August 1):21A-22.

Murray, Charles. 1984. *Losing Ground.* New York: Basic Books.

Murray, Jim. 1976. "Vocabulary Takes on a Ruddy-Faced Look," *Rocky Mountain News* (December 9):150.

Muwakkil, Salim. 1994. "Dangerous Curve," *In These Times* (November 28):22–24.

Mydans, Seth. 1991. "Vote in a 'Melting Pot' of Los Angeles May Be Mirror of California's Future," *New York Times* (June 2):16.

Myers, Jerome K., and Lee L. Bean. 1968. *A Decade Later: A Follow-Up of Social Class and Mental Illness.* New York: John Wiley.

Myrdal, Gunnar. 1944. *An American Dilemma.* New York: Pantheon. National Center for Education Statistics. 1980. Cited in "Bilingual Hispanics Do Better in School," *Phi Delta Kappan* 62 (December).

National Conference of Catholic Bishops. 1986. *Economic Justice for All: Pastoral Letter on Catholic Social Teaching and the U.S. Economy.* Washington, DC: United States Catholic Conference, Inc.

Navarro, Vincente. 1991. "Class and Race: Life and Death Situations," *Monthly Review* 43 (September):1–13.

Nelson, Lars-Erik. 1994. "Ending Corporate Welfare: A Worthy Goal," *Denver Post* (November 29):B9.

Nesbitt, Paula J. 1996. "Women Clergy," in *Women and Work: A Handbook,* Paula J. Dubeck and Kathryn Borman (eds.). New York: Garland Publishing, pp. 181–184.

Nettler, Gwynn. 1974. *Explaining Crime.* New York: McGraw-Hill.

Newman, Katherine S. 1988. *Falling from Grace: The Experience of Downward Mobility in the American Middle Class.* New York: Free Press.

———. 1993. *Declining Fortunes: The Withering of the American Dream.* New York: Basic Books.

———. 1996. "Working Poor, Working Hard," *The Nation* (July 29):20–23.

News Report. 1989. "Slow Economy, Discrimination Block Opportunity for Blacks," (August/September):2–6.

Newsweek. 1975. "The FBI's 'Black-Bag Boys' " (July 28):18, 21.

———. 1975. "Project Minaret" (November 10):31–32.

New York Times. 1993. "Study Says Gay Bashing Up" (March 13):9.

———. 1995. "California Immigrants Make Fast Economic Gains, Study Finds." *New York Times* (November 5):13.

———. 1996. *The Downsizing of America.* New York: Times Books.

Niebuhr, R. Gustav. 1995. "Where Shopping Mall Culture Gets a Big Dose of Religion," *New York Times* (April 16): A1, A12.

Nielson, Joyce McCarl. 1990. *Sex and Gender in Society.* Prospect Heights, IL: Waveland Press.

North, C. C., and Paul K. Hatt. 1947. "Jobs and Occupations: A Popular Evaluation," *Public Opinion News* 9 (September):3–13.

Nottingham, Elizabeth K. 1954. *Religion and Society.* New York: Random House.

Novak, Viveca. 1991. "Why Workers Can't Win," *Common Cause Magazine* 17 (July/August):28–32.

Oakes, Jeannie. 1985. *Keeping Track: How Schools Structure Inequality.* New Haven, CT: Yale University Press.

O'Dea, Thomas. 1966. *The Sociology of Religion.* Englewood Cliffs, NJ: Prentice-Hall.

Ogbu, John U. 1982. "Minority Education and Caste," in *Majority and Minority,* 3rd ed., Norman R. Yetman and C. Hoy Steele (eds.). Boston: Allyn and Bacon, pp. 426–439.

O'Hare, William P. 1985. "Poverty in America: Trends and New Patterns," *Population Bulletin* 40 (June):entire issue.

———. 1987. "America's Welfare Population: Who Gets What?" *Population Trends and Public Policy* 13 (September):entire issue.

———. 1990. "A New Look at Asian Americans," *American Demographics* 13 (October):26–31.

———. 1992. "America's Minorities: The Demographics of Diversity," *Population Bulletin* 47 (December):entire issue.

———. 1993. "Diversity Trend: More Minorities Looking Less Alike," *Population Today* 21 (April):1–2.

———. 1996. "A New Look at Poverty," *Population Bulletin* 51 (September):entire issue.

———, and Brenda Curry-White. 1992. "Is There a Rural Underclass?" *Population Today* 20 (March):6–8.

————, Kelvin M. Pollard, Taynia L. Mann, and Mary M. Kent. 1991. "African Americans in the 1990s," *Population Bulletin* 46 (July):entire issue.

O'Kelly, Charlotte. 1980. *Women and Men in Society,* New York: Van Nostrand.

Olsen, Marvin E. 1976. *The Process of Social Organization,* 2nd ed. New York: Holt, Rinehart and Winston.

Omi, Michael, and Howard Winant. 1983. "By the Rivers of Babylon: Race in the United States, Part One," *Socialist Review* 71 (September-October):31–66.

————. 1983. "By the Rivers of Babylon: Race in the United States, Part Two," *Socialist Review* 72 (November-December):35–68.

————. 1986. *Racial Formation in the United States.* London: Routledge and Kegan Paul.

————. 1994. *Racial Formation in the United States,* 2nd ed. New York: Routledge.

O'Reilly, Brian. 1992. "Your New Global Work Force," *Fortune* (December 14):52–66.

Ortner, Sherry B. 1974. "Is Female to Male as Nature Is to Culture?" in *Women, Culture, and Society,* Michelle Zimbalist Rosaldo and Louise Lamphere (ed.). Stanford, CA: Stanford University Press, pp. 66–88.

Orwell, George. 1946. *Animal Farm.* New York: Harcourt, Brace.

Osmond, Marie Withers, and Barrie Thorne. 1993. "Feminist Theories: The Social Construction of Gender in Families and Society," in *Sourcebook of Family Theories and Methods: A Contextual Approach,* P. G. Boss, W. J. Doherty, R. LlaRossa, W. R. Schumm, and S. K. Steinmetz (eds.). New York: Plenum Press, pp. 591–623.

Ottinger, Cecilia, and Robin Sikula. 1993. "Women in Higher Education: Where Do We Stand?" *Research Briefs* 4 (American Council of Education).

Outtz, Janice Hamilton. 1995. "Higher Education and the New Demographic Reality," *Educational Record* 76 (Spring/Summer):65–69.

Pachon, Harry P., and Joan W. Moore. 1981. "Mexican Americans," *The Annals of the American Academy of Political and Social Sciences* (March):111–124.

Parenti, Michael. 1978. *Power and the Powerless,* 2nd ed. New York: St. Martin's Press.

————. 1980. *Democracy for the Few,* 3rd ed. New York: St. Martin's Press.

————. 1986. *Inventing Reality: The Politics of the Mass Media.* New York: St. Martin's Press.

————. 1988. *Democracy for the Few,* 5th ed. New York: St. Martin's Press.

————. 1992. *Make-Believe Media: The Politics of Entertainment.* New York: St. Martin's Press.

————. 1993. *Inventing Reality: The Politics of the News Media,* 2nd ed. New York: St. Martin's Press.

————. 1994. *Land of Idols: Political Mythology in America.* New York: St. Martin's Press.

————. 1995. *Democracy for the Few,* 6th ed. New York: St. Martin's Press.

Parlee, Mary Brown. 1979. "Conversational Politics," *Psychology Today* 12 (May):48–56.

Parry, Robert. 1995. "The Lord's Work," *In These Times* (November 27):14–16.

Parsons, Talcott, Robert F. Bales, et al. 1955. *Family, Socialization and Interaction Process.* New York: Free Press.

Pascale, Celine-Marie. 1995. "Normalizing Poverty," *Z Magazine* 8 (June):38–42.

Pear, Robert. 1993. "Poverty Is Cited as Divorce Factor," *New York Times* (January 15):A 6.

Pearce, Diana. 1978. "The Feminization of Poverty: Women, Work, and Welfare," *The Urban and Social Change Review* 11:28–36.

Peter, Laurence F., and Raymond Hull, 1969. *The Peter Principle.* New York: Morrow.

Peterson, Linda, and Elaine Enarson. 1974. "Blaming the Victim in the Sociology of Women: On the Misuse of the Concept of Socialization," Paper presented at the Pacific Sociological Association, San Jose, CA (March).

Peterson, Richard R. 1996. "A Re-evaluation of the Consequences of Divorce," *American Sociological Review* 61 (June):528–536.

Philippus, M. J. 1989. "Hispanics Fail Tests Because Tests Fail Them," *Rocky Mountain News* (June 15):59.

Phillips, Kevin. 1990. *The Politics of Rich and Poor: Wealth and the American Electorate in the Reagan Aftermath.* New York: Random House.

Piernard, Richard V., and Robert D. Linder. 1988. *Civil Religion and the Presidency.* Grand Rapids, MI: Zondervan Publishing House.

Piore, Michael J. 1975. "Notes for a Theory of Labor Market Stratification," in *Labor Market Segmentation,* Richard L. Edwards, et al. (eds.). Lexington, MA: DC Heath.

Piven, Frances Fox. 1996. "Welfare and the Transformation of Electoral Politics," *Dissent* 43 (Fall):61–67.

————, and Richard A. Cloward. 1971. "The Relief of Welfare," *Transaction* 8 (May).

————, and Richard A. Cloward. 1993. *Regulating the Poor,* updated edition. New York: Random House.

Plagens, Peter. 1991. "Violence in Our Culture," *Newsweek* (April 1):46–52.

Pleck, Joseph. 1977. "The Work-Family Role System," *Social Problems* 24 (April):417–427.

————. 1981. "Prisoners of Manliness," *Psychology Today* 15 (September).

Pollard, Kelvin. 1992. "Income Down, Poverty Up," *Population Today* 20 (November):5, 9.

Pope, Liston. 1942. *Millhands and Preachers.* New Haven, CT: Yale University Press.

Portes, Alejandro. 1992. "Immigration and the Reshaping of America," *The Baltimore Sun* (May 13).

Poulantzas, Nicos. 1974. *Classes in Contemporary Capitalism.* London: New Left Books.

Powell, Walter W. 1987. "Explaining Technological Change," *American Journal of Sociology* 93 (July):185–197.

Powers, Edwin, and Helen Witmer. 1951. *An Experiment in the Prevention of Delinquency.* New York: Columbia University Press.

Powledge, Fred. 1991. *Free at Last? The Civil Rights Movement and the People Who Made It.* Boston: Little, Brown.

Price, Sharon J., and Patrick C. McKenry. 1988. *Divorce.* Beverly Hills, CA: Sage.

Progressive, The. 1976. "Voting for What We Want" (November).

————. 1980a. "Out of the Bottle," 44 (August):8.

————. 1980b. An Editorial 44 (August):27–28.

————. 1981. "Merger Madness," 45 (September):10–11.

Puente, Maria. 1993. "Hispanics Debating Their Destiny in USA," *USA Today* (July):10A.

————, and Sandra Sanchez. 1995. "Experts Call Educational Gap National Threat," *USA Today* (September 6):A1-A2.

Quadagno, D. M., R. Briscoe, and J. S. Quadagno. 1977. "Effect of Perinatal Gonadal Hormones on Selected Nonsexual Behavior Patterns," *Psychological Bulletin* 84:62–80.

Quinney, Richard. 1970. *The Social Reality of Crime.* Boston: Little, Brown.

————. 1973. *Critique of Legal Order: Crime Control in Capitalist Society.* Boston: Little, Brown.

————. 1974. *Criminal Justice in America: A Critical Understanding.* Boston: Little, Brown.

Rachlin, Jill. 1989. "The Label That Sticks," *U.S. News & World Report* (July 3):51–52.

Ramirez, Blandina. 1992. "Minority Students Make Some Gains," *USA Today* (January 20):11A.

Randall, Eric D., Janet L. Fix, and Donna Rosato. 1993. "Takeovers in '90s: Kinder, Strategic," *USA Today* (September 2):3B.

Rankin, Robert A. 1995. "GOP Targets Welfare to Poor, Not Industry," *Denver Post* (May 28):A28.

Rapp, Rayna. 1982. "Family and Class in Contemporary America," in *Rethinking the Family: Some Feminist Questions,* Barrie Thorne and Marilyn Yalom (eds.). New York: Longman.

Record, Jane C., and Wilson Record. 1965. "Ideological Forces and the Negro Protest," *The Annals* 357 (January):89–96.

Reed, Adolph Jr. 1990. "The Underclass as Myth and Symbol: The Poverty of Discourse about Poverty," *Radical America* 24 (January/March):21–40.

————. 1994. "Looking Backward," The Nation (November 28):654–662.

Reiman, Jeffrey H. 1995. *The Rich Get Richer and the Poor Get Prison: Ideology, Class, and Criminal Justice,* 3rd ed. New York: Macmillan.

Religious News Service. 1995. "Vatican Declares 'Infallible' Its Ban on Women Priests."

Renshaw, Patrick. 1968. *The Wobblies.* Garden City, NY: Doubleday.

Renzetti, Claire M., and Daniel J. Curran. 1992. *Women, Men, and Society,* 2nd ed. Boston: Allyn and Bacon.

————. 1995. *Women, Men, and Society,* 3rd ed. Boston: Allyn and Bacon.

Reskin, Barbara F., and Irene Padavic. 1994. *Women and Men at Work.* Thousand Oaks, CA: Pine Forge Press.

————, and Patricia A. Roos. 1990. *Job Queues, Gender Queues.* Philadelphia: Temple University Press.

Richardson, Laurel Walum. 1981. *The Dynamics of Sex and Gender,* 2nd ed. Boston: Houghton Mifflin.

Riche, Martha Farnsworth. 1991. "We're All Minorities Now," *American Demographics* 13 (October):26–31.

Richmond, Julius B. 1994. "Give Children an Earlier Head Start," *USA Today* (April 12):13A.

Richmond-Abbott, Marie. 1992. *Masculine and Feminine: Sex Roles over the Life Cycle,* 2nd ed. New York: McGraw-Hill.

Riesman, David. 1950. *The Lonely Crowd.* New Haven, CT: Yale University Press.

Rifkin, Jeremy. 1996. "Civil Society in the Information Age," *The Nation* (February 26):11–16.

Ritzer, George. 1995. *Expressing America: A Critique of the Global Credit Card Society.* Thousand Oaks, CA: Pine Forge Press.

———. 1996. *The McDonaldization of Society,* rev. ed. Thousand Oaks, CA: Pine Forge Press.

Rizvi, Haider. 1995. "Slaves to Fashion," *Multinational Monitor* 16 (October):6–7.

Robins, Natalie. 1987. "The Defiling of Writers," *The Nation* (October 10):367–372.

———. 1992. "The Secret War against American Writers," *Esquire* 117 (March):106–109, 158–160.

Rogers, Susan Carol. 1978. "Women's Place: A Critical Review of Anthropological Theory," *Comparative Studies in Society and History* 20 (1):123–162.

Rohter, Larry. 1993. "Revisiting Immigration and the Open-Door Policy," *New York Times* (September 19):E4.

Ropers, Richard H. 1991. *Persistent Poverty.* New York: Insight Books.

Rosaldo, Michele Zimbalist. 1974. "Women, Culture and Society: A Theoretical Overview," in *Women, Culture, and Society,* Michele Zimbalist Rosaldo and Louise Lamphere (eds.). Palo Alto, CA: Stanford University Press, pp. 17–42.

———. 1980. "The Use and Abuse of Anthropology," *Signs* 5 (Spring):389–417.

Rosenblum, Karen E., and Toni-Michelle C. Travis. 1996. In *The Meaning of Difference,* Karen E. Rosenblum and Toni-Michelle C. Travis (eds.). New York: McGraw-Hill, pp. 1–34.

Rosenthal, Robert, and Lenore Jacobsen. 1968. *Pygmalion in the Classroom: Teacher Expectations and Pupils' Intellectual Development.* New York: Holt, Rinehart and Winston.

Ross, Catherine E., John Mirowsky, and Karen Goldsteen. 1991. "The Impact of the Family on Health: The Decade in Review," in *Contemporary Families: Looking Forward, Looking Back,* Alan Booth (ed.). Minneapolis: National Council on Family Relations, pp. 341–360.

Ross, I. 1980. "How Lawless Are Big Companies?" *Fortune* 102 (December 1):56–64.

Rossie, Dave. 1994. "Pendulum Swings in Florida," *Fort Collins Coloradoan* (May 19):B6.

Rotello, Gabriel. 1996. "To Have and To Hold: The Case for Gay Marriage," *The Nation* (June 24):11–18.

Rothfeder, Jeffrey. 1992. *Privacy for Sale: How Computerization Has Made Everyone's Life an Open Secret.* New York: Simon & Schuster.

Rubenstein, Richard E. 1970. *Rebels in Eden: Mass Political Violence in the United States.* Boston: Little, Brown.

Rubin, Lillian B. 1973. *Worlds of Pain.* New York: Basic Books.

———. 1983. *Intimate Strangers.* New York: Harper and Row.

Rubington, Earl, and Martin S. Weinberg. 1973. *Deviance: The Interactionist Perspective,* 2nd ed. New York: Macmillan.

Rukeyser, Louis, and John Cooney. 1991. *Louis Rukeyser's Business Almanac.* New York: Simon & Schuster.

Rumbaut, Ruben G. 1992. "The Americans: Latin American and Caribbean Peoples in the United States," in *Americas: New Interpretive Essays,* Alfred Stepan (ed.). New York: Oxford University Press, pp. 275–307.

Ryan, Joanna. 1972. "IQ—The Illusion of Objectivity," in *Race and Intelligence,* Ken Richardson and David Spears (eds.). Baltimore: Penguin.

Ryan, Mary P. 1983. *Womanhood in America: From Colonial Times to the Present,* 3rd ed. New York: Franklin Watts.

Ryan, William. 1970. "Is Banfield Serious?" *Social Policy* 1 (November-December):74–76.

———. 1972. "Postscript: A Call to Action," *Social Policy* 3 (May-June).

———. 1976. *Blaming the Victim,* rev. ed. New York: Pantheon.

Sacks, Karen. 1974. "Engels Revisited: Women, the Organization of Production, and Private Property," in *Woman, Culture, and Society,* Michele Zimbalist Rosaldo and Louise Lamphere (eds.). Stanford, CA: Stanford University Press, pp. 207–222.

Sacks, Oliver. 1993. "To See and Not See," *The New Yorker* (May 5):59–73.

Sadker, Myra, and David Sadker. 1994. *Failing at Fairness: How Schools Shortchange Girls.* New York: Charles Scribner's Sons.

Salvatore, Nick. 1992. "The Decline of Labor," *Dissent* 39 (Winter):86–92.

Samuels, Patrice Duggan. 1996. "Who's Reading Your E-Mail? Maybe the Boss," *New York Times* (May 12):F11.

Sandefur, Gary. 1989. "American Indian Reservations: The First Underclass Areas?" *Focus* 12 (Spring):37–41.

———. 1990. "Census Volume on the American Indian," *Social Science Research Council Items* 44 (June/September):37–40.

Sanders, Bernard. 1993a. "A Workers' Bill of Rights," *Zeta Magazine* 6 (March):17.

———. 1993b. "Clinton Must Go to the People," *The Nation* (June 21):865–867.

Sanderson, Stephen K. 1988. *Macrosociology: An Introduction to Human Societies.* New York: Harper and Row.

Sapiro, Virginia. 1994. *Women in American Society,* 3rd ed. Palo Alto, CA: Mayfield.

Scanzoni, John. 1980. "Resurgent Fundamentalism: Marching Backward into the '80s?" *The Christian Century* (September 10):847–849.

Scarpitti, Frank R., and Margaret L. Andersen. 1992. *Social Problems,* 2nd ed. New York: HarperCollins.

Schafer, Walter E., Carol Olexa, and Kenneth Polk. 1972. "Programmed for Social Class," in *Schools and Delinquency,* Kenneth Polk and Walter E. Schafer (eds.). Englewood Cliffs, NJ: Prentice-Hall.

Scheff, Thomas J. 1966. *Mentally Ill.* Chicago: Aldine.

Schlegal, Alice. 1977. *Sexual Stratification: A Cross-Cultural View.* New York: Columbia University Press.

Schlosser, Eric. 1995. "In the Strawberry Fields." *Atlantic Monthly* 276 (November):80–108.

Schneider, David M., and Raymond T. Smith. 1973. *Class Differences and Sex Roles in American Family and Kinship Structure.* Englewood Cliffs, NJ: Prentice-Hall.

Schor, Juliet B. 1991. *The Overworked American: The Unexpected Decline of Leisure.* New York: Basic Books.

Schorr, Lisbeth B, with Daniel Schorr. 1988. *Within Our Reach: Breaking the Cycle of Disadvantage.* New York: Doubleday Anchor Press.

Schultz, Ellen E. 1993. "More Equal Benefits Go to Some Top Executives," *Wall Street Journal* (May 25):1C, 19C.

Schur, Edwin. 1971. *Labeling Deviant Behavior: Its Sociological Implications.* New York: Harper & Row.

———. 1973. *Radical Non-Intervention: Rethinking the Delinquency Problem.* Englewood Cliffs, NJ: Prentice-Hall.

———. 1980. *The Politics of Deviance.* Englewood Cliffs, NJ: Prentice-Hall.

Schwartz, Herman. 1983. "Reagan's Bullish on Bugging," *The Nation* (June 4):697–699.

Schwarz, John E., and Thomas J. Volgy. 1993. "Above the Poverty Line—But Poor," *The Nation* (February 15):191–192.

See, Katherine O'Sullivan, and William J. Wilson. 1988. "Race and Ethnicity," in *Handbook of Sociology,* Neil J. Smelser (ed.). Newbury Park, CA: Sage.

Sennett, Richard, and Jonathan Cobb. 1973. *The Hidden Injuries of Class.* New York: Random House Vintage.

Sesser, Stan. 1992. "A Nation of Contradictions," *New Yorker* (January 13):37–68.

Shanas, Ethel. 1980. "Old People and Their Families: The New Pioneers," *Journal of Marriage and the Family* 42:9–15.

Shanker, Albert. 1991. "Improving Our Schools," *New York Times* (May 17):E7.

———. 1992. "How Far Have We Come?" *New York Times* (August 16):E9.

Shapiro, Judith. 1981. "Anthropology and the Study of Gender," in *A Feminist Perspective in the Academy,* Elizabeth Langland and Walter Gove (eds.). Chicago: University of Chicago Press, pp. 110–129.

Sheler, Jeffrey L. 1995. "The Era of Collective Repentence," *U.S. News & World Report* (July 3):10–11.

Sherif, Muzafer. 1958. "Group Influences upon the Formation of Norms and Attitudes," in *Readings in Social Psychology,* 3rd ed. Eleanor E. Maccoby, Theodore M. Newcomb, and Eugene L. Hartley (eds.). New York: Holt, Rinehart and Winston, pp. 219–232.

———, and Carolyn W. Sherif. 1966. *Groups in Harmony and Tension.* New York: Farrar, Straus & Giroux.

Sherrill, Robert. 1990. "S & Ls, Big Banks and Other Triumphs of Capitalism," *The Nation* (November 19): 589–623.

Shils, Edward A., and Morris Janowitz. 1948. "Cohesion and Disintegration in the Wehrmacht in World War II," *Public Opinion Quarterly* 12 (Summer 1948):280–315.

Shipp, E. R. 1991. "After Scandals, TV Preachers See Empty Pews," *New York Times* (March 3):1, 17.

Shortridge, Kathleen. 1989. "Poverty Is a Women's Problem," in *Women, A Feminist Perspective,* 4th ed., Jo Freeman (ed.). Palo Alto, CA: Mayfield, pp. 482–491.

Shreve, Anita. 1984. "The Working Mother as Role Model," *New York Times Magazine* (September 9):43.

Sidel, Ruth. 1994. *Battling Bias.* New York: Penguin Books.

———. 1996. *Keeping Women and Children Last: America's War on the Poor.* Baltimore: Penguin.

Silberman, Charles E. 1970. *Crisis in the Classroom.* New York: Random House.

Simon, David R., and D. Stanley Eitzen. 1993. *Elite Deviance,* 4th ed. Boston: Allyn and Bacon.

Simon, Julian. 1989. *The Economic Consequences of Immigration.* Cambridge, MA: Basil Blackwell.

Simon, Rita J., Angela J. Scanlan, and Pamela Madell. 1993. "Rabbis and Ministers: Women of the Book and Cloth," *Sociology of Religion* 54 (1):115–122.

Sims, Calvin. 1990. "As Token Lines Lengthen, Fare-Beating Rises," *New York Times* (June 24):E22.

Skinner, B. F. 1972. *Beyond Freedom and Dignity.* New York: Alfred A. Knopf.

Sklar, Holly. 1992. "Reaffirmative Action," *Z Magazine* 5 (May/June):9–15.

———. 1993a. "The Upperclass and Mothers N and Hood," *Z Magazine* 6 (March):22–36.

———. 1993b. "Young and Guilty by Stereotype," *Z Magazine* 6 (July/August):52–61.

———. 1995a. "The Snake Oil of Scapegoating." *Z Magazine* 8 (May):49–56.

———. 1995b. "Back to the Raw Deal." *Z Magazine* 8 (November):19–24.

Skolnick, Arlene S. 1979. "Public Images, Private Realities: The American Family in Popular Culture and Social Science," in *Changing Images of the Family,* Virginia Tufte and Barbara Meyerhoff (eds.). New Haven, CT: Yale University Press, pp. 297–315.

———. 1991. *Embattled Paradise: The American Family in an Age of Uncertainty.* New York: Basic Books.

———, and Jerome H. Skolnick (eds.). 1983. *Family in Transition,* 4th ed. Boston: Little, Brown.

Skolnick, Jerome. 1969. *The Politics of Protest.* New York: Ballantine Books.

———, and Elliott Currie. 1970. "Approaches to Social Problems," in *Crisis in American Institutions,* Jerome H. Skolnick and Elliott Currie (eds.). Boston: Little, Brown.

Slater, Philip. 1970. *The Pursuit of Loneliness: American Culture at the Breaking Point.* Boston: Beacon Press.

Smelser, Neil. 1962. *Theory of Collective Behavior.* New York: Free Press.

Smith, Lee. 1993. "What the Boss Knows About You," *Fortune* (August 9):88–93.

Snell, Bradford. 1974. "GM and the Nazis," *Ramparts* (June):14–16.

Snipp, Matthew. 1989. *American Indians: The First of This Land.* New York: Russell Sage.

———. 1992. "Sociological Perspectives on American Indians," *Annual Review of Sociology* 18:351–371.

———. 1996. "The First Americans: American Indians," in *Origins and Destinies: Immigration, Race, and Ethnicity in America,* Silvia Pedraza and Ruben G. Rumbaut (eds.). Belmont, CA: Wadsworth, pp. 390–403.

Snyder, Eldon. 1972. "Athletic Dressing Room Slogans and Folklore," *International Review of Sport Sociology* 7:89–102.

Sociologists for Women in Society. 1986. "Facts about Pay Equity," (April). East Lansing: Department of Sociology, Michigan State University.

Sontag, Deborah. 1993. "Muslims in the United States Fear an Upsurge in Hostility," *New York Times* (March 7):1,19.

Southern Poverty Law Center. 1996. "Klanwatch: Monitoring Hate and Fighting for Justice," *Southern Poverty Law Center Report* (March):12–13.

Sowell, Thomas. 1981a. *Ethnic America: A History.* New York: Basic Books.

———. 1981b. "Culture—Not Discrimination—Decides Who Gets Ahead," *U.S. News & World Report* (October 12):74.

Spring, Joel H. 1972. *Education and the Rise of the Corporate State.* Boston: Beacon Press.

Stacey, Judith. 1990. *Brave New Families: Stories of Domestic Upheaval in Late Twentieth-Century America.* New York: Basic Books.

———. 1991. "Backward Toward the Postmodern Family: Reflections on Gender, Kinship, and Class in the Silicon Valley," in *America at Century's End,* Alan Wolfe (ed.). Berkeley, CA: University of California Press, pp. 17–34.

———. 1994. "The New Family Values Crusaders," *The Nation* (July 25/August 1):119–122.

Stack, Carol B. 1990. "Different Voices, Different Visions: Gender, Culture, and Moral Reasoning," in *Uncertain Terms: Negotiating Gender in American Culture,* Faye Ginsburg and Anna Lowenhaupt Tsing (eds.). Boston: Beacon, pp. 19–27.

Stallard, Karin, Barbara Ehrenreich, and Holly Sklar. 1983. *Poverty in the American Dream.* Boston: Institute for New Communications, South End Press.

Stein, Peter J., Judith Richman, and Natalie Hannon. 1977. *The Family: Functions, Conflicts, and Symbols.* Reading, MA: Addison-Wesley.

Steinberg, David. n.d. "Racism in America: Definition and Analysis," in *People against Racism.* Detroit.

Steinmetz, Suzanne K. 1977. "Wifebeating, Husbandbeating—A Comparison of the Use of Violence between Spouses to Resolve Marital Conflicts," in *Battered Women: A Psychological Study of Domestic Violence,* Marina Roy (ed.). New York: Van Nostrand.

———. 1977–78. "The Battered Husband Syndrome," *Victimology* 2, nos. 3–4:449–509.

Stephens, William N. 1967. "Family and Kinships," in *Sociology,* Neil J. Smelser (ed.). New York: John Wiley.

Stern, Philip. M. 1988. *The Best Congress Money Can Buy.* New York: Pantheon.

Stevens, William K. 1989. "Racial Differences Found in Kind of Medical Care Americans Get," *New York Times* (January 1):1.

Stivers, Richard. 1975. "Introduction to the Social and Cultural Control of Deviant Behavior," in *The Collective Definition of Violence,* F. James Davis and Richard Stivers (eds.). New York: Free Press.

Stone, Andrea. 1991. "Asian Growth: 105% in 10 Years," *USA Today* (February 27):11A.

———. 1994. "There is No One Kind of Muslim," *USA Today* (January 27):A1-A2.

Stone, Marvin, 1978. "Political Spending Running Wild," *U.S. News & World Report* (October 23):112.

Straus, Murray A. 1974a. "Leveling, Civility, and Violence in the Family," *Journal of Marriage and the Family* 36:13–27.

———. 1974b. "Sexual Inequality, Cultural Norms, and Wife Beating," *Journal of Marriage and the Family* 36 (February):13–30.

———. 1977. "A Sociological Perspective on the Prevention and Treatment of Wifebeating," in *Battered Women,* Maria Roy (ed.). New York: Van Nostrand.

———, and Richard J. Gelles. 1985. "Societal Change and Change in Family Violence from 1975 to 1985 as Revealed by Two National Surveys," paper presented at the American Society of Criminology, San Diego (November). Published by the Family Violence Research Program, University of New Hampshire, Durham.

———, and Suzanne K. Steinmetz. 1980. *Behind Closed Doors: Violence in the American Family.* New York: Anchor Books.

Sutherland, Edwin H., and Donald R. Cressey. 1966. *Principles of Criminology,* 7th ed. Philadelphia: J. B. Lippincott.

Swartz, Steve. 1989. "Why Mike Milken Stands to Qualify for Guinness Book," *Wall Street Journal* (March 31):1, 4.

Sweeney, John J. 1996. *America Needs a Raise.* Boston: Houghton Mifflin.

Swinton, David. 1987. "Economic Status of Blacks 1986," in *The Status of Black America 1987.* New York: National Urban League.

Sykes, Gresham M. 1974. "Criminology: The Rise of Critical Criminology," *The Journal of Criminal Law and Criminology* 65 (June).

Szasz, Thomas. 1974. *Ceremonial Chemistry.* Garden City, NY: Doubleday.

Szymanski, Albert. 1978. *The Capitalist State and the Politics of Class.* Cambridge, MA: Winthrop.

Takaki, Ronald. 1993. *A Different Mirror: A History of Multicultural America.* Boston: Little, Brown.

Tannen, Deborah. 1990. *You Just Don't Understand: Women and Men in Conversation.* New York: Ballantine Books.

———. 1991. "Teachers' Classroom Strategies Should Recognize That Men and Women Use Language Differently," *The Chronicle of Higher Education* 37, no. 40:B3.

Terkel, Studs. 1975. *Working: People Talk about What They Do All Day and How They Feel about What They Do.* New York: Avon Books.

Thomas, Rich. 1993. "The Economic Cost of Immigration," *Newsweek* (August 9):18–19.

Thorne, Barrie. 1982. "Feminist Rethinking of the Family: An Overview," in *Rethinking the Family: Some Feminist Questions,* Barrie Thorne and Marilyn Yalom (eds.). New York: Longman.

———. 1993. *Gender Play: Girls and Boys in School.* New Brunswick, NJ: Rutgers University Press.

Thornton, Russell. 1996. "North American Indians and the Demography of Contact," in *Origins and Destinies: Immigration, Race, and Ethnicity in America,* Silvia Pedraza and Ruben G. Rumbaut (eds.). Belmont, CA: Wadsworth, pp. 43–59.

Thurm, Scott. 1995. "Hispanic Employment Slips," *Denver Post* (January 27):E1,E5.

Thurow, Lester. 1995. "Companies Merge: Families Break Up," *New York Times* (September 3):A11.

———. 1995. "Why Their World Might Crumble," *New York Times Magazine* (November 19):78–79.

Tiefer, Leonore. 1978. "The Kiss," *Human Nature* 1 (July):28–30.

Tienda, Marta, and Jennifer Glass. 1985. "Household Structure and Labor Force Participation of Black, Hispanic, and White Mothers," *Demography* 22:381–394.

Tifft, Susan. 1989. "The Big Shift in School Finance," *Time* (October 16):48.

Time. 1980. "Unmanning the Holy Bible" (December 8):128.

———. 1982. "Bishops and the Bomb" (November 29):77.

Timmer, Doug A., and D. Stanley Eitzen (eds.). 1989. *Crime in the Streets and Crime in the Suites.* Boston: Allyn and Bacon.

———, and D. Stanley Eitzen. 1992. "The Root Causes of Urban Homelessness in the United States," *Humanity and Society* 16 (May):159–175.

———, and D. Stanley Eitzen. 1993. "Government Policies and the Middle-Class" (unpublished).

————. D. Stanley Eitzen, and Kathryn D. Talley. 1994. *Paths to Homelessness in Urban America.* Boulder, CO: Westview Press.

Topolnicki, Denise M. 1995. "No More Pity for the Poor," *Money* 24 (May):122–127.

Treas, Judith. 1995. "Older Americans in the 1990s and Beyond," *Population Bulletin* 50 (May):entire issue.

————, and Ramon Torrecilha. 1995. "The Older Population," in *State of the Union, America in the 1990s,* Vol. 2: "Social Trends," Reynolds Farley (ed.). New York: Russell Sage, pp. 47–92.

Tribe, Lawrence H. 1996. "Toward a Less Perfect Union," *New York Times* (May 26):E11.

TRB. 1975. "The Case for More Planning," *Rocky Mountain News* (March 30):2.

Troeltsch, Ernst. 1931. *The Social Teaching of the Christian Churches,* Olive Wyon (trans.). New York: Macmillan.

Tufte, Virginia, and Barbara Meyerhoff (eds.). 1979. *Changing Images of the Family.* New Haven, CT: Yale University Press.

Tumin, Melvin M. 1953. "Some Principles of Stratification," *American Sociological Review* 18 (August):387–393.

————. 1973. *Patterns of Society.* Boston: Little, Brown.

Turner, Ronny. n.d. Personal communication.

————, and John R. Brouillette. 1992. Personal communication.

Uchitelle, Louis. 1993. "Fewer Jobs Filled as Factories Rely on Overtime Pay," *New York Times* (May 16):1, 15.

————, and N. R. Kleinfield. 1996. "The Price of Jobs Lost," in New York Times, *The Downsizing of America.* New York: Times Books, pp. 3–36.

Unnithan, N. Prabha. 1996. "Divisions and Violence in India," unpublished manuscript. Fort Collins: Colorado State University.

USA Today. 1989. "Kids' Health: The Obstacles" (March 3):D1.

————. 1991a. "Let Stockholders Vote on Executive Pay" (May 23):10A.

————. 1991b. "USA at Home: Streets Still Isolate Races" (November 11):1–2.

————. 1992a. "Middle Class 'Pulling Apart' to Rich, Poor" (February 20):A1.

————. 1992b. "Equal Justice under Law Must Be Blind to Race" (May 1):14A.

————. 1992c. "Plight of Cities Worsens" (May 5):13A.

————. 1992d. "Band-Aids Won't Do; Treat Riot's Roots of Despair" (May 7):10A.

————. 1992e. "Minority Majorities in One of Six Cities" (June 9):10A.

————. 1992f. "Unemployment" (July 7):2B.

————. 1992g. "Income Inequality Gap Widens for Minorities" (July 24):A3.

————. 1992h. "Minorities in Majority" (December 4):8A.

————. 1992i. "1990s Wedding Bell Blues" (December 9):12A.

————. 1993a. "From Honolulu to Detroit, Homeowners Pay More" (May 6):10B.

————. 1993b. "Whose 'Objectivity' Are We Getting?" (September 1):11A.

————. 1994. "Population Growing at a Furious Rate" (July 19): A1–A2.

————. 1996. "Majority Oppose Gay Marriage" (September 11):A4.

U.S. Bureau of the Census. 1991a. "The Black Population in the United States: March 1990 and 1989," *Current Population Reports,* Series P-20, No. 448. Washington, DC: Government Printing Office.

————. 1991b. "The Hispanic Population in the United States: March 1990," *Current Population Reports,* Series P-20, No. 449. Washington, DC: Government Printing Office.

————. 1991c. "Educational Attainment in the United States: March 1989 and 1988," *Current Population Reports,* Series P-20, No. 451. Washington, DC: Government Printing Office.

————. 1991d. "Population Profile of the United States: 1991," *Current Population Reports,* Series P-23, No. 173. Washington, DC: Government Printing Office.

————. 1992a. "Workers with Low Earnings: 1964 to 1990," *Current Population Reports,* Series P-60, No. 178. Washington, DC: Government Printing Office.

————. 1992b. "Educational Attainment in the United States: March 1991 and 1990," *Current Population Reports,* Series P-20, No. 462. Washington, DC: Government Printing Office.

————. 1992c. "Poverty in the United States: 1991," *Current Population Reports,* Series P-60, No. 181. Washington, DC: Government Printing Office.

————. 1992d. "Marital Status and Living Arrangements," *Current Population Reports,* Series P-20, No. 468. Washington, DC: Government Printing Office.

————. 1992e. "Money Income of Households, Families, and Persons in the U.S.: 1991," *Current Population Reports,* Series P-60, No. 180. Washington, DC: Government Printing Office.

————. 1992f. *Statistical Abstract of the United States,* 112th ed. Washington, DC: Government Printing Office.

U.S. Bureau of the Census. 1993. "We the American . . . Foreign Born," (September). Washington, DC: Government Printing Office.

————. 1994. "Household and Family Characteristics: March 1993," Series P20, No. 477. Washington, DC: U.S. Government Printing Office.

————. 1995a. "Population Profile of the United States: 1995." *Current Population Reports,* Series P23, No. 189. Washington, DC: Government Printing Office.

————. 1995b. *Statistical Abstracts of the United States,* 115th ed. Washington, DC: Government Printing Office.

————. 1996a. "Income, Poverty, and Valuation of Non-Cash Benefits, 1994." *Current Population Reports,* Series P-60, No. 189. Washington, DC: Government Printing Office.

————. 1996b. "Current Population Survey: Poverty 1995." Reported on World Wide Web (September 26).

U.S. Department of Health, Education and Welfare. 1966. *Equality of Educational Opportunity.* Washington, DC: Government Printing Office.

U.S. Department of Health and Human Services. 1991. *Health United States: 1990.* Washington, DC: Public Health Service.

U.S. Department of Justice. 1990. *Crime and Justice Facts, 1990.* Washington, DC: Department of Justice.

U.S. Department of Labor. 1965. *The Negro Family: The Case for National Action.* Washington, DC: Office of Policy Planning and Research.

————. 1988. "Twenty Facts on Women Workers," Office of the Secretary. Women's Bureau. Washington, DC: Government Printing Office.

————. 1990. "Earnings Differences between Women and Men," Facts on Working Women. Washington, DC: U.S. Department of Labor, Women's Bureau.

————. 1992. "Employment in Perspective: Women in the Labor Force," Report No. 831. Washington, DC: Division of Labor Statistics.

————. 1993. "Earnings Difference between Women and Men, Facts on Working Women." Washington, DC: U.S. Department of Labor, Women's Bureau.

————. 1995. "Employment and Earnings." Washington, DC: U.S. Government Printing Office.

U.S. News & World Report. 1996. "The Divorce Dilemma" (September 30):58–60.

Usdansky, Margaret L. 1991. "Minorities a Majority in 51 Cities," *USA Today* (September 17):A1, A9.

————. 1992. "Immigrant Tide Surges in the 80s." USA Today (May 22):A8.

Useem, Michael. 1983. "Equity and the Draft," *Working Papers* 10 (January-February):62–64.

U.S. Senate, 1978. Committee on Governmental Affairs, *Interlocking Directorates among the Major United States Corporations.* Washington, DC: Government Printing Office.

Valdivieso, Rafael, and Cary Davis. 1988. *U.S. Hispanics: Changing Issues for the 1990s.* Population Reference Bureau, No. 17 (December): entire issue.

van den Berghe, Pierre L. 1963. "Dialectics and Functionalism: Toward a Theoretical Synthesis," *American Sociological Review* 28 (October):697–705.

————. 1967. *Race and Racism: A Comparative Perspective.* New York: John Wiley.

Vanneman, Reeve, and Lynn Weber Cannon. 1987. *The American Perception of Class.* Philadelphia: Temple University Press.

Vecoli, Rudolph J. 1964. "Contadini in Chicago: A Critique of the Uprooted," *Journal of American History* 51:405–417.

Vedder, Richard and Lowell Gallaway. 1993. "Declining Black Employment," *Society* 31 (July/August):57–63.

Verhovek, Sam Howe. 1993. "Rich Schools, Poor Schools, Never-Ending Legislation," *New York Times* (May 30):3E.

Waldron, Ingred, and Jerry A. Jacobs. 1988. "Effects of Labor Free Participation on Women's Health," *Journal of Occupational Medicine* 30: 977–983.

Waldrop, Judith. 1990. "You'll Know It's the 21st Century When . . . ," *American Demographics* 13 (December): 22–27.

————, and Thomas Exter. 1991. "The Legacy of the 1980's," *American Demographics* (March):32–38.

Wali, Alaka. 1992. "Multiculturalism: An Anthropological Perspective," *Report from the Institute for Philosophy and Public Policy,* University of Maryland, Vol. 12 (Spring/ Summer):6–8.

Walker, Leonore E. 1979. *The Battered Woman.* New York: Harper & Row.

Walley, Dean. n.d. *What Boys Can Be.* Kansas City: Hallmark.

———. n.d. *What Girls Can Be.* Kansas City: Hallmark.

Wall Street Journal. 1992a. "Breast Cancer Takes Bigger Toll among Poor" (June 19):1B.

———. 1992b. "TV Violence Measured" (August 17):B6.

Walton, John. 1990. *Sociology and Critical Inquiry: The Work, Tradition, and Purpose.* Belmont, CA: Wadsworth.

Warner, W. Lloyd, and Paul S. Lunt. 1941. *The Social Life of a Modern Community.* New Haven, CT: Yale University Press.

Warren, Carol A. B., and John M. Johnson. 1973. "A Critique of Labeling Theory from the Phenomenological Perspective," in *Theoretical Perspectives on Deviance,* Jack D. Douglas and Robert Scott (eds.). New York: Basic Books.

Warriner, Charles K. 1956. "Groups Are Real: A Reaffirmation," *American Sociological Review* 21 (October):549–554.

Wartzman, Rick. 1992. "Segment of Full-Time Workers Earning Very Low Wages Surged in Past Decade." *Wall Street Journal* (May 12):A2.

Waters, Mary C. 1996. "Optional Ethnicities: For Whites Only?" in *Origins and Destinies: Immigration, Race, and Ethnicity in America,* Silvia Pedraza and Ruben G. Rumbaut (eds.). Belmont, CA: Wadsworth.

Weber, Max. 1947. *The Theory of Social and Economic Organization,* A. M. Henderson and Talcott Parsons, trans. New York: Free Press.

———. 1958. *The Protestant Ethic and the Spirit of Capitalism,* Talcott Parsons, trans. New York: Scribner's.

———. 1963. *The Sociology of Religion,* Ephraim Fischoff, trans. Boston: Beacon Press.

Weinstein, Deena, and Michael Weinstein. 1974. *Living Sociology: A Critical Introduction.* New York: David McKay.

Weistart, John C. 1996. "Can Gender Equity Find a Place in Commercialized College Sports?" *Duke Journal of Gender Law & Policy* 3 (Spring):191–264.

Weitzman, Lenore J. 1979. "Sex Role Socialization," in *Women: A Feminist Perspective,* 2nd ed., Jo Freeman (ed.). Palo Alto, CA: Mayfield.

———. 1984. "Sex-Role Socialization: A Focus on Women," in *Women: A Feminist Perspective,* 3rd ed., Jo Freeman (ed.). Palo Alto, CA: Mayfield, pp. 157–237.

———. 1985. *The Divorce Revolution: The Unexpected Social and Economic Consequences for Women and Children in America.* New York: The Free Press.

———. 1996. "Comment: Consequences of Divorce Are Still Unequal." *American Sociological Review* 61 (June):537–538.

———, Deborah Eifler, Elizabeth Hokada, and Catherine Ross. 1972. "Sex-Role Socialization in Picture Books for Preschool Children," *American Journal of Sociology* 77 (May):1125–1150.

Wellman, David T. 1977. *Portraits of White Racism.* Cambridge: Cambridge University Press.

West, Candace, and Don Zimmerman. 1987. "Doing Gender," *Gender and Society* 1:125–151.

Westhues, Kenneth. 1982. *First Sociology.* New York: McGraw-Hill.

Wheelis, Allen. 1958. *The Quest for Identity.* New York: W. W. Norton.

White, Daphne Siev. 1983. "Unemployment's Children: They're Growing Up Old," *On Campus* 2 (April):1, 8–9.

Whitman, David. 1990. "The Rise of the 'Hyper-Poor,'" *U.S. News & World Report* (October 15):40–41.

Whorf, B. L. 1956. "Science and Linguistics," in *Readings in Social Psychology,* E. E. Maccoby, T. M. Newcomb, and E. L. Hartley (eds.). New York: Holt.

Whyte, William Foote. 1956. *Street Corner Society: The Social Structure of an Italian Slum,* rev. ed. Chicago: University of Chicago Press.

———. 1988. *City: Rediscovering the Center.* New York: Doubleday.

Wicker, Tom. 1996. "Deserting the Democrats," *The Nation* (June 17):11–15.

Williams, David R. 1990. "Socioeconomic Differentials in Health: A Review and Redirection," *Social Psychology Quarterly* 53 (June):81–99.

———. 1996. "The Health of the African American Population," in *Origins and Destinies: Immigration, Race, and Ethnicity in America,* Silvia Pedraza and Ruben G. Rumbaut (eds.). Belmont, CA: Wadsworth, pp. 404–416.

Williams, J. Allen, JoEtta A. Vernon, Martha C. Williams, and Karen Malecha. 1987. "Sex Role Socialization in Picture Books: An Update," *Social Science Quarterly* 68 (March):148–156.

Williams, Juan. 1994. "The New Segregation," *Modern Maturity* 37 (April/May):24–33.

Williams, Robin M., Jr. 1970. *American Society: A Sociological Interpretation,* 3rd ed. New York: Alfred A. Knopf.

Wilson, William J. 1987. *The Truly Disadvantaged: The Inner City, the Underclass, and Public Policy.* Chicago: University of Chicago Press.

———. 1996. *When Work Disappears: The World of the New Urban Poor.* New York: Knopf.

————, and Kathryn M. Neckerman. 1986. "Poverty and Family Structure: The Widening Gap between Evidence and Public Policy Issues," in *Fighting Poverty,* Sheldon H. Danzinger and Daniel H. Weinberg (eds.). Cambridge, MA: Harvard University Press, pp. 209–231.

Winant, Howard. 1994. *Racial Conditions, Politics, Theory, Comparisons.* Minneapolis: University of Minnesota Press.

Wise, Arthur E., and Tamar Gendler. 1989. "Rich Schools, Poor Schools: The Persistence of Unequal Education," *The College Board Review,* No. 151 (Spring):12–17, 36–37.

Wolfe, Alan (ed.). 1991. *America at Century's End.* Berkeley: University of California Press.

Wolff, Edward N. 1995. *Top Heavy: A Study of Increasing Inequality of Wealth in America.* New York: The Twentieth Century Fund Press.

Woller, Barbara. 1991. "Women Earn Less Than Men Despite Equal Pay Legislation," *Lansing State Journal* (Nov. 8):4B.

Woodward, Kenneth L. 1990. "Young beyond Their Years," *Newsweek* Special Issue on the Family (November):54–60.

————. 1993. "Dead End for the Mainline?" *Newsweek* (August 9):46–48.

Wright, Erik Olin, David Hachen, Cynthia Costello, and Joey Sprague. 1982. "The American Class Structure," *American Sociological Review* 47 (December):709–726.

Wrong, Dennis. 1969. "The Oversocialized Conception of Man in Modern Sociology," in *Sociological Theory,* 3rd ed., Lewis A. Coser and Bernard Rosenberg (eds.). New York: Macmillan.

Yates, Michael D. 1994. *Longer Hours, Fewer Jobs: Employment & Unemployment in the United States.* New York: Monthly Review Press.

Yetman, Norman R. (ed.). 1985. *Majority and Minority,* 3rd ed. Boston: Allyn and Bacon.

————. 1991. "Introduction," in *Majority and Minority: The Dynamics of Race and Ethnicity in American Life,* Norman R. Yetman (ed.). Boston: Allyn and Bacon, pp. 1–29.

Yinger, J. Milton. 1961. *Sociology Looks at Religion.* New York: Macmillan.

————. 1962. "Contraculture and Subculture," *American Sociological Review* 25 (October): 625–635.

Yorburg, Betty. 1983. *Families and Societies: Survival or Extinction?* New York: Columbia University Press.

Z Magazine. 1995. "Bought and Paid For," 8 (June):5.

Zaldivar, R. A. 1987. "Illegal U.S. Planting of Articles Told," *Des Moines Register* (October 5):1.

Zaretsky, Eli. 1976. *Capitalism, The Family, and Personal Life.* New York: Harper Colophon.

Zeitlin, Maurice, Kenneth G. Lutterman, and James W. Russell. 1977. "Death in Vietnam: Class, Poverty, and the Risks of War," in *American Society, Inc.,* 2nd ed., Maurice Zeitlin (ed.). Chicago: Rand McNally, pp. 143–155.

Zimbardo, Philip G. 1972. "Pathology of Imprisonment," *Society* 9 (April).

Zinn, Howard. 1980. *A People's History of the United States.* New York: Harper & Row.

Zinn, Laura. 1992. "Move Over Boomers: The Busters Are Here—and They're Angry," *Business Week* (December 14):74–82.

Zuckerman, Mortimer B. 1990. "Who Stole Our Future?" *U.S. News & World Report* (May 7):78.

Zwerling, L. Steven. 1995. "Commentary: Redefining One-Third of a Nation," *Educational Record* 76 (Spring/Summer):19–21.

NAME INDEX

SUBJECT INDEX

protest, 64, 65
social control and, 136, 138, 140, 152, 159, 295, 459–460
Life chances, 240, 259, 304, 310, 320, 441, **535**
definition, **222–223**, **256–257**, **425**
of the poor, 56, 262, 278, 446, 494
Lifestyle, 3, 62–63, 84, 105, 396, 440, 495
choice, 177, 224, 233
class level, 163, 240, 425
reduction in, 202, 215, 380
social class and, 250–252, 256, 258, 378
Literacy, 419, 522
Little League programs, 137, 524–525
Lobbyists, 375, 385, 525
Looking-glass self, 115, 127–128, 172, **535**
Lower class, 162, 164, 184, 250, 252, 255–256
criminal activities, 106, 168–169, 259, 369
deficiency theories and, 233–234, 292
education and, 459, 462, 474
family dynamics of, 258, 425, 433
religion, 495
social control of, 137
Lutherans, 494, 497–498, 500

McDonaldization, 37, **535**
Machismo (macho), **535**
Macro level, of process of social organization, 27, 188, 214–215, 223, 225, 305, **535**
agency and, 513, 527
the family, 427, 445
gender inequality, 315
Majority group, 72, 105, 115, 187, 215, **282, 535**
deciding deviance, 165, 183
in a democracy, 386, 389
minority relations, 207, 224, 312
political power and, 401, 404, 413
status quo and, 61, 62, 147, 222
Majority-minority relations, 283, 292–293
Male chauvinism, **319**, 320, 344, **535**
Male dominance, 121, 315, 317–324, **319**, 345, 349, **535**
family dynamics, 433, 445
gender roles and, 326, 329, 339, 351, 375
reinforcement of, 331–336
sports and, 523, 526, 527
Manifest consequence, **54**, 101, **535**
Marginality, 328, 426, **535**
Marital power, **433**, 443, **535**
Marriage, 14, 34, 39, 65, 157, 198, 430–436
disruptions, 258, 269–270, 272, 291, 308, 418, 434–436
educational system and, 477

gendered role in, 321, 323, 334, 420, 431
remarriage, 434–436, 443, 446
social stratification, 221, 222, 425
types of, 30, 45, 63, 284, 448, 520, 528
Marxist theory, 22, 54, 74, 253, 520, 528
capitalism, 379, 382
ideology, 11, 452, 515
political power, 393, 401, 414
Masculinity, 316–317, 319, 323, 326, 332, 348–349
Mass media, 3, 11, 121–122, 176, 227, 250, 253
as agent for social control, 16, 133, 138–139, 152, 393, 398, 403
minority protrayal of, 291, 295
reflecting gender assumptions, 329, 332–333, 337, 350, 352, 523, 527
religion and, 502–505
social integration, 54, 67, 73–76, 521
socializing agent, 118, 120–123, 126, 128
value system and, 95, 104, 440
Materialism, 94, 104, 122, 124, 137, 524
Material technology, **86**, 89, 101–102, **535**
Maternity leaves, 438–439
Matriarchal family, 165, 288, **535**
Matrix of domination, **225–226**, **535**
Means of production, 54, 253–254, 278, 356, 358, 382
Medicaid, 142, 257, 274–276, 370
Medicare, 273, 370
Megachurch, 502–503, **535**
Mennonites, 34, 64, 135
Mental illness, 17, 21, 57, 140–142, 152, 172–173
deviance and, 158–161, 167–168, 172–174
Meritocracy, 8, 227, **229**, 261, 458, 478, **535**
Methodist Church, 36, 136, 334, 494, 499–500
Mexican Americans, 208, 211, 252, 283, 286–287, 295, 308. *See also* Hispanics, Latinos
demographics, 206
racial inequality of, 304–305
Micro level, of process of social organization, 25–43, 87, 223, 445, 527, **535**
Middle class, 99, 191, 256, 259, 265, 292, 512
classification, 250–252, 255
declining, 422, 425
deviance and, 163–165, 168–169, 173, 183
economic resources, 409, 412
education, 233, 259, 261, 288, 458–459, 462, 467
family dynamics, 421–422, 425–426, 428, 432–433
gender roles of, 324, 326–327

minorities and, 290, 294, 297, 306–308
mobility, 426
religion and, 493, 495, 496
school experience, 470, 472–474
shrinking, 74, 141, 197–202, 213, 215, 278
stratification and, 89, 224, 231, 234, 237
threat to, 246, 264, 371, 378, 380, 382
upper, 251, 389
Militarism, 138–139, 508
Military, 36, 62–63, 226, 379, 392, 394–400, 410
draft, 258–259, 278, 411–412, 524
interventionism, 488, 508
segregated, 521
Military-industrial complex, 21, 410–411, 414, **535**
Mill's pyramid of power, 394–400, 414
Minority group, 102–103, 119, 121, 277, 288, 382, 517
by size, 286–287, 289–290
characteristics of, 115, 165, 169–171, 441
deficiency theories and, 231, 236–237, 292–293, 295, 312
definition, **282–283**, **535**
discrimination, 177–178, 224, 228, 264, 294, 298, 310–312
economic displacement, 297, 303–305, 308–311
education and, 134, 262–263, 300, 302–303, 330
in labor force, 197, 199, 304, 372, 421
population share, 206–209, 215–216
power inequalities, 69, 215, 282, 336, 411
roadblocks to success for, 57, 59, 61–62, 65, 70, 308
school experience, 454, 461–462, 467, 471–473, 475, 477
six common beliefs, 16–19
social control and, 139–140, 142, 147
status and, 89, 176, 224, 252, 312
Minor vs. *Happerset*, 335
Modal personality type, 123, **124**, 125, **535**
Model, **52**, 76, **536**
Modern family, **427–428**, **536**
Monogamy, 16, 45, 58, 323, **536**
Monopolistic capitalism, 359–361, 405, **536**
Monopoly, 102, 277, 359–361, 380, 382, **536**
Montgomery bus boycott, 519, 528
Morality, 15, 118, 121, 126, 163–164, 177–178
culture/values and, 4, 28, 81, 84, 87, 94–95, 105
religion and, 505, 508
Morals, 53–54, 73, 128, 274, 291, 370
criteria for judging, 27, 357

Photo Credits